A CITY IN COREA.

COREA

THE HERMIT NATION

I.—ANCIENT AND MEDIÆVAL HISTORY
II.—POLITICAL AND SOCIAL COREA
III.—MODERN AND RECENT HISTORY

BY

WILLIAM ELLIOT GRIFFIS

FORMERLY OF THE IMPERIAL UNIVERSITY OF TOKIO, JAPAN
AUTHOR OF "THE MIKADO'S EMPIRE"

NINTH EDITION, REVISED AND ENLARGED

AMS PRESS
NEW YORK

Reprinted from the edition of 1911, New York

First AMS EDITION published 1971

Manufactured in the United States of America

International Standard Book Number: 0-404-02916-7

Library of Congress Number: 74-158615

AMS PRESS INC.
NEW YORK, N.Y. 10003

TO

ALL COREAN PATRIOTS:

WHO SEEK

BY THE AID OF SCIENCE, TRUTH, AND PURE RELIGION,

TO ENLIGHTEN

THEMSELVES AND THEIR FELLOW-COUNTRYMEN,

TO RID

THEIR LAND OF SUPERSTITION, BIGOTRY, DESPOTISM, AND
PRIESTCRAFT—BOTH NATIVE AND FOREIGN—

AND TO PRESERVE

THE INTEGRITY, INDEPENDENCE, AND HONOR, OF THEIR COUNTRY;

THIS UNWORTHY SKETCH

OF

THEIR PAST HISTORY AND PRESENT CONDITION

IS DEDICATED.

PREFACE TO THE NINTH EDITION.

THE year 1910 saw the Land of the Plum Blossom and the Islands of the Cherry Blooms united. In this ninth edition of a work which for nearly thirty years has been a useful hand-book of information—having, by their own unsought confession, inspired not a few men and women to become devoted friends and teachers of the Corean people—I have made some corrections and added a final chapter, "Chō-sen: A Province of Japan." Besides outlining in brief the striking events from 1907 to 1911, I have analyzed the causes of the extinction of Corean sovereignty, aiming in this to be a disinterested interpreter rather than a mere annalist.

Although the sovereignty of Corea, first recognized and made known to the world by the Japanese in their treaty of 1876, has been, through the logic of events, destroyed, I doubt not that the hopes of twelve millions of people will be increasingly fulfilled under the new arrangement. Not in haste, but only after long compulsion, did the statesmen of Japan assume a responsibility that may test to the full their abilities and those of their successors. The severe criticisms, in Japan itself, of the policy of the Tokio government bear witness to the sensitiveness of the national conscience in regard to the treatment of their colonies. In this respect, as in so many other points of public ethics, the Japanese are ranging themselves abreast with the leading nations that are making a world-conscience.

In sending forth what may be the final edition of a work, with the title of which time has had its revenges, while the contents are still of worth, the author thanks heartily all who, from 1876, when the work was planned, until the present time, have assisted in making this book valuable to humanity.

W. E. G.

ITHACA, N. Y., June 27, 1911.

PREFACE TO THE EIGHTH EDITION.

WHEN in October, 1882, the publishers of " Corea the Hermit Nation " presented this work to the public of English-speaking nations, they wrote :

" Corea stands in much the same relation to the traveller that the region of the pole does to the explorer, and menaces with the same penalty the too inquisitive tourist who ventures to penetrate its inhospitable borders."

For twenty-four years, this book, besides enjoying popular favor, has been made good use of by writers and students, in Europe and America, and has served even in Corea itself as the first book of general information to be read by missionaries and other new comers.   In this eighth edition, I have added to the original text, ending with Chapter XLVIII (September, 1882), five fresh chapters : on The Economic Condition of Corea ; International Politics : Chinese and Japanese ; The War of 1894 : Corea an Empire ; Japan and Russia in Conflict ; and Corea a Japanese Protectorate, bringing the history down to the late autumn of 1906.

Within the brief period of time treated in these new chapters, the centre of the world's politics has shifted from the Atlantic and the Mediterranean to the waters surrounding Corea, the strange anomaly of dual sovereignty over the peninsular state has been eliminated, and the military reputation of China ruined, and that of Russia compromised.   The rise of Japan, within half a century of immediate contact with the West, to the position of a modern state, able first to humiliate China and then to grapple successfully with Russia, has vitally affected Corea, on behalf of whose independence Japan a second time went to war with a Power vastly greater in natural resources than herself.   In this period also, the United States of America has become one of the great Powers interested in the politics of Asia, and with which the would-be conquerors of Asiatic peoples must reckon.

The present or eighth edition shows in both text and map, not only the swift, logical results both of Japan's military and naval successes in Manchuria and on the sea of Japan and of her signal diplomatic victory at Portsmouth, but more. It makes clear the reasons why Corea, as to her foreign relations, has lost her sovereignty.

The penalty laid upon the leaders of the peninsular kingdom for making intrigue instead of education their work, and class interests instead of national welfare their aim, is also shown to be pronounced—less by the writer than by the events themselves—in the final failure of intriguing Yang-banism, in May, 1906. The Japanese, in the administration of Corea, are like the other protecting nations, British, American, French, German, now on a moral trial before the world.

In again sending forth a work that has been so heartily welcomed, I reiterate gladly my great obligations to the scholars, native and foreign, who have so generously aided me by their conversation, correspondence, criticism, and publications, and the members of the Korean Branch of the Royal Asiatic Society, who have honored me with membership in their honorable body. My special obligations are due to our late American Minister, H. N. Allen, for printed documents and illustrative matter; to Professor Homer B. Hulbert, Editor of *The Korea Review*, from the pages of which I have drawn liberally, and to the Editor of *The Japan Mail*, the columns of which are rich in correspondence from Corea. I would call attention also to the additions made upon the map at the end of the volume.

I beg again the indulgence of my readers, especially of those who by long residence upon the soil, while so thoroughly able to criticize, have been so profuse in their expression of appreciation. From both sides of the Atlantic and Pacific have come these gratifying tokens, and to them as well as to my publishers, I make glad acknowledgments in sending forth this eighth edition.

W. E. G.

ITHACA, N. Y., December 12, 1906.

PREFACE TO THE FIRST EDITION.

In the year 1871, while living at Fukui, in the province of Echizen, Japan, I spent a few days at Tsuruga and Mikuni, by the sea which separates Japan and Corea. Like "the Saxon shore" of early Britain, the coast of Echizen had been in primeval times the landing-place of rovers, immigrants, and adventurers from the continental shore opposite. Here, at Tsuruga, Corean envoys had landed on their way to the mikado's court. In the temple near by were shrines dedicated to the Corean Prince of Mimana, and to Jingu Kōgō, Ojin, and Takénouchi, whose names in Japanese traditions are associated with "The Treasure-land of the West." Across the bay hung a sweet-toned bell, said to have been cast in Corea in A.D. 647; in which tradition— untested by chemistry— declared there was much gold. Among the hills not far away, nestled the little village of Awotabi (Green Nook), settled centuries ago by paper-makers, and visited a millenium ago by tribute-bearers, from the neighboring peninsula; and famous for producing the crinkled paper on which the diplomatic correspondence between the two nations was written. Some of the first families in Echizen were proud of their descent from Chō-sen, while in the villages, where dwelt the Eta, or social outcasts, I beheld the descendants of Corean prisoners of war. Everywhere the finger of tradition pointed westward across the waters to the Asian mainland, and the whole region was eloquent of "kin beyond sea." Birds and animals, fruits and falcons, vegetables and trees, farmers' implements and the potter's wheel, names in geography and thing-in the arts, and doctrines and systems in religion were in some way connected with Corea.

The thought often came to me as I walked within the moss-grown feudal castle walls—old in story, but then newly given up to schools of Western science and languages—why should Corea be sealed and mysterious, when Japan, once a hermit, had opened her doors and come out into the world's market-place ? When would Corea's awakening come? As one diamond cuts another, why should not Chō-ka (Japan) open Chō-sen (Corea) ?

Turning with delight and fascination to the study of Japanese history and antiquities, I found much that reflected light upon the neighbor country. On my return home, I continued to search for materials for the story of the last of the hermit nations. No master of research in China or Japan having attempted the task, from what Locke calls "the roundabout view," I have essayed it, with no claim to originality or profound research, for the benefit of the general reader, to whom Corea " suggests," as an American lady said, "no more than a sea-shell." Many ask "What's in Corea ?" and "Is Corea of any importance in the history of the world?"

My purpose in this work is to give an outline of the history of the Land of Morning Calm—as the natives call their country—from before the Christian era to the present year. As " an honest tale speeds best, being plainly told," I have made no attempt to embellish the narrative, though I have sought information from sources from within and without Corea, in maps and charts, coins and pottery, the language and art, notes and narratives of eye-witnesses, pencil-sketches, paintings and photographs, the standard histories of Japan and China, the testimony of sailor and diplomatist, missionary and castaway, and the digested knowledge of critical scholars. I have attempted nothing more than a historical outline of the nation and a glimpse at the political and social life of the people. For lack of space, the original manuscript of " Recent and Modern History," part III., has been greatly abridged, and many topics of interest have been left untouched.

The bulk of the text was written between the years 1877 and

1880 ; since which time the literature of the subject has been enriched by Ross's "Corea" and "Corean Primer," besides the Gram-
mar and Dictionary of the Corean language made by the French
missionaries.   With these linguistic helps I have been able to get
access to the language, and thus clear up doubtful points and obtain much needed data.   I have borrowed largely from Dallet's
"Histoire d'Eglise de Corée," especially in the chapters devoted to
Folk-lore, Social Life, and Christianity.   In the Bibliography following the Preface is a list of works to which I have been more
or less indebted.

Many friends have assisted me with correspondence, advice, or
help in translation, among whom I must first thank my former students, Haségawa, Hiraii, Haraguchi, Matsui, and Imadatté, and my
newer Japanese friends, Ohgimi and Kimura, while others, alas !
will never in this world see my record of acknowledgment—K.
Yaye' and Egi Takato—whose interest was manifested not only in
discussion of mooted points, but by search among the book-shops
in Kióto and Tōkiō, which put much valuable standard matter in my
hands.   I also thank Mr. Charles Lanman, Secretary of the Legation
of Japan in Washington, for four ferrotypes taken in Seoul in 1878
by members of the Japanese embassy ; Mr. D. R. Clark, of the
United States Transit of Venus Survey, for four photographs of
the Corean villages in Russian Manchuria ; Mr. R. Idéura, of Tōkiō,
for a set of photographs of Kang-wa and vicinity, taken in 1876,
and Mr. Ozawa Nankoku, for sketches of Corean articles in Japanese
museums.   To Lieutenant Wadhams, of the United States Navy,
for the use of charts and maps made by himself while in Corea in
1871, and for photographs of flags and other trophies, now at
Annapolis, captured in the Han forts ; to Fleet-Surgeon H. O. Mayo,
and other officers of the United States Navy, for valuable information, I hereby express my grateful appreciation of kindness shown.
I would that Admiral John Rodgers, Commodore H. C. Blake, and
Minister F. F. Low were living to receive my thanks for their
courtesies personally shown me, even though, in attempting to
write history, I have made criticisms also.   To Lieutenant N. Y.
Yanagi, of the Hyrographic Bureau, of the Japanese Navy, for a

set of charts of the coast of Corea ; to Mr. Metcalfe, of Milwaukee, for photographs of Coreans ; to Miss Marshall, of New York, for making colored copies of the battle-flags captured by our naval battalion in 1871, and for the many favors of correspondents—in St. Petersburg, Mr. Hoffman Atkinson ; in Peking, Jugoi Arinori Mori ; in Tōkiō, Dr. D. B. McCartee, Hon. David Murray, Rev. J. L. Amerman, and others whose names I need not mention. To Gen. George W. McCullum, Vice-President, and to Mr. Leopold Lindau, Librarian, of the American Geographical Society, I return my warmest thanks ; as well as to my dear wife and helpmeet, for her aid in copying, proof-reading, suggestions, and criticism during the progress of the work.

In one respect, the presentation of such a subject by a compiler, while shorn of the fascinating element of personal experience, has an advantage even over the narrator who describes a country through which he has travelled. With the various reports of many witnesses, in many times and places, before him, he views the whole subject and reduces the many impressions of detail to unity, correcting one by the other. Travellers usually see but a portion of the country at one time. The compiler, if able even in part to control his authorities, and if anything more than a tyro in the art of literary appraisement, may be able to furnish a hand-book of information more valuable to the general reader.

In the use of my authorities I have given heed to Bacon's advice—tasting some, chewing others, and swallowing few. In ancient history, original authorities have been sought, and for the story of modern life, only the reports of careful eye-witnesses have been set down as facts ; while opinions and judgments of alien occidentals concerning Corean social life are rarely borrowed without due flavoring of critical salt.

Corean and Japanese life, customs, beliefs, and history are often reflections one of the other. Much of what is reported from Corea, which the eye-witnesses themselves do not appear to understand, is perfectly clear to one familiar with Japanese life and history. China, Corea, and Japan are as links in the same chain of civilization. Corea, like Cyprus between Egypt and Greece, will yet supply many missing details to the comparative student of language, art, science, the development of civilization, and the distribution of life on the globe.

Some future writer, with more ability and space at command than the undersigned, may discuss the question as to how far the opening of Corea to the commerce of the world has been the result of internal forces ; the scholar, by his original research, may prepare the materials for a worthy history of Corea during the two or three thousand years of her history ; the geologist or miner may determine the question as to how far the metallic wealth of Corea will affect the monetary equilibrium of the world.   The missionary has yet to prove the full power of Christianity upon the people—and before Corean paganism, any form of the religion of Jesus, Roman, Greek or Reformed, should be welcomed ; while to the linguist, the man of science, and the political economist, the new country opened by American diplomacy presents problems of profound interest.

                                                        W. E. G.

Schenectady, N. Y., October 2, 1882.

BIBLIOGRAPHY.

THE following is a list of books and papers containing information about Corea. Those of primary value to which the compiler of this work is specially indebted are marked with an asterisk (*) ; those to which slight obligation, if any, is acknowledged with a double asterisk ; and those which he has not consulted, with a dagger (†). See also under THE COREAN LANGUAGE and CARTOGRAPHY, in the Appendix.

* History of the Eastern Barbarians. "Book cxv. contains a sketch of the tribes and nations occupying the northeastern seaboard of China, with the territory now known as Manchuria and Corea." This extract from a History of the Later Han Dynasty (25–220 A.D.), by a Chinese scholar of the fifth century, has been translated into English by Mr. Alexander Wylie, and printed in the Revue de l'Extrême Orient, No. 1, 1882. Du Halde and De Mailla, in French, and Ross, in English, have also given the substance of the Chinese writer's work, which also furnishes the basis of Japanese accounts of Corean history previous to the fourth century.

† The Subjugation of Chaou-seen, by A. Wylie. (Atti del IV. Cong. int. degli Orient, ii., pp. 309–315, 1881.) This fragment is a translation of the 95th book of the History of the Former Han Dynasty of China.

* Empire de la Chine et la Tartarie Chinoise, par P. du Halde.

* The Kōjiki and Nihongi, written in Japan during the eighth century, throws much light on the early history of Corea.

* Wakan-San-sai Dzuyé. Article on Chō-sen in this great Japanese Encyclopædia.

† Tong-Kuk Tong-Kan (General View of the Eastern Kingdom), a native Corean history written in Chinese.

* Zenrin Koku Hoki (Precious Jewels from a Neighboring Country), by Shiuho. Japan, 1586.

* Corea, its History, Manners, and Customs, by John Ross. 1 vol., pp. 404. Illustrations and maps. Paisley, 1880.

* The Chinese Reader's Manual, by W. Fred. Mayers. 1 vol., pp. 440. Shanghae, 1874. An invaluable epitome of Chinese history, biography, chronology, bibliography, and whatever is of interest to the student of Chinese literature.

* Kō-chō Rekidai Enkaku Zukai. Historical Periods and Changes of the Japanese Empire, with maps and notes, by Otsuki Tōyō.

** San Koku Tsu-ran To-setsu. Mirror of the Three [Tributary] Kingdoms, Chō-sen, Riu kiu, and Yezo, by Rin Shihei, 1785. This work, with its maps, was translated into French by J. Klaproth, and published in Paris, 1832. 1 vol. 8vo, pp. 288, of which pp. 158 relate to Chō-sen. Digested also in Siebold's Archiv.

** Archiv zur Bescriebung von Japan, by Franz von Siebold. This colossal work contains much matter in text and illustrations relating to Corea, and the digest of several Japanese books, in the part entitled Nachrichten uber Korai, Japan's Bezüge mit der Koraischen Halbinsel und mit Schina.

** Corea und dessen Einfluss auf die Bevölkerung Japans. Zeit. für Ethnologie, Zitzungbericht VIII. p. 78, 1876. P. Kempermann.

** O Dai Ichi Ran. This work, containing the annals of the emperors of Japan, is a bird's-eye view of the principal events in Japanese history, written in the style of an almanac, which Titsingh copied down from translations made by Japanese who spoke Dutch. Klaproth revised and corrected Titsingh's work, and published his own version in 1834. Paris and London, 8vo, pp. 460. This work contains many references to Corea and the relations of the two countries, transcribed from the older history.

** Tableaux Historiques de l'Asie, depuis la monarchie de Cyrus jusque nos jours, accompagnes de recherches historiques et ethnographiques, etc. Par J. Klaproth, Paris, 1826. Avec un atlas in folio. This manual of the political geography of Asia is very useful, but not too accurate.

† A Heap of Jewels in a Sea of Learning (Gei Kai Shu Jin ; Jap. pron.). A chapter from this Chinese book treats of Corea.

† Chō-sen Hitsu Go-shin. A collection of conversations with the pen, with a Corean who could not speak Japanese. By Ishikawa Rokuroku Sanjin, Yedo.

* The Classical Poetry of the Japanese. By Basil Hall Chamberlain. London, 1880.

** An Outline History of Japanese Education, New York, 1876. This monograph, prepared for the Centennial Exposition at Philadelphia, reviews the educational influences of Corea upon Japan. The information given is, with other data, from Klaproth, utilized in Pickering's Chronological History of Plants, by Charles Pickering, M.D., Boston, 1879.

* Japanese Chronological Tables. By William Bramsen, Tōkiō, 1880. An invaluable essay on Japanese chronology, which was, like the Corean, based on the Chinese system. We have used this work of the lamented scholar (who died a few months after it was published) in rendering dates expressed in terms of the Chinese into those of the Gregorian or modern system.

** History of the Mongols 3 vols. pp. 1827. London, 1876. By Henry Howorth. This portly work is full of the fruits of research concerning the people led by Genghis Khan. It contains excellent maps of Asia, and of Mongolia, and of Manchuria, illustrating the Mongol conquests.

† Chō-sen Ki-che. (Memorandum upon Corean Affairs.) The Chinese ambassador sent by the Ming emperor in 1450, gives in this little work an account of his journey, which throws light upon the political and geographical situation of Chō-sen and China at that time. Quoted by M. Scherzer, but not translated.

* Nihon Guaishi. Military History of Japan, by Rai Sanyo. This is the Japanese standard history. It was published in 1827 in twenty-two volumes. It covers the period from the Taira and Minamoto families to that of the Tokugawa in the seventeenth century. The first part of this work was translated into English by Mr. Ernest Satow, and published in The Japan Mail at Yokohama, 1872–74. In the latter portion the invasion of Chō-sen, 1592–97, is outlined.

* Chō-sen Seito Shimatsŭki. A work in five volumes, giving an account of the embassies, treaties, documents relating to the invasion of 1592–97, with an outline of the war, geographical notes, with nine maps by Yamazaki Masanagi and Miura Katsuyoshi.

* Illustrated History of the Invasion of Chō-sen. Written by Tsuruminé Hikoichiro. Illustrations by Hashimoto Giokuron. 20 vols. Yedo, 1853. This popular work, besides an outline of Corean history from the beginning, condensed from local legends and Chinese writers, details the operations of war and diplomacy relating to Hidéyoshi's invasion. It is copiously illustrated with first-class wood engravings. It has not been translated.

* Chō-sen Monogatari. A Diary and Narrative of the Japanese Military Operations in Chō-sen during the Campaign of 1594–97, by Okoji Hidémoto. Copied out and published in 1672, and again in 1849. This narrative of an eye-witness was written by the author at the time of the events described, and afterward copied by his own son and deposited in the temple at which his ancestors worshipped. This vivid and spirited story of the second invasion of Chō-sen by Hidéyoshi has been translated into German by Dr. A. Pfizmaier, under the title Der Feldzug der Japaner gegen Corea, im Jahre, 1597. 2 vols. Vienna, 1875 : 4to, pp. 98 ; 1876 : 4to, pp. 58.

** Chohitsuroku. History of the Embassies, Treaties, and War Operations during the Japanese Invasion. This work is by a Corean author, who was one of the ministers of the king throughout the war. It is written in Chinese, has a map, and gives the Corean side of the history of affairs from about 1585 to 1598. 3 vols.

* Three Severall Testimonies Concerning the mighty Kingdom of Coray, tributary to the Kingdom of China, and bordering upon her Northeastern Frontiers, and called by the Portugales, Coria, etc., etc., collected out of Portugale yeerely Japonian Epistles, dated 1590, 1592, 1594. In Hakluyt, London, 1600.

* Hidéyoshi's Invasion of Korea. Trans. Asiatic Society of Japan. By W. G. Aston. In these papers Mr. Aston gives the results of a study of the campaign of 1592–97, as found in Japanese and Corean authors.

** Lettre Annuelle de Mars 1593, ecrite par le P. Pierre Gomez au P. Claude Acquavira, general de la Compagnie de Jesus. Milan, 1597, p. 112 et suiv. In Hakluyt.

* Histoire de la Religion Chr'tienne au Japon. Par Leon Pages. 2 vols., text and documents. Paris, 1869.

** Histoire des deux Conquerans Tartares, qui ont subjugé la Chine, par le R. P. Pierre Joseph D'Orliens.

* Chō-sen Monogatari (Romantic Narrative of Travels in Corea), by two Men from Mikuni, in Echizen, cast ashore in Tartary in 1645. This work is digested in Siebold's Archiv.

* Narrative of an Unlucky Voyage and Imprisonment in Corea, 1653–1667. In Astley's and Pinkerton's Voyages. By Hendrik Hamel.

* Imperial Chinese Atlas, containing maps of China and each of the Provinces, including Shing-king and the neutral strip.

* Histoire de l'Eglise de Corée, par Ch. Dallet. 2 vols. 8vo, pp. 982. Paris, 1874. This excellent work contains 192 pages of introduction, full of accurate information concerning the political social life, geography, and language of Corea, and a history of the introduction and progress of Roman Christianity, and the labors of the French missionaries, from 1784–1866. It contains also a map and four charts of Corean writing.

* Une Expedition en Corée. In la Tour du Monde for 1873 there is an article of 16 pp. (401–417) with illustrations, by M. H. Zuber, a French naval officer, who was in Corea in 1866 under Admiral Roze. An excellent descriptive paper by an eye-witness.

* Diary of a Chinese Envoy to Corea (Journal d'une Mission en Corée), by Koei Ling, Ambassador of his Majesty the Emperor of China, to the court of Chō-sen in 1866. Translated from the Chinese into French by F. Scherzer, Interpreter to the French Legation at Peking. 8vo, pp. 77. Paris, 1882. This journal of the last Chinese ambassador to Seoul is well rendered, and is copiously supplied with explanatory notes, and a colored map of the author's route from Peking through Chili, Shing-King, *via* Mukden, and through three provinces of Corea to Seoul.

† Many memoirs and special papers prepared by French officers in the expedition to Corea in 1866 were prepared and read before local societies at Cherbourg, Lyons, etc.

† Expedition de Corée. Revue maritime et coloniale, February, 1867, pp. 474–481.

† Paris Moniteur, 1866–67.

** Lettre sur la Corée et son Eglise Chrétienne. Bulletin de la Société Geographique de Lyon, 1876, pp. 278–282, and June, 1870, pp. 417–422, and map.

** The Corean Martyrs. By Canon Shortland. 1 vol., pp. 115. London. Compiled from the letters of the French missionaries.

**Nouvelle Geographie Universelle. This superb treasury of geographical science, still unfinished, contains a full summary of our knowledge of Corea, especially showing the prominent part which French navigators, scholars, and missionaries have taken in its exploration. Paris.

** Voyage of Discovery to the North Pacific Ocean and Round the World. By William R. Broughton. 2 vols. 4to, with atlas. London, 1804.

** Voyage Round the World. By Jean François de Gallou de La Perouse. London, 1799.

** Voyages to the Eastern Seas in the year 1818. By Basil Hall. New York, London, and revised by Captain Hall in 1827. Jamaica, N. Y.

* Narrative of a Voyage in His Majesty's late Ship Alceste, to the Yellow Sea, along the Coast of Corea, and through its numerous hitherto undiscovered Islands, etc., etc. By John McLeod, Surgeon of the Alceste. 1 vol., pp. 288 (see pp. 38–53). London, 1877. A witty and lively narrative.

** Voyages along the Coast of China (Corea), etc. By Charles Gutzlaff. 1 vol., pp. 332. New York, 1833. (From July 17, to August 17, 1832 ; pp. 254–287.)

* Narrative of the Voyage of H.M.S. Samarang, during the years 1843–46. By Captain Sir E. Belcher. 2 vols. 8vo, pp. 574–378. London, 1848. Vol. i. pp. 324–358 ; vol. ii., pp. 444–466, relate to Corea.

* American Commerce with China. By Gideon Nye, Esq. In the Far East. Shanghae, 1878. A history of the commercial relations of the United States with China, especially before 1800.

* Diplomatic Correspondence of the United States, China, and Japan, 1866–81.

* Report of the Secretary of the Navy to Congress, pp. 275–313. 1872.

* Private Notes, Charts, and Maps of Officers of the United States Navy who were in Corea in 1871.

** A Summer Dream of '71. A Story of Corea. By T. G. The Far East. Shanghae, April, 1878.

* Journey through Eastern Mantchooria and Korea. By Walton Grinnell. Journal American Geographical Society, 1870–71, pp. 283–300.

* Japan and Corea. A valuable monograph in six chapters, by Mr. E. H. House, in The Tōkiō Times, 1877.

** On a Collection of Crustacea made in the Corean and Japanese Seas. J. Muirs, 1879. London Zoological Society's Proceedings (pp. 18–81, pls. 1–113). Reviewed by J. S. Kingsley. Norwich, N. Y. American Naturalist.

** A Private Trip in Corea. By Frank Cowan, M.D. The Japan Mail, 1880.

† The Leading Men of Japan. By Charles Lanman. Boston, 1882. Contains a chapter on Corea.

* Manuscript volume of pencil notes made by Kawamura Kuanshiu, an officer on the Japanese gunboat Unyo-kuan, during her cruise and capture of the Kang-wa Fort, 1875. Partly printed in the Japan Mail.

* Journals of Japanese Military and Diplomatic Officers who have visited Corea, and Correspondence of the Japanese newspapers, from Seoul, Fusan, Gensan, etc. These have been partly translated for the English press at Yokohama.

* Correspondence, Notes, Editorials, etc., in the English and French newspapers published in China and Japan.

** Maru-maru Shimbun (Japanese Punch).

* Chō-sen : Its Eight Administrative Divisions. 1 vol. Tōkiō, Japan, 1882.

* Cho-sen Jijo. A short Account of Corea, its History, Productions, etc. 2 vols. Tōkiō, 1875.

* Chō-sen Bunkenroku (Things Seen and Heard concerning Corea). By Sato Hakushi. 2 vols. Tōkiō, 1875.

* Travels of a Naturalist in Japan [Corea] and Manchuria. By Arthur Adams. 1 vol., pp. 334. London, 1870. See chaps. x., xi., pp. 125–166.

** Ueber die Reise der Kais. Corvette Hertha, in besondere nach Corea. Kramer, Marine Prediger. Zeit. für Ethnologie, 1873. Verhandlungen, pp. 49–54.

** A Forbidden Land. By Ernest Oppert. 1 vol., pp. 349. Illustrations, charts, etc. New York, 1880.

** Journeys in North China. By Rev. A. Williamson. 2 vols. 16mo. London, 1870. Besides a chapter on Corea, this work contains an excellent map of the country north and east of Chō-sen

** The Middle Kingdom. By S. Wells Williams.

** Consular Reports in the Blue Books of the British Government, especially
the Reports of Mr. McPherson, Consul at Niu-chwang. January, 1866.
˟ Handbook for Central and Northern Japan, with maps and plans. Satow
and Hawes. 1 vol. 16mo, pp. 489. This work, which leaves nothing to
be desired as a guide-book, contains several references to Corean art and
history.
** The Wild Coasts of Nipon. By Captain H. C. St. John (who surveyed some
parts of Southern Corea in H.B.M.S. Sylvia). See chap. xii., pp. 235-255,
with a map of Corea.
** Darlegun aus der Geschichte und Geographie Coreas. Pfizmaier. 8vo, pp.
56. Vienna, 1874.
† Petermann's Mittheilungen, No. 1, Carte No. 19, 1871.
** Das Konigreich Korea. Von Kloden. Aus allen Welth., x., Nos. 5 u. 6.
⁑ Corea. Geographical Magazine. (S. Mossman.) vi. p. 148, 1877.
† Corea. By Captain Allen Young, Royal Geographical Society. Vol. ix., No.
6, pp. 296-300.
** China, with an Appendix on Corea. By Charles Eden. 1 vol., pp. 281-
322. London. A popular compilation.
** Korea and the Lost Tribes, and Map and Chart of Korea. Text and illus-
trations. The title of this work is sufficient. Even the bibliography of
Corea has a comic side.
** Chi-shima (Kurile Islands) and Russian Invasion. A lecture delivered in
Japanese, before the Tōkiō United Geographical Society, February 24,
1882. By Admiral Enomoto. This valuable historical treatise, translated
for the Japan Mail and Japan Herald, contains much information about
Russian operations in the countries bordering the North Pacific and the
Coreans north of the Tumen.
† Bulletin de la Société Geographique, 1875. Corean villages in the Russian
possessions described.
** Ravensteins, The Russians on the Amoor. London, 1861.
† Die Insel Quelpart. Deutsche Geogr. Blätter, 1879. iii., No. 1, S. 45-46.
† A Trip to Quelpaert. Nautical Magazine, 1870, No. 4, p. 321-325.
** The Edinburgh Review of 1872, and Fortnightly Review of 1875, contain
articles on Corea.
* The Missionary Record of the United Presbyterian Church of Scotland,
Edinburgh, containing the Correspondence and Notes of the Missionaries
laboring among the Chinese and Coreans, and who have translated the
New Testament into Corean.
† La Corée, par M. Paul Tournafond, editor of L'Exploration, a geographical
journal published in Paris, which contains frequent notes on Corea.
† La Corée, ses Ressources, son avenir commercial, par Maurice Jametel.
L'Economiste Français, Juillet 23, 1881.
* The Japan Herald, The Japan Mail, The Japan Gazette, L'Echo du Japan,
of Yokohama, and North China Herald, Shanghae, have furnished much
information concerning recent events in Corea.
Corea, the Last of the Hermit Nations. Sunday Magazine, New York, May,1878.
Corea and the United States. The Independent, New York, Nov. 17, 1881.
Corea, the Hermit Nation. Bulletin of the American Geographical Society,
New York, 1881, No. 3.

Chautauqua Text-Books, No. 34. Asiatic History ; China, Corea, Japan. 16mo, pp. 86. New York, 1881.

Library of Universal Knowledge, articles Corea, Fusan, Gensan, Kang-wa, etc. New York, 1880.

Cyclopædia of Political Science, etc., article Corea. Chicago, 1881.

The Corean Origin of Japanese Art. Century Magazine. December, 1882. By Wm. Elliot Griffis.

ORTHOGRAPHY AND PRONUNCIATION.

IN the transliteration of Corean names into English, an attempt has been made to render them in as accurate and simple a manner as is, under the circumstances, possible. The Coreans themselves have no uniform system of spelling proper names, nor do the French missionaries agree in their renderings—as a comparison of their maps and writings shows. Our aim in this work has been to use as few letters as possible.

Japanese words are all pronounced according to the European method—*a* as in *father*, *é* as in *prey*, *e* as in *men*, *i* as in *machine*, *o* as in *bone*, *u* as in *tune*, *ŭ* as in *sun* ; *ai* as in *aisle*, *ua* as in *quarantine*, *ei* as in *feign*, and *iu* is sounded as *yu* ; *g* is always hard ; and *c* before a vowel, *g* soft, *l*, *q*, *s* used as *z*, *x*, and the combinations *ph* and *th* are not used. The long vowel, rather diphthong *o*, or *oho*, is marked *ō*.

The most familiar Chinese names are retained in their usual English form.

Corean words are transliterated on the same general principles as the Japanese, though ears familiar with Corean will find the obscure sound between *o* and short *u* is written with either of these letters, as Chan-yon, or In-chiŭn, or Kiung-sang. *Ch* may sometimes be used instead of *j* ; and *e* where *o* or *a* or *u* might more correctly be used, as in Kang-wen, or Wen-chiu. Instead of the French ou, or ho, we have written *W*, as in Whang-hai, Kang-wa, rather than Hoang-hai, Kang-hoa, Kang-ouen, Tai-ouen Kun, etc. ; and in place of *ts* we have used *ch*, as Kwang-chiu rather than Kwang-tsiu, and Wen-chiu than Ouen-tsiu.

MAPS AND PLANS.

CONTENTS.

PART I.

ANCIENT AND MEDIÆVAL HISTORY.

PART II.

POLITICAL AND SOCIAL COREA.

CONTENTS.

PART III.

MODERN AND RECENT HISTORY.

CONTENTS.

LIST OF ILLUSTRATIONS.

I.

ANCIENT AND MEDIÆVAL HISTORY

COREA:

THE HERMIT NATION.

CHAPTER I.

THE COREAN PENINSULA.

COREA, though unknown even by name in Europe until the sixteenth century, was the subject of description by Arab geographers of the middle ages. Before the peninsula was known as a political unit, the envoys of Shinra, one of the three Corean states, and those from Persia met face to face before the throne of China. The Arab merchants trading to Chinese ports crossed the Yellow Sea, visited the peninsula, and even settled there. The youths of Shinra, sent by their sovereign to study the arts of war and peace at Nanking, the mediæval capitol of China, may often have seen and talked with the merchants of Bagdad and Damascus. The Corean term for Mussulmans is *hoi-hoi*, "round and round" men. Corean art shows the undoubted influence of Persia.

A very interesting passage in the chronicles of Japan, while illustrating the sensitive regard of the Japanese for the forms of etiquette, shows another point of contact between Corean and Saracen civilization. It occurs in the Nihon O Dai Ichi Ran, or "A View of the Imperial Family of Japan." "In the first month of the sixth year of Tempiō Shōhō [February, 754 A.D.], the Japanese nobles Ohan no Komaro and Kibi no Mabi returned from China, in which country they had left Fujiwara no Seiga. The former reported that at the audience which they had of the Emperor Gen-sho, on New Year's Day [January 18th], the ambassadors

of Towan [Thibet] occupied the first place to the west, those from
Shinra the first place to the east, and that the second place to the
west had been destined for them (the Japanese envoys), and the
second place to the east for the ambassadors of the Kingdom
of Dai Shoku [Persia, then part of the empire of the Caliphs].
Komaro, offended with this arrangement, asked why the Chinese
should give precedence over them to the envoys of Shinra, a state
which had long been tributary to Japan. The Chinese officials,
impressed alike with the firmness and displeasure exhibited by
Komaro, assigned to the Japanese envoys a place above those of
Persia and to the envoys of Shinra a place above those of Thibet."

Thus the point at issue was settled, by avoiding it, and assign-
ing equal honor to Shinra and Japan.

This incident alone shows that close communications were kept
up between the far east and the west of Asia, and that Corea was
known beyond Chinese Asia. At that time the boundaries of the
two empires, the Arab and the Chinese, touched each other.

The first notice of Corea in western books or writings occurs in
the works of Khordadbeh, an Arab geographer of the ninth century,
in his Book of Roads and Provinces. He is thus quoted by Richthofen in his work on China (p. 575, note):

"What lies on the other side of China is unknown land. But
high mountains rise up densely across from Kantu. These lie over
in the land of Sila, which is rich in gold. Mussulmans who visit
this country often allow themselves, through the advantages of the
same, to be induced to settle here. They export from thence ginseng, deerhorn, aloes, camphor, nails, saddles, porcelain, satin,
zimmit (cinnamon?) and galanga (ginger?)."

Richthofen rightly argues that Sila is Shinra and Kantu is the
promontory province of Shantung. This Arabic term "Sila" is a
corruption of Shinra—the predominant state in Corea at the time
of Khordadbeh.

The name of this kingdom was pronounced by the Japanese,
Shinra, and by the Chinese, Sinlo—the latter easily altered in
Arabic mouths to Sila.

The European name Corea is derived from the Japanese term
Korai (Chinese Kaoli), the name of another state in the peninsula,
rival to Shinra. It was also the official title of the nation from the
eleventh to the fourteenth century. The Portuguese, who were the
first navigators of the Yellow Sea, brought the name to Europe,
calling the country Coria, whence the English Corea.

The French Jesuits at Peking Gallicized this into Corée. Fol-lowing the genius of their language, they call it La Corée, just as they speak of England as L'Angleterre, Germany as L'Allemande, and America as L'Amerique. Hence has arisen the curious desig-nation, used even by English writers, of this peninsula as "the Corea." But what is good French in this case is very bad English, and we should no more say "the Corea" than "the Germany," "the England," or "the America." English usage forbids the employment of the definite article before a proper name, and those writers who persist in prefixing the definite article to the proper name Corea are either ignorant of the significance of the word, or knowingly violate the laws of the English language. The native name of the country is Chō-sen (Morning Calm or Fresh Morning), which French writers, always prodigal in the use of vowels, spell Tsio-sen, Teo-cen, or Tchao-sian. The Chinese call it Tung-kwo (Eastern Kingdom), and the Manchius, Sol-ho or Solbo.

The peninsula, with its outlying islands, is nearly equal in size to Minnesota or to Great Britain. Its area is between eighty and ninety thousand square miles. Its coast line measures 1,740 miles. In general shape and relative position to the Asian Continent it resembles Florida. It hangs down between the Middle Kingdom and the Sunrise Land, separating the sea of Japan and the Yellow Sea, between the 34th and 43d parallels of north latitude. In its general configuration, when looked at from the westward on a good map, especially the magnificent one made by the Japanese War Department, Chō-sen resembles the outspread wings of a headless butterfly, the lobes of the wings being toward China, and their tops toward Japan.

Legend, tradition, and geological indications lead us to believe that anciently the Chinese promontory and province of Shantung and the Corean peninsula were connected, and that dry land once covered the space filled by the waters joining the Gulf of Pechili and the Yellow Sea. These waters are so shallow that the eleva-tion of their bottoms but a few feet would restore their area to the land surface of the globe. On the other side, also, the sea of Japan is very shallow, and the straits of Corea, at their greatest depth, have but eighty-three feet of water. That portion of the Chinese province of Shing King, or Southern Manchuria, bordering the sea, is a great plain, or series of flats elevated but a few feet above tide water, which becomes nearly impassable during heavy rains.

A marked difference is noted between the east and west coasts of the peninsula. The former is comparatively destitute of harbors, and the shore is high, monotonous, and but slightly indented or fringed with islands. It contains but three provinces. On the west coast are five provinces, and the sea is thickly strewn with islands, harbors and landing places, while navigable rivers are more numerous. The " Corean Archipelago " contains an amazing number of fertile and inhabited islands and islets rising out of deep water. They are thus described by the naturalist Arthur Adams :

" Leaving the huge, cone-like island of Quelpaert in the distance, the freshening breeze bears us gallantly toward those unknown islands which form the Archipelago of Korea. As you approach them you look from the deck of the vessel and you see them dotting the wide, blue, boundless plain of the sea—groups and clusters of islands stretching away into the far distance. Far as the eye can reach, their dark masses can be faintly discerned, and as we close, one after another, the bold outlines of their mountain peaks stand out clearly against the cloudless sky. The water from which they seem to arise is so deep around them that a ship can almost range up alongside them. The rough, gray granite and basaltic cliffs, of which they are composed, show them to be only the rugged peaks of submerged mountain masses which have been rent, in some great convulsion of nature, from the peninsula which stretches into the sea from the main land. You gaze upward and see the weird, fantastic outline which some of their torn and riven peaks present. In fact, they have assumed such peculiar forms as to have suggested to navigators characteristic names. Here, for example, stands out the fretted, crumbling towers of one called Windsor Castle, there frowns a noble rock-ruin, the Monastery, and here again, mounting to the skies, the Abbey Peak.

" Some of the islands of this Archipelago are very lofty, and one was ascertained to boast of a naked granite peak more than two thousand feet above the level of the sea. Many of the summits are crowned with a dense forest of conifers, dark trees, very similar in appearance to Scotch firs."

The king of Corea may well be called " Sovereign of Ten Thousand Isles."

Almost the only striking feature of the inland physical geography of Chō-sen, heretofore generally known, is that chain of mountains which traverses the peninsula from North to South, not in a straight line, but in an exceedingly sinuous course, similar to the tacking of a ship when sailing in the eye of the wind. As the Coreans say, "it winds out and in ninety-nine times."

Striking out from Manchuria it trends eastward to the sea at Cape Bruat on the 41st parallel, thence it strikes southwest about eighty miles to the region west of Broughton's Bay (the narrowest part of Corea), whence it bears westward to the sea at the 37th parallel, or Cape Pelissier, where its angle culminates in the lofty mountain peaks named by the Russians Mount Popoff—after the inventor of the high turret ships. From this point it throws off a fringe of lesser hills to the southward while the main chain strikes southwest, and after forming the boundary between two most southern provinces reaches the sea near the Amherst Isles. Nor does its course end here, for the uncounted islands of the Archipelago, with their fantastic rock-ruins and perennial greenery, that suggest deserted castles and abbeys mantled with ivy, are but the wave-worn and shattered remnants of this lordly range.

This chief feature in the physical geography of the peninsula determines largely its configuration, climate, river system and watershed, political divisions, and natural barriers. Speaking roughly, Eastern Corea is a mountainous ridge of which Western Corea is but the slope.

No river of any importance is found inside the peninsula east of these mountains, except the Nak-tong, which drains the valley formed by the interior and the sea-coast ranges, while on the westward slope ten broad streams collect the tribute of their melted snows to enrich the valleys of five provinces.

Through seven parallels of latitude this range fronts the sea of Japan with a coast barrier which, except at Yung-hing Bay, is nearly destitute of harbors. Its timbered heights present a wall of living green to the mariner sailing from Vladivostok to Shanghai.

Great differences of climate in the same latitude are observed on opposite sides of this mountain range, which has various local epithets. From their height and the permanence of their winter covering, the word "white" forms an oft-recurring part of their names.

The division of the country into eight dō, or provinces, which are grouped in southern, central, and northern, is based mainly on the river basins. The rainfall in nearly every province finds an outlet on its own sea-border. Only the western slopes of the two northeastern provinces are exceptions to this rule, since they discharge part of their waters into streams emptying beyond their boundaries. The Yalu, and the Han—"the river"—are the only streams whose sources lie beyond their own provinces. In rare instances are the rivers known by the same word along their whole length, various local names being applied by the people of different neighborhoods. On the maps in this work only the name most commonly given to each stream near its mouth is printed.

In respect to the sea basins, three provinces on the west coast form one side of the depression called the Yellow Sea Basin, of which Northeastern China forms the opposite rim. The three eastern dō, or circuits, lining the Sea of Japan, make the concave in the sea basin to which Japan offers the corresponding edge. The entire northern boundary of the peninsula from sea to gulf, except where the colossal peak Paik-tu ('White Head') forms the water-shed, is one vast valley in which lie the basins of the Yalu and Tumen.

Corea is, in reality, an island, as the following description of White Head Mountain, obtained from the Journal of the Chinese Ambassador to Seoul, shows. This mountain has two summits, one facing north, the other east. On the top is a lake thirty *ri* around. In shape the peak is that of a colossal white vase open to the sky, and fluted or scolloped round the edge like the vases of Chinese porcelain. Its crater, white on the outside, is red, with whitish veins, inside. Snow and ice clothe the sides, sometimes as late as June. On the side of the north, there issues a runnel, a yard in depth, which falls in a cascade and forms the source of the (Tumen) river. Three or four *ri* from the summit of the mountain the stream divides into two parts; one is the source of the Yalu River.

In general, it may be said to dwellers in the temperate zone that the climate of Corea is excellent, bracing in the north, and in the south tempered by the ocean breezes of summer. The winters in the higher latitudes are not more rigorous than in the State of New York; while, in the most southern, they are as delightful as those in the Carolinas. In so mountainous and sea-girt a country there are, of course, great climatic varieties even in the same provinces.

As compared with European countries of the same latitude, Corea is much colder in winter and hotter in summer. In the north, the Tumen River is usually frozen during five months in the year. The Han River at Seoul may be crossed on ice during two or three months. Even in the southern provinces, deep snows cover the mountains, though the plains are usually free, rarely holding the snow during a whole day. The lowest point to which the mercury fell, in the observation of the French missionaries, was at the 35th parallel of latitude 8° and at the 37th parallel 15° (F.). The most delightful seasons in the year are spring and autumn. In summer, in addition to the great heat, the rain falls often in torrents that blockade the roads and render travelling and transport next to impossible. Toward the end of September occurs the period of tempests and variable winds.

A glance at the fauna of Corea suggests at once India, Europe, Massachusetts, and Florida. In the forests, especially of the two northern circuits, tigers of the largest size and fiercest aspect abound. When food fails them, they attack human habitations, and the annual list of victims is very large. The leopard is common. There are several species of deer, which furnish not only hides and venison, but horns which, when "in velvet," are highly prized as medicine. In the fauna are included bears, wild hogs and the common pigs of stunted breed, wild cats, badgers, foxes, beavers, otters, several species of martens. The salamander is found in the streams, as in western Japan.

Of domestic beasts, horses are very numerous, being mostly of a short, stunted breed. Immense numbers of oxen are found in the south, furnishing the meat diet craved by the people who eat much more of fatty stuff than the Japanese.

Goats are rare. Sheep are imported from China only for sacrificial purposes. The dog serves for food as well as for companionship and defence. Of birds, the pheasant, falcon, eagle, crane, and stork, are common.

Corea has for centuries successfully carried out the policy of isolation. Instead of a peninsula, her rulers have striven to make her an inaccessible island, and insulate her from the shock of change. She has built not a Great Wall of masonry, but a barrier of sea and river-flood, of mountain and devastated land, of palisades and cordons of armed sentinels. Frost and snow, storm and winter, she hails as her allies. Not content with the sea-border she desolates her shores lest they tempt the mariner to land. Between her Chinese neighbor and herself, she has placed a neutral space of unplanted, unoccupied land. This strip of forests and desolated plains, twenty leagues wide, stretches between Corea and Manchuria. To form it, four cities and many villages were suppressed three centuries ago, and left in ruins. The soil of these solitudes is very good, the roads easy, and the hills not high.

For centuries, only the wild beasts, fugitives from justice, and outlaws from both countries, have inhabited this fertile but forbidden territory. Occasionally, borderers would cultivate portions of it, but gather the produce by night or stealthily by day, venturing on it as prisoners would step over the "dead line." Of late years, the Chinese Government has respected the neutrality of this barrier less and less. One of those recurring historical phenomena peculiar to Manchuria—the increase and pressure of population—has within a generation caused the occupation of large portions of this neutral strip. Parts of it have been surveyed and staked out by Chinese surveyors, and the Corean Government has been too feeble to prevent the occupation. Though no towns or villages are marked on the map of this "No-man's land," yet already, a considerable number of small settlements exist upon it.

As this once neutral territory is being gradually obliterated, so the former lines of palisades and stone walls on the northern border which, two centuries and more ago, were strong, high, guarded and kept in repair, have year by year, during a long era of peace, been suffered to fall into decay. They exist no longer, and should be erased from the maps.

The pressure of population in Manchuria upon the Corean border is a portentous phenomenon. For Manchuria, which for ages past has, like a prolific hive, swarmed off masses of humanity into other lands, seems again preparing to send off a fresh cloud. Already her millions press upon her neighbors for room.

The clock of history seems once more about to strike, perhaps to order again another dynasty on the oft-changed throne of China.

From mysterious Mongolia, have gone out in the past the various hordes called Tartars, or Tâtars, Huns, Turks, Kitans, Mongols, Manchius. Perhaps her loins also are already swelling with a new progeny. This marvellous region gave forth the man-children who destroyed the Roman Empire ; who extinguished Christianity in Asia and Africa, and nearly in Europe ; who, after conquering India and China threatened Christendom, and holding Russia for two centuries, created the largest empire ever known on earth ; and finally reared "the most improvable race in Asia" that now holds the throne and empire of China.

Chō-sen since acting the hermit policy of ancient Egypt and mediæval China, has preserved two loopholes at Fusan and Ai-chiu, the former on the sea toward Japan, and the latter in the northwest, on the Chinese border. What in time of peace is a needle's eye, is in time of war a flood-gate for enemies. From the west, the invading armies of China have again and again marched around over the Gulf of Liao Tung and entered the peninsula to plunder and to conquer, while Chinese fleets from Shan-tung have over and over again arched their sails in the Yellow Sea to furl them again in Corean Rivers. From the east, the Japanese have pushed across the sea to invade Corea as enemies, to help as allies against China, to levy tribute and go away enriched, or anon to send their grain-laden ships to their starving neighbors.

From a political point of view the geographical position of this country is most unfortunate. Placed between two rival nations, aliens in blood, temper, and policy, Chō-sen has been the rich grist between the upper and nether millstones of China and Japan. Out of the north, rising from the vast plains at Manchuria, the conquering hordes, on their way to the prize lying south of the Great Wall, have over and over again descended on Corean soil to make it their granary. From the pre-historic forays of the tribes beyond the Sungari, to the last new actors on the scene, the Russians, who stand with their feet on the Tumen, looking over the border on her helpless neighbor, Corea has been threatened or devastated by her eager enemies.

Nevertheless Corea has always remained Corea, a separate country ; and the people are Coreans, more allied to the Japanese than the Chinese, yet in language, politics, and social customs, different from either. As Ireland is not England or Scotland, neither is Chō-sen China nor Japan.

In her boasted history of "four thousand years," the little kingdom has too often been the Ireland of China, so far as misgovernment on the one side, and fretful and spasmodic resistance on the other, are considered. Yet ancient Corea has also been an Ireland to Japan, in the better sense of giving to her the art, letters, science, and ethics of continental civilization. As of old, went forth from Tara's halls to the British Isles and the continent, the bard and the monk to elevate and civilize Europe with the culture of Rome and the religion of Christianity, so for centuries there crossed the sea from the peninsula a stream of scholars, artists, and missionaries who brought to Japan the social culture of Chō-sen, the literature of China, and the religion of India. A grateful bonze of Japan has well told the story of Corea's part in the civilization of his native country in a book entitled "Precious Jewels from a Neighbor Country."

Corea fulfils one of the first conditions of national safety in having "scientific frontiers," or adequate natural boundaries of river, mountain, and sea. But now what was once barrier is highway. What was once the safety of isolation, is now the weakness of the recluse. Steam has made the water a surer path than land, and Japan, once the pupil and anon the conqueror of the little kingdom, has in these last days become the helpful friend of Corea's people, and the opener of the long-sealed peninsula.

Already the friendly whistle of Japanese steamers is heard in the harbors of two ports in which are trading settlements. At Fusan and Gensan, the mikado's subjects hold commercial rivalry with the Coreans, and through these two loopholes the hermits of the peninsula catch glimpses of the outer world that must waken thought and create a desire to enter the family of nations. The ill fame of the native character for inhospitality and hatred of foreigners belongs not to the people, nor is truly characteristic of them. It inheres in the government which curses country and people, and in the ruling classes who, like those in Old Japan, do not wish the peasantry to see the inferiority of those who govern them.

Corea cannot long remain a hermit nation. The near future will see her open to the world. Commerce and pure Christianity will enter to elevate her people, and the student of science, ethnology, and language will find a tempting field on which shall be solved many a yet obscure problem. The forbidden land of to-day is, in many striking points of comparison, the analogue of Old Japan. While the last of the hermit nations awaits some gallant Perry of the future, we may hope that the same brilliant path of progress on which the Sunrise Kingdom has entered, awaits the Land of Morning Calm.

We add a postscript. As our manuscript turns to print, we hear of the treaty successfully negotiated by Commodore Shufeldt.

Corean Coin—'' Eastern Kingdom, Precious Treasure.''

CHAPTER II.

THE OLD KINGDOM OF CHŌ-SEN.

LIKE almost every country on earth, whose history is known, Corea is inhabited by a race that is not aboriginal. The present occupiers of the land drove out or conquered the people whom they found upon it. They are the descendants of a stock whose ancestral seats were beyond those ever white mountains which buttress the northern frontier.

Nevertheless, for the origins of their national history, we must look to one whom the Coreans of this nineteenth century still call the founder of their social order. The scene of his labors is laid partly within the peninsula, and chiefly in Manchuria, on the well watered plains of Shing-king, formerly called Liao Tung.

The third dynasty of the thirty-three or thirty-four lines of rulers who have filled the oft-changed throne of China, is known in history as the Shang (or Yin). It began B.C. 1766, and after a line of twenty-eight sovereigns, ended in Chow Sin, who died B.C. 1122. He was an unscrupulous tyrant, and has been called "the Nero of China."

One of his nobles was Ki Tsze, viscount of Ki (or Latinized, Kicius). He was a profound scholar and author of important portions of the classic book, entitled the Shu King. He was a counsellor of the tyrant king, and being a man of upright character, was greatly scandalized at the conduct of his licentious and cruel master.

The sage remonstrated with his sovereign hoping to turn him from his evil ways. In this noble purpose he was assisted by two other men of rank named Pi Kan and Wei Tsze. All their efforts were of no avail, and finding the reformation of the tyrant hopeless, Wei Tsze, though a kinsman of the king, voluntarily exiled himself from the realm, while Pi Kan, also a relative of Chow Sin, was cruelly murdered in the following manner:

The king, mocking the wise counsellor, cried out, "They say

that a sage has seven orifices to his heart; let us see if this is the case with Pi Kan." This Chinese monarch, himself so much like Herod in other respects, had a wife who in her character resembled Herodias. It was she who expressed the bloody wish to see the heart of Pi Kan. By the imperial order the sage was put to death and his body ripped open. His heart, torn out, was brought before the cruel pair. Ki Tsze, the third counsellor, was cast into prison.

Meanwhile the people and nobles of the empire were rising in arms against the tyrant whose misrule had become intolerable. They were led on by one Wu Wang, who crossed the Yellow River, and met the tyrant on the plains of Muh. In the great battle that ensued, the army of Chow Sin was defeated. Escaping to his palace, and ordering it to be set on fire, he perished in the flames.

Among the conqueror's first acts was the erection of a memorial mound over the grave of Pi Kan, and an order that Ki Tsze should be released from prison, and appointed Prime Minister of the realm.

But the sage's loyalty exceeded his gratitude. In spite of the magnanimity of the offer, Ki Tsze frankly told the conqueror that duty to his deposed sovereign forbade him serving one whom he could not but regard as a usurper. He then departed into the regions lying to the northeast. With him went several thousand Chinese emigrants, mostly the remnant of the defeated army, now exiles, who made him their king. It is not probable that in his distant realm he received investment from or paid tribute to King Wu. Such an act would be a virtual acknowledgment of the righteousness of rebellion and revolution. It would prove that the sage forgave the usurper. Some Chinese historians state that Ki Tsze accepted a title from Wu Wang. Others maintain that the investiture "was a euphemism to shield the character of the ancestor of Confucius." The migration of Ki Tsze and his followers took place 1122 B.C.

Ki Tsze began vigorously to reduce the aboriginal people of his realm to order. He policed the borders, gave laws to his subjects, and gradually introduced the principles and practice of Chinese etiquette and polity throughout his domain. Previous to his time the people lived in caves and holes in the ground, dressed in leaves, and were destitute of manners, morals, agriculture and cooking, being ignorant savages. The divine being, Dan Kun, had partially civilized them, but Kishi, who brought 5,000 Chinese colonists with him, taught the aborigines letters, reading and writing, medicine, many of the arts, and the political principles of feudal China. The Japanese pronounce the founder's name Kishi, and the Coreans Kei-tsa or Kysse.

The name conferred by Kishi, the civilizer, upon his new domain is that now in use by the modern Coreans—Chō-sen or Morning Calm.

This ancient kingdom of Chō-sen, according to the Coreans, comprised the modern Chinese province of Shing-king, which is now about the size of Ohio, having an area of 43,000 square miles, and a population of 8,000,000 souls. It is entirely outside and west of the limits of modern Corea.

In addition to the space already named, the fluctuating boundaries of this ancient kingdom embraced at later periods much territory beyond the Liao River toward Peking, and inside the line now marked by the Great Wall. To the east the modern province of Ping-an was included in Chō-sen, the Ta-tong River being its most stable boundary. "Scientific frontiers," though sought for in those ancient times, were rather ideal than hard and fast. With all due allowance for elastic boundaries, we may say that ancient Chō-sen lay chiefly within the Liao Tung peninsula and the Corean province of Ping-an, that the Liao and the Ta-tong Rivers enclosed it, and that its northern border lay along the 42d parallel of latitude.

The descendants of Ki Tsze are said to have ruled the country until the fourth century before the Christian era. Their names and deeds are alike unknown, but it is stated that there were forty-one generations, making a blood-line of eleven hundred and thirty-one years. The line came to an end in 9 A.D., though they had lost power long before this time.

By common consent of Chinese and native tradition, Ki Tsze is the founder of Corean social order. If this tradition be true, the civilization of the hermit nation nearly equals, in point of time, that of China, and is one of the very oldest in the world, being contemporaneous with that of Egypt and Chaldea. It is certain that the natives plume themselves upon their antiquity, and that the particular vein of Corean arrogance and contempt for western civilization is kindred to that of the Hindoos and Chinese. From the lofty height of thirty centuries of tradition, which to them is unchallenged history, they look with pitying contempt upon the upstart nations of yesterday, who live beyond the sea under some other heaven. When the American Admiral, John Rodgers, in

1871, entered the Han River with his fleet, hoping to make a treaty, he was warned off with the repeated answer that "Corea was satisfied with her civilization of four thousand years, and wanted no other." The perpetual text of all letters from Seoul to Peking, of all proclamations against Christianity, of all death-warrants of converts, and of the oft-repeated refusals to open trade with foreigners is the praise of Ki Tsze as the founder of the virtue and order of "the little kingdom," and the loyalty of Corea to his doctrines.

In the letter of the king to the Chinese emperor, dated November 25, 1801, the language following the opening sentence is as given below :

"His Imperial Majesty knows that since the time when the remnants of the army of the Yin dynasty migrated to the East [1122 B.C.], the little kingdom has always been distinguished by its exactness in fulfilling all that the rites prescribe, justice and loyalty, and in general by fidelity to her duties," etc., etc.

In a royal proclamation against the Christian religion, dated January 25, 1802, occurs the following sentence :

"The kingdom granted to Ki Tsze has enjoyed great peace during four hundred years [since the establishment of the ruling dynasty], in all the extent of its territory of two thousand *ri* and more," etc.

These are but specimens from official documents which illustrate their pride in antiquity, and the reverence in which their first law giver is held by the Coreans.

Nevertheless, though Kishi may possibly be called the founder of ancient Chō-sen, and her greatest legislator, yet he can scarcely be deemed the ancestor of the people now inhabiting the Corean peninsula. For the modern Coreans are descended from a stock of later origin, and quite different from the ancient Chō-senese. From Ki Tsze, however, sprang a line of kings, and it is possible that his blood courses in some of the noble families of the kingdom.

As the most ancient traditions of Japan and Corea are based on Chinese writings, there is no discrepancy in their accounts of the beginning of Chō-sen history.

Ki Tsze and his colonists were simply the first immigrants to the country northeast of China, of whom history speaks. He found other people on the soil before him, concerning whose origin nothing is known in writing. The land was not densely populated, but of their numbers, or time of coming of the aborigines, or whether of the same race as the tribes in the outlying islands of Japan, no means yet in our power can give answer.

Even the story of Ki Tsze, when critically examined, does not satisfy the rigid demands of modern research. Mayers, in his "Chinese Reader's Manual" (p. 369), does not concede the first part of the Chow dynasty (1122 B.C.–255 A.D.) to be more than semi-historical, and places the beginning of authentic Chinese history between 781 and 719 B.C., over four centuries after Ki Tsze's time. Ross (p. 11) says that "the story of Kitsu is not impossible, but it is to be received with suspicion." It is not at all improbable that the Chō-sen of Ki Tsze's founding lay in the Sungari valley, and was extended southward at a later period.

It is not for us to dissect too critically the tradition concerning the founder of Corea, nor to locate exactly the scene of his labors. Suffice it to say that the general history, prior to the Christian era, of the country whose story we are to tell, divides itself into that of the north, or Chō-sen, and that of the south, below the Ta-tong River, in which region three kingdoms arose and flourished, with varying fortunes, during a millennium.

We return now to the well-established history of Chō-sen. The Great Wall of China was built by Cheng, the founder of the Tsin dynasty (B.C. 255–209), who began the work in 239 A.D. Before his time, China had been a feudal conglomerate of petty, warring kingdoms. He, by the power of the sword, consolidated them into one homogeneous empire and took the title of the "First Universal Emperor" (Shi Whang Ti). Not content with sweeping away feudal institutions, and building the Great Wall, he ordered all the literary records and the ancient scriptures of Confucius to be destroyed by fire. Yet the empire, whose perpetuity he thought to secure by building a rampart against the barbarians without, and by destroying the material for rebellious thought within, fell to pieces soon after, at his death, when left to the care of a foolish son, and China was plunged into bloody anarchy again.

One of these petty kingdoms that arose on the ruins of the empire was that of Yen, which began to encroach upon its eastern neighbor Chō-sen.

In the later days of the Ki Tsze family, great anarchy prevailed, and the last kings of the line were unable to keep their domain in order, or guard its boundaries.

Taking advantage of its weakness, the king of Yen began boldly and openly to seize upon Chō-sen territory, annexing thousands of

square miles to his own domain.　By a spasmodic effort, the successors of Ki Tsze again became ascendant, reannexing a large
part of the territory of Yen, and receiving great numbers of her
people, who had fled from civil war in China, within the borders of
Chō-sen for safety and peace.

Thus the spoiler was spoiled, but, later on, the kingdom of Yen
was again set up, and the rival states fixed their boundaries and
made peace.　The Han dynasty in B.C. 206 claimed the imperial
power, and sent a summons to the king of Yen to become vassal.
On his refusing, the Chinese emperor despatched an army against
him, defeated his forces in battle, extinguished his dynasty, and annexed his kingdom.

One of the survivors of this revolt, named Wei-man, with one
thousand of his followers, fled to the east.　Dressing themselves
like wild savages they entered Chō-sen, pretending, with Gibeoni-
tish craft, that they had come from the far west, and begged to be
received as subjects.

Kijun, the king, like another Joshua, believing their professions, welcomed them and made their leader a vassal of high rank,
with the title of 'Guardian of the Western Frontier.'　He also set
apart a large tract of land for his salary and support.

In his post at the west, Wei-man played the traitor, and collecting a number of his former countrymen from the Yen province,
suddenly sent to Kijun a messenger, informing him that a large
Chinese army of the conquering Han was about to invade Chō-sen.
At the same time, he suggested that he should be called to the
royal side and be made Protector of the Capital.　His desire being
granted, he hastened with his forces and suddenly appearing before
the royal castle, attacked it.　Kijun was beaten, and fled by sea,
escaping in a boat to the southern end of the peninsula.

Wei-man then proclaimed himself King of Chō-sen, 194 B.C.　He
set out on a career of conquest and seized several of the neighboring provinces, and Chō-sen again expanded her boundaries to cover
an immense area.　Wei-man built a city somewhere east of the Ta-
tong River.　It was named Wang-hien.

Two provinces of modern Corea were thus included within Chō-
sen at this date.　The new kingdom grew in wealth, power, and
intelligence.　Many thousands of the Chinese gentry, fleeing before
the conquering arms of the Han "usurpers," settled within the limits of Chō-sen, adding greatly to its prosperity.

During the reign of Yukio (Chinese, Yow Jin), the grandson of

Wei-man, he received a summons to become vassal to the Chinese emperor, who sublimely declared that henceforward the eastern frontier of China should be the Ta-tong River—thus virtually wiping out Chō-sen with a proclamation. In B.C. 109, a Chinese ambassador sailed over from China, entered the Ta-tong River, and visited Yukio in his castle. He plead in vain with Yukio to render homage to his master.

Nevertheless, to show his respect for the emperor and his envoy, Yukio sent an escort to accompany the latter on his way. The sullen Chinaman, angry at his defeat, accepted the safe conduct of the Chō-sen troops until beyond the Ta-tong River, and then treacherously put their chief to death. Hurrying back to his master, he glossed over his defeat, and boasted of his perfidious murder. He was rewarded with the appointment of the governorship of Liao Tung.

Smarting at the insult and menace of this act, Yukio, raising an army, marched to the west and slew the traitor. Having thus unfurled the standard of defiance against the mighty Han dynasty, he returned to his castle, and awaited with anxious preparation the coming of the invading hosts which he knew would be hurled upon him from China.

The avenging expedition, that was to carry the banners of China farther toward the sunrise than ever before, was despatched both by land and sea, B.C. 108. The horse and foot soldiers took the land route around the head of Liao Tung Gulf, crossed on the ice of the Yalu River, and marched south to the Ta-tong, where the Chō-sen men attacked their van and scattered it.

The fleet sailed over from Shantung, and landed a force of several thousand men on the Corean shore, in February or March, B.C. 107. Without waiting for the entire army to penetrate the country, Yukio attacked the advance guards and drove them to the mountains in disorder.

Diplomacy was now tried, and a representative of the emperor was sent to treat with Yukio. The latter agreed to yield and become vassal, but had no confidence in the general whom he had just defeated. His memory of Chinese perfidy was still so fresh, that he felt unable to trust himself to his recently humbled enemies, and the negotiations ended in failure. As usual, with the unsuccessful, the Chinaman lost his head.

Recourse was again had to the sword. The Chinese crossed the Ta-tong River on the north, and defeating the Chō-sen army,

2

marched to the king's capital, and laid siege to it in conjunction with the naval forces. In spite of their superior numbers, the invaders were many months vainly beleaguering the fortress. Yet, though the garrison wasted daily, the king would not yield. Knowing that defeat, with perhaps a cruel massacre, awaited them, four Chō-sen men, awaiting their opportunity, during the fighting, discharged their weapons at Yukio, and leaving him dead, opened the gates of the citadel, and the Chinese entered.

With the planting of the Han banners on the city walls, B.C. 107, the existence of the kingdom of Chō-sen came to an end. Henceforth, for several centuries, Liao Tung and the land now comprised within the two northwestern provinces of Corea, were parts of China.

The conquered territory was at once divided into four provinces, two of which comprised that part of Corea north of the Ta-tong River. The other two were in Liao Tung, occupying its eastern and its western half. Within the latter was the district of Kokorai, or Kaokuli, at whose history we shall now glance.

Coin of Modern Chō-sen.   "Chō-sen, Current Treasure."

CHAPTER III.

SOMEWHERE north of that vast region watered by the Sungari River, itself only a tributary to the Amur, there existed, according to Chinese tradition, in very ancient times, a petty kingdom called Korai, or To-li. Out of this kingdom sprang the founder of the Corean race. Slightly altering names, we may say in the phrase of Genesis: "Out of Korai went forth Ko and builded Corea," though what may be sober fact is wrapped up in the following fantastic legend.

Long, long ago, in the kingdom called To-li, or *Korai* (so pronounced, though the characters are not those for the Korai of later days), there lived a king, in whose harem was a waiting-maid. One day, while her master was absent on a hunt, she saw, floating in the atmosphere, a glistening vapor which entered her bosom. This ray or tiny cloud seemed to be about as big as an egg. Under its influence, she conceived.

The king, on his return, discovered her condition, and made up his mind to put her to death. Upon her explanation, however, he agreed to spare her life, but at once lodged her in prison.

The child that was born proved to be a boy, which the king promptly cast among the pigs. But the swine breathed into his nostrils and the baby lived. He was next put among the horses, but they also nourished him with their breath, and he lived. Struck by this evident will of Heaven, that the child should live, the king listened to its mother's prayers, and permitted her to nourish and train him in the palace. He grew up to be a fair youth, full of energy, and skilful in archery. He was named "Light of the East," and the king appointed him Master of his stables.

One day, while out hunting, the king permitted him to give an exhibition of his skill. This he did, drawing bow with such unerring aim that the royal jealousy was kindled, and he thought of nothing but how to compass the destruction of the youth. Knowing that he would be killed if he remained in the royal service, the young archer fled the kingdom. He directed his course to the southeast, and came to the borders of a vast and impassable river, most probably the Sungari. Knowing his pursuers were not far behind him he cried out, in a great strait,

The Founder of Fuyu Crossing the Sungari River. (Drawn by G. Hashimoto, Yedo, 1853.)

"Alas! shall I, who am the child of the Sun, and the grandson of the Yellow River, be stopped here powerless by this stream."

So saying he shot his arrows at the water.

Immediately all the fishes of the river assembled together in a thick shoal, making so dense a mass that their bodies became a floating bridge. On this, the young prince (and according to the

Japanese version of the legend, three others with him), crossed the stream and safely reached the further side. No sooner did he set foot on land than his pursuers appeared on the opposite shore, when the bridge of fishes at once dissolved. His three companions stood ready to act as his guides. One of the three was dressed in a costume made of sea-weeds, a second in hempen garments, and a third in embroidered robes. Arriving at their city, he became the king of the tribe and kingdom of Fuyu, which lay in the fertile and well-watered region between the Sungari River and the Shan Alyn, or Ever-White Mountains. It extended several hundred miles east and west of a line drawn southward through Kirin, the larger half lying on the west.

Fuyu, as described by a Chinese writer of the Eastern Han dynasty (25 B.C.–190 A.D.), was a land of fertile soil, in which "the five cereals" (wheat, rice, millet, beans, and sorghum) could be raised. The men were tall, muscular, and brave, and withal generous and courteous to each other. Their arms were bows and arrows, swords, and lances. They were skilful horsemen. Their ornaments were large pearls, and cut jewels of red jade. They made spirits from grain, and were fond of drinking bouts, feasting, dancing, and singing. With many drinkers there were few cups. The latter were rinsed in a bowl of water, and with great ceremony passed from one to another. They ate with chopsticks, out of bowls, helping themselves out of large dishes.

It is a striking fact that the Fuyu people, though living so far from China, were dwellers in cities which they surrounded with palisades or walls of stakes. They lived in wooden houses, and stored their crops in granaries.

In the administration of justice, they were severe and prompt. They had regular prisons, and fines were part of their legal system. The thief must repay twelve-fold. Adultery was punished by the death of both parties. Further revenge might be taken upon the woman by exposing her dead body on a mound. Certain relatives of a criminal were denied burial in a coffin. The other members of the family of a criminal suffering capital punishment were sold as slaves. Murderers were buried alive with their victims.

The Fuyu religion was a worship of Heaven, their greatest festival being in the eleventh month, when they met joyfully together, laying aside all grudges and quarrels, and freeing their prisoners. Before setting out on a military expedition they worshipped Heaven, and sacrificed an ox, examining the hoof, to obtain an omen. If the cloven part remained separated, the portent was evil, if the hoof closed together, the omen was auspicious.

The Fuyu chief men or rulers were named after the domestic beasts, beginning with their noblest animal, the horse, then the ox, the dog, etc. Rulers of cities were of this order. Their king was buried at his death in a coffin made of jade.

Evidently the Fuyu people were a vigorous northern race, well clothed and fed, rich in grain, horses and cattle, possessing the arts of life, with considerable literary culture, and well advanced in social order and political knowledge. Though the Chinese writers classed them among barbarians, they were, in contrast with their immediate neighbors, a civilized nation. Indeed, to account for such a high stage of civilization thus early and so far fom China, Mr. Ross suggests that the scene of the Ki Tsze's labors was in Fuyu, rather than in Chō-sen. Certain it is that the Fuyu people were the first nation of Manchuria to emerge from barbarism, and become politically well organized. It is significant, as serving to support the conjecture that Ki Tsze founded Fuyu, that we discern, even in the early history of this vigorous nation, the institution of feudalism. We find a king and nobles, with fortified cities, and wealthy men, with farms, herds of horses, cattle, and granaries. We find also a class of serfs, created by the degradation of criminals or their relatives. The other Manchurian people, or barbarians, surrounding China, were still in the nomadic or patriarchal state. Why so early beyond China do we find a well-developed feudal system and high political organization?

It was from feudal China, the China of the Yin dynasty, from which Ki Tsze emigrated to the northeast. Knowing no other form of government, he, if their founder, doubtless introduced feudal forms of government.

Whatever may be thought of the theory there suggested, it is certainly surprising to find a distinctly marked feudal system, already past the rudimentary stage, in the wilderness of Manchuria, a thousand miles away from the seats of Chinese culture, as early as the Christian era.

As nearly the whole of Europe was at some time feudalized, so China, Corea, and Japan have each passed through this stage of political life.

The feudal system in China was abolished by Shi Whang Ti,

the first universal Emperor, B.C. 221, but that of Japan only after an interval of 2,000 years, surviving until 1871. It lingers still in Corea, whose history it has greatly influenced, as our subsequent narrative will prove. In addition to the usual features of feudalism, the existence of serfdom, in fact as well as in form, is proved by the testimony of Dutch and French observers, and of the language itself. The richness of Corean speech, in regard to every phase and degree of servitude, would suffice for a Norman landholder in mediæval England, or for a Carolina cotton-planter before the American civil war.

Out of this kingdom of Fuyu came the people who are the ancestors of the modern Coreans. In the same Chinese history which describes Fuyu, we have a picture of the kingdom of Kokorai (or Kao-ku-li), which had Fuyu for its northern and Chō-sen for its southern neighbor. "The land was two thousand *li* square, and contained many great mountains, and deep valleys." There was a tradition among the Eastern barbarians that they were an offshoot from Fuyu. Hence their language and laws were very much alike. The nation was divided into five families, named after the four points of the compass, with a yellow or central tribe.

Evidently this means that a few families, perhaps five in number, leaving Fuyu, set out toward the south, and in the valleys west of the Yalu River and along the 42d parallel, founded a new nation. Their first king was Ko, who, perhaps, to gain the prestige of ancient descent, joined his name to that of Korai (written however with the characters which make the sound of modern Korai) and thus the realm of Kokorai received its name.

A Japanese writer derives the term Kokorai from words selected out of a passage in the Chinese classics referring to the high mountains. The first character Ko, in Kokorai, means high, and it was under the shadows of the lofty Ever White Mountains that this vigorous nation had its cradle and its home in youth. Here, too, its warriors nourished their strength until their clouds of horsemen burst upon the frontiers of the Chinese empire, and into the old kingdom of Chō-sen. The people of this young state were rich in horses and cattle, but less given to agriculture. They lived much in the open air, and were fierce, impetuous, strong, and hardy. They were fond of music and pleasure at night. Especially characteristic was their love of decoration and display. At their public gatherings they decked themselves in

dresses embroidered with gold and silver. Their houses were also
adorned in various ways. Their chief display was at funerals,
when a prodigal outlay of precious metals, jewels, and embroi-
deries was exhibited.

In their religion they sacrificed to Heaven, to the spirits of the
land, and of the harvests, to the morning star, and to the celestial
and invisible powers. There were no prisons, but when crimes
were committed the chiefs, after deliberation, put the criminal to
death and reduced the wives and children to slavery. In this way
serfs were provided for labor. In their burial customs, they
made a cairn, and planted fir-trees around it, as many Japanese
tombs are made.

In the general forms of their social, religious, and political life,
the people of Fuyu and Kokorai were identical, or nearly so;
while both closely resemble the ancient Japanese of Yamato.

The Chinese authors also state that these people were already
in possession of the Confucian classics, and had attained to an unusual degree of literary culture. Their officials were divided into
twelve ranks, which was also the ancient Japanese number. In
the method of divination, in the wearing of flowery costumes, and
in certain forms of etiquette, they and the Japanese were alike.
As is now well known, the ancient form of government of the
Yamato Japanese (that is, of the conquering race from Corea and
the north) was a rude feudalism and not a monarchy. Further,
the central part of Japan, first held by the ancestors of the mikado, consists of *five* provinces, like the Kokorai division, into five
clans or tribes.

At the opening of the Christian era we find the people of Kokorai already strong and restless enough to excite attention from
the Chinese court. In 9 A.D. they were recognized as a nation
with their own "kings," and classified with Huentu, one of the
districts of old Chō-sen. One of these kings, in the year 30, sent
tribute to the Chinese emperor. In 50 A.D. Kokorai, by invitation,
sent their warriors to assist the Chinese army against a rebel horde
in the northwest. In A.D. 70 the men of Kokorai descended upon
Liao Tung, and having now a taste for border war and conquest,
they marched into the petty kingdom of Wei, which lay in what is
now the extreme northeast of Corea. Absorbing this little country, they kept up constant warfare against the Chinese. Though
their old kinsmen, the Fuyu men, were at times allies of the Han,
yet they gradually spread themselves eastward and southward, so

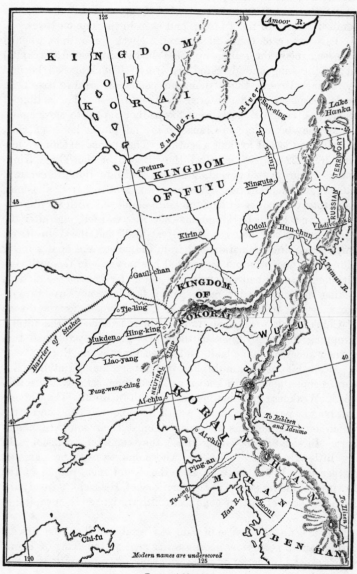

Fuyu and Manchiu.

that by 169 A.D. the Kokorai kingdom embraced the whole of the territory of old Chō-sen, or of Liao Tung, with all the Corean peninsula north of the Ta-tong, and even to the Tumen River.

This career of conquest suffered a check for a time, when a Chinese expedition, sailing up the Yalu River, invested the capital city of the king and defeated his army. The king fled beyond the Tumen River. Eight thousand people are said to have been made prisoners or slaughtered by the Chinese. For a time it seemed as though Kokorai were too badly crippled to move again.

Anarchy broke out in China, on the fall of the house of Han, A.D. 220, and lasted for half a century. That period of Chinese history, from 221 to 277, is called the "Epoch of the Three Kingdoms." During this period, and until well into the fifth century, while China was rent into "Northern" and "Southern" divisions, the military activities of Kokorai were employed with varying results against the petty kingdoms that rose and fell, one after the other, on the soil between the Great Wall and the Yalu River. During this time the nation, free from the power and oppression of China, held her own and compacted her power. In the fifth century her warriors had penetrated nearly as far west as the modern Peking in their cavalry raids. Wily in diplomacy, as brave in war, they sent tribute to both of the rival claimants for the throne of China which were likely to give them trouble in the future. Dropping the family name of their first king, they retained that of their ancestral home-land, and called their nation Korai.

Meanwhile, as they multiplied in numbers, the migration of Kokorai people, henceforth known as Korai men, set steadily southward. Weakness in China meant strength in Korai. The Chinese had bought peace with their Eastern neighbors by titles and gifts, which left the Koraians free to act against their southern neighbors. In steadily displacing these, they came into collision with the little kingdom of Hiaksai, whose history will be narrated farther on. It will be seen that the Korai men, people of the Fuyu race, finally occupied the territory of Hiaksai. Already the Koraians, sure of further conquest southward, fixed their capital at Ping-an.

In 589 A.D. the house of Sui was established on the dragon throne, and a portentous message was sent to the King of Korai, which caused the latter to make vigorous war preparations. Evidently the Chinese emperor meant to throttle the young giant of the north, while the young giant was equally determined to live.

The movement of a marauding force of Koraians, even to the inside of the Great Wall, gave the bearded dragon not only the pretext of war but of annexation.

For this purpose an army of three hundred thousand men and a fleet of several hundred war-junks were prepared. The latter were to sail over from Shantung, and enter the Ta-tong River, the goal of the expedition being Ping-an city, the Koraian capital.

The horde started without provisions, and arrived in mid-summer at the Liao River in want of food. While waiting, during the hot weather, in this malarious and muddy region, the soldiers died by tens of thousands of fever and plague. The incessant rains soon rendered the roads impassable and transport of provisions an impossibility. Disease melted the mighty host away, and the army, reduced to one-fifth its numbers, was forced to retreat. The war-junks fared no better, for storms in the Yellow Sea drove them back or foundered them by the score.

Such a frightful loss of life and material did not deter the next emperor, the infamous Yang (who began the Grand Canal), from following out the scheme of his father, whom he conveniently poisoned while already dying. In spite of the raging famines and losses by flood, the emperor ordered magazines for the armies of invasion to be established near the coast, and contingents of troops for the twenty-four corps to be raised in every province. All these preparations caused local famines and drove many of the people into rebellion.

This army, one of the greatest ever assembled in China, numbered over one million men. Its equipment consisted largely of banners, gongs, and trumpets. The undisciplined horde began their march, aiming to reach the Liao River before the hot season set in. They found the Koraian army ready to dispute their passage. Three bridges, hastily constructed, were thrown across the stream, on which horse and foot pressed eagerly toward the enemy. The width of the river had, however, been miscalculated and the bridges were too short, so that many thousands of the Chinese were drowned or killed by the Koraians, at unequal odds, while fighting on the shore. In two days, however, the bridges were lengthened and the whole force crossed over. The Chinese van pursued their enemy, slaughtering ten thousand before they could gain the fortified city of Liao Tung. Once inside their walls, however, the Korai soldiers were true to their reputation of being splendid garrison fighters. Instead of easy victory the

Chinese army lay around the city unable, even after several
months' besieging, to breach the walls or weaken the spirit of the
defenders.

Meanwhile the other division had marched northward and
eastward, according to the plan of the campaign. Eight of these
army corps, numbering 300,000 men, arrived and went into camp
on the west bank of the Yalu River. In spite of express orders to
the contrary, the soldiers had thrown away most of the hundred
days' rations of grain with which they started, and the commissariat was very low. The Koraian commander, carrying out the
Fabian policy, tempted them away from their camp, and led them
by skirmishing parties to within a hundred miles of Ping-an.
The Chinese fleet lay within a few leagues of the invading army,
but land and sea forces were mutually ignorant of each other's vicinity. Daring not to risk the siege of a city so well fortified by
nature and art as Ping-an, in his present lack of supplies, the Chinese general reluctantly ordered a retreat, which began in late
summer, the nearest base of supplies being Liao Tung, four hundred miles away and through an enemy's country.

This was the signal for the Koraians to assume the offensive,
and like the Cossacks, upon the army of Napoleon, in Russia, they
hung upon the flanks of the hungry fugitives, slaughtering thousands upon thousands.

When the Chinese host were crossing the Chin-chion River,
the Koraian army fell in full force upon them, and the fall of the
commander of their rear-guard turned defeat into a rout. The
disorderly band of fugitives rested not till well over and beyond
the Yalu River. Of that splendid army of 300,000 men only a
few thousand reached Liao Tung city. The weapons, spoil, and
prisoners taken by the Koraians were "myriads of myriads of
myriads." The naval forces in the river, on hearing the amazing
news of their comrades' defeat, left Corea and crept back to China.
The Chinese emperor was so enraged at the utter failure of his
prodigious enterprise, that he had the fugitive officers publicly
put to death as an example.

In spite of the disasters of the previous year, the emperor
Yang, in 613, again sent an army to besiege Liao Tung city. On
this occasion scaling ladders, 150 feet long, and towers, mounted
on wheels, were used with great effect. Just on the eve of the
completion of their greatest work and tower the Chinese camp
was suddenly abandoned, the emperor being called home to put

down a formidable rebellion. So cautious were the besieged and
so sudden was the flight of the besiegers, that it was noon before
a Koraian ventured into camp, and two days elapsed before they
discovered that the retreat was not feigned. Then the Koraian
garrison attacked the Chinese rear-guard with severe loss.

The rebellion at home having been put down the emperor
again cherished the plan of crushing Korai, but other and greater
insurrections broke out that required his attention; for the three
expeditions against Corea had wasted the empire even as they had
sealed the doom of the Sui dynasty. Though no land forces could
be spared, a new fleet was sent to Corea to lay siege to Ping-an city.
Even with large portions of his dominions in the hands of rebels,
Yang never gave up his plan of humbling Korai. This project
was the cause of the most frightful distress in China, and seeing
no hope of saving the country except by the murder of the infamous emperor, coward, drunkard, tyrant, and voluptuary, a band
of conspirators, headed by Yü Min, put him to death and Korai
had rest.

To summarize this chapter. It is possible that Ki Tsze was
the founder of Fuyu. The Kokorai tribes were people who had
migrated from Fuyu, and settled north and west of the upper
waters of the Yalu River. They entered into relations with the
Chinese as early as 9 A.D., and coming into collision with them by
the year 70, they kept up a fitful warfare with them, sustaining
mighty invasions, until the seventh century, while in the mean-
time Korai, instead of being crushed by China, grew in area and
numbers until the nation had spread into the peninsula, and overrun it as far as the Han River.

Thus far the history of Corea has been that of the northern
and western part of the peninsula, and has been derived chiefly
from Chinese sources. We turn now to the southern and eastern
portions, and in narrating their history we shall point out their
relations with Japan as well as with China, relying largely for our
information upon the Japanese annals.

CHAPTER IV.

SAM-HAN, OR SOUTHERN COREA.

AT the time of the suppression of Chō-sen and the incorpora-
tion of its territory with the Chinese Empire, B.C. 107, all Corea

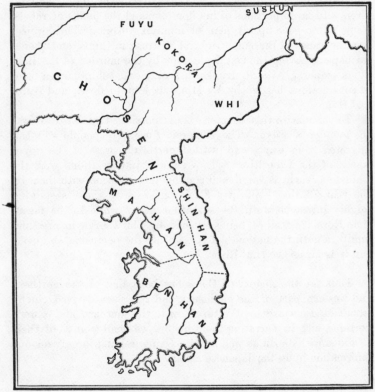

Map of Sam-han in Southern Corea.

south of the Ta-tong River was divided into three *han,* or geographical divisions. Their exact boundaries are uncertain, but
their general topography may be learned from the map.

MA-HAN AND BEN-HAN.

This little country included fifty-four tribes or clans, each one independent of the other, and living under a sort of patriarchal government. The larger tribes are said to have been composed of ten thousand, and the smaller of a thousand, families each. Round numbers, however, in ancient records are worth little for critical purposes.

South of the Ma-han was the Ben-han, in which were twelve tribes, having the same manners and customs as the Ma-han, and speaking a different yet kindred dialect. One of these clans formed the little kingdom of Amana, from which came the first visit of Coreans recorded in the Japanese annals.

After the overthrow of his family and kingdom by the traitor Wei-man, Kijun, the king of old Chō-sen escaped to the sea and fled south toward the archipelago. He had with him a number of his faithful adherents, their wives and children. He landed among one of the clans of Ma-han, composed of Chinese refugees, who, not wishing to live under the Han emperors, had crossed the Yellow Sea. On account of their numbering, originally, one hundred families, they called themselves Hiaksai. Either by conquest or invitation Kijun soon became their king. Glimpses of the manner of life of these early people are given by a Chinese writer.

The Ma-han people were agricultural, dwelling in villages, but neither driving nor riding oxen or horses, most probably because they did not possess them. Their huts were made of earth banked upon timber, with the door in the roof. They went bareheaded, and coiled or tied their hair in a knot. They set no value on gold, jewels, or embroidery, but wore pearls sewed on their clothes and hung on their necks and ears. Perhaps the word here translated "pearl" may be also applied to drilled stones of a cylindrical or curved shape, like the *magatama*, or "bent jewels," of the ancient Japanese. They shod their feet with sandals, and wore garments of woven stuff. In etiquette they were but slightly advanced, paying little honor to women or to the aged. Like our Indian bucks, the young men tested their endurance by torture. Slitting the skin of the back, they ran a cord through the flesh, upon which was hung a piece of wood. This was kept suspended till the man, unable longer to endure it, cried out to have it taken off.

After the field work was over, in early summer, they held drinking bouts, in honor of the spirits, with songs and dances. Scores of men, quickly following each other, stamped on the ground to beat time as they danced. In the late autumn, after harvests, they repeated these ceremonies. In each clan there was a man, chosen as ruler, to sacrifice to the spirits of heaven. On a great pole they hung drums and bells for the service of the heavenly spirits. Perhaps these are the originals of the tall and slender pagodas with their pendant wind-bells at the many eaves and corners.

Among the edible products of Ma-han were fowls with tails five feet in length. These "hens with tails a yard long" were evidently pheasants—still a delicacy on Corean tables. The large apple-shaped pears, which have a wooden taste, half way between a pear and an apple, were then, as now, produced in great numbers. The flavor improves by cooking.

As Kijun's government was one of vigor, his subjects advanced in civilization, the Hiaksai people gradually extended their authority and influence. The clan names in time faded away or became symbols of family bonds instead of governmental authority, so that by the fourth century Hiaksai had become paramount over all the fifty-four tribes of Ma-han, as well as over some of those of the other two *han*.

Thus arose the kingdom of Hiaksai (called also Kudara by the Japanese, Petsi by the Chinese, and Baiji by the modern Coreans), which has a history extending to the tenth century, when it was extinguished in name and fact in united Corea.

Its relations with Japan were, in the main, friendly, the islanders of the Sunrise Kingdom being comrades in arms with them against their invaders, the Chinese, and their hostile neighbors, the men of Shinra—whose origin we shall now proceed to detail.

SHIN-HAN.

After the fall of the Tsin dynasty in China, a small body of refugees, leaving their native seats, fled across the Yellow Sea toward the Sea of Japan, resting only when over the great mountain chain. They made settlements in the valleys and along the sea-coast. At first they preserved their blood and language pure, forming one of the twelve clans or tribes into which the han or country was divided.

This name Shin (China or Chinese), which points to the origin of the clan, belonged to but one of the twelve tribes in eastern Corea. As in the case of Hiaksai, the Shin tribe, being possessed of superior power and intelligence, extended their authority and boundaries, gradually becoming very powerful. Under their twenty-second hereditary chief, or "king," considering themselves paramount over all the clans, they changed the name of their country to Shinra, which is pronounced in Chinese Sinlo.

Between the years 29 and 70 A.D., according to the Japanese histories, an envoy from Shinra arrived in Japan, and after an audience had of the mikado, presented him with mirrors, swords, jade, and other works of skill and art. In this we have a hint as to the origin of Japanese decorative art. It is evident from these gifts, as well as from the reports of Chinese historians concerning the refined manners, the hereditary aristocracy, and the fortified strongholds of the Shinra people, that their grade of civilization was much higher than that of their northern neighbors. It was certainly superior to that of the Japanese, who, as we shall see, were soon tempted to make descents upon the fertile lands, rich cities, and defenceless coasts of their visitors from the west.

How long the Chinese colonists who settled in Shin-han preserved their language and customs is not known. Though these were lost after a few generations, yet it is evident that their influence on the aborigines of the country was very great. From first to last Shinra excelled in civilization all the petty states in the peninsula, of which at first there were seventy-eight. Unlike the Ma-han, the Shin-han people lived in palisaded cities, and in houses the doors of which were on the ground and not on the roof. They cultivated mulberry-trees, reared the silk-worm, and wove silk into fine fabrics. They used wagons with yoked oxen, and horses for draught, and practised "the law of the road." Marriage was conducted with appropriate ceremony. Dancing, drinking, and singing were favorite amusements, and the lute was played in addition to drums. They understood the art of smelting and working iron, and used this metal as money. They carried on trade with the other *han*, and with Japan. How far these arts owed their encouragement or origin to traders, or travelling merchants from China, is not known. Evidently Shinra enjoyed leadership in the peninsula, largely from her culture, wealth, and knowledge of iron. The curious custom, so well known among

3

American savages, of flattening the heads of newly born infants, is noted among the Shin-han people.

Neither Chinese history nor Japanese tradition, though they give us some account of a few hundred families of emigrants from China who settled in the already inhabited Corean peninsula, throws any light on the aborigines as to whence or when they came. The curtain is lifted only to show us that a few people are already there, with language and customs different from those of China. The descendants of the comparatively few Chinese settlers were no doubt soon lost, with their language and ancestral customs, among the mass of natives. These aboriginal tribes were destined to give way to a new people from the far north, as we shall learn in our further narrative. The Japanese historians seem to distinguish between the San Han, the three countries or confederacies of loosely organized tribes, and the San Goku, or Three Kingdoms. The Coreans, however, speak only of the Sam-han, meaning thereby the three political divisions of the peninsula, and using the word as referring rather to the epoch. The common "cash," or fractional coin current in the country, bears the characters meaning "circulating medium of the Three Kingdoms," or Sam-han. These were Korai in the north, Shinra in the southeast, and Hiaksai in the southwest. Other Japanese names for these were respectively Komé, Shiriaki, and Kudara, the Chinese terms being Kaoli, Sinlo, and Pe-tsi.

Like the three kingdoms of England, Scotland, and Wales, called also Britannia, Caledonia, and Cambria, these Corean states were distinct in origin, were conquered by a race from without, received a rich infusion of alien blood, struggled in rivalry for centuries, and were finally united into one nation, with one flag and one sovereign.

Coin of the Sam-han or the Three Kingdoms. " Sam-han, Current Treasure."

CHAPTER V.

THE history of the peninsular states from the time in which it is first known until the tenth century, is that of almost continuous civil war or border fighting. The boundaries of the rival kingdoms changed from time to time as raid and reprisal, victory or defeat, turned the scale of war. A series of maps of the peninsula expressing the political situation during each century or half-century would show many variations of boundaries, and resemble those of Great Britain when the various native and continental tribes were struggling for its mastery. Something like an attempt to depict these changes in the political geography of the peninsula has been made by the Japanese historian, Otsuki Tōyō, in his work entitled "Historical Periods and Changes of the Japanese Empire."

Yet though our narrative, through excessive brevity, seems to be only a picture of war, we must not forget that Hiaksai, once lowest in civilization, rapidly became, and for a while continued, the leading state in the peninsula. It held the lead in literary culture until crushed by China. The classics of Confucius and Mencius, with letters, writing, and their whole train of literary blessings, were introduced first to the peninsula in Hiaksai. In 374 A.D. Ko-ken was appointed a teacher or master of Chinese literature, and enthusiastic scholars gathered at the court. Buddhism followed with its educational influences, becoming a focus of light and culture. As early as 372 A.D. an apostle of northern Buddhism had penetrated into Liao Tung, and perhaps across the Yalu. In 384 A.D. the missionary Marananda, a Thibetan, formally established temples and monasteries in Hiaksai, in which women as well as men became scholastics. Long before this new element of civilization was rooted in Shinra or Korai, the faith of India was established and flourishing in the little kingdom of Hiaksai, so that its influences were felt as far as Japan. The first teacher of Chinese letters and ethics in Nippon was a Corean named Wani, as was also the first missionary who carried the images and sutras of northern Buddhism across the Sea of Japan. To Hiaksai more than to any other Corean state Japan owes her first impulse toward the civilization of the west.

Hiaksai came into collision with Kokorai as early as 345 A.D., at which time also Shinra suffered the loss of several cities. In the fifth century a Chinese army, sent by one of the emperors of the Wei dynasty to enforce the payment of tribute, was defeated by Hiaksai. Such unexpected military results raised the reputation of "the eastern savages" so high in the imperial mind, that the emperor offered the King of Hiaksai the title of "Great Protector of the Eastern Frontier." By this act the independence of the little kingdom was virtually recognized. In the sixth century, having given and received Chinese aid and comfort in alliance with Shinra against Korai, Hiaksai was ravaged in her borders by the troops of her irate neighbor on the north. Later on we find these two states in peace with each other and allied against Shinra, which had become a vassal of the Tang emperors of China.

From this line of China's rulers the kingdoms of Korai and Hiaksai were to receive crushing blows. In answer to Shinra's prayer for aid, the Chinese emperor, in 660, despatched from Shantung a fleet of several hundred sail with 100,000 men on board. Against this host from the west the Hiaksai army could make little resistance, though they bravely attacked the invaders, but only to be beaten. After a victory near the mouth of the Rin-yin River, the Chinese marched at once to the capital of Hiaksai and again defeated, with terrible slaughter, the provincial army. The king fled to the north, and the city being nearly empty of defenders, the feeble garrison opened the gates. The Tang banners fluttered on all the walls, and another state was absorbed in the Chinese empire. For a time Hiaksai, like a fly snapped up by an angry dog, is lost in China.

Not long, however, did the little kingdom disappear from sight. In 670 a Buddhist priest, fired with patriotism, raised an army of monks and priests, and joining Fuku-shin (Fu-sin), a brave general, they laid siege to a city held by a large Chinese garrison. At the same time they sent word to the emperor of Japan praying for succor against the "robber kingdom." They also begged that Hōsho (Fung), the youthful son of the late king, then a hostage and pupil at the mikado's court, might be invested with the royal title and sent home. The mikado despatched a fleet of 400 junks and a large body of soldiers to escort the royal heir homeward. On his arrival Hōsho was proclaimed king.

Meanwhile the priest-army and the forces under Fuku-shin had reconquered nearly all their territory, when they suffered a severe defeat near the sea-coast from the large Chinese force hastily despatched to put down the rebellion. The invaders marched eastward and effected a junction with the forces of Shinra. The prospects of Hiaksai were now deplorable.

For even among the men of Hiaksai there was no unity of purpose. Fuku-shin had put the priest-leader to death, which arbitrary act so excited the suspicions of the king that he in turn ordered his general to be beheaded. He then sent to Japan, appealing for reinforcements. The mikado, willing to help an old ally, and fearing that the Chinese, if victorious, might invade his own dominions, quickly responded. The Japanese contingent arrived and encamped near the mouth of the Han River, preparatory to a descent by sea upon Shinra. Unsuspecting the near presence of an enemy, the allies neglected their usual vigilance. A fleet of war-junks, flying the Tang streamers, suddenly appeared off the camp, and while the Japanese were engaging these, the Chinese land forces struck them in flank. Taken by surprise, the mikado's warriors were driven like flocks of sheep into the water and drowned or shot by the Chinese archers. The Japanese vessels were burned as they lay at anchor in the bloody stream, and the remnants of the beaten army got back to their islands in pitiable fragments. Hōsho, after witnessing the destruction of his host, fled to Korai, and the country was given over to the waste and pillage of the infuriated Chinese. The royal line, after thirty generations and nearly seven centuries of rule, became extinct. The sites of cities became the habitations of tigers, and once fertile fields were soon overgrown. Large portions of Hiaksai became a wilderness.

Though the Chinese Government ordered the bodies of those killed in war and the white bones of the victims of famine to be buried, yet many thousands of Hiaksai families fled elsewhere to find an asylum and to found new industries. The people who remained on their fertile lands, as well as all Southern Corea, fell under the sway of Shinra.

The fragments of the beaten Japanese army gradually returned to their native country or settled in Southern Corea. Thousands of the people of Hiaksai, detesting the idea of living as slaves of China, accompanied or followed their allies to Japan. On their arrival, by order of the mikado, 400 emigrants of both sexes were located in the province of Omi, and over 2,000 were distributed in the Kuantō, or Eastern Japan. These colonies of Coreans founded potteries, and their descendants, mingled by blood with the Japanese, follow the trade of their ancestors.

In 710 another body of Hiaksai people, dissatisfied with the poverty of the country and tempted by the offers of the Japanese, formed a colony numbering 1,800 persons and emigrated to Japan. They were settled in Musashi, the province in which Tōkiō, the modern capital, is situated. Various other emigrations of Coreans to Japan of later date are referred to in the annals of the latter country, and it is fair to presume that tens of thousands of emigrants from the peninsula fled from the Tang invasion and mingled with the islanders, producing the composite race that inhabit the islands ruled by the mikado. Among the refugees were many priests and nuns, who brought their books and learning to the court at Nara, and thus diffused about them a literary atmosphere. The establishment of schools, the awakening of the Japanese intellect, and the first beginnings of the literature of Japan, the composition of their oldest historical books, the Kojiki and the Nihongi—all the fruits of the latter half of the seventh and early part of the eighth century—are directly traceable to this influx of the scholars of Hiaksai, which being destroyed by China, lived again in Japan. Even the pronunciation of the Chinese characters as taught by the Hiaksai teachers remains to this day. One of them, the nun Hōmiō, a learned lady, made her system so popular among the scholars that even an imperial proclamation against it could not banish it. She established her school in Tsushima, A.D. 655, and there taught that system of [Chinese] pronunciation [*Go-on*] which still holds sway in Japan, among the ecclesiastical literati, in opposition to the *Kan-on* of the secular scholars. The Go-on, the older of the two pronunciations, is that of ancient North China, the Kan-on is that of mediæval Southern China (Nanking). Corea and Japan having phonetic alphabets have preserved and stereotyped the ancient Chinese pronunciation better than the Chinese language itself, since the Chinese have no phonetic writing, but only ideographic characters, the pronunciation of which varies during the progress of centuries.

Hiaksai had given Buddhism to Japan as early as 552 A.D., but opposition had prevented its spread, the temple was set on fire, and the images of Buddha thrown in the river. In 684 one Sayéki brought another image of Buddha from Corea, and Umako, son of Inamé, a minister at the mikado's court, enshrined it in a chapel on his own grounds. He made Yeben and Simata, two Coreans, his priests, and his daughter a nun. They celebrated a festival, and henceforth Buddhism[1] grew apace.

The country toward the sunrise was then a new land to the peninsulars, just as "the West" is to us, or Australia is to England; and Japan made these fugitives welcome. In their train came industry, learning, and skill, enriching the island kingdom with the best infusion of blood and culture.

Hiaksai was the first of the three kingdoms that was weakened by civil war and then fell a victim to Chinese lust of conquest.

The progress and fall of the other two kingdoms will now be narrated. Beginning with Korai, we shall follow its story from the year 613 A.D., when the invading hordes of the Tang dynasty had been driven out of the peninsula with such awful slaughter by the Koraians.

---

[1] There are colossal stone images at Pe-chiu (Pha-jiu) in the capital province, and at Un-jin in Chung-chong Dō. The former, discovered by Lieutenant J. G. Bernadon, U.S.N., are in the midst of a fir-wood, and are carved in half-figure out of bowlders in place, the heads and caps projecting over the tops of the trees. One wears a square cap and the other a round one, from which Mr. G. W. Aston conjectures that they symbolize the male and female elements in nature (p. 329). At Un-jin in Chung-chong Dō Mr. G. C. Foulke, U.S.N., saw, at a distance of fifteen miles, what seemed to be a lighthouse. On approach, this half-length human figure proved to be a pinnacle of white granite, sixty-four feet high, cut into a representation of Buddha. Similar statues may perhaps be discovered elsewhere. Coreans call such figures *mi-ryek* (stone men, as the Chinese characters given in the French-Corean dictionary read), or *miriok*, from the Chinese *Mi-lē*, or Buddha. (In Japanese, the Buddha to come is *Miroku-butsu*—a verbal coincidence.) Professor Terrien de Lacouperie has written upon this theme with great learning. Besides the lop-ears, forehead-mark, and traditional countenance seen in the Buddhas of Chinese Asia, there is on the Un-jin figure a very high double cap, on which are set two slabs of stone joined by a central column, suggesting both the ceremonial cap of ancient Chinese ritual and the Indian pagoda-like umbrella. These *miriok* stand in what was once Hiaksai. In his "Life in Corea," Mr. Carles gives a picture of the one at Un-jin. Smaller ones exist near monasteries and temples.

CHAPTER VI.

EPOCH OF THE THREE KINGDOMS.—KORAI.

AFTER the struggle in which the Corean tiger had worsted the Western Dragon, early in the seventh century, China and Korai were for a generation at peace. The bones of the slain were buried, and sacrificial fires for the dead soothed the spirits of the victims. The same imperial messenger, who in 622 was sent to supervise these offices of religion, also visited each of the courts of the three kingdoms. So successful was he in his mission of peaceful diplomacy, that each of the Corean states sent envoys with tribute and congratulation to the imperial throne. In proof of his good wishes, the emperor returned to his vassals all his prisoners, and declared that their young men would be received as students in the Imperial University at his capital. Henceforth, as in many instances during later centuries, the sons of nobles and promising youth from Korai, Shinra, and Hiaksai went to study at Nanking, where their envoys met the Arab traders.

Korai having been divided into five provinces, or circuits, named respectively the Home, North, South, East, and West divisions, extended from the Sea of Japan to the Liao River, and enjoyed a brief spell of peace, except always on the southern border ; for the chronic state of Korai and Shinra was that of mutual hostility. On the north, beyond the Tumen River, was the kingdom of Pu-hai, with which Korai was at peace, and Japan was in intimate relations, and China at jealous hostility.

The Chinese court soon began to look with longing eyes on the territory of that part of Korai lying west of the Yalu River, believing it to be a geographical necessity that it should become their scientific frontier, while the emperor cherished the hope of soon rectifying it. Though unable to forget the fact that one of his predecessors had wasted millions of lives and tons of treasure in vainly attempting to humble Kokorai, his ambition and pride spurred him on to wade through slaughter to conquest and revenge. He waited only for a pretext.

This time the destinies of the Eastern Kingdom were profoundly influenced by the character of the feudalism brought into it from ancient times, and which was one of the characteristic institutions of the Fuyu race.

The Government of Korai was simply that of a royal house, holding, by more or less binding ties of loyalty, powerful nobles, who in turn held their lands on feudal tenure. In certain contingencies these noble land-holders were scarcely less powerful than the king himself.

In 641 one of these liegemen, whose ambition the king had in vain attempted to curb and even to put to death, revenged himself by killing the king with his own hands. He then proclaimed as sovereign the nephew of the dead king, and made himself prime minister. Having thus the control of all power in the state, and being a man of tremendous physical strength and mental ability, all the people submitted quietly to the new order of things, and were at the same time diverted, being sent to ravage Shinra, annexing all the country down to the 37th parallel. The Chinese emperor gave investiture to the new king, but ordered this Corean Warwick to recall his troops from invading Shinra, the ally of China. The minister paid his tribute loyally, but refused to acknowledge the right of China to interfere in Corean politics. The tribute was then sent back with insult, and war being certain to follow, Korai prepared for the worst. War with China has been so constant a phenomenon in Corean history that a special term, Ho-ran, exists and is common in the national annals, since the "Chinese wars" have been numbered by the score.

Again the sails of an invading fleet whitened the waters of the Yellow Sea, carrying the Chinese army of chastisement that was to land at the head of the peninsula, while two bodies of troops were despatched by different routes landward. The Tang emperor was a stanch believer in Whang Ti, the Asiatic equivalent of the European doctrine of the divine right of kings to reign—a tenet as easily found by one looking for it in the Confucian classics, as in the Hebrew scriptures. He professed to be marching simply to vindicate the honor of majesty and to punish the regicide rebel, but not to harm nobles or people. The invaders soon overran Liao Tung, and city after city fell. The emperor himself accompanied the army and burned his bridges after the crossing of every river. In spite of the mud and the summer rains he steadily pushed his way on, helping with his own hands in the works at the sieges of the walled cities—the ruins of which still litter the plains of Liao Tung. In one of these, captured only after a protracted investment, 10,000 Koraians are said to have been slain. In case of submission on summons, or after a slight defence, the besieged were leniently and even kindly treated. By July all the country west of the Yalu was in possession of the Chinese, who had crossed the river and arrived at Anchiu, only forty miles north of Ping-an city.

By tremendous personal energy and a general levy in mass, an army of 150,000 Korai men was sent against the Chinese, which took up a position on a hill about three miles from the city. The plan of the battle that ensued, made by the Chinese emperor himself, was skilfully carried out by his lieutenants, and a total defeat of the entrapped Koraian army followed, the slain numbering 20,000. The next day, with the remnant of his army, amounting to 40,000 men, the Koraian general surrendered. Fifty thousand horses and 10,000 coats of mail were among the spoils. The foot soldiers were dismissed and ordered home, but the Koraian leaders were made prisoners and marched into China.

After so crushing a loss in men and material, one might expect instant surrender of the besieged city. So far from this, the garrison redoubled the energy of their defence. In this we see a striking trait of the Corean military character which has been noticed from the era of the Tangs, and before it, down to Admiral Rodgers. Chinese, Japanese, French, and Americans have experienced the fact and marvelled thereat. It is that the Coreans are poor soldiers in the open field and exhibit slight proof of personal valor. They cannot face a dashing foe nor endure stubborn fighting. But put the same men behind walls, bring them to bay, and the timid stag amazes the hounds. Their whole nature seems reinforced. They are more than brave. Their courage is sublime. They fight to the last man, and fling themselves on the bare steel when the foe clears the parapet. The Japanese of 1592 looked on the Corean in the field as a kitten, but in the castle as a tiger. The French, in 1866, never found a force that could face rifles, though behind walls the same men were invincible. The American handful of tars kept at harmless distance thousands of black heads in the open, but inside the fort they met giants in bravery. No nobler foe ever met American steel. Even when disarmed they fought their enemies with dust and stones until slain to the last man. The sailors found that the sheep in the field were lions in the fort.

The Coreans themselves knew both their forte and their foible, and so understood how to foil the invader from either sea. Shut out from the rival nations on the right hand and on the left by the treacherous sea, buttressed on the north by lofty mountains, and separated from China by a stretch of barren or broken land, the peninsula is easily secure against an invader far from his base of supplies. The ancient policy of the Coreans, by which they over and over again foiled their mighty foe and finally secured their independence, was to shut themselves up in their well-provisioned cities and castles, and not only beat off but starve away their foes. In their state of feudalism, when every city and strategic town of importance was well fortified, this was easily accomplished. The ramparts gave them shelter, and their personal valor secured the rest. Reversing the usual process of starving out a beleaguered garrison, the besiegers, unable to fight on empty stomachs, were at last obliged to raise the siege and go home. Long persistence in this resolute policy finally saved Corea from the Chinese colossus, and preserved her individuality among nations.

Faithful to their character, as above set forth, the Koraians held their own in the city of Anchiu, and the Chinese could make no impression upon it. In spite of catapults, scaling ladders, movable towers, and artificial mounds raised higher than the walls, the Koraians held out, and by sorties bravely captured or destroyed the enemy's works. Not daring to leave such a fortified city in their rear, the Chinese could not advance further, while their failing provisions and the advent of frost showed them that they must retreat.

Hungrily they turned their faces toward China.

In spite of the intense chagrin of the foiled Chinese leader, so great was his admiration for the valor of the besieged that he sent the Koraian commander a valuable present of rolls of silk. The Koraians were unable to pursue the flying invaders, and few fell by their weapons. But hunger, the fatigue of crossing impassable oceans of worse than Virginia mud, cold winds, and snow storms destroyed thousands of the Chinese on their weary homeward march over the mountain passes and quagmires of Liao Tung. The net results of the campaign were great glory to Korai;

and besides the loss of ten cities, 70,000 of her sons were captives in China, and 40,000 lay in battle graves.

According to a custom which Californians have learned in our day, the bones of the Chinese soldiers who died or were killed in the campaign were collected, brought into China, and, with due sacrificial rites and lamentations by the emperor, solemnly buried in their native soil. Irregular warfare still continued between the two countries, the offered tribute of Korai being refused, and the emperor waiting until his resources would justify him in sending another vast fleet and army against defiant Korai. While thus waiting he died.

After a few years of peace, his successor found occasion for war, and, in 660 A.D., despatched the expedition which crushed Hiaksai, the ally of Korai, and worried, without humbling, the latter state. In 664 Korai lost its able leader, the regicide prime minister—that rock against which the waves of Chinese invasion had dashed again and again in vain.

His son, who would have succeeded to the office of his father, was opposed by his brother. The latter, fleeing to China, became guide to the hosts again sent against Korai "to save the people and to chastise their rebellious chiefs." This time Korai, without a leader, was doomed. The Chinese armies having their rear well secured by a good base of supplies, and being led by skilful commanders, marched on from victory to victory, until, at the Yalu River, the various detachments united, and breaking the front of the Korai army, scattered them and marched on to Ping-an. The city surrendered without the discharge of an arrow. The line of kings of Korai came to an end after twenty-eight generations, ruling over 700 years.

All Korai, with its five provinces, its 176 cities, and its four or five millions of people, was annexed to the Chinese empire. Tens of thousands of Koraian refugees fled into Shinra, thousands into Pu-hai, north of the Tumen, then a rising state; and many to the new country of Japan. Desolated by slaughter and ravaged by fire and blood, war and famine, large portions of the land lay waste for generations. Thus fell the second of the Corean kingdoms, and the sole dominant state now supreme in the peninsula was Shinra, an outline of whose history we shall proceed to give.

CHAPTER VII.

EPOCH OF THE THREE KINGDOMS.—SHINRA.

WHEN Shinra becomes first known to us from Japanese tradition, her place in the peninsula is in the southeast, comprising portions of the modern provinces of Kang-wen and Kiung-sang. The people in this warm and fertile part of the peninsula had very probably sent many colonies of settlers over to the Japanese Islands, which lay only a hundred miles off, with Tsushima for a stepping-stone. It is probable that the "rebels" in Kiushiu, so often spoken of in old Japanese histories, were simply Coreans or their descendants, as, indeed, the majority of the inhabitants of Kiushiu originally had been. The Yamato tribe, which gradually became paramount in Japan, were probably immigrants of old Kokorai stock, that is, men of the Fuyu race, who had crossed from the north of Corea over the Sea of Japan, to the land of Sunrise, just as the Saxons and Engles pushed across the North Sea to England. They found the Kumaso, or Kiushiu "rebels," troublesome, mainly because these settlers from the west, or southern mainland of Corea, considered themselves to be the righteous owners of the island rather than the Yamato people. At all events, the pretext that led the mikado Chiu-ai, who is said to have reigned from 192 to 200 A.D., to march against them was, that these people in Kiushiu would not acknowledge his authority. His wife, the Amazonian queen Jingu, was of the opinion that the root of the trouble was to be found in the peninsula, and that the army should be sent across the sea. Her husband, having been killed in battle, the queen was left to carry out her purposes, which she did at the date said to be 202 A.D. She set sail from Hizen, and reached the Asian mainland probably at the harbor of Fusan. Unable to resist so well-appointed a force, the king of Shinra submitted and became the declared vassal of Japan. Envoys from Hiaksai and another of the petty kingdoms also came to the Japanese camp and made friends with the invaders. After a two months' stay, the victorious fleet, richly laden with precious gifts and spoil, returned.

How much of truth there is in this narrative of Jingu it is difficult to tell. The date given cannot be trustworthy. The truth seems at least this, that Shinra was far superior to the Japan of the early Christian centuries. Buddhism was formally established in Shinra in the year 528 ; and as early as the sixth century a steady stream of immigrants—traders, artists, scholars, and teachers, and later Buddhist missionaries—passed from Shinra into Japan, interrupted only by the wars which from time to time broke out. The relations between Nippon and Southern Corea will be more fully related in another chapter, but it will be well to remember that the Japanese always laid claim to the Corean peninsula, and to Shinra especially, as a tributary nation. They supported that claim not only whenever embassies from the two nations met at the court of China, but they made it a more or less active part of their national policy down to the year 1876. Many a bloody war grew out of this claim, but on the other hand many a benefit accrued to Japan, if not to Shinra.

Meanwhile, in the peninsula the leading state expanded her borders by gradual encroachments upon the little "kingdom" of Mimana to the southwest and upon Hiaksai on the north. The latter, having always considered Shinra to be inferior, and even a dependant, war broke out between the two states as soon as Shinra assumed perfect independence. Korai and Hiaksai leagued themselves against Shinra, and the game of war continued, with various shifting of the pieces on the board, until the tenth century. The three rival states mutually hostile, the Japanese usually friends to Hiaksai, the Chinese generally helpers of Shinra, the northern nations beyond the Tumen and Sungari assisting Korai, varying their operations in the field with frequent alliances and counterplots, make but a series of dissolving-views of battle and strife, into the details of which it is not profitable to enter. Though Korai and Hiaksai felt the heaviest blows from China, Shinra was harried oftenest by the armies of her neighbors and by the Japanese. Indeed, from a tributary point of view, it seems questionable whether her alliances with China were of any benefit to her. In times of peace, however, the blessings of education and civilization flowed freely from her great patron. Though farthest east from China, it seems certain that Shinra was, in many respects, the most highly civilized of the three states. Especially was this the case during the Tang era (618–905 A.D.), when the mutual relations between China and Shinra were closest, and arts, letters, and customs were borrowed most liberally by the pupil state. Even at the present time, in the Corean idiom, "Tang-yang" (times of the Tang and Yang dynasties) is a synonym of prosperity. The term for "Chinese," applied to works of art, poetry, coins, fans, and even to a certain disease, is "Tang," instead of the ordinary word for China, since this famous dynastic title represents to the Corean mind, as to the student of Kathayan history, one of the most brilliant epochs known to this longest-lived of empires. What the names of Plantagenet and Tudor represent to an Anglo-Saxon mind, the terms Tang and Sung are to a Corean.

During this period, Buddhism was being steadily propagated, until it became the prevailing cult of the nation. Reserving the story of its progress for a special chapter, we notice in this place but one of its attendant blessings. In the civilization of a nation, the possession of a vernacular alphabet must be acknowledged to be one of the most potent factors for the spread of intelligence and culture. It is believed by many linguists that the Choctaws and Coreans have the only two perfect alphabets in the world. It is agreed by natives of Chō-sen that their most profound scholar and ablest man of intellect was Chul-chong, a statesman at the court of Kion-chiu, the capital of Shinra. This famous penman, a scholar in the classics and ancient languages of India as well as China, is credited with the invention of the Nido, or Corean syllabary, one of the simplest and most perfect "alphabets" in the world. It expresses the sounds of the Corean language far better than the *kata-kana* of Japan expresses Japanese. Chul-chong seems to have invented the *Nido* syllabary by giving a phonetic value to a certain number of selected Chinese characters, which are ideographs expressing ideas but not sounds. Perhaps the Sanskrit alphabet suggested the model both for manner of use and for forms of letters. The Nido is composed almost entirely of straight lines and circles, and the letters belonging to the same class of labials, dentals, etc., have a similarity of form easily recognized. The Coreans state that the Nido was invented in the early part of the eighth century, and that it was based on the Sanskrit alphabet. It is worthy of note that, if the date given be true, the Japanese kata-kana, invented a century later, was perhaps suggested by the Corean.

One remarkable effect of the use of phonetic writing in Corea and Japan has been to stereotype, and thus to preserve, the ancient sounds and pronunciation of words of the Chinese, which the latter have lost. These systems of writing outside of China have served, like Edison's phonographs, in registering and reproducing the manner in which the Chinese spoke, a whole millennium ago. This fact has already opened a fertile field of research, and may yet yield rich treasures of discovery to the sciences of history and linguistics.

Certainly, however, we may gather that the Tang era was one of learning and literary progress in Corea, as in Japan—all countries in pupilage to China feeling the glow of literary splendor in which the Middle Kingdom was then basking. The young nobles were sent to obtain their education at the court and schools of Nanking, and the fair damsels of Shinra bloomed in the harem of the emperor. Imperial ambassadors frequently visited the court of this kingdom in the far east. Chinese costume and etiquette were, for a time, at least, made the rigorous rule at court. On one occasion, in 653 A.D., the envoy from Shinra to the mikado came arrayed in Chinese dress, and, neglecting the ceremonial forms of the Japanese court, attempted to observe those of China. The mikado was highly irritated at the supposed insult. The premier even advised that the Corean be put to death; but better counsels prevailed. During the eighth and ninth centuries this flourishing kingdom was well known to the Arab geographers, and it is evident that Mussulman travellers visited Shinra or resided in the cities of the peninsula for purposes of trade and commerce, as has been shown before.

Kion-chiu, the capital of Shinra, was a brilliant centre of art and science, of architecture and of literary and religious light. Imposing temples, grand monasteries, lofty pagodas, halls of scholars, magnificent gateways and towers adorned the city. In campaniles, equipped with water-clocks and with ponderous bells and gongs, which, when struck, flooded the valleys and hill-tops with a rich resonance, the sciences of astronomy and horoscopy were cultivated. As from a fountain, rich streams of knowledge flowed from the capital of Shinra, both over the peninsula and to the court of Japan. Even after the decay of Shinra's power in the political unity of the whole peninsula, the nation looked upon Kion-chiu as a sacred city. Her noble temples, halls, and towers stood in honor and repair, enshrining the treasures of India, Persia, and China, until the ruthless Japanese torch laid them in ashes in 1596.

The generation of Corean people during the seventh century, when the Chinese hordes desolated large portions of the peninsula and crushed out Hiaksai and Korai, saw the borders of Shinra extending from the Everlasting White Mountains to the Island of Tsushima, and occupying the entire eastern half of the peninsula. From the beginning of the eighth until the tenth century, Shinra is the supreme state, and the political power of the Eastern Kingdom is represented by her alone. Her ambition tempted, or her Chinese master commanded, her into an invasion of the kingdom of Pu-hai beyond her northern border, 733 A.D. Her armies crossed the Tumen, but met with such spirited resistance that only half of them returned. Shinra's desire of conquest in that direction was appeased, and for two centuries the land had rest from blood.

Until Shinra fell, in 934 A.D., and united Corea rose on the ruins of the three kingdoms, the history of this state, as found in the Chinese annals, is simply a list of her kings, who, of course, received investiture from China. On the east, the Japanese, having ceased to be her pupils in civilization during times of peace, as in time of war they were her conquerors, turned their attention to Nanking, receiving directly therefrom the arts and sciences, instead of at second-hand through the Corean peninsula. They found enough to do at home in conquering all the tribes in the north and east and centralizing their system of government after the model of the Tangs in China. For these reasons the sources of information concerning the eighth and ninth centuries fail, or rather it is more exact to say that the history of Shinra is that of peace instead of war. In 869 we read of pirates from her shores descending upon the Japanese coast to plunder the tribute ships from Buzen province, and again, in 893, that a fleet of fifty junks, manned by these Corean rovers, was driven off from Tsushima by the Japanese troops, with the loss of three hundred slain. Another descent of "foreign pirates," most probably Coreans, upon Iki Island, in 1019, is recorded, the strangers being beaten off by reinforcements from the mainland. The very existence of these marauders is, perhaps, a good indication that the power of the Shinra government was falling into decay, and that lawlessness within the kingdom was preparing the way for some mighty hand to not only seize the existing state, but to unite all Corea into political, as well as geographical, unity. In the far north another of those great intermittent movements of population was in process, which, though destroying the kingdom of Puhai beyond the Tumen, was to repeople the desolate land of Korai, and again call a dead state to aggressive life. From the origin to the fall of Shinra there were three royal families of fifty-five kings, ruling nine hundred and ninety-three years, or seven years less than a millennium.

Despite the modern official name of the kingdom, Chō-sen, the people of Corea still call their country Gaoli, or Korai, clinging to the ancient name. In this popular usage, unless we are mistaken, there is a flavor of genuine patriotism. Chō-sen does indeed mean Morning Calm, but the impression made on Western ears, and more vividly upon the eye by means of the Chinese characters, is apt to mislead. The term is less a reflection of geographical position than of the inward emotions of those who first of all were more Chinese than Corean in spirit, and of a desire for China's favor. The term Chō-sen savors less of dew and dawn than of policy and prosy fact. It is probable, despite the Corean's undoubted love of nature and beautiful scenery, that Americans and Europeans have been led astray as to the real significance of the phrase "morning calm." At the bottom, it means rather peace with China than the serenity of dewy morning. Audience of the Chinese emperor to his vassals is always given at daybreak, and to be graciously received after the long and tedious prostrations is an auspicious beginning as of a day of heaven upon earth. To the founder of Corea, Ki Tsze, the gracious favor of the Chow emperor was as "morning calm;" and so to Ni Taijo, in 1392 A.D., was the sunshine of the Ming emperor's favor. In both instances the name Chō-sen given to their realm had, in reality, immediate reference to the dayspring of China's favor, and "the calm of dawn" to the smile of the emperor.

CHAPTER VIII.

JAPAN AND COREA.

I⊤ is as nearly impossible to write the history of Corea and ex-
clude Japan, as to tell the story of mediæval England and leave
out France. Not alone does the finger of sober history point directly westward as the immediate source of much of what has been
hitherto deemed of pure Japanese origin, but the fountain-head of
Japanese mythology is found in the Sungari valley, or under the
shadows of the Ever-White Mountains. The first settler of Japan,
like him of Fuyu, crosses the water upright upon the back of a
fish, and brings the rudiments of literature and civilization with
him. The remarkable crocodiles and sea-monsters, from which
the gods and goddesses are born and into which they change, the
dragons and tide-jewels and the various mystic symbols which
they employ to work their spells, the methods of divination and
system of prognostics, the human sacrifices and the manner of
their rescue, seem to be common to the nations on both sides of
the Sea of Japan, and point to a common heritage from the same
ancestors. Language comes at last with her revelations to furnish
proofs of identity.

The mischievous Susanoō, so famous in the pre-historic legends,
told in the Kojiki, half scamp, half benefactor, who planted all
Japan with trees, brought the seeds from which they grew from
Corea. His rescue of the maiden doomed to be devoured by the
eight-headed dragon (emblem of water, and symbolical of the sea
and rivers) reads like a gallant fellow saving one of the human
beings who for centuries, until the now ruling dynasty abolished
the custom, were sacrificed to the sea on the Corean coast fronting Japan. In Kiōto, on Gi-on Street, there is a temple which
tradition declares was "founded in 656 A.D. by a Corean envoy in
honor of Susanoō, to whom the name of Go-dzu Tenno (Heavenly
King of Go-dzu) was given, because he was originally worshipped
in Go-dzu Mountain in Corea."

Dogs are not held in any honor in Japan, as they were anciently in Kokorai. Except the silk-haired, pug-nosed, and large-eyed *chin*, which the average native does not conceive as canine, the dogs run at large, ownerless, as in the Levant; and share the work of street scavenging with the venerated crows. Yet there are two places of honor in which the golden and stone effigies of this animal—highly idealized indeed, but still *inu*—are enthroned.

The *ama-inu*, or heavenly dogs, in fanciful sculpture of stone or gilt wood, represent guardian dogs. They are found in pairs guarding the entrances to miya or temples. As all miya (the name also of the mikado's residence) were originally intended to serve as a model or copy of the palace of the mikado and a reminder of the divinity of his person and throne, it is possible that the *ama-inu* imitated the golden Corean dogs which support and guard the throne of Japan. Access to the shrine was had only by passing these two heavenly dogs. These creatures are quite distinct from the "dogs of Fo," or the "lions" that flank the gateways of the magistrate's office in China. Those who have had audience of the mikado in the imperial throne-room, as the writer had in January, 1873, have noticed at the foot of the throne, serv. ing as legs or supports to the golden chair, on which His Majesty sits, two dogs sitting on their haunches, and upright on their forelegs. These fearful-looking creatures, with wide-open mouths, hair curled in tufts, especially around the front neck, and with tails bifurcated at their upright ends, are called "Corean dogs." For what reason placed there we know not. It may be in witness of the conquest of Shinra by the empress Jingu, who called the king of Shinra "the dog of Japan," or it may point to some forgotten symbolism in the past, or typify the vassalage of Corea—so long a fundamental dogma in Japanese politics. It is certainly strange to see this creature, so highly honored in Fuyu and dishonored among the vulgar in Japan, placed beneath the mikado's throne.

The Japanese laid claim to Corea from the second century until the 27th of February, 1876. On that day the mikado's minister plenipotentiary signed the treaty, recognizing Chō-sen as an independent nation. Through all the seventeen centuries which, according to their annals, elapsed since their armies first compelled the vassalage of their neighbor, the Japanese regarded the states of Corea as tributary. Time and again they enforced their claim with bloody invasion, and when through a more enlightened policy the rulers voluntarily acknowledged their former enemy as an equal, the decision cost Japan almost immediately afterward seven months of civil war, 20,000 lives, and fifty millions of dollars in treasure. The mainspring of the "Satsuma rebellion" of 1877 was the official act of friendship by treaty, and the refusal of the Tōkiō Government to make war on Corea.

From about the beginning of the Christian era until the fifteenth century the relations between the two nations were very close and active. Alternate peace and war, mutual assistance given, and embassies sent to and fro are recorded with lively frequency in the early Japanese annals, especially the Nihongi and Kojiki. A more or less continual stream of commerce and emigration seems to have set in from the peninsula. Some writers of high authority, who are also comparative students of the languages of the two countries, see in these events the origin of the modern Japanese. They interpret them to mean nothing less than the peopling of the archipelago by continental tribes passing through the peninsula, and landing in Japan at various points along the coast from Kiushiu to Kaga. Some of them think that Japan was settled wholly and only by Tungusic races of Northeastern Asia coming from or through .Corea. They base their belief not only on the general stream and tendency of Japanese tradition, but also and more on the proofs of language.

The first mention of Corea in the Japanese annals occurs in the fifth volume of the Nihongi, and is the perhaps half-fabulous narrative of ancient tradition. In the 65th year of the reign of the tenth mikado, Sujin (97–30 B.C.), a boat filled with people from the west appeared off the southern point of Chō-shiu, near the modern town of Shimonoséki. They would not land there, but steered their course from cape to cape along the coast until they reached the Bay of Keji no Wara in Echizen, near the modern city of Tsuruga. Here they disembarked and announced themselves from Amana Sankan (Amana of the Three Han or Kingdoms) in Southern Corea. They unpacked their treasures of finely wrought goods, and their leader made offerings to the mikado Sujin. These immigrants remained five years in Echizen, not far from the city of Fukui, till 28 B.C. Before leaving Japan, they presented themselves in the capital for a farewell audience. The mikado Mimaki, having died three years before, the visitors were requested on their return to call their country Mimana, after their patron, as a memorial of their stay in Japan. To this they assented, and on their return named their district Mimana.

Some traditions state that the first Corean envoy had a horn growing out of his forehead, and that since his time, and on account of it, the bay near which he dwelt was named Tsunaga (Horn Bay) now corrupted into Tsuruga.

It may be added that nearly all mythical characters or heroes in Japanese and Chinese history are represented as having one or more very short horns growing out of their heads, and are so delineated in native art.

Six years later an envoy from Shinra arrived, also bringing presents to the mikado. These consisted of mirrors, jade stone, swords, and other precious articles, then common in Corea but doubtless new in Japan.

According to the tradition of the Kojiki (Book of Ancient Legends) the fourteenth mikado, Chiu-ai (A.D. 192–200) was holding his court at Tsuruga in Echizen, in A.D. 194, when a rebellion broke out in Kiushiu. He marched at once into Kiushiu, against the rebels, and there fell by disease or arrow. His consort, Jingu Kōgō, had a presentiment that he ought not to go into Kiushiu, as he would surely fail if he did, but that he should strike at the root of the trouble and sail at once to the west.

After his death she headed the Japanese army and, leading the troops in person, quelled the revolt. She then ordered all the available forces of her realm to assemble for an invasion of Shinra. Japanese modern writers have laid great stress upon the fact that Shinra began the aggressions which brought on war, and in this fact justify Jingu's action and Japan's right to hold Corea as an honestly acquired possession.

All being ready, the doughty queen regent set sail from the coast of Hizen, in Japan, in the tenth month A.D. 202, and beached the fleet safely on the coast of Shinra. The King of Shinra, accustomed to meet only with men from the rude tribes of Kiushiu, was surprised to see so well-appointed an army and so large a fleet from a land to the eastward. Struck with terror he resolved at once to submit. Tying his hands in token of submission and in presence of the queen Jingu, he declared himself the slave of Japan. Jingu caused her bow to be suspended over the gate of the palace of the king in sign of his submission. It is even said that she wrote on the gate "The King of Shinra is the dog of Japan." Perhaps these are historic words, which find their meaning to-day in the two golden dogs forming part of the mikado's throne, like the Scotch "stone of Scone," under the coronation chair in Westminster Abbey.

The followers of Jingu evidently expected a rich booty, but after so peaceful a conquest the empress ordered that no looting should be allowed, and no spoil taken except the treasures constituting tribute. She restored the king to the throne as her vassal, and the tribute was then collected and laden on eighty boats with hostages for future annual tribute. The offerings comprised pictures, works of elegance and art, mirrors, jade, gold, silver, and silk fabrics.

Preparations were now made to conquer Hiaksai also, when Jingu was surprised to receive the voluntary submission and offers of tribute of this country.

The Japanese army remained in Corea only two months, but this brief expedition led to great and lasting results. It gave the Japanese a keener thirst for martial glory, it opened their eyes to a higher state of arts and civilization. From this time forth there flowed into the islands a constant stream of Corean emigrants, who gave a great impulse to the spirit of improvement in Japan. The Japanese accept the story of Jingu and her conquest as sound history, and adorn their greenback paper money with pictures of her foreign exploits. Critics reject many elements in the tradition, such as her controlling the waves and drowning the Shinra army by the jewels of the ebbing and the flowing tide,[1] and the delay of her accouchement by a magic stone carried in her girdle. The Japanese ascribe the glory of victory to her then unborn babe, afterward deified as Ojin, god of war, and worshipped by Buddhists as Hachiman or the Eight-bannered Buddha. Yet many temples are dedicated to Jingu, one especially famous is near Hiōgo, and Koraiji (Corean village) near Oiso, a few miles from Yokohama, has another which was at first built in her honor. Evidently the core of the narrative of conquest is fact.

At the time when the faint, dim light of trustworthy tradition dawns, we find the people inhabiting the Japanese archipelago to be roughly divided, as to their political status, into four classes.

In the central province around Kiōto ruled a kingly house—

---

[1] The story, told in full in the *Heiké Monogatari*, is given in English in "Japanese Fairy World."

the mikado and his family—with tributary nobles or feudal chiefs holding their lands on military tenure. This is the ancient classic land and realm of Yamato. Four other provinces adjoining it have always formed the core of the empire, and are called the Go-Kinai, or five home provinces, suggesting the five clans of Kokorai.

To the north and east stretched the little known and less civilized region, peopled by tribes of kindred blood and speech, who

Map of Ancient Japan and Corea.

spoke nearly the same language as the Yamato tribes, and who had probably come at some past time from the same ancestral seats in Manchuria, and called the Kuan-tō, or region east (tō) of the barrier (kuan) at Ozaka; or poetically Adzuma.

Still further north, on the main island and in Yezo, lived the Ainos or Ebisŭ, probably the aborigines of the soil—the straight-eyed men whose descendants still live in Yezo and the Kuriles.

The northern and eastern tribes were first conquered and thoroughly subdued by the Yamato tribes, after which all the far north was overrun and the Ainos subjugated.

In the extreme south of the main island of Japan and in Kiushiu, then called Kumaso by the Yamato people, lived a number of tribes of perhaps the same ethnic stock as the Yamato Japanese, but further removed. Their progenitors had probably descended from Manchuria through Corea to Japan. Their blood and speech, however, were more mixed by infusions from Malay and southern elements. Into Kiushiu—it being nearest to the continent—the peninsulars were constantly coming and mingling with the islanders.

The allegiance of the Kiushiu tribes to the royal house of Yamato was of a very loose kind. The history of these early centuries, as shown in the annals of Nihon, is but a series of revolts against the distant warrior mikado, whose life was chiefly one of war. He had often to leave his seat in the central island to march at the head of his followers to put down rebellions or to conquer new tribes. Over these, when subdued, a prince chosen by the conqueror was set to rule, who became a feudatory of the mikado.

The attempts of the Yamato sovereign to wholly reduce the Kiushiu tribes to submission, were greatly frustrated by their stout resistance, fomented by emissaries from Shinra, who instigated them to "revolt," while adventurers from the Corean mainland came over in large numbers and joined the "rebels," who were, in one sense, their own compatriots.

From the time of Jingu, if the early dates in Japanese history are to be trusted, may be said to date that belief, so firmly fixed in the Japanese mind, that Corea is, and always was since Jingu's time, a tributary and dependency of Japan. This idea, akin to that of the claim of the English kings on France, led to frequent expeditions from the third to the sixteenth century, and which, even as late as 1874, 1875, and 1877, lay at the root of three civil wars.

All these expeditions, sometimes national, sometimes filibustering, served to drain the resources of Japan, though many impulses to development and higher civilization were thus gained, especially in the earlier centuries. It seemed, until 1877, almost impossible to eradicate from the military mind of Japan the conviction that to surrender Corea was cowardice and a stain on the national honor. But time will show, as it showed centuries ago in England, that the glory and prosperity of the conqueror were increased, not diminished, when Japan relinquished all claim on her continental neighbor and treated her as an equal.

The Coreans taught the Japanese the arts of peace, while the Coreans profited from their neighbors to improve in the business of war. We read that, in 316 A.D., a Corean ambassador, bringing the usual tribute, presented to the mikado a shield of iron which he believed to be invulnerable to Japanese arrows. The mikado called on one of his favorite marksmen to practice in the presence of the envoy. The shield was suspended, and the archer, drawing bow, sent a shaft through the iron skin of the buckler to the astonishment of the visitor. In all their battles the Coreans were rarely able to stand in open field before the archers from over the sea, who sent true cloth-yard shafts from their oak and bamboo bows.

The paying of tribute to a foreign country is never a pleasant duty to perform, though in times of prosperity and good harvests it is not difficult. In periods of scarcity from bad crops it is well nigh impossible. To insist upon its payment is to provoke rebellion. Instances are indeed given in Japanese history where the conquerors not only remitted the tribute but even sent ship loads of rice and barley to the starving Coreans. When, however, for reasons not deemed sufficient, or out of sheer defiance, their vassals refused to discharge their dues, they again felt the iron hand of Japan in war. During the reign of Yuriaki, the twenty-second mikado (A.D. 457–477), the three states failed to pay tribute. A Japanese army landed in Corea, and conquering Hiaksai, compelled her to return to her duty. The campaign was less successful in Shinra and Korai, for after the Japanese had left the Corean shores the "tribute" was sent only at intervals, and the temper of the half-conquered people was such that other expeditions had to be despatched to inflict chastisement and compel payment.

The gallant but vain succor given by the Japanese to Hiaksai during the war with the Chinese, in the sixth century, which resulted in the destruction of the little kingdom, has already been detailed. Among the names, forever famous in Japanese art and tradition, of those who took part in this expedition are Saté-hiko and Kasi-wadé. The former sailed away from Hizen in the year 536, as one of the mikado's body-guard to assist their allies the men of Hiaksai. A poetical legend recounts that his wife, Sayo-

himé, climbed the hills of Matsura to catch the last glimpse of his
receding sails. Thus intently gazing, with straining eyes, she
turned to stone. The peasants of the neighborhood still discern
in the weathern-worn rocks, high up on the cliffs, the figure of a
lady in long trailing court dress with face and figure eagerly bent
over the western waves. Not only is the name Matsura Sayohimé
the symbol of devoted love, but from this incident the famous
author Bakin constructed his romance of "The Great Stone Spirit
of Matsura."

Kasiwadé, who crossed over to do "frontier service" in the
peninsula a few years later, was driven ashore by a snow squall at
an unknown part of the coast. While in this defenceless condition his camp was invaded by a tiger, which carried off and devoured his son, a lad of tender age. Kasiwadé at once gave chase
and followed the beast to the mountains and into a cave. The
tiger leaping out upon him, the wary warrior bearded him with
his left hand, and buried his dirk in his throat. Then finish-
ing him with his sabre, he skinned the brute and sent home the
trophy. From olden times Chō-sen is known to Japanese children only as a land of tigers, while to the soldier the "marshal's
baton carried in his knapsack" is a tiger-skin scabbard, the emblem
and possession of rank.

As the imperial court of Japan looked upon Shinra and Hiaksai as outlying vassal states, the frequent military movements
across the sea were reckoned under "frontier service," like that
beyond the latitude of Sado in the north of the main island, or in
Kiushiu in the south. "The three countries" of Corea were far
nearer and more familiar to the Japanese soldiers than were Yezo
or the Riu Kiu Islands, which were not part of the empire till
several centuries afterward. Kara Kuni, the country of Kara
(a corruption of Korai?), as they now call China, was then applied to Corea. Not a little of classic poetry and legend in
the Yamato language refers to this western frontier beyond the
sea. The elegy on Ihémaro, the soldier-prince, who died at Iki
Island on the voyage over, and that on the death of the Corean
nun Riguwan, have been put into English verse by Mr. Chamberlain (named after the English explorer and writer on Corea,
Basil Hall), in his "Classical Poetry of the Japanese." This
Corean lady left her home in 714, and for twenty-one years found
a home with the mikado's Prime Minister, Otomo, and his wife, at
Nara. She died in 735, while her hosts were away at the mineral

springs of Arima, near Kobé; and the elegy was written by their daughter. One stanza describes her life in the new country.

> " And here with aliens thou didst choose to dwell,
>   Year in, year out, in deepest sympathy;
> And here thou builtest thee a holy cell,
>   And so the peaceful years went gliding by."

An interesting field of research is still open to the scholar who will point out all the monuments of Corean origin or influence in the mikado's empire, in the arts and sciences, household customs, diet and dress, or architecture; in short, what by nature or the hand of man has been brought to the land of Sunrise from that of Morning Calm. One of the Corean princes, who settled in Japan early in the seventh century, founded a family which afterward ruled the famous province of Nagatō or Chōshiu. One of his descendants welcomed Francis Xavier, and aided his work by gifts of ground and the privilege of preaching. Many of the temples in Kiōto still contain images, paintings, and altar furniture brought from Corea. The "Pheasant Bridge" still keeps its name from bygone centuries; in a garden near by pheasants were kept for the supply of the tables of the Corean embassies. The Arab and Persian treasures of art and fine workmanship, in the imperial archives and museums of Nara, which have excited the wonder of foreign visitors, are most probably among the gifts or purchases from Shinra, where these imports were less rare. A Buddhist monk named Shiuho has gathered up the traditions and learning of the subject, so far as it illustrated his faith, and in "Precious Jewels from a Neighboring Country," published in 1586, has written a narrative of the introduction of Buddhism from Corea and its literary and missionary influences upon Japan.

Under the chapters on Art and Religion we shall resume this topic. As earnestly as the Japanese are now availing themselves of the science and progress of Christendom in this nineteenth century, so earnestly did they borrow the culture of the west, that is of Corea and China, a thousand years ago.

The many thousands of Coreans, who, during the first ten centuries of the Christian era, but especially in the seventh, eighth, and ninth, settled in Japan, lived peaceably with the people of their adopted country, and loyally obeyed the mikado's rule. An exception to this course occurred in 820, when seven hundred men who some time before had come from Shinra to Tōtōmi and Suruga revolted, killed many of the Japanese, seized the rice in the store-houses, and put to sea to escape. The people of Musashi and Sagami pursued and attacked them, putting many of them to death.

The general history of the Coreans in Japan divides itself into two parts. Those who came as voluntary immigrants in time of peace were in most cases skilled workmen or farmers, who settled in lands or in villages granted them, and were put on political and social equality with the mikado's subjects. They founded industries, intermarried with the natives, and their identity has been lost in the general body of the Japanese people.

With the prisoners taken in war, and with the laborers impressed into their service and carried off by force, the case was far different. These latter were set apart in villages by themselves— an outcast race on no social equality with the people. At first they were employed to feed the imperial falcons, or do such menial work, but under the ban of Buddhism, which forbids the destruction of life and the handling of flesh, they became an accursed race, the "Etas" or pariahs of the nation. They were the butchers, skinners, leather-makers, and those whose business it was to handle corpses of criminals and all other defiling things. They exist to-day, not greatly changed in blood, though in costume, language, and general appearance, it is not possible to distinguish them from Japanese of purest blood. By the humane edict of the mikado, in 1868, granting them all the rights of citizenship, their social condition has greatly improved.

From the ninth century onward to the sixteenth, the relations of the two countries seem to be unimportant. Japan was engaged in conquering northward the barbarians of her main island and Yezo. Her intercourse, both political and religious, grew to be so direct with the court of China, that Corea, in the Japanese annals, sinks out of sight except at rare intervals. Nihon increased in wealth and civilization while Chō-sen remained stationary or retrograded. In the nineteenth century the awakened Sunrise Kingdom has seen her former self in the hermit nation, and has stretched forth willing hands to do for her neighbor now, what Corea did for Japan in centuries long gone by.

Still, it must never be forgotten that Corea was not only the bridge on which civilization crossed from China to the archipelago, but was most probably the pathway of migration by which the rulers of the race now inhabiting Nihon reached it from their ancestral seats around the Sungari and the Ever-White Mountains.

True, it is not absolutely certain whether the homeland of the mikado's ancestors lay southward in the sea, or westward among the
mountains, but that the mass of the Corean and Japanese people
are more closely allied in blood than either are with the Chinese,
Manchius, or Malays, seems to be proved, not only by language
and physical traits, but by the whole course of the history of both
nations, and by the testimony of the Chinese records.   Both Coreans and Japanese have inherited the peculiar institutions of their
Fuyu ancestors—that race which alone of all the peoples sprung
from Manchuria migrated toward the rising, instead of toward the
setting, sun.

CHAPTER IX.

KORAI, OR UNITED COREA.

The fertile and well-watered region drained by the Amur River and its tributaries, stretching from the Pacific Ocean to Lake Baikal, covers the ancestral seats of many nations, and is perhaps the home of nations yet to arise. It may be likened to a great intermittent geyser-spring which, at intervals, overflows with terrific force and volume. The movements of population southward seem, on a review of Chinese and Corean history, almost as regular as a law of nature. As the conquerors from the central Asian plateaus have over and over again descended into India, as the barbarians overran the Roman empire, so out of the region drained by the Amur and its tributaries have burst forth, time and again, floods of conquest to overwhelm the rich plains of China. Or, if we regard the flowery and grassy lands of Manchuria and beyond as a great hive, full of busy life which, from the pressure of increasing numbers, must swarm off to relieve the old home, we shall have a true illustration. Time and again have clouds of human bees, with the sting of their swords and the honey of their new energy, issued from this ancient hive. The swarms receive different names in history : Hun, Turk, Tartar, Mongol, Manchiu, but they all emerge from the same source, giving or receiving dynastic names, but being in reality Tungusic people of the same basic stock.

A tribe inhabiting one of the ravines or rich river flats of the Sungari region increases in wealth and numbers. A powerful chief leads them to war and victory. Tribes and lands are annexed. Martial valor, wealth, and strength increase. Ambition and the pressure of numbers tempt to farther conquest. Over and beyond the Great Wall is the ever-glittering prize—teeming China. The march begins southward. After many a battle, and only, it may be, after a generation of war against the imperial legions beyond the frontiers, the goal is reached. The Middle Kingdom is conquered and a new dynasty sits on the Dragon

Throne, until long peace enervates and luxury weakens. Then out of the old northern seats of population rolls a new flood of conquest, and a new swarm of conquerors is hived off.

Thus we see the original land embracing the Amur and Sungari valleys has had its periods of power and decay, of historical and unhistorical life. Unity and movement make history, disintegration and apathy cause the page of history to be blank. But the land is still there with the people and the possibilities of the future.

In spite of the associations of hoary antiquity that cluster around Asiatic countries, the reader of history does not expect to hear of single empires enduring through many centuries. With the exception of Japan, no nation of Asia can show a dynastic line extending through a millennium. The empires founded by Asiatic conquerors are short-lived. The countries and the people remain, but the rulers constantly change, and the building up, flourishing, decay, and dissolution suggest the seasons rather than the centuries. No enduring political fabrics, like those of Rome or Britain, are known in Asia. Though China and India abide like the oak, their rulers change like the leaves. Socially, these countries are the symbols of petrifaction, politically they are as the kaleidoscope. From this law of continuous political mutation, Corea has not been free.

In one of these epochs of historical movement, at the opening of the eighth century, there arose the kingdom of Puhai, the capital of which was the present city of Kirin. Its northern boundaries first touched the Sungari, and later the Amur, shifting to the Sungari again. Its southern border was at first the Tumen River, and later the modern province of Ham-kiung was included in it. Lines drawn southwardly through Lake Hanka on the east, and Mukden on the west, would enclose its longitude. Its life lasted from about 700 to 925 A.D. This kingdom was continually on bad terms with China, and the Tang emperors for nearly a century attempted to crush it into vassalage. Puhai made brave resistance, being aided not only by the large numbers of Koraians, who had fled when beaten by the Chinese across the Tumen River, but also by the Japanese, whose supremacy they acknowledged by payment of tribute. With the latter their relations were always of a peaceful and pleasant nature, and the correspondence and other documents of the visiting embassies to the mikado's court are still preserved in Japan.

Yet though Puhai was able to resist China and hold part of the old territory of Korai, it fell before the persistent attacks of the Kitan tribes, whose empire, lasting from 907 to 1125 A.D., stretched from west of Lake Baikal to the Pacific Ocean. In the early part of the tenth century this Puhai kingdom, whose age was scarcely two centuries, melted away again into tribes and villages, each with its chief. The country being without political unity returned to unhistorical obscurity, as part of the Kitan empire. Without crossing the Tumen, to enter China by way of Corea, the Kitans marched at once around the Ever-White Mountains and down the Liao Tung valley into China.

The breaking up of Puhai was not without its influence on the Corean peninsula. As early as the ninth century thousands of refugees, driven before the Kitans or dissatisfied with nomad life on the plains, recrossed the Tumen and a great movement of emigration set into Northern Corea, which again became populous, cultivated, and rich. With increasing prosperity better government was desired. The worthlessness of the rulers and the prospect of a successful revolution tempted the ambition of a Buddhist monk named Kung-wo who, in 912 A.D., left his monastery and raised the flag of rebellion. He set forth to establish another political fabric of mushroom duration, which was destined to make way for a more permanent kingdom, and, in the end, united Corea.

With his followers, Kung-wo attacked the city of Kaichow (in the modern Kang-wen province), and was so far successful as to enter it and proclaim himself king. His personal success was of short duration. His lieutenant, Wang-ken, that is Wang the founder, was a descendant of the old kingly house of Korai. During all the time of Chinese occupancy, or Shinra supremacy, his family had kept alive their spirit, traditions, and claims. Think ing he could rule better than a priest, Wang put the ex-monk to death and proclaimed himself the true sovereign of Korai. All this went on without the interference of China, which at this time was torn by internal disorder and the ravages of the same Kitan tribes that had destroyed Puhai. Wang made Ping-an and Kaichow the capitals of his kingdom, and resolved to take full advantage of his opportunity to conquer the entire peninsula and unite all its parts under his sceptre.

Circumstances made this an easy task. With China passive, Shinra weak, through long absorption in luxury and the arts of peace, and with most part of the population of the peninsula of Korain blood and descent, the work was easy. The whole country, from the Ever-White Mountains to Quelpart Island, was overrun and welded into unity. The name of Shinra was blotted out after a line of fifty-six kings and a life of nine hundred and ninety-three years. For the first time the peninsula became a political unit, and the name Korai, springing to life again like the Arabian phœnix out of its ashes, became the symbol alike of united Corea and of the race which peopled it. Even yet the name Korai (Gauli or Gori in the vernacular) is generally used by the people.

The probabilities are that the people of the old Fuyu race, descendants of the tribes of Kokorai, as the more vigorous stock, had already so far supplanted the old aboriginal people inhabiting Southern Corea as to make conquest by Wang, who was one of their own blood, easy. This is shown in a series of maps representing the three kingdoms of Corea from 201 to 655 A.D., by the Japanese scholar Otsuki Tōyō. At the former date the Kokorai people beyond that part of their domain conquered by China have occupied the land as far south as the Han River, or to the 37th parallel. Later, Shinra, in 593, and again in 655, backed by Chinese armies, had regained her territory a degree or two northward, and in the eighth and ninth centuries, acting as the ally of China, ruled all the country to the Tumen River. Yet, though Shinra held the land, the inhabitants were the same, namely, the stock of Korai, ready to rise against their rulers and to annihilate Shinra in a name and monarchy that had in it nationality and the prestige of their ancient freedom and greatness.

Thoroughly intent on unifying his realm, Wang chose a central location for the national capital. Kion-chiu, the metropolis of Shinra, was too far south, Ping-an, the royal seat of old Korai, was too far north ; but one hundred miles nearer "the river" Han, was Sunto. This city, now called Kai-seng, is twenty-five miles from Seoul and equally near the sea. Wang made Sunto what it has been for over nine centuries, a fortified city of the first rank, the chief commercial centre of the country, and a seat of learning. It remained the capital until 1392 A.D. Wang-ken or Wang, the founder of the new dynasty under which the people were to be governed for over four hundred years, was an ardent Buddhist. Spite of his having put the monk to death to further personal ends, he became the defender of the India faith and made it the official religion. Monasteries were founded and temples built in great numbers. To furnish revenues for the support of these, tracts of land were set apart as permanent endowment. The four centuries of the house of Korai are the palmy days of Corean Buddhism.

From China, which at this time was enjoying that era of literary splendor, for which the Sung dynasty was noted, there came an impulse both to scholastic activity and to something approaching popular education.

The Nido, or native syllabary, which had been invented by Chul-chong, the statesman of Shinra, now came into general use. While Chinese literature and the sacred books of Buddhism were studied in the original Sanscrit, popular works were composed in Corean and written out in the Nido, or vernacular syllables. The printing press, invented by the Sung scholars, was introduced and books were printed from cut blocks. The Japanese are known to have adopted printing from Corea as early as the twelfth century, when a work of the Buddhist canon was printed from wooden blocks. "A Corean book is known which dates authentically from the period 1317–1324, over a century before the earliest printed book known in Europe." The use of metal type, made by moulding and casting, is not distinctly mentioned in Corea until the year 1420, and the invention and use of the Unmun, a true native alphabet, seems to belong to the same period. The eleven vowels and fourteen consonants serve both as an alphabet and a syllabary, the latter being the most ancient system, and the former an improvement on it.

The unifier of Corea died in 945 and was succeeded by his son Wu. Fifteen years later the last of the five weak dynasties that had rapidly succeeded each other in China, fell. The Chinese emperor proposing, and the Corean king being willing, the latter hastened to send tribute, and formed an alliance of friendship with the imperial Sung, who swayed the destinies of China for the next 166 years (960–1101).

Korai soon came into collision with the Kitans in the following manner. The royal line of united Corea traced their descent directly from the ancient kings of Kokorai, and therefore claimed relationship with the princes of Puhai. On the strength of this claim, the Koraian king asserted his right to the whole of Liao Tung, which had been formerly held by Puhai. The Kitans, having matters of greater importance to attend to at the time, allowed its temporary occupation by Korai troops. Nevertheless the king thought it best to send homage to the Kitan emperor, in order to get a clear title to the territory. In 1012 he despatched an embassy acknowledging the Kitan supremacy. This verbal message did not satisfy the strong conqueror, who demanded that the Koraian king should come in person and make obeisance. The latter refused. A feud at once broke out between them, which led to a war, in which Korai was worsted and stripped of all her territory west of the Yalu River.

Palladius has pointed out the interesting fact that a little village about twenty miles north of Tie-ling, and seventy miles north of Mukden, called Gauli-chan (Korai village) still witnesses by its name to its former history, and to the possession by Corea of territory west of the Yalu.

The Kitans, not satisfied with recovering Liao Tung, crossed the river and invaded Korai, in 1015. By this time a new nation, under the name of Nüjun or Ninchi, had formed around Lake Hanka, in part of the territory of extinct Puhai. With their new frontagers the Koraians made an alliance "as solid as iron and stone," and with their aid drove back the Kitan invaders.

Henceforth the boundaries of Corea remained stationary, and have never extended beyond the limits with which the western world is familiar.

An era of peace and prosperity set in, and a thriving trade sprang up between the Nüjun and Korai. The two nations, cemented in friendship through a common fear of the Kitans, grew apace in numbers and prosperity.

The Kitans were known to Chinese authors as early as the fifth century, seven nomad tribes being at that time confederate under their banners. At the beginning of the tenth century, these wanderers had been transformed into hordes of disciplined cavalry. Their wealth and intelligence having increased by conquest, they formed a great empire in 925, which extended from the Altai Mountains to the Pacific Ocean, and from within the Great Wall to the Yablonoi Mountains, having Peking for one of its capitals. It flourished until the twelfth century (A.D. 1125), when it gave way to the Kin empire, which held Mongolia and still more territory than the Kitans possessed within what is now China proper.

This Kin empire was founded by the expansion of the Nüjun, who, from their seats north of the Tumen and east of the Sungari, had gradually widened, and by conquest absorbed the Kitans. Aguta, the founder of the new empire, gave it the name of the

Golden Dominion.   During its existence Corea was not troubled
by her great neighbor, and for two hundred years enjoyed peace
within her borders.   Her commerce now flourished at all points
of the compass, both on land, with her northern and western
neighbors, with the Japanese on the east, and the Chinese south
and west.   Much direct intercourse in ships, guided by the magnetic needle, "the chariot of the south," took place between
Ningpo and Sunto.   Mr. Edkins states that the oldest recorded
instance of the use of the mariner's compass is that in the Chinese
historian's account of the voyage of the imperial ambassador to
Corea, from Nanking by way of Ningpo, in a fleet of eight vessels,
in the year 1122.

The Arabs, who about this time were also trading with the
Coreans, and had lived in their country, soon afterward introduced
this silent friend of the mariner into their own country in the
west, whence it found its way into Europe and to the hands of
Columbus.   To the eye of the Corean its mysterious finger pointed
to the south.   To the western man it pointed to the lode-star.

The huge wide-open eyes which the sailors of Chinese Asia
paint at the prow of their ship, to discover a path in the sea,
became more than ever an empty fancy before this unerring path-
finder.   As useless as the ever-open orbs on a mummy lid, these
lidless eyes were relegated to the domain of poetry, while the
swinging needle opened new paths of science and discovery.

Coin of Korai.   "Ko-ka" (Name of Year-Period).   "Current Money."

CHAPTER X.

CATHAY, ZIPANGU, AND THE MONGOLS.

AFTER a long breathing-spell—as one, in reading history, might call it—the old hive in the north was again ready to swarm. It was to be seen once more how useless was the Great Wall of China in keeping back the many-named invaders, known in history by the collective term Tâtars. A new people began descending from their homeland, which lay near the northern and eastern shores of Lake Baikal. This inland sea—scarcely known in the school geographies, or printed in the average atlas in such proportionate dimensions as to suggest a pond—is one of the largest lakes in the world, being 370 miles long and covering 13,300 square miles of surface. Its shores are now inhabited by Russian colonists and its waters are navigated by whole fleets of ships and steamers. It lies 1,280 feet above the sea.

Beginning their migrations from this point, in numbers and bulk that suggest only the snowball, the Mongol horsemen moved with resistless increase and momentum, consolidating into their mass tribe after tribe, until their horde seemed an avalanche of humanity that threatened to crush all civilization and engulph the whole earth. These mounted highlanders from the north were creatures who seemed to be horse and man in one being, and to actualize the old fable of the Centaurs. With a tiger-skin for a saddle, a thong loop with only the rider's great toe thrust in it for a stirrup, a string in the horse's lower jaw for a bridle, armed with spear and cimeter, these conquerors who despised walls went forth to level cities and slaughter all who resisted. In their raids they found food ever ready in the beasts they rode, for a reeking haunch of horse-meat, cut from the steed whose saddle had been emptied by arrow or accident, was usually found slung to their pommels. A slice of this, raw or warmed, served to sustain life for these hard riders, who lived all day in the saddle and at night slept with it wrapped around them.

For a century the power of these nomads was steadily growing, before they emerged clearly into history and loomed up before the frontiers of the empire. The master mind and hand that moulded them into unity was Genghis Khan (1160–1227 A.D.).

Who was Genghis Khan? A Japanese writer, who is also a traveller in Corea and China, has written in English a thesis which shows, with strong probability, at least, that this unifier of Asia was Gen-Ghiké, or Yoshitsuné. This Japanese hero, born in 1159, was the field-marshal of the army of the Minamoto who annihilated the Taira family.[1] In 1189, having fled from his jealous brother, Yoritomo, he reached Yezo and thence crossed, it is believed, to Manchuria. His was probably the greatest military mind which Japan ever produced.

That Yoshitsuné and Genghis Khan were one person is argued by Mr. Suyematz,[2] who brings a surprising array of coincidences to prove his thesis. These are in names, titles, ages, dates, personal characteristics, flags and banners, myths and traditions, nomenclature of families, localities and individuals, and Japanese relics, coins, arms, and fortresses in Manchuria. Without reaching the point of demonstration, it seems highly probable that this wonderful personality, this marvellous intellect, was of Japanese origin.

Whoever this restless spirit was, it is certain that he gathered tribes once living in freedom like the wild waves into the unity of the restless sea. Out from the grassy plains of Manchuria rolled a tidal-wave of conquest that swept over Asia, and flung its last drops of spray alike over Japan, India, and Russia. Among the nations completely overrun and overwhelmed by the Mongol hordes was Corea.

In 1206, Yezokai—the word in Japanese means Yezo Sea—the leader of the Mongols, at the request of his chieftains, took the name of Genghis Khan and proclaimed himself the ruler of an empire. He now set before himself the task of subduing the Kitans and absorbing their land and people, preparatory to the conquest of China. This was accomplished in less than six years. Liao Tung was invaded and, in 1213, his armies were inside the Great Wall. Three mighty hosts were now organized, one to overrun all China to Nepal and Anam, one to conquer Corea and Japan, and one to bear the white banners of the Mongols across Asia into Europe. This work, though not done in a day, was nearly completed before

---

[1] The Mikado's Empire, Chapters XIII. and XIV.
[2] The Identity of the Great Conqueror, Genghis Khan, with the Japanese Hero Yoshitsuné, by K. Suyematz of Japan. London, 1879.

a generation passed.[1] Genghis Khan led the host that moved to the west. In 1218 the Corean king declared himself a vassal of Genghis. In 1231 the murder of a Mongol envoy in Corea was the cause of the first act of war. The Mongols invaded the country, captured forty of the principal towns, received the humiliation of the king, who had fled to Kang-wa Island, and began the abolition of Corean independence by appointing seventy-two Mongol prefects to administer the details of local government. The people, exasperated by the new and strange methods of their foreign conquerors, rose against them and murdered them all. This was the signal for a second and more terrible invasion. A great Mongol army overran the country in 1241, fought a number of pitched battles, defeated the king, and again imposed heavy tribute on their humbled vassal. In 1256 the Corean king went in person to do homage at the court of the conqueror of continents.

In the details of the Mongol rule kindness and cruelty were blended. The most relentless military measures were taken to secure obedience after the conciliatory policy failed. By using both methods the great Khan kept his hold on the little peninsula, although the Coreans manifested a constant disposition to revolt.

About this time began a brilliant half century of intercourse between Europe and Cathay, which has been studied and illustrated in the writings of Colonel H. Yule. The two Franciscan monks Carpinini and Rubruquis visited China, and the camps of the great Khan, between the years 1245 and 1253. By their graphic narratives, in which the wars of Genghis were described, they made the name of Cathay (from Kitai, or Kitan) familiar in Europe. Matteo, Nicolo, and Marco Polo, who came later, as representatives of the commerce which afterward flourished between Venice and Genoa, and Ningpo and Amoy, were but a few among many merchants and travellers. Embassies from the Popes and the Khan exchanged courtesies at Avignon and Cambaluc (Peking). Christian churches were established in Peking and other cities by the Franciscan monks. The various Europeans who have saved their own names and a few others from oblivion, and have left us a romantic, but in the main a truthful, picture of mediæval China and the Mongols, were probably only the scribes among a host who traded or travelled, but never told their story. Among the marvels of the empire of the Mongols, in which one might walk safely from Corea to Russia, was religious toleration. When, however, the Mongols

---

[1] See Howorth's History of the Mongols, London, 1876.

of central Asia embraced the creed of Islam, bigotry closed the highway into Europe, and communications ceased. Cathay, Zipangu, and Corea again sunk from the eyes of Europe into the night of historic darkness.

Khublai Khan having succeeded his grandfather, Genghis, and being now ruler of all the Asiatic mainland, resolved, in 1266, to conquer Japan. He wrote a letter to the mikado, but the envoys were so frightened by the Corean's exaggerated account of the difficulties of reaching the empire in the sea, that they never sailed. Other embassies were despatched in 1271 and 1273, and Khublai began to prepare a mighty flotilla and army of invasion. One hundred of the ships were built on Quelpart Island. His armada, consisting of 300 vessels and 15,000 men, Chinese, Mongols, and Coreans, sailed to Japan and was met by the Japanese off the island of Iki. Owing to their valor, but more to the tempest that arose, the expedition was a total loss, only a few of the original number reaching Corea alive.

Evidently desirous of conquering Japan by diplomacy, the great Khan despatched an embassy which reached, not the mikado's, but only the shō-gun's court in 1275. His ambassadors were accompanied by a large retinue from his Corean vassals. The Japanese allowed only three of the imposing number to go to Kamakura, twelve miles from the modern Tōkiō, and paid no attention to the Khan's threatening letters. So irritated were the brave islanders that when another ambassador from the Khan arrived, in the following year, he disembarked as a prisoner and was escorted, bound, to Kamakura, where he was thrown into prison, kept during four years, and taken out only to be beheaded.

Upon hearing this, Khublai began the preparation of the mightiest of his invading hosts. To be braved by a little island nation, when his sceptre ruled from the Dnieper to the Yellow Sea, was not to be thought of. Various fleets and contingents sailed from different ports in China and made rendezvous on the Corean coast. The fleet was composed of 3,500 war junks, of large size, having on board 180,000 Chinese, Mongols, and Coreans. Among their engines of war were the catapults which the Polos had taught them to make. They set sail in the autumn of 1281.

From the very first the enterprise miscarried. The general-in-chief fell sick and the command devolved on a subordinate, who had no plan of operation. The various divisions of the force became separated. It is probable that the majority of them never reached the mainland of Japan. The Mongol and Corean contingent reached the province of Chikuzen, but were not allowed to make a successful landing, for the Japanese drove them back with sword and fire. The Chinese division, arriving later, was met by a terrible tempest that nearly annihilated them and destroyed the ships already engaged. The broken remnant of the fleet and armies, taking refuge on the island of Iki, were attacked by the Japanese and nearly all slain, imprisoned, or beheaded in cold blood. Only a few reached Corea to tell the tale.

The "Mongol civilization," so-called, seems to have had little influence on Corea. The mighty empire of Genghis soon broke into many fragments. The vast fabric of his government melted like a sand house before an incoming wave, and that wave receding left scarcely a sediment recognizable on the polity or social life of Corea. Marco Polo in his book hardly mentions the country, though describing Zipangu or Japan quite fully. One evil effect of their forced assistance given to the Mongols, was that the hatred of the Japanese and Coreans for each other was mutually intensified. After the Mongolian invasion begins that series of piratical raid on their coast and robbery of their vessels at sea, by Japanese adventurers, that made navigation beyond sight of land and shipbuilding among the Coreans almost a lost art.

The centuries following the Mongol invasion were periods of anarchy and civil war in Japan, and the central government authority being weak the pirates could not be controlled. Building or stealing ships, bands of Japanese sailors or ex-soldiers put to sea, capturing Corean boats, junks, and surf-rafts. Landing, they harried the shores and robbed and murdered the defenceless people. Growing bolder, the marauders sailed into the Yellow Sea and landed even in China and in Liao Tung. They kept whole towns and cities in terror, and a chain of coast forts had to be built in Shan-tung to defend that province.

The fire-signals which, in the old days of "the Three Kingdoms," had flashed upon the headlands to warn of danger seaward, were now made a national service. The system was perfected so as to converge at the capital, Sunto, and give notice of danger from any point on the coast. By this means better protection against the sea-rovers was secured.

All this evil experience with the piratical Japanese of the middle ages has left its impress on the language of the Coreans. From this period, perhaps even long before it, date those words of sinister omen of which we give but one or two examples which have the prefix *wai* (Japan) in them. A *wai-kol*, a huge, fierce man, of gigantic aspect, with a bad head, though perhaps with good heart, a kind of ogre, is a Japanese *kol* or creature. A destructive wind or typhoon is a Japanese wind. As western Christendom for centuries uttered their fears of the Norse pirates, "From the fury of the Northmen, Good Lord, deliver us," so the Korai people,

Two-Masted Corean Vessel (from a Photograph taken in 1871).

along the coast, for many generations offered up constant petition to their gods for protection against these Northmen of the Pacific.

This chronic danger from Japanese pirates, which Korai and Chō-sen endured for a period nearly as extended as that of England from the Northmen, is one of the causes that have contributed to make the natives dread the sea as a path for enemies, and in Corea we see the strange anomaly of a people more than semi-civilized whose wretched boats scarcely go beyond tide-water.

CHAPTER XI.

NEW CHŌ-SEN.

It will be remembered that the first Chinese settler and civilizer of Corea, Ki Tsze, gave it the name of Chō-sen. Coming from violence and war, to a land of peace which lay eastward of his old home, Ki Tsze selected for his new dwelling-place a name at once expressive of its outward position and his own inward emotions—Chō-sen, or Morning Calm.

For eleven centuries a part of Manchuria, including, as the Coreans believe, the northern half of the peninsula, bore this name. From the Christian era until the tenth century, the names of the three kingdoms, Shinra, Hiaksai, and Kokorai, or Korai, express the divided political condition of the country. On the fall of these petty states, the united peninsula was called Korai. Korai existed from A.D. 934 until A.D. 1392, when the ancient name of Chō-sen was restored. Though the Coreans often speak of their country as Korai (Gauli, or Gori), it is as the English speak of Britain—with a patriotic feeling rather than for accuracy. Chō-sen is still the official and popular designation of the country. This name is at once the oldest and the newest.

The first bestowal of this name on the peninsula was in poetic mood, and was the symbol of a peaceful triumph. The second gift of the name was the index of a political revolution not unaccompanied with bloodshed. The latter days of the dynasty founded by Wang were marked by licentiousness and effeminacy in the palace, and misrule in the country. The people hated the cruelties of their monarch, the thirty-second of his line, and longed for a deliverer. Such a one was Ni Taijo (Japanese, Ri Seiki), who was born in the region of Broughton's Bay, in the Ham-kiung province. It is said of him that from his youth he surpassed all others in virtue, intelligence, and skill in manly exercises. He was especially fond of hunting with the falcon.

One day, while in the woods, his favorite bird, in pursuing its quarry, flew so far ahead that it was lost to the sight of its master. Hastening after it the young man espied a shrine at the roadside into which he saw his hawk fly. Entering, he found within a hermit priest. Awed and abashed at the weird presence of the white-bearded sage, the lad for a moment was speechless; but the old man, addressing him, said: "What benefit is it for a youth of your abilities to be seeking a stray falcon? A throne is a richer prize. Betake yourself at once to the capital."

Acting upon the hint thus given him, and leaving the falcon behind, Taijo wended his way westward to Sunto, and entered the military service of the king. He soon made his mark and rapidly rose to high command, until he became lieutenant-general of the whole army. He married and reared children, and through the espousal of his daughter by the king, became father-in-law to his sovereign.

The influence of Taijo was now immense. While with his soldierly abilities he won the enthusiastic regard of the army, his popularity with the people rested solely on his virtues. Possessed of such influence with the court, the soldiers, and the country at large, he endeavored to reform the abuse of power and to curb the cruelties of the king. Even to give advice to a despot is an act of bravery, but Taijo dared to do it again and again. The king, however, refused to follow the counsel of his father-in-law or to reform abuses. He thus daily increased the odium in which he was held by his subjects.

Such was the state of affairs toward the end of the fourteenth century, when everything was ripe for revolution.

In China, great events, destined to influence "the little kingdom," were taking place. The Mongol dynasty, even after the breaking up of the empire founded by Genghis Khan, still held the dragon throne; but during the later years of their reign, when harassed by enemies at home, Corea was neglected and her tribute remained unpaid. A spasmodic attempt to resubdue the lapsed vassal, and make Corea a Mongol castle of refuge from impending doom, was ruined by the energy and valor of Ni Taijo. The would-be invaders were driven back. The last Mongol emperor fell in 1341, and the native Ming, or "Bright," dynasty came into power, and in 1368 was firmly established.

Their envoys being sent to Corea demanded pledges of vassalage. The king neglected, finally refused, and ordered fresh levies to be made to resist the impending invasion of the Chinese. In

this time of gloom and bitterness against their own monarch, the
army contained but a pitifully small number of men who could be
depended on to fight the overwhelming host of the Ming veterans.
Taijo, in an address to his followers, thus spoke to them:

"Although the order from the king must be obeyed, yet the
attack upon the Ming soldiers, with so small an army as ours, is
like casting an egg against a rock, and no one of the army will
return alive. I do not tell you this from any fear of death, but
our king is too haughty. He does not heed our advice. He has
ordered out the army suddenly without cause, paying no attention
to the suffering which wives and children of the soldiers must
undergo. This is a thing I cannot bear. Let us go back to the
capital and the responsibility shall fall on my shoulders alone."

Thereupon the captains and soldiers being impressed with the
purity of their leader's motives, and admiring his courage, resolved
to obey his orders and not the king's. Arriving at Sunto, he
promptly took measures to depose the king, who was sent to
Kang-wa, the island so famous in modern as in ancient and mediæval history.

The king's wrath was very great, and he intrigued to avenge
himself. His plot was made known, by one of his retainers, to
Taijo, who, by a counter-movement, put forth the last radical
measure which, in Chinese Asia means, for a private person, disin-
heritance; for a king, deposition; and for a royal line, extinction.
This act was the removal of the tablets of the king's ancestors from
their shrine, and the issue of an order forbidding further continuance of sacrifice to them. This Corean and Chinese method of
clapping the extinguisher upon a whole dynasty was no sooner ordered than duly executed.

Ni Taijo was now made king, to the great delight of the people. He sent an embassy to Nanking to notify the Ming emperor
of affairs in the "outpost state," to tender his loyal vassalage, to
seek the imperial approval of his acts, and to beg his investiture
as sovereign. This was graciously granted. The ancient name of
Chō-sen was revived, and at the petitioner's request conferred upon
the country by the emperor, who profited by this occasion to enforce upon the Coreans his calendar and chronology—the reception of these being in itself alone tantamount to a sufficient declaration of fealty. Friendship being now fully established with
the Mings, the king of Chō-sen sent a number of youths, sons of
his nobles, to Nanking to study in the imperial Chinese college.

The dynasty thus established is still the reigning family in Corea, though the direct line came to an end in 1864. The Coreans in their treaty with Japan, in 1876, dated the document according to the 484th year of Chō-sen, reckoning from the accession of Ni Taijo to the throne. One of the first acts of the new dynasty was to make a change in the location of the national capital. The new dynasty made choice of the city of Han Yang,

The Walls of Seoul (from a Photograph, 1876).

situated on the Han River, about fifty miles from its mouth. The king enlarged the fortifications, enclosed the city with a wall of masonry of great extent, extending over the adjacent hills and valleys. On this wall was a rampart pierced with port-holes for archers and over the streams were built arches of stone. He organized the administrative system which, with slight modification, is still in force at the present time. The city being well situated, soon grew in extent, and hence became the *seoul* or capital (pronounced by the Chinese *king*, as in Nanking and Peking, and the Japanese *kio*, as in Kiōto and Tōkiō). He also re-divided the kingdom into eight *dō* or provinces. This division still maintains. The names, formed each of two Chinese characters joined to that of *dō* (circuit or province), and approximate meanings are given below.[1] With such names of bright omen, "the eight provinces" entered upon an era of peace and flourishing prosperity. The people found out that something more than a change of masters was meant by the removal of the capital to a more central situation. Vigorous reforms were carried out, and changes were made, not only in political administration, but in social life, and even in religion. In all these the influence of the China of the Ming emperors is most manifest.

Buddhism, which had penetrated into every part of the country, and had become, in a measure, at least, the religion of the state, was now set aside and disestablished. The Confucian ethics and the doctrines of the Chinese sages were not only more diligently studied and propagated under royal patronage, but were incorporated into the religion of the state. From the early part of the fifteenth century, Confucianism flourished until it reached the point of bigotry and intolerance ; so that when Christianity was discovered by the magistrates to be existing among the people, it was put under the band of extirpation, and its followers thought worthy of death.

---

[1] Beginning at the most northern and eastern, and following the sea line south around up to the northeast, they are :

COREAN.	JAPANESE.	ENGLISH.
1. Ham-kiung, or	Kan-kiō dō.	Perfect Mirror, or Complete View Province.
2. Kang-wen, or	Ko-gen dō.	Bay Meadow Province.
3. Kiung-sang, or	Kei-shō dō.	Respectful Congratulation Province.
4. Julla, or	Zen-ra dō.	Completed Network Province.
5. Chung-chong, or	Chiu-sei dō.	Serene Loyalty Province.
6. Kiung-kei, or	Kei-ki dō.	The Capital Circuit, or Home Province.
7. Whang-hai, or	Ko-kai dō.	Yellow Sea Province.
8. Ping-an, or	Hei-an dō	Peace and Quiet Province.

In this table we have given the names in English which approximate the sounds of the Chinese characters, with which names of the provinces are written, and as they are heard to-day in Chō-sen. The modern Coreans use the modern Chinese sounds of the characters, while the Japanese cling to the ancient Chinese pronunciation of the same characters as they received them through Hiaksai and Shinra, eleven or twelve centuries ago. The old pure Corean sounds were Teru-ra tai for Zen-ra dō, Tsiku-shaku tai for Chiu-sei dō, Keku-shaku tai for Kei-ki dō, etc.

Magistrate and Servant.

Whatever may have been the motive for supplanting Buddhism, whether from sincere conviction of the paramount truth of
the ancient ethics, or a desire to closely imitate the Middle Kingdom in everything, even in religion, or to obtain easy and great
wealth by confiscating the monastery and temple lands, it is certain
that the change was sweeping, radical, and thorough. All observers testify that the cult of Shaka in Corea is almost a shadow. On
the other hand, in many cities throughout the land, are buildings
and halls erected and maintained by the government, in which sit
in honor the statues of Confucius and his greatest disciples.

One great measure that tended to strengthen and make popular the new religious establishment, to weaken the old faith, to
give strength and unity to the new government, to foster education and make the Corean literary classes what they are to-day—
critical scholars in Chinese—was what Americans would call " civil
service reform." Appointment to office on the basis of merit, as
shown in the literary examinations, was made the rule. Modelled
closely upon the Chinese system, three grades of examinations
were appointed, and three degrees settled. All candidates for
military or civil rank and office must possess diplomas, granted
by the royal or provincial examiners, before appointment could be
made or salary begun. The system, which is still in vogue, is
more fully described in the chapter on education.

Among the changes in the fashion of social life, introduced
under the Ni dynasty, was the adoption of the Ming costume. To
the Chinese of to-day the Corean dress and coiffure, as seen in
Peking, are subjects for curiosity and merriment. The lack of a
long queue, and the very different cut, form, and general appearance of these eastern strangers, strike the eye of mandarin and
street laborer alike, very much as a gentleman in knee-breeches,
cocked hat, and peruke, or the peasant costumes at Castle Garden,
appear to a New Yorker, stepping from the elevated railway, on
Broadway.

Yet from the fourteenth to the seventeenth century, the Chinese
gentleman dressed like the Corean of to-day, and the mandarin of
Canton or Nanking was as innocent of the Tartar hair-tail as is the
citizen of Seoul. The Coreans simply adhere to the fashions prevalent during the Ming era. The Chinese, in the matter of garb,
however loath foreigners may be to credit it, are more progressive
than their Corean neighbors.

To the house of Ni belongs also the greater honor of abolishing at least two cruel customs which had their roots in superstition. Heretofore the same rites which were so long in vogue in Japan, traces of which were noticed even down to the seventeenth century, held unchallenged sway in Corea. *Ko-rai-chang*, though not fully known in its details, was the habit of burying old men alive. *In-chei* was the offering up of human sacrifices, presumably to the gods of the mountains and the sea. Both of these classes of rites, at once superstitious and horrible, were anciently very frequent; nor was Buddhism able to utterly abolish them. In the latter case, they choked the victims to death, and then threw them into the sea. The island of Chansan was especially noted as the place of propitiation to the gods of the sea.

The first successors of the founder of the house of Ni held great power, which they used for the good of the people, and hence enjoyed great popularity. The first after Taijo reigned two years, from 1398 to 1400. Hetai-jong, who came after him, ruled eighteen years, and among other benefits conferred, established the *Sin-mun-ko*, or box for the reception of petitions addressed directly to the king. Into this coffer, complaints and prayers from the people could lawfully and easily be dropped. Though still kept before the gate of the royal palace in Seoul, it is stated that access to it is now difficult. It seems to exist more in name than in fact. Among the first diplomatic acts of King Hetai-jong was to unite with the Chinese emperor, in a complaint to the mikado of Japan, against the buccaneers, whom the authorities of the latter country were unable to control. Hence the remonstrance was only partially successful, and the evil, which was aggravated by Corean renegades acting as pilots, grew beyond all bounds. These rascals made a lucrative living by betraying their own countrymen.

Siei-jong, who succeeded to the throne on the death of his father, Hetai-jong, enjoyed a long reign of thirty-two years, during which the fortifications of the capital were added to and strengthened. The Manchius beyond the Ever-white Mountains were then beginning to rise in power, and Liao Tung was disturbed by the raids of tribes from Mongolia, which the Ming generals were unable to suppress. When the fighting took place within fifty miles of her own boundary river, Chō-sen became alarmed, and looked to the defence of her own frontier and capital. In 1450, on the death of the king, who " in time of peace prepared for war," Mun-jong, his son, succeeded to royal power. As usual on the accession of a new sovereign, a Chinese ambassador was despatched from Peking, which had been the Ming capital since 1614, to Seoul, to confer the imperial patent of investiture. This dignitary, on his return, wrote a book recounting his travels, under the title of "Memŏrandum concerning the Affairs of Chō-sen." According to this writer, the military frontier of Corea at that time was at the Eastern Mountain Barrier, a few miles north-west of the present Border Gate. Palladius, the Russian writer, also states that, during the Ming dynasty, three grades of fortresses were erected on the territory between the Great Wall and the Yalu River, "to guard against the attacks of the Coreans."

It is more in accordance with the facts to suppose that the Chinese erected these fortifications to guard against invasion from the Manchius and other northern tribes that were ravaging Liao Tung, rather than against the Coreans. These defences did not avail to keep back the invasion which came a generation or two later, and "the Corean frontier," which the Chinese traveller, in 1450, found much further west than even the present "wall of stakes," shows that the neutral territory was then already established, and larger than it now is. Of this strip of rich forest and ginseng land, with many well-watered and arable valleys, once cultivated and popu-lous, but since the fifteenth century desolate, we shall hear again. In Chinese atlases the space is blank, with not one village marked where, until the removal by the Chinese government of the inhabi-tants westward, there was a population of 300,000 souls. The de-population of this large area of fertile soil was simply a Chinese measure of military necessity, which compelled her friendly ally Chō-sen, for her own safety, to post sentinels as far west of her boundary river as the Eastern Mountain Barrier, described by the imperial envoy in 1450.

The century which saw America discovered in the west, was that of Japan's greatest activity on the sea. On every coast within their reach, from Tartary to Tonquin, and from Luzon to Siam, these bold marauders were known and feared. The Chinese learned to bitterly regret the day when the magnetic needle, in-vented by themselves, got into the hands of these daring island-ers. The wounded eagle that felt the shaft, which had been feath-ered from his own plumes, was not more to be pitied than the Chinese people that saw the Japanese craft steering across the Yellow Sea to ravage and ruin their cities, guided by the compass bought in China. They not only harried the coasts, but went far up the rivers. In 1523, they landed even at Ningpo, and in the fight the chief mandarin of the city was killed.

Yet, with the exception of incursions of these pirates, Chō-sen enjoyed the sweets of peace, and two centuries slipped away in Morning Calm. The foreign vessels from Europe which first, in 1530, touched at the province of Bungo, in Southern Japan, may possibly have visited some part of the Corean shores. Between

The Neutral Territory (from a Chinese Atlas).

1540 and 1546 four arrivals of "black ships" from Portugal, are known to have called at points in Japan. It was from these the Japanese learned how to make the gunpowder and firearms which, before the close of the century, were to be used with such deadly effect in Corea.

Now came back to Europe accounts of China and Japan—which were found to be the old Kathay, and Zipangu of Polo and the Franciscans—and of " Coria," which Polo had barely mentioned. It was from the Portuguese, that Europe first learned of this middle land between the mighty domain of the Mings, and the empire in the sea. Stirred by the spirit of adventure and enterprise, and unwilling that the Iberian peninsulars should gain all the glory, an English " Society for the Discovery of Unknown Lands" was formed in 1555. A voyage was made as far as Novaia Zemlia and Weigatz, but neither Corea nor Cathay was reached. Other attempts to find a northeast passage to India failed, and Asia remained uncircumnavigated until our own and Nordensköld's day. The other attempts to discover a northwest passage to China around the imaginary cape, in which North America was supposed to terminate, and through the equally fictitious straits of Anian, resulted in the discoveries of the Cabots, and of Hudson and Frobisher—of the American continent from the Hudson River to Greenland, but the way to China lay still around Africa.

From Japan, the only possibility of danger during these two centuries was likely to come. In the north, west, and south, on the main land, hung the banners of the Ming emperors of China, and, as the tribute enforced was very light, the protection of her great neighbor was worth to Chō-sen far more than the presents she gave. From China there was nothing to fear.

At first the new dynasty sent ships, embassies, and presents regularly to Japan, which were duly received, yet not at the mikado's palace in Kiōto, but at the shō-gun's court at Kamakura, twelve miles from the site of the modern Japanese capital, Tōkiō. But as the Ashikaga family became effeminate in life, their power waned, and rival chiefs started up all over the country. Clan fights and chronic intestine war became the rule in Japan. Only small areas of territory were governed from Kamakura, while the mikado became the tool and prey of rival daimiōs. One of these petty rulers held Tsushima, and traded at a settlement on the Corean coast called Fusan, by means of which some intercourse was kept up between the two countries. The Japanese government had always made use of Tsushima in its communications with the Coreans, and the agency at Fusan was composed almost exclusively of retainers of the feudal lord of this island. The journey by land and sea from Seoul to Kamakura, often consumed two or three months, and with civil wars inland and piracy on the water, intercourse between the two countries became less and less. The last embassy from Seoul was sent in 1460, but after that, owing to continued intestine war, the absence of the Coreans was not noticed by the Ashikagas, and as the Tsushima men purposely kept their customers ignorant of the weakness of their rulers at Kamakura and Kiōto, lest the ancient vassals should cease to fear their old master, the Coreans remained in profound ignorance of the real state of affairs in Japan. As they were never summoned, so they never came. Giving themselves no further anxiety concerning the matter, they rejoiced that such disagreeable duties were no longer incumbent upon them. It is even said in Corean histories that their government took the offensive, and under the reign of the king Chung-jong (1506–1544) captured Tsushima and several other Japanese islands, formerly tributary to Corea. Whatever fraction of truth there may be in this assertion, it is certain that Japan afterward took ample revenge on the score both of neglect and of reprisal.

So, under the idea that peace was to last forever, and the morning calm never to know an evening storm, the nation relaxed all vigilance. Expecting no danger from the east, the military resources were neglected, the army was disorganized, and the castles were allowed to dilapidate into ruin. The moats filled and became shallow ditches, choked with vegetation, the walls and ramparts crumbled piecemeal, and the barracks stood roofless. As peace wore sweeter charms, and as war seemed less and less probable, so did all soldierly duties become more and more irksome. The militia system was changed for the worse. The enrolled men, instead of being called out for muster at assigned camps, and trained to field duty and the actual evolutions of war, were allowed to assemble at local meetings to perform only holiday movements. The muster rolls were full of thousands of names, but off paper the army of Corea was a phantom. The people, dismissing all thought of possibility of war, gave themselves no concern, leaving the matter to the army officials, who drew pay as though in actual war. They, in turn, devoted themselves to dissipation, carousing, and sensual indulgence. It was while the country was in such a condition that the summons of Japan's greatest conqueror came to them and the Coreans learned, for the first time, of the fall of Ashikaga, and the temper of their new master.

CHAPTER XII.

EVENTS LEADING TO THE JAPANESE INVASION.

CHINA and Japan are to each other as England and the United States. The staid Chinaman looks at the lively Japanese with feelings similar to those of John Bull to his American " cousin." Though as radically different in blood, language, and temperament as are the Germans and French, they are enough alike to find food for mutual jealousy. They discover ground for irritation in causes, which, between nations more distant from each other, would stir up no feeling whatever. China considers Japan a young, vain, and boasting stripling, whose attitude ought ever to be that of the pupil to the teacher, or the child to the father. Japan, on the contrary, considering China as an old fogy, far behind the age, decayed in constitution and fortune alike, and more than ready for the grave, resents all dictation or assumption of superiority. Even before their adoption of the forces of occidental civilization in this nineteenth century, something of this haughty contempt for China influenced the Japanese mind. Japan ever refused to become vassal or tributary to China, and the memory of one of her military usurpers, who accepted the honorary title of Nihon-O, or King of Japan, from the Chinese Emperor, is to this day loaded with increasing execration. It has ever been the practice of the Japanese court and people cheerfully to heap upon their mikado all the honors, titles, poetical and divine appellations which belong also to the Chinese emperor.

To conquer or humble their mighty neighbor, to cross their slender swords of divine temper with the clumsy blades of the continental braves, has been the ambition of more than one Japanese captain. But Hidéyoshi alone is the one hero in Japanese annals who actually made the attempt.

As the Mongol conquerors issuing from China had used Corea as their point of departure to invade Japan, so Hidéyoshi resolved to make the peninsula the road for his armies into China. After two centuries of anarchy in Japan, he followed up the work which Nobunaga had begun until the proudest daimiō had felt the weight of his arm, and the empire was at peace.

Yet, although receiving homage and congratulations from his feudal vassals, once proud princes, Hidéyoshi was irritated that Chō-sen, which he, with all Japanese, held to be a tributary province, failed to send like greetings. Since, to the Ashikagas, she had despatched tribute and embassies, he was incensed that similar honors were not awarded to him, though, for over a century, all official relations between the two countries had ceased.

On the 31st day of July, 1585, Hidéyoshi was made Kuambaku, or Regent, and to celebrate his elevation to this, the highest office to which a subject of the mikado's could aspire, he shortly afterward gave a great feast in Kiôto, and proclaimed holiday throughout the empire. This feast was graced by the presence of his highest feudatories, lords, and captains, court nobles and palace ladies in their richest robes. Among others was one Yasuhiro, a retainer of the lord of Tsushima. Hidéyoshi's memory had been refreshed by his having had read to him, from the ancient chronicles, the account of Jingu Kōgō's conquests in the second century. He announced to his captains that, though Chōsen was from ancient times tributary to Japan, yet of late years her envoys had failed to make visits or to send tribute. He then appointed Yasuhiro to proceed to Seoul, and remind the king and court of their duty.

The Japanese envoy was a bluff old campaigner, very tall, and of commanding mien. His hair and beard had long since turned white under years and the hardships of war. His conduct was that of a man accustomed to command and to instant obedience, and to expect victory more by brute courage than by address. On his journey to Seoul he demanded the best rooms in the hotels, and annoyed even the people of rank and importance with haughty and strange questions. He even laughed at and made sarcastic remarks about the soldiers and their weapons. This conduct, so different from that of previous envoys, greatly surprised the Corean officials. Heretofore, when a Japanese officer came to Fusan, native troops escorted him from Fusan to Seoul, overawing him by their fierceness and insolence. Yasuhiro, accustomed to constant war under Hidéyoshi's gourd-banner, rode calmly on his horse, and, amid the lines of lances drawn up as a guard of honor, spoke to his followers in a loud voice, telling them to watch the escort and note any incivility. In a certain village he joked with a Corean soldier about his spear, saying, with a pun, that it was too short and unfit for use. At this, all the Japanese laughed out loud. The Coreans could not understand the language, but hearing the laugh were angry and surprised at such boldness. At another town he insulted an aged official who was entertaining him, by remarking to his own men that his hair and that of the Japanese grew gray by years, or by war and manly hardships ; " but what," cried he, " has turned this man's hair gray who has lived all his life amid music and dancing ? " This sarcastic fling, at premature and sensual old age, stung the official so that he became speechless with rage. At the capital, credentials were presented and a feast given, at which female musicians sang and wine flowed. During the banquet, when all were well drunk, the old hero pulled out a gourd full of pepper seeds and began to hand them around. The singing-girls and servants grabbed them, and a disgraceful scuffle began. This was what Yasuhiro wanted. Highly disgusted at their greedy behavior, he returned to his quarters and poured out a tirade of abuse about the manners of the people, which his Corean interpreter duly retailed to his superiors. Yasuhiro made up his mind that the country was in no way prepared for invasion ; the martial spirit of the people was very low, and the habits of dissipation and profligacy among them had sapped the vigor of the men.

To the offensive conduct of the envoy was added the irritation produced by the language of Hidéyoshi's summons ; for in his letter he had used the imperial form of address, " we," the plural of majesty. Yasuhiro asked for a reply to these letters, that he might return speedily to Japan. There was none given him, and the Coreans, pleading the flimsy excuse of the difficulty of the voyage, refused to send an embassy to Japan.

Hidéyoshi was very angry at the utter failure of Yasuhiro's mission. He argued that for an envoy to be content with such an answer was sure proof that he favored the Coreans. Some of Yasuhiro's ancestors, being daimiōs of Tsushima, had served as envoys to Chō-sen, and had enjoyed a monopoly of the lucrative commerce, and even held office under the Corean government. Reflecting on these things, Hidéyoshi commanded Yasuhiro and all his family to be put to death.

He then despatched a second envoy, named Yoshitoshi, himself the daimiō of Tsu Island, who took with him a favorite retainer, and a priest, named Genshō, as his secretary. They reached Seoul in safety, and, after the formal banquet, demanded the despatch of an envoy to Japan. The Corean dignitaries did not reply at once, but unofficially sent word, through the landlord of the hotel, that they would be glad to agree to the demand if the Japanese would send back the renegades who piloted the Japanese pirates in their raids upon the Corean coasts. Thereupon, Yoshitoshi despatched one of his suite to Japan. With amazing promptness he collected the outlaws, fourteen in number, and produced them in Seoul. These traitors, after confessing their crime, were led out by the executioners and their heads knocked off. Meanwhile, having tranquillized "all under Heaven" (Japan), even to Yezo and the Ainos, and finding nothing "within the four seas" worth capturing, Hidéyoshi cast his eyes southward to the little kingdom well named Riu Kiu, or the Sleepy Dragon without horns. The people of these islands, called Loo Choo, on old maps, are true Japanese in origin, language, and dynasty. They speak a dialect kindred to that of Satsuma, and their first historical ruler was Sunten, a descendant of Tamétomo, who fled from Japan in the twelfth century. Of the population of 120,000 people, one-tenth were of the official class, who lived from the public granaries. Saving all expense in war equipment, and warding off danger from the two great powers between which they lay, they had kept the good will of either by making their country act the part of the ass which crouches down between two burdens. They made presents to both, acknowledging Japan as their father, and China as their mother. From early times they had sent tribute-laden junks to Ningpo, and had introduced the Chinese classics, and social and political customs. When the Ming dynasty came into power, the Chinese monarch bestowed on the Prince of Riu Kiu a silver seal, and a name for his country, which meant "hanging balls," a reference to the fact that their island chain hung like a string of tassels on the skirt of China. Another of their ancient native names was Okinawa, or "long rope," which stretches as a cable between Japan and Formosa. Sugar and rice are the chief products. Hidéyoshi, wishing to possess this group of isles as an ally against China, and acting on the principle of baiting with a sprat in order to catch a mackerel, sent word to Riu Kiu to pay tribute hereafter only to him.

The young king, fearing the wrath of the mighty lord of Nippon, sent a priest as his envoy, and a vessel laden with tribute offerings. Arriving in the presence of the august parvenu, the priest found himself most graciously received. Hidéyoshi entered into a personal conversation with the bonze, and set forth the benefits of Riu Kiu's adherence to Japan alone, and her ceasing to send tribute to China. At the same time he gave the priest clearly to understand that, willing or unwilling, the little kingdom was to be annexed to the mikado's empire. When the priest returned to Riu Kiu and gave the information to the king, the latter immediately despatched a vessel to China to inform the government of the designs of Japan.

Meanwhile, the court at Seoul, highly gratified with the action of the Japanese government in the matter of the renegade pilots, gave a banquet to the embassy. Yoshitoshi had audience of the king, who presented him with a horse from his own stables. An embassy was chosen which left Seoul, in company with Yoshitoshi and his party, and their musicians and servants, in April, 1590, and, after a journey and voyage of three months, arrived at Kiōto during the summer of 1590. At this time Hidéyoshi was absent in Eastern Japan, not far from the modern city of Tōkiō, besieging Odawara Castle and reducing "the second Hōjō" family to submission. Arriving at Kiōto in the autumn, he postponed audience with the Coreans in order to gain time for war preparations, for his heart was set on conquests beyond sea.

Finally, after five months had passed, they were accorded an interview. They were allowed to ride in palanquins under the gateway of the palace without dismounting—a mark of deference to their high rank—all except nobles of highest grade being compelled to get out and walk. As usual, their band of musicians accompanied them.

They report Hidéyoshi as a man of low appearance, but with eyes that shot fire through their souls. All bowed before him, but his conduct in general was of a very undignified character. This did not raise him in the estimation of his guests, who had already discovered his true position, which was that of a subject of the mikado, whose use of the imperial " we " in his letters was, in their eyes, a preposterous assumption of authority. They delivered the king's letter, which was addressed to Hidéyoshi on terms of an equal as a Koku O (king of a nation, in distinction from the title of Whang Ti, by which title the Heavenly Ruler, or Emperor—the Mikado of Japan, or the Emperor of China—is addressed). The letter contained the usual commonplaces of friendly greeting, the names of the envoys, and a reference to the list of accompanying presents.

The presents—spoken of in the usual terms of Oriental mock modesty—consisted of two ponies and fifteen falcons, with harness for bird and beast, rolls of silk, precious drugs, ink, paper, pens, and twenty magnificent tiger-skins. The interview over, Hidéyoshi wished the envoys to go home at once. This they declined to do, but, leaving Kiōto, waited at the port of Sakai. A letter to the king finally reached them, but couched in so insolent a tone that the ambassadors sent it back several times to be purged. Even in its improved form it was the blustering threat of a Japanese bully. All this consumed time, which was just what Hidéyoshi wished.

Some years before this, some Portuguese trading ships had landed at the island of Tané, off the south of Japan. The Japanese, for the first time, saw Europeans and heard their unintelligible language. At first all attempts to understand them were in vain. A Chinese ship happened to arrive about the same time, on which were some sailors who knew a little Portuguese, and thus communications were held. The foreigners, being handsomely treated, gave their hosts some firearms, probably pistols, taught their use, and how to make powder. These "queer things, able to vomit thunder and lightning, and emitting an awful smell," were presented to Shimadzŭ, the daimiō of Satsuma, who gave them to Hidéyoshi. Among the presents, made in return to Chōsen, were several of these new weapons made by Japanese. They were most probably sent as a hint, like that of the Pequot's offering of the arrows wrapped in snake-skin. With them were pheasants, stands of swords and spears, books, rolls of paper, and four hundred gold *koban* (a coin worth about $5.00).

With the returning embassy, Hidéyoshi sent the priest and a former colleague of Yoshitoshi to Seoul. They were instructed to ask the king to assist Hidéyoshi to renew peaceful relations between Japan and China. These, owing to the long continued piratical invasions from Japan, during the anarchy of the Ashikaga, had been suspended for some years past.

The peaceful influences of Christianity's teachings now came between these two pagan nations, in the mind and person of Yoshitoshi, who had professed the faith of Jesus as taught by the Roman Catholic missionaries from Portugal, then in Japan. Be this as it may, Yoshitoshi, who had been in Seoul, and lived in Tsushima, being well acquainted with the military resources of the three countries, knew that war would result in ruin to Chō-sen, while, in measuring their swords with China, the Japanese were at fearful odds. Animated by a desire to prevent bloodshed, he resolved to mediate with the olive branch. He started on an independent mission, at his own cost, to persuade the Coreans to use their good offices at mediation between Japan and China, and tʰus prevent war. Arriving at Fusan, in 1591, he forwarded his petition to Seoul, and waited in port ten days in hopes of the answer he desired. But all was in vain. He received only a letter containing a defiant reply to his master's bullying letter. In sadness he returned to Kiōto, and reported his ill-success. Surprised and enraged at the indifference of the Coreans, Hidéyoshi pushed on his war preparations with new vigor. He resolved to test to its utmost the military strength of Japan, in order to humble China as well as her vassal. Accustomed to victory under the gourdbanner in almost every battle during the long series of intestine wars now ended, an army of seasoned veterans heard joyfully the order to prepare for a campaign beyond sea.

Hidéyoshi, during this year, nominally resigned the office of Kuambaku, in favor of his son, and, according to usage, took the title of Taikō, by which name (Taikō Sama) he is popularly known, and by which we shall refer to him. Among the Coreans, even of to-day, he is remembered by the title which still inspires their admiration and terror—Kuambaku. Chinese writers give a grotesque account of Hidéyoshi, one of whose many names they read as Ping-syew-kye. They call him "the man under a tree," in reference to his early nickname of Kinomoto. He is also dubbed "King of Taikō." The Jesuit missionaries speak of him in their letters as Quabacundono (His Lordship the Kuambaku), or by one of his personal names, Faxiba (Hashiba).

The Coreans were now in a strait. Though under the protectorate of China, they had been negotiating with a foreign power. How would China like this? Should they keep the entire matter secret, or should they inform their suzerain of the intended invasion of China? They finally resolved upon the latter course, and despatched a courier to Peking. About the same time the messenger from Riu Kiu had landed, and was on his way with the same tidings. The Riukiuan reached Peking first, and the Corean arrived only to confirm the news. Yet, in spite of such overwhelming evidence of the designs of Japan, the colossal " tortoise " could, at first, scarce believe " the bee " would attempt to sting.

CHAPTER XIII.

THE INVASION—ON TO SEOUL.

For the pictures of camps, fleets, the details of armory and commissariat, and all the pomp and circumstance that make up the bright side of Japanese war preparations in 1591 and 1592, we are indebted, not only to the Japanese writers, but to those eye witnesses and excellent "war correspondents," the Portuguese missionaries then in Kiushiu, and especially to Friar Louis Frois. He tells us of the amplitude, vigor, and brilliancy of Taikō's measures for invasion, and adds that the expenses therefor greatly burdened the "ethniques" or daimiōs who had to pay the cost. Those feudatories, whose domain bordered the sea, had to furnish a mighty fleet of junks, while to man them, the quota of every hundred houses of the fishing population was ten sailors.

The land and naval forces assembled at Nagoya, in Hizen, now called Karatsu, and famous for being the chief place for the manufacture of Hizen porcelain. Here a superb castle was built, while huge inns or resting-places were erected all along the road from Kiōto. The armies gathered here during the war numbered 500,-000 men ; of whom 150,000 formed the army of invasion, 60,000 the first reserve, while 100,000 were set apart as Taikō's bodyguard ; the remainder were sailors, servants, camp followers, etc.

Beside the old veterans were new levies of young soldiers, and a corps of matchlock men, who afterward did good execution among the Coreans. The possession of this new and terrible weapon gave the invaders a mighty advantage over their enemies. Though firearms had been known and manufactured in Japan for a half century, this was the first time they were used against foreign enemies, or on a large scale. Taikō also endeavored to hire or buy from the Portuguese two ships of war, so as to use their artillery ; but in this he failed, and the troops were despatched in native-built vessels. These made a gallant display as they crowded together by hundreds. At the signal, given by the firing of can-

non, the immense fleet hoisted sail and, under a fresh breeze, bore
away to the west.

Their swelling sails, made of long sections of canvass laced
together, vertically, at their edges, from stem to boom (thus differing from the Chinese, which are laced horizontally), were inscribed with immense crests and the heraldic devices of feudalism, many feet in diameter. Near the top were cross-wise bands
or stripes of black. The junks of Satsuma could be distinguished
by the white cross in a circle; those of Higo by the broad-banded
ring. On one were two crossed arrow-feathers, on others the
chess-board, the "cash" coin and palm-leaves, the butterfly, the
cloisonné symbol, the sun, the fan, etc. Innumerable banners,
gay with armorial designs or inscribed with Buddhist texts, hung
on their staves or fluttered gaily as flags and streamers from the
mastheads. Stuck into the back of many of the distinguished
veterans, or officers, were the *sashi-mono*, or bannerets. Kato
Kiyomasa, being a strict Buddhist, had for the distinctive blazon
of his back-pennant, and on the banners of his division, the prayer
and legend of his sect, the Nichirenites, "NAMU MIYO HO RENGÉ KIŌ"
(Glory to the Holy Lotus, or Glory to the salvation-bringing book
of the Holy Law of Buddha). On the forward deck were ranged
heavy shields of timber for the protection of the archers. These,
at close quarters, were to be let down and used as boarding
planks, when the sword, pike, and grappling-hook came into play.
Huge tassels, dangling from the prows like the manes of horses,
tossed up and down as the ships rode over the waves. Each junk
had a huge eye painted at the prow, to look out and find the path in
the sea. With the squadron followed hundreds of junks, laden with
salt meat, rice-wine, dried fish, and rice and beans, which formed
the staple of the invaders commissariat for man and horse. Transport junks, with cargoes of flints, arrows, ball, powder, wax can-
dles, ship and camp stores, "not forgetting a single thing," sailed
soon after, as well as the craft containing horses for the cavalry.

Taikō did not go to Corea himself, being dissuaded by his
aged mother. The court also wished no weaker hand than his to
hold the reins of government while the army was on foreign
shores. The men to whom he entrusted the leadership of the expedition, were Konishi Yukinaga and Kato Kiyomasa. To the
former, he presented a fine war horse, telling him to "gallop over
the bearded savages" with it, while to the latter he gave a battle-
flag. Konishi was an impetuous young man, only twenty-three years

of age. He was a favorite of Taikō, and sprung like the latter from the common people, being the son of a medicine dealer. His crest or banner was a huge, stuffed, white paper bag, such as druggists in Japan use as a shop sign. In this he followed the example of his august chief, who, despising the brocade banners of the imperial generals, stuck a gourd on a pole for his colors. For every victory he added another gourd, until his immense cluster contained as many proofs of victory as there are bamboo sticks in an umbrella. The " gourd-banner " became the emblem of infallible victory. Konishi also imitated his master in his tactics—impetuous attack and close following up of victory.

Konishi was a Christian, an ardent convert to the faith of the Jesuit fathers, by whom he had been baptized in 1584. In their writings, they call him " Don Austin "—a contraction of Augustine. Other Christian lords or daimiōs, who personally led their troops in the field with Konishi, were Arima, Omura, Amakusa, Bungo, and Tsushima. The personal name of the latter, a former envoy to Corea, of whom we have read before, was Yoshitoshi. He was the son-in-law of Konishi. Kuroda, as Mr. Ernest Satow has shown, is the "Kondera" of the Jesuit writers.

Kato Kiyomasa was a noble, whose castle seat was at Kumamoto in Higo. From his youth he had been trained to war, and had a reputation for fierce bravery. It is said that Kato suggested to Taikō the plan of invading Corea. His crest was a broad-banded circle, and his favorite weapon was a long lance with but one cross-blade instead of two. Kato is the "Toronosqui" of the Jesuit fathers, who never weary of loading his memory with obloquy. This " vir ter execrandus " was a fierce Buddhist and a bitter foe to Christianity. A large number of fresh autographic writings had been made by the bonzes in the monasteries expressly for Kato's division. The silk pennon, said to have been inscribed by Nichiren himself and worn by Kato during the invasion, is now in Tōkiō, owned by Katsu Awa, and is six centuries old.

With such elements at work between the two commanders, bitterness of religious rivalry, personal emulation, the desire to earn glory each for himself alone, the contempt of an old veteran for a young aspirant, harmony and unity of plan were not to be looked for. Nevertheless, the personal qualities of each general were such as to inspire his own troops with the highest enthusiasm, and the army sailed away fully confident of victory.

7

What were the objects of Taikō in making this war? Evidently his original thought was to invade and humble China. Then followed the determination to conquer Chō-sen. Ambition may have led him to rival Ojin Tennō, who, in his mother's womb, made the conquest of Shinra, and, as the deified Hachiman, became the Japanese god of war. Lastly, the Jesuit fathers saw in this expedition a plot to kill off the Christian leaders in a foreign land, and thus extirpate Christianity in Japan. To ship the Christians off to a foreign soil to die of wounds or disease, was easier than to massacre them. They make Taikō a David, and his best generals Uriahs—though Coligny, slain twenty years before, might have served for a more modern illustration.

Certain it is that it was during the absence of the Christian leaders that the severest persecutions at home took place. It is probable, also, that his jealousy of the success and consequent popularity of the Christian generals created irresolution in Taikō's mind, leading him to neglect the proper support of the expedition and thus to bring about a gigantic failure.

Finally, we must mention the theory of a Japanese friend, Mr. Egi Takato, who held that Taikō, having whole armies of unemployed warriors, all jealous of each other, was compelled, in order to ensure peace in Japan, to find employment for their swords. His idea was to send them on this distant "frontier service," and give them such a taste of home-sickness that peaceful life in Japan would be a desideratum ever afterward.

The Coreans, by their own acknowledgment, were poorly prepared for a war with the finest soldiers in Asia, as the Japanese of the sixteenth century certainly were. Nor had they any leader of ability to direct their efforts. Their king, Sien-jo, the fifteenth of the house of Ni, who had already reigned twenty-six years, was a man of no personal importance, addicted entirely to his own pleasures, a drunkard, and a debauchee. Though the royal proclamation was speedily issued, calling on the people to fortify their cities, to rebuild the dilapidated castles, and to dig out the moats, long since choked by mud and vegetation, the people responded so slowly, that few of the fortresses were found in order, when their enemies laid siege to them. Weapons were plentiful, but there were no firearms, save those presented as curiosities by the Taikō to the king. There was little or no military organization, except on paper, while the naval defences were in a sad plight. However, they began to enroll and drill, to lay up stores

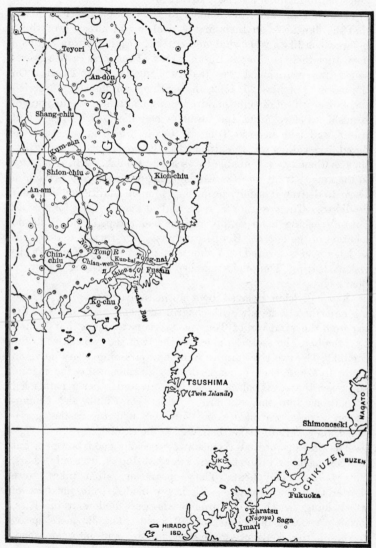

Map of the Japanese Military Operations of 1592.

of fish and grain for the army, to build ships, to repair their walls, and even to manufacture rude firearms.

Yet even the most despondent of the Coreans never dreamed that the Japanese, on their first arrival, would sweep everything before them like a whirlwind, and enter the capital within eighteen days after their landing at Fusan. One of the first castles garrisoned and provisioned was that of Tong-nai, near Fusan. On the morning of May 25, 1592, the sentinels on the coast descried the Japanese fleet of eight hundred ships, containing the division of Konishi. Before night the invaders had disembarked, captured Fusan, and laid siege to Tong-nai Castle, which at once surrendered. So sudden was the attack that the governor of the district, then in the city, was unable to escape. Konishi, writing a letter to the king, gave it into the hands of the governor, and made him swear to deliver it safely, promising him unconditional liberty if he did so. The governor agreed, and at once set out for Seoul ; but on reaching it he simply said he had escaped, and made no mention of the letter. His perjury was not to remain undetected, as later events proved. Without an hour's delay Konishi's division, leaving Tong-nai, marched up the Nak-tong valley to Shang-chiu.

Kato's division, delayed by a storm, arrived next day. Landing immediately, he saw with chagrin the pennons of his rival flying from the ramparts of Tong-nai. Angry at being left behind by "the boy," he took the more northerly of the two routes to the capital. The two rival armies were now straining every nerve on a race to Seoul, each eager to destroy all enemies on the march, and reach the royal palace first. Kuroda and other generals led expeditions into the southern provinces of Chulla and Chung-chong. These provinces being subdued, and the castles garrisoned, they were to make their way to the capital.

The Coreans proved themselves especially good bowmen, but inexpert at other weapons, their swords being of iron only, short, clumsy, and easily bent. Their spears, or rather pikes, were shorter than the Japanese, with heavy blades, from the base of which hung tassels. The iron heads were hollow at the base, forming a socket, in which the staff fitted. The Japanese spearheads, on the contrary, were riveted down and into the wood, which was iron-banded for further security, making a weapon less likely to get out of order, while the blades were steel-edged. The Corean cavalry had heavy, three-pronged spears, which were extremely formidable to look at, but being so heavy as to be unwieldly at close quarters, they did little execution. Many of their suits of armor were handsomely inlaid, made of iron and leather.

Corean Knight of the Sixteenth Century.

but less flexible and more vulnerable than those of the Japanese. which were of interlaced silk and steel on a background of tough buckskin, with sleeves of chain mail. The foot soldiers on either side were incased in a combination of iron chain and plate armor, but the Coreans had no glaves, or cross-blades on their pikes, and thus were nearly helpless against their enemy's cavalry. The Japanese were smooth-shaven, and wore stout helmets, with ear-guards and visors, but the Coreans, with open helmets, without visors, and whiskered faces, were dubbed "hairy barbarians." They were beginning to learn the use of powder, which, however, was so badly mixed as to be exasperatingly slow in burning. Their very few firearms were of the rudest and most cumbrous sort. They used on their ramparts a kind of wooden cannon, made of bamboo-hooped timber, from which they shot heavy wooden darts, three feet long, pointed with sharp-bladed, Y-shaped iron heads. The range of these clumsy missiles was very short. The Japanese, on the contrary, had at several sieges pieces of light brass ordnance, with which they quickly cleared the walls of the castles, and then scaled them with long and light ladders, made of bamboo, and easily borne by men on a run. The Japanese were not only better equipped, but their tactics were superior. Their firearms frightened the Corean horses, and the long spears and halberds of their cavalry were used with fearful effect while pursuing the fugitives, who were pierced or pulled off their steeds, or sabred in droves. Few bodies of native troops faced the invaders in the field, while fire-arrows, gunpowder, and ladders quickly reduced the castles. Not a few of the Corean officers were killed inside their fortresses by the long range fire of the sharp-shooters in the matchlock corps.

The greater share of glory fell to Konishi, the younger man. Taking the southern route, he reached the castle of Shang-chiu, in the northwestern part of Kiung-sang, and captured it. Leaving a garrison, he pushed on to Chiun-chiu. This fortress of Chiun-chiu is situated in the northeastern part of Chung-chong province, and on the most northerly of the two roads, over which Kato was then marching. It was at that time considered to be the strongest castle in the peninsula. On it rested the fate of the capital. It lay near one of the branches of the Han River, which flows past Seoul. At this point the two high roads to the capital, on which the two rivals were moving, converged so as to nearly touch. Chiun-chiu castle lay properly on Kato's route, but Konishi, being in the advance, invested it with his forces and, after a few days' siege, captured the great stronghold. The loss of the Coreans thus far in the three fortresses seized by Konishi, as reported by Friar Frois, was 5,000 men, 3,000 of whom fell at Chiun-chiu; while the

Japanese had lost but 100 killed and 400 wounded. After such a victory, " Konishi determined to conquer all Corea by himself."

Kato and his army, arriving a few days after the victory, again saw themselves outstripped. Konishi's pennons floated from every tower, and the booty was already disposed of. The goal of both armies was now " the Miaco of the kingly city of Coray." Straining every nerve, Kato pressed forward so rapidly that the two divisions of the Japanese army entered Seoul by different gates on the same day. No resistance was offered, as the king, court, and army had evacuated the city three days before. The brilliant pageant of the Japanese army, in magnificent array of gay silk and glittering armor, was lost on the empty streets of deserted Seoul.

When Taikō heard of the success of his lieutenants in Corea, especially of Konishi's exploits, he was filled with joy, and cried out, " Now my own son seems risen from the dead."

CHAPTER XIV.

THE CAMPAIGN IN THE NORTH.

THE court at Seoul had been too much paralyzed by the sudden invasion to think of or carry out any effective means of resistance. Konishi had sent letters from Fusan and Shang-chiu, but these, through official faithlessness and the accidents of war, had failed in their purpose. Konishi was too fast for them. When the news reached Seoul, of the fall of Chiun-chiu castle, the whole populace, from palace to hut, was seized with a panic which, in a few hours, emptied the city. The soldiers deserted their post, and the courtiers their king, while the people fled to the mountains. His Majesty resolved to go with his court into Liao Tung, but to send the royal princes into the northern provinces, that the people might realize the true state of affairs. So hurried were the preparations for flight, which began June 9th, that no food was provided for the journey. The only horses to be obtained were farm and pack animals, as the royal stables had been emptied by the runaway soldiers. The rain fell heavily, in perpendicular streams, soon turning the roads to mire, and drenching the women and children. The Corean dress, in wet weather, is cold and uncomfortable, and when soaked through, becomes extremely heavy, making a foot journey a severe tax on the strength. To add to the distress of the king, as the cortege passed, the people along the road clamored, with bitter tears, that they were being abandoned to the enemy. Tortured with hunger and fatigue, the wretched party floundered on.

Their first day's journey was to Sunto, or Kai Seng, thirty miles distant. Darkness fell upon them long before they reached the Rin-yin River, a tributary of the Han, which joins it a few miles above Kang-wa Island. The city lay beyond it, and the crossing of the stream was done in the light of the conflagration kindled behind them. The king had ordered the torch to be applied to the barracks and fortifications which guarded the southern bank of the river. Another motive for this incendiary act was to deprive their pursuers of ready materials to ferry themselves across the river. It was not until near midnight that the miserable fugitives, tortured with hunger and almost dead with fatigue, entered the city. Though feeling safe for the moment, since the Japanese pursuers could not cross the river without boats or rafts, most of the king's household were doomed still to suffer the pangs of hunger. The soldiers had stolen the food provided for the party, and the king had a scant supper, while his household remained hungry until the next day, when some of the military gave them a little rice. The march was resumed on the following morning and kept up until Ping-an was reached. Here they halted to await the progress of events.

The king ordered his scattered forces to rally at the Rin-yin River, and, on its northern bank, to make a determined stand.

Kato and Konishi, remaining but a short time in the capital, united their divisions and pressed forward to the north. Reaching the Rin-yin River, they found the Corean junks drawn up on the opposite side in battle array. The Japanese, being without boats, could not cross, and waited vainly during several days for something to turn up. Finally they began a feigned retreat. This induced a portion of the Corean army to cross the river, when the Japanese turned upon them and cut them down with terrible slaughter. With the few rafts and boats used by the enemy, the Japanese matchlock men rapidly crossed the stream, shot down the sailors and the remaining soldiers in the junks, and thus secured the fleet by which the whole army·crossed and began the march on Ping-an.

The rival Japanese commanders, Kato and Konishi, who had hitherto refrained from open quarrel, now found it impossible to remain longer together, and drew lots to decide their future fields of action in the two northern provinces. Ham-kiung fell to Kato, who immediately marched eastward with his division, taking the high road leading to Gensan. Konishi, to whom the province of Ping-an fell, pushed on to Ping-an City, arriving on the south bank of the river toward the end of July, or about three weeks after leaving Seoul. Here he went into camp, to await the reinforcements under Kuroda and Yoshitoshi. These soon afterward arrived, having traversed the four provinces bordering on the Yellow Sea.

The great need of the Japanese was floating material; next to this, their object was to discover the fords of the river. On

July 20th they made a demonstration against the fleet of junks along the front of the city, by sending out a few detachments of matchlock men on rafts. Though unsuccessful, the Corean king was so frightened that he fled with his suite to Ai-chiu. The garrison still remained alert and defiant.

Delay made the Japanese less vigilant. The Corean commanders, noticing this, planned to surprise their enemy by a night attack. Owing to bad management and delay, the various detachments did not assemble on the opposite side of the river until near daylight. Then forming, they charged furiously upon Konishi's camp, and, taking his men by surprise, carried off hundreds of prisoners and horses, the cavalry suffering worse than the infantry. Kuroda's division came gallantly to their support, and drove the Coreans back to the river. By this time it was broad daylight, and the cowardly boat-keepers, frightened at the rout of their countrymen, had pushed off into mid-stream. Hundreds of the Coreans were drowned, and the main body, left in the lurch, were obliged to cross by the fords. This move gave the Japanese the possession of the coveted secret. Flushed with victory, the entire army crossed over later on the same day and entered the city. Dispirited by their defeat, the garrison fled, after flinging their weapons into the castle moats and ditches of the city ; but all the magazines of grain, dried fish, etc., were now in the' hands of the invaders. Frois reports, from hearsay, that 80,000 Coreans made the attack on Konishi's camp, 8,000 of whom were slain.

The news of the fall of Ping-an City utterly demoralized the Coreans, so that, horses being still numerous, the courtiers deserted the king, and the villagers everywhere looted the stores of food provided for the army. Many of the fugitives did not cease their flight until they had crossed the Yalu River, and found themselves on Chinese territory. These bore to the Governor of Liao Tung province, who had been an anxious observer of events, the news of the fall of Ping-an, and the irresistible character of the invasion. The main body of the Corean army went into camp at Sun-an, between An-ton and Sun-chon. In Japan, there was great rejoicing at the news received from the frontier, because, as Frois wrote, Konishi, " in twenty days, hath subdued so mighty a kingdom to the crown of Japan." Taikō sent the brilliant young commander a two-edged sword and a horse—" pledges of the most peerless honor that can possibly be done to a man."

The Japanese soldiers felt so elated over their victory that they

expected immediate orders to march into China. With this purpose in view, Konishi sent word to the fleet at Fusan to sail round
the western coast, into Ta-tong River, in order to co-operate with
the victorious forces at Ping-an. Had this junction taken place,
it is probable China would have been invaded by Japanese armies, and a general war between these rival nations might have

Map illustrating the Campaign in the North, 1592–93.

turned the current of Asiatic history. This, however, was not to
be. Corean valor, with the aid of gunpowder and improved naval
construction, prevented this, and kept three hundred miles of distance, in a mountainous country, between the Japanese and their
base of supplies.

Oriental rhetoric might describe the situation in this wise : the
eastern dragon of invasion flew across the sea in winged ships, and

speedily won the crystal of victory. But on land the dragon must go upon its belly. The Corean navy snatched the jewel from the very claws of the dragon, and left it writhing and hungry.

In cool western phrase, sinister, but significant, Konishi was soon afterward obliged to " make a change of base." The brilliant success of the army seems to have impressed the Japanese naval men with the idea that there was nothing for them to do. On the contrary, the Chō-sen people set to work to improve the architecture of their vessels by having them double-decked. They also provided for the safety of their fighting men, by making heavy bulwarks, and rearing, along the upper deck, a line of strong planks, set edgewise, and bolted together. Behind these, archers discharged their missiles without danger, while from port-holes below they fired their rude, but effective, cannon. Appearing off the inlet, in which the Japanese fleet lay at anchor, they at first feigned retreat, and thus enticed their enemies into pursuit. When well out on the open sea, they turned upon their pursuers, and then their superior preparation and equipment were evident at once.

Lively fighting began, but this time the Coreans seemed invulnerable. They not only gained the advantage by the greater length of their lances and grappling-hooks, with which, using them like long forks, they pulled their enemies into the sea, but they sunk a number of the Japanese junks, either by their artillery or by ramming them with their prows. The remnant of the beaten fleet crept back to Fusan, and all hope of helping the army was given up. The moral effect of the victory upon the Corean people was to inspire them to sacrifice and resistance, and in many skirmishes they gained the advantage. They now awaited hopefully the approach of Chinese reinforcements.

To the Chinese it seemed incredible that the capture of the strongest castles, the capital, and the chief northern city, could be accomplished without the treasonable connivance of the Coreans. In order to satisfy his own mind, the Chinese mandarin sent a special agent into Corea to examine and report. The government at Peking were even more suspicious, but after some hesitation, they despatched, not without misgiving, a small body of Chinese soldiers to act as a body-guard to the Corean king. These braves crossed the frontier ; but while on their way to Ping-an, heard of the fall of the city, and, facing about, marched back into Liao Tung. The king and the fragments of his court now sent courier after courier with piteous appeals to Peking for aid, even offering to become the subjects of China in return for succor rendered. A force of 5,000 men was hastily recruited in Liao Tung, who marched rapidly into Corea. Early in August the Japanese pickets first descried the yellow silk banners of the Chinese host. These were inscribed with the two characters Tai-Ming (Great Brightness), the distinctive blazon of the Ming dynasty. For the first time, in eight centuries, the armies of the rival nations were to meet in pitched battle.

The Chinese seemed confident of success, and moved to the attack on Ping-an with neither wariness nor fear. Having invested the city, they began the assault on August 27th. The Japanese allowed them to enter the city and become entangled in its narrow lanes. They then attacked them from advantageous positions, which they had occupied previously, assailing them with showers of arrows, and charging them with their long lances. One body of the Ming soldiers attempted to scale the wall of a part of the fortifications, which seemed to have been neglected by the Japanese, when near the top, the whole face of the castle being covered with climbing men, the garrison, rushing from their hiding-places, tumbled over or speared their enemies, who fell down and into the mass of their comrades below. Those not killed by thrusts or the fall, were shot by the gunners on the ramparts, and the Chinese now received into their bosoms a shower of lead, against which their armor of hide and iron was of slight avail. In this fight the Ming commander was slain. The rout of the Chinese army was so complete, that the fugitives never ceased their retreat until safely over the border, and into China.

The government at Peking now began to understand the power of the enemy with whom they had to deal. An army of 40,000 men was raised to meet the invaders, and, in order to gain time, a man, named Chin Ikei, was sent, independently of the Coreans, to treat with Konishi and propose peace. Some years before the Japanese pirates had carried off a Chinaman to Japan, where he was kept captive for many years. Returning to China, he made the acquaintance of Chin Ikei, and gave him much information concerning the country and people of his captivity. Chin Ikei was evidently a mercenary adventurer, who could talk Japanese, and hoped for honors and promotion by acting as a go-between. He had no commission or any real authority. The Chinese seem to have used him only as a cat's-paw.

Arriving at the Corean camp, at Sun-an, early in October, and fully trusting the honor of the Japanese commander, Chin Ikei ventured, in spite of the warnings of the frightened Coreans, and to their intense admiration, within the Japanese lines, and had a conference with Konishi, Yoshitoshi, and Genshō. The Chinese agent agreed to proceed to Peking, and, returning to Ping-an after fifty days, to report the approval or disapproval of his government. To this Konishi agreed, and there was a truce. The conditions of peace, insisted on by Konishi, were that the Japanese ancient territory in the peninsula, namely, those portions covered by the old states of Shinra and Hiaksai, should be delivered over to Japan, to be held as vassal provinces. This demand virtually claimed all Corea south of the Ta-tong River, in right of ancient possession and recent conquest and occupation.

Arriving in Peking, Chin Ikei found the Chinese army nearly ready to march, and, as their government disowned his right to treat with the Japanese, nothing, except the time gained for the Chinese, resulted from the negotiations. Meanwhile Kato Kiyomasa, with his troops, had overran the whole extent of Hamkiung, the longest and largest province of Corea, occupying also parts of Kang-wen. No great pitched battle in force was fought, but much hard fighting took place, and many castles were taken after bloody sieges. In one of these, the two royal princes, sent north by their father on his flight from Seoul, and many men of rank were captured. Among his prisoners, was " a young girl reputed to be the most beautiful in the whole kingdom." In the pursuit of the fugitives the Japanese were often led into wild and lonely regions and into the depths of trackless mountains and forests, in which they met, not only human foes, but faced the tiger disturbed from his lair. They were often obliged to camp in places where these courageous beasts attacked the sentries or the sleeping soldiers. Kato himself slew a tiger with his lance, after a desperate struggle. After a hard campaign, the main body of the troops fixed their camp at Am-pen, near Gensan, but closer to the southern border of the province. Nabéshima's camp was in Kang-wen, three days' journey distant. From a point on the seacoast near by, in fair weather, the island cone of Dagelet is visible. To the question of Kato, some Corean prisoners falsely answered that this was Fujiyama—the worshipped mountain of the home-land, and " the thing of beauty and a joy forever " to the Japanese people. Immediately the Japanese reverently uncovered their heads

and, kneeling on the strand, gazed long and lovingly with home-
sick hearts—a scene often portrayed in Japanese decorative art.

Thus the year 1592 drew near its close ; the Japanese, necessarily inactive, and the spirit of patriotism among the Coreans
rising. Collecting local volunteer troops and forming guerilla
bands, they kept the Japanese camps, along the road from Fusan
to Ping-an, constantly vigilant. They ferreted out the spies who
had kept the Japanese informed of what was going on, and
promptly cut off their heads. Isolated from all communication,
Konishi remained in ignorance of the immense Chinese army that
was marching against him. The discovery, by the Japanese, of the
existence of the regular Chinese troops in Corea, was wholly a
matter of accident. According to Chinese report, the commander
of the Ming army, Li-yu-son (Japanese, Ri Jo Shō), was a valiant
hero fresh from mighty victories over the rising Manchiu tribes
in the north. The march of his host of 60,000 men through
Liao Tung in winter, especially over the mountain passes, was a
severe one, and the horses are said to have sweated blood. Evidently the expectation of the leader was to drive out the invaders and annex the country to China. When the Corean mountains appeared, as they reached the Yalu River, the leader cried
out, " There is the place which it depends on our valor to recover
as our hereditary possessions." On the sixth day, after crossing
the frontier, he arrived at Sun-an. It was then near the last of January, 1592, and the New Year was close at hand. Word was sent
to Konishi that Chin Ikei had arrived and was ready to reopen
negotiations, with a favorable reply. Konishi promptly despatched
a captain, with a guard of twenty men, to meet Chin Ikei and escort
him within the lines. It being New Year's Day, February 2, 1593,
the guard sallied out amid the rejoicings of their comrades who,
tired of desolate Chō-sen, longed for peace and home. The treacherous Chinamen received the Japanese with apparent cordiality,
and feasted them until they were well drunk. Then the unsuspi-
cious Japanese were set upon while their swords were undrawn in
their scabbards. All were killed except two or three. According to another account, they fell into an ambuscade, and fought
so bravely that only three were taken alive. From the survivors
Konishi first learned of the presence of the Ming army. The pretext, afterward given by the lying Chinaman, was that the interpreters misunderstood each other, and began a quarrel. The
gravity of the situation was now apparent. A Chinese army, of

whose numbers the Japanese were ignorant, menaced them in front, while all around them the natives were gathering in numbers and in courage to renew the struggle for their homes and country. The new army from China was evidently well equipped, disciplined, and supplied, while the Japanese forces were far in an enemy's country, distant from their base of supplies, and with a desolate territory in the rear. Under this gloomy aspect of affairs, the faces of the soldiers wore a dispirited air.

Konishi's alternative lay between the risk of a battle and retreat to Kai-seng. He was not long in resolving on the former course, for, in six days afterward, the Ming host, gay with gleaming arms, bright trappings, and dragon-bordered silk banners, appeared within sight of the city's towers. Konishi anxiously watched their approach, having posted his little force to the best advantage. The city was defended on the west by a steep mountainous ridge, on the north by a hill, and on the south by a river. The Japanese occupying the rising ground to the north, which they had fortified by earthworks and palisades.

At break of day, on February 10th, the allies began a furious assault along the whole line. The Japanese at first drove back their besiegers with their musketry fire, but the Chinese, with their scaling ladders, reached the inside of the works, where their numbers told. When night fell on the second day of the siege, all the outworks were in their possession, and nearly two thousand of the Japanese lay dead. The citadel seemed now an easy prize to the Corean generals; but the Chinese commander, seeing that the Japanese were preparing to defend it to the last, and that his own men were exhausted, gave the order to return to camp, expecting to renew the attack next morning.

Konishi had despatched a courier to Otomo, the Japanese officer in command at Hozan, a small fortress in Whang-hai, to come to his aid. So far from obeying, the latter, frightened at the exaggerated reports of the numbers of the Chinese, evacuated his post and marched back to Seoul. Unable to obtain succor from the other garrisons, and having lost many men by battle and disease, while many more were disabled by wounds and sickness, Konishi gave orders to retreat. One of his bravest captains was put in command of the rear-guard, and the castle was silently deserted at midnight. In this masterly retreat, little was left behind but corpses. Crossing, upon the ice, the river, which was then frozen many feet in thickness, their foes were soon left behind.

Next day the allied army, surprised at seeing no enemy to meet them, entered the castle, finding neither man nor spoil of any kind. The Coreans wished to pursue their enemy, but the Chinese commander, not only forbade it, but glad of a pretext by which he could shift the blame on some other person, cashiered the Corean general for allowing the Japanese to escape so easily. Konishi, without stopping at Kai-seng, was thus enabled to reach Seoul, now the headquarters of all the invading forces. Fully expecting the early advance of the Chinese, the men were now set to work in fortifying the city.

In the flush of success, Li-yu-sung, the Ming commander, sent an envoy with a haughty summons of surrender to Kato and Nabéshima. To this Kato answered in a tone of defiance, guarded his noble prisoners more vigilantly, and with his own hand, in sight of the envoy, put the beautiful Corean girl to death, by transfixing her, with a spear, from waist to shoulder, while bound to a tree. He immediately sent reinforcements to the castle of Kié-chiu, then threatened by the enemy.

The Corean patriots, who organized small detachments of troops, began to attack or repel the invaders in several places, and even to lay siege to castles occupied by Japanese wherever they suspected the garrison was weak. The possession of a few firearms and even rude artillery made them very daring. They compelled the evacuation of one fortress held by Kato's men by the following means. A Corean, named Richosun, says a Japanese author, invented bombs, or *shin-ten-rai* (literally, heaven-shaking thunder), containing poison. Going secretly to the foot of the castle, he discharged the bombs out of a cannon into the castle. As soon as they fell or touched anything they burst and emitted poisonous gas, and every one within reach fell dead. The first of these balls fell into the garden of the castle, and the Japanese soldiers did not know what it was. They gathered around to examine it, and while doing so, the powder in the ball exploded. The report shook heaven and earth. The ball was rent into a thousand pieces, which scattered like stars. Every man that was hit instantly fell, and thus more than thirty men were killed. Even those who were not struck fell down stunned, and the soldiers lost their courage. Many balls were afterward thrown in, which finally compelled the evacuation of the castle.

From the above account it seems that the Coreans actually invented bombs similar to the modern iron shells. They may have been fired from a heavy wooden cannon, a sort of howitzer, made

8

by boring out a section of tree trunk and hooping it along its whole length with stout bamboo. Such cannon are often used in Japan. They will shoot a ten or twenty pound rocket or case of fireworks many hundred feet in the air. The Corean most probably selected a spot so distant from the castle that a sortie for its capture could not be successfully made. Corean gunpowder is proverbially slow in burning, which accounts for the fact that the Japanese had time to gather round it. The bomb was most probably a thin shell of iron, loaded only with gunpowder, which, like the Chinese mixture, contains an excess of sulphur. The military customs of the Japanese required every man disabled by a wound to commit hara-kiri, so that the number of actual deaths must have been swelled by the suicides that followed wounds inflicted by the iron fragments. The Japanese were so completely demoralized that they evacuated the castle.

Two other castles at Kinzan and Kishiu, being beleagured by the patriots, Kato started to succor the slender garrisons. The Coreans, hearing this, redoubled their efforts to capture them before Kato should arrive. They had so far succeeded that the Japanese officer in the citadel, having lost nearly all his men, went into the keep, or fireproof storehouse, in the centre of the castle, and opened his bowels, preferring to die by his own hands rather than allow a Corean the satisfaction of killing him. Just at that moment the black rings of Kato's banners appeared in sight. The Coreans, setting the castle on fire, and giving loud yells of defiance and victory, disappeared.

Kato and Nabéshima had received an urgent message from Seoul to come with their troops, and thus unite all the Japanese forces in a stand against the Chinese. Kato disliked exceedingly to obey this order because he knew it came from Konishi, but he finally set out to march across the country. Thorough discipline was maintained on the march, and the rivers were safely crossed. Cutting down trees, the soldiers, in companies of five or ten, holding on abreast of logs, forded or floated over the most impetuous torrents, while the cavalry kept the Coreans at bay. Though annoyed by attacks of guerilla parties on their flanks, the Japanese succeeded in reaching Seoul without serious loss.

By the retreat of the Japanese armies, and their concentration in Seoul, the four northern provinces, comprising half the kingdom, were virtually lost to them. At the fall of Ping-an the war found its pivot, for the Japanese never again retrieved their fortunes in Chō-sen.

CHAPTER XV.

THE RETREAT FROM SEOUL.

THE allies, after looking well to their commissariat, began their march on Seoul, about the middle of February, with forces which the Japanese believed to number two hundred thousand men. The light cavalry formed the advance guard. The main body, after floundering through the muddy roads, arrived, on February 26th, about forty miles northwest of Seoul.

In the first skirmish, which took place near the town shortly afterward, the allies drove back the Japanese advance detachment with heavy loss. Li-yo-sun, the commander-in-chief, now ordered the army to move against the capital.

In the council of war, held by the Japanese generals, Ishida, who, like Konishi, was a Christian in faith, advised the evacuation of Seoul. This, of course, provoked Kato, who rose and angrily said : "It is a shame for us to give up the capital before we have seen even a single banner of the Ming army. The Coreans and our people at home will call us cowards, and say we were afraid of the Chinamen." Hot words then passed between the rival generals, but Otani and others made peace between them. All concluded that, in order to guard against treason, the Coreans in the capital must be removed. Thereupon, large portions of the city were set on fire, and houses, gates, bridges, public and private buildings, were soon a level waste of ashes. The people, old and young, of both sexes, sick and well, were driven out at the point of the lance. To the stern necessities of war were added the needless carnage of massacre, and hundreds of harmless natives were cruelly murdered. Only a few lusty men, to be used as laborers and burden-bearers, were spared.

Years after, the memory of this frightful and inhuman slaughter, burdening the conscience of many a Japanese soldier, drove him a penitent suppliant into the monasteries. There, exiled from the world, with shaven head and priestly robe, he spent his days

in fasting, vigils, and prayers for pardon, seeking to obtain Nirvana with the Eternal Buddha.

Meanwhile the work of fortification went on. The advance
guard of the Chinese host were now within a few miles of the city,
and daily skirmishes took place. The younger Japanese officers
clamored to lead the van against the Chinese, but Kobayékawa,
an elderly general, was allowed to arrange the order of battle, and
the Japanese army marched out from the capital to the attack in
three divisions, Kobayékawa leading the third, or main body of ten
thousand men, the others having only three thousand each. In the
battle that ensued the Japanese were at first unable to hold their
ground against the overwhelming forces of their enemies. The Chinese and Coreans drove back their first and second divisions with
heavy loss. Then, thinking victory certain, they began a pursuit
with both foot soldiers and cavalry, which led them into disorder and
exhausted their strength. When well wearied, Kobayékawa, having
waited till they were too far distant from their camp to receive
reinforcements, led his division in a charge against the allies. The
battle then became a hand-to-hand fight on a gigantic scale. The
Chinese were armed mainly with swords, which were short, heavy,
and double-edged. The allies had a large number of cavalry engaged, but the ground being miry from the heavy rains, they were
unable to form or to charge with effect. Their advantage in other
respects was more than counterbalanced by the length of the Japanese swords, the strength of their armor, and their veteran valor and
coolness. Even the foot soldiers wielded swords having blades
usually two, but sometimes three and four, feet long.

The Japanese have ever prided themselves upon the length,
slenderness, temper, and keen edge of their blades, and look with
unmeasured contempt upon the short and clumsy weapons of the
continental Asiatics. They proudly call their native land " The
country ruled by a slender sword." Marvellous in wonder and
voluminousness are their legends, literature, and exact history
concerning *ken* (two-edged, short falchion), and *katana* (two-handed
and single-edged sabre). In this battle it was the sword alone
that decided the issue, though firearms lent their deadly aid. The
long, cross-bladed spears of their foot soldiers were also highly
effective, first, in warding off the sabre strokes of the Chinese cavalry, and then unhorsing them, either by thrust or grapple. One
general of high rank was pulled off his steed and killed.

The Japanese leaders were in their best spirits, as well as in their finest equipments. One was especially noticeable by his gilded helmet that flashed and towered conspicuously. It was probably that of Kato, whose head-gear was usually of incredible height and dazzling splendor.

After a long struggle and frightful slaughter, the allies were beaten back in confusion. Ten thousand Chinese and Coreans, according to Japanese accounts, were slaughtered on this bloodiest day and severest pitched battle of the first invasion.

The Chinese suffered heavily in officers, and their first taste of war in the field with such veterans as the soldiers of Taikō was discouraging in the extreme. Li-yo-sun drew off his forces and soon after retired to Sunto. Not knowing that Kato had got into Seoul, and fearing an attack from the rear, on Ping-an, he drew off his main body to that city, leaving a garrison at Sunto. Tired, disgusted, and scared, the redoubtable Chinaman, like "the beaten soldier that fears the top of the tall grass," sent a lying report to Peking, exaggerating the numbers of the Japanese, and asking for release from command, on the usual Oriental plea of poor health. As for the Japanese, they had lost so heavily in killed, that they were unable to follow up the victory, if victory it may be called. A small force, however, pressed forward and occupied Kai-jo, while the main body prepared to pass a miserable winter in the desolate capital.

The Corean stronghold of An-am was also assaulted. This castle was built on a precipitous steep, having but one gate and flank capable of access, and that being a narrow, almost perpendicular, cutting through the rocks. The attacking force entered the gloomy valley shut in from light by the luxuriant forest, which darkened the path even in the daytime. At the tops, and on the ledges of the rocks beetling over the entrance-way, the Corean archers took up advantageous positions, while others of the garrison, with huge masses of rock and timber piled near the ledge, stood ready to hurl these upon the invaders.

Awaiting in silence the approach of their enemies, they soon saw the Japanese fan-standards and paper-strip banners approach, when these were directly beneath them, every bow twanged, and a shower of arrows rained upon the invaders, while volleys of stones fell into their ranks, crushing heads and helmets together. The besiegers were compelled to draw off and arrange a new attack ; but in the night the garrison withdrew. Next day the Japanese entered, garrisoned the castle, and decorated it with their streamers.

The long-continued abandonment of the soil, owing to the war and the presence of three large armies, bore their natural fruits, and turned fertile Corea into a land of starvation. Famine began its ravages of death on friend and foe alike. The peasants petitioned their government for food, but none was to be had. Thousands of the poor people died of starvation. The fathers suffered in camp, while the dead mothers lay unburied in the houses, and the children, tortured with hunger, cried for food. One day a captain in the Chinese army found, by the roadside, an emaciated infant vainly seeking for nourishment from the cold and rigid breast of its dead mother. Touched with compassion, the warrior took the child and reared him to manhood under his own care.

Some rice was distributed to the wretched people from the government store-houses in certain places, but still the groans and cries of the starving filled the air. Pestilence entered the Japanese camp, and thousands of the home-sick soldiers died ingloriously. The long winter rains made the living despondent and gloomy enough to commit hara-kiri, while the state of the roads and the dashing courage of the guerillas, who pushed their raids to the very gates of the camps, made foraging an unpopular duty among the men. In such discomfort, winter wore away, and tardy spring approached. In this state of affairs the Japanese were willing to listen, and the allies ready to offer, terms of peace. A Corean soldier, named Rijunchin, by permission of his superior officer, had penetrated into Seoul to visit the two captive princes. On his return to the camp, he stated that the Japanese generals were very homesick and heartily tired of the war. At the same time, a letter was received from Konishi, stating his readiness to receive terms of peace. Chin Ikei was again chosen to negotiate. Reaching the Japanese lines at Kai-jo, he held an interview with Konishi, and the following points of agreement were made :

1. Peace between the three countries.

2. Japan to remain in possession of the three southern provinces of Chō-sen.

3. Corea to send tribute to Japan as heretofore.

4. Hidéyoshi to be recognized as King of Corea. The three other articles drawn up were not made public, but the acknowledgment of Taikō as the equal of the Emperor of China was evidently one of them. The Japanese, on their part, were to return the two captive princes, withdraw all their armies to Fusan, and evacuate the country when the stipulations were carried out.

Both parties were weary of the war. The Ming commander had requested to be relieved of his command and to return to China, while the three old gentlemen, who were military advisers in the Japanese camp, yearning for the pleasures of Kiōto, wrote to Taikō, asking leave to come home, telling him the object of his ambition was on the eve of attainment, and that he was to receive investiture from the Chinese emperor, and recognition as an equal.

Scholarship and literature were not at a very high premium at that time among the Japanese military men. The martial virtues and accomplishments occupied the time and thoughts of the warriors to the exclusion of book learning and skill at words. The sword for the soldier, and the pen for the priest, was the rule. The bluff warrior in armor looked with contempt, not unmingled with awe, upon the shaven-pated man of ink and brush. One of the bonzes from the monastery was usually of necessity attached to the service of each commander. It was by reason of the ignorance, as well as the vanity, of the illiterate Japanese generals that such a mistake, in supposing that Taikō was to be recognized as equal to the Emperor of China, was rendered possible. The wily Chin Ikei, who drove a lucrative trade as negotiator, hoodwinked Konishi, who would not have been thus outwitted if he had had a bonze present to inspect the writing. Being a Christian, however, he was on bad terms with the bonzes.

In both camps there were those who bitterly opposed any peace short of that which the sword decided. The Corean generals chafed at the time wasted in parley, and wished to march on the Japanese at once, whose ranks they knew were decimated with sickness, and their spirit and discipline relaxed under the idea of speedy return home. An epidemic had also broken out among their horses, probably owing to scant provender. Thus crippled and demoralized, victory would certainly follow a well-planned attack in force. Within the camp of the invaders Achilles and Agamemnon were as far as ever from harmony. Kato sullenly refused to entertain the idea of peace, partly because Konishi proposed it, but mainly because, if the two princes were given up, his achievements would be brought to naught, and all the glory of the war would redound to his rival. Only after the earnest representation by his friends of the empty granaries, and the danger of impending starvation, the great sickness among the troops, and the fearful loss of horses, was he induced to agree with the other commanders that Seoul should be evacuated.

Meanwhile, the allies were advancing toward the capital.

On May 22, 1593, the Japanese, with due precautions, evacuated the city, and the vanguard of the Chinese army entered on the same day. The retreat of the Japanese was effected in good order, and, to guard against treachery, they bivouacked in the open air, avoiding sleeping in the houses or villages, and rigidly kept up the vigilance of their sentinels and the discipline of the divisions. In this way the various detachments of the army safely reached Fusan, Tong-nai, Kinka, and other places near the coast. Here, after fortifying their camps, they rested for a space from the alarms of war, almost within sight of their native land. The allies later on marched southward and went into camp a few leagues to the northward. Since crossing the Yalu River, the Chinese had lost by the sword and disease twenty thousand men.

CHAPTER XVI.

CESPEDES, THE CHRISTIAN CHAPLAIN

THE aspect of affairs had now changed from that of a triumphal march through Corea into China and to Peking, to long and tedious camp life, with uncertain fortunes in the field, which promised a long stay in the peninsula. Konishi had now breathing time and space for reflection. Being an ardent Christian—after the faith and practice of the Portuguese Jesuits—he wished for himself and his fellow-believers the presence and ministrations of one of the European friars to act as chaplain. He therefore sent, probably when at or near Fusan, a message to the superior of the Mission in Japan, asking for a priest.

Toward the end of 1593, the Vice-Provençal of the Company of the Jesuits despatched Father Gregorio de Cespedes and a Japanese convert named "Foucan Eion" to the army in Chō-sen. They left Japan and spent the winter in Tsushima, the domain of Yoshitoshi, one of the Christian lords then in the field. Early in the spring of 1594 they reached Corea, arriving at Camp Comangai (most probably a name given by the Japanese after the famous hero Kumagayé), at which Konishi made his headquarters. The two holy men immediately began their labors among the Japanese armies. They went from castle to castle, and from camp to camp, preaching to the pagan soldiers, and administering the rite of baptism to all who professed the faith, or signed themselves with the cross. They administered the sacraments to the Christian Japanese, comforted and prayed with the sick, reformed abuses, assisted the wounded, and shrived the dying. New converts were made and old ones strengthened. Dying in a foreign land, of fever or of wounds, the soul of the Japanese man-at-arms was comforted with words of hope from the lips of the foreign priest. Held before his glazing eyes gleamed the crucifix, on which appeared the image of the world's Redeemer. The home-sick warrior, pining for wife and babe, was told of the "House not made with hands."

The two brethren seem to have been very popular among the
Japanese soldiers. Perhaps they already dreamed of planting the
faith in Corea, when, suddenly, their work was arrested at its height
by Kato, whose jealousy of Konishi was only equalled by his fanatical zeal for the Buddhist faith. Being in Japan he denounced the
foreign priest to Taikō, declaring that these zealous endeavors to
propagate the Christian faith only concealed a vast conspiracy
against himself and the power of the mikado. At this time Taikō
was dealing with the Jesuits in Japan, and endeavoring to rid the
country of their presence by shipping them off to China. He
fully believed that they were political as well as religious emissaries, and that their aim was at temporal power. These suspicions,
as every student of Japan knows, were more than well founded.

Besides accusing Cespedes, Kato insinuated that Konishi himself was leading the conspiracy. The cry of chō-téki (rebel, or
enemy of the mikado) in Japan is enough to blacken the character
of the bravest man and greatest favorite. Treason against the mikado being the supreme crime, Konishi found it necessary to
return to Kiōto, present himself before Taikō, and cleanse his reputation even from suspicion. This the lull in the active operations,
occasioned by the negotiations of Chin Ikei, enabled him to do.

Immediately sending back the priest, he shortly afterward
crossed the straits, and, meeting Taikō, succeeded in fully ingratiating himself and allaying all suspicion.

The wife of Konishi had also embraced the Christian faith, her
baptized name being Marie. To her, while in camp, he had sent
two Corean lads, both of whom were of rank and gentle blood, the
elder being called in the letters of the Jesuits " secretary to the
Corean king." He was the son of a brave captain in the army,
and was thirteen years old. The lady, Marie, touched by their
misfortune, kept the younger to be educated in the faith under
her own direction, and sent the elder to the Jesuit seminary in
Kiōto. Of this young man's career we catch some glimpses from
the letters of the missionaries. At the college he was a favorite,
by reason of his good character, gentle manners, and fine mind.
Professing the faith, he was baptized in 1603, taking the name of
Vincent. He began his religious work by instructing and cate-
chising Japanese and his numerous fellow Coreans at Nagasaki.
When about thirty-three years old, the Jesuits, wishing to establish a mission in Corea, proposed to send him to his native land as
missionary ; but not being able, on account of the persecution

then raging in Japan, he was chosen by the Father Provençal to go to Peking, communicate with the Jesuits there, and enter Corea from China. At Peking he remained four years, being unable to enter his own country by reason of the Manchius, who then held control of the northern provinces of Manchuria and were advancing on Peking, to set on the throne that family which is still the ruling dynasty of the Middle Kingdom. Vincent was recalled to Japan in 1620, where, in the persecutions under Iyémitsŭ, the third Tokugawa shō-gun, he fell a victim to his fidelity, and was martyrized in 1625, at the age of about forty-four.

Warned of the dangers of patronizing the now proscribed religion, there was no farther return of zeal on Konishi's part, or that of the other Christian princes, and no farther opportunity was given to plant the seeds of the faith in the desolated land.

Of the large numbers of Corean prisoners sent over to Japan, from time to time, many of those living in the places occupied by the missionaries became Christians. Many more were sold as slaves to the Portuguese. In Nagasaki, of the three hundred or more living there, most of them were converted and baptized. They easily learned the Japanese language so as to need no interpreter at the confessional—a fact which goes to prove the close affinity of the two languages.

Others, of gentle blood and scholarly attainments, rose to positions of honor and eminence under the government, or in the households of the daimiōs. Many Corean lads were adopted by the returned soldiers or kept as servants. When the bloody persecutions broke out, by which many thousand Japanese found death in the hundred forms of torture which hate and malice invented, the Corean converts remained steadfast to their new-found faith, and suffered martyrdom with fortitude equal to that of their Japanese brethren. But, by the army in Corea, or by Cespedes, no seed of Christianity was planted or trace of it left, and its introduction was postponed by Providence until two centuries later.

CHAPTER XVII.

DIPLOMACY AT KIŌTO AND PEKING.

THE Chinese ambassadors, with whom was Chin Ikei, set sail from Fusan, and reached Nagoya, in Hizen, on June 22d. Taikō received them in person, and entertained them in magnificent style. His lords imitated the august example set them, and both presents and attentions were showered upon the guests. Among other entertainments in their honor was a naval review, in which hundreds of ships, decorated with the heraldry of feudalism, were ranged in line. The boats moved in procession; the men, standing up as they worked the sculls, sang in measured chorus. The sheaves of glittering weapons, spears, and halberds arranged at their bows, were inlaid with gold and pearl. The cabins were arranged with looped brocades and striped canvas, with huge crests and imperial chrysanthemums of colossal size. The ambassadors were delighted, both with the lovely scenery and the attentions paid them, and so remained until August.

Little, however, came of this mission. Taikō sent orders to Kato to release the Corean princes and nobles; and Chin Ikei, who usually went off like a clumsy blunderbuss, at half-cock, hied back to Chō-sen to tell the news and get the credit of having secured this concession. The Coreans were made to bear the blame of the war, and the envoys of China, in good humor, returned to Peking in company with a Japanese ambassador.

Yet Taikō, though willing to be at peace with China, did not intend to spare unhappy Chō-sen. To soothe the spirit of Kato, the order was given to capture the castle of Chin-chiu, forty miles west of Fusan, which had not yet been taken by the Japanese, though once before invested.

Alarmed at the movements of the invaders, the Coreans tried to revictual and garrison the devoted fortress, and even to attack the enemy on the way. Unable, however, to make a stand against their foes, they were routed with frightful carnage. Kato led the besieging force, eager to make speedy capture so as to irritate the Coreans and prevent the peace he feared.

He invested the castle which the Coreans had not been able to reinforce, but the vigorous resistance of the garrison, who threw stones and timber upon the heads of his assaulting parties, drove him to the invention of Kamé-no-kosha, or tortoise-shell wagons, which imitated the defensive armor of that animal. Collecting together several hundred green hides, and dry-hardening them in the fire, he covered four heavily built and slant-roofed wagons with them. These vehicles, proof against fire, missiles, or a crushing weight, and filled with soldiers, were pushed forward to the foot of the walls. While the matchlock men in the lines engaged those fighting on the ramparts, the soldiers, under the projecting sheds of the tortoise wagons, that jutted against the walls, began to dig under the foundations. These being undermined, the stones were pried out, and soon fell in sufficient number to cause a breach. Into this fresh soldiers rushed and quickly stormed the castle. The slaughter inside was fearful.

The news of the fall of this most important fortress fell like a clap of thunder in Peking, and upon the Corean king, who was preparing to go back to Seoul. The Chinese government appointed fresh commissioners of war, and ordered the formation of a new and larger army.

The immediate advance of the invaders on the capital was expected, but Kato, having obeyed Taikō's orders, left a garrison in the castle and fell back on Fusan.

The Chinese general, upbraiding Chin Ikei for his insincerity, sent him to Konishi again. Their interview was taken up mainly with mutual charges of bad faith. Chin Ikei, returning, tried to persuade the Chinese commander to evacuate Corea, or, at least, retire to the frontier. Though he refused, being still under orders to fight, the Chinese army moved back from Seoul toward Manchuria, while Konishi, on his own responsibility, despatched a letter to the Chinese emperor. Large detachments of the Japanese army actually embarked at Fusan, and returned to Japan. In the lull of hostilities, negotiations were carried on at Peking and Kiōto, as well as between the hostile camps. The pen took the place of the matchlock, and the ink-stone furnished the ammunition.

A son was born to Taikō, and named Hidéyori. A great pageant, in honor of the infant, was given at the newly built and splendid castle of Fushimi, near Kiōto, which was graced by a large number of the commanders and veterans of Corea, who had returned home on furlough, while negotiations were pending. The result of the Japanese mission to Peking was the despatch of an ambassador extraordinary, named Rishosei, with one of lesser rank, to Japan, by way of Fusan.

On his arrival, he requested to see Konishi, who, however, evaded him, excusing himself on the plea of expecting to hear from Taikō, after which he promised to hold an interview. Konishi then departed for Japan, taking Chin Ikei with him. On his return he still avoided the Chinese envoy, for he had no definite orders, and the other generals refused to act without direct word from their master in Kiōto. Meanwhile Chin Ikei, consumed with jealousy, and angry at the Peking mandarins for ignoring him and withholding official recognition and honors, planned revenge against Rishosei; for Chin Ikei believed himself to have done great things for Chō-sen and China, and yet he had received neither thanks, pay, nor promotion for his toils, while Rishosei, though a young man, with no experience, was honored with high office solely on account of being of rank and in official favor at Peking. Evidently with the intent of injuring Rishosei, Chin Ikei gave out that Taikō did not wish to be made King of Chō-sen, but had sent an envoy to China merely to have a high ambassador of China come to Japan, that he might insult or rather return the insult of the sovereign of China, in the person of his envoy, by making him a prisoner or putting him to death. Konishi and Chin Ikei again crossed to Japan to arrange for the reception of the Chinese envoys.

The reports started by Chin Ikei, coming to the ears of Rishosei, so frightened him that he fled in disguise from Fusan, and absconded to China. His colleague denounced him as a coward, and declaring that the Chinese government desired only "peace with honor," sailed with his retinue and two Corean officers to Japan. "And Satan [Chin Ikei], came also among them." All landed safely at Sakai, near Ozaka, October 8, 1596.

Audience was duly given with pomp and grandeur in the gorgeous castle at Fushimi, on October 24th. The ambassador brought the imperial letter, the patent of rank, a golden seal, a crown, and silk-embroidered robes of state. At a banquet, given next day, these robes were worn by Taikō and his officers.

Formalities over, the Ming emperor's letter was delivered to

Taikō, who at once placed it in the hands of three of the most learned priests, experts in the Chinese language, and ordered them to translate its contents literally.

To Konishi, then at Kiōto, came misgivings of his abilities as a diplomatist. Visiting the bonzes, he earnestly begged them to soften into polite phrase anything in the letter that might irritate Taikō. But the priests were inflexibly honest, and rendered the text of the letter into the exact Japanese equivalent. In it the patent of nobility first granted to the Ashikaga shō-gun (1403–1425) was referred to; and the gist of this last imperial letter was: "We, the Emperor of China, appoint you, Taikō, to be the King of Japan" (Nippon O). In other words, the mighty Kuambaku of Japan was insulted by being treated no better than one of the Ashikaga generals!

This was the mouse that was born from so great a mountain of diplomacy. The rage of Taikō was so great that, with his own hands, he would have slain Konishi, had not the bonzes plead for his life, claiming that the responsibility of the negotiations rested upon three other prominent persons. As usual, the "false-hearted Coreans" were made to bear the odium of the misunderstanding.

The Chinese embassy, dismissed in disgrace, returned in January, 1596, and made known their humiliation at Peking; while the King of Corea, who had been living in Seoul during the negotiations, appealed at once for speedy aid against the impending invasion. Hidéyoshi again applied himself with renewed vigor to raising and drilling a new army, and obtaining ships and supplies. A grand review of the forces of invasion, consisting of one hundred and sixty-three thousand horse and foot soldiers, was held under his inspection. Kuroda, Nagamasa, and other generals, with their divisions, sailed away for Fusan, January 7, 1597, and joined the army under Konishi and Kato.

The new levies from China, which had been waiting under arms, crossed the Yalu and entered from the west at about the same time. Marching down through Ping-an and Seoul, a division of ten thousand garrisoned the castle of Nan-on, in Chulla. The Coreans, meanwhile, fitted out a fleet, under the command of Genkai, expecting a second victory on the water.

An extinguisher was put on Chin Ikei, who was suspected of being in the pay of Konishi. Genkai, a Chinese captain, had long believed him to be a dangerous busybody, without any real powers from the Peking government, but only used by them as a decoy duck, while, in reality, he was in the pay of the Japanese, and the chief hinderance to the success of the allied arms.   On the other hand, this volunteer politician, weary and disappointed at not receiving from China the high post and honors which his ambition coveted, was in a strait.   Taikō urged him to secure from China the claim of Japan to the southern half of Corea.   China, on the contrary, ordered him to induce the Japanese generals to leave the country.   Thus situated, Chin Ikei knew not what to do.   He sent a message, through a priest, to Kato, urging him to make peace or else meet an army of one hundred thousand Chinamen. The laconic reply of the Japanese was : "I am ready to fight.   Let them come."

Bluffed in his last move, and aware of the plots of Genkai, his enemy, Chin Ikei, at his wits' end, resolved to escape to Konishi's camp. The spies of Genkai immediately reported the fact to their master, who lay in wait for him.   Suddenly confronting his victim, they demanded his errand.   "I am going to treat with Kato, the Japanese general ; I shall be back in one month," answered Chin Ikei.   He was seized and, on being led back, was thrown into prison.   A searching party was then despatched at once to his house.   There they found gold, treasure, and jewels "mountain high," and his wife living in luxury.   Believing all these to have been purchased by Japanese gold, and the fruits of bribery, the Chinese confiscated the spoil and imprisoned the traitor's family.

This ended all further negotiations until the end of the war. Henceforth, on land and water, by the veterans of both armies, with fresh levies, both of allies and invaders, the issue was tried by sword and siege.

CHAPTER XVIII.

THE SECOND INVASION.

THE plan of the second invasion was to land all the Japanese forces at Fusan, and then to divide them into three columns, which were to advance by the south to Nan-on castle in Chulla, and by two roads, northward and westward, to the capital. As before, Konishi and Kato Kiyomasa were the two field commanders, while Hidéaki, a noble lad, sixteen years old, was the nominal commander-in-chief.

The Coreans had made preparations to fight the Japanese at sea as well as on land. Their fleet consisted of about two hundred vessels of heavy build, for butting and ramming, as well as for accommodating a maximum of fighting men. They were two hundred and fifty or three hundred feet in length, with huge sterns, having enormous rudders, the tillers of which were worked by eight men. Their high, flat prows were hideously carved and painted to represent the face and open jaws of a dragon, or demon, ready to devour. Stout spars or knotted logs, set upright along the gunwale, protected the men who worked the catapults, and heavily built roofed cabins sheltered the soldiers and gave the archers a vantage ground. The rowers sat amidships, between the cabins and the gunwales, or rather over on these latter, in casements made of stout timber. The catapults were on deck, between the bows. They were twenty-four feet long, made of tree-trunks a yard in circumference. Immense bows, drawn to their notches by windlasses, shot iron-headed darts and bolts six feet long and four inches thick. On some of the ships towers were erected, in which cannon, missile-engines, and musketeers were stationed, to shoot out fire-arrows, stones, and balls. At close quarters the space at the bows—about one-third of the deck—was free for the movements of the men wielding spear and sword, and for those who plied the grappling hooks or boarding planks. The decks crowded with men in armor, the glitter of steel and flash of oars, the blare

9

of the long Corean trumpets, and the gay fluttering of thousands
of silken flags and streamers made brilliant defiance.

The Japanese accepted the challenge, and, sailing out, closed
with the enemy. Wherever they could, they ran alongside and
gave battle at the bows. Though their ships were smaller, they
were more manageable. In some cases, they ran under the high
sterns and climbed on board the enemy's ships. Once at hand to
hand fight, their superior swordsmanship quickly decided the day.
Their most formidable means of offence which, next to their cannon, won them the victory, were their rockets and fire-arrows,
which they were able to shoot into the sterns, where the dry
wood soon caught fire, driving the crews into the sea, where they
drowned. Two hours fighting sufficed, by which time one hundred and seventy-four Corean ships had been burned or taken.
News of this brilliant victory was at once sent by a swift vessel to
Japan.

Endeavors were made to strengthen the garrison at Nan-on,
but the Japanese general, Kato Yoshiakira, meeting the reinforcements on their way, prevented their design. Kato Kiyomasa,
changing his plans, also marched to Nan-on, resolving to again,
if possible, snatch an honor from his rival. As usual, the younger
man was too swift for him. Konishi now moved his entire command in the fleet up the Sem River, in Chulla province, and landing, camped at a place called Uren, eighteen *ri* from Nan-on castle.
He rested here five days in the open meadow land to allow the
horses to relax their limbs after the long and close confinement in
the ships. From a priest, whom they found at this place, they
learned that the garrison of Nan-on numbered over 20,000 Chinese and Coreans, the reinforcements in the province, and on their
way, numbered 20,000 more, while in the north was another Chinese corps of 20,000.

At the council of war held, it was resolved to advance at once
to take the castle before succor came. In spite of many lame
horses, and the imperfect state of the commissariat, the order to
march was given. Men and beasts were in high spirits, but many
of the horses were ridden to death, or rendered useless by the
forced march of the cavalry. Early on the morning of September
21st, the advance guard camped in the morning fog at a distance of
a mile from the citadel. The main body, coming up, surrounded
it on all sides, pitched their camp, threw out their pickets, set up
their standards, and proceeded promptly to fortify their lines.

Nan-on castle was of rectangular form, enclosing a space nearly two miles square, as each side was nine thousand feet long. Its

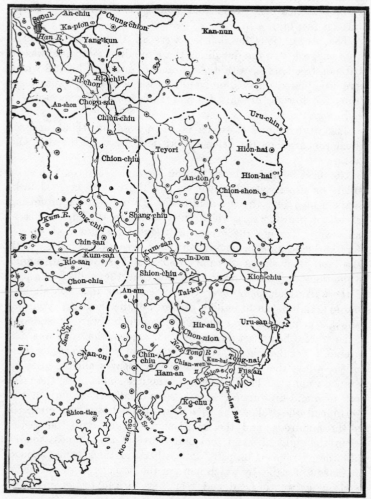

Map of the Operations of the Second Invasion.

walls, which were twelve feet high, were built of great stones, laid together without cement. Though no mortar had been used on wall or tower, shell-lime had been laid over the outside, in which glistened innumerable fragments of nacre and the enamel of shells, giving the structure the appearance of glittering porcelain. At the angles, and at intervals along the flanks, were towers, two or three stories high. The four ponderous gates were of stone, fourteen feet high.

The preparations for defence were all that Chinese science could suggest. In the dry ditch, three hundred feet wide, was an abatis of tree-trunks, with their branches outward, behind which were iron-plated wagons, to be filled with archers and spearmen. From the towers, fire-missiles and shot from firearms were in readiness.

The weak points, at which no enemy was expected, and for which preparations for defence were few, were on the east and west.

No effect being produced during the first two days, either by bullets or fire-arrows, Konishi, on the third, sent large detachments of men into the rice-fields, then covered with a promising harvest of growing rice, which the farmers, in the hope of peace, had sown. Reaping the green, juicy stalks, the hundreds of soldiers gathered an enormous quantity of sheaves and waited, with these and their stacks of bamboo poles and ladders, until night. In the thick darkness, and in perfect silence, they moved to a part of the wall which, being over twenty feet high, was but slightly guarded, and began to build a platform of the sheaves. Four Japanese, reaching the top by climbing, raised the war-cry, and one of the towers being set on fire by their arrows, the work was discovered. Yet the matchlock men kept the walls swept by their bullets, while the work of piling fresh sheaves and bundles of bamboo went on. The greenness of the rice-stalks made the mass both firm and fire-proof. At last the mound was so high that it overtopped the wall. The men now climbed over the ramparts by the hundreds, and the swordsmen, leaping into the castle, began the fight at hand to hand. Most of the Chinese fought with the courage of despair, while others, in their panic, opened the gates to escape, by which more of the besiegers entered. The garrison, smitten in front and rear, were driven to the final wall by Konishi's troops. On the other side a body of picked men, from Kato's army, joined in the slaughter. They had entered the castle at the rear, by scaling a rugged mountain path known only to the Corean prisoners, whose treachery they had purchased by the promise of their lives. Between the two attacking forces the

Coreans and Chinese, who could not escape, were slain by thousands.

Among many curious incidents narrated by Ogawuchi, who
tells the story of this siege and attack, was this. As he entered
the castle, amid the smoke and confusion, in which he saw some
of the panic-stricken garrison destroying themselves, he cut off the
heads of two enemies, and then, suddenly recollecting that this
fifteenth day of the eighth month was the day sacred to Hachiman, the god of war and Buddha of the Eight Banners, he flung
down his bloody sword, put his red palms together, and bowing
his head, prayed devoutly toward his adored Japan. His devo-
tions ended, he sliced off the noses from the heads of the two
enemies he had slain, wrapped them in paper, twisted the package to his girdle, and sprang forward to meet, with but three men,
the charge of fifty horsemen. The first sweep of the Japanese
sabre severed the leg of the nearest rider, who fell to the earth on
the other side of his horse, and Ogawuchi's companions killing each
his man, the enemy fled. The fires of the burning towers now
lighted up the whole area of the castle, while the autumn moon
rose red and clear. Ogawuchi slew, with his own hand, Kéku-
shiu, one of the Chinese commanders. His body, in rich armor,
lined with gold brocade, was stripped, and the trappings secured
as trophies to be sent home, while his head was presented for
Konishi's inspection next morning.

According to the barbarous custom of the victors, they severed
the heads of the bodies not already decapitated in fight, until the
castle space resembled a great slaughter-yard. Collecting them
into a great heap, they began the official count. The number of
these ghastly trophies, or " glory-signs," was three thousand seven
hundred and twenty-six. The ears and noses of the slain were
then sheared off, and with the commander's head, were packed
with salt and quick lime in casks, and sent to Japan to form the
great ear-tomb now in Kiōto, the horrible monument of a most
unrighteous war.

A map of the castle and town, with the list of the most meritorious among 'the victors, was duly sent back to Taikō. Then
the walls and towers, granaries, and barracks were destroyed.
This work occupied two days.

Promptly on September 30th the army moved on to Teru-shiu,
the cavalry riding day and night, and reaching the castle only to
find it deserted, the garrison having fled toward Seoul. The Jap-

anese remained here ten days, levelling the fortress with fire and hammer.

As the cold weather was approaching, the Japanese commanders, after council, resolved at once to march to the capital. Katsuyoshi and Kiyomasa had joined them, and the advance northward was at once began. By October 19th they were within seventeen miles of Seoul.[1]

The successes on land, brilliant though they were, were balanced by the defeat of the Japanese navy off the southern coast. The Chinese admiral Rishinshin, in conjunction with the Coreans, won an important victory over Kuroda's naval forces a few days after the fall of Nan-on. In this instance, the Chinese ships were not only heavy enough to be formidable as rams, but were made more manageable by numerous rowers sitting in well-defended timber casements, apparently covered with metal. The warriors, too, seem to have been armed with larger lances. The Chinese commanders, having improved their tactics, so managed their vessels that the Japanese fleet was destroyed or driven away.

This event may be said to have decided the fate of the campaign. Bereft of their fleet, which would, by going round the west coast, have afforded them a base of supplies, they were now obliged to advance into a country nearly empty of forage, and with no store of provisions. As in the opening of the war, so again, the loss of the fleet at a critical period made retreat necessary even at the moment of victory.

Meanwhile, the Chinese general Keikai, thoroughly disliking the rigors of a camp in a Corean winter, and feeling deeply for his soldiers suffering from exposure in a desolate land, determined on closing the war as soon as possible. Erecting an altar, in presence of the army, he offered sacrifices to propitiate the spirits of Heaven and Earth, and prayed for victory against the invaders. Then, after seeing well to commissariat and equipment, he gave orders for a general movement of all the allied forces, with the design of ending the war by a brief and decisive campaign. The Japanese generals at Koran, by means of their spies and advance parties, kept themselves well informed of the movements of the enemy. At a

---

[1] Their line of march, as shown in the Japanese histories, was to Sen-ken, October 11th; to Kumu-san, where they experienced the first frost; to Kumui, October 12th; to Chin-zon; to Funki; to Shaku-shiu; to Koran; to Chin-zen. These are names of places in Chulla and Chung-chong, expressed in the Japanese and old Corean pronunciation.

skirmish at Chin-zen the Chinese advance guard was defeated with heavy loss, but the Japanese at once began their retreat. Shishida and Ota, who were further east, learning of the overwhelming odds against them, fell back into Uru-san, which was already manned by a detachment of Kato's corps.

While Kato and Katsuyoshi were at Chin-zen, a grand tiger hunt was proposed and carried out, in which a soldier was bitten in two places and died. The army agreed that tiger-hunting required much nerve and valor. Besides the tiger steaks, which they ate, much fresh meat was furnished by the numerous crane, pheasants, and "the ten thousand things different from those in Japan," which they made use of to eke out their scanty rations.

To remain in camp until the Han River was frozen over, and could be crossed easily, or to press on at once, was the question now considered by the Japanese. While thus debating, word came that the Chinese armies had made junction at Seoul, and numbered one hundred thousand men. The Japanese "felt cold in their breasts" when they heard this. Far from their base of supplies, their fleet destroyed, and they at the threshold of winter in a famine-stricken land, they were forced, reluctantly, again to retreat into Kiung-sang.

This turning their backs on Seoul was, in reality, the beginning of their march homeward. The invaders, therefore, enriched themselves with the spoil of houses and temples as they moved toward the coast—gold and silver brocades, rolls of silk, paintings, works of art, precious manuscripts, books written with gold letters on azure paper, inlaid weapons and armor, rich mantles, and whatever, in this long-settled and wealthy province, pleased their fancy. On the boundaries of roads and provinces they noticed large dressed stone columns of an octagonal form, with inscriptions upon them. Their route lay from Chin-zen, which they left in ashes, on October 25th, to Chin-nan ; to Ho-won ; to Hokin ; to Karon ; reaching Kion-chiu, the old capital of Shinra, after some fighting along the way.

The Japanese were impressed with the size and grandeur of the buildings in this old seat of the civilization and learning of Shinra and Korai. Here, in ancient days, was the focus of the arts, letters, religion, and science which, from the west, the far off mysterious land of India, and the nearer, yet august, empire of China, had been brought to Corea. Here, too, their own ancient mikados had sent embassies, and from this historic city had radia-

ted the influences of civilization into Japan. As Buddhism had
been the dominant faith of Shinra and Korai, this was the old
sacred city of the peninsula, and among the historic edifices still
standing and most admired were the halls and pagodas of the
Eternal Buddha. Kion-chiu was to the Japanese very much what
London is to an American, Geneva to a Protestant, or Dordrecht
to a Hollander. Yet, in spite of all classic associations, the city
was wantonly destroyed. On the morning of November 2d, beginning at the magnificent temples, the whole city was given to
the torch. Three hundred thousand dwellings were burned, and
the flames lighted up the long night with the glare of day.

The next morning, turning their backs on the gray waste of
ashes, they resumed their march. Kokiō, Kunoi, Sin-né were
passed through. Skirmishing and the destruction of castles, and
the burning of granaries, were the pastimes enjoyed between
camps. On November 18th the army reached a river, where the
Coreans made an unsuccessful night attack, repeating the same in
the morning, while the Japanese were crossing the stream, with
the same negative results.

Thence through Yei-tan, they came to Kéku-shiu, another
famous old seat of Shinra's ancient grandeur. The beautiful situation and rich appearance of the city charmed the invaders, who
lingered long in the deserted streets before applying the torch.
The "three hundred thousand houses of the people" were clustered around the great Buddhist temple in the centre. The clock-
tower, eighteen stories high, was especially admired. The massive
swinging beam by which the tongueless bells, or gongs, of the
Far East are made to boom out the hours, struck against a huge
bronze lotus eight or nine feet in diameter. This sacred flower
of the Buddhist emblem of peace and calm in Nirvana had in
Corean art taken the place of the suspended bell, being most
probably a cup-shaped mass of metal set with mouth upright, or
like a bell turned upside down—such being the form often seen
in the temples of Chinese Asia. Again did antiquity, religion, or
the promptings of mercy fail to restrain the invaders. Securing
what spoils they cared for, everything else was burned up.

After camping at Kiran, they reached the sea-coast, at Uru-san,
November 18th.

CHAPTER XIX.

THE SIEGE OF URU-SAN CASTLE.

THE Japanese now took up the spade as their immediate weapon of defence against the infuriated Coreans and the avenging Chinese. A force of twenty-three thousand men was at once set to work, "without regard to wind or rain," along the lines marked out by the Japanese engineers. To furnish the wood for towers, gates, huts, and engines, a party of two thousand axemen and laborers, guarded by twenty-eight mounted pickets and three hundred matchlock men, with seven flags, went daily into the forest.

The winter huts were hastily erected, walls thrown up, ditches dug, towers built, and sentinels and watch stations set. The work went on from earliest daybreak till latest twilight, the carpenters so suffering from the cold that "their finger nails dropped off." By the first part of January the castle was almost completed. From the eleventh day the garrison took rest.

The fortress was three-sided, the south face lying on the sea. The total line of works was about three and a half miles, pierced by three gates. The inner defences were in three parts, or *maru*. The third *maru*, or enclosure, had stone walls, one tower and one gate ; the second had two towers, two gates ; and the first or chief citadel had stone walls, forty-eight feet high, with two towers and two gates.

The war operations, which had hitherto covered large spaces of the country, now found the pivot at this place situated in Kiung-sang, on the sea-coast, thirty-five miles north of Fusan. Another commander, Asano, marched to assist the garrison and entered the castle before the Ming army arrived. His advance guard, while reconnoitring, was defeated by the Coreans, yet he succeeded, by an impetuous charge, in entering the castle.

The Chinese, smarting under their losses at Chin-sen, and stung by the gibes of the Coreans, now hastened to Uru-san, to swallow up the Japanese. The Corean army, which had been collecting around the Japanese camps, were soon joined by the advance guard of the Ming army. The arrival of the Chinese forces was made known in the following manner.

A Japanese captain commanded one of the advance pickets,

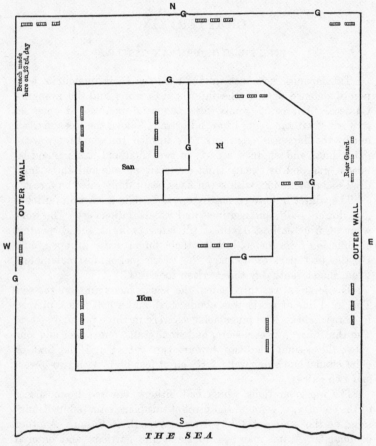

Plan of Uru-san Castle.—Explanation : Hon, First Enclosure ; Ni, Second ; San, Third ; G, Gates ; ▭▭▭ Bodies of Troops.

which had their quarters in the cloisters of Ankokuji (Temple of the Peaceful Country). One night a board, inscribed with Chinese characters, was set up before the gate of the camp. The soldiers, seeing it in the morning, but unable to read Chinese, car-

ried it to their captain, who handed it to his priest-secretary. The
board contained a warning that the Chinese were near and would
soon attack Uru-san. Betraying no emotion and saying nothing,
the captain soon after declared himself on the sick-list, and secretly absconded to Fusan. The truth was, that an overwhelming Ming army was now in front of them and their purpose to in-
vest the castle was thus published. The entire Japanese forces
were now gathered close under the walls, or inside the castle, and
the sentinels were doubled.

On the morning of January 30th the Ming army suddenly assaulted the castle. A small detachment, evidently a decoy and
forlorn hope, attempting to scale the walls, was driven back by the
matchlock men and began to retreat. Seeing this, the Japanese
recklessly opened the barbican gate and began pursuit of their
enemies, thinking they were only Coreans. Lured on to a distance, they suddenly found themselves encircled by a mighty host
By their black and yellow standards, and their excellent tactics,
the Japanese officers saw that they were Ming soldiers. The dust
raised by the horses of the oncoming enemy seemed to the garrison as high as Atago Mountain in Japan. They now knew that
eighty thousand Chinese were before their gates. Only after hard
fighting, was the remnant of the Japanese sortie enabled to get
back within the castle, while the allies, surrounding the walls,
fought as fiercely as if they intended to take it by immediate assault. Some of the bravest leaders of the garrison fell outside,
but no sooner were the gates locked than Katsuyoshi, without ex-
tracting the two arrows from his wounds, or stanching the blood,
posted the defenders on the walls in position. Ogawuchi had per-
formed the hazardous feat of sallying out and firing most of the
outside camps. He re-entered the castle with arrows in his clothes,
but received no wounds. The battle raged until night, when the
Chinese drew off.

The Japanese had suffered fearfully by the first combat beyond
and on the walls. "There was none but had been shot at by five
or ten or fifteen arrows." One of their captains reckoned their
loss at eighteen thousand three hundred and sixty men, which
left them but a garrison of five thousand fighting men. A large
number of non-combatants, including many of the friendly people
of the neighborhood, had crowded into the fortifications, and had
to be fed.

Food growing scarcer, and danger increasing, Asano sent word to Kato for help. On a fleet horse the messenger arrived, after a ride of two days. Kato had, in Japan, taken oath to Asano's father to help him in every strait. Immediately, with seventy picked companions, he put out to sea in seven boats, and, after hard rowing, succeeded in entering the castle.

On January 31, 1598, the war-conch sounded in the Ming camp, as the signal of attack, and the ears of the besieged were soon deafened by the yells of the "eighty thousand" besiegers. The Japanese were at first terrified at the clouds of dust, through which the awful sight of ranks of men, twenty deep, were on all sides visible. The enemy, armed with shields shaped like a fowl's wings, upon which they received the missiles of the garrison, charged on the outer works, but when into and on the slope of the ditch, flung their shields away, and plied axe, knife, sword, and lance. Though seven attacks were repulsed, the wall was breached, the outer works were gained by overwhelming numbers, and the garrison was driven into the inner enclosure.

Night fell upon the work of blood, but at early morn, the enemy waked the garrison with showers of arrows, and with ladders and hurdles of bamboo, tried to scale the walls. In four hours, seven attacks in force had been repulsed, yet the fighting went on. In spite of the intense cold, the soldiers perspired so that the sweat froze on their armor. Over their own heaps of corpses the Chinese attempted to force one of the gates, while, from the walls of the inner citadel, and from the higher gate above them, the Japanese smote them. The next day the carnage ceased from the third to the ninth hour. On February 3d, the Chinese, with their ladders, were again repulsed. At night their sentinels "gathered hoar-frost on their helmets," while guarding the night long against the sortie, which they feared. Another attack from the clouds of enemies kept up the work of killing. Some of the Japanese warriors now noticed that their stockings and greave-bands kept slipping down, though adjusted repeatedly. The fact was their flesh had shrunk until their bones were nearly visible, and "their legs were as lean as bamboo sticks." Another warrior, taking off his helmet and vizor, was seen to have a face so thin and wizen that he reminded his comrades of one of those hungry demons of the nether world, which they had seen so often depicted in temple pictures at home.

On February 5th, the Ming generals, who had looked upon the reduction of Uru-san as a small affair to be settled by the way, and

vexed at not having been able to take it by one assault, tried negotiation. In fact, they were suffering from lack of provisions.
The Japanese sent back a defiant answer, and some of them profited by the lull in the fighting to make fires of broken arrows and
lances, to strip the armor from the dead and frozen carcasses of
their steeds, and enjoy a dinner of hot horse-meat. The vast number of shafts that had fallen within the walls, were gathered into
stacks, and those damaged were reserved for fuel. Outside the
citadel, they lay under the wall in heaps many feet high.

The next day, February 6th, was one of quiet, but it was intensely cold, and many of the worn out soldiers of the garrison
died. Sitting under the sunny side of the towers for warmth, they
were found in this position frozen to death. Yet amid all the suffering, the Japanese jested with each other, poured out mutual
compliments, and kept light hearts and defiant spirits.

A council of war had been held February 2d, at Fusan, and a
messenger sent to encourage the garrison. By some means he was
able to communicate with his beleaguered brethren. With helmets
off, the leaders listened to the words of cheer and praise, and
promised to hold out yet longer.

While the lull or truce was in force, the Chinese were, according to Ogawuchi, plotting to entrap the Japanese leaders. This
they learned from one Okomoto, a native of Japan, who had lived
long in China, and was a division commander of eight thousand
men in the Chinese army. He it was who first brought the offers
of accommodation from the Ming side. The Chinese proposed to
get the Japanese leaders to come out of their citadel, leave their
horses and weapons at a certain place, and go to the altar to
swear before Heaven to keep the peace. Then the Chinese were
to surround and make prisoners of the Japanese. Okomoto's soul
recoiled at the perfidy. Going by night to the side of the castle
near the hills, he was admitted in the citadel, and exposing the
plot, gave warning of the danger. A profound impression was
produced on the grateful leaders, who immediately made a plan to
show their gratitude to Okomoto. They swore by all the gods to
reward also his sons and daughters who were still living in Japan.
When this fact was made known to him, he burst into tears and
said he had never forgotten his wife or children ; though he saw
them often in his dreams, yet " the winds brought him no news."

On the following morning a Chinese officer, coming to the foot
of the wall, made signs with his standard, and offered the same

terms in detail which Okomoto had exposed. The Japanese lead.
ers excused themselves on the plea of sickness, and the parley
came to nothing.

Yet the sufferings of the Japanese were growing hourly se-
verer. To half rations and hunger had succeeded famine, and
with famine came actual death from starvation. Unfortunately
there was no well in the castle, so the Japanese had at first sallied
out, under cover of the night, and carried water from the mountain
brooks. The Chinese, discovering this, posted archers in front of
every accessible stream, and thus cut off all approach by night or
day. To hunger was added the torture of thirst. The soldiers
who fought by day stole out at night and licked the wounds of
their slain enemies and even secretly chewed the raw flesh sliced
from the corpses of the Chinese. Within the castle, ingenuity was
taxed to the utmost to provide sustenance from the most unprom-
ising substances. The famished soldiers chewed paper, trapped
mice and ate them, killed horses and devoured every part of them.
Braving the arrows of the Chinese pickets, they wandered at night
wherever their dead enemies lay, and searched their clothes for
stray grains of parched rice. On one occasion the Chinese, lying
in wait, succeeded in capturing one hundred of the garrison, that
were prowling like ghouls around the corpses of the slain. After
this the commanders forbade any soldier, on pain of death, to
leave the castle. Yet famine held revel within, and scores of
starved and frozen multiplied into hundreds, until room for the
corpses was needed.

Tidings of the straits of the dwindling garrison at Uru-san having reached the other Japanese commanders, Nabéshima and Kuroda, they marched to the relief of their compatriots. One of the
Chinese generals, Rijobai, leaving camp, set out to attack them.

The foiled Chinese commander-in-chief, angry at the refusal of
the Japanese to come to his camp, ordered a fresh attack on the castle. This time fresh detachments took the places of others when
wearied. The day seemed shut out by the dust of horses, the smoke
of guns, the clouds of arrows, and the masses of flags. Again the
scaling ladders were brought, but made useless by the vigilant defenders in armor iced with frozen sweat, and chafing to the bone.
Their constant labor made "three hours seem like three years."
The attack was kept up unceasingly until February 12th, when
the exhausted garrison noticed the Chinese retreating. The van
of the reinforcements from Fusan had attacked the allies in the

rear, and a bloody combat was raging. At about the same time the fleet, laden with provisions, was on its way and near the starving garrison.

Next morning the keen eyes of their commander noticed flocks of wild birds descending on the Chinese camp. The careful scrutiny of the actions of wild fowl formed a part of the military education of all Japanese, and they inferred at once that the camp was empty and the birds, attracted by the refuse food, were feeding without fear. Orders were immediately given to a detachment to leave the castle and march in pursuit. Passing through the deserted Ming camp, they came up with the forces of Kuroda and Nabéshima, who had gained a great victory over the allies. In this battle of the river plain of Gisen, February 9, 1598, the Japanese had eighteen thousand men engaged. Their victory was complete, thirteen thousand two hundred and thirty-eight heads of Coreans and Chinese being collected after the retreat of the allies. The noses and ears were, as usual, cut off and packed for shipment to Kiōto.

The sufferings of the valiant defenders were now over. Help had come at the eleventh hour. For fourteen days they had tasted neither rice nor water, except that melted from snow or ice. The abundant food from the relief ships was cautiously dealt out to the famished, lest sudden plenty should cause sudden death. The fleet men not only congratulated the garrison on their brave defence, but decorated the battered walls with innumerable flags and streamers, while they revictualed the magazines. On the ninth, the garrison went on the ships to go to Sezukai, another part of the coast, to recruit their shattered energies. With a feeling as if raised from the dead, the warriors took off their armor. The reaction of the fearful strain coming at once upon them, they found themselves lame and unable to stand or sit. Even in their dreams, they grappled with the Ming, and, laying their hand on their sword, fought again their battles in the land of dreams. For three years afterward they did not cease these night visions of war.

According to orders given, the number of the dead lying on the frozen ground, within two or three furlongs of the castle, was counted, and found to be fifteen thousand seven hundred and fifty-four. Of the Japanese, who had starved or frozen to death, eight hundred and ninety-seven were reported.

In the camp of the allies, crimination and recrimination were going on, the Coreans angry at being foiled before Uru-san, and the

Chinese mortified that one fortress, with its garrison, could not have been taken. They made their plans to go back and try the siege anew, when the explosion of their powder magazine, which killed many of their men, changed their plans. For his failure the Chinese commander-in-chief was cashiered in disgrace.

On May 10th the soldiers of the garrison, now relieved, left for their homes in Japan.

Thus ended the siege of Uru-san, after lasting an entire year.

After this nothing of much importance happened during the war. The invaders had suffered severely from the cold and the climate, and from hunger in the desolated land. Numerous skirmishes were fought, and a continual guerilla war kept up, but, with the exception of another naval battle between the Japanese and Chinese, in which artillery was freely used, there was nothing to influence the fortunes of either side. In this state of inaction, Hidéyoshi fell sick and died, September 9, 1598, at the age of sixty-three. Almost his last words were, "Recall all my troops from Chō-sen." The governors appointed by him to carry out his policy at once issued orders for the return of the army. The orders to embark for home were everywhere gladly heard in the Japanese camps by the soldiers whose sufferings were now to end. Before leaving, however, many of the Japanese improved every opportunity to have a farewell brush with their enemies.

It is said, by a trustworthy writer, that 214,752 human bodies were decapitated to furnish the ghastly material for the "ear-tomb" mound in Kiōto. Ogawuchi reckons the number of Corean heads gathered for mutilation at 185,738, and of Chinese at 29,014 ; all of which were despoiled of ears or noses. It is probable that 50,000 Japanese, victims of wounds or disease, left their bones in Corea.

Thus ended one of the most needless, unprovoked, cruel, and desolating wars that ever cursed Corea, and from which it has taken her over two centuries to recover.

CHAPTER XX.

CHANGES AFTER THE INVASION.

THE war over, and peace again in the land, the fugitives returned to their homes and the farmers to their fields. The whole country was desolate, the scars of war were everywhere visible, and the curse of poverty was universal. From the king and court, in the royal city, of which fire had left little but ashes, and of which war and famine had spared few inhabitants, to the peasant, who lived on berries and roots until his scanty seed rose above the ground and slowly ripened, all now suffered the woful want which the war had bred. Kind nature, however, ceased not her bountiful stores, and from the ever-ready and ever-full treasuries of the ocean, fed the stricken land.

The war was a fruitful cause of national changes in Corean customs and institutions. The first was the more thorough organization of the military, the rebuilding and strengthening of old castles, and the erection of new ones ; though, like most measures of the government, the proposed reforms were never properly carried out. The coasts were guarded with fresh vigilance. Upon one of the Corean commanders, who had been many times successful against the Japanese, a new title and office was created, and the coast defence of the three southern provinces was committed to him. This title was subsequently conferred upon three officials whose headquarters were at points in Kiung-sang. Among the literary fruits of the leisure now afforded was the narrative, in Chinese, of the events leading to the war with the Japanese, written by a high dignitary of the court, and covering the period from about 1586 to 1598. This is, perhaps, the only book reprinted in Japan, which gives the Corean side of the war. In his preface the excessively modest author states that he writes the book "because men ought to look at the present in the mirror of the past." The Chinese style of this writer is difficult for an ordinary Japanese to read. The book (Chōhitsuroku) contains a curious map of the eight provinces.

10

In Japan the energies of the returned warriors were fully employed at home after their withdrawal from Corea. The adherents of Taikō and those of Iyéyasŭ, the rising man, came to blows, and at the great battle of Sékigahara, in October, 1600, Iyéyasŭ crushed his foes. Many of the heroes of the peninsular campaign fell on the field ; or, as beaten men, disembowelled themselves, according to the Japanese code of honor.

Konishi, being a Christian, and unable, from conscientious scruples, to commit suicide by *hara kiri*, was decapitated. The humbled spirit and turbulent wrath of Satsuma were appeased, and given a valve of escape in the permission accorded them to make definite conquest of Riu Kiu. This was done by a well-planned and vigorously executed expedition in 1609, by which the little archipelago was made an integral part of the Japanese empire. When retiring from Chō-sen, in 1597, the daimiō and general Nabéshima requited himself for the possible loss of further military glory, by bringing over and settling in Satsuma a colony of Corean potters. He builded better than he knew, for in founding these industries in his own domain, he became the prime author of that delight of the æsthetic world, "old Satsuma faïence." Other daimiōs, in whose domains were potteries, likewise transported skilled workers in clay, who afterward brought fame and money to their masters. On the other hand, Iyéyasŭ sent back the Corean prisoners in Japan to their own homes.

The spoil brought back from the peninsular campaign—weapons, flags, brocades, porcelains, carvings, pictures, and manuscripts was duly deposited, with certifying documents, in temples and storehouses, or garnished the home of the veterans for the benefit of posterity. Some, with a literary turn, employed their leisure in writing out their notes and journals, several of which have survived the wreck of time. Some, under an artistic impulse, had made valuable sketches of cities, scenery, battle-fields, and castles, which they now finished. A few of the victors shore off their queues and hair, and became monks. Others, with perhaps equal piety, hung up the arrow-pierced helmet, or corslet slashed by Chinese sabre, as ex-voto at the local shrines. The writer can bear personal witness to the interest which many of these authentic relics inspired in him while engaged in their study. In 1878, a large collection of various relics of the Corean war of 1592–1597 came into the possession of the mikado's government in Tōkiō, from the heirs or descendants of the veterans of Taikō. In

Kiōto, besides the Ear-monument, the Hall of the Founder, in one of the great Buddhist temples, rebuilt by the widow of Taikō, was ceiled with the choice wood of the war junk built for the hero.

Though the peninsula was not open to trade or Christianity, it was not for lack of thought or attention on the part of merchant or missionary.

In England, a project was formed to establish a trading-station in Japan, and, if there was a possibility, in Corea also, or, at least, to see what could be done in "the island"—as Corea then, and for a long time afterward, was believed to be. Through the Dutch, the Jesuits, and their countryman, Will Adams, in Japan, they had heard of the Japanese war, and of Corea. Captain Saris arrived off Hirado Island about the middle of June, 1613, with a cargo of pepper, broadcloth, gunpowder, and English goods. In a galley, carrying twenty-five oars and manned by sixty men furnished by the daimiō, Saris and his company of seventeen Englishmen set out to visit the Iyéyasŭ at Yedo, by way of Suruga (now Shidzuoka). After two days' rowing along the coast, they stopped for dinner in the large and handsome city of Hakata (or Fukuoka), the city being, in reality, double. As the Englishmen walked about to see the sights, the boys, children, and worse sort of idle people would gather about them, crying out, "Coré, Coré, Cocoré Waré" (Oh you Coreans, Coreans, you Kokorai men), taunting them by these words as Coreans with false hearts, whooping, holloaing, and making such a noise that the English could hardly hear each other speak. In some places, the people threw stones at these "Corean" Englishmen. Hakata was one of the towns at which the embassy from Seoul stopped while on its way to Yedo, and the incident shows clearly that the Japanese urchins and common people had not forgotten the reputed perfidy of the Coreans, while they also supposed that any foreigner, not a Portuguese, with whom they were familiar, must be a Corean. In the same manner, at Nankin, for a long while all foreigners, even Americans, were called "Japanese."

Nothing was done by Saris, so far as is known, to explore or open Corea to Western commerce, although the last one of the eight clauses of the articles of license to trade, given him by Iyéyasŭ, was, "And that further, without passport, they may and shall set out upon the discovery of Yeadzo (Yezo), or any other part in and about our empire." By the last clause any Japanese would un-

derstand Corea and Riu Kiu as being land belonging to, but outside of "civilized" Nippon.

After leaving Nagasaki, and calling at Bantam, Saris took in a
load of pepper, and sailed for England, reaching Plymouth September 27, 1614.

An attempt was also made by the Dominican order of friars to
establish a mission in Corea. Vincent (Caun), the ward of Konishi, who had been educated and sent over by the Jesuits to plant
Christianity among his countrymen, reached Peking and there
waited four years to accomplish his purposes, but could not,
owing to the presence of the hostile Manchius in Liao Tung. But
just as he was returning to Japan, in 1618, another attempt was
made by the Dominican friars to penetrate the sealed land. Juan
de Saint Dominique, a Castilian Spaniard, who had labored as a
missionary in the Philippine Islands since 1601, was the chosen
man. Having secured rapid mastery of the languages of the
Malay archipelago, he was selected as one well fitted to acquire
Corean. With two others of the same fraternity he embarked for
the shores of Morning Calm. For some reason, not known, they
could not land in Corea, and so passed over to Japan, where the
next year, March 19th, having met persecution, Dominique died
in prison. The ashes of his body, taken from the cremation furnace, were cast in the sea ; but his followers, having been able to
save from the fire a hand and a foot, kept the ghastly remnants as
holy relics.

The exact relations of "the conquering and the vassal state,"
as the Japanese would say, that is, of Nihon and Chō-sen, were not
definitely fixed, nor the menace of war withdrawn, until the last
of the line of Taikō died, and the family became extinct by the
death of Hidéyori, the son of Taikō, in 1612.

There is not a particle of evidence that the conquerors ever exacted an annual tribute of "thirty human hides," as stated by a
recent French writer. While Iyéyasŭ had his hands full in Japan,
he paid little attention to the country which Taikō had used as a
cockpit for the Christians. Iyéyasŭ dealt with the Jesuit, the
Christian, and the foreigner, in a manner different from, and for
obvious reasons with success greater than, that of Taikō. He uni-
fied Japan, re-established the dual system of mikado and shō-gun,
with two capitals and two centres of authority, Kiōto and Yedo.
He cleared the ground for his grandson Iyémitsŭ, who at once
summoned the Coreans to renew tributary relations and pay hom-

age to him at Yedo. Magnifying his authority, he sent, in 1623, a letter to the King of Corea, in which he styles himself Tai-kun ("Tycoon"), or Great Prince. This is the equivalent in Chinese pronunciation of the pure Japanese O-gimi, an ancient title applied only to the mikado. No assumption or presumption of pomp and power was, however, scrupled at by the successors of Iyéyasŭ.

The title "Tycoon," too, was intended to overawe the Coreans, as being even higher than the title *Koku O* (king of a [tributary] country), which their sovereign and the Ashikaga line of rulers held by patents from the Emperor of China, and which Taikō had scornfully refused.

The court at Seoul responded to the call, and, in 1624, sent an embassy with congratulations and costly presents. The envoys landed in Hizen, and made their journey overland, taking the same route so often traversed by the Hollanders at Déshima, and described by Kaempfer, Thunberg, and others. A sketch by a Yedo artist has depicted the gorgeous scene in the castle of the "Tycoon." Seated on silken cushions, on a raised dais, behind the bamboo curtains, with sword-bearer in his rear, in presence of his lords, all in imitation of the imperial throne room in Kiōto, the haughty ruler received from the Corean envoy the symbol of vassalage—a gohei or wand on which strips of white paper are hung. Then followed the official banquet.

Since the invasion, Fusan, as before, had been held and garrisoned by the retainers of the daimiō of Tsushima. At this port all the commerce between the two nations took place. The interchange of commodities was established on an amicable basis. Japanese swords, military equipments, works of art, and raw products were exchanged for Corean merchandise. Having felt the power of the eastern sword-blades, and unable to perfect their own clumsy iron hangers, either in temper, edge, or material, they gladly bought of the Japanese, keeping their sword-makers busy. Kaempfer, who was at Nagasaki from September 24, 1690, to November, 1692, tells us that the Japanese imported from Fusan scarce medicinal plants, especially ginseng, walnuts, and fruits; the best pickled fish, and some few manufactures; among which was "a certain sort of earthen pots made in Japij and Ninke, two Tartarian provinces." These ceramic oddities were "much esteemed by the Japanese, and bought very dear."

From an American or British point of view, there was little trade done between the two countries, but on the strength of even this small amount, Earl Russell, in 1862, tried to get Great Britain included as a co-trader between Japan and Corea. He was not successful. Provision was also made for those who might be cast, by the perils of the sea, upon the shore of either country. At the expense of the Yedo government a *Chō-sen Yashiki* (Corean House), was built at Nagasaki. From whatever part of the Japanese shores the waifs were picked up, they were sent to Nagasaki, fed and sheltered until a junk could be despatched to Fusan. These unfortunates were mostly fishermen, who, in some cases, had their wives and children with them. It was from such that Siebold obtained the materials for his notes, vocabulary, and sketches in the Corean department of his great *Archiv*.

The possession of Fusan by the Japanese was, until 1876, a perpetual witness of the humiliating defeat of the Coreans in the war of 1592–1597, and a constant irritation to their national pride. Their popular historians, passing over the facts of the case, substitute pleasing fiction to gratify the popular taste. The subjoined note of explanation, given by Dallet, attached to a map of Corea of home manufacture, thus accounts for the presence of the foreigners. The substance of the note is as follows : During the sixteenth century many of the barbarous inhabitants of Tsushima left that island, and, coming over to Corea, established themselves on the coast of Corea, in three little ports, called Fusan, Yum, and Chisi, and rapidly increased in numbers. About five years after Chung-chong ascended the throne, the barbarians of Fusan and Yum made trouble. They destroyed the walls of the city of Fusan, and killed also the city governor, named Ni Utsa. Being subdued by the royal troops, they could no longer live in these ports, but were driven into the interior. A short time afterward, having asked pardon for their crimes, they obtained it and came and established themselves again at the ports. This was only for a short time, for a few years afterward, a little before the year 1592, they all returned to their country, Tsushima. In the year 1599 the king, Syen-cho, held communication with the Tsushima barbarians. It happened that he invited them to the places which they had quitted on the coast of Corea, built houses for them, treated them with great kindness, established for their benefit a market during five days in each month, beginning on the third day of the month, and when they had a great quantity of merchandise on hand to dispose of he even permitted them to hold it still oftener.

This is a good specimen of Corean varnish-work carried into

history. The rough facts are smoothed over by that well-applied native lacquer, which is said to resemble gold to the eye. The official gloss has been smeared over more modern events with equal success, and even defeat is turned into golden victory.

Yet, with all the miseries inflicted upon her, the humble nation learned rich lessons and gained many an advantage even from her enemy. The embassies, which were yearly despatched to yield homage to their late invaders, were at the expense of the latter. The Japanese pride purchased, at a dear rate, the empty bubble of homage, by paying all the bills. We may even suspect that a grim joke was practised upon the victors by the vanquished. Year by year they swelled the pomp and numbers of their train until, finally, it reached the absurd number of four hundred persons. With imperturbable effrontery they devastated the treasury of their "Tycoon." To receive an appointment on the embassy to Yedo was reckoned a rich sinecure. It enabled the possessor to enjoy an expensive picnic of three months, two of which were at the cost of the entertainers. Landing in Chikuzen, or Hizen, they slowly journeyed overland to Yedo, and, after their merry-making in the capital, leisurely made their jaunt back again. For nearly a century the Yedo government appeared to relish the sensation of having a crowd of people from across the sea come to pay homage and bear witness to the greatness of the Tokugawa family. In 1710 a special gateway was erected in the castle at Yedo to impress the embassy from Seoul, who were to arrive next year, with the serene glory of the shō-gun Iyénobu. From a pavilion near by the embassy's quarters, the Tycoon himself was a spectator of the feats of archery, on horseback, in which the Coreans excelled. The intolerable expense at last compelled the Yedo rulers to dispense with such costly vassalage, and to spoil what was, to their guests, a pleasant game. Ordering them to come only as far as Tsushima, they were entertained by the So family of daimiōs, who were allowed by the "Tycoon" a stipend in gold kobans for this purpose.

A great social custom, that has become a national habit, was introduced by the Japanese when they brought over the tobacco plant and taught its properties, culture, and use. The copious testimony of all visitors, and the rich vocabulary of terms relating to the culture, curing, and preparation of tobacco show that the crop that is yearly raised from the soil merely for purposes of waste in smoke is very large. In the personal equipment of every male Corean, and often in that of women and children, a tobacco pouch and materials for firing forms an indispensable part. The smoker does not feel " dressed " without his well-filled bag. Into the forms of hospitality, the requisites of threshold gossip and social enjoyment, and for all other purposes, real or imaginary, which nicotine can aid or abet, tobacco has entered not merely as a luxury or ornament, but as a necessity.

Another great change for the better, in the improvement of the national garb, dates from the sixteenth century, and very probably from the Japanese invasion. This was the introduction of the cotton plant. Hitherto, silk for the very rich, and hemp and sea grass for the middle and poorer classes, had been the rule. In the north, furs were worn to a large extent, while plaited straw for various parts of the limbs served for clothing, as well as protection against storm and rain. The vegetable fibres were bleached to give whiteness. Cotton now began to be generally cultivated and woven.

It is true that authorities do not agree as to the date of the first use of this plant. Dallet reports that cotton was formerly unknown in Corea, but was grown in China, and that the Chinese, in order to preserve a market for their textile fabrics within the peninsula, rigorously guarded, with all possible precautions, against the exportation of a single one of the precious seeds.

One of the members of the annual embassy to Peking, with great tact, succeeded in procuring a few grains of cotton seed, which he concealed in the quill of his hat feather. Thus, in a manner similar to the traditional account of the bringing of silkworms' eggs inside a staff to Constantinople from China, the precious shrub reached Corea about five hundred years ago. It is now cultivated successfully in the peninsula in latitude far above that of the cotton belt in America, and even in Manchuria, the most northern limit of its growth.

It is evident that a country which contains cotton, crocodiles, and tigers, cannot have a very bleak climate. It seems more probable that though the first seeds may have been brought from China, the cultivation of this vegetable wool was not pursued upon a large scale until after the Japanese invasion. Our reasons for questioning the accuracy of the date given in the common tradition is, that it is certain that cotton was not known in Northern China five hundred years ago. It was introduced into Central China from Turkestan in the fourteenth century, though known in the extreme

south before that time.   The Chinese pay divine honors to one
Hwang Tao Po, the reputed instructress in the art of spinning and
weaving the "tree-wool."   She is said to have come from Hainan
Island.

Though cotton was first brought to Japan by a Hindoo, in the
year 799, yet the art of its culture seems to have been lost during
the long civil wars of the middle ages.   The fact that it had
become extinct is shown in a verse of poetry composed by a court
noble in 1248. "The cotton-seed, that was planted by the foreigner
and not by the natives, has died away."   In another Japanese book,
written about 1570, it is stated that cotton had again been introduced and planted in the southern provinces.

The Portuguese, trading at Nagasaki, made cotton wool a familiar object to the Japanese soldiers.   While the army was in
Corea a European ship, driven far out of her course and much
damaged by the storm, anchored off Yokohama.   Being kindly
treated while refitting, the captain, among other gifts to the
daimiō of the province, gave him a bag of cotton seeds, which
were distributed.   The yarn selling at a high price, the culture of
the shrub spread rapidly through the provinces of Eastern and
Northern Japan, being already common in the south provinces.
Even if the culture of cotton was not introduced into Corea by
the Japanese army, it is certain that it has been largely exported
from Japan during the last two centuries.   The increase of general comfort by this one article of wear and use can hardly be estimated.   Not only as wool and fibre, but in the oil from its seeds,
the nation added largely to the sum of its blessings.

Paper, from silk and hemp, rice stalk fibres, mulberry bark,
and other such raw material, had long been made by the Chinese,
but it is probable that the Coreans, first of the nations of Chinese
Asia, made paper from cotton wool.   For this manufacture they
to-day are famed.   Their paper is highly prized in Peking and
Japan for its extreme thickness and toughness.   It forms part of
the annual tribute which the embassies carry to Peking.   It is
often thick enough to be split into several layers, and is much
used by the tailors of the Chinese metropolis as a lining for the
coats of mandarins and gentlemen.   It also serves for the covering
of window-frames, and a sewed wad of from ten to fifteen thicknesses of it make a kind of armor which the troops wear.   It will
resist a musket-ball, but not a rifle-bullet.

CHAPTER XXI.

THE ISSACHAR OF EASTERN ASIA.

THE Shan-yan Alin, or Ever-White Mountains, stand like a wall along the northern boundary of the Corean peninsula. Irregular mountain masses and outjutting ranges of hills form its buttresses, while, at intervals, lofty peaks rise as towers. These are all over-topped by the central spire Paik-tu, or Whitehead, which may be over ten thousand feet high. From its bases flow out the Yalu, Tumen, and Hurka Rivers.

From primeval times the dwellers at the foot of this mountain, who saw its ever hoary head lost in the clouds, or glistening with fresh-fallen snow, conceived of a spirit dwelling on its heights in the form of a virgin in white. Her servants were animals in white fur and birds in white plumage.

When Buddhism entered the peninsula, as in China and Japan, so, in Corea, it absorbed the local deities, and hailed them under new names, as previous incarnations of Buddha before his avatar in India, or the true advent of the precious faith through his mis-sionaries. They were thenceforth adopted into the Buddhist pan-theon, and numbered among the worshipped Buddhas. The spirit of the Ever-White Mountains, the virgin in ever-white robes, named Manchusri, whose home lay among the unmelting snows, was one of these. Perhaps it was from this deity that the Man-chius, the ancestors of the ruling dynasty of China, the wearers of the world-famous hair tails, took their name.

According to Manchiu legend, as given by Professor Douglas, it is said that "in remote ages, three heaven-born virgins dwelt beneath the shadow of the Great White Mountains, and that, while they were bathing in a lake which reflected in its bosom the snowy clad peaks which towered above it, a magpie dropped a blood red fruit on the clothes of the youngest. This the maiden instinctively devoured, and forthwith conceived and bore a son, whose name they called Ai-sin Ghioro, which being interpreted is

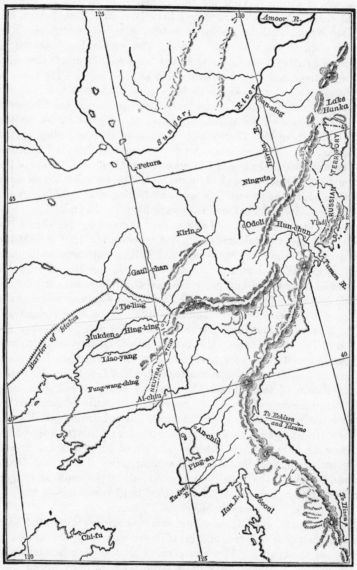

Home of the Manchius, and Their Migrations.

the 'Golden Family Stem,' and which is the family name of the emperors of China. When his mother had entered the icy cave of
the dead, her son embarked on a little boat, and floated down the
river Hurka, until he reached a district occupied by three families
who were at war with each other. The personal appearance of
the supernatural youth so impressed these warlike chiefs that they
forgot their enmities, and hailed him as their ruler. The town of
O-to-le [Odoli] was chosen as his capital, and from that day his
people waxed fat and kicked against their oppressors, the Chinese."

The home of the Manchius was, as this legend shows, on the
north side of the Ever-White Mountains, in the valley of the
Hurka. From beyond these mountains was to roll upon China and
Corea another avalanche of invasion. Beginning to be restless in the
fourteenth century, they had, in the sixteenth, consolidated so many
tribes, and were so strong in men and horses, that they openly defied the Chinese. The formidable expeditions of Li-yu-sun, previous
to the Japanese invasion of Corea, kept them at bay for a time, but
the immense expenditure of life and treasure required to fight the
Japanese, drained the resources of the Ming emperors, while their
attention being drawn away from the north, the Manchiu hordes
massed their forces and grew daily in wealth, numbers, discipline,
and courage. The invasion of Chō-sen by the Japanese veterans was
one of the causes of the weakness and fall of the Ming dynasty.

To repress the rising power in the north, and to smother the
life of the young nation, the Peking government resorted to barbarous cruelties and stern coercion, in which bloodshed was continual. Unable to protect the eastern border of Liao Tung, the entire
population of three hundred thousand souls, dwelling in four
cities and many villages, were removed westward and resettled on
new lands. Fortresses were planned, but not finished, in the deserted land, to keep back the restless cavalry raiders from the north.
Thus the foundation of the neutral strip of fifty miles was unconsciously laid, and ten thousand square miles of fair and fertile
land, west of the Yalu, was abandoned to the wolf and tiger.
What it soon became, it has remained until yesterday—a howling
wilderness. (See map on page 155.)

Unable to meet these cotton-armored raiders in the field, the
Ming emperor ordered, and in 1615 consummated, the assassination of their king. This exasperated all the Manchiu tribes to
vengeance, and hostilities on a large scale at once began by a
southwest movement into Liao Tung.

China had now again to face an invasion greater than the Japanese, for this time a whole nation was behind it. Calling on her vassal, the Eastern Kingdom, to send an army of twenty thousand men, she ordered them to join the imperial army at Hingking. This city, now called Yen-den, lies about seventy miles west of the Yalu River, near the 42d parallel, just beyond what was "the neutral strip," and inside the palisades erected later. In the battle, which ensued, the Coreans first faced the Manchius. The imperial legions were beaten, and the Coreans, seeing which way the victory would finally turn, deserted from the Chinese side to that of their enemy. This was in 1619.

The Manchiu general sent back some of the runaway Coreans to their king, intimating that, though the Coreans were acting gratefully in assisting the Chinese, who had formerly helped the Coreans against the Japanese, yet it might hereafter be better to remain neutral. So far from taking any notice of this letter, the government at Seoul allowed the king's subjects to cross the Yalu and assist the people of Liao Tung against the Manchius, who were making Hing-king their capital. At the same time the Chinese commander was permitted to enter Corea, and thence to make expeditions against the Manchius, by which they inflicted great damage upon the enemy. This continued until the winter of 1827, when the Manchius, having lost all patience with Corea, prepared to invade the peninsula. Compelling two refugees to act as their guides, they crossed the frozen Yalu in four divisions, in February, and at once attacked the Chinese army, which was defeated, and retreated into Liao Tung. They then began the march to Seoul. Ai-chiu was the first town taken, and then, after crossing the Ching-chong River, followed in succession the cities lining the high road to Ping-an. Thence, over the Tatong River, they pressed on to Seoul, the Coreans everywhere flying before them. Thousands of dwellings and magazines of provisions were given to the flames, and their trail was one of blood and ashes. Among the slain were two Hollanders, who were captives in the country.

Heretofore a line of strong palisades had separated Corea from Manchuria, on the north, but large portions of it were destroyed at this time in the constant forays along the border. Those parts which stood yet intact were often seen by travellers along the Manchurian side as late as toward the end of the last century. Since then this wooden wall, a pigmy imitation of China's colossal embargo in masonry, has gradually fallen into decay.

The Manchius invested Seoul and began its siege in earnest. The queen and ladies of the court had already been sent to Kang-wa Island. The king, to avoid further shedding of blood, sent tribute offerings to the invaders, and concluded a treaty of peace by which Chō-sen again exchanged masters, the king not only acknowledging from the Manchiu sovereign the right of investiture, but also direct authority over his person, that is, the relation of master and subject.

The Coreans now waited to see whether events were likely to modify their new relations, so reluctantly entered into, for the Chinese were far from beaten as yet. When free from the presence of the invading army the courage of the ministers rose, and by their advice the king, by gradual encroachments and neglect, annulled the treaty.

No sooner were the Manchius able to spare their forces for the purpose, than, turning from China, they marched into Corea, one hundred thousand strong, well supplied with provisions and baggage-wagons. Entering the peninsula, both at Ai-chiu and by the northern pass, they reached Seoul, and, after severe fighting, entered it. Being now provided with cannon and boats, they took Kang-wa, into which all the royal, and many of the noble, ladies had fled for safety.

The king now came to terms, and made a treaty in February, 1637, in which he utterly renounced his allegiance to the Ming emperor, agreed to give his two sons as hostages, promised to send an annual embassy, with tribute, to the Manchiu court, and to establish a market at the Border Gate, in Liao Tung. These covenants were ratified by the solemn ceremonial of the king, his sons and his ministers confessing their crimes and making "kowtow" (bowing nine times to the earth). Tartar and Corean worshipped together before Heaven, and the altar erected to Heaven's honor. A memorial stone, erected near this sacred place, commemorates the clemency of the Manchiu conqueror.

In obedience to the orders of their new masters, the Coreans despatched ships, loaded with grain, to feed the armies operating against Peking, and sent a small force beyond the Tumen to chastise a tribe that had rebelled against their conquerors. A picked body of their matchlock men was also admitted into the Manchiu service.

After the evacuation of Corea, the victors marched into China, where bloody, civil war was already raging. The imperial army was badly beaten by the rebels headed by the usurper Li-tse-ching. The Manchius joined their forces with the Imperialists, and defeated the rebels, and then demanded the price of their victory. Entering Peking, they proclaimed the downfall of the house of Ming. The Tâtar (vassal) was now a "Tartar." The son of their late king was set upon the dragon-throne and proclaimed the Whang Ti, the Son of Heaven, and the Lord of the Middle Kingdom and all her vassals. The following tribute was fixed for Chō-sen to pay annually :

100 ounces of gold, 1,000 ounces of silver, 10,000 bags of rice, 2,000 pieces of silk, 300 pieces of linen, 10,000 pieces of cotton cloth, 400 pieces of hemp cloth, 100 pieces of fine hemp cloth, 10,000 rolls (fifty sheets each) of large paper, 1,000 rolls small sized paper, 2,000 knives (good quality), 1,000 ox-horns, 40 decorated mats, 200 pounds of dye-wood, 10 boxes of pepper, 100 tiger skins, 100 deer skins, 400 beaver skins, 200 skins of blue (musk ?) rats.

When, as it happened the very next year, the shō-gun of Japan demanded an increase of tribute to be paid in Yedo, the court of Seoul plead in excuse their wasted resources consequent upon the war with the Manchius, and their heavy burdens newly laid upon them. Their excuse was accepted.

Twice, within a single generation, had the little peninsula been devastated by two mighty invasions that ate up the land. Between the mountaineers of the north, and "the brigands" from over the sea, Corea was left the Issachar among nations. The once strong ass couched down between two burdens. "And he saw that the rest was good, and the land that it was pleasant, and bowed his shoulder to bear, and became a servant unto tribute."

The Manchius, being of different stock and blood from the Chinese, yet imposed their dress and method of wearing the hair upon the millions of Chinese people, but here their tyranny seemed to stop. Hitherto, the Chinese and Corean method of rolling the hair in a knot or ball, on the top of the head, had been the fashion for ages. As a sign of loyalty to the new rulers, all people in the Middle Kingdom were compelled to shave the fore-front of the head and allow their hair to grow in a queue, or pigtail, behind on their back. At first they resisted, and much blood was shed before all submitted ; but, at length, the once odious mark of savagery and foreign conquest became the national fashion, and the Chinaman's pride at home and abroad. Even in foreign lands, they cling to this mark of their loyalty as to life and country. The object of the recent queue-cutting plots, fomented by the political, secret societies of China, is to insult the imperial family at Peking by robbing the Chinese of their loyal appendage, and the special sign of the Tartar dominion.

As a special favor to the Coreans who first submitted to the new masters of Kathay, they were spared the infliction of the queue, and allowed to dress their hair in the ancient style.

The Corean king hastened to send congratulations to the emperor, Shun Chi, which ingratiated him still more in favor at Peking. In 1650 a captive Corean maid, taken prisoner in their first invasion, became sixth lady in rank in the imperial household. Through her influence her father, the ambassador, obtained a considerable diminution of the annual tribute, fixed upon in the terms of capitulation in 1637. In 1643, one-third of this tribute had been remitted, so that, by this last reduction, in 1650, the tax upon Corean loyalty was indeed very slight. Indeed it has long been considered by the Peking government that the Coreans get about as much as they give, and the embassy is one of ceremony rather than of tribute-bringing. Their offering is rather a percentage paid for license to trade, than a symbol of vassalage. Nevertheless, the Coreans of the seventeenth and eighteenth centuries found out, to their cost, that any lack of due deference was an expensive item of freedom. Every jot and tittle, or tithe of the mint or anise of etiquette, was exacted by the proud Manchius. In 1695, the king of Chō-sen was fined ten thousand ounces of silver for the omission of some punctilio of vassalage. At the investiture of each sovereign in Seoul, two grandees were sent from Peking to confer the patent of royalty. The little bill for this costly favor was about ten thousand taels, or dollars, in silver. The Coreans also erected, near one of the gates of Seoul, a temple, which still stands, in honor of the Manchius general commanding the invasion, and to whom, to this day, they pay semi-divine honors. Yet to encourage patriotism it was permitted, by royal decree, to the descendants of the minister who refused, at the Yalu River, to allow the Manchius to cross, and who thereby lost his life, to erect to his memory a monumental gate, a mark of high honor only rarely granted.

The Jesuits at Peking succeeded in ingratiating themselves with the conquerors, and Shun-chi, the emperor, was a pupil of Adam Schall, a German Jesuit, who became President of the Board

Styles of Hair-dressing in Corea.

of Mathematicians. Nevertheless, in the troubles preceding the
peace, many upright men lost their lives, and hundreds of scholars who hated the Tâtar conquerors of their beloved China—as
the Christians of Constantinople hated the Turks—fled to Corea
and Japan, conferring great literary influence and benefit. In
both countries their presence greatly stimulated the critical study
of Chinese literature. With the Mito and Yedo scholars in Japan,
they assisted to promote the revival of learning, so long neglected
during the civil wars. At Nagasaki, a Chinese colony of merchants,
and trade between the two countries, were established, after the
last hope of restoring the Mings had been extinguished in Koku-
senya (Coxinga), who also drove the Dutch from Formosa. This
exodus of scholars was somewhat like the dispersion of the Greek
scholars through Europe after the fall of the Byzantine empire.

To the Jesuits in Peking, who were mostly Frenchmen, belongs
the credit of beginning that whole system of modern culture, by
which modern science and Christianity are yet to transform the
Chinese mind, and recast the ideas of this mighty people concerning nature and Deity. They now began to make known in
Europe much valuable information about China and her outlying
tributary states. They sent home a map of Corea—the first seen
in Europe. Imperfect, though it was, it made the hermit land
more than a mere name. In "China Illustrata," written by the
Jesuit Martini, and published in 1649, in Amsterdam—the city of
printing presses and the Leipsic of that day—there is a map of
Corea. The same industrious scholar wrote, in Latin, a book, entitled "De Bello inter Tartaros et Seniensis" (On the War between
the Manchius and the Chinese), which was issued at Antwerp in
1654, and in Amsterdam in 1661. It was also translated into
English, French, and Spanish, the editions being issued at London, Donay, and Madrid. The English title is "Bellum Tartari-
cum ; or, the Conquest of the Great and Most Renowned Empire
of China by the Invasion of the [Manchiu] Tartars," London, 1654,
octavo.

The Dutch had long tried to get a hand in the trade of China,
and, in 1604, 1622, and 1653, had sent fleets of trading vessels to
Chinese ports, but were in every instance refused. The Russians,
however, were first allowed to trade on the northern frontier of
China before the same privileges were granted to other Europeans.
The Cossacks, when they first crossed the Ural Mountains, in 1579,
with their faces set toward the Pacific, never ceased their advance

till they had added to the Czar's domain a portion of the earth's surface as large as the United States, and half of Europe. Once on the steppes, there began that long duel between Cossack and Tartar, which never ended until the boundaries of Russia touched those of Corea, Japan, and British America. Cossacks discovered, explored, conquered, and settled this triple-zoned region of frozen moss, forest land and fertile soil, bringing over six million square miles of territory under the wings of the double-headed eagle. They brought reports of Corea to Russia, and it was from Russian sources that Sir John Campbell obtained the substance of his "Commercial History of Chorea and Japan" in his voyages and travels, printed in London, 1771.

In 1645, a party of Japanese traversed Chō-sen from Ai-chiu to Fusan, the Dan and Beersheba of the peninsula. Returning from their travels, one of them wrote a book called the "Romance of Corea" (Chō-sen Monogatari). Takéuchi Tosaémon and his son, Tozo, and shipmaster Kunida Hisosaémon, on April 26, 1645, left the port of Mikuni in the province of Echizen—the same place to which the first native of Corea is said to have reached Japan in the legendary period. With three large junks, whose crews numbered fifty-eight men, they set sail for the north on a trading voyage. Off the island of Sado a fearful storm broke upon them, which, after fifteen days, drove them on the mountain coast of Tartary, where they landed, May 12th, to refit and get fresh water. At first the people treated them peacefully, trading off their ginseng for the *saké*, or rice-beer, of the Japanese. Later on, the Japanese were attacked by the natives, and twenty-five of their number slain. The remainder were taken to Peking, where they remained until the winter of 1646. Honorably acquitted of all blame, they were sent homeward, into the Eastern Kingdom, under safe conduct of the Chinese emperor Shun-chi. They began the journey December 18th, and, crossing the snow-covered mountains and frozen rivers of Liao Tung, reached Seoul, after twenty-eight days travel, February 3, 1647.

The Japanese were entertained in magnificent style in one of the royal houses with banquets, numerous servants, presents, and the attendance of an officer, named Kan-shun, who took them around the city and showed them the sights. The paintings on the palace walls, the tiger-skin rugs, the libraries of handsomely bound books, the festivities of New Year's day, the evergreen trees and fine scenery, were all novel and pleasing to the Japanese, but still they longed to reach home. Leaving Seoul, February 12th, they passed through a large city, where, at sunset and sunrise, they heard the trumpeters call the laborers to begin and cease work. They noticed that the official class inscribed on their walls the names and dates of reign and death of the royal line from the founder of the dynasty to the father of the ruling sovereign. This served as an object lesson in history for the young. The merchants kept in their houses a picture of the famous Tao-jō-kung, who, by skill in trade, accumulated fortunes only to spend them among his friends. On February 21st, they passed through Shang-shen (or Shang-chiu ?), where the Japanese gained a great victory.

In passing along the Nak-tong River, they witnessed the annual trial of archery for the military examinations. The targets were straw mannikins, set up on boats, in the middle of the river. On March 6th they reached Fusan. The Japanese settlement, called *Nippon-machi*, or Japan Street, was outside the gates of the town, a guard-house being kept up to keep the Japanese away. Only twice a year, on August 15th and 16th, were they allowed to leave their quarters to visit a temple in the town. The Coreans, however, were free to enter the Japanese concession to visit or trade. The waifs were taken into the house of the daimiō of Tsushima, and glad, indeed, were they to talk with a fellow countryman. Sailing to Tsushima, they were able there to get Japanese clothes, and, on July 19th, they reached Ozaka, and finally their homes in Echizen. One of their number wrote out an account of his adventures.

Among other interesting facts, he states that he saw, hanging in the palace at Peking, a portrait of Yoshitsuné, the Japanese hero, who, as some of his countrymen believe, fled the country and, landing in Manchuria, became the mighty warrior Genghis Khan. Whether mistaken or not, the note of the Japanese is interesting.

Mr. Leon Pages, in his "Histoire de la Religion Chretienne au Japon," says that these men referred to above found established in the capital a Japanese commercial factory, but with the very severe restrictions similar to those imposed upon the Hollanders at Deshima. This is evidently a mistake. There was no trading mart in the capital, but there was, and had been, one at Fusan, which still exists in most flourishing condition.

The Manchius, from the first, showed themselves "the most improvable race in Asia." In 1707, under the patronage of the

renowned emperor Kang Hi, the Jesuits in Peking began their
great geographical enterprise—the survey of the Chinese Empire,
including the outlying vassal kingdoms. From the king's palace,
at Seoul, Kang Hi's envoy obtained a map of Corea, which was reduced, drawn, and sent to Europe to be engraved and printed.
From this original, most of the maps and supposed Corean names
in books, published since that time, have been copied. Having
no Corean interpreter at hand, the Jesuit cartographers gave the
Chinese sounds of the characters which represent the local names.
Hence the discrepancies between this map and the reports of the
Dutch, Japanese, French, and American travellers, who give the

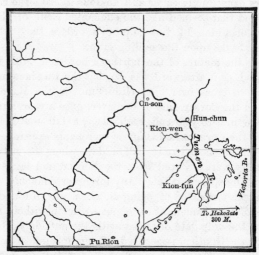

Map illustrating the Jesuit Survey of 1709.

vernacular pronunciation. To French genius and labor, from first
to last, we owe most of what is known in Europe concerning the
secluded nation. The Jesuits' map is accurate as regards the latitude and longitude of many places, but lacking in true coast lines.

While making their surveys, the party of missionaries, whose
assignment of the work was to Eastern Manchuria, caught something like a Pisgah glimpse of the country which, before a century
elapsed, was to become a land of promise to French Christianity. In
1709, as they looked across the Tumen River, they wrote: "It was a
new sight to us after we had crossed so many forests, and coasted
so many frightful mountains to find ourselves on the banks of the

river Tumen-ula, with nothing but woods and wild beasts on one side, while the other presented to our view all that art and labor could produce in the best cultivated kingdoms. We there saw walled cities, and placing our instruments on the neighboring heights, geometrically determined the location of four of them, which bounded Korea on the north." The four towns seen by the Jesuit surveyors were Kion-wen, On-son, and possibly Kion-fun and Chon-shon.

The Coreans could not understand the Tartar or Chinese companions of the Frenchmen, but, at Hun-chun, they found interpreters, who told them the names of the Corean towns. The French priests were exceedingly eager and anxious to cross the river, and enter the land that seemed like the enchanted castle of Thornrose, but, being forbidden by the emperor's orders, they reluctantly turned their backs upon the smiling cities.

This was the picture of the northern border in 1707, before it was desolated, as it afterward was, so that the Russians might not be tempted to cross over. At Hun-chun, on the Manchiu, and Kion-wen, on the Corean side of the river, once a year, alternately, that is, once in two years, at each place, a fair was held up to 1860, where the Coreans and Chinese merchants exchanged goods. The lively traffic lasted only half a day, when the nationals of either country were ordered over the border, and laggards were hastened at the spear's point. Any foreigner, Manchiu, Chinese, or even Corean suspected of being an alien, was, if found on the south side of the Tumen, at once put to death without shrift or pity. Thus the only gate of parley with the outside world on Corea's northern frontier resembled an embrasure or a muzzle. When at last the Cossack lance flashed, and the Russian schoolhouse rose, and the church spire glittered with steady radiance beyond the Tumen, this gateway became the terminus of that "underground railroad," through which the Corean slave reached his Canada beyond, or the Corean Christian sought freedom from torture and dungeons and death.

CHAPTER XXII.

THE DUTCHMEN IN EXILE.

THE old saw which tells us that "truth is stranger than fiction " receives many a new and unexpected confirmation whenever a traveller into strange countries comes back to tell his tale. Marco Polo was denominated "Signor Milliano" (Lord Millions) by his incredulous hearers, because, in speaking of China, he very properly used this lofty numeral so frequently in his narratives. Mendez Pinto, though speaking truthfully of Japan's wonders, was dubbed by a pun on his Christian name, the "Mendacious," because he told what were thought to be very unchristian stories. In our own day, when Paul Du Chaillu came back from the African wilds and told of the gorilla which walked upright like a man, and could dent a gun-barrel with his teeth, most people believed, as a college professor of belles lettres, dropping elegant words for the nonce, once stated, that "he lied like the mischief." When lo! the once mythic gorillas have come as live guests at Berlin and Philadelphia, while their skeletons are commonplaces in our museums. Even Stanley's African discoveries were, at first, discredited.

The first European travellers in Corea, who lived to tell their tale at home, met the same fate as Polo, Pinto, Du Chaillu, and Stanley. The narratives were long doubted, and by some set down as pure fiction. Like the Indian braves that listen to Red Cloud and Spotted Tail, who, in the lodges of the plains, recount the wonders of Washington and civilization, the hearers are sure that they have taken "bad medicine." Later reports or personal experience, however, corroborate the first accounts, and by the very commonplaceness of simple truth the first reports are robbed alike of novelty and suspicion.

The first known entrance of any number of Europeans into Corea was that of Hollanders, belonging to the crew of the Dutch ship Hollandra, which was driven ashore in 1627. In those days the Dutch were pushing their adventurous progress in the eastern seas as well as on the American waters. They had forts, trading settlements, or prosperous cities in Java, Sumatra, the Spice Islands, Formosa, and the ports of Southern Japan. The shores of these archipelagoes and continents being then little known, and slightly surveyed, shipwrecks were very frequent. The profits of a prosperous voyage usually repaid all losses of ships, though it is estimated that three out of five were lost. The passage between China and Japan and up the seas south of Corea, has, from ancient times, been difficult, even to a Chinese proverb.

A big, blue-eyed, red-bearded, robust Dutchman, named John Wetterree, whose native town was Rip, in North Holland, volunteered on board the Dutch ship Hollandra in 1626, in order to get to Japan. In that wonderful country, during the previous seventeen years, his fellow-countrymen had been trading and making rich fortunes, occasionally fighting on the seas with the Portuguese and other buccaneers of the period.

The good ship, after a long voyage around the Cape of Good Hope, and through the Indian and Chinese Seas, was almost in sight of Japan. Coasting along the Corean shores, Mr. John Wetterree and some companions went ashore to get water, and there were captured by the natives. The Coreans were evidently quite willing to have such a man at hand, for use rather than ornament. After the Japanese invasions a spasm of enterprise in the way of fortification, architecture, and development of their military resources possessed them, and to have a big-nosed and red-bearded foreigner, a genuine "Nam-ban," or barbarian of the south, was a prize. To both Coreans and Japanese, the Europeans, as coming in ships from the southward, were called "Southerners," or "Southern savages." Later on, after learning new lessons in geography, they called them "Westerners," or "Barbarians from the West."

Like the black potentates of Africa, who like to possess a white man, believing him to be a "spirit," or a New Zealand chief, who values the presence of a "paheka Maori" (Englishman), the Coreans of that day considered their western "devil" a piece of property worth many tiger skins. It may be remembered—and the Coreans may have borrowed the idea thence—that the Japanese, then beginning their hermit policy, had also a white foreigner in durance for their benefit. This was the Englishman Will Adams, who had been a pilot on a Dutch ship that sailed from the same

Texel River. Perhaps the boy Wetterree had seen and talked with the doughty Briton on the wharves of the Dutch port. Adams served the Japanese as interpreter, state adviser, ship architect, mathematician, and in various useful ways, but was never allowed to leave Japan. It is highly probable that the ambassadors from Seoul, while in Yedo, saw Will Adams, since he spent much of his time in public among the officials and people, living there until May, 1620.

The magnates of Seoul probably desired to have a like factotum, and this explains why Wetterree was treated with kindness and comparative honor, though kept as a prisoner. When the Manchius invaded Corea, in 1635, his two companions were killed in the wars, and Wetterree was left alone. Having no one with whom he could converse, he had almost forgotten his native speech, when after twenty-seven years of exile, in the fifty-ninth year of his age, he met some of his fellow-Hollanders and acted as interpreter to the Coreans, under the following circumstances :

In January, 1653, the Dutch ship Sparwehr (Sparrowhawk) left Texel Island, bound for Nagasaki. Among the crew was Hendrik Hamel, the supercargo, who afterward became the historian of their adventures. After nearly five months' voyage, they reached Batavia, June 1st, and Formosa July 16th. From this island they steered for Japan, fortunately meeting no "wild Chinese" or pirates on their course. Off Quelpart Island, a dreadful storm arose, and, being close on a lee shore with death staring all in the face, the captain ordered them "to cut down the mast and go to their prayers." The ship went to pieces, but thirty-six out of the sixty-four men composing the crew reached the shore alive. The local magistrate, an elder of some seventy years of age, who knew a little Dutch, met them with his retainers, and learned their plight, who they were, and whence they came. The Hollanders were first refreshed with rice-water. The Coreans then collected the pieces of the broken ship, and all they could get from the hulk, and burned them for the sake of the metal. One of the iron articles happened to be a loaded cannon, which went off during the firing. The liquor casks were speedily emptied into the gullets of the wreckers, and the result was a very noisy set of heathen.

The old leader, however, evidently determined to draw the line between virtue and vice somewhere. He had several of the thieves seized and spanked on the spot, while others were bambooed on the soles of their feet, one so severely that his toes dropped off.

On October 29th the survivors were brought by the officials to be examined by the interpreter Wetterree. The huge noses, the red beards and white faces were at once recognized by the lone exile as belonging to his own countrymen. Wetterree was very "rusty" in his native language, after twenty-seven years' nearly complete disuse, but in company with the new arrivals he regained it all in a month.

Of course, the first and last idea of the captives was how to escape. The native fishing-smacks were frequently driven off to Japan, which they knew must be almost in sight. One night they made an attempt to reach the sea-shore. They at first thought they were secure, when the dogs betrayed them by barking and alarming the guards.

It is evident that the European body has an odor entirely distinct from a Mongolian. The Abbé Huc states that even when travelling through Thibet and China, in disguise, the dogs continually barked at him and almost betrayed him, even at night. In travelling, and especially when living in the Japanese city of Fukui, the writer had the same experience. In walking through the city streets at night, even when many hundred yards off, the Japanese dogs would start up barking and run toward him. This occurred repeatedly, when scores of native pedestrians were not noticed by the beasts. The French missionaries in Corea, even in disguise, report the same facts.

The baffled Hollanders were caught and officially punished after the fashion of the nursery, but so severely that some had to keep their beds for a month, in order to heal their battered flanks. Finally they were ordered to proceed to the capital, which the Dutchmen call Sior (Seoul).

Hamel gives a few names of the places through which he passed. These are in the pronunciation of the local dialect, and written down in Dutch spelling. Most of them are recognizable on the map, though the real sound is nearly lost in a quagmire of Dutch letters, in which Hamel has attempted to note the quavers and semi-demi-quavers of Corean enunciation. He writes *Coeree* for Corea, and *Tyocen-koeck* for Chō-sen kokŭ, and is probably the first European to mention Quelpart Island, on which the ship was wrecked.

The first city on the mainland to which they came was Heynam (Hai-nam), in the extreme southwest of Chulla. This was about the last of May. Thence they marched to Jeham, spending the night

at Na-diou (Nai-chiu). The gunner of the ship died at Je-ham, or
Je-ban. They passed through San-siang (Chan-shon), and came
to Tong-ap (Chon-wup ?), after crossing a high mountain, on the
top of which was the spacious fortress of Il-pam San-siang. The
term "San-siang," used twice here, means a fortified stronghold
in the mountains, to which, in time of war, the neighboring villagers may fly for refuge. Teyn (Tai-in), was the next place arrived
at, after which, "having baited at the little town of Kuniga"
(Kumku), they reached Khin-tyo (Chon-chiu), where the governor
of Chillado (Chulla dô) resided. This city, though a hundred miles
from the sea, was very famous, and was a seat of great traffic.
After this, they came to the last town of the province, Jesan, and,
passing through Gunun and Jensan, reached Konsio (Kong-chiu),
the capital of Chung-chong province. They reached the border of
Kiung-kei by a rapid march, and, after crossing a wide river (the
Han), they traversed a league, and entered Sior (Seoul). They
computed the length of the journey at seventy-five leagues. This,
by a rough reckoning, is about the distance from Hainam to Seoul,
as may be seen from the map.

In the capital, as they had been along the road, the Dutchmen
were like wild beasts on show. Crowds flocked to see the white-
faced and red-bearded foreigners. They must have appeared to
the natives as Punch looks to English children. The women were
even more anxious than the men to get a good look. Every one
was especially curious to see the Dutchmen drink, for it was generally believed that they tucked their noses up over their ears
when they drank. The size and prominence of the nasal organ of
a Caucasian first strikes a Turanian with awe and fear. Thousands of people no doubt learned, for the first time, that the western "devils" were men after all, and ate decent food and not
earthworms and toads. Some of the women, so Hamel flattered
himself, even went so far as to admire the fair complexions and
ruddy cheeks of the Dutchmen. At the palace, the king (Yo-
chong, who reigned from 1648 to 1658) improved the opportunity
for a little fun. It was too good a show not to see how the animals could perform. The Dutchmen laughed, sang, danced, leaped,
and went through miscellaneous performances for His Majesty's
benefit. For this they were rewarded with choice drink and
refreshments. They were then assigned to the body-guard of
the king as petty officers, and an allowance of rice was set apart
for their maintenance. Chinese and Dutchmen drilled and com-

manded the palace troops, who were evidently the flower of the army. During their residence at the capital the Hollanders learned many things about the country and people, and began to be able to talk in the "Coresian" language.

The ignorance and narrowness of the Coreans were almost incredible. They could not believe what the captives told them of the size of the earth. "How could it be possible," said they, in sneering incredulity, "that the sun can shine on all the many countries you tell us of at once?" Thinking the foreigners told exaggerated lies, they fancied that the "countries" were only counties and the "cities" villages. To them Corea was very near the centre of the earth, which was China.

The cold was very severe. In November the river was frozen over, and three hundred loaded horses passed over it on the ice.

After they had been in Seoul three years, the "Tartar" (Manchiu) ambassador visited Seoul, but before his arrival the captives were sent away to a fort, distant six or seven leagues, to be kept until the ambassador left, which he did in March. This fort stood on a mountain, called Numma, which required three hours to ascend. In time of war the king sought shelter within it, and it was kept provisioned for three years. Hamel does not state why he and his companions were sent away, but it was probably to conceal the fact that foreigners were drilling the royal troops. The suspicions of the new rulers at Peking were easily roused.

When the Manchiu envoy was about to leave Seoul, some of the prisoners determined to put in execution a plan of escape. They put on Dutch clothes, under their Corean dress, and awaited their opportunity. As the envoy was on the road about to depart, some of them seized the bridle of his horse, and displaying their Dutch clothing, begged him to take them to Peking. The plan ended in failure. The Dutchmen were seized and thrown into prison. Nothing more was ever heard of them, and it was believed by their companions that they had been put to death. This was in March.

In June there was another shipwreck off Quelpart Island, and Wetterree being now too old to make the journey, three of the Hollanders were sent to act as interpreters. Hamel does not give us the result of their mission.

The Manchiu ambassador came again to Seoul in August. The nobles urged the king to put the Hollanders to death, and have no more trouble with them. His Majesty refused, but sent

them back into Chulla, allowing them each fifty pounds of rice a
month for their support.

They set out from Seoul in March, 1657, on horseback, passing
through the same towns as on their former journey. Reaching
the castle-city of "Diu-siong," they were joined by their three
comrades sent to investigate the wreck at Quelpart, which made
their number thirty-three. Their chief occupation was that of
keeping the castle and official residence in order—an easy and
congenial duty for the neat and order-loving Dutchmen.

Hamel learned many of the ideas of the natives. They represented their country as in the form of a long square, "in shape like
a playing-card"—perhaps the Dutchmen had a pack with them to
beguile the tedium of their exile. Certain it is that they still kept
the arms and flag of Orange, to be used again.

The exiles were not treated harshly, though in one case, after
a change of masters, the new magistrate "afflicted them with
fresh crosses." This "rotation in office" was evidently on account
of the change on the throne. Yo-chong ceased to reign in 1658,
and "a new king arose who knew not Joseph." Yen-chong succeeded his father, reigning from 1658 to 1676.

Two large comets appearing in the sky with their tails toward
each other, frightened the Coreans, and created intense alarm.
The army was ordered out, the guards were doubled, and no fires
were allowed to be kindled along the coast, lest they might attract
or guide invaders or a hostile force. In the last few decades,
comets had appeared, said the Coreans, and in each case they had
presaged war. In the first, the Japanese invasions from the east,
and, in the second, the Manchius from the west. They anxiously
asked the Dutchmen how comets were regarded in Holland, and
probably received some new ideas in astronomy. No war, however, followed, and the innocent comets gradually shrivelled up
out of sight, without shaking out of their fiery hair either pestilence or war.

The Dutchmen saw many whales blowing off the coast, and in
December shoals of herring rushed by, keeping up an increasing
stream of life until January, when it slackened, and in March
ceased. The whales made sad havoc in these shoals, gorging
themselves on the small fry. These are the herring which arrive
off the coast of Whang-hai, and feed on the banks and shoals during the season. The catching of them affords lucrative employment to hundreds of junks from North China.

From their observations, the Dutchmen argued—one hundred and twenty years before La Perouse demonstrated the fact—that there must be a strait north of Corea, connecting with the Arctic Ocean, like that of Waigats (now called the Strait of Kara), between Nova Zemla and the island lying off the northwestern end of Russia. They thus conjectured the existence of the Straits of Tartary, west of Saghalin, before they appeared on any European map. Waigats was discovered by the Englishman, Stephen Burroughs, who had been sent out by the Muscovy company to find a northwest passage to China. Their mention of it shows that they were familiar with the progress of polar research, since it was discovered in 1556, only seven years before they left Holland. It had even at that time, however, become a famous hunting-place for whalers and herring fishers.

These marine studies of the captives, coupled with the fact that they had before attempted to escape, may have aroused the suspicions of the government. In February, 1663, by orders from Seoul, they were separated and put in three different towns. Twelve went to " Saysiano," five to Siun-schien, and five to Namman, their numbers being now reduced to twenty-two. Two of these places are easily found on the Japanese map. During all the years of their captivity, they seem not to have known anything of the Japanese at Fusan, nor the latter of them.

Though thus scattered, the men were occasionally allowed to visit each other, which they did, enjoying each other's society, sweetened with pipes and tobacco, and Hamel devoutly adds that " it was a great mercy of God that they enjoyed good health." A new governor having been appointed over them, evidently was possessed with the idea of testing the skill of the bearded foreigners, with a view of improving the art productions of the country. He set the Dutchmen to work at moulding clay—perhaps to have some pottery and tiles after Dutch patterns, and the Delft system of illustrating the Bible at the fireplace. This was so manifestly against the national policy of making no improvements on anything, that the poor governor lost his place and suffered punishment. The spies informed on him to the king. An explosion of power took place, the ex-governor received ninety strokes on his shin-bones, and was disgraced from rank and office. The quondam improvers of the ceramic art of Corea were again set to work at pulling up grass and other menial duties about the official residence.

As the years passed on, the poor exiles were in pitiful straits. Their clothing had been worn to tatters, and they were reduced even to beggary. They were accustomed to go off in companies to seek alms of the people, for two or three weeks at a time. Those left at home, during these trips, worked at various odd jobs to earn a pittance, especially at making arrows. The next year, 1664, was somewhat easier for them, their overseer being kind and gentle; but, in 1665, the homesick fellows tried hard to escape. In 1666, they lost their benefactor, the good governor. Now came the time for flight.

All possible preparations were made, in the way of hoarding provisions, getting fresh water ready, and studying well the place of exit. They waited for the sickness or absence of their overseer, to slacken the vigilance of their guards.

In the latter part of August, or early in September, 1667, as the fourteenth year of their captivity was drawing to a close, the governor fell sick. The Dutchmen, taking time by the forelock, immediately, as soon as dark, on the night of September 4th, climbed the city wall, and reaching the seaside succeeded, after some parleying, in getting a boat. "A Corean, blinded by the offer of double the value of it," sold them his fishing craft. They returned again to the city. At night they crept along the city wall, and this time the dogs were asleep, absent, or to windward, though the Dutchmen's hearts were in their mouths all the time. They carried pots of rice and water, and that darling of a Dutchman— the frying-pan. Noiselessly they slipped the wood and stone anchor, and glided out past the junks and boats in the harbor, none of the crews waking from their mats.

They steered directly southeast, and on the 6th found themselves in a current off the Goto Islands. They succeeded in landing, and cooked some food. Not long after, some armed natives (probably from the lingering influence of the comet) approached them cautiously, as the Japanese feared they were Coreans, and forerunners of an invading band.

Hamel at once pulled out their flag, having the arms and colors of the Prince of Orange. Surrendering themselves, they stated their history, and condition, and their desire of getting home. The Japanese were kind, "but made no return for the gifts" of the Dutchmen. They finally got to Nagasaki in Japanese junks, and met their countrymen at Déshima. The annual ship from Batavia was then just about to return, and in the nick of time the waifs got on board, reached Batavia November 20th, sailed for Holland December 28th, and on July 20, 1668, stepped ashore at home.

Hamel, the supercargo of the ship, wrote a book on his return, recounting his adventures in a simple and straightforward style. It was written in Dutch and shortly after translated into French, German, and English. Four editions in Dutch are known. The English version may be found in full in the Astley, and in the Pinkerton, Collections of Voyages and Travels.

The French translator indulges in skepticism concerning Hamel's narrative, questioning especially his geographical statements. Before a map of Corea, with the native sounds even but approximated, it will be seen that Hamel's story is a piece of downright unembroidered truth. It is indeed to be regretted that this actual observer of Corean life, people, and customs gave us so little information concerning them.

The fate of the other survivors of the Sparrowhawk crew was never known. Perhaps it never will be learned, as it is not likely that the Coreans would take any pains to mark the site of their graves. Yet as the tomb of Will Adams was found in Japan, by a reader of Hildreth's book, so perhaps some inquiring foreigner in Corea may discover the site of the graves of these exiles, and mark their resting-places.

There is no improbability in supposing that other missing vessels, previous to the second half of the nineteenth century, shared the fate of the Sparrowhawk. The wrecks, burned for the sake of the iron, would leave no trace; while perhaps many ship-wrecked men have pined in captivity, and dying lonely in a strange land have been put in unmarked graves.

At this point, we bring to an end our sketch of the ancient and mediæval history of Corea. Until the introduction of Christianity into the peninsula, the hermit nation was uninfluenced by any ideas which the best modern life claims as its own. As with the whole world, so with its tiny fraction Corea, the door of ancient history shut, and the gate of modern history opened, when the religion of Jesus moved the hearts and minds of men. We now glance at the geography, politics, social life, and religion of the Coreans; after which we shall narrate the story of their national life from the implanting of Christianity until their rivulet of history flowed into the stream of the world's history.

II.

POLITICAL AND SOCIAL
COREA.

POLITICAL AND SOCIAL COREA.

CHAPTER XXIII.

THE EIGHT PROVINCES.

PING-AN, OR THE PACIFIC.

THIS province bears the not altogether appropriate name of Peaceful Quiet. It is the border land of the kingdom, containing what was for centuries the only acknowledged gate of entrance and outlet to the one neighbor which Corea willingly acknowledged as her superior. It contains, probably, the largest area of any province, unless it be Ham-kiung. Its northern, and a great part of its western, frontier is made by the Yalu River, called also the Ap-nok, the former name referring to its sinuous course, meaning "dragon's windings," and the latter after its deep green color.

The Yalu is the longest river in Corea. Its source is found near the 40th parallel. Flowing northwardly, for about eighty miles, the stream forms the boundary between Ping-an and Ham-kiung. Then, turning to the westward, it receives on the Manchurian side twelve tributaries, which run down the gorges of the Ever-White Mountains. Each of these streams is named, beginning westwardly, after the numerals of arithmetic. The waters of so many valleys on the west, as well as on the north and east, emptying into the Yalu, make it, in spring and fall, a turbulent stream, which sinuates like the writhing of a dragon; whence its name. In the summer, its waters are beautifully clear, and blue or green—the Coreans having no word to distinguish between these two colors. It empties by three mouths into the Yellow Sea, its deltas, or islands, being completely submerged during the melting of the snows. It is easily navigable for junks to the town of Chan-son, a noted trading place, sixty miles from the sea. The valley of the Yalu is extremely fertile, and well wooded, and the scenery is superb. Its navigation was long interdicted to the Chinese, but steamers and gunboats have entered it, and access to the fertile valley and the trade of the region will be gained by other nations. The Tong-kia River drains the neutral strip.

The town nearest the frontier, and the gateway of the kingdom, is Ai-chiu. It is situated on a hill overlooking the river, and surrounded by a wall of light-colored stone. The annual embassy always departed for its overland journey to China through its gates. Here also are the custom-house and vigilant guards, whose chief business it was to scrutinize all persons entering or leaving Corea by the high road, which traverses the town. A line of patrols and guard-houses picketed the river along a length of over a hundred miles.

Nevertheless, most of the French missionaries have entered the mysterious peninsula through this loophole, disguising themselves as wood-cutters, crossing the Yalu River on the ice, creeping through the water-drains in the granite wall, and passing through this town. Or they have been met by friends at appointed places along the border, and thence have travelled to the capital.

Through this exit also, Corea sent to Peking or Mukden the waifs and sailors cast on her shores. A number of shipwrecked Americans, after kind treatment at the hands of the Coreans, have thus reached their homes by way of Mukden. This prosperous city, having a population of over two hundred thousand souls, and noted for its manufactures, especially in metal, is the capital of the Chinese province of Shing-king, formerly Liao Tong. It is surrounded by a long wall pierced with eight gates, one of which —that to the northeast—is called "the Corean Gate." Niuchwang has also a "Corean Gate."

Fifty miles beyond the Corean frontier is the "Border Gate" (Pien-mun), at which there was a fair held three or four times a year, the chief markets being at the exit and return of the Corean embassy to China. The value of the products here sold annually averaged over five hundred thousand dollars. In the central apartment of a building inhabited at either end by Chinese and Corean mandarins respectively, the customs-officers sat to collect taxes on the things bartered. The Corean merchants were obliged to pay "bonus" or tribute of about four hundred dollars to the mandarin of Fung-wang Chang, the nearest Chinese town, who came in person to open the gates of the building for the spring fair. For the privilege of the two autumn fairs, the Coreans were mulcted but half the sum, as the gates were then opened by an underling

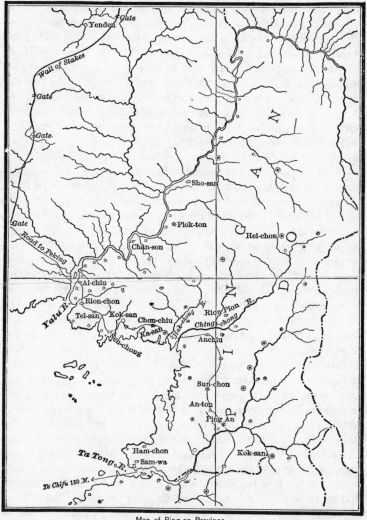

Map of Ping-an Province.

Manchiu official. The winter fair was but of slight importance. For the various Chinese goods, and European cottons, the Coreans bartered their furs, hides, gold dust, ginseng, and the mulberry paper used by Chinese tailors for linings, and for windows.

Ping-an has the reputation of being very rich in mineral and metallic wealth. Gold and silver by report abound, but the natives are prohibited by the government from working the mines. The neutrality of the strip of territory, sixty miles wide and about three hundred miles long, and drained by the Tong-kia River, between Chō-sen and Chin, was respected by the Chinese government until 1875, when Li Hung Chung, on complaint of the king of Corea, made a descent on the Manchiu outlaws and squatters settled on the strip. Having despatched a force of troops, with gunboats up the Yalu, to co-operate with them, he found the region overspread with cultivators. The eyes of the viceroy being opened to the fertility of this land, and the navigability of the river, he proposed, in a memorial to Peking, that the land be incorporated in the Chinese domain, but that a wall and ditch be built to isolate Corea, and that all Chinese trespassers on Corean ground be handed over to the mandarins to be sent prisoners to Mukden, and to be there beheaded, while Chinese resisting capture should be lawfully slain by Coreans. To this the Seoul government agreed. By this clever diplomacy the Chinese gained back a huge slice of valuable land, probably without the labor of digging ditches or building palisades. The old wall of stakes still remains, in an extremely dilapidated condition. Off the coast are a few islands, and a number of shallow banks, around which shell- and scale-fish abound. Chinese junks come in fleets every year in the fishing season, but their presence is permitted only on condition of their never setting foot on shore. In reality much contraband trade is done by the smugglers along the coast. A group of islands near the mouth was long the nest of Chinese pirates, but these have been broken up by Li Hung Chang's gunboats. Next to the Yalu, the most important river of the province is the Ta-tong or Ping-an, which discharges a great volume of fresh water annually into the sea. A number of large towns and cities are situated on or near its banks, and the high road follows the course of the river. It is the Rubicon of Chō-sen history, and at various epochs in ancient times was the boundary river of China, or of the rival states within the peninsula. About fifty miles from its mouth is the city of Ping-an, the metropolis of the province, and the royal seat of authority, from before the Christian era, to the tenth century. Its situation renders it a natural stronghold. It has been many times besieged by Chinese and Japanese armies, and near it many battles have been fought. "The General Sherman affair," in 1866, in which the crew of the American schooner were murdered—which occasioned the sending of the United States naval expedition in 1871—took place in front of the city of Ping-an. Commander J. C. Febiger, in the U. S. S. Shenandoah, visited the mouths of the river in 1869, and while vainly waiting for the arrest of the murderers, surveyed the inlet, to which he gave the name of "Shenandoah."

By official enumeration, Ping-an contains 293,400 houses, and the muster-rolls give 174,538 as the number of men capable of military duty. The governor resides at Ping-an.

There is considerable diversity of character between the inhabitants of the eight provinces. Those of the two most northern, particularly of Ping-an, are more violent in temper than the other provincials. Very few nobles or official dignitaries live among them, hence very few of the refinements of the capital are to be found there. They are not over loyal to the reigning dynasty, and are believed to cherish enmity against it. The government keeps vigilant watch over them, repressing the first show of insubordination, lest an insurrection difficult to quell should once gain headway. It is from these provinces that most of the refugees into Russian territory come. It was among these men that the "General Sherman affair" took place, and it is highly probable that even if the regent were really desirous of examining into the outrage, he was afraid to do so, when the strong public sentiment was wholly on the side of the murderers of the Sherman's crew.

THE YELLOW-SEA PROVINCE.

All the eight circuits into which Chō-sen is divided are maritime provinces, but this is the only one which takes its name from the body of water on which its borders lie, jutting out into the Whang-hai, or Yellow Sea, its extreme point lies nearest to Shantung promontory in China. Its coast line exceeds its land frontiers. In the period anterior to the Christian era, Whang-hai, was occupied by the tribes called the Mahan, and from the second to the sixth century, by the kingdom of Hiaksai. It has been the camping-ground of the armies of many nations. Here, besides the border forays which engaged the troops of the rival kingdoms, the Japanese, Chinese, Mongols, and Manchius, have contended

for victory again and again. The ravages of war, added to a somewhat sterile soil, are the causes of Whang-hai being the least
populated province of the eight in the peninsula. From very ancient times the Corean peninsula has been renowned for its pearls.
These are of superior lustre and great size. Even before the
Christian era, when the people lived in caves and mud huts, and
before they had horses or cattle, the barbaric inhabitants of this
region wore necklaces of pearls, and sewed them on their clothing, row upon row. They amazed the invading hordes of the
Han dynasty, with such incongruous mixture of wealth and savagery ; as the Indians, careless of the yellow dust, surprised by
their indifference to it the gold-greedy warriors of Balboa. Later
on, the size and brilliancy of Corean pearls became famous all
over China. They were largely exported. The Chinese merchant
braved the perils of the sea, and of life among the rude Coreans, to win lustrous gems of great price, which he bartered
when at home for sums which made him quickly rich. In the
twelfth century the fame of these "Eastern pearls," as they were
then called, and which outrivalled even those from the Tonquin
fisheries, became the cause of an attempted conquest of the peninsula, the visions of wealth acting as a lure to the would-be invaders. It may even be that the Corean pearl fisheries were known by
fame to the story-tellers of the "Arabian Nights Entertainments."
Much of the mystic philosophy of China concerning pearls is held
also by the Coreans. The Corean Elysium is a lake of pearls. In
burying the dead, those who can afford it, fill the mouth of the
corpse with three pearls, which, if large, will, it is believed, preserve the dead body from decay. This emblem of three flashing
pearls, is much in vogue in native art. The gems are found on
the banks lying off the coast of this province, as well as in the
archipelago to the south, and at Quelpart. The industry is, at
present, utterly neglected. The pearls are kept, but no use seems
to be made of the brilliant nacre of the mussel-shells, which are
exported to Japan, to be used in inlaying.

More valuable to the modern people than the now almost abandoned pearl mussel-beds, are the herring fisheries, which, during
the season, attract fleets of junks and thousands of fishermen from
the northern coast provinces of China. Opposite, at a distance of
about eighty miles as the crow flies, measuring from land's end to
land's end, is the populous province of Shantung, or "Country
east of the mountains." On the edge of this promontory are the

cities of Chifu and Teng Chow, while further to the east is Tientsin, the seaport of Peking. From the most ancient times, Chinese armadas have sailed, and invading armies have embarked for Corea from these ports. Over and over again has the river Tatong been crowded with fleets of junks, fluttering the dragon-banners at their peaks. From the Shantung headlands, also, Chinese pirates have sailed over to the tempting coasts and green islands of Corea, to ravage, burn, and kill. To guard against these invaders, and to notify the arrival of foreigners, signal fires are lighted on the hill-tops, which form a cordon of flame and speed the alarm from coast to capital in a few hours. These pyrographs or fire

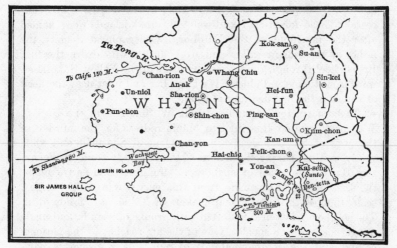

Map of the Yellow-sea Province.

signals are called "Pong-wa." At Mok-mie' san, a mountain south of the capital, the fire-messages of the three southern provinces are received. By day, instead of the pillars of fire, are clouds of smoke, made by heaping wet chopped straw or rice-husks on the blaze. Instantly a dense white column rises in the air, which, to the sentinels from peak to peak, is eloquent of danger. In more peaceful times, Corean timber has been largely exported to Chifu, and tribute-bearing ships have sailed over to Tientsin. The Chinese fishermen usually appear off the coast of this province in the third month, or April, remaining until June, when their white sails, bent homeward, sink from the gaze of the vigilant sentinels

on the hills, who watch continually lest the Chinese set foot on
shore. This they are forbidden to do on pain of death. In spite
of the vigilance of the soldiers, however, a great deal of smuggling
is done at night, between the Coreans and Chinese boatmen, at
this time, and the French missionaries have repeatedly passed the
barriers of this forbidden land by disembarking from Chifu junks
off this coast. The island of Merin (Merin-to) has, on several
occasions, been trodden by the feet of priests who afterward
became martyrs. At one time, in June, 1865, four Frenchmen entered "the lion's den" from this rendezvous. There is a great
bank of sand and many islands off the coast, the most important
of the latter being the Sir James Hall group, which was visited,
in 1816, by Captains Maxwell and Hall, in the ships Lyra and Alceste. These forest-clad and well-cultivated islands were named
after the president of the Edinburgh Geographical Society, the
father of the gallant sailor and lively author who drove the first
British keel through the unknown waters of the Yellow Sea. Eastward from this island cluster is a large bay and inlet near the head
of which is the fortified city of Chan-yon.

In January, 1867, Commander R. W. Shufeldt, in the U. S. S.
Wachusett, visited this inlet to obtain redress for the murder of
the crew of the American schooner General Sherman, and while
vainly waiting, surveyed portions of it, giving the name of Wachusett Bay to the place of anchorage. Judging from native maps,
the scale of the chart made from this survey was on too large a
scale, though the recent map-makers of Tōkiō have followed it.
The southern coast also is dotted with groups of islands, and made
dangerous by large shoals. One of the approaches to the national
capital and the commercial city of Sunto, or Kai-seng, is navigable for junks, through a tortuous channel which threads the vast
sand-banks formed by the Han River. Hai-chiu, the capital, is
near the southern central coast, and Whang-chiu, an old baronial
walled city, is in the north, on the Ta-tong River, now, as of old,
a famous boundary line.

Though Whang-hai is not reckoned rich, being only the sixth
in order of the eight circuits, yet there are several products of
importance. Rock, or fossil salt, is plentiful. Flints for fire-arms
and household use were obtained here chiefly, though the best
gun-flints came from China. Lucifer matches and percussion
rifles have destroyed, or will soon destroy, this ancient industry.
One district produces excellent ginseng, which finds a ready sale,

and even from ancient times Whang-hai's pears have been celebrated. Splendid yellow varnish, almost equal to gilding, is also
made here. The native varnishers are expert and tasteful in its
use, though far behind the inimitable Japanese. Fine brushes
for pens, made of the hair of wolves' tails, are also in repute
among students and merchants.

The high road from the capital, after passing through Sunto,
winds through the eastern central part, and crosses a range of
mountains, the scenery from which is exceedingly fine. Smaller
roads thread the border of the province and the larger towns, but
a great portion of Whang-hai along its central length, from east
to west, seems to be mountainous, and by no means densely
populated. There are, in all, twenty-eight cities with magistrates.

Whang-hai was never reckoned by the missionaries as among
their most promising fields, yet on their map we count fifteen
or more signs of the cross, betokening the presence of their converts, and its soil, like that of the other provinces, has more than
once been reddened by the blood of men who preferred to die for
their convictions, rather than live the worthless life of the pagan
renegade. Most of the victims suffered at Hai-chiu, the capital,
though Whang-chiu, in the north, shares the same sinister fame
in a lesser degree. The people of Whang-hai are said, by the
Seoul folks, to be narrow, stupid, and dull. They bear an ill
name for avarice, bad faith, and a love of lying quite unusual even
among Coreans. The official enumeration of houses and men fit
for military duty, is 103,200 of the former and 87,170 of the
latter.

KIUNG-KEI, OR THE CAPITAL PROVINCE.

Kiung-kei, the smallest of the eight circuits, is politically the
royal or court province, and physically the basin of the largest
river inside the peninsula. The tremendous force of its current,
and the volume of its waters bring down immense masses of silt
annually. Beginning at a point near the capital, wide sand-banks
are formed, which are bare at low water, but are flooded in time
of rain, or at the melting of the spring snows. The tides rise to
the height of twenty or thirty feet, creating violent eddies and
currents, in which the management of ships is a matter of great
difficulty. The Han is navigable for foreign vessels, certainly as
far as the capital, as two French men-of-war proved in 1866, and
it may be ascended still farther in light steamers. The causes

of the violence, coldness, and rapidity of the currents of Han
River (called Salt or Salée on our charts), which have baffled
French and American steamers, will be recognized by a study of
its sources. The head waters of this stream are found in the distant province of Kang-wen, nearly the whole breadth of the peninsula from the mouth. Almost the entire area of this province of
the river-sources, including the western watershed of the mountain range that walls the eastern coast, is drained by the tributaries which form the river, which also receives affluents from two
other provinces. Pouring their united volume past the capital,
shifting channels and ever new and unexpected bars and flats are

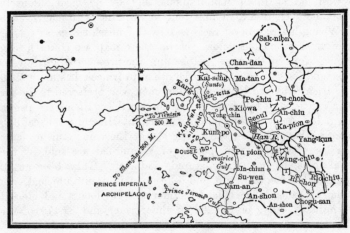

Map of the Capital Province.

formed, rendering navigation, and especially warlike naval opera-
tions, very difficult. Its channel is very hard to find from the sea.
The French, in 1845, attempting its exploration, were foiled.
Like most rivers in Chō-sen, the Han has many local names.

The city of Han-Yang, or Seoul, is situated on the north side of
the river, about thirty-five miles from its mouth, measuring by a
straight line, or fifty miles if reckoned by the channel of the river.
It lies in 37° 30' north latitude, and 127° 4' longitude, east from
Greenwich. The name Han-yang, means "the fortress on the
Han River." The common term applied to the royal city is *Seoul*,
which means "the capital," just as the Japanese called the capital
of their country Miako, or Kiō, instead of saying Kiōto. Seoul is

properly a common noun, but by popular use has become a proper name, which, in English, may be correctly written with a capital initial. According to the locality whence they come, the natives pronounce the name *Say'-ool, Shay'-ool,* or *Say'-oor.* The city is often spoken of as "the king's residence," and on foreign maps is marked "King-ki Taö," which is the name of the province. The city proper lies distant nearly a league from the river bank, but has suburbs, extending down to the sand-flats. A pamphlet lately published in the city gives it 30,723 houses, which, allowing five in a house, would give a population of over 150,000 souls. The natural advantages of Seoul are excellent. On the north a high range of the Ho Mountain rises like a wall, to the east towers the Ridge of Barriers, the mighty flood of the Han rolls to the south, a bight of which washes the western suburb.

The scenery from the capital is magnificent, and those walking along the city walls, as they rise over the hill-crests and bend into the valleys, can feast their eyes on the luxuriant verdure and glorious mountain views for which this country is noted. The walls of the city are of crenellated masonry of varying height, averaging about twenty feet, with arched stone bridges spanning the watercourses, as seen in the reproduced photograph on page 79. The streets are narrow and tortuous. The king's castle is in the northern part. The high roads to the eight points of the compass start from the palace, through the city gates. Within sight from the river are the O-pong san, and the Sam-kak san or three-peaked mountain, which the French have named Cock's Comb. North of the city is Chō-kei, or tide-valley, in which is a waterfall forty feet high. This spot is a great resort for tourists and picnic parties in the spring and summer. From almost any one of the hills near the city charming views of the island-dotted river may be obtained, and the sight of the spring floods, or of the winter ice breaking up and shooting the enormous blocks of ice with terrific force down the current, that piles them up into fantastic shapes or strews the shores, is much enjoyed by the people. Inundations are frequent and terrible in this province, but usually the water subsides quickly. Not much harm is done, and the floods enrich the soil, except where they deposit sand only. There are few large bridges over the rivers, but in the cities and towns, stone bridges, constructed with an arch and of good masonry, are built. The islands in the river near the capital are inhabited by fishermen, who pay their taxes in fish. Another large stream which joins its waters with the Han, within a few miles from its mouth near Kang-wa Island, is the Rin-chin River, whose head waters are among the mountains at the north of Kang-wen, within thirty miles of the newly-opened port of Gen-san on the eastern coast. Several important towns are situated on or near its banks, and it is often mentioned in the histories which detail the movements of the armies, which from China, Japan, and the teeming North, have often crossed and recrossed it.

Naturally, we expect to find the military geography of this province well studied by the authorities, and its strategic points strongly defended. An inspection of the map shows us that we

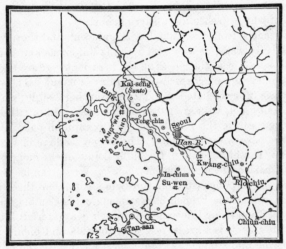

Military Geography of Seoul.

are not mistaken. Four great fortresses guard the approaches to the royal city. These are Suwen to the south, Kwang-chiu to the southeast, Sunto or Kai-seng to the north, and Kang-wa to the west. All these fortresses have been the scene of siege and battle in time past. On the walls of the first three, the rival banners of the hosts of Ming from China and of Taikō from Japan were set in alternate succession by the victors who held them during the Japanese occupation of the country, between the years 1592 and 1597. The Manchiu standards in 1637, and the French eagles in 1866, were planted on the ramparts of Kang-wa. Besides these castled cities, there are forts and redoubts along the river banks, crowning most of the commanding headlands, or points of vantage. Over these the stars and stripes floated for three days, in 1871, when the American forces captured these strongholds. In most cases the walls of cities and forts are not over ten feet high, though, in those of the first order, a height of twenty-five feet is obtained. None of them would offer serious difficulty to an attacking force possessing modern artillery.

Kai-seng, or Sunto, is one of the most important, if not the chief, commercial city in the kingdom, and from 960 to 1392, it was the national capital. The chief staple of manufacture and sale is the coarse cotton cloth, white and colored, which forms the national dress. Kang-wa, on the island of the same name at the mouth of the Han River, is the favorite fortress, to which the royal family are sent for safety in time of war, or are banished in case of deposition. Kang-wa means "the river-flower." During the Manchiu invasion, the king fled here, and, for a while, made it his capital. Kwang-chiu was anciently the capital of the old kingdom of Hiaksai, which included this province, and flourished from the beginning of the Christian era until the Tang dynasty of China destroyed it in the seventh century. Kwang-chiu has suffered many sieges. Other important towns near the capital are Tong-chin, opposite Kang-wa, Kum-po, and Pupion, all situated on the high road. In-chiŭn, situated on Imperatrice Gulf, is the port newly opened to foreign trade and residence. The Japanese pronounce the characters with which the name is written, Nin-sen, and the Chinese Jen-chuan. At this place the American and Chinese treaties were signed in June, 1882 ; Commodore Shufeldt, in the steam corvette Swatara, being the plenipotentiary of the United States. Situated on the main road from the southern provinces, and between the capital and the sea, the location is a good one for trade, while the dangerous channel of the Han River is avoided.

Most of the islands lying off the coast are well wooded; many are inhabited, and on a number of them shrines are erected, and hermits live, who are regarded as sacred. Their defenceless position offer tempting inducements to the Chinese pirates, who have often ravaged them. Kiung-kei has been the scene of battles and contending armies and nations and the roadway for migrations from the pre-historic time to the present decade. The great highways of the kingdom converge upon its chief city. In it also Christianity has witnessed its grandest triumphs and bloodiest defeats. Over and over again the seed of the church has been planted in the blood of its martyrs. Ka-pion, east of Seoul, is the cradle of the faith, the home of its first convert.

For political purposes, this "home province" is divided into the left and right divisions, of which the former has twenty-two, and the latter fourteen districts. The *kam-sa*, or governor, lives at the capital, but outside of the walls, as he has little or no authority in the city proper. His residence is near the west gate. The enumeration of houses and people gives, exclusive of the capital, 136,000 of the former, and 680,000 of the latter, of whom 106,573 are enrolled as soldiers. The inhabitants of the capital province enjoy the reputation, among the other provincials, of being light-headed, fickle, and much given to luxury and pleasure. "It is the officials of this province," they say, "who give the cue to those throughout the eight provinces, of rapacity, prodigality, and love of display." Official grandees, nobles, literary men, and professionals generally are most numerous in Kiung-kei, and so, it may be added, are singing and dancing girls and people who live to amuse others. When fighting is to be done, in time of war, the government usually calls on the northern provinces to furnish soldiers. From a bird's-eye view of the history of this part of Corea, we see that the inhabitants most anciently known to occupy it were the independent clans called the Ma-han, which about the beginning of the Christian era were united into the kingdom of Hiaksai, which existed until its destruction by the Tang dynasty of China, in the seventh century. From that time until 930 A.D. it formed a part of the kingdom of Shinra, which in turn made way for united Korai, which first gave political unity to the peninsula, and lasted until 1392, when the present dynasty with Chō-sen, or Corea, as we now know it, was established. The capital cities in succession from Hiaksai to Chō-sen were, Kwang-chiu, Sunto, and Han-yang.

CHUNG-CHONG, OR SERENE LOYALTY.

The province of Serene Loyalty lies mostly between the thirty-sixth and thirty-seventh parallel. Its principal rivers are the Keum, flowing into Basil's Bay, and another, which empties into Prince Jerome Gulf. Its northeast corner, is made by the Han River bending in a loop around the White Cloud (Paik Un) Mountain. Fertile flats and valleys abound. The peninsula of Nai-po (within the waters), in the northwestern corner, is often called the "Granary of the Kingdom." Most of the rice of the Nai-po, and the province generally, is raised for export to the capital and the north. In the other circuits the rice lands are irrigated by leading the water from the streams through each field, which is divided from the other by little walls or barriers of earth, while in this region, and in Chulla, the farmers more frequently make great reservoirs or ponds, in which water is stored for use in dry weather. The mountains are the great reservoirs of moisture, for in all the peninsula there is not a lake of noticeable size. The coast line is well indented with bays and harbors, and the run to Shantung across the Yellow Sea is easily made by junks, and even in open boats. On this account the native Christians and French missionaries have often chosen this province as their gate of entry into the "land of martyrs."

In the history of Corean Christianity this province will ever be remembered as the nursery of the faith. Its soil has been most richly soaked with the blood of the native believers. With unimportant exceptions, every town along its northern border, and especially in the Nai-po, has been sown with the seeds of the faith. The first converts and confessors, the most devoted adherents of their French teachers, the most gifted and intelligent martyrs, were from Nai-po, and it is nearly certain that the fires of Roman Christianity still smoulder here, and will again burst into flame at the first fanning of favorable events. The three great highways from Fusan to the capital cross this province in the northeastern portion. Over these roads the rival Japanese armies of invasion, led by Konishi and Kato, passed in jealous race in 1592, reaching the capital, after fighting and reducing castles on the way, in eighteen days after disembarkation. Chion-Chiu, the fortress on whose fate the capital depended, lies in the northeast, where two of the roads converge. The western, or sea road, that comes up from the south, hugs the shore through the entire length of the province. Others, along which the Japanese armies marched in 1592, and again in 1597, traverse the central part. Along one of these roads, the captive Hollanders, almost the first Europeans in Corea, rode in 1663, and one of the cities of which Hamel speaks, Konsio (Kong-Chiu), is the capital and residence of the provincial governor.

The bays and islands, which have been visited by foreign navigators, retain their names on European or Japanese charts. Some

13

of these are not very complimentary, as Deception Bay, Insult Island, and False River. At Basil's Bay, named after Captain Basil Hall, Gutzlaff also landed in 1832, planted potatoes, and left seeds and books. The archipelago to the northwest was, in 1866, named after the Prince Imperial, who met his death in Zululand in 1878. Prince Jerome's Gulf is well known as the scene of the visits of the Rover and the Emperor, with the author of "A Forbidden Land" on board. Haimi, a town several times mentioned by him, is at the head of Shoal Gulf, which runs up into the Nai-po. Two other bays, named Caroline and Deception, indent the Nai-po peninsula.

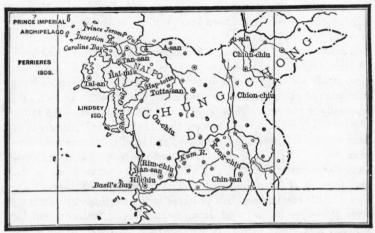

Map of Chung-chong Province.

The large shoal off the coast is called Chasseriau. Other wide and dangerous shoals line parts of the coast, making navigation exceedingly difficult. Fogs are frequent and very dense, shrouding all landmarks for hours. The tides and currents are very strong, rising in some places even as high as sixty feet. The international body-snatching expedition, undertaken by a French priest, a German merchant, and an American interpreter, in 1867, to obtain the bones or ancestral relics of the Regent, was planned to take advantage of a certain "nick of time." The river emptying into the Prince Jerome Gulf, runs some thirty miles inland, and can be ascended by a barge, or very light-draught steamer, only within the period of thirty hours during spring tides, when the water rises to a height of three feet at the utmost, while during the rest of the month it dries up completely. On account of delays, through grounding, miscalculated distances, and the burglar-proof masonry of Corean tombs, the scheme failed. The narrative of this remarkable expedition is given in a certain book on Corea, and in the proceedings of the United States Consular Court at Shanghae, China, for the year 1867.

The flora is a brilliant feature of the summer landscape. Tiger-lilies and showy compositæ, asters, cactus plants, cruciferæ, labiatæ, and many other European species abound side by side with tropical varieties. The air is full of insects, and the number and variety of the birds exceed those of Japan. Pigeons, butcher-birds, fly-catchers, woodpeckers, thrushes, larks, blackbirds, king-fishers, wrens, spoonbills, quail, curlew, titmouse, have been noticed. The ever-present black crows contrast with the snowy heron, which often stand in rows along the watercourses, while on the reefs the cormorant, sea-gulls, and many kinds of ducks and diving birds, many of them being of species differing from those in Europe, show the abundance of winged life. The archipelago and the peninsula alike, are almost virgin soil to the student of natural history and the man of science will yet, in this secluded nook of creation, solve many an interesting problem concerning the procession of life on the globe. So far as known, the Coreans seem far behind the Japanese in the study and classification of animate nature.

The Coreans are not a seafaring people. They do not sail out from land, except upon rare occasions. A steamer is yet, to most Coreans, a wonderful thing. The common folks point to one, and call it "a divine ship." The reason of this is, that they think the country of steamships so utterly at the ends of the earth, that to pass over ten million leagues, and endure the winds and waves, could not be done by human aid, and therefore such a ship must have, in some way, the aid of the gods. The prow and stern of fishing-boats are much alike, and are neatly nailed together with wooden nails. They use round stems of trees in their natural state, for masts. The sails are made of straw, plaited together with cross-bars of bamboo. The sail is at the stern of the boat. They sail well within three points of the wind, and the fishermen are very skilful in managing them. In their working-boats, they do not use oars, but sculls, worked on a pivot in the gunwale or an outrigger. The sculls have a very long sweep, and are worked

by two, three, and even ten men. For narrow rivers this method
is very convenient, and many boats can easily pass each other, or
move side by side, taking up very little room. For fishing among
the rocks, or for landing in the surf, rafts are extensively used all
along the coasts. These rafts have a platform, capable of holding
eight or ten persons. The boats or barges, which are used for
pleasure excursions and picnic parties, have high bows and ornamental sterns, carved or otherwise decorated. Over the centre a
canopy stretched on four poles, tufted with horsehair, shelters the
pleasure-seekers from the sun as they enjoy the river scenery. In
the cut we see three officials, or men of rank, enjoying themselves
at a table, on which may be tea, ginseng infusion, or rice spirit,

A Pleasure-party on the River.

with fruits in dishes. They sit on silken cushions, and seem to be
pledging each other in a friendly cup. Perhaps they will compose
and exchange a pedantic poem or two on the way. In the long, high
bow there is room for the two men to walk the deck, while with
their poles they propel the craft gently along the stream, while the
steersman handles the somewhat unwieldy rudder The common
people use a boat made of plain unpainted wood, neatly joined
together, without nails or metal, the fastenings being of wood, the
cushions of straw matting and the cordage of sea grass.

By official reckoning Chung-chong contains 244,080 houses,
with 139,201 men enrolled for military service, in fifty-four
districts. It contains ten walled cities, and like every other one
of the eight provinces is divided into two departments, Right and
Left.

CHULLA, OR COMPLETE NETWORK.

This province, the most southern of the eight, is also the warmest and most fertile. It is nearest to Shang-hae, and to the track of foreign commerce. Its island-fringed shores have been the scene of many shipwrecks, among which were the French frigates, whose names Glory and Victory, were better than their inglorious end, on a reef near Kokun Island.

Until the voyage of Captains Maxwell and Basil Hall, in the Alceste and Lyra, in 1816, "the Corean archipelago" was absolutely unknown in Europe, and was not even marked on Chinese charts. In the map of the empire, prepared by the Jesuits at Peking in the seventeenth century, the main land was made to extend out over a space now known to be covered by hundreds of islands, and a huge elephant—the conventional sign of ignorance of the map-makers of that day—occupied the space. In these virgin waters, Captain Hall sailed over imaginary forests and cities, and straight through the body of the elephant, and for the first time explored an archipelago which he found to be one of the most beautiful on earth. A later visitor, and a naturalist, states that from a single island peak, one may count one hundred and thirty-five islets. Stretching far away to the north and to the south, were groups of dark blue islets, rising mistily from the surface of the water. The sea was covered with large picturesque boats, which, crowded with natives in their white fluttering robes, were putting off from the adjacent villages, and sculling across the pellucid waters to visit the stranger ship.

On these islands, as Arthur Adams tells us, the seals sport, the spoonbill, quail, curlew, titmouse, wagtail, teal, crane and innumerable birds thrive. The woody peaks are rich in game, and the shores are happy hunting-grounds for the naturalist. Sponges are very plentiful, and in some places may be gathered in any quantity. There are a number of well-marked species. Some are flat and split into numerous ribbon-like branches, others are round and finger-shaped, some cylindrical, and others like hollow tubes. Though some have dense white foliations, hard or horny, others are loose and flexible, and await only the hand of the diver. The Corean toilet requisites perhaps do not include these useful articles, which lie waste in the sea. The coral-beds are also very splendid in their living tints of green, blue, violet, and yellow,

and appear, as you look down upon them through the clear transparent water, to form beautiful flower-gardens of marine plants.
In these submarine parterres, amid the protean forms of the
branched corals, huge madrepores, brain-shaped, flat, or headed
like gigantic mushrooms, are interspersed with sponges of the
deepest red and huge star-fishes of the richest blue. Seals sport
and play unharmed on many of the islands, and the sea-beach is
at times blue with the bodies of lively crabs. An unfailing storehouse of marine food is found in this archipelago.

The eight provinces take their names from their two chief cities,
as Mr. Carles has shown. Whang Hai Dō, for instance, is formed
by uniting the initial syllables of the largest cities, Whang-chiu and
Hai-chiu. In the case of Chulla-Dō, the Chon and Nai in Chon-
chiu and Nai-chiu (or Chung-jiu and Na-jiu) become, by euphony,
Chulla or Cholla. Hamel tells of the great cayman or "alligator,"
as inhabiting this region, asserting that it was "eighteen or twenty
ells long," with "sixty joints in the back," and able to swallow a
man.[1]

The soil of Chulla is rich and well cultivated, and large quantities of rice and grain are shipped to the capital. The wide valleys afford juicy pasture for the herds of cattle that furnish the beef
diet which the Coreans crave more than the Japanese. The visiting or shipwrecked foreign visitors on the coast speak in terms of
highest praise of fat bullocks, and juicy steaks which they have
eaten. Considerable quantities of hides, bones, horns, leather,
and tallow now form a class of standard exports to Japan, whose
people now wear buttons and leather shoes. As a beef market,
Corea exceeds either China or Japan—a point of importance to
the large number of foreigners living at the ports, who require a
flesh diet. Troops of horses graze on the pasture lands.

Chulla is well furnished with ports and harbors for the junks
that ply northward. The town of Mopo, in latitude 34° 40', has
been looked upon by the Japanese as a favorable place for trade
and residence, and may yet be opened under the provisions of
the treaty of 1876. This region does not lack sites of great
historic interest. The castle of Nanon, in the eastern part, was

---

[1] Mr. Pierre L. Jouy, of the Smithsonian Institute, who in 1884 spent six
months in Corea in zoological collecting and research, says: "No monkeys or
alligators are found in Corea. I am at a loss to understand how the alligator
story originated." Was the alleged animal the giant salamander, or the *aké?*
Japanese art and legend refer often to alligators.

the scene of a famous siege and battle between the allied Coreans
and Chinese and the Japanese besiegers, during the second inva-

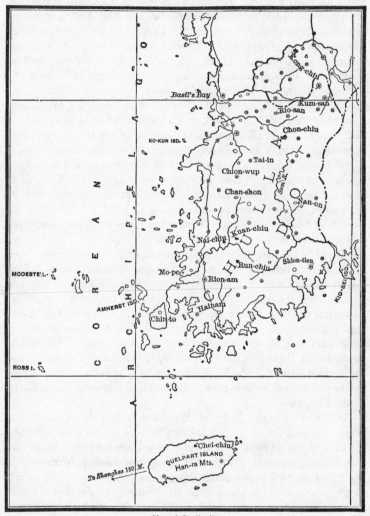

Map of Chulla-dō.

sion, in 1597. The investment lasted many weeks, and over five
thousand men were slaughtered. It was in this province also
that the crew of the Dutch ship Sparrowhawk were kept prison-

ers, some for thirteen years, some for life, of whom Hendrik Hamel wrote so graphic a narrative. For two centuries his little work afforded the only European knowledge of Corea accessible to inquirers. Among other employments, the Dutch captives were set to making pottery, and this province has many villages devoted to the fictile art. The work turned out consists, in the main, of those huge earthern jars for holding water and grains, common to Corean households, and large enough to hold one of the forty thieves of Arabian Nights story.

Through the labors of the French missionaries, Christianity has penetrated into Chulla-dō, and a large number of towns, especially in the north, still contain believers who are the descendants or relatives of men and women who have exchanged their lives for a good confession. The tragedy and romance of the Christian martyrs, of this and other provinces, have been told by Dallet. Most of the executions have taken place at the capital city of Chon-chiu. Many have been banished to Quelpart, or some of the many islands along the coast, where it is probable many yet live and pine.

Three large, and several small rivers drain the valleys. Two of these flow into the Yellow Sea and one into the sea of Japan. The main highway of this province traverses the western portion near the sea, the other roads being of inferior importance. Fortified cities or castle towns are numerous in this part of Corea, for this province was completely overrun by the Japanese armies in 1592–1597, and its soil was the scene of many battles. By official enumeration there are 290,550 houses, and 206,140 males enrolled for service in war. The districts number fifty-six. The capital is Chon-chiu, which was once considered the second largest city in the kingdom.

If Corea is "the Italy of the East," then Quelpart is its Sicily. It lies about sixty miles south of the main land. It may be said to be an oval, rock-bound island, covered with innumerable conical mountains, topped in many instances by extinct volcanic craters, and "all bowing down before one vast and towering giant, whose foot is planted in the centre of the island, and whose head is lost in the clouds." This peak, called Mount Auckland, or Han-ra san, by the people, is about 6,500 feet high. On its top are three extinct craters, within each of which is a lake of pure water. Corean children are taught to believe that the three first-created men of the world still dwell on these lofty heights.

The whole surface of the island, including plains, valleys, and mountain flanks, is carefully and beautifully cultivated. The fields are neatly divided by walls of stone. It contains a number of towns and three walled cities, but there are no good harbors. As Quelpart has long been used as a place for the banishment of convicts, the islanders are rude and unpolished. They raise excellent crops of grain and fruit for the home provinces. The finely-plaited straw hats, which form the staple manufacture, are the best in this land of big hats, in which the amplitude of the head-coverings is the wonder of strangers. Immense droves of horses and cattle are reared, and one of the outlying islands is called Bullock Island. This island has been known from ancient times, when it formed an independent kingdom, known as Tam-na. About 100 A.D., it is recorded that the inhabitants sent tribute to one of the states on the main land. The origin of the high central peak, named Mount Auckland, is thus given by the islanders. " Clouds and fogs covered the sea, and the earth trembled with a noise of thunder for seven days and seven nights. Finally the waves opened, and there emerged a mountain more than one thousand feet high, and forty *ri* in circumference. It had neither plants nor trees upon it, and clouds of smoke, widely spread out, covered its summit, which appeared to be composed chiefly of sulphur." A learned Corean was sent to examine it in detail. He did so, and on his return to the main land published an account of his voyage, with a sketch of the mountain thus born out of the sea. It is noticeable that this account coincides with the ideas of navigators, who have studied the mountain, and speculated on its origin.

KIUNG-SANG, OR RESPECTFUL CONGRATULATION.

Kiung-sang dō, or the Province of Respectful Congratulation, is nearest to Japan, and consists chiefly of the valleys drained by the Nak-tong River and its tributaries. It admirably illustrates the principle of the division of the country on the lines furnished by the river basins. One of the warmest and richest of the eight provinces, it is also the most populous, and the seat of many historical associations with Japan, in ancient, mediæval, and modern times. Between the court of Kion-chiu, the capital of Shinra, and that of Kiōto, from the third to the tenth century, the relations of war and peace, letters, and religion were continuous and fruitful. When the national capital was fixed at Sunto, and later at

Seoul, this province was still the gateway of entrance and exit to the Japanese. Many a time have they landed near the mouth of the Nak-tong River, which opens as a natural pass in the mountains which wall in the coast. Rapidly seizing the strategic points, they have made themselves masters of the country. The influence of their frequent visitations is shown in the language, manners, and local customs of southern Chō-sen. The dialect of Kiung-sang differs to a marked degree from that of Ping-an, and much more closely resembles that of modern Japanese. Kiung-sang seems to show upon its surface that it is one of the most ancient seats of civilization in the peninsula. This is certainly so if roads and facilities for travelling be considered. The highways and footpaths and the relays and horses kept for government service, and for travellers, are more numerous than in any other province. It also contains the greatest number of cities having organized municipal governments, and is the most densely populated of the eight provinces. It is also probable that in its natural resources it leads all the others. The province is divided into seventy-one districts, each having a magistrate, in which are 421,500 houses, and 310,440 men capable of military duty. Two officials of high rank assist the governor in his functions, and the admirals of the "Sam-nam," or three southern provinces, have their headquarters in Kiung-sang. This title and office, one of the most honorable in the military service, was created after the Japanese war of 1592–1597, in honor of a Corean commander, who had successfully resisted the invaders in many battles. There are five cities of importance, which are under the charge of governors. Petty officials are also appointed for every island, who must report the arrival or visit of all foreigners at once to their superiors. They were always in most favor at court who succeeded in prevailing upon all foreign callers to leave as soon as possible. Fusan has been held by the Japanese from very ancient times. Until 1868 it was a part of the fief of the daimiō of Tsushima. It lies in latitude 35° 6′ north, and longitude 129° 1′ east from Greenwich, and is distant from the nearest point on the Japan coast, by a straight line, about one hundred and fifty miles. It was opened to the Japanese by the treaty of 1876, and is now a bustling mart of trade. The name means, not "Gold Hill," but Pot or Skillet Mountain.

The approach to the port up the bay is through very fine scenery, the background of the main land being mountainous and the bay studded with green islands. The large island in front of the settlement, to the southward, called Tetsuyé, or the Isle of Enchanting View, has hills eight hundred feet high. Hundreds of horses were formerly reared here, hence it is often called Maki, or island of green pastures. The fortifications of Fusan, on the northern side, are on a hill, and front the sea. The soil around Fusan is of a dark ruddy color, and fine fir trees are numerous. The fort is distant about a league from the settlement, and Tong-nai city and castle, in which the Corean governor resides, are about two leagues farther. Tai-ku, the capital, lies in the centre of the province. Shang-chiu, in the northwestern part, is one of the fortified cities guarding the approach to the capital from the southeast. It was captured by Konishi during his brilliant march, in eighteen days, to the capital in 1592. In recent years, much Christian blood has been shed in Shang-chiu, though the city which justly claims the bad eminence in slaughtering Christians is Tai-ku, the capital of the province. Uru-san, a few miles south, is a site rich in classic memories to all Japanese, for here, in 1597, the Chinese and Corean hosts besieged the intrepid Kato and the brave, but not over-modest, Ogawuchi for a whole year, during which the garrison were reduced, by straits of famine, to eat human flesh. When the Chinese retreated, and a battle was fought near by, between them and the relieving forces, ten thousand men were slain.

Foreign navigators have sprinkled their names along the shore. Cape Clonard and Unkoffsky Bay are near the thirty-sixth parallel. Chō-san harbor was named by Captain Broughton, who on asking the name of the place in 1797, received the reply "Chō-san," which is the name of the kingdom instead of the harbor. Other names of limited recognition are found on charts made in Europe. Many inhabited islands lie off the coast, some of which are used as places of exile to Christians and other offenders against the law. Christianity in this province seems to have flourished chiefly in the towns along the southern sea border. Nearly the whole of the coast consists of the slopes of the two mountain ranges which front the sea, and is less densely inhabited than the interior, having few or no rivers or important harbors. The one exception is at the mouth of the Nak-tong River, opposite Tsushima. This is the gateway into the province, and the point most vulnerable from Japan. The river after draining the whole of Kiung-sang, widens into a bay, around which are populous cities and towns, the port of Fusan and the two great roads to Seoul. Tsushima (the Twin

Islands) lies like a stepping-stone between Corea and Japan, and was formerly claimed by the Coreans, who call it Tu-ma. Its port of Wani-ura is thirty miles distant from Fusan, and often shelters

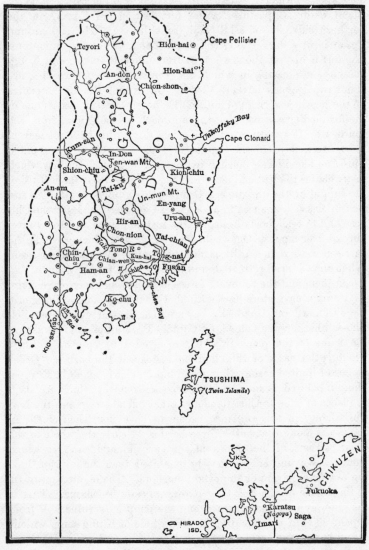

Map of the Province nearest Japan.

the becalmed or storm-stayed junks which, with fair wind and weather, can make the run between the two countries in a single day.

From a strategic military point of view, the Twin Islands are invaluable to the mikado's empire, guarding, as they do, the sea of Japan like a sentinel. The Russians who now own the long island at the upper end of the sea, attempted, in 1859, to obtain a footing on Tsushima. They built barracks and planted seed, with every indication of making a permanent occupation. The timely appearance on the scene of a fleet of British ships, under Sir James Hope, put an end to Russian designs on Tsushima.

A Japanese writer reports that the Kiung-sang people are rather more simple in their habits, less corrupted in their manners, and their ancient customs are more faithfully preserved than in some of the other provinces. There is little of luxury and less of expensive folly, so that the small estates or property are faithfully transmitted from father to son, for many generations, in the same families. Studious habits prevail, and literature flourishes. Often the young men, after toiling during the day, give the evening to reading and conversation, for which admirable practice the native language has a special word. Here ladies of rank are not so closely shut up in-doors as in other provinces, but often walk abroad, accompanied by their servants, without fear of insult. In this province also Buddhism has the largest number of adherents. Kion-chiu, the old capital of Shinra, was the centre of the scholastic and missionary influences of the Buddha doctrine in Corea, and, though burned by the Japanese in 1597, its influence still survives.

The people are strongly attached to their superstitions, and difficult to change, but to whatever faith they are once converted they are steadfast and loyal. The numerous nobles who dwell in this province, belong chiefly to the Nam In party.

KANG-WEN, THE RIVER-MEADOW PROVINCE.

Kang-wen fronts Japan from the middle of the eastern coast, and lies between Ham-kiung and Kiung-sang. Its name means River Meadow. Within its area are found the sources of "the river" of the realm. Though perhaps the most mountainous of all the provinces, it contains several fertile plains, which are watered by streams flowing mainly to the west, forming the Han River, which crosses the entire peninsula, and empties into the Yellow Sea. The main mountain chain of the country, called here the Makira, runs near the coast, leaving the greater area of the province to the westward. The larger part of the population, the most important high roads, and the capital city Wen-chiu, are in the western division, which contains twenty-six districts, the eastern division having seventeen. The official census gives the number of houses at 93,000, and of men capable of bearing arms, 44,000.

Some of the names of mountains in this province give one a general idea of the geographical nomenclature of the kingdom, reflecting, as it does, the ideas and beliefs of the people. One peak is named Yellow Dragon, another the Flying Phœnix, and another the Hidden Dragon (not yet risen up from the earth on his passage to the clouds or to heaven). Hard Metal, Oxhead, Mountain facing the Sun, Cool Valley, Wild Swamp, White Cloud, and Peacock, are other less heathenish, and perhaps less poetical names. One range is said to have twelve hundred peaks, and from another, rivers fall down like snow for several hundred feet. These "snowy rivers" are cataracts. Deer are very plentiful, and the best hartshorn for the pharmacy of China comes from these parts. Out in the sea, about a degree and a half from the coast, lies an island, called by the Japanese Matsu-shima, or Pine Island, by the Coreans U-lon-to, and by Europeans, Dagelet This island was first discovered by the French navigator, La Perouse, in June, 1787. In honor of an astronomer, it was named Dagelet Island. "It is very steep, but covered with fine trees from the sea-shore to the summit. A rampart of bare rock, nearly as perpendicular as a wall, completely surrounds it, except seven sandy little coves at which it is possible to land." The grand central peak towers four thousand feet into the clouds. Firs, sycamores, and juniper trees abound. Sea-bears and seals live in the water, and the few poor Coreans who inhabit the island dry the flesh of the seals and large quantities of petrels and haliotis, or sea-ears, for the markets or the main land. The island is occasionally visited by Japanese junks and foreign whaling ships, as whales are plentiful in the surrounding waters. The Japanese obtained the timber for the public and other buildings at their new settlement at Gensan from this island.

The Land of Morning Calm is, by all accounts of travellers, a land of beauty, and the customs and literature of the people prove that the superb and inspiring scenery of their peninsula is fully appreciated by themselves. Not only are picnics and pleasure gatherings, within the groves, common to the humbler classes, but the wealthy travel great distances simply to enjoy the beauty of marine or mountain views. Scholars assemble at chosen seats, having fair landscapes before them, poets seek inspiration under waterfalls, and the bonzes, understanding the awe-compelling influence of the contemplation of nature's grandeur, plant their monasteries and build their temples on lofty mountain heights. These favorite haunts of the lovers of natural beauty are as well known to the Coreans as Niagara and Yo Semite are to Americans, or Chamouni to all Europe. The places in which the glory of the Creator's works may be best beheld are the theme of ardent discussion and competing praise with the people of each province. The local guide-books, itineraries, and gazetteers, descant upon the merits of the scenery, for which each of the eight divisions is renowned. In the River-meadow province, the eight most lovely " sceneries " are all located along the coast. Beginning at the south, and taking them in order toward the north, they are the following :

1. The house on Uru-chin, a town below the thirty-seventh parallel of latitude. The inn is called " The House of the Emerging Sun," because here the sun seems to rise right out of the waters of the ocean. In front of the coast lies an island, set like a gem in the sea. The view of the rising sun, the tints of sky, river, waves, land, and mountains form a vision of gorgeous magnificence.

2. Hion-hai (Tranquil Sea). Out in the sea, in front of this village, are many small islands. When the moon rises, they seem to be floating in a sea of molten silver. The finest effect is enjoyed just before the orb is fully above the horizon. In many of the dwellings of the men of rank and wealth, there is a special room set apart for the enjoyment of the scenery, upon which the apartment looks. Especially is this the case, with the houses of public entertainment. At Hion-hai, one of the inns from which the best view may be obtained is called the " House Fronting the Moon." In it are several " looking-rooms."

3. One of the finest effects in nature is the combination of fresh fallen snow on evergreens. The pure white on the deep green is peculiarly pleasing to the eye of the Japanese, who use it as a popular element in their decorative art, in silver and bronze,

in embroidery, painting, and lacquer. The Coreans are equally happy in gazing upon the snow, as it rests on the deep shadows of the pine, or the delicate hue of the giant grass called bamboo. Near the large town of San-cho is a tower or house, built within view of a stream of water, which flows in winding course over the rocks, sparkling beneath the foliage. It has a scene-viewing room to which people resort to enjoy the "chikusetsu," or snow and bamboo effect.

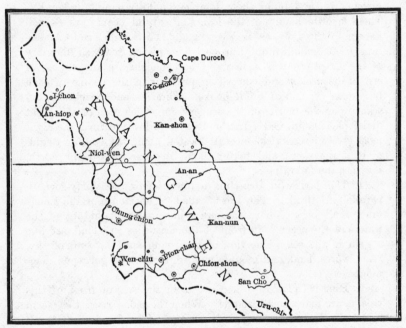

Map of Kang-wen Province.

4. From an elevation near the town of Kan-nun, or Bay Hill, one may obtain a pretty view of the groves and shrubbery growing upon the rocks. During the spring showers, when the rain falls in a fine mist, and the fresh vegetation appears in a new rich robe of green, the sight is very charming.

5. Beneath the mound at An-an the river flows tranquilly, tinted by the setting sun. The sunsets at this place are of exquisite beauty.

6. At the old castle town of Kan-nun, there is a room named

"The Chamber between the Strong Fortress and the Tender Verdure." Here the valley is steep, and in the bosom of the stream of water lie "floating islands"—so called because they seem to swim on the surface of the water.

7. Near Ko-sion, or High Fortress, is "Three Days Bay," to which lovers of the picturesque resort on summer mornings, to see the sun rise, and on autumnal evenings, to watch the moonlight effects. The fishers' boats gliding to and fro over the gleaming waters delight the eye.

8. At Tsu-sen is the "Rock-loving Chamber." Here, among some steep rocks, grow trees of fantastic form. The combination of rock-scenery and foliage make the charm of this place, to which scholars, artists, and travellers resort. In spring and autumn, literary parties visit the chamber dedicated to those who love the rocks. There, abandoning themselves to literary revels, they compose poems, hold scholarly reunions, or ramble about in search of health or pleasure.

The people of Kang-wen are industrious and intelligent, with less energy of body than the southern provincials, but like their northern countrymen, they have the reputation of being bold, obstinate, and quarrelsome. In time of bad harvests or lax government, "tramps" form bands of thirty or fifty, and roam the country, stealing food or valuables from the villages. Local thieves are sufficiently abundant. During the heavy snows of winter, people travel the mountain paths on snow-shoes, and in exceptional places, cut tunnels under the snow for communication from house to house. Soldiers test their strength by pulling strong bows, and laborers by carrying heavy burdens on their shoulders. Strong men shoulder six hundred pounds of copper, or two bales of white rice (260 pounds each.) The women of this province are said to be the most beautiful in Corea. Even from ancient times, lovely damsels from this part of the peninsula, sent to the harem of the Chinese emperor, were greatly admired. Christianity has made little progress in Kang-wen, only a few towns in the southern part being marked with a cross on the French missionary map. In the most ancient times the Chinhan tribes occupied this portion of Corea. From the Christian era, until the tenth century, it was alternately held by Kokorai, or Korai, and by Shinra.

14

HAM-KIUNG, OR COMPLETE VIEW.

Ham-kiung is that part of Corean territory which touches the boundary of Russia. Only a few years ago all the neighbors along the land frontiers of Chō-sen were Chinese subjects. Now she has the European within rifle-shot of her shores. Only the Tumen River separates the Muscovites from the once hermits of the peninsula. The southern boundary of Russia in Asia, which had been thrown farther south after every European war with China,

Corean frontier facing Manchuria and Russia.

touched Corea in 1858. What was before an elastic line, has in each instance become the Czar's "scientific frontier." By the supplementary treaty of Aigun, March 28, 1858, Count Mouravieff "rectified" the far eastern line of the Czar's domain, by demanding and obtaining that vast and fertile territory lying south of the Amur River, and between the Gulf of Tartary and the river Usuri, having a breadth of one hundred and fifty miles. This remote, but very desirable, slice of Asia, is rich in gold and silk, coal and cotton, rice and tobacco. With energy and enterprise, the Russian government at once encouraged emigration, placed steamers built in New York on the Usuri River and Lake Hanka, laid out

Corean Village in Russian Territory.

the ports of Vladivostok, and Possiet, constructed a telegraph from the Baltic Sea to the Pacific Ocean, and enforced order among the semi-civilized and savage tribes. The name of the new Russian territory between the Amur River and the Sea of Okhotsk, is Primorskaïa, with Vladivostok for the capital, which is finely situated on Peter the Great or Victoria Bay. Immense fortifications have been planned, and the place is to be made the Sebastopol of the Czar's Pacific possessions. This gigantic work was begun under the charge of the late Admiral Popoff, whose name has been given to the iron-turreted war vessels of which he was the inventor, and to a mountain in Central Corea. Possiet is within twenty-five miles of the Corean frontier. It is connected with Nagasaki by electric cable. In the event of a war between China and Russia, or even of Anglo-Russian hostilities, the Czar would most probably make Corea the basis of operations against China; for Corea is to China as Canada is to the United States, or, as the people say, "the lips of China's teeth."

Russia needs a coast line in the Pacific with seaports that are not frozen up in winter, and her ambition is to be a naval power. While England checks her designs in the Mediterranean, and in Europe, her desire is great and her need is greater to have this defenceless peninsula on her eastern borders. The Coreans know too well that the possession of their country by "Russia the ravenous" is considered a necessity of the absorption policy of Peter the Great's successors. The Tumen River, which rises at the foot of the Ever-White Mountains and separates Corea from Russia, is about two hundred miles in length. It drains a mountainous and rainy country. Ordinarily it is shallow and quiet; but in spring, or after heavy rains, and swollen by a great number of tributaries, its current becomes very turbulent and powerful. In winter it is frozen over during several months, and hence is easily crossed. Thousands of Coreans fleeing from famine, or from the oppression of government officials, Christians persecuted for their faith, criminals seeking to escape the clutches of the law, emigrants desirous of bettering their condition, have crossed this river and settled in Primorskaïa, until they now number, in all, about eight thousand. The majority of them are peasants from Ham-kiung, and know little of the southern parts of their country. There is, however, an "underground railroad" by which persecuted Christians can fly for refuge to Russian protection. Their houses are built of stout timbers, wattled with

cane, plastered with mud, and surrounded with a neat fencing
of interlaced boughs. They cover their houses with strips of
bamboo, well fastened down by thatching. The chimney is detached from the house, and consists of a hollow tree. Under the
warmed floor is the usual system of flues, by which the house is
kept comfortable in winter, and every atom of fuel utilized. Their
food is millet, corn, venison, and beef. They pare and dry melon-
like fruits, cutting them up in strips for winter use. They dress
in the national color, white, using quilted cotton clothes. They
make good use of bullock-carts, and smoke tobacco habitually.
The national product—thick strong paper—is put to a great variety of uses, and a few sheets dressed with oil, serve as windows.

Some of the Russian merchants have married Corean women,
who seem to make good wives. Their offspring are carefully brought
up in the Christian faith. Some of these Corean children have
been sent to the American Home at Yokohama, where the ladies
of the Woman's Union Missionary Society of America have given
them an education in English. Through the Russian possessions,
the Corean liberal, Kin Rinshio, made his escape. From this
man the Japanese officials learned so much of the present state of
the peninsula, and by his aid those in the War Department at
Tōkiō were enabled to construct and publish so valuable a map
of Corea, the accuracy of which astonishes his fellow-countrymen. The Russians have taken the pains to educate the people in
schools, and, judging from the faces and neat costumes, as seen in
photographs taken on the spot, they enjoy being taught. The
object of instruction is not only to civilize them as loyal subjects
of the Czar, but also to convert them to the Russian form of Christianity. In this work the priests and schoolmasters have had considerable success. There are but few Coreans north of the Tumen
who cannot read and write, and the young men employed as
clerks are good linguists. A number of them are fishermen, living near the coast. Most of the converts to the Greek church
are gathered at Vladivostok.

So great has been the fear and jealousy felt by Corea toward
Russia, that during the last two generations the land along the
boundary river has been laid desolate. The banks were picketed
with sentinels, and death was the penalty of crossing from shore
to shore. Many interesting relics of the ancient greatness of
Corea still abound in Manchuria and on Russian soil. Travellers
have visited these ruins, now overgrown with large forest trees,

and have given descriptions and measurements of them. One fortification was found to cover six acres, with walls over thirty feet in height, protected by a moat and two outer ditches, with gateways guarded by curtains. In the ruins were elaborately carved fragments of columns, stone idols or statues, with bits of armor and weapons. Some of these now silent ruins have sustained famous sieges, and once blazed with watch-fires and echoed to battle-shouts. They are situated on spurs or ends of mountain chains, commanding plains and valleys, testifying to the knowledge of strategic skill possessed by their ancient builders.

The Shan-yan Alin, range on range, visible from the Corean side of the river, are between eight thousand and twelve thousand feet high, and are snow-covered during most of the year. The name means Long-white, or Ever-White Mountains, the Chinese Shang-bai, meaning the same thing. Two of the peaks are named after Chinese emperors. Paik-tu, or White Head, is a sacred mountain famous throughout the country, and is the theme of enthusiastic description by Chinese, Japanese, and Corean writers, the former comparing it to a vase of white porcelain, with a scolloped rim. Its flora is mostly white, and its fauna are reputed to be white-haired, never injuring or injured by man. It is the holy abode of a white-robed goddess, who presides over the mountain. She is represented as a woman holding a child in her arms, after a legendary character, known in Corean lore and Chinese historical novels. Formerly a temple dedicated to her spirit was built, and for a long time was presided over by a priestess. The Corean Buddhists assign to this mountain, the home of Manchusri, one of their local deities, or incarnations of Buddha. Lying in the main group of the range, over eight thousand feet above the sea, is a vast lake surrounded by naked rocks, probably an extinct crater. Large portions of the mountain consist of white limestone, which, with its snow, from which it is free only during two months of the year, gives it its name.

Another imposing range of mountains follows the contour of the coast, and thus presents that lofty and magnificent front of forest-clad highland which strikes the admiration of navigators. Other conspicuous peaks are named by the natives, Continuous Virtue, The Peak of the Thousand Buddhas, Cloud-toucher, Sword Mountain, Lasting Peace, Heaven-reaching.

Twenty-four rivers water and drain this mountainous province. The coast of Ham-kiung down to the fortieth parallel is devoid of any important harbors. A glance at a foreign chart shows that numerous French, Russian, and English navigators have visited it, and gained precarious renown by sprinkling foreign names upon its capes and headlands. At the south, Yung-hing, or Broughton's Bay, so named by the gallant British captain in 1797, is well known for its fine harbors and its high tides. It contains a small archipelago, while the country around it is the most populous and fertile portion of the province. Port Lazareff, east of

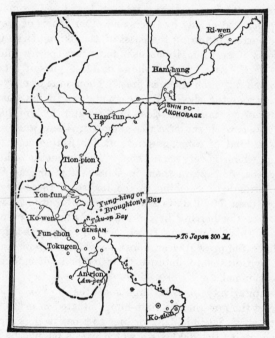

Southern part of Ham-kiung.

Yon-fun, near the mouth of the Dungan River, and west of Virginie Bay, is well known. A large Japanese army under Kato occupied this territory during the year 1592.

By the recent treaty with Japan, the port of Gensan, fronting on the south of Broughton's Bay, was opened for trade and commerce, from May 1, 1880. Gensan lies near the thirty-ninth parallel of latitude. Near the shore is the island of Chotoku, and within the twenty-five mile circuit allowed to Japanese merchants for general travel, or free movement, is the old castle-town of To-kugen. The tomb of the founder of the reigning dynasty of Chō-sen is situated near the bay and is a highly venerated spot. As the dragon is in native ideas the type of all that is strong, mighty, and renowned, the place is named the "Rise of the Dragon." One of the high roads of the kingdom traverses the strip of land skirt-ing the sea from north to south throughout the province, touch-ing the water at certain places. The greater part of the people dwelling in the province live along this road. The interior, being a mass of mountains, is thinly inhabited, and the primeval for-ests are populated chiefly by tigers and other beasts of prey.

In the current scouring the coast of Ham-kiung swim unnum-bered shoals of herring, ribbon fish, and other species inhabiting the open seas. After these follow in close pursuit schools of whales, which fatten on them as prey. Thousands of natives from the interior and the shore villages come down in the season and fish. They often stand knee-deep in the water, looking like long rows of the snowy heron of a rice-swamp, in their white clothes. They use a kind of catamaran or raft for fishing and for surf navigation, which is very serviceable. They sometimes hunt the whales at sea, or capture them in shoal water, driving them in shore till stranded. Sticking in the bodies of these huge crea-tures have been found darts and harpoons of European whalers. This chase of the herring by the whales was noticed, even in the extreme south of Corea, by Hamel, and by shipwrekced Dutch-men. Since the present year, Japanese whale-hunters have been engaged by Coreans to improve their methods of catching this huge sea-mammal.

The capital city of this largest of the provinces, and the residence of the governor, is Ham-hung, situated near the fortieth parallel of north latitude. According to a native geography this province contains 103,200 houses, which gives a population varying from 309,600 to 516,000 souls. There are enrolled and capable of military service (on paper) 87,170 men. For administrative pur-poses the province is divided into divisions, the northern and the southern. There are fifteen walled cities.

Formerly, and until the Russians occupied the Primorskaia territory, an annual or bi-annual fair was held at the Corean city of Kion-wen, which lies close to the border. The Manchiu and Chi-nese merchants bartered tea, rice, pipes, gold, and furs for the Corean ginseng, hides, and household implements. Furs of a thousand sorts, cotton stuff, silks, artificial flowers, and choice woods, changed hands rapidly, the traffic lasting but two or three days, and sometimes only one day, from noon until sunset. Such was the bustle and confusion that these fairs often terminated in a free fight, which reminds one of the famous Donnybrook. One of the articles most profitable to the Coreans was their cast-off hair. Immense quantities cut from the heads of young persons, and especially by those about to be married, were and are still sold by the Chinese to lengthen out their " pig-tails "—that mark of subjection to their Manchiu conquerors. During the time of trade no Chinese or Manchiu was allowed to enter a Corean house, all the streets and doorways being guarded by soldiers, who at the end of the fair drove out any lingering Chinese, who, if not soon across the border, were forced to go at the point of the spear. Any foreigner found inside the border at other seasons might be, and often was, ruthlessly murdered.

The nearest town beyond the frontier, at which the Chinese merchants were wont to assemble, is Hun-chun.[1] This loophole of entrance into Corea, corresponded to Ai-chiu at the Yalu River in the west. As at the latter place, foreigners and Christian natives have attempted to penetrate the forbidden country at Kion-wen, but have been unsuccessful.

An outline of the political history of the part of the peninsula now called Ham-kiung shows that many masters have in turn been its possessors. When the old kingdom of Chō-sen, which comprehended Liao Tung and that part of the peninsula between the Ta-tong and the Tumen Rivers, was broken up toward the end of the first century, the northern half of what is now Ham-kiung was called Oju or Woju, the southern portion forming part of the little state of Wei, or Whi. These were both conquered by Kokorai, which held dominion until the seventh century, when it was crushed by the Chinese emperors of the Han dynasty, and the land fell under the sway of Shinra, whose borders extended in the ninth and tenth centuries, from Eastern Sea to the Tumen River. After Shinra, arose Korai and Chō-sen, the founders of both states being sprung from this region and of the hardy race inhabiting it. From very ancient times, the boundaries of this province, being almost entirely natural and consisting of mountain, river, and sea, have remained unchanged.

---

[1] Hun-chun is in Chinese Manchuria. The Russian possessions south of Victoria Bay extend but a few miles from the mouth of the Tumen.

CHAPTER XXIV.

THE KING AND ROYAL PALACE.

THE title of majesty in Chō-sen is Hap-mun. In full robes of state the sovereign wears a silken garment, the gift of his suzerain, the Emperor of China. It is embroidered with dragons, the emblems of regal power. His throne has *riong* or dragons sculptured around it. The steps leading to it are called "the staircase of jade." The cord which is used to tie criminals has a dragon's head at the ends, to signify that the officers act in obedience to the royal command. Chief of the regalia of Corean sovereignty is the Great Seal, the possession of which makes the holder the actual sovereign of Chō-sen. This seal, of which we shall hear again, seems to have been captured by the French in 1866. In time of war or public danger, the royal library, archives and regalia are sent to Kang-wa Island for safety. Ridel wrote in 1866 :

"In another case, they found a marble tortoise, sculptured in perfect art, upon the pedestal of which was the great seal of state. This royal cartouche was to the simple Corean folk neither visible nor approachable, the possession of which has sufficed many times to transfer the royal authority and to terminate revolutions. It was the regalia of Corean sovereignty. The one which he saw was new and appeared never to have been used."

The sovereign, in speaking of himself, uses the term "Hap-mun," which is the equivalent of the imperial "We" of Asiatic state documents. The word is somewhat similar to that employed by, or for, other rulers—Pharaoh, Sublime Porte, Mikado, all of which mean the Grand, Chief, or First, Gate of all the gates in the country. The first character in Hap-mun is, however, different from that in Mikado, or Honorable Gate, but the *hap* is honorific. No other person in the land, official or private, is allowed to use this compound word in speech or writing as applying to anyone except the king. Even in transcribing the term *hap*, a stroke must be omitted out of respect to the august personage to whom alone it is applied. At his death, three cups of rice are set out in the households *in memoriam.* This ceremony must not be imitated for any other person. So also, if the character with which the name of the ruling emperor of China is written be found in that of a public person, a gateway, a palace or edifice in Seoul, the graphic sign must be temporarily changed, though the pronunciation remains the same. This same system of graduated honors, of which, in Corea, the king is the culmination, slopes down to the common people, and is duly protected by law.

The sovereign's person is hedged round with a divinity that has an antipathy to iron. This metal must never touch his august body, and rather than have an abscess lanced, the king Cheng-jong, in 1800, died from the effects of the disease. No ordinary mortal must touch him, and if by accident this is done, the individual must ever afterward wear a red silk cord. Notwithstanding such regulated veneration for the Hap-mun's person, the royal harem numbers several hundred inmates, duly presided over by eunuchs. None but the king can drink out of a cup made of gold, and a heavy penalty is visited upon all who presume to do so. When outside the palace, the three signs of the sovereign's power of life and death over his subjects, are the axe, sabre, and trident. The huge violet fan and red umbrella are likewise borne before him. The Chinese envoy is always escorted by soldiers bearing the three emblems, and by a band of musicians. When the Hap-mun, or king, is in his minority, the queen, who is regent, sits behind a curtain in the council of ministers, and takes part in the discussions. When she is pregnant, the slaughter of beeves is prohibited during the space of three months. This is done in order "to honor heaven by abstinence," and may also be ordered to procure rain. Once every year, the queen entertains at her palace some worthy woman in humble life, who has reached the advanced age of eighty years. The king likewise shows favor to old men in the lower walks of life. Whenever an auspicious event happens, or good fortune befalls the kingdom, all the officials over seventy, and the common people over eighty years of age, are feasted at the expense of the government. When the first male child is born to the king, criminals are pardoned, and general festivity is observed. The birthdays of the royal pair are celebrated every year. The royal princes are supposed to have nothing whatever to do with politics, and any activity in matters of government on their part is jealously resented by the nobles, who form the political parties.

The Royal Castle contains over three acres (15,202 square yards), surrounded by a wall twenty feet high, and formerly by a moat, now filled up, measuring fifty feet wide or less. It is crossed by stone bridges in several places. This castled palace is called the "Place of Government," and is divided into two parts called the "East and West" palace. The East, or Lower Palace, is the residence of the king and is so called because situated on level land. The Western palace is used for the reception of the Chinese ambassadors. The gates of the outer city proper, and inner city, or palace, are named in high-sounding phrase, such as "Beneficent Reception," "Exalted Politeness," "Perfect Change," "Entrance of Virtue," and the throne-room is styled "The Hall of the Throne of the Humane Government." The Chinese ambassador of 1866 spent the night in that part of the royal residence called "The Palace Reserved for the South,"—"the south" here evidently referring to the imperial favor, or the good graces, of the emperor.

A marked difference concerning "the freedom of the city" is noticed in the relative treatment of the two embassies. While the entire body of Coreans, dignitaries, servants, merchants, and cartmen enter Peking, and all circulate freely in the streets among the people, the Chinese envoy to Seoul, must leave his suite at the frontier, and proceed to the capital with but a few servants, and while there dwell in seclusion. After the long and rough journey through Shin-king and Corea, the Chinese envoy in 1866 stayed less than three days in Seoul, and most of the time in-doors. The Japanese who, in 1646, were feasted in some part of the Eastern palace, describe it as being handsomely furnished, with the walls gilded and painted with landscapes, beasts, birds, and flowers, with artistic effects in gold-dust and leaf. The royal family live each in separate buildings, those above the ninth degree of relationship reside inside the enclosure, all others live beyond the wall in the city. When the wife of the king has a child, she dwells apart in a separate building. The queen is selected from among the old and most loyal families of the nobility. The palace pages, who attend the king day and night, number thirty. There are also three hundred court ladies, and eunuchs are among the regularly-appointed officers of the court. The royal archives and library form an interesting portion of the royal residence. Part of this library, when removed to Kang-wa in 1866, was captured by the French. Bishop Ridel wrote of it, "The library is very rich, consisting of two or three thousand books printed in Chinese.

with numerous illustrations upon beautiful paper, all well labeled, for the most part in many volumes hooped together with copper bands, the covers being of green or crimson silk. I notice among other things the ancient history of Corea in sixty volumes. What was most curious of all was a book formed of tablets of marble, with characters in gold encrusted in the marble, folding upon one another like the leaves of a screen, upon hinges of gilded copper, and each tablet protected by a cushion of scarlet silk, the whole placed in a handsome casket made of copper, which was in its turn enclosed in a box of wood painted red, with chased ornaments in gilt copper. These square tablets formed a volume of a dozen pages. They contain, as some say, the moral laws of the country, but according to others, whose opinion is more probable, the honors accorded the kings of Corea by the Emperor of China. The Coreans set great store by it."

A custom, similar to the old "curfew" of England prevails in the capital. The great city bell is struck at sunset, after which male citizens are not allowed to go out of their houses even to visit their neighbors. If such nocturnal prowlers are caught, they run the risk of receiving the bastinado on their legs. At eight o'clock another three strokes are given on the bell. At the hours of midnight, and at two and four A.M. the drum is struck, and the brass cymbals sounded. At these signals the watchmen or guards of the palace are relieved. The night-watch consists of ten reliefs of eighteen each. Twenty stand guard at midnight, thirty at two A.M., twenty at four A.M., and ten at six A.M. There are also extra reliefs with their officers ready. The sentinels change after giving the pass-word. The military garrison of the city is divided into five portions, or four in addition to the household or palace troops. This is the modern form of the old division of Kokorai, into five tribes or clans.

There are several noted holidays, on which the curfew law is suspended, and the people are allowed to be out freely at night. These are the first and the last day of the year, the fourteenth and fifteenth day of the first month, and the fifteenth of August.

Even under a despotism there are means by which the people win and enjoy a certain measure of liberty. The monarch hears the complaints of his subjects. Close communication between the palace and populace is kept up by means of the pages employed at the court, or through officers, who are sent out as the king's spies all over the country. An *E-sa*, or commissioner, who is to

be sent to a distant province to ascertain the popular feeling, or
to report the conduct of certain officers, is also called "The Messenger on the Dark Path." He receives sealed orders from the
king, which he must not open till beyond the city walls. Then,
without even going to his own house, he must set out for his destination, the government providing his expenses. He bears the
seal of his commission, a silver plate having the figure of a horse
engraved on it. In some cases he has the power of life and death
in his hands. Yet, even the Messenger of the Dark Path is not
free from espionage, for after him forthwith follows his "double"
—the *yashi* or Night Messenger, who reports on the conduct of
the royal inspector and also on the affairs of each province
through which he passes. The whereabouts of these emissaries
are rarely discoverable by the people, as they travel in strict disguise, and unknown. This system corresponds almost exactly to
that of the ométsuké (eye-appliers), for many centuries in use in
Japan, but abolished by the mikado's government at the revolution of 1868. It was by means of these *E-sa* or spies that many
of the Corean Christians of rank were marked for destruction.
The system, though abominable in free countries, is yet an excellent medium between the throne and the subject, and serves as a
wholesome check on official rapine and cruelty.

The king rarely leaves the palace to go abroad in the city or
country. When he does, it is a great occasion which is previously
announced to the public. The roads are swept clean and guarded
to prevent traffic or passage while the royal cortége is moving.
All doors must be shut and the owner of each house is obliged to
kneel before his threshold with a broom and dust-pan in his hand
as emblems of obeisance. All windows, especially the upper ones,
must be sealed with slips of paper, lest some one should look
down upon his majesty. Those who think they have received
unjust punishment enjoy the right of appeal to the sovereign.
They stand by the roadside tapping a small flat drum of hide
stretched on a hoop like a battledore. The king as he passes
hears the prayer or receives the written petition held in a split
bamboo. Often he investigates the grievance. If the complaint
is groundless the petitioner is apt to lose his head. The procession for pleasure or a journey, as it leaves the palace, is one of the
grandest spectacles the natives ever witness. His body-guard and
train amount to many thousand persons. There are two sedan
chairs made exactly alike, and in which of them the king is riding

no one knows except the highest ministers. They must never be turned round, but have a door to open at both ends. The music used on such occasions is—to a Corean ear—of a quiet kind, and orders are given along the line by signals made with pennons. In case of sudden emergencies, when it is neccessary to convey an order from the rear to the front or far forward of the line, the message is sent by means of an arrow, which, with the writing attached, is shot from one end of the line to the other.

Five caparisoned horses with embroidered saddles precede the royal sedan. The great dragon-flag, which is about fourteen feet square, mounted in a socket and strapped on the back of a strong fresh horse—with four guy ropes held by footmen, like banner-string boys in a parade—forms the most conspicuous object in the procession. Succession to the throne is at the pleasure of the sovereign, who may nominate his legitimate son, or any one of his natural male offspring, or his cousin, or uncle, as he pleases. A son of the queen takes precedence over other sons, but the male child of a concubine becomes king when the queen is childless, which, in Corean eyes, is virtually the case when she has daughters only. Since the founding of the present dynasty in 1392, there have been twenty-nine successors to the founder, among whom we find nephews, cousins, or younger sons, in several instances. Four were *kun*, princes, or king's son only, and not successors in the royal line. They are not styled *wang*, or kings, but only *kun*, or princes, in the official light. One of these four *kun*, degraded from the throne, was banished after eleven years, and another was served in like manner after fourteen years, reign. The heir to the throne holds the rank of *wang* (Japanese Ō), king, while the younger sons are *kun*, princes. From 1392 to 1882, the average reign of the twenty sovereigns of Corea who received investiture is very nearly sixteen and a half years.

CHAPTER XXV.

POLITICAL PARTIES.

During the past three centuries the nobles have been steadily gaining political power, or rather we might say have been regaining their ancient prestige at court. They have compelled the royal princes to take the position of absolute political neutrality, and the policy of the central government is dictated exclusively by them. Those who hold no office are often the most powerful in influence with their own party.

The origin of the political parties, which have played such an influential part in the history of modern Corea, is referred to about the time of the discovery of America. During the reign of Sien-chong (1469–1494), the eleventh sovereign of the house of Ni, a dispute broke out between two of the most powerful of the nobles. The court had bestowed upon one of them a high dignity, to which his rival laid equal claim. As usual in feudalism everywhere, the families, relatives, retainers, and even servants, of either leader took part in the quarrel. The king prudently kept himself neutral between the contending factions, which soon formed themselves into organized parties under the names of "Eastern" and "Western." Later on, from a cause equally trivial to an alien eye, two other parties formed themselves under the names "Southern" and "Northern." Soon the Easterners joined themselves to the Southerners, and the Northerners, who were very numerous, split into two divisions, called the Great North and the Little North. In one of those unsuccessful palace intrigues, called conspiracies, the Great North party was mixed up with the plot, and most of its members were condemned to death. The survivors hastened to range themselves under the banner of the Little North. The next reaction which arranged the parties on new lines, occurred during the reign of Suk-chong (1676–1720), and well illustrates that fanaticism of pedantry to which the literary classes in time of peace formerly devoted their energies. The father of a young noble named Yun, who belonged to the Western party, having died, the young man composed an epitaph. His tutor, an influential man of letters, not liking the production of his pupil, proposed another. Unable to agree upon the proper text, a lively controversy arose, and out of a literary acorn sprang up a mighty oak of politics. The Western party split into the Sho-ron, and No-ron, in which were found the adherents of the pupil and master. A free translation of the correlative terms *sho* and *no*, would be "Old Corea" and "Young Corea," or Conservative and Progressive, or radical. There were now four political parties.

The *Shi-seik*, or "the four parties," are still in existence, and receive illustration better from French than from British politics. Every noble in the realm is attached to one or the other of the four parties, though "trimmers" are not unknown. These *Tuhil-poki*, or "right and left men," are ever on the alert for the main chance, and on the turn of the political vane promptly desert to the winning side.

However trivial the causes which led to their formation, as Western eyes see, the objects kept in view by the partisans are much the same as those of parties in European countries and in the United States. Nominally the prime purpose of each faction is to advance the interests of the country. Actual and very powerful motives have reference to the spoils of office. Each party endeavors to gain for its adherents as many of the high appointments and dignities as possible. Their rallying-point is around the heirs apparent, or possible, to the throne. When a strong and healthy king holds the reins of power, political activity may be cool. When the sovereign dies and the succession is uncertain, when a queen or royal concubine is to be chosen, when high ministers of state die or resign, the Corean political furnace is at full blast. When king Suk-chong was reigning in 1720, having no son to succeed him, the four parties coalesced into two, the Opposition and the Court or royal party. The former supported in this case one who proved the successful candidate, a brother of the king; the latter party urged the claims of an expected heir to the reigning king, which, however, was not born, as the king died childless. To secure the throne to their nominee, the brother of the childless king, the opposition secretly despatched a courier to Peking to obtain the imperial investiture. The other party sent assassins to waylay or overtake the courier, who was murdered before he had crossed the frontier.

15

Yeng-chong, the nominee of the Opposition, mounted the throne after the death of his brother, and reigned from 1724 to 1776. He was an able ruler, and signalized his reign by abolishing many of the legal tortures until then practised, especially the branding of criminals. Yet personally he was cruel and unscrupulous. Public rumor credited him with having found a road to power by means of a double crime. By the use of various drugs he made it impossible for his brother to have an heir, after which he poisoned him.

Stung by these reports, he began, as soon as he was made sovereign, to send to the block numbers of the opposite party whom he knew to be his enemies. Some years after, his eldest son having died, he nominated his second son, Sato, to be his heir, and associated him with himself in the government of the kingdom. This young and accomplished prince endeavored to make his father forget his bitter hatred against the *Si-pai* party, to proclaim general amnesty, and to follow out a frank policy of reconciliation. The king, irritated by his son's reproaches, and hounded on by his partisans, resolved to put the prince out of the way. By the royal command a huge chest of wood was made, into which the young prince was ordered to sleep while living. The ponderous lid was put on during one of his slumbers and sealed with the royal seal. They then covered this sarcophagus with leaves and boughs, so that in a short time the young prince was smothered. This horrible crime served only to exasperate the party of the prince, and they demanded that his name should be enrolled in the list of sovereigns. Their opponents refused, and this question is still a burning one. The king's defenders, to this day decline to rehabilitate the character of the smothered prince. The others demand that historic justice be done. Though other questions have since arisen, of more immediate moment, this particular moot point makes its distinct hue in the opposing colors of Corean politics. This, however, does not take on the features of an hereditary feud, for oftentimes in the same family, father and son, or brothers may hold varying views on this historical dispute, nor does it affect marriage between holders of diverse views. The Corean Romeo and Juliet may woo and wed without let or danger. In general, it may be said that the *Piek-pai* are radical and fiery, the *Si-pai* are conservative and conciliatory.

Cheng-chong, who ruled from 1776 to 1800, a wise, moderate, and prudent prince, and a friend of learning, favored the men of merit among the Southern *Si-pai*, and is also noted for having revised the code of laws.

Among the more radical of the partisans, the object in view is not only to gain for their adherents the public offices, but also to smite their rivals hip and thigh, and prevent their getting appointments. Hence the continual quarrels and the plots, which often result in the death of one or other of the leaders. Assassination and murderous attacks are among the means employed, while to supplant their enemies the king is besought to order them to death or exile. Concessions are made by the dominant party to the other only to avoid violent outbreaks, and to keep the peace. With such a rich soil for feuds, it is not wonderful that Corea is cursed with elements of permanent disturbance like those in mediæval Scotland or Italy. As each of the noble families have many retainers, and as the feuds are hereditary, the passions of human nature have full sway. All manner of envy and malice, with all uncharitableness flourish, as in a thicket of interlacing thorns. The Southern and No-ron parties have always been the most numerous, powerful, and obstinate. Between them marriages do not take place, and the noble who in an intrigue with one of his enemies loses caste, his honors, or his life, hands down to his son or his nearest relative his demand for vengeance. Often this sacred duty is associated with an exterior and visible pledge. He may give to his son, for instance, a coat which he is never to take off until revenge is had. The kinsman, thus clad with vengeance as with a garment, must wear it, it may be until he dies, and then put it upon his child with the same vow. It is not rare to see noblemen clad in rags and tatters during two or three generations. Night and day these clothes call aloud to the wearer, reminding him of the debt of blood which he must pay to appease the spirits of his ancestors.

In Corea, not to avenge one's father is to be disowned, to prove that one is illegitimate and has no right to bear the family name, it is to violate, in its fundamental point, the national religion, which is the worship of ancestors. If the father has been put to death under the forms of law, it behooves that his enemy or his enemy's son should die the same death. If the father has been exiled, his enemy's exile must be secured. If the parent has been assassinated, in like manner must his enemy fall. In these cases, public sentiment applauds the avenger, as fulfilling the holy dictates of piety and religion.

The pretext of accusation most often employed by the rival factions is that of conspiracy against the life of the king. Petitions and false evidence are multiplied and bribery of the court ministers is attempted. If, as is often the case, the first petitioners are thrown in jail, beaten, or condemned to mulct or exile, the partisans assess the fine among themselves and pay it, or manage by new methods, by the favor or venality of the court ministers, or the weakness of the king, at last to compass their ends, when those of the vanquished party are ousted from office, while the victors use and abuse their positions to enrich themselves and ruin their enemies, until they in their turn are supplanted.

It is no wonder that a Corean liberal visiting in Tōkiō, in 1882, declared to a Japanese officer his conviction that Corea's dfficulties in the way of national progress were greater than those of which Japan had rid herself, mighty as these had been. By the revolutions of 1868, and later, the ripened fruits of a century of agitation and the presence of foreigners, Japan had purged from her body politic feudalism and caste, emancipating herself at once from the thrall of the priest and the soldier ; but Corea, with her feudalism, her court intrigues, her Confucian bigotry, and the effete products of ages of seclusion and superstition has even a more hopeless task to attempt. The bearing of these phases of home politics will be further displayed when the new disturbing force of Christianity enters to furnish a lever to ambition and revenge, as well as to affection and philanthropy.

A native caricature, which was published about a generation ago, gives even a foreigner a fair idea of the relative position of each party at that epoch. At a table gorgeously furnished, a No-ron is seated at his ease, disposing of the bountiful fare. A Sho-ron seated beside him, yet in the rear, graciously performs the office of servant, receiving part of the food as reward for his attendance. The Little North, seeing that the viands are not for him, is also seated, but with a more sedate and serious visage. Last of all the Southern, covered with rags, keeps far in the rear, behind the No-ron, who does not notice him, while he, in vexation, grinds his teeth and shakes his fist like a man who means to take burning vengeance. Such was the political situation before 1850, as some native wit pictured it for the amusement of the Seoulians.

It requires a ruler of real ability to be equal to the pressure brought upon him by the diverse and hostile political parties. Nominally sovereign of the country, he is held in check by powerful nobles intrenched in privileges hoary with age, and backed by all the reactionary influences of feudalism. The nobles are the powerful middle term in the problem of Corean politics, who control both king and commons. The nobles have the preponderance of the government patronage, and fill the official positions with their liegemen to an extent far beyond what the theory of the law, as illustrated in the literary examinations, allows them. A native caricature thus depicts the situation. Chō-sen is represented as a human being, of whom the king is the head, the nobles the body, and the people the legs and feet. The breast and belly are full, while both head and lower limbs are gaunt and shrunken. The nobles not only drain the life-blood of the people by their rapacity, but they curtail the royal prerogative. The nation is suffering from a congestion, verging upon a dropsical condition of over-officialism.

The disease of Corea's near neighbor, old Japan, was likewise a surplus of government and an excess of official patronage, but the body politic was purged by revolution. The obstructions between the throne and the people were cleared away by the removal of the shō-gunate and the feudal system. Before the advent of foreigners, national unity was not the absolute necessity which it became the instant that aliens fixed their dwelling on the soil. Now, the empire of the mikado rejoices in true political unity, and has subjects in a strong and not over-meddlesome government. The people are being educated in the rudiments of mutual obligations—their rights as well as their duties. The mikado himself took the oath of 1868, and his own hand shaped the august decree of 1881, which will keep his throne unshaken, not because it was won by the bows and arrows of his divine ancestors, but because it will rest broad-based upon the peoples' will. So in Chō-sen the work of the future for intelligent patriots is the closer union of king and people, the curtailment of the power of the nobles, and the excision of feudalism. Already, to accomplish this end, there are Coreans who are ready to die. During the last decade, the pressure from Japan, the jealousy of China, the danger from Russia, the necessity, at first shrunk from and then yielded to, of making treaties with foreign nations, has altered the motives and objects of Corean politics. Old questions have fallen out of sight, and two great parties, Progressionists and Obstructionists, or Radical and Conservative, have formed for the solution of the problems thrust upon them by the nineteenth century.

CHAPTER XXVI.

ORGANIZATION AND METHODS OF GOVERNMENT.

NEXT in authority to the king are the three *chong* or high min-isters. The chief of these (Chen-kun) is the greatest dignitary in the kingdom, and in time of the minority, inability, or imbecility of the king, wields royal authority in fact if not in name. Another term applied to him when the king is unable to govern, is "Foun-dation-stone Minister," upon whom the king leans and the state rests as a house upon its foundation-stone. The title of Tai-wen-kun, which suggests that of the "Tycoon" of Japan, seems to have been a special one intended for the emergency. It was given to the Regent who is the father of the present King, and who ruled with nearly absolute power from 1863 to 1874, when the king reached his majority. In the troubles in Seoul in July, 1882, his title, written in Japanese as Tai-in kun, became familiar to western newspapers.

After the king, and the three prime ministers, come the six ministries or boards of government, the heads of which rank next to the three *chong* or ministers forming the Supreme Council. In the six departments, the heads are called *pan-cho*, and these are assisted by two other associates, the *cham-pan*, or substitutes, and the *cham-é*, or counsellor. These four grades and twenty-one dignitaries constitute the royal council of *dai-jin* (great ministers), though the actual authority is in the supreme council of the three *chong*. The six boards, or departments of the government, are: 1, Office and Public Employ; 2, Finance; 3, Ceremonies; 4, War; 5, Justice; 6, Public Works. The heads of these tribunals make a daily report of all affairs within their province, but refer all matters of importance to the Supreme Council. There are also three chamberlains, each having his assistants, who record every day the acts and words of the king. A daily government gazette, called the Chō-po, is issued for information on official matters. The general cast and method of procedure in the court and gov-ernment is copied after the great model in Peking.

Each of the eight provinces is under the direction of a *kam-sa*, or governor. The cities are divided into six classes (*yin, mu, fu, ki, ling,* and *hilu*), and are governed by officers of corresponding rank. The towns are given in charge of the petty magistrates, there being twelve ranks or dignities in the official class. In theory any male Corean able to pass the government examinations is eligible to office, but the greater number of the best positions are secured by nobles and their friends.

From the sovereign to the beggar, the gate, both figuratively and actually, is very prominent in the public economy and in family relationships. A great deal of etiquette is visible in the gates. At the entrance to the royal palace are, or were formerly, two huge effigies, in wood, of horses, painted red. Only high officials can pass these mute guardians. All persons riding past the palace must dismount and walk. To the houses of men of rank there are usually two, sometimes three, gates. The magistrate himself enters by the largest, his parents and nearer friends by the eastern, and servants by the west or smallest. When a visitor of equal grade calls upon an officer or noble, the host must come all the way to the great or outer gate to receive him, and do likewise on dismissing him. If he be of one degree lower rank, the host comes only to the outside of the middle gate. If of third or fourth rank, the caller is accompanied only to the space inside the middle gate. The man of fifth and sixth rank finds that etiquette has so tapered off that the lord of the mansion walks only to the piazza. In front of a magistrate's office, at the gateway, are ranged the symbols of authority, such as spears and tridents. The gates are daily opened amid the loud cries of the underlings, and their opening and closing with a vocal or instrumental blast is a national custom, illustrated as well at the city as at the office. The porters who close them at sunset and open them at dawn execute a salvo on their trumpets, often lasting a quarter of an hour. This acoustic devastation, so distressing to foreign ears, is considered good music to the native tympanum.

In sitting, the same iron tongue upon the buckle of custom holds each man to his right hole in the social strap. People of equal rank sit so that the guest faces to the east and the host to the west. In ordinary easy style, the visitor's nose is to the south, as he sits eastward of his host. A commoner faces north. In social entertainments, after the *yup*, or bows with the head and hands bent together, have been made, wine is sipped or drunk three or five times, and then follows what the Coreans call music.

The sumptuary laws of the kingdom are peculiar, at many points amusing to occidentals. To commit *pem-ram* is to violate these curious regulations. What may be worn, or sat upon, is solemnly dictated by law. Nobles sit on the *kan-kio*, or better kind of chairs. Below the third rank, officers rest upon a bench made of ropes. Chairs, however, are not common articles of use, nor intended to be such. At entertainments for the aged, in time of rich harvests, local feasts, archery tournaments, and on public occasions, these luxuries are oftener used. In short, the chair seems to be an article of ceremony, rather than a constant means of use or comfort.

Only men above the third rank are allowed to put on silk. Petty officials must wear cotton. Merchants and farmers may not imitate official robes, but don tighter or more economical coats and trowsers. A common term for officials is "blue clouds," in reference to their blue-tinted garments. To their assistants, the people apply the nickname, not sarcastic, but honorable, of "crooked backs," because they always bend low in talking to their employers.

The magistrates lay great stress on the trifles of etiquette, and keep up an immense amount of fuss and pomp to sustain their dignity, in order to awe the common folks. Whenever they move abroad, their servants cry out "chii-wa," "chii-wa," "get down off your horse," "get down off your horse," to riders in sight. The Il-san, or large banner or standard in the form of an umbrella, is borne at the head of the line. To attempt to cross one of their processions is to be seized and punished, and anyone refusing to dismount, or who is slow about slipping off his horse, is at once arrested, to be beaten or mulcted. When permission is given to kill an ox, the head, hide, and feet usually become the perquisites of the magistrate or his minions. The exuberant vocabulary in Corean, for the various taxes, fines, mulcts, and squeezes of the understrappers of the magistrate, in gross and in detail, chief and supplementary, testify to the rigors and expenses of being governed in Chō-sen.

Overreaching magistrates, through whose injustice the people are goaded into rebellion, are sometimes punished. It seems that one of the penalties in ancient times was that the culpable official should be boiled in oil. Now, however, the condemned man is exiled, and only rarely put to death, while a commutation of justice

—equivalent to being burned in effigy—is made by a pretended boiling in oil. Good and upright magistrates are often remembered by *mok-pi*, or inscribed columns of wood, erected on the public road by the grateful people. In many instances, this testimonial takes the form of sculptured stone. A number of the public highways are thus adorned. These, with the *tol-pi*, or monumental bourne, which marks distances or points out the paths to places of resort, are interesting features of travel in the peninusla, and more pleasant to the horseman than the posts near temples and offices on which one may read "Dismount." At the funeral of great dignitaries of the realm, a life-sized figure of a horse, made of bamboo, dragged before the coffin, is burned along with the clothes of the deceased, and the ashes laid beside his remains.

As the magistrates are literary men, their official residences often receive poetic or suggestive names, which, in most cases, reflect the natural scenery surrounding them. "Little Flowery House," "Rising Cloud," "Sun-greeting," "Sheet of Resplendent Water," "Water-that-slides-as-straight-as-a-sword Dwelling," "Gate of Lapis-lazuli," "Mansion near the Whirlpool," are some of these names, while, into the composition of others, the Morning-star, the Heaven-touching, the Cave-spirit, and the Changing-cloud Mountain, or the Falling-snow Cataract may enter. Passionately fond of nature, the Corean gentleman will erect a tablet in praise of the scenery that charms his eye. One such reads, "The beauty of its rivers, and of its mountains, make this district the first in the country."

If, as the French say, "Paris is France," then Seoul is Corea. An apparently disproportionate interest centres in the capital, if one may judge from the vast and varied vocabulary relating to Seoul, its people and things, which differentiate all else outside its wall. Three thousand official dignitaries are said to reside in the capital, and only eight hundred in all the other cities and provinces. Seoul is "the city," and all the rest of the peninsula is "the country." A provincial having cultivated manners is called "a man of the capital." "Capital and province" means the realm.

The rule of the local authorities is very minute in all its ramifications. The system of making every five houses a social unit is universal. When a crime is committed, it is easy to locate the group in which the offender dwells, and responsibility is fixed at once. Every subject of the sovereign except nobles of rank, must possess a passport or ticket testifying to his personality, and all

must "show their tickets" on demand. For the people, this cer-
tificate of identity is a piece of branded or inscribed wood, for the
soldiers of horn, for the literary class and government officials of
bone. Often, the tablet is in halves, the individual having one-
half, and the government keeping its tally. The people who cannot read or write have their labels carefully tied to their clothing.
When called upon to sign important documents, or bear witness
on trial, they make a blood-signature, by rudely tracing the signs
set before them in their own blood. The name, residence of the
holder, and the number of the group of houses in which he lives,
are branded or inscribed on the *ho-pai*, or passport.

The actual workings of Corean justice will be better understood when treating of Christianity—an element of social life
which gave the pagan tribunals plenty of work. Civil matters are
decided by the ordinary civil magistrate, who is judge and jury at
once; criminal cases are tried by the military commandant. Very
important cases are referred to the governor of the province. The
highest court of appeal is in the capital. Cases of treason and rebellion, and charges against high dignitaries, are tried in the
capital before a special tribunal instituted by the king.

The two classes of assistants to the magistrate, who are called
respectively *hai-seik* and *a-chen*, act as constables or sheriffs,
police messengers, and jailers. French writers term them "pre-
torians" and "satellites." These men have practically the administration of justice, and the details and spirit of local authority are
in their power. The *hai-seik*, or constables, form a distinct class
in the community, rarely intermarrying with the people, and
handing down their offices, implements, and arts from father to
son. The *a-chen*, who are the inferior police, jailers, and torturers,
are from the very lowest classes, and usually of brutal life and
temper.

The vocabulary of torture is sufficiently copious to stamp Chō-
sen as still a semi-civilized nation. The inventory of the court and
prison comprises iron chains, bamboos for beating the back, a
paddle-shaped implement for inflicting blows upon the buttocks,
switches for whipping the calves till the flesh is ravelled, ropes
for sawing the flesh and bodily organs, manacles, stocks, and
boards to strike against the knees and shin-bones. Other punishments are suspension by the arms, tying the hands in front of the
knees, between which and the elbows is inserted a stick, while the
human ball is rolled about. An ancient but now obsolete mode

of torture was to tie the four limbs of a man to the horns of as many oxen, and then to madden the beasts by fire, so that they tore the victim to fragments. The punishment of beating with paddles often leaves scars for life, and causes ulcers not easily healed. One hundred strokes cause death in most cases, and many die under forty or fifty blows. For some crimes the knees and shin-bones are battered. A woman is allowed to have on one garment, which is wetted to make it cling to the skin and increase the pain. The chief of the lictors, or public spanker, is called *siu-kiŏ*. With the long, flexible handle swung over his head, he plies the resounding blows, planting them on the bare skin just above the knee-joint, the victim being held down by four gaolers. The method of correction is quite characteristic of paternal government, and is often inflicted upon the people openly and in public, at the whim of the magistrate. The bastinado was formerly, like hundreds of other customs common to both countries, in vogue in Japan. As in many other instances, this has survived in the less civilized nation.

When an offender in the military or literary class is sentenced to death, decapitation is the rather honorable method employed. The executioner uses either a sort of native iron hatchet-sword or cleaver, or one of the imported Japanese steel-edged blades, which have an excellent reputation in the peninsula.

Undoubtedly the severity of the Corean code has been mitigated since Hamel's time. According to his observations, husbands usually killed their wives who had committed adultery. A wife murdering her husband was buried to the shoulders in the earth at the road side, and all might strike or mutilate her with axe or sword. A serf who murdered his master was tortured, and a thief might be trampled to death. The acme of cruelty was produced, as in old Japan, by pouring vinegar down the criminal's throat, and then beating him till he burst. The criminal code now in force is, in the main, that revised and published by the king in 1785, which greatly mitigated the one formerly used. One disgraceful, but not very severe, mode of correction is to tie a drum to the back of the offender and publicly proclaim his transgression, while the drum is beaten as he walks through the streets. Amid many improvements on the old barbarous system of aggravating the misery of the condemned, there still survives a disgraceful form of capital punishment, in which the cruelty takes on the air of savage refinement. The *cho-reni-to-ta* appears only in extreme cases. The criminal's face is smeared with chalk, his hands are tied behind him, a gong is tied on his back, and an arrow is thrust through either ear. The executioner makes the victim march round before the spectators, while he strikes the gong, crying out, "This fellow has committed [adultery, murder, treason, etc.]. Avoid his crime." The French missionaries executed near Seoul were all put to death in this barbarous manner.

Officials often receive furloughs to return home and visit their parents, for filial piety is the supreme virtue in Chinese Asia. The richest rewards on earth and brightest heaven hereafter await the filial child. Curses and disgrace in this life and the hottest hell in the world hereafter are the penalties of the disobedient or neglectful child. The man who strikes his father is beheaded. The parricide is burned to death. Not to mourn long and faithfully, by retiring from office for months, is an incredible iniquity.

Coreans, like Japanese, argue that, if the law punishes crime, it ought also to reward virtue. Hence the system which prevails in the mikado's empire and in Chō-sen of publicly awarding prizes to signal exemplars of filial piety. These in Japan may be in the form of money, silver cups, rolls of silk, or gewgaws. In Corea, they are shown in monumental columns, or dedicatory temples, or by public honors and promotion to office. Less often are the rewarded instances of devotion to the mother than to the father.

Official life has its sunshine and shadows in this land as elsewhere, but perhaps one of the hardest tasks before the Corean ruling classes of this and the next generation is the duty of diligently eating their words. Accustomed for centuries to decry and belittle the foreigner from Christendom, they must now, as the people discern the superiority of westerners, "rise to explain" in a manner highly embarrassing. In intellect, government, science, social customs, manual skill, refinement, and possession of the arts and comforts of life, the foreigner will soon be discovered to be superior. At the same time the intelligent native will behold with how little wisdom, and how much needless cruelty, Chō-sen is governed. The Japanese official world has passed through such an experience. If we may argue from a common ancestry and hereditary race traits, we may forecast the probability that to Corea, as to Japan, may come the same marvellous revolution in ideas and customs.

CHAPTER XXVII.

FEUDALISM, SERFDOM, AND SOCIETY.

IT is remarked by Palladius that the Fuyu race, the ancestors of the modern Coreans, was the first to emerge from the desert under feudal forms of organization. The various migrations of new nations rising out of northern and eastern Asia were westward, and were held together under monarchical systems of government. The Fuyu tribes who, by turning their face to the rising, instead of the setting sun, were anomalous in the direction of their migration, were unique also in their political genius. Those emigrants who, descending from the same ancestral seats in Manchuria, and through the peninsula, crossed toward Nippon, or Sunrise, and settled Japan, maintained their feudalism until, through ambitious desire to rival great China, they borrowed the centralized system of court and monarchy from the Tang dynasty, in the seventh century. The mikado, by means of boards or ministries like the Chinese, ruled his subjects until the twelfth century. Then, through the pride and ambition of the military clans, which had subdued all the tribes to his sway, feudalism, which had spread its roots, lifted its head. By rapid growths, under succeeding military regents, it grew to be the tree overspreading the empire. It was finally uprooted and destroyed only by the revolution of 1868, and the later victories of united Japan's imperial armies, at an awful sacrifice of life and treasure.

That branch of the Fuyu migration which remained in the Corean peninsula likewise preserved the institution of feudalism which had been inherited from their ancestors. In their early history, lands were held on the tenure of military service, and in war time, or on the accession of a new dynasty, rewards were made by parcelling out the soil to the followers of the victor. Provision for a constant state of servitude among one class of the political body was made by the custom of making serfs of criminals or their kindred. A nucleus of slavery being once formed, debt, famine, capture in war, voluntary surrender, would serve to increase those whose persons and labor were wholly or partly owned by another. To social prosperity, religion, and the increase of general intelligence, we may look as elements for the amelioration of serfdom and the elevation of certain classes of bondsmen into free people. The forms of Corean society, to this day, are derived from feudal ranks and divisions, and the powers, status, divisions, and practical politics of the nobles have their roots in the ancient feudalism which existed even " before the conquest." Its fruit and legacy are seen in the serfdom or slavery which is Corea's " domestic " or " peculiar " institution.

Speaking in general terms, the ladder of society has four rungs, the king, nobles, and the three classes of society, in the last of which are " the seven low callings." In detail, the grades may be counted by the tens and scores. In the lowest grade of the fourth class are " the seven vile callings," viz. : the merchant, boatman, jailor, postal or mail slave, monk, butcher, and sorcerer.

The " four classes of society " include the literary men or officials, the farmers, the artisans, and the traders. Among the nobility are various ranks, indicated by titles, high offices at court, or nearness of relationship to the king. He is " neither ox nor horse " is the native slang for one who is neither noble nor commoner. The nobles are usually the serf-proprietors or slave-holders, many of them having in their households large numbers whom they have inherited along with their ancestral chattels. The master has a right to sell or otherwise dispose of the children of his slaves if he so choose. The male slave is called *chong-nom*. A free man may marry a female slave, in which case he is termed a *pi-pu*. The male children by this marriage are free, but the female offspring belong to the master of the mother, and may be sold. A•liberated slave is called *pal-sin*, and he speaks of his former master as *ku-siang*. The native vocabulary for the slave in his various relations is sufficiently copious. " Fugitive " slaves, " slave-hunters," and " slave-drivers," are as common to the Corean ear, as to the American in the long-ago days of "before the war." A *pan-no* is a bondsman trying to escape, and to attempt *chiu-ro* is to hunt the fugitive and bring him back. The *in-chang* is the public slave of the village. Yet such a thing as the bondsman's servile love of place, rising into swollen and oppressive pride that looks down on the poor freeman, is a common thing, and cruel and overbearing treatment of the peasantry by the minions of a noble is too frequently witnessed in Corea. "*Tek-pun-ai*" ("By your favor," equivalent to "Let me live, I pray you") is a cry, more than once heard by French missionaries, from a man beaten by the swaggering serfs of some nobleman. It is not exactly the feeling of the sleek and well-bred black slave of old-time Virginia for "the poor white trash," since in Corea slavery has no color-line; yet, in essentials of circumstance, it is the same. Such a phase of character is more likely to be developed among the serfs of the old barons or landed proprietors who have longest occupied their hereditary possessions, and who keep up a petty court within their castles or semi-fortified mansions.

Slavery or serfdom in Corea is in a continuous state of decline, and the number of slaves constantly diminishing. In the remote provinces it is practically at an end. The greater number of serfs are to be found attached to the estates of the great noble families of the central provinces. The slaves are those who are born in a state of servitude, those who sell themselves as slaves, or those who are sold to be such by their parents in time of famine or for debt. Infants exposed or abandoned that are picked up and educated become slaves, but their offspring are born free. The serfdom is really very mild. Only the active young men are held to field labor, the young women being kept as domestics. When old enough to marry, the males are let free by an annual payment of a sum of money for a term of years. Often the slaves marry, are assigned a house apart, and bound only to a fixed amount of labor. Although the master has the power of life and death over his slaves, the right is rarely exercised unjustly, and the missionaries report that there were few cases of excessive cruelty practised. An unjust master could be cited before the tribunals, and the case inquired into. Often the actual condition of the serfs is superior to that of the poor villagers, and instances are common in which the poor, to escape the rapacity and cruelty of the nobles, have placed themselves under the protection of a master known to be a kind man, and thus have purchased ease and comfort at the sacrifice of liberty.

Outside of private ownership of slaves, there is a species of government slavery, which illustrates the persistency of one feature of ancient Kokorai perpetuated through twenty centuries. It is the law that in case of the condemnation of a great criminal, the ban of *Ui-ro-ui-pi* shall fall upon his wife and children, who at once become the slaves of the judge. These unfortunates do not have the privilege of honorably serving the magistrate, but usually pass their existence in waiting on the menials in the various departments and magistracies. Only a few of the government slaves are such by birth, most of them having become so through judicial condemnation in criminal cases; but this latter class fare far worse than the ordinary slaves. They are chiefly females, and are treated very little better than beasts. They are at the mercy not only of the officers but even of their satellites, servants, and grooms, or to whomever they are sold for an hour. Nothing can equal the contempt in which they are held, and for an honest or an innocent woman, such a fate is worse than many deaths. In the earliest written account of the Kokorai people, the ancestors of the modern Coreans, we find this same feature of ancient feudalism by which a class of serfs may be continually provided. To Christian eyes it is a horrible relic of barbarism.

The penal settlements on the sea-coast, and notably Quelpart Island, are worked by colonies of these male government slaves or convicts. The females are not usually sent away from the place of their parents or their own crime.

In ancient times of Kokorai and Korai there were only two classes of people, the nobles and their free retainers, and the serfs or slaves. The nobles were lords of cities and castles, like the daimiōs of Japan, and were very numerous. The whole country was owned by them, or at least held in the king's name under tenure of military service—a lien which length of time only strengthened. In the long centuries of peace, many of these old families—weakly descendants of vigorous founders—have died out, and the land reverting to the sovereign, or possessed by the people, is now owned by a more numerous and complex class, while nearly all the cities and towns are governed by officers sent out by the central authority at Seoul. The ancient class of serfs has, by industry and intelligence and accumulation of rights vested in their special occupations, developed into the various middle classes. The nobles are now in a minority, though at present their power is on the increase, and their ancestral landholds comprise but a small portion of the soil.

As in mediæval Europe, so in Corea, where feudalism, which rests on personal loyalty to a reigning sovereign, or a particular royal line, prevails, a more or less complete revolution of titles and possessions takes place upon a change of dynasty. On the accession of the present royal house in 1392, the old Korai nobility were impoverished and the partisans of the founder of the Ni, and all who had aided him to the throne, became at once the nobility of the kingdom, and were rewarded by gifts of land. To the victors belonged the spoils. The honors, riches, and the exclusive right to fill many of the most desirable public offices were awarded in perpetuity to the aristocracy. The mass of the people were placed or voluntarily put themselves under the authority of the nobles. The agricultural class attached to the soil simply changed masters and landlords, while the cities and towns people and sea-coast dwellers became, only in a nominal sense, the tenantry of the nobles. Gradually, however, those who had ability and address obtained their full liberty, so that they were in no way bound to pay tithe or tax to the nobles, but only to the central government. Under peace, with wealth, intelligence, combination, trade-unions, and guilds, and especially by means of the literary examinations, the various classes of the people emerged into independent existence, leaving but a few of the lowest of the population in the condition of serfs or slaves. Between the accounts of Hamel in 1653, and of the French missionaries in the last decade, there are many indications of progress. Laborers, artisans, merchants, soldiers, etc., now have a right to their own labor and earnings, and the general division of the commonwealth is into three classes—nobles, common people, and serfs or slaves.

Speaking generally, the peculiar institution of Chō-sen is serfdom rather than slavery, and is the inheritence of feudalism; yet, as Russia has had her Alexander, America her Lincoln, and Japan her Mutsŭhito, we may hope to see some great liberator yet arise in the "Land of Morning Calm."

Under absolute despotisms, as most Asiatic governments are, it is a wonder to republicans how the people enjoy any liberty at all. If they have any, it is interesting to study how they have attained it, and how they hold it. Politically, they have absolutely no freedom. They know nothing of government, except to pay taxes and obey. Their political influence is nothing. In Chō-sen, according to law, any person of the common people may compete at the public examinations for civil or military employment, but, in point of fact, his degree is often worthless, for he is not likely to receive office by it. In a country where might and wealth make right, and human beings are politically naught, being but beasts of burden or ciphers without a unit, how do the people

16

protect themselves and gain any liberty? How does it come to pass that serfs may win their way to social freedom?

It is by union and organization. The spirit of association, so natural and necessary, is spread among the Coreans of all classes, from the highest families to the meanest slaves. All those who have any kind of work or interest in common form guilds, corporations, or societies, which have a common fund, contributed to by all for aid in time of need. Very powerful trade-unions exist among the mechanics and laborers, such as porters, ostlers, and pack-horse leaders, hat-weavers, coffin-makers, carpenters, and masons. These societies enable each class to possess a monopoly of their trade, which even a noble vainly tries to break. Sometimes, they hold this right by writ purchased or obtained from government, though usually it is by prescription. Most of the guilds are taxed by the government for their monopoly enjoyed. They have their chief or head man, who possesses almost despotic power, and even, in some guilds, of life and death. New members or apprentices may be admitted by paying their rate and submitting to the rules of the guild. In the higher grades of society we see the same spirit of association. The temple attendants, the servants of the nobles, the gardeners, messengers, and domestics of the palace, the supernumeraries and government employés, all have their "rings," which an outsider may not break. Even among the noble families the same idea exists in due form. The villages form each a little republic, and possess among themselves a common fund to which every family contributes. Out of this money, hid in the earth or lent out on interest, are paid the public taxes, expenses of marriage and burial, and whatever else, by custom and local opinion, is held to be a public matter. Foreigners, accustomed to the free competition of English-speaking countries, will find in Chō-sen, as they found in Japan, and even more so, the existence of this spirit of protective association and monopoly illustrated in a hundred forms which are in turn amusing, vexatious, or atrocious. A man who in injustice, or for mere caprice, or in a fit of temper, discharges his ostler, house-servant, or carpenter, will find that he cannot obtain another good one very easily, even at higher wages, or, if so, that his new one is soon frightened off the premises. To get along comfortably in Chinese Asia, one must, willy-nilly, pay respect to the visible or invisible spirit of trade-unionism that pervades all society in those old countries.

One of the most powerful and best organized guilds is that of the porters. The interior commerce of the country being almost entirely on the backs of men and pack-horses, these people have the monopoly of it. They number about ten thousand, and are divided by provinces and districts under the orders of chiefs, sub-chiefs, censors, inspectors, etc. A large number of these porters are women, often poor widows, or those unable to marry. Many of them are of muscular frame, and their life in the open air tends to develop robust forms, with the strength of men. They speak a conventional language, easily understood among themselves, and are very profuse in their salutations to each other. They have very severe rules for the government of their guild, and crimes among them are punished with death, at the order of their chief. They are so powerful that they pretend that even the government dare not interfere with them. They are outside the power of the local magistrate, just as a German University student is responsible to the Faculty, but not to the police. They are honest and faithful in their business, delivering packages with certainty to the most remote places in the kingdom. They are rather independent of the people, and even bully the officers. When they have received an insult or injustice, or too low wages, they "strike" in a body and retire from the district. This puts a stop to all travel and business, until these grievances are settled or submission to their own terms is made.

Owing to the fact that the country at large is so lacking in the shops and stores so common in other countries, and that, instead, fairs on set days are so numerous in the towns and villages, the guild of pedlers and hucksters is very large and influential. The class includes probably 200,000 able-bodied adult persons, who in the various provinces move freely among the people, and are thus useful to the government as spies, detectives, messengers, and, in time of need, soldiers. It was from this class that the Corean battalions which figured prominently in the affair of December 4–6, 1887, were recruited.

CHAPTER XXVIII.

SOCIAL LIFE.—WOMAN AND THE FAMILY.

ACCORDING to the opinions of the French missionaries, who were familiar with the social life of the people, a Corean woman has no moral existence. She is an instrument of pleasure or of labor; but never man's companion or equal. She has no name. In childhood she receives indeed a surname by which she is known in the family, and by near friends, but at the age of puberty, none but her father and mother employ this appellative. To all others she is "the sister" of such a one, or "the daughter" of so-and-so. After her marriage her name is buried. She is absolutely nameless. Her own parents allude to her by employing the name of the district or ward in which she has married. Her parents-in-law speak of her by the name of the place in which she lived before marriage, as women rarely marry in the same village with their husbands. When she bears children, she is "the mother" of so-and-so. When a woman appears for trial before a magistrate, in order to save time and trouble, she receives a special name for the time being. The women below the middle class work very hard. Farm labor is done chiefly by them. Manure is applied by the women, rarely by the men. The women carry lunch to the laborers in the field, eating what is left for their share. In going to market, the women carry the heavier load. In their toilet, the women use rouge, white powders, and hair oil. They shave the eyebrows to a narrow line—that is, to a perfectly clean arch, with nothing straggling. They have luxuriant hair, and, in addition, use immense switches to fill out large coiffures.

In the higher classes of society, etiquette demands that the children of the two sexes be separated after the age of eight or ten years. After that time the boys dwell entirely in the men's apartments, to study and even to eat and drink. The girls remain secluded in the women's quarters. The boys are taught that it is a shameful thing even to set foot in the female part of the house.

The girls are told that it is disgraceful even to be seen by males, so that gradually they seek to hide themselves whenever any of the male sex appear. These customs, continued from childhood to old age, result in destroying the family life. A Corean of good taste only occasionally holds conversation with his wife, whom he regards as being far beneath him. He rarely consults her on anything serious, and though living under the same roof, one may say that husband and wife are widely separated. The female apartments among the higher classes resemble, in most respects, the zenanas of India. The men chat, smoke, and enjoy themselves in the outer rooms, and the women receive their parents and friends in the interior apartments. The same custom, based upon the same prejudice, hinders the common people in their moments of leisure from remaining in their own houses. The men seek the society of their male neighbors, and the women, on their part, unite together for local gossip. In the higher classes, when a young woman has arrived at marriageable age, none even of her own relatives, except those nearest of kin, is allowed to see or speak to her. Those who are excepted from this rule must address her with the most ceremonious reserve. After their marriage, the women are inaccessible. They are nearly always confined to their apartments, nor can they even look out in the streets, without permission of their lords. So strict is this rule that fathers have on occasions killed their daughters, husbands their wives, and wives have committed suicide when strangers have touched them even with their fingers. The common romances or novels of the country expatiate on the merits of many a Corean Lucretia. In some cases, however, this exaggerated modesty produces the very results it is intended to avoid. If a bold villain or too eager paramour should succeed in penetrating secretly the apartments of a noble lady, she dare not utter a cry, nor oppose the least resistance which might attract attention; for then, whether guilty or not, she would be dishonored forever by the simple fact that a man had entered her chamber. Every Corean husband is a Cæsar in this respect. If, however, the affair remains a secret, her reputation is saved.

There is, however, another side. Though counting for nothing in society, and nearly so in their family, they are surrounded by a certain sort of exterior respect. They are always addressed in the formulas of honorific language. The men always step aside in the street to allow a woman to pass, even though she be of the

poorer classes. The apartments of females are inviolable even to
the minions of the law. A noble who takes refuge in his wife's
room may not be seized. Only in cases of rebellion is he dragged
forth, for in that case his family are reckoned as accomplices in
his guilt. In other crimes the accused must in some way be enticed outside, where he may be legally arrested. When a pedler
visits the house to show his wares, he waits until the doors of the
women's apartments are shut. This done, his goods are examined
in the outer apartments, which are open to all. When a man
wishes to mend, or go up on his roof, he first notifies his neighbors, in order that they may shut their doors and windows, lest
he risk the horrible suspicion of peeping at the women. As the
Coreans do not see a "man in the moon," but only a rabbit
pounding drugs, or a lady banished there for a certain fault,
according as they are most familiar with Sanskrit or the Chinese
story, the females are not afraid of this luminary, nor are the men
jealous of her, the moon being female in their ideas of gender.

Marriage in Chō-sen is a thing with which a woman has little
or nothing to do. The father of the young man communicates,
either by call or letter, with the father of the girl whom he wishes
his son to marry. This is often done without consulting the tastes
or character of either, and usually through a middle-man or go-
between. The fathers settle the time of the wedding after due
discussion of the contract. A favorable day is appointed by the
astrologers, and the arrangements are perfected. Under this aspect
marriage seems an affair of small importance, but in reality it is
marriage only that gives one any civil rank or influence in society. Every unmarried person is treated as a child. He may
commit all sorts of foolishness without being held to account.
His capers are not noticed, for he is not supposed to think or act
seriously. Even the unmarried young men of twenty-five or thirty
years of age can take no part in social reunions, or speak on affairs
of importance, but must hold their tongues, be seen but not heard.
Marriage is emancipation. Even if mated at twelve or thirteen
years of age, the married are adults. The bride takes her place
among the matrons, and the young man has a right to speak
among the men and to wear a hat. The badge of single or of
married life is the hair. Before marriage, the youth, who goes
bareheaded, wears a simple tress, hanging down his back. The
nuptial tie is, in reality, a knot of hair, for in wedlock the hair is
bound up on the top of the head and is cultivated on all parts of

the scalp. According to old traditions, men ought never to clip a single hair; but in the capital the young gallants, in order to add to their personal attractions—with a dash of fashionable defiance—trim their locks so that their coiffure will not increase in size more than a hen's egg. The women, on the contrary, not only preserve all their own hair, but procure false switches and braids to swell their coiffures to fashionable bulk. They make up two large tresses, which are rolled to the back and top of the head, and secured by a long pin of silver or copper. The common people roll their plaits around their heads, like a turban, and shave the front of the scalp. Young persons who insist on remaining single, or bachelors arrived at a certain or uncertain age, and who have not yet found a wife, secretly cut off their hair, or get it done by fraud, in order to pass for married folks and avoid being treated as children. Such a custom, however, is a gross violation of morals and etiquette. (See illustration, page 161.)

On the evening before the wedding, the young lady who is to be married invites one of her friends to change her virginal coiffure to that of a married woman.

The bridegroom-to-be also invites one of his acquaintance to "do up" his hair in manly style. The persons appointed to perform this service are chosen with great care, and as changing the hair marks the turning-point in life, the hair-dresser of this occasion is called the "hand of honor," and answers to the bridesmaid and groomsman of other countries.

On the marriage-day, in the house of the groom, a platform is set up and richly adorned with decorative woven stuffs. Parents, friends, and acquaintances assemble in a crowd. The couple to be married—who may never have seen or spoken to each other— are brought in and take their places on the platform, face to face. There they remain for a few minutes. They salute each other with profound obeisance, but utter not a word. This constitutes the ceremony of marriage. Each then retires, on either side; the bride to the female, the groom to the male apartments, where feasting and amusement, after fashions in vogue in Chō-sen, take place. The expense of a wedding is considerable, and the bridegroom must be unstinting in his hospitality. Any failure in this particular may subject him to unpleasant practical jokes.

On her wedding-day, the young bride must preserve absolute silence, both on the marriage platform and in the nuptial chamber. Etiquette requires this at least among the nobility. Though overwhelmed with questions and compliments, silence is her duty. She must rest mute and impassive as a statue. She seats herself in a corner clothed in all the robes she can bear upon her person. Her husband may disrobe her if he wishes, but she must take no part or hinder him. If she utters a word or makes a gesture, she is made the butt of the jokes and gossip of her husband's house or neighborhood. The female servants of the house place themselves in a peeping position to listen or look through the windows, and are sure to publish what they see and hear amiss. Or this may be done to discover whether the husband is pleased with his wife, or how he behaves to her, as is the case in Japan. A bit of gossip—evidently a stock story—is the following from Dallet:

A newly married Corean groom spent a whole day among his male friends, in order to catch some words from his wife at their first interview, after their hours of separation. His spouse was informed of this, and perhaps resolved to be obstinate. Her husband, having vainly tried to make her speak, at last told her that on consulting the astrologers they had said that his wife was mute from birth. He now saw that such was the case, and was resolved not to keep for his wife a dumb woman. Now in a Corean wedding, it is quite possible that such an event may take place. One of the contracting parties may be deaf, mute, blind, or impotent. It matters not. The marriage exists. But the wife, stung by her husband's words, broke out in an angry voice, "Alas, the horoscope drawn for my partner is still more true. The diviner announced that I should marry the son of a rat." This, to a Corean, is a great insult, as it attaints father and son, and hence the husband and his father. The shouts of laughter from the eavesdropping female servants added to the discomfiture of the young husband, who had gained his point of making his bride use her tongue at a heavy expense, for long did his friends jeer at him for his bravado, and chaff him at catching a Tartar.

From the language, and from Japanese sources, we obtain some side-lights on the nuptial ceremony and married life. In Corean phrase *hon-sang* (the wedding and the funeral) are the two great events of life. Many are the terms relating to marriage, and the synonyms for conjugal union. "To take the hat," "to clip the hair," "to don the tuft," "to sit on the mat," are all in use among the gentlemen of the peninsula to denote the act or state of marriage. The hat and the hair play an important part in the transition from single to double blessedness. All who wear their locks *ta-rai*, or in a tress behind, are youths and maidens. Those with the tuft or top-knot are married. At his wedding and during the first year, the bridegroom wears a cap, made of a yellow herb, which is supposed to grow only near Sunto. Other honeymoon caps are melon-shaped, and made of sable skin. Ater the *chung-mai*, or middle-man, has arranged the match, and the day is appointed for the *han-sa*, or wedding, the bride chooses two or three maiden friends as "bridesmaids." If rich, the bride goes to her future husband's house in a palanquin; if poor, she rides on horseback. Even the humblest maid uses a sort of cap or veil, with ornaments on the breast, back, and at the girdle. When she cannot buy, she borrows. The prominent symbolic figure at the wedding is a goose, which, in Corean eyes, is the emblem of conjugal fidelity. Sometimes this *mok-an* is of gilded wood, sometimes it is made out of a fish for eating, again it is a live bird brought in a cloth with the head visible. If in the house, as is usual, the couple ascend the piled mats or dais and the reciprocal prostrations, or acts of mutual consent, form the sacramental part of the ceremony, and constitute marriage. The bride bows four times to her father-in-law and twice to the groom. The groom then bows four times to the bride. Other symbolic emblems are the fantastic shapes of straw (*otsuka*) presented to bride and groom alike. Dried pheasant is also brought in and cut. A gourd-bottle of rice-wine, decorated or tied with red and blue thread, is handed by the bride to the groom. The bridesmaids standing beside the couple pour the liquid and pass for exchange the one little "cup of the wine of mutual joy," several times filled and emptied.

Then begins the wedding-feast, when the guests drink and make merry. The important document certifying the fact of wedlock is called the *hon-se-chi*, and is signed by both parties. When the woman is unable to write, she makes "her mark" (*siu-pon*) by spreading out her hand and tracing with a pencil the exact profile of palm, wrist, and fingers. Sometimes the groom, in addition to his four prostrations, which are significant of fidelity to the bride, gives to his father-in-law a written oath of constancy to his daughter. Faithfulness is, however, a typical feminine, rather than masculine, virtue in the hermit nation. The *pong-kang*, a kind of wild canary bird, is held up to the wife as her model of conjugal fidelity. Another large bird, somewhat exceeding a duck in size, and called the *ching-kiong*, is said never to remate after the death of its consort. Corean widows are expected to imitate this virtuous fowl. In some places may be seen the vermilion arch or monumental gateway erected to some widow of faithful memory who wedded but once. Married women wear two rings on the ring finger. Sixty years, or a cycle, completes the ideal length of marital life, and "a golden wedding" is then celebrated.

Among the most peculiar of women's rights in Chō-sen is the curious custom forbidding any males in Seoul from being out after eight o'clock in the evening. When this Corean curfew sounds, all men must hie in-doors, while women are free to ramble abroad until one A.M. To transgress this law of *pem-ya* brings severe penalty upon the offender. In-doors, the violation of the privacy of the woman's quarters is punishable by exile or severe flagellation.

The following story, from Dallet, further illustrates some phases of their marriage customs, and shows that, while polygamy is not allowed, concubinage is a recognized institution:

A noble wished to marry his own daughter and that of his deceased brother to eligible young men. Both maidens were of the same age. He wished to wed both well, but especially his own child. With this idea in view he had already refused some good offers. Finally he made a proposal to a family noted alike for pedigree and riches. After hesitating some time which of the maidens he should dispose of first, he finally decided upon his own child. Without having seen his future son-in-law, he pledged his word and agreed upon the night. Three days before the ceremony he learned from the diviners that the young man chosen was silly, exceedingly ugly, and very ignorant. What should he do? He could not retreat. He had given his word, and in such a case the law is inflexible. In his despair he resolved upon a plan to render abortive what he could not avert. On the day of the marriage, he appeared in the women's apartments, and gave orders in the most imperative manner that his niece, and not his daughter, should don the marriage coiffure and the wedding-dress, and mount the nuptial platform. His stupefied daughter could not but acquiesce. The two cousins being of about the same height, the substitution was easy, and the ceremony proceeded according to the usual forms. The new bridegroom passed the afternoon in the men's apartments, where he met his supposed father-in-law. What was the amazement of the old noble to find that far from being stupid and ugly, as depicted by the diviners, the young man was good-looking, well-formed, intelligent, highly educated, and amiable in manners. Bitterly regretting the loss of so accomplished a son-in-law, he determined to repair the evil. He secretly ordered that, instead of his niece, his daughter should be introduced as the bride. He knew well that the young man would suspect nothing, for during the salutations the brides are always so muffled up with dresses and loaded with ornaments that it is impossible to distinguish their countenances.

All happened as the old man desired. During the two or three days which he passed with the new family, he congratulated himself upon obtaining so excellent a son-in-law. The latter, on his part, showed himself more and more charming, and so gained the heart of his supposed father-in-law that, in a burst of confidence, the latter revealed to him all that had happened. He told of the diviners' reports concerning him, and the successive substitutions of niece for daughter and daughter for niece.

The young man was at first speechless, then, recovering his composure, said: "All right, and that is a very smart trick on your part. But it is clear that both the two young persons belong to me, and I claim them. Your niece is my lawful wife, since she has made to me the legal salute, and your daughter—introduced by yourself into my marriage-chamber—has become of right and law my concubine." The crafty old man, caught in his own net, had nothing to answer. The two young women were conducted to the house of the new husband and master, and the old noble was jeered at both for his lack of address and his bad faith.

It is the reciprocal salutation before witnesses on the wedding-dais that constitutes legitimate marriage. From that moment a husband may claim the woman as his wife. If he repudiates or divorces her, he may not marry another woman while his former wife is living, but he is free to take as many concubines as he can support. It is sufficient that a man is able to prove that he has had intimate relations with a maiden or a widow; she then becomes his legal property. No person, not even her parents, can claim her if the man persists in keeping her. If she escape, he may use force to bring her back to his house. Conjugal fidelity—obligatory on the woman—is not required of the husband, and a wife is little more than a slave of superior rank. Among the nobles, the young bridegroom spends three or four days with his bride, and then absents himself from her for a considerable time, to prove that he does not esteem her too highly. Etiquette dooms her to a species of widowhood, while he spends his hours of relax-ation in the society of his concubines. To act otherwise would be considered in very bad taste, and highly unfashionable. Instances are known of nobles who, having dropped a few tears at the death of their wives, have had to absent themselves from the saloons of their companions to avoid the torrent of ribaldry and jeers at such weakness. Such eccentricity of conduct makes a man the butt of long-continued railery.

Habituated from infancy to such a yoke, and regarding them-selves as of an inferior race, most women submit to their lot with exemplary resignation. Having no idea of progress, or of an in-fraction of established usage, they bear all things. They become devoted and obedient wives, jealous of the reputation and well-being of their husbands. They even submit calmly to the tyranny and unreason of their mothers-in-law. Often, however, there is genuine rebellion in the household. Adding to her other faults of character, violence and insubordination, a Corean wife quarrels with her mother-in-law, makes life to her husband a burden, and in-cessantly provokes scenes of choler and scandal. Among the lower classes, in such cases, a few strokes of a stick or blows of the fist bring the wife to terms. In the higher classes it is not proper to strike a woman, and the husband has no other course than that of divorce. If it is not easy for him to marry again, he submits. If his wife, not content with tormenting him, is unfaithful to him, or, deserting his bed, goes back to her own house, he can lead her before the magistrate, who after administering a beating with the paddles, gives her as a concubine to one of his underlings.

Women of tact and energy make themselves respected and con-quer their legitimate position, as the following example shows. It is taken by Dallet from a Corean treatise on morals for the youth of both sexes:

Toward the end of the last century a noble of the capital, of high rank, lost his wife, by whom he had had several children. His advanced age rendered a second marriage difficult. Never-theless, the middle-men (or marriage-brokers employed in such cases) decided that a match could be made with the daughter of a poor noble in the province of Kiung-sang. On the appointed day he appeared at the mansion of his future father-in-law, and the couple mounted the stage to make the salute according to custom. Our grandee, casting his eyes upon his new wife, stopped for the moment thunderstruck. She was very fat, ugly, hump-backed, and appeared to be as slightly favored with gifts of mind as of body.

But he could not withdraw, and he played his part firmly. He resolved neither to take her to his house nor to have anything to do with her. The two or three days which it was proper to pass in his father-in-law's house being spent, he departed for the capital and paid no further attention to his new relatives.

The deserted wife, who was a person of a great deal of intelligence, resigned herself to her isolation and remained in her father's house, keeping herself informed, from time to time, of what happened to her husband. She learned, after two or three years, that he had become minister of the second rank, and that he had succeeded in marrying his two sons very honorably. Some years later, she heard that he proposed to celebrate, with all proper pomp, the festivities of his sixtieth birthday. Immediately, without hesitation and in spite of the remonstrances and opposition of her parents, she took the road to the capital. There hiring a palanquin, she was taken to the house of the minister and announced herself as his wife. She alighted, entered the vestibule, and presented herself with an air of assurance and a glance of tranquillity at the women of the united families. Seating herself at the place of honor, she ordered some fire brought, and with the greatest calmness lighted her pipe before the amazed domestics. The news was carried to the outer apartments of the gentlemen, but, according to etiquette, no one appeared surprised.

Finally the lady called together the household slaves and said to them, in a severe tone, "What house is this? I am your mistress, and yet no one comes to receive me. Where have you been brought up? I ought to punish you severely, but I shall pardon you this time." They hastened to conduct her into the midst of all the female guests. "Where are my sons-in-law?" she demanded. "How is it that they do not come to salute me? They forget that I am without any doubt, by my marriage, the mother of their wives, and that I have a right, on their part, to all the honors due to their own mothers."

Forthwith the two daughters-in-law presented themselves with a shamed air, and made their excuses as well as they were able. She rebuked them gently, and exhorted them to show themselves more scrupulous in the accomplishment of their duties. She then gave different orders in her quality as mistress of the house.

Some hours after, seeing that neither of the men appeared, she called a slave to her, and said to him : "My two sons are surely not absent on such a day as this. See if they are in the men's apartments, and bid them come here." The sons presented themselves before her, much embarrassed, and blundered out some excuses. "How?" said she, "you have heard of my arrival for several hours and have not come to salute me? With such bad bringing up, and an equal ignorance of principles of action, how will you make your way in the world? I have pardoned my slaves and my daughters-in-law for their want of politeness, but for you who are men I cannot let this fault pass unpunished." With this she called a slave and bade him give them some strokes on the legs with a rod. Then she added, "For your father, the minister, I am his servant, and I have not had orders to yield to him ; but, as for you, henceforth do you act so as not to forget proprieties." Finally the minister himself, thoroughly astonished at all that had passed, was obliged to come to terms and to salute his wife. Three days after, the festivities being ended, he returned to the palace. The king asked familiarly if all had passed off happily. The minister narrated in detail the history of his marriage, the unexpected arrival of his wife, and how she had conducted herself. The king, who was a man of sense, replied : "You have acted unjustly toward your wife. She appears to me to be a woman of spirit and extraordinary tact. Her behavior is admirable, and I don't know how to praise her enough. I hope you will repair the wrongs you have done her." The minister promised, and some days later solemnly conferred upon his wife one of the highest dignities of the court.

The woman who is legally espoused, whether widow or slave, enters into and shares the entire social estate of her husband. Even if she be not noble by birth she becomes so by marrying a noble, and her children are so likewise. If two brothers, for example, espouse an aunt and a niece, and the niece falls to the lot of the elder, she becomes thereby the elder sister, and the aunt will be treated as a younger sister. This relation of elder and younger sisters makes an immense difference in life, position, and treatment, in all Chinese Asia.

It is not proper for a widow to remarry. In the higher classes a widow is expected to weep for her deceased husband, and to wear mourning all her life. It would be infamy for her, however young, to marry a second time. The king who reigned 1469–1494 excluded children of remarried widows from competition at the public examinations, and from admittance to any official employment. Even to the present day such children are looked upon as illegitimate.

Among a people so passionate as Coreans, grave social disorders result from such a custom. The young noble widows who cannot remarry become, in most cases, secretly or openly the concubines of those who wish to support them. The others who strive to live chastely are rudely exposed to the inroads of passion. Sometimes they are made intoxicated by narcotics which are put in their drink, and they wake to find themselves dishonored. Sometimes they are abducted by force, during the night, by the aid of hired bandits. When they become victims of violence, there is no remedy possible. It often happens that young widows commit suicide, after the death of their husbands, in order to prove their fidelity and to secure their honor and reputation beyond the taint of suspicion. Such women are esteemed models of chastity, and there is no end to their praises among the nobles. Through their influence, the king often decrees a memorial gateway, column, or temple, intended to be a monument of their heroism and virtue. Thus it has often happened that Christian widows begged of the missionary fathers permission to commit suicide, if attempts were made to violate their houses or their persons ; and it was with difficulty that they could be made to comprehend the Christian doctrine concerning suicide.

The usual method of self-destruction is *ja-mun*, or cutting the throat, or opening the abdomen with a sword. In this the Coreans are like the Japanese, neck-cutting or piercing being the feminine, and *hara-kiri* (belly-cutting) the masculine, method of ending life at one's own hands.

Among the common people, second marriages are forbidden neither by law nor custom, but wealthy families endeavor to imitate the nobles in this custom as in others. Among the poor, necessity knows no law. The men must have their food prepared for them, and women cannot, and do not willingly die of famine when a husband offers himself. Hence second marriages among the lowly are quite frequent.

Most of the facts stated in this chapter are drawn from Dallet's "History of the [Roman Catholic] Church in Corea." Making due allowance for the statements of celibate priests, who are aliens in religion, nationality, and civilization, the picture of the social life of Chŏ-sen is that of abominable heathenism.

CHAPTER XXIX.

CHILD LIFE.

JUDGING from a collection of the toys of Corean children, and from their many terms of affection and words relating to games and sports, festivals and recreation, nursery stories, etc., the life of the little Kim or Ni must be a pleasant one. For the blessings of offspring the parents offer rice to the god of the household (*sam-sin-hang*), whose tiny shrine holds a place of honor in some ornamental niche in the best room. When the baby begins to grow, cradles being unknown, the mother puts the infant to sleep by *to-tak, to-tak*—patting it lightly on the stomach. When it is able to take its first step across the floor—the tiger-skin rug being ready to ease its possible fall—this important household event, spoken of with joy as the *ja-pak, ja-pak*, is described to the neighbors. As the child grows up and is able to walk and run about, the hair is mostly shaved off, so that only a "button of jade" is left on the top of the head. This infantile tuft takes its name from the badge or togle worn on the top of the men's caps in winter. A child, "three feet high," very beautiful and well formed, docile and strong, if a son, is spoken of "as a thousand-mile horse"—one who promises to make an alert and enduring man. A child noted for filial piety will even cheerfully commit *tan-ji*—cutting his finger to furnish his blood as a remedy for the sickness of father or mother. Should the child die, a stone effigy or statue of itself is set up before his grave.

In the capital and among the higher classes, the children's toys are very handsome, ranking as real works of art, while in every class the playthings of the tiny Corean humanity form but a miniature copy of the life of their elders. Among the living pets, the monkey is the favorite. These monkeys are fitted with jackets, and when plump and not too mischievous make capital pets for the boys. Puppies share the affections of the nursery with the tiger on wheels. Made of paper pulp and painted, this harmless effigy of the king of beasts is pulled about with a string. A jumping-jack is but a copy of the little boy who pulls it. A jerk of the string draws in the pasteboard tongue, and sends the trumpet to his mouth. Official life is mirrored in the tasselled umbrella, the fringed hats, and the toy-chariot with fancy wheels. Other toys, such as rattles, flags, and drums, exactly imitate the larger models with which the grown-up men and women amuse themselves. All these are named, fashioned, and decorated in a style peculiarly Corean. Among the most common of the children's plays are the following : A ring is hidden in a heap of sand, and the urchins poke sticks into and through the pile to find it. Whoever transfixes the circlet wins the game, suggesting our girls' game of grace-hoop, though often taking a longer time. Rosettes or pinwheels of paper are made and fastened on the end of sticks. Running before the breeze, the miniature windmills afford hilarious delight.

The children's way of bringing rain is to move the lips up and down, distending the cheeks and pressing the breath through the lips. Playing " dinner " with tiny cups and dishes, and imitating the ponderous etiquette of their elders, is a favorite amusement. See-saw is rougher and more exhilarating. Games of response are often played with hands, head, or feet, in which one watches the motions of his rival, opens or shuts his hands, and pays a forfeit or loses the game when a false move is made. For the coast-dwellers, the sea-shore, with the rocks which are the refuge of the shell-fish, is the inexhaustible playground of the children. Looking down in the clear deep water of the archipelago they see the coral reefs, the bright flower-gardens of marine plants, and shoals of striped, banded, crimson-tailed, and green-finned fish, which, in the eastern seas, glitter with tints of gold and silver. The children, half naked, catch the crabs and lobsters, learning how to hold their prizes after many a nab and pinch, which bring infantile tears and squalls. One of the common playthings of Corean children, the "baby's rattle," is the dried leathery egg of the skate, which with a few pebbles inside makes the infant, if not its parents, happy with the din.

Besides a game of patting and dabbling in the water—*chal-pak, chal-pak*—boys amuse themselves by fishing with hook and line or net. One method is to catch fish by means of the *yek-kui*. This is a plant of peppery taste, which poisons or stupefies the fish that bite the tempting tip, making them easy prey. More serious indoor games played by women and children are *pa-tok*, or back-

17

gammon ; *sang-pi-yen,* dominoes ; *siu-tu-chen,* game of eighty cards ; and *chang-keui,* or chess. All these pastimes are quite different from ours of the same name, yet enough like them to be recognized as belonging to the species named. The festivals most intensely enjoyed by the children are those of "Treading the Bridges," "The Meeting of the Star Lovers," and the "Mouse Fire." There is one evening in the year in which men and children, as well as women, are allowed to be out in the streets of the capital. The people spend the greater part of the night in passing and repassing upon the little bridges of stone. It is a general "night out" for all the people. Comedians, singers, harlequins, and merrymakers of all kinds are abroad, and it being moonlight, all have a good time in "treading the bridges." On the seventh day of the seventh month, the festival honored in China, Corea, and Japan takes place, for which children wait, in expectation, many days in advance. Sweetmeats are prepared, and bamboos strung with strips of colored paper are the symbols of rejoicing. On this night the two stars Capricornus and Alpha Lyra (or the Herd-boy and Spinning Maiden) are in conjunction in the milky way [1] (or the River of Heaven), and wishes made at this time are supposed to come true.

Chu-pul, or the Mouse Fire, occurs in the twelfth month, on the day of the Mouse (or rat). Children light brands or torches of dry reeds or straw, and set fire to the dry herbage, stubble, and shrubbery on the borders of the roads, in order to singe the hair of the various field or ground-burrowing animals, or burn them out, so as to obtain a plentiful crop of cotton.

At school, the pupils study according to the method all over Asia, that is, out loud, and noisily. This *kang-siong,* or deafening buzz, is supposed to be necessary to sound knowledge. Besides learning the Chinese characters and the vernacular alphabet, with tongue, ear, eye, and pen, the children master the *ku-ku* ("nine times nine"), or the multiplication table, and learn to work the four simple rules of arithmetic, and even fractions, involution, and evolution on the *chon-pan,* or sliding numeral frame. A "red mark" is a vermilion token of a good lesson, made by the examiner ; and for a good examination passed rewards are given in the form of a first-rate dinner, or one or all of "the four friends of the study table"—pens, ink, paper, and inkstand, or brushes, sticks of "India" ink, rolls of unsized paper, and an inkstone

---

[1] See "The Meeting of the Star Lovers," in Japanese Fairy World.

or water-dropper. Writing a good autograph signature—"one's own pen"—is highly commended. Sometimes money is given for encouragement, which the promising lad saves up in an earthen savings-bank. Not a few of the youth of the humbler classes, who work in the fields by day and study the characters by night, rise to be able officers who fill high stations.

The French missionaries assure us that the normal Corean is fond of children, especially of sons, who in his eyes are worth ten times as much as daughters. Such a thing as exposure of children is almost unknown. In times of severe famine this may happen after failure to give away or sell for a season, that they may be bought back. Parents rarely find their family too numerous.

The first thing inculcated in a child's mind is respect for his father. All insubordination is immediately and sternly repressed. Far different is it with the mother. She yields to her boy's caprices and laughs at his faults and vices without rebuke. The child soon learns that a mother's authority is next to nothing. In speaking of his father a lad often adds the words "severe," "terrible," implying the awe and profound respect in which he holds his father. (Something of the same feeling prevails as in Japan, where the four dreadful things which a lad most fears, and which are expressed in a rhyming proverb, are: "Earthquake, wind, fire, and father," or "daddy.") On the contrary, in speaking of his mother, he adds the words "good," "indulgent," "I'm not afraid of her," etc. A son must not play nor smoke in his father's presence, nor assume free or easy posture before him. For lounging, there is a special room, like a nursery. The son waits on his father at meals and gets his bed ready. If he is old or sickly, the son sleeps near him and does not quit his side night or day. If he is in prison the son takes up his abode in the vicinity, to communicate with his parent and furnish him with luxuries. In case of imprisonment for treason, the son at the portal, on bended knees day and night, awaits the sentence that will reduce himself to slavery. If the accused is condemned to exile, the son must at least accompany his father to the end of the journey, and, in some cases, share banishment with him. Meeting his father in the street, the son must make profound salute on his knees, in the dust, or in the ditch. In writing to him, he must make free use of the most exaggerated honorifics which the Corean knows.

The practice of adoption is common, as it is abnormally so in all countries where ancestral worship is prevalent and underlies all religions.   The preservation of the family line is the supreme end and aim of life.   In effect all those persons are descendants of particular ancestors who will keep up the ancestral sacrifices, guard the tablets and observe the numerous funeral and mourning ceremonies which make life such a burden in Eastern Asia.   Daughters are not adopted, because they cannot accomplish the prescribed rites.   When parents have only a daughter, they marry her to an adopted son, who becomes head of the family so adopted into.   Even the consent of the adopted, or of his parents, is not always requisite, for as it is a social, as well as a religious necessity, the government may be appealed to, and, in case of need, forces acceptance of the duty.   In this manner, as in the patriarchal age of biblical history, a man may be coerced into "raising up seed" to defunct ancestors.

Properly, an adoption, to be legal, ought to be registered at the office of the Board of Rites, but this practice has fallen into disuse, and it is sufficient to give public notice of the fact among the two families concerned.   An adoption once made cannot be void except by a decree from the Tribunal of Rites, which is difficult to obtain.   In practice, the system of adoption results in many scandals, quarrels, jealousies, and all the train of evils which one familiar with men and women, as they are, might argue a priori without the facts at hand.   The iron fetters of Asiatic institutions cannot suppress human nature.

Primogeniture is the rigid rule.   Younger sons, at the time of their marriage, or at other important periods of life, receive paternal gifts, now more, now less, according to usage, rank, the family fortune, etc., but the bulk of the property belongs to the oldest son, on whom the younger sons look as their father.   He is the head of the family, and regards his father's children as his own.   In all Eastern Asia the bonds of family are much closer than among Caucasian people of the present time.   All the kindred, even to the fifteenth or twentieth degree, whatever their social position, rich or poor, educated or illiterate, officials or beggars—form a clan, a tribe, or more exactly one single family, all of whose members have mutual interests to sustain.   The house of one is the house of the other, and each will assist to his utmost another of the clan to get money, office, or advantage.   The law recognizes this system by levying on the clan the imposts and debts which individuals of it cannot pay, holding the sodality responsible for the indivdual.   To this they submit without complaint or protest.

Instead of the family being a unit, as in the west, it is only the fragment of a clan, a segment in the great circle of kindred. The number of terms expressing relationship is vastly greater and much more complex than in English. One is amazed at the exuberance of the national vocabulary in this respect. The Coreans are fully as clannish as the Chinese, and much more so than the Irish; and in this, as in the Middle Kingdom, lies one great obstacle to Christianity or to any kind of individual reform. Marriage cannot take place between two persons having the same family cognomen. There are in the kingdom only one hundred and forty or fifty family, or rather clan names. Yet many of these names are widespread through the realm. All are formed of a single Chinese letter, except six or seven, which are composed of two characters. To distinguish the different families who bear the same patronymic, they add the name which they call the *pu*, or Gentile name, to indicate the place whence the family originally came. In the case of two persons wishing to marry, if this *pu* is the same, they are in the eyes of the law relatives, and marriage is forbidden. If the *pu* of each is different, they may wed. The most common names, such as Kim and Ni—answering to our Smith and Jones—have more than a score of *pu*, which arise from more than twenty families, the place of whose origin is in each case different. The family name is never used alone. It is always followed by a surname; or only the word *so-pang*, junior, *sang-wen*, senior, lord, sir, etc.

Male adults usually have three personal names, that given in childhood, the common proper name, and the common legal name, while to this last is often added the title. Besides these, various aliases, nicknames, fanciful and punning appellatives, play their part, to the pleasure or vexation of their object. This custom is the source of endless confusion in documents and common life. It was formerly in vogue in Japan, but was abolished by the mikado's government in 1872, and now spares as much trouble to tongue, tpyes, and pens, as a reform in our alphabet and spelling would save the English-speaking world. As in Nippon, a Corean female has but one name from the cradle to the grave. The titles "Madame," or "Madame widow," are added in mature life. As in old Japan, the common people do not, as a rule, have distinguishing individual names, and among them nicknames are very common. Corean etiquette forbids that the name of father, mother, or uncle be used in conversation, or even pronounced aloud.

CHAPTER XXX.

HOUSEKEEPING, DIET, AND COSTUME.

COREAN architecture is in a very primitive condition. The cas-tles, fortifications, temples, monasteries and public buildings can-not approach in magnificence those of Japan or China. The country, though boasting hoary antiquity, has few ruins in stone. The dwellings are tiled or thatched houses, almost invariably one story high. In the smaller towns these are not arranged in regu-lar streets, but scattered here and there. Even in the cities and capital the streets are narrow and tortuous.

In the rural parts, the houses of the wealthy are embosomed in beautiful groves, with gardens surrounded by charming hedges or fences of rushes or split-bamboo. The cities show a greater display of red-tiled roofs, as only the officials and nobles are allowed this sumptuary honor. Shingles are not much used. The thatching is of rice or barley straw, cut close, with ample eaves, and often finished with great neatnesss.

A low wall of uncemented stone, five or six feet high, sur-rounds the dwelling, and when kept in repair gives an air of neat-ness and imposing solidity to the estate. Often a pretty rampart of flat bamboo or rushes, plaited in the herring-bone pattern, sur-mounts the wall, which may be of pebbles or stratified rock and mortared. Sometimes the rampart is of wattle, covered with smooth white plaster, which, with the gateway, is also surmounted by an arched roofing of tiles. Instead of regular slanting lines of gables, one meets with the curved and pagoda-like roofs seen in China, with a heavy central ridge and projecting ornaments of fire-hardened clay, like the "stirrup" or "devil" tiles of Japan. These curves greatly add to the beauty of a Corean house, because they break the monotony of the lines of Corean architecture.

Doors, windows, and lintels are usually rectangular, and are set in regularly, instead of being made odd to relieve the eye, as in Japan. Bamboo is a common material for window-frames.

The foundations are laid on stone set in the earth, and the floor of the humble is part of the naked planet. People one grade above the poorest cover the hard ground with sheets of oiled paper, which serve as rugs or a carpet. For the better class a floor of wood is raised a foot or so above the earth, but in the sleeping- and sitting-room of the average family, the "kang" forms a vaulted floor, bed, and stove.

The kang is characteristic of the human dwelling in north-eastern Asia. It is a kind of tubular oven, in which human beings, instead of potatoes, are baked. It is as though we should make a bedstead of bricks, and put foot-stoves under it. The floor is bricked over, or built of stone over flues, which run from the fireplace, at one end of the house, to the chimney at the other. The fire which boils the pot or roasts the meat is thus utilized to warm those sitting or sleeping in the room beyond. The difficulty is to keep up a regular heat without being alternately chilled or smothered. With wood fuel this is almost impossible, but by dint of tact and regulated draught may be accomplished. As in the Swedish porcelain stove, a pail of live coals keeps up a good warmth all night. The kangs survive in the *kotatsù* of Japan.

The "fire" in sentiment and fact is the centre of the Corean home, and the native phrase, "he has put out his fire," is the dire synonym denoting that a man is not only cold and fasting, but in want of the necessities of life.

Bed-clothes are of silk, wadded cotton, thick paper, and tiger, wolf, or dog skins, the latter often sewn in large sheets like a carpet. Comfort, cleanliness, and luxury make the bed of the noble on the warm brick in winter, or cool matting in summer; but with the poor, the cold of winter, and insects of summer, with the dirt and rags, make sleeping in a Corean hut a hardship. Cushions or bags of rice-chaff form the pillows of the rich. The poor man uses a smooth log of wood or slightly raised portion of the floor to rest his head upon. "Weariness can snore upon the flint when resty sloth finds the down pillow hard."

Three rooms are the rule in an average house. These are for cooking, eating, and sleeping. In the kitchen the most noticeable articles are the *ang-pak*, or large earthen jars, for holding rice, barley, or water. Each of them is big enough to hold a man easily. The second room, containing the kang, is the sleeping apartment, and the next is the best room or parlor. Little furniture is the rule. Coreans, like the Japanese, sit, not cross-legged,

but on their heels. Among the well-to-do, dog-skins, or *kat-tei*,
cover the floor for a carpet, or splendid tiger-skins serve as rugs.
Matting is common, the best being in the south.

As in Japan, the meals are served on the floor on low *sang*, or
little tables, one for each guest, sometimes one for a couple. The
best table service is of porcelain, and the ordinary sort of earthen-
ware with white metal or copper utensils. The table-cloths are of
fine glazed paper and resemble oiled silk. No knives or forks are
used ; instead, chopsticks, laid in paper cases, and, what is more
common than in China or Japan, spoons are used at every meal.

Table Spread for Festal Occasions.

The climax of æsthetic taste occurs when a set of historic porcelain and faience of old Corean manufacture and decoration, with
the tall and long-spouted teapot, are placed on the pearl-inlaid
table and filled with native delicacies.

The walls range in quality of decoration from plain mud to colored plaster and paper. The Corean wall-paper is of all grades,
sometimes as soft as silk, or as thick as canvas. *Sa-peik* is a favorite reddish earth or mortar which serves to rough-cast in rich
color tones the walls of a room.

Pictures are not common ; the artistic sense being satisfied with scrolls of handsome Chinese characters containing moral and literary gems from the classics, or the caligraphic triumph of some king, dignitary, or literary friend. To possess a sign-manual or autograph scrap of Yung, Hong, or O, the three most renowned men of Chō-sen, is reckoned more than a golden manuscript on azure paper.

The windows are square and latticed without or within, and covered with tough paper, either oiled or unsized, and moving in grooves—the originals of the Japanese sliding-doors and windows. In every part of a Corean house, paper plays an important and useful part.

Very fine venetian blinds are made of threads split from the ever-useful bamboo, which secures considerable variety in window decoration. The doors are of wood, paper, or plaited bamboo. Glass was, till recently, a nearly unknown luxury in Corea among the common people. Even with the nobles, it is rather a curiosity. The windows being made of oiled or thin paper, glass is not a necessity. This fact will explain the eagerness of the people to possess specimens of this transparent novelty. Even old porter and ale bottles, which sailors have thrown away, are eagerly picked up, begged, bought, or stolen. An old medicine-vial, among the Coreans, used to fetch the price of a crystal goblet among us. The possessor of such a prize as a Bass' ale bottle will exhibit it to his neighbor as a rare curio from the Western barbarians, just as an American virtuoso shows off his last new Satsuma vase or box of Soochow lacquer. When English ship captains, visiting the coast, gave the Coreans a bottle of wine, the bottle, after being emptied, was always carefully returned with extreme politeness as an article of great value. The first Corean visitor to the American expedition of 1871, went into ecstacies, and his face budded into smiles hitherto thought impossible to the grim Corean visage, because the cook gave him an arm-load of empty ale-bottles. The height of domestic felicity is reached when a Corean householder can get a morsel of glass to fasten into his window or sliding-door, and thus gaze on the outer world through this "loophole of retreat." This not only saves him from the disagreeable necessity of punching a finger-hole through the paper to satisfy his curiosity, but gives him the advantage of not being seen, and of keeping out the draft. When a whole pane has been secured, it is hard to state whether happiness or pride reigns uppermost in the owner's bosom.

Candlesticks are either tall and upright, resting on the floor in the Japanese style, or dish-lamps of common oil are used.

Flint and steel are used to ignite matches made of chips of wood dipped in sulphur, by which a "fire-flower" is made to blossom, or in more prosaic English, a flame is kindled. Phosphorus matches, imported from Japan, are called by a word signifying "fire-sprite," "will-of-the-wisp," or *ignis-fatuus*.

Usually in a gentlemen's house there is an ante-room or vestibule, in which neighbors and visitors sit and talk, smoke or drink. In this place much freedom is allowed and formalities are laid aside. Here are the facilities and the atmosphere which in Western lands are found in clubs, coffee- and ale-houses, or obtained from newspapers. One such, of which the picture is before us, has in it seats, and looks out on a garden or courtyard. On a ledge or window-seat are vases of blossoms and cut flowers; a smaller vase holds fans, and another is presumably full of tobacco or some other luxury. Short eave-curtains and longer drapery at the side, give an air of inviting comfort to these free and easy quarters, where news and gossip are exchanged. These *oi-tiang*, or outer apartments, are for strangers and men only, and women are never expected or allowed to be present.

The Ching-ja is a small house or room on the bank of a river, or overlooking some bit of natural scenery, to which picnic parties resort, the Coreans most heartily enjoying out-door festivity, in places which sky, water, and foliage make beautiful to the eye.

There are often inscribed on the portals, in large Chinese characters, moral mottoes or poetical sentiments, such as "Enter happiness, like breezes bring the spring, and depart evil spirit as snow melts in water." Before a new house is finished, a sheet of pure white paper, in which are enclosed some *nip*, or "cash," with grains of rice which have been steeped in wine, is nailed or fastened on the wall, over the door, and becomes the good spirit or genius of the house, sacrifices being duly offered to it. In more senses than one, the spirit that presides over too many Corean households is the alcohol spirit.

The Corean liquor, by preference, is brewed or distilled from rice, millet, or barley. These alcoholic drinks are of various strength, color, and smell, ranging from beer to brandy. In general their beverages are sufficiently smoky, oily, and alcoholic to Western tastes, as the fusel-oil usually remains even in the best products of their stills. No trait of the Coreans has more impressed their numerous visitors, from Hamel to the Americans, than their love of all kinds of strong drink, from ale to whiskey. The common verdict is, "They are greatly addicted to the worship of Bacchus." The Corean vocabulary bears ample witness to the thorough acquaintance of the people with the liquor made from grain by their rude processes. The inhabitants of the peninsula were hard drinkers even in the days of Fuyu and Kokorai. No sooner were the ports of modern Chō-sen open to commerce than the Chinese established liquor-stores, while European wines, brandies, whiskeys, and gins have entered to vary the Corean's liquid diet and increase the national drunkenness.

Strange as it may seem, the peasant, though living between the two great tea-producing countries of the world—Japan and China— and in the latitude of tea-plantations, scarcely knows the taste of tea, and the fragrant herb is as little used as is coffee in Japan. The most common drink, after what the clouds directly furnish, is the water in which rice has been boiled. Infusions of dried ginseng, orange-peel, or ginger serve for festal purposes, and honey when these fail; but the word "tea," or *cha*, serves the Corean, as it does the typical Irishman, for a variety of infusions and decoctions. With elastic charity the word covers a multitude of sins, chiefly of omission; all that custom or euphony requires is to prefix the name of the substance used to "cha" and the drink is tea—of some kind.

The staple diet has in it much more of meat and fat than that of the Japanese. The latter acknowledge that the average Corean can eat twice as much as himself. Beef, pork, fowls, venison, fish, and game are consumed without much waste in rejected material. Nearly everything edible about an animal is a tidbit, and a curious piece of cookery, symbolical of a generous feast, is often found at the board of a liberal host. This *tang-talk* (which often becomes the "town-talk") is a chicken baked and served with its feathers, head, claws, and inwards intact. "To treat to an entire fowl" is said of a liberal host, and is equivalent to "killing the fatted calf."

Fish are often eaten raw from tail to head, especially if small, with only a little seasoning. *Ho-hoi*, or fish-bone salad, is a delicacy. Dog-flesh is on sale among the common butchers' meats, and the Coreans enjoy it as our Indians do. In the first month of the year, however, owing to religious scruples, no dog-meat is eaten, or dishes of canine origin permitted.

The state dinner, given to the Japanese after the treaty, consisted of this bill of fare : two-inch squares of pastry, made of flour, sugar, and oil ; heaps of boiled eggs ; pudding made of flour, sesame, and honey ; dried persimmons ; " pine-seeds," honey-like food covered with roasted rice colored red and white ; maccaroni soup with fowl ; boiled legs of pork, and wine, rice or millet spirit with everything. It is customary to decorate the tables on grand occasions with artificial flowers, and often the first course is intended more for show than for actual eating. For instance, when the Japanese party, feasted at Seoul in 1646, first sat down to the table, one of them began to help himself to fish, of which he was very fond. The dish seemed to contain a genuine cooked carp basted with sauce, but, to the embarrassment of the hungry guest, the fish would not move. He was relieved by the servant, who told him that it was put on the table only for show. The courses brought on later contained more substantial nourishment, such as fish, flesh, fowl, vegetables, soups, cakes, puddings and tea. Judging from certain words in the language, these show-dishes form a regular feature at the opening of banquets. The women cook rice beautifully, making it thoroughly soft by steaming, while yet retaining the perfect shape of each grain by itself. Other well-known dishes are barley, millet, beans, *taro* (potato cooked in a variety of ways), lily-bulbs, sea-weeds, acorns, *dai-kon* (radishes), turnips, and potatoes. Maccaroni and vermicelli are used for soups and refreshing lunches. Apples, pears, plums, grapes, persimmons, and various kinds of berries help to furnish the table, though the flavor of these is inferior to the same fruits grown in our gardens.

All kinds of condiments, mustard, vinegar, pepper, and a variety of home-made sauces, are much relished. Itinerant food-sellers are not so common as in China, but butcher-shops and vermicelli stands are numerous. Two solid meals, with a light breakfast, is the rule. *Opan*, or midday rice, is the dinner. *Tai-sik* is a regular meal. The appearance of the evening star is the signal for a hearty supper, and the planet a synonym for the last meal of the day. At wakes or funeral feasts, and on festal days, the amount of victuals consumed is enormous, while a very palatable way of remembering the dead is by the *yum-pok*, or drinking of sacrificial wine. The Coreans understand the preservative virtues of ice, and in winter large quantities of this substance are cut and stored away for use in the summer, in keeping fresh meat and fish. Their ice-houses are made by excavating the ground and covering over the store with earth and sod, from which in hot weather they use as may be necessary. These ice stores are often under the direction of the government, especially when large quantities of fish are being preserved for rations of the army in time of war. Those who oversee the work are called "Officers of the Refrigerator."

One striking fault of the Coreans at the table is their voracity, and to this trait of their character Japanese, French, Dutch, and Chinese bear witness. It might be supposed that a Frenchman, who eats lightly, might make a criticism where an Englishman would be silent; but not so. All reports concerning them seem to agree. In this respect there is not the least differ- ence between the rich and poor, noble or plebeian. To eat much is an honor, and the merit of a feast consists not in the quality but in the quantity of the food served. Little talking is done while eating, for each sentence might lose a mouthful. Hence, since a capacious stomach is a high accomplishment, it is the aim from infancy to develop a belly having all possible elasticity. Often the mothers take their babies upon their knees, and after stuffing them with rice, like a wad in a gun, will tap them from time to time with the paddle of a ladle on the stomach, to see that it is fully spread out or rammed home, and only cease gorg- ing when it is physically impossible for the child to swell up more. A Corean is always ready to eat; he attacks whatever he meets with, and rarely says, "Enough." Even between meals, he will help himself to any edible that is offered. The ordinary portion of a laborer is about a quart of rice, which when cooked makes a good bulk. This, however, is no serious hindrance to his devouring double or treble the quantity when he can get it. Eat- ing matches are common. When an ox is slaughtered, and the beef is served up, a heaping bowl of the steaming mess does not alarm any guest. Dog-meat is a common article of food, and the canine sirloins served up in great trenchers are laid before the guests, each one having his own small table to himself. When fruits, such as peaches or small melons, are served, they are devoured without peeling. Twenty or thirty peaches is considered an ordinary allowance, which rapidly disappears. Such a prodi- gality in victuals is, however, not common, and for one feast there are many fastings. Beef is not an article of daily food with the peasantry. Its use is regulated by law, the butcher being a sort of government official; and only under extraordinary circumstances, as when a grand festival is to be held, does the king allow an ox to be killed in each village. The Coreans are neither fastidious in their eating nor painstaking in their cooking. Nothing goes to waste. All is grist that comes to the mill in their mouths.

They equal Japanese in devouring raw fish, and uncooked food of all kinds is swallowed without a wry face. Even the intestines pass among them for delicate viands. Among the poorer classes, a cooked fish is rarely seen on the table ; for no sooner is it caught than it is immediately opened and devoured. The raw viands are usually eaten with a strong seasoning of pepper or mustard, but they are often swallowed without condiment of any sort. Often in passing along the banks of a river, one may see men fishing with rod and line. Of these some are nobles who are not able, or who never wish to work for a living, yet they will fish for food and sport. Instead of a bag or basket to contain the game, or a needle to string it upon, each fisher has at his side a jar of diluted pepper, or a kind of soy. No sooner is a fish hooked, than he is drawn out, seized between the two fingers, dipped into the sauce, and eaten without ceremony. Bones do not scare them. These they eat, as they do the small bones of fowls.

Nationally, and individually, the Coreans are very deficient in conveniences for the toilet. Bath-tubs are rare, and except in the warmer days of summer, when the river and sea serve for immersion, the natives are not usually found under water. The Japanese in the treaty expedition in 1876 had to send bath-tubs on shore from their ships. Morning ablutions are made in a copper basin. The sponges which grow on the west coast seem to find no market at home. This neglect of more intimate acquaintance with water often makes the lowest classes "look like mulattos," as Hamel said. Gutzlaff, Adams, and others, especially the Japanese, have noted this personal defect, and have suggested the need of soap and hot water. It may be that the contrast between costume and cuticle tempts to exaggeration. People who dress in white clothing have special need of personal cleanliness. Perhaps soap factories will come in the future.

The men are very proud of their beards, and the elders very particular in keeping them white and clean. The lords of creation honor their beard as the distinctive glory and mark of their sex. A man is in misery if he has only just enough beard to distinguish him from a woman. A full crop of hair on cheek and chin insures to its possessor unlimited admiration, while in Corean billingsgate there are numerous terms of opprobrium for a short beard. Europeans are contemptuously termed "short-hairs"—with no suspicion of the use of the word in New York local politics. Old gentlemen keep a little bag in which they assiduously collect the combings of their hair, the strokings of their beard and parings of their nails, in order that all that belongs to them may be duly placed in their coffin at death.

The human hair crop is an important item in trade with China, to which country it is imported and sold to piece out the hair-tails which the Chinese, in obedience to their Manchiu conquerors, persist in wearing. Some of this hair comes from poor women, but the staple product is from the heads of boys who wear their hair parted in the middle, and plaited in a long braid, which hangs down their backs. At marriage, they cut this off, and bind what remains in a tight, round knot on the top of the scalp, using pins or not as they please.

The court pages and pretty boys who attend the magnates, usually rosy-cheeked, well fed, and effeminate looking youths, do not give any certain indication of their sex, and foreigners are often puzzled to know whether they are male or female. Their beardless faces and long hair are set down as belonging to women. Most navigators have made this mistake in gender, and when the first embassy from Seoul landed in Yokohama, the controversy, and perhaps the betting, as to the sex of these nondescripts was very lively. Captain Broughton declared that the whole duty of these pages seemed to be to smooth out the silk dresses of the grandees. Officials and nobles cover their top-knots with neat black nets of horse-hair or glazed thread. Often country and town people wear a fillet or white band of bark or leaves across the forehead to keep the loose hair in order, as the ancient Japanese used to do. Women coil their glossy black tresses into massive knots, and fasten them with pins or golden, silver, and brass rings. The heads of the pins are generally shaped like a dragon. They oil their hair, using a sort of vegetable pomatum. Among the court ladies and female musicians the styles of coiffure are various ; some being very pretty, with loops, bands, waves, and "bangs," as the illustration on page 161 shows.

Corea is decidedly the land of big hats. From their amplitude these head-coverings might well be called "roofs," or, at least, "umbrellas." Their diameter is so great that the human head encased in one of them seems but as a hub in a cart-wheel. They

would probably serve admirably as parachutes in leaping from a
high place. Under his wide-spreading official hat a magistrate
can shelter his wife and family. It serves as a numeral, since a
company is counted by hats, instead of heads or noses. How the
Corean dignitary can weather a gale remains a mystery, and, perhaps, the feat is impossible and rarely attempted. A slim man is
evidently at a disadvantage in a "Japanese wind" or typhoon.
The personal avoirdupois, which is so much admired in the peninsula, becomes very useful as ballast to the head-sail. Corean
magnates, cast away at sea, would not lack material for ship's canvas. In shape, the gentleman's hat resembles a flower-pot set on
a round table, or a tumbler on a Chinese gong. Two feet is a
common diameter, thus making a periphery of six feet. The top
or cone, which rises nine inches higher, is only three inches
wide. This chimney-like superstructure serves as ornament and
ventilator. Its purpose is not to encase the head, for underneath
the brim is a tight-fitting skull-cap, which rests on the head and
is held on by padded ties under the ears. The average rim for
ordinary people, however, is about six inches in radius. The
huge umbrella-hat of bleached bamboo is worn by gentlemen in
mourning. After death it is solemnly placed on the bier, and
forms a conspicuous object at the funeral. The native name for
hat is *kat* or *kat-si*.

The usual material is bamboo, split to the fineness of a thread,
and woven so as to resemble horse-hair. The fabric is then var-
nished or lacquered, and becomes perfectly weather-proof, resisting
sun and rain, but not wind. The prevalence of cotton clothing,
easily soaked and rendered uncomfortable, requires the ample protection for the back and shoulders, which these umbrella-like
hats furnish. In heavy rain, the *kat-no* is worn, that is, a cone
of oiled paper, fixed on the hat in the shape of a funnel. Indeed,
the umbrella in Corea is rather for a symbol of state and dignity
than for vulgar use, and is often adorned with knobs and strips.
Quelpart Island is the home of the hatters, whose fashionable
wares supply the dandies and dignitaries of the capital and of the
peninsula. The highest officers of the government have the cone
truncated or rounded at the vertex, and surmounted by a little
figure of a crane in polished silver, very handsome and durable.
This long-legged bird is a symbol of civil office. "To confer the
hat," means as much to an officer high in favor at the court of
Seoul as to a cardinal in the Vatican, only the color is black, not

red. It is Corean etiquette to keep the hat on, and in this respect, as well as in their broad brims, the hermits resemble the Quakers. Marriage and mourning are denoted also by the hat.

A variety of materials is employed by other classes. Soldiers wear large black or brown felt hats, resembling Mexican sombreros, which are adorned with red horse-hair or a peacock's feather, swung on a swivel button.

Suspended from the sides, over the ears and around the neck, are strings of round balls of blue porcelain, cornelian, amber, or what resembles kauri gum. Sometimes these ornaments are tubular, reminding one of the millinery of a cardinal's hat.

For the common people, plaited straw or rushes of varied shapes serve for summer, while in winter shaggy caps of lynx, wolf, bear, or deer-skin are common, made into Havelock, Astrachan, Japanese, and other shapes, some resembling wash-bowls, some being fluted or fan-like, winged, sock-shaped, or made like a nightcap. Variety seems to be the fashion.

The head-dress of the court nobles differs from that of the vulgar as much as the Pope's tiara differs from a cardinal's *rubrum*. It is a crown or helmet, which, eschewing brim, rises in altitude to the proportions of a mitre. Without earstrings or necklaces of beads, it is yet highly ornamental. One of these consists of a cap, with a sort of gable at the top. Another has six lofty curving folds or volutes set in it. On another are designs from the *pa-kwa*, or sixty-four mystic diagrams, which are supposed to be sacred symbols of the Confucian philosophy, and of which fortune-tellers make great use.

The wardrobe of the gentry consists of the ceremonial and the house dress. The former, as a rule, is of fine silk, and the latter of coarser silk or cotton. These "gorgeous Corean dresses" are of pink, blue, and other rich colors. The official robe is a long garment like a wrapper, with loose, baggy sleeves. This is embroidered with the stork or phœnix for civil, and with the kirin, lion, or tiger for military officers. Buttons are unknown and form no part of a Corean's attire, male or female, thus greatly reducing the labor of the wives and mothers who ply the needle, which in Corea has an "ear" instead of an "eye." Strings and girdles, and the shifting of the main weight of the clothing to the shoulders, take the place of these convenient, but fugitive, adjuncts to the Western costume. There are few tailors' shops, the women of each household making the family outfit.

18

Soldiers in full dress wear a sleeveless, open surcoat for display. The under dress of both sexes is a short jacket with tight sleeves, which for men reaches to the thighs, and for women only to the waist, and a pair of drawers reaching from waist to ankle, a little loose all the way down for the men, and tied at the ankles, but for the women made tight and not tied. The females wear a petticoat over this garment, so that the Coreans say they dress like Western women, and foreign-made hosiery and under-garments are in demand. Although they have a variety of articles of apparel easily distinguishable to the native eye, yet their general style of costume is that of the wrapper, stiff, wide, and inflated with abundant starch in summer, but clinging and baggy in winter. The rule is tightness and economy for the working, amplitude and richness of material for the affluent, classes. The women having no pockets in their dresses, wear a little bag suspended from their girdle. This is worn on the right side, attached by cords. These contain their bits of jewelry, scissors, knife, a tiger's claw for luck, perfume-bottle or sachet, a tiny chess-board in gold or silver, etc. Besides the rings on their fingers the ladies wear hair-pins of gold ornamented with bulbs or figures of birds. Many of them dust *pun*, or white powder, on their faces, and employ various other cosmetics, which are kept in their *kiong-tai*, or mirror toilet-stands ; in which also may be their *so-hak*, or book containing rules of politeness.

The general type of costume is that of China under the Ming dynasty. To a Chinaman a Corean looks antiquated, a curiosity in old clothes ; a Japanese at a little distance, in the twilight, is reminded of ghosts, or the snowy heron of the rice-fields, while to the American the Corean swell seems compounded chiefly of bed-clothes, and in his most elaborate costume to be still in his under-garments.

Plenty of starch in summer, and no stint of cotton in winter, are the needs of the Corean. His white dress makes his complexion look darker than it really is. The monotonous dazzle of bleached garments is relieved by the violet robes of the magistrate, the dark blue for the soldiers, and lighter shades of that color in the garb of the middle class ; the blue strip which edges the coat of the literary graduates, and the pink and azure clothes of the children. Less agreeable is the nearness which dispels illusion. The costume, which seemed snowy at a distance, is seen to be dingy and dirty, owing to an entire ignorance of soap.

The Corean dress, though simpler than the Chinese, is not entirely devoid of ornament. The sashes are often of handsome blue silk or brocaded stuff. The official girdles, or flat belts a few inches wide, have clasps of gold, silver, or rhinoceros horn, and are decorated with polished ornaments of gold or silver. For magistrates of the three higher ranks these belts are set with blue stones ; for those of the fourth and fifth grade with white stones, and for those below the fifth with a substance resembling horn. Common girdles are of cotton, hemp cloth, or rope.

Fans are also a mark of rank, being made of various materials,

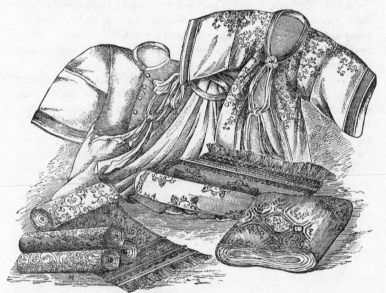

Gentlemen's Garments and Dress Patterns.

especially silk or cloth, stretched on a frame. The fan is an instrument of etiquette. To hide the face with one is an act of politeness. The man in mourning must have no other kind than that in which the pin or rivet is of cow's horn. Oiled paper fans serve a variety of purposes. In another kind, the ribs of the frame are bent back double. The finer sort for the nobility are gorgeously inlaid with pearl or nacre.

A kind of flat wand or tablet, seen in the hands of nobles, ostensibly to set down orders of the sovereign, is made of ivory for officers above, and of wood for those below the fourth grade.

Another badge of office is the little wand, half way between a toy whip and a Mercury's caduceus, of black lacquered wood, with cords of green silk. This is carried by civil officers, and may be the original of the Japanese baton of command, made of lacquered wood with pendant strips of paper.

Canes are carried by men of the literary or official class when in mourning. These tall staves, which, from the decks of European vessels sailing along the coast, have often looked like spears, are the *sang-chang*, or smooth bamboo staves, expressive of ceremonial grief, and nothing more.

As the Coreans have no pockets, they make bags, girdles, and their sleeves serve instead. The women wear a sort of reticule hung at the belt, and the men a smoking outfit, consisting of an oval bag to hold his flint and steel, some fine-cut tobacco, and a long, narrow case for his pipe.

Foot-gear is either of native or of Chinese make. The laborer contents himself with sandals woven from rice-straw, which usually last but a few days. A better sort is of hempen twine or rope, with many strands woven over the top of the foot. A man in mourning can wear but four cords on the upper part. Socks are too expensive for the poor, except in the winter. Shoes made of cotton are often seen in the cities, having hempen or twine soles. The low shoes of cloth, or velvet, and cowhide, upturned at the toe, worn by officials, are imported from China. Small feet do not seem to be considered a beauty, and the foot-binding of the Chinese is unknown in Chō-sen, as in Japan.

CHAPTER XXXI.

MOURNING AND BURIAL.

THE fashion of mourning, the proper place and time to shed tears and express grief according to regulations, are rigidly prescribed in an official treatise or "Guide to Mourners," published by the government. The corpse must be placed in a coffin of very thick wood, and preserved during many months in a special room prepared and ornamented for this purpose. It is proper to weep only in this death-chamber, but this must be done three or four times daily. Before entering it, the mourner must don a special weed, which consists of a gray cotton frock coat, torn, patched, and as much soiled as possible. The girdle must be of twisted straw and silk, made into a rope of the thickness of the wrist. Another cord, the thickness of the thumb, is wound round the head, which is covered with dirty linen, each of the rope's ends falling upon the cheek. A special kind of sandals is worn, and a big knotty stick completes the costume of woe. In the prescribed weeds the mourner enters the death-chamber in the morning on rising, and before each meal. He carries a little table filled with food, which he places upon a tray at the side of the coffin. The person who is master of the mourners presides at the ceremonies. Prostrate, and struck by the stick, he utters dolorous groans, sounding "ai-kō" if for a parent. For other relatives he groans out "oi, oi." According to the noise and length of the groans and weeping, so will the good opinion of the public be. The lamentations over, the mourner retires, doffs the mourning robes, and eats his food. At the new and the full moon, all the relatives are invited and expected to assist at the ceremonies. These practices continue more or less even after burial, and at intervals during several years. Often a noble will go out to weep and kneel at the tomb, passing a day, and even a night, in this position. In some instances, mourners have built a little house before the grave, and watched there for years, thus winning a high reputation for filial piety.

Among the poor, who have not the means to provide a death-chamber and expensive mourning, the coffin is kept outside their houses covered with mats until the time of sepulture.

Though cremation, or "burying in the fire," is known in Chō-sen, the most usual form of disposing of the dead is by inhumation. Children are wrapped up in the clothes and bedding in which they die, and are thus buried. As unmarried persons are reckoned as children, their shroud and burial are the same. With the married and adult, the process is more costly, and the ceremonial more detailed and prolonged. This, which is described very fully in Ross' "Corea," and with which Hamel's curt notes agree, consists of minute ceremonial and mourning among the living and the washing, combing, nail-paring, robing, and laying out in state of the dead, with calling of the spirits, and with screens, lights, and offerings, according to Confucian ritual. In many interesting features, the most ancient rites of China have survived in the peninsula after they have become obsolete in the former country. The very old tombs opened, and the painted coffins, coated with many layers of silicious paint, dug up near Shanghai recently, are much like those of the Coreans.

The coffin, which fits the body, is made air-tight with wax, resin, or varnish, and is borne on a bier to the grave by men who make this their regular business. Often there are two coffins, one inside the other. Sons follow the body of their father on foot, relatives ride in palanquins or on horseback. Prominent at the head of the procession is the red standard containing the titles and honors of the deceased. This banner, or *sa-jen*, has two points on it to frighten away the spirits, and at the funeral of a high officer, a man wears a hideous mask for the same purpose. When there are no titles, only the name of the deceased is inscribed upon the banner.

The selection of a proper site for a tomb is a matter of profound solicitude, time, and money; for the geomancers must be consulted with a fee. The *pung-sui* superstition requires for the comfort of both living and dead that the right site should be chosen. Judging from the number of times the word "mountain" enters into terms relating to burial, most interments are on the hillsides. If these are not done properly, trouble will arise, and the bones must then be dug up, collected, and re-buried, often at heavy expense. Thousands of professional cheats and self-duped people live by working upon the feelings of the bereaved through this superstition.

The tombs of the poor consist only of the grave and a low mound of earth. These mounds, subjected to the forces of nature, and often trampled upon by cattle, disappear after the lapse of a few years, and oblivion settles over the spot.

With the richer class monuments are of stone, sometimes neat or even imposing, sometimes grotesque. Some, as the *pi-popi*, are shaped like a house or miniature temple ; or, two stones, cut in the form of a ram and a horse respectively, are placed before the sepulchre. The *man-tu*, " gazing headstone," consists of two monoliths or columns of masonry, flanking the tomb on either side, so that the soul of the dead, changed into a bird, may repose peacefully. In the graveyards are many tombs paved with granite slabs around the temple model, but for the most part a Corean cemetery is filled with little obelisks, or tall, square columns, either pointed at the top or surmounted with the effigy of a human head, or a rudely sculptured stone image, which strangely reminds a foreigner of " patience on a monument, smiling at grief." This apparition of a human head rising above the tall grass of the burial-ground may be the original of Japanese pictures of the ghosts and spirits which seem to rise dark and windblown out of the wet grass. Often the carving in Corean grave-yards is so rude as to be almost indistinguishable.

Mourning is of many degrees and lengths, and is betokened by dress, abstinence from food and business, visits to the tomb, offerings, tablets, and many visible indications, detailed even to absurdity. Pure, or nearly pure white is the mourning color, as a contrast to red, the color of rejoicing. Even the rivets of the fan, the strings on the shoes, and the carrying of a staff in addition to the mourning-hat, betoken the uniform of woe.

When noblemen don the peaked hat, which covers the face as well as the head, they are as dead to the world—not to be spoken to, molested, or even arrested if charged with crime. This Corean mourning hat proved " the helmet of salvation" to Christians, and explains the safety of the French missionaries who lived so long in disguise, unharmed in the country where the police were as lynxes and hounds ever on their track. The Jesuits were not slow to see the wonderful shelter promised for them, and availed themselves of it at once and always.

The royal sepulchres within the peninsula have attracted more than one unlawful descent upon the shores of Chō-sen. The various dynasties of sovereigns during the epoch of the Three Kingdoms in the old capitals of these states, the royal lines of Kokorai at Ping-an, of Korai at Sunto, and of the ruling house at Seoul, have made Corea during her two thousand years of history rich in royal tombs. These are in various parts of the country, and those which are known are under the care of the government.

Are these mausoleums filled with gold or jewels? Foreign grave-robbers have believed so, and shown their faith by their works, as we shall see. French priests in the country have said so. The ancient Chinese narratives descriptive of the customs of the Fuyu people, confirm the general impression. Without having the facts at hand to demonstrate what eager foreigners have believed, we know that vast treasures have been spent upon the decoration of the royal sepulchres, and the erection of memorial buildings over them, and that the fear of their violation by foreign or native outlaws has been for centuries ever before the Corean people. That these fears have too often been justified, we shall find when we read of that memorable year, A.D. 1866. The profuse vocabulary of terms relating to burial, mourning, and memorial tablets in Corea show their intense loyalty to the Confucian doctrines, the power of superstition, and the shocking waste of the resources of the living upon the dead.

The voluble Corean envoys when in Tōkiō, visited the Naval College, and on learning that in certain emergencies the students from distant provinces were not allowed to go home to attend the funeral of their parents, nor to absent themselves from duty on account of mourning, were amazed beyond measure, and for a few moments literally speechless from surprise. It is hard for a Corean to understand the sayings of Jesus to the disciple who asked, "Lord, suffer me first to go and bury my father," and "Let the dead bury their dead."

From the view-point of political economy, this lavish expense of time, energy, money, and intellect upon corpses and superstition is beneficial. Without knowing of Malthus or his theories, the Chō-senese have hit upon a capital method of limiting population, and keeping the country in a state of chronic poverty.

The question has been asked the writer, "How can a people, pent in a little mountainous peninsula like Corea, exist for centuries without overpopulating their territory?"

Wars, famine, pestilence, ordinary poverty answer the question in part. The absurd and rigorous rules of mourning, requiring frightful expense, postponement of marriage to young people—who even when betrothed must mourn three years for parents and grandparents, actual and expected, the impoverishing of the people, and the frequent hindrances to marriage at the proper season, serve to keep down population. This fact is an often chosen subject for native anecdotes and romances. The vexations and delays often caused by the long periods of idle mourning required by etiquette, are well illustrated by the following story, from the "Grammaire Coréene," which is intended to show the sympathy of the king Cheng-chong (1776 to 1800) with his subjects. It is entitled "A Trait of Royal Solicitude."

It was about New Year's that Cheng-chong walked about here and there within the palace enclosure. Having come to the place reserved for the candidates at the literary examinations, he looked through a crack in the gate. The competitors had nearly all gone away to spend the New Year holidays at home, and there remained only two of them, who were talking together.

"Well, all the others have gone off to spend New Year's at home; isn't it deplorable that we two, having no place to go to, must be nailed here?"

"Yes, truly," said the other; "you have no longer either wife, children, or house. How is this?"

"Listen to my story," said the first man. "My parents, thinking of my marriage, had arranged my betrothal, but some time before the preparations were concluded, my future grandfather died, and it became necessary to wait three years. Hardly had I put off mourning, when I was called on to lament the death of my poor father. I was now compelled to wait still three years. These three years finished, behold my mother-in-law who was to be died, and three years passed away. Finally, I had the misfortune to lose my poor mother, which required me to wait again three years. And so, three times four—a dozen years—have elapsed, during which we have waited the one for the other. By this time she, who was to be my wife, fell ill. As she was upon the point of death, I went to make her a visit. My intended brother-in-law came to see me, found me, and said, 'Although the ceremonies of marriage have not been made, they may certainly consider you as married, therefore come and see her.' Upon his invitation I entered her house, but we had hardly blown a puff of smoke, one before the other, than she died.

"Seeing this, I have no more wished even to dream at night.

Thatched House near Seoul. (From a photograph, 1876.)

I am not yet married. You may understand, then, why I have neither wife, children, nor home."

In his turn the other thus spoke : "My house was extremely poor. Our diet looked like fasting. We had no means of freeing ourselves from embarrassment. When the day of the examination came I presented myself. During my absence my wife contrived in such a manner, that putting in the brazier a farthing's worth of charcoal, she set a handful of rice to cook in a skillet, and settled herself to wait for me. She served this to me every time I came back. But I never obtained a degree. The day on which I was at last received as a bachelor of arts, on returning after examination, I found that she had as before lighted the charcoal, put to boil a dish of soup, and seating herself before the fire, she waited. In this position she was dead.

"At sight of this my grief was without bounds. Having no desire to contract a new union, I have never re-married."

Hearing these narratives, Cheng-chong was touched with pity. Entering the palace, seating himself upon the throne, and having had the two scholars brought in, he said to them :

"All the other scholars have gone to their homes to spend New Year's. Why have not you two gone also?" They answered, "Your servants having no house to go to, remained here."

"What does that mean?" said Cheng-chong. "The fowls and the dogs, oxen and horses have shelter. The birds have also a hole to build their nests in. Can it be that men have no dwelling? There should be a reason for this. Speak plainly." One of the scholars answered : "Your servant's affairs are so-and-so. I have come even till now without re-marriage. It is because I have neither wife, child, nor family."

The story being exactly like that which he had heard before, the king cried out, "Too bad!"

Then addressing the other, he put this question : "And you, how is it that you are reduced to this condition?" He answered . "My story is almost the same."

"What do you wish? Speak!" replied the king.

"The circumstances being such and such, I am at this moment without wife and without food. That is my condition."

As there was in all this nothing different from the preceding, the king, struck with compassion, bestowed upon them immediately lucrative offices.

If he had not examined for himself, how could he have been able to know such unfortunate men, and procure for them so happy a position in the world? In truth, the goodness of his Majesty Cheng-chong has become celebrated.

CHAPTER XXXII.

OUT-DOOR LIFE.—CHARACTERS AND EMPLOYMENTS.

Six public roads of the first class traverse the peninsula and centre at the capital. They are from twenty to thirty feet in width, with ditches at the side for drainage. One of these begins near the ocean, in Chulla Dō, and in general follows the shores of the Yellow Sea through three provinces to Tong-chin opposite Kang-wa Island, and enters the capital by branch roads. Another highway passes through the interior of the three provinces bordering the Yellow Sea, and enters Seoul by the southern gate. Hamel and his fellow-captives journeyed by this road. The road by which the annual embassy reaches Peking, after leaving the capital, passes through Sunto and Ping-an and Ai-chiu, crosses the Neutral Strip, and enters Manchuria for Peking by way of Mukden. This was the beaten track of the French missionaries, and the shipwrecked men from the United States and Japan, and is the military road from China. It is well described, with a good map, in Koei-Ling's "Journal of a Mission into Corea," which Mr. F. Scherzer has translated for us.

From Fusan and Tong-nai, in the southeast, Seoul is reached by no less than three roads. One strikes westward through Chung-chong, and joins the main road coming up from the south. Another following the Nak-tong River basin, crosses the mountains to Chulla, and enters Seoul by the south gate. Eight river crossings must be made by this road, over which Konishi marched in 1593. The third route takes a more northerly trend, follows the sea-coast to Urusan, and passing through Kion-chiu, enters the capital by the east gate.

The fifth great road issuing from the north gate of the capital passes into Kang-wen, and thence upward to Gensan, and to the frontiers at the Tumen River.

The roads of the second class are eight or nine feet wide, and without side ditches. They ramify through all the provinces, but are especially numerous in the five southern. The three northern circuits, owing to their mountainous character, are but poorly furnished with highways, and these usually follow the rivers.

The third class roads, which are nothing more than bridle-paths, or trails, connect the villages.

The hilly nature of the country, together with the Asiatic apathy to bestowing much care on the public highways, makes travelling difficult. Inundations are frequent, though the water subsides quickly. Hence in summer the road-beds are dust, and in winter a slough of mud. Macadamized, or paved roads, are hardly known, except for short lengths. Few of the wide rivers are bridged, which necessitates frequent fordings and ferriages. Stone bridges, built with arches, are sometimes seen over streams not usually inundated, but few of the wooden bridges are over one hundred and eighty feet long.

In one respect the roads are well attended to. The distances are well marked. At every *ri* is a small, and at every three *ri* a large mound, surmounted with an inscribed post or " mile-stone," called *chang-sung*. They are two, six, and even ten feet in length.

In ancient times, it is said, there was a man named Chang-sung, who killed his servant and wife. When punished, his head was placed on a small mound. Legend even declares that it was successively exposed on all the distance mounds in the kingdom. This is said to be the origin of the bournes or distance-mounds, which suggests, as Mr. Adams has shown, the *termini* of the Romans. When of stone, they are called *pio-sek*, but they are often of wood, rudely carved or hacked out of a whole tree by an axe into the exaggerated form of a man, and are of a ludicrous or absurd appearance. The face is meant to be that of the murderer Chang-sung. The author of " A Forbidden Land " mistook these for " village idols," and was surprised to find the boys in some cases sacrilegiously kicking about some that had rotted down or fallen. The " gods of the roads " may, however, have their effiges, which are worshipped or profaned.

All distances in every direction are measured from the front gate of the magistrates' offices, the standard of all being the palace at Seoul. Not the least interesting sights to the traveller are the memorial stones set up and inscribed with a view to commemorate local or national worthies, or the events of war, famine, or philanthropy. The Coreans are " idolaters of letters," and the erection of memorial tablets or columns occasionally becomes a passion. Sometimes the inscriptions are the means of stirring up patriotism, as the following inscription shows. It was graven on a stone in front of a castle erected after the French and American expeditions, and was copied by a Japanese correspondent.

"It is nothing else than selling the kingdom into slavery, in order to avoid war, to make peace without fighting when any Western nation comes to attack it; such should never be done even by our descendants thousands of years hence."

In this country, in which sumptuary laws prevent the humbler classes from travelling on horseback, and where wagons and steam-roads are unknown, the roads are lively with numerous foot-passengers. Palanquins are used by the better classes and the wealthy. The rambling life of many of the people, the goodly numbers of that character not unknown in Christendom—the tramp—the necessities of trade, literary examinations, government service, and holy pilgrimages, prevent too many weeds from growing in the highways. In travelling over the high roads one meets a variety of characters that would satisfy a Corean Dickens, or the Japanese author who wrote the *Tokaidō Hizakurigé* (Leg-hair, *i.e.*, "Shanks' mare," on the East Sea Road). Bands of students on their way to the capital or provincial literary examinations, some roystering youths in the full flow of spirits, are hastening on, others, gray-headed and solemn, are wending their way to fail for the twentieth time. Pompous functionaries in umbrella-hats, on horseback, before whom ordinary folks dismount or kneel or bow, brush past with noisy attendants. Pilgrims in pious garb are on their way to some holy mountain or famous shrine, men to pray for success in business, women to beseech the gods for offspring. Here hobbles along the lame or rheumatic, or the pale-faced invalid is borne to the hot springs. Here is a party of pic-nickers, or poets intent on the joys of drink, verse, and scenery. Here a troop of strolling players or knot of masqueraders are in peripatetic quest of a livelihood, toiling fearfully hard in order to escape settled industry. Nobles in mourning pass with their faces invisible. Postal slaves, women doing the work of express agents in forwarding parcels, pass the merchant with his loaded pack-horses returning from Sunto, or going to Gensan. There a packman is doing horse's work in transportation. Here an ox laden with brushwood is led by a woman. Beggars, corpses, *kang-si*, or men dead of hunger in times of famine, make the lights and shadows of life on the road.

There are other methods of travel besides those of horseback, on foot, and sedan chair, for oxen are often straddled by the men, and poor women travel on an ox, in a sort of improvised palanquin having four poles recurved to centre and covered with robe or cloak. In winter, among the mountains not only in the north, but even in Chulla, the people go on racquettes or snow-shoes. These are in shape like a battledore, and are several feet long. At regular distances are *yek*, or relays or offices, at which sit clerks or managers under government auspices, with hered-itary slaves or serfs, porters, guides, mail-couriers, and pack-horses. These await the service of the traveller, especially of official couriers, the finer beasts being reserved for journeying dignitaries.

All these throughout a certain district, of which there are sev-eral in each province, are under the direction of the *Tsal-peng*, or Director of Posts. Kiung-sang, the province having the greatest number of roads, has also the best equipment in the way of post-officers, relays, and horses. The following table from Dallet shows the equipment of the eight provinces :

	Post Superin-tendents.	Relays.	Horses.
Kiung-Kei	6	47	449
Chung-chong	5	62	761
Chulla	6	53	506
Kiung-sang	11	115	1,700
Kang-wen	4	78	447
Wang hei	3	28	396
Ham-kiung	3	58	792
Ping-an	2	30	311
	40	471	5,362

Yet with this provision for locomotion, the country is very deficient in houses for public accommodation. Inns are to be found only along the great highways, and but rarely along the smaller or sequestered roads. This want arises, perhaps, not so much from the poverty of the people, as from the fact that their proverbial hospitality does away with the necessity of numerous inns. The Coreans have been so often represented, or rather mis-

represented, as inhospitable, fierce, and rude by foreigners, that
to give an inside view of them as seen through information gathered from the French missionaries in Corea is a pleasant task.
From them we may learn how much the white-coated peninsulars
are like their cousins, the Japanese, and that human nature in
good average quantity and quality dwells under the big hats of
the Coreans. The traveller usually takes his provisions along with
him, but he need not eat it out-doors. As he sits along the way-
side, he will be invited into some house to warm his food. When
obliged to go some distance among the mountains to cut wood or
make charcoal, a man is sure to find a hut in which he can lodge.
He has only to bring his rice. The villagers will cook it for him,
after adding the necessary pickles or sauces. Even the oxen,
except during the busy season, are easily obtained on loan.

The great virtue of the Coreans is their innate respect for and
daily practice of the laws of human brotherhood. Mutual assistance and generous hospitality among themselves are distinctive
national traits. In all the important events of life, such as marriages and funerals, each one makes it his duty to aid the family
most directly interested. One will charge himself with the duty
of making purchases ; others with arranging the ceremonies. The
poor, who can give nothing, carry messages to friends and relatives in the near or remote villages, passing day and night on foot
and giving their labors gratuitously. To them, the event is not a
mere personal matter, but an affair of public interest.

When fire, flood, or other accident destroys the house of one
of their number, neighbors make it a duty to lend a hand to rebuild. One brings stone, another wood, another straw. Each, in
addition to his gifts in material, devotes two or three days' work
gratuitously. A stranger, coming into a village, is always assisted
to build a dwelling.

Hospitality is considered as one of the most sacred duties. It
would be a grave and shameful thing to refuse a portion of one's
meal with any person, known or unknown, who presents himself
at eating-time. Even the poor laborers, who take their noon-meal
at the side of the roads, are often seen sharing their frugal nourishment with the passer-by. Usually at a feast, the neighbors
consider themselves invited by right and custom. The poor man
whose duty calls him to make a journey to a distant place does
not need to make elaborate preparatons. His stick, his pipe,
some clothes in a packet hung from his shoulder, some cash in

his purse, if he has one, and his outfit is complete. At night, instead of going to a hotel with its attendant expense, he enters some house, whose exterior room is open to any comer. There he is sure to find food and lodging for the night. Rice will be shared with the stranger, and, at bed-time, a corner of the floor-mat will serve for a bed, while he may rest his head on a foot-length of the long log of wood against the wall, which serves as a pillow. Even should he delay his journey for a day or two, little or nothing to his discredit will be harbored by his hosts. In Corea, the old proverb concerning fish and company after three days does not seem to hold good.

As may be imagined, such a system is prolific in breeding beggars, tramps, blackmailers, and lazy louts, who "sponge" upon the benevolently disposed. Rich families are often bored by these self-invited parasites, who eat with unblushing cheek at their tables for weeks at a time. They do not even disdain—nay, they often clamor for—clothing as well. To refuse would only result in bringing down calumny and injury. Peddlers, strolling players, astrologers, etc., likewise avail themselves of the opportunities, and act as plundering harpies. Often whole bands go round quartering themselves on the villages, and sometimes the government is called upon to interpose its authority and protect the people.

Corea is full of Micawbers, men who are as prodigal as avaricious, who when they have plenty of money, scatter it quickly. When flush they care only to live in style, to treat their friends, to satisfy their caprices. When poverty comes, they take it without complaint, and wait till the wheel of fortune turns again to give them better days. When by any process they have made some gain by finding a root of ginseng, a bit of gold ore, a vein of crystal, what matters it? Let the future take care of itself. Hence it happens that the roads are full of men seeking some stroke of luck, hoping to discover at a distance what they could not find at home, to light upon some treasure not yet dug up or to invent some new means of making money. People forever waiting for something to turn up emigrate from one village to another, stop a year or two, and then tramp on, seeking better luck, but usually finding worse.

Strolling companies of mountebanks, players and musicians, in numbers of five, six, or more, abound in Chō-sen. They wander up and down through the eight circuits, and, in spring and sum-

19

mer, earn a precarious and vagabond livelihood. Their reputation among the villagers is none of the best, being about on a par with that of the gypsies, or certain gangs of railroad surveyors of our own country. They often levy a sort of blackmail upon the people. They are jugglers, acrobats, magicians, marionette players, and performers on musical instruments. Some of them display an astonishing amount of cleverness and sleight of hand in their feats. In the villages crowds of gaping urchins are their chief spectators, but in the large cities they are invited to private houses to give exhibitions and are paid for it. When about to begin a performance, they secure attention by whistling on the nail of their little finger. On the occasion of the anniversary of some happy event, a public fête day, a marriage or a social company, the lack of what we call society—that is, social relations between gentlemen and ladies—is made up, and amusement is furnished by these players, engaged for an evening or two. The guests fully appreciate the "hired music," and "best talent" thus secured for a variety entertainment. The company of one class of these "men of society," or *pang-tang*, a kind of "professional diner-out," is so desirable that several are taken along by the ambassadors to China to amuse them on their long and tedious journey, especially at nights. The *chang-pu* are character-comedians, who serenade the baccalaureates that have passed successfully the government examinations. They play the flute and other instruments of music, forming the escort which accompanies the graduate on his visits to relatives and officials. A band of performers is always attached to the suite of ambassadors to China and Japan, or when visiting a foreign vessel.

A character common to Corea and Japan is the singing-girl, who is also a great aid in making life endurable to the better class of Coreans, whose chief business it is to kill time. The singing-girl is the one poem and picture in the street life of the humbler classes, whose poverty can rarely, if ever, allow them to purchase her society or enjoy her charms and accomplishments. Socially, her rank is low, very low. She is herself the child of poverty and toil. Her parents are poor people, who gladly give up their daughter, if of pretty face and form, to a life of doubtful morals, in order that she may thereby earn her own support and assist her parents. She herself gladly leaves the drudgery of the kitchen, and the abject meanness of the hovel, to shine in the palace and the mansion. Her dress is of finest fabric, her luxuriant black hair is bound with skill and grace, her skin is whitened by artificial cosmetics as far as possible, and with powder, paint, and pomatum, she spends much of her life before the looking-glass, studying in youth to increase, and in womanhood to retain, her charms. At home, she practises her music, occasionally enlivening a party of her humble neighbors. As she passes along the street, fresh, clean, bright, and pretty, she may dispense smiles for popularity's sake, but her errand is to the houses of the wealthy, and especially to the official, who, for his own amusement as he dines alone, or for his friends in social gathering, may employ from two to twenty *geishas* (as the Japanese call them). Most Corean cities have these geishas, who form themselves into a sort of guild for fixed prices, etc. Often they organize complete bands or choirs, by which music may be had in mass and volume. At a feast they serve the wine, fill and pass the dishes, and preside generally at the table. When eating has fairly begun, they sing (chant), play the guitar, recite in pantomine or vocally, and furnish general amusement. The dancing is usually not of an immoral character. Such a life, however, amid feast and revel, wine and flattery, makes sad wreck of many of them, morally and physically. A large proportion of the most beautiful girls become concubines to wealthy men or officials, or act as ladies of the chamber (brevet wives) to young men and widowers. Not a few join the business of prostitutes with that of musicians. Nevertheless, it is quite possible for a respectable family to enjoy a pleasant and harmless evening by the aid of the lively geishas. Of course, Seoul is the chief headquarters of the fairest and most accomplished geishas, who are, as a class, the best educated of their sex in Corea.

The theatre, proper, does not seem to exist in Corea. The substitute and nearest approach to it is recitation in monologue of certain events or extracts from the standard or popular histories, a single individual representing the successive rôles. The histrionic artist pitches his tabernacle of four posts in some popular street or corner. He spreads mats for a roof or shade from the sun in front, and for a background in the rear. A platform, and a box to squat on, with a small reading-desk, and a cup of gingery water to refresh his palate, complete his outfit.

A few rough benches or mats constitute all the accommodation for the audience. A gaping crowd soon collects around him, his auditors pull out their pipes, and refreshment venders improve the occasion for the chance sale of their viands. With his voice trained to various tones and to polite and vulgar forms of speech, he will hold dialogues and conversations, and mimic the attitude and gestures of various characters. The trial of a criminal before a magistrate, the bastinado, a quarrel between husband and wife, scenes from high life and low life will be in turn rendered. He will imitate the grave tones and visage of the magistrate, the piteous appeals, the cries and groans and contortions of the victim under torture, the angry or grumbling voice of the husband, the shrill falsetto of the scolding shrew or the shower of tears and the piteous appeals of the wife. Smiles, frowns, surprise, sorrow, and all the emotions are simulated, and the accompaniment of voice is kept up with jokes, puns, bon-mots, irony, or well-expressed pathos. In short, the reciter is a theatrical stock company, and a band of minstrels, rolled into one person. For the use of beginners, and the mediocrity of the profession, there are a number of "jest-books," collections of jokes and anecdotes, more or less threadbare, and of varying moral quality, from which speakers may prime for the occasion. With the advanced of the profession, however, most of the smart sayings are original and off-hand. The habitués of the booths have their "star" favorite, as theatre-goers with us go into raptures over their actors. Able men make a good living at the business, as they "pass round the hat" to take up a collection in the audience. This usually comes at the most telling point of the narrative, when the interest of the hearers is roused to the highest pitch (or when it is to be "continued in our next," as the flash newspapers say). Sometimes the speaker will not go on till the collection is deemed by the tyrant a sufficient appreciation of his talents. In addition to their public street income, the best of them are often invited to perform in private houses, at family reunions, social parties, and as a rule, in visits to dignitaries by candidates who have won degrees.

The Corean gamut, differing from the scale used in European countries, makes a fearful and wonderful difference in effect upon our ears. Some of their melodies upon the flute are plaintive and sweet, but most of their music is distressing to the ear and desolating to the air. One hearer describes their choicest pieces as "the most discordant sounds that ever were emitted under the name of music from brass tubes." Some of the flute music, however, is very sweet. As most of the ancient music of Japan is of Corean origin, one can get a fair idea of the nature of the sounds that delight a Corean ear from the music of the imperial band of

Tōkiō, which plays the classical scores. Yet it is evident that the modern tunes of Seoul are not melodious to Japanese auditory nerves. One would think that, as the mikado's subjects "hear themselves as others hear them" when Corean musicians play, they would be delighted. On the contrary, Corean music seems to horrify and afflict the Japanese ear. Evidently, in the course of centuries the musical scales of the two countries, originally identical, have altered in tone and interval. Wan-ka is the father of Corean music—though the mere fact that he belonged to antiquity would secure his renown. The various stringed musical instruments known are the *kemunko*, a kind of large guitar ; the *kanyakko*, mandolin ; the *ko-siul*, or guitar of twenty-five strings ; and the five-stringed harp or violin. The wind instruments comprise a whole battery of flutes, long and short trumpets, while cymbals, drums, and other objects of percussion are numerous. Ambassadors and other high officers at home, and when on duty to foreign countries, are accompanied by a band of musicians. Laborers on government works are summoned to begin and end work by music, but the full effect of a musical salvo is attained at the opening and closing of the city gates. Then the sound is most distressing—or most captivating, according as the ears are to the manner born, or receive their first experience of what tortures the air may be made to vibrate.

The chief out-door manly sport in Corea is, by excellence, that of archery. It is encouraged by the government for the national safety in war, and nobles stimulate their retainers to excellence by rewards. Most gentlemen have targets and arrow-walks for practice in their gardens. At regular times in the year contests of skill are held, at which archers of reputation compete, the expense and prizes being paid for out of the public purse. Hamel says the great men's retainers have nothing to do but to learn to shoot. The grandees rival each other in keeping the most famous archers, as an Englishman might his fox-hounds or as the daimiōs of Japan formerly vied with each other in patronizing the fattest and most skilful wrestlers. Other manly sports are those of boxing and fist-fights. Young men practice the "manly art" in play with each other, and at times champions are chosen by rival villages and a set-to between the bruisers is the result, with more or less of broken heads and pulpy faces. In large cities the contestants may come from different wards of the same city. In Seoul, usually in the first month, there are some lively tussles between picked champions, with betting and cheering of the backers of either party. Often these trials of skill degenerate into a free fight, in which clubs and stones are used freely; cracked skulls and loss of life are common. The magistrates do not usually interfere, but allow the frolic to spend itself.

Another class of men worthy of notice, and identified with out-door life, are the sportsmen. The bird-hunters never shoot on the wing. They disguise themselves in skins, feathers, straw, etc., and lurk in some coigne of vantage to bring down the game that comes within their range. The skilled fowler understands perfectly how to imitate the cries of the various birds, particularly that of the pheasant calling his mate. By this means most of the female pheasants are captured. The call used is an iron whistle, shaped like the apricot-stone, and simliar to that used by the Japanese hunters. The method of hunting the deer is as follows: During the months of June and July deer-horn commands a very high price, for it is at this season that the deer-horns are developing, and the "spike-bucks" are special prizes. A party of three or four hunters is formed. They beat up the mountain sides during several days, and, at night, when obliged to cease for awhile, they have a wonderful instinct for detecting the trail of the game, except when the earth is too dry. Usually they come up to their game on the third day, which they bring down with a gunshot. The horn is sold to the native physicians or is exported to China and Japan, where hartshorn and valuable medicines are concocted from it. A successful deer-hunt usually enables a hunter to live on his profits for a good part of the year, and in some cases individuals make small fortunes. Those who hunt bears wait for the occasion when the mother bear leads her cubs to the seashore to feast them on the crabs. Then the hunters bide their time till they see the mother lifting up the heavy rocks on edge, while the little cubs eat the crabs. The hunters usually rush forward and assault the bear, which, frightened, lets fall the rock, which crushes the cub. When on the open field or shore they do not fire at the she-bear, unless sure of killing her. For the various parts of the animal good prices await the hunter who sells. In addition to the proceeds from hide, flesh, fat, and sinews, the liver and gall of the brute, supposed to possess great potency in medicine, are sold for their weight in silver. In another chapter we have written of the tiger-hunters and their noble game.

Gambling and betting are fearfully common habits in Corea, and kite-flying gives abundant occasion for money to change hands. The two months of the winter, during which the north wind blows, is "kite time." The large and strong kites are flown with skill, requiring stout cords and to be held by young men. A large crowd usually collects to witness the battle of the kites, when the kites are put through various evolutions in the air, by which one seeks to destroy, tear, or saw off the string of the other.

Resources for in-door amusement are chiefly in the form of gossip, story-telling, smoking, lounging, and games of hazard, such as chess, checkers, and backgammon. The game of chess is the same as that played in Japan and China. Card-playing, though interdicted by law, is habitual among the common people. The nobles look upon it as vulgar amusement beneath their dignity. The people play secretly or at night, often gambling to a ruinous extent. It is said that the soldiers, especially those on guard, and at the frontiers, are freely allowed to play cards, as that is the surest way to keep them awake and alert in the presence of enemies, and as safeguards against night attacks. They shuffle and cut the cards as we do. Games with the hands and fingers, similar to those in Japan, are also well known.

In pagan lands, where a Sabbath, or anything like it, is utterly uknown alike to the weary laborer, the wealthy, and the men of leisure, some compensation is afforded by the national and religious holidays. These in Corea consist chiefly of the festal occasions observed in China, the feasts appropriate to the seasons, planting, and harvest, the Buddhist saints' anniversaries, the king's birthday, and the new year.

Among the poorer classes the families celebrate the birthday of the head of the family only, but among the noble and wealthy, each member of the family is honored with gifts and a festal gathering of friends. There are certain years of destiny noticed with extra joy and congratulations, but the chief of all is the sixty-first year. With us, the days of man are three score years and ten, but in the hermit kingdom the limit of life is three score years and one, and the reason is this: The Coreans divide time according to the Chinese cycle of sixty years, which is made up of two series of ten and twelve each respectively. Every year has a name after the zodiacal sign, or one of the five elements. The first birthday occurring after the entire revolution of the cycle is a very solemn event to a sexagenarian, and the festival commemorative of it is

called *Wan-kap*. All, rich and poor, noble and vulgar, observe
this day, which definitely begins old age, when man, having passed
the acknowledged limit of life, must remember and repose. When
it happens—a rare event—that the sixty-first anniversary of a
wedding finds both parties alive, there are extraordinary rejoicings, and the event is celebrated like our "diamond weddings."
For both these feasts children and friends must strain every
nerve, and spend all their cash to be equal to the occasion and to
spread the table for all comers ; for at such a time, not only the
neighbors, but often the whole country folk round are interested.
A silk robe for the honored aged, new clothes for themselves,
and no end of wine and good cheer for friends, acquaintances,
hangers-on, country cousins, and strangers from afar, must be
provided without stint. Poems are recited, games and sports
enjoyed, minstrels sing and dance, and recitations are given. All
come with compliments in their mouths—and a ravenous appetite.
All must be fed and none turned away, and the children of the
honored one must be willing to spend their last coin and econo-
mize, or even starve, for a year afterward. It is often as dreadful
an undertaking as a funeral pageant in other lands. In the event
of the queen, royal mother, or king, reaching the sixty-first birthday the profusion and prodigality of expense and show reaches a
height of shameful extravagance. All the prisons are opened by
general amnesty, and the jail-birds fly free. An extraordinary
session of examiners is held to grant degrees. In the capital all
the grandees present themselves before the king with gifts and
homage. In all the rural districts, a large picture of the king is
hung up in a noted place. The chief magistrate, preceded by
music and followed by his satellites, and all the people proceed to
the place and prostrate themselves before the effigy, offering their
congratulations. In the capital the soldiers receive gifts from the
court, and the day is a universal holiday for the entire nation.

Almost as matter of course, the festivals are used as means of
extortion and oppression of the people by the officials, who grind
the masses mercilessly to provide the necessary resources for the
waste and luxury of the capital and the court. New Year's day is
not only the greatest of all Corean feasts in universal observance,
but is also the only real Sabbath time of the year, when for days
together all regular employments cease and rejoicing reigns supreme. All debts must be paid and accounts squared up, absen-
tees must return, and children away from home must rejoin the

family. The magistrates close the tribunals, no arrests are made, and prisoners held to answer for slight offences are given leave of absence for several days, after which they report again as prisoners. All work, except that of festal preparation, ought to cease during the last three days of the old year. It is etiquette to begin by visits on New Year's Eve, though this is not universal.

On New Year's morning salutations or calls are made on friends, acquaintances, and superiors. To this rule there must be no exception, on pain of a rupture of friendly relations. The chief ceremony of the day is the sacrifice at the tablets of ancestors. Proceeding to the family tombs, if near the house, or to the special room or shelf in the dwelling itself, the entire family make prostrations. Costly ceremonies, with incense-sticks, etc., regulated according to the family purse, follow. This is the most important filial and religious act of the year. In cases where the tombs are distant, the visit must not be postponed later than during the first month. After the ancestral sacrifices, comes the distribution of presents, which are enclosed in New Year's boxes. These consist of new dresses, shoes, confectionery, jewelry for the boys and girls, and various gifts, chiefly cooked delicacies, for neighbors, friends, and acquaintances. For five days the festivities are kept up by visits, social parties, and entertainments of all sorts. The ordinary labors of life are resumed on the sixth day of the new year, but with many, fun, rest, and frolic are prolonged during the month.

The tenth day of the second month is the great house-cleaning day of the year, when mats are taken up and shaken, the pots, kettles, and jars scoured, and the clothing renovated.

Tomb-cleaning day occurs in the third month. On this occasion they make offerings of food to their ancestors, and cleanse tombs and tablets. It is a busy time in the graveyards, to which women transfer their straw scrubbers, dippers, and buckets, when monuments and idols are well soused and scoured. It is more like a picnic, with fun and work in equal proportions.

The third day of the third month comes in spring, and is the great May-day and merrymaking. The people go out on the river with food and drink, and spend the day in feasting and frolic. Others wander in the peach-orchards to view the blossoms. Others so inclined, enjoy themselves by composing stanzas of poetry.

On the eighth day of the fourth month the large cities are illuminated with paper lanterns of many colors, and people go out on hills and rivers to view the gay sights and natural scenery.

The fifth day of the fifth month is a great festival day, on which the king presents fans to his courtiers.

On the fifteenth day of the seventh month occurs the ceremony of distributing seed. The king gives to his officials one hundred kinds of seed for the crops of the next year.

On the fifteenth day of the eighth month sacrifices are offered at the graves of ancestors and broken tombs are repaired.

The chrysanthemum festival is one of much popular interest. Among the most brilliant flowers of the peninsula are the chrysanthemums, which are cultivated with great pride and care by gentlemen and nobles. The flower is brought to unusual perfection by allowing but a single flower to grow upon one stem. They are often cultivated apart, under oiled paper frames. On the ninth day of the ninth month the perfected blossoms are in their glory, and the owner of a crop of brilliant chrysanthemums invites his friends to his house to feast and enjoy the sight of the blooms. The florists exhibit their triumphs, and picnic parties enjoy the scenery from the bridges and on the mountains.

The article chiefly used for pastry among oblique-eyed humanity is what the Japanese call *mochi*, a substance made by boiling rice and pounding it into a tough mass resembling pie-crust. Like oysters, it may be eaten "in every style," raw, warmed, baked, toasted, boiled, or fried. It occupies an important place in ceremonial offerings to the dead, in the temple, and in household festal decoration. It is made in immense quantities, and eaten especially at New Year's time, and on the two equinoctial days of the year. Another favorite mixed food for festive occasions is "red rice" and beans. The Corean housewife takes as much pains to color the rice properly as a German lavishes upon his meerschaum, and if the color fails, or is poor, it is a sign of bad luck.

The fourteenth day of the first month a person who is entering upon a critical year of his life makes an effigy of straw, dresses it up with his own clothing at evening, and casts it out on the road, and then feasts merrily during the whole night. Whatever happens to the man of straw thus kicked out of the house, is supposed to happen to the man's former self, now gone into the past; and Fate is believed to look upon the individual in new clothes as another man.

The fifth, fifteenth, and twenty-fifth of each month are called "broken days," on which they avoid beginning anything new. These are the "Fridays" of Chō-sen. In the beginning of each of the four seasons of the year they post up on the doors of their houses slips of paper, on which are written mottoes, such as "Longevity is like the South Mountain," "Wealth is like the Eastern Sea," etc.   Certain years in each person's life are supposed to be critical, and special care as to health, food, clothing, new ventures, etc., must be taken during these years, which are ended with a feast, or, what is more economical, a sigh of relief.

The fifteenth day of the first month is called "Stepping on the Bridge."   A man and woman go out together over the bridge at the rising of the moon and view the moonlit scenery, indulging meanwhile in refreshments, both of the solid and liquid sort.   It is believed that if one crosses over seven bridges on this night, he will be free from calamities during the year.

Not the least interesting of the local or national festivals, are those held in memory of the soldiers slain in the service of their country on famous battle-fields.   Besides holding annual memorial celebrations at these places, which fire the patriotism of the people, there are temples erected to soothe the spirits of the slain.   Especially noteworthy are these monumental edifices, on sites made painful to the national memory by the great Japanese invasion of 1592–97, which keep fresh the scars of war.   A revival of these patriotic festivals has been stimulated by the fanatical haters of Japan, since this neighbor country broke away from Asiatic traditions.

Though much has been written concerning the population of Corea, we consider all conjectures of persons alike unfamiliar with the interior and the true sources of information as worthless. These random figures vary from 250,000 (!) to 6,000,000.   Dallet presumes a population of 10,000,000.   A rude enumeration made thirty years ago gives the number of houses at 1,700,000, and of the people at 7,000,000.   Our own opinion, formed after a study of the map and official lists of towns and cities, is that there are at least 12,000,000 souls in Chō-sen.   A Japanese correspondent of the Tōkiō *Hochi Shimlun*, writing from Seoul, states that a census made last year (1881) shows that there are 3,480,911 houses and 16,227,885 persons in the kingdom.

CHAPTER XXXIII.

SHAMANISM AND MYTHICAL ZOÖLOGY.

SHAMANISM is the worship of a large number of primitive North Asiatic tribes, having no idols except a few fetishes and some rude ancestral images or representations of the spirits of the earth and air. It is a gross mixture of sorcery and sacrificial ceremonies for the propitiation of evil spirits. These malignant beings are supposed to populate the earth, the clouds, and the air, and to be the cause of most of the ills suffered by man. They take various forms, chiefly those of animals whose structure and anatomy are more or less imaginary, each imp or demon being a composite creature, compiled from the various powers of locomotion, destruction, and defence possessed by the real creatures that inhabit water, earth, and air. Some of them, however, are gentle and of lovely form and mien. Their apparition on earth is welcomed with delight as the harbinger of good things to come. Confucius, the teacher, hailed by the Chinese as their holiest sage, and to whom even divine honors are paid, believed firmly in these portents and appearances. Chief among these mythic creatures are the phœnix, the kirin, the dragon, besides a variety of demons of various sizes, colors, habits, and character. Much of the mythology of Chō-sen is that common to Chinese Asia. Instead of a gallery of beautiful human, or partially human, presences like that of Greece, the mythology of China deals largely with mythic animals, though legendary heroes, sages, and supernatural beings in human form are not lacking. The four chief ideal creatures are the dragon, phœnix, tortoise, and kirin.

There is another animal which, though a living reality, the Coreans have idealized and gifted with powers supernatural and supra-animal, almost as many in number as those with which the Japanese have endowed the white fox. This is the tiger. They not only ascribe to him all the mighty forces and characteristics of which he is actually possessed, but popular superstition attributes to him the powers of flying, of emitting fire and hurling lightning. He is the symbol of strength and ubiquity, the standard of comparison with all dangers and dreadful forces, and the paragon of human courage. On the war-flags this animal is painted or embroidered in every posture, asleep, leaping, erect, couchant, winged, and holding red fire in his fore-paw. On works of art, cabinets, boxes, and weapons the tiger is most frequently portrayed and is even associated as an equal with the four supernatural beings. In ancient time he was worshipped.

The riong, or dragon, whose figure, as depicted in Corean art, is perhaps nothing more than a highly idealized form of an extinct geological species of saurian, is one of the four supernatural or spiritually endowed creatures. He is an embodiment of all the forces of motion, change, and power for offence and defence in animal life, fin, wing, tusk, horn, claws, with the mysterious attributes of the serpent. There are many varieties of the species dragon, which is the chief of scaly monsters. It possesses the gift of transformation and of rendering itself visible or invisible at will. In the spring it ascends to the skies and in the autumn buries itself in the watery depths.

It is this terrific manifestation of movement and power which the Corean artist loves to depict—always in connection with water, clouds, or the sacred jewel of which it is the guardian, and for which it battles, causing commotion in heaven and earth. The dragon is synonymous in Chinese philosophy with the third of the four creative influences and indicative of the East and Springtime, the blue dragon being the guardian of the East.

Another cycle of popular notions and artistic ideas is suggested by its change of bulk, for this omnipotent monster "becomes at will reduced to the size of a silkworm or swollen till it fills the space of heaven and earth. It desires to mount, and it rises until it affronts the clouds ; to sink, and it descends until hidden below the fountains of the deep." The dragon is the embodiment of the watery principle of the atmosphere, and its Protean shapes are but the varied ideal expression of the many forms and forces of water. Moisture in its fertilizing or destructive aspects—from the silent dew to the roaring tempest, from the trickling of a rill to the tidal wave that engulphs cities—blessed, terrible, gentle, irresistible, is symbolized by the dragon. The functions of the celestial dragon are to guard the mansions of the gods in heaven, so that they do not fall ; of the spiritual, to cause the wind to blow and produce rain for the benefit of mankind ; of the terrestrial, to mark out the courses of rivers and streams, while another watches over the hidden treasures concealed from mortals. This last is the dragon that presides over mines and gems, and which mortals must propitiate or overcome in order to gain the precious metals and minerals out of the earth. Intense belief in the dragon is one of the chief reasons why the mines in Chō-sen are so little worked, and the metals disturbed. The dragon pursuing the invaders of their sanctuaries or fighting each other to gain possession of the jewel balls or sacred crystals is a favorite subject in all art of Chinese parentage. Rarely is the whole figure of the writhing creature exposed. Partly hidden in clouds or water, he seems ever in motion. There are also four dragon-kings, who have their palaces in the world under the sea, one ruling in the northern, one in the eastern, one in the southern, and one in the western sea. The ministers and messengers of these four monarchs are the terrible dragons whose battles in the air and in the deep are the causes of the commotion of the elements. There is also a dragon without horns, and another that never ascends to the skies. The yellow dragon is reckoned the most honorable of his tribe. In common belief the dragon carries on his forehead a pear-shaped pearl, supposed to possess wondrous virtues of healing and power. Whoever possesses these jewels will be invincible, and the power of his descendants endure.

From its divine origin and character the dragon is symbolical of all that pertains to the emperor of Great China. Hence it is made use of not only by him, but by his vassal, the king of Chō-sen, and by his rival the mikado of Japan. Hence the significance of the trio of these sacred jewels on ornaments and instruments belonging to the royal family, whether embroidered on the robes of state worn by the king, surmounting the large drum of his musicians, or glistening in golden embroidery on the banners of his body-guard. The "dragon robe" and "dragon's bed," "dragon standard," refer to the mantle, throne, and flag of the king. In the popular speech, whatever is most excellent is compared to a dragon. A "dragon-child" is a paragon, a "dragon horse" is one of extraordinary speed. When "the fish has been metamorphosed into the dragon," some happy change or promotion has taken place—the student-competitor has received his degree of doctorate, or the office-holder has been told by royal appointemnt to "come up higher."

The kirin (kilin or lin) is another of the four supernatural creatures of Chinese philosophy and mythology, believed in by the Coreans, and depicted in Corean art especially as a symbol of peace and joy, and on articles used on auspicious and happy occasions. This beast, which to the Corean is a "living creature," has the body of a deer and the tail of an ox, usually highly curled and twisted in a manner to suggest the work of a hair-dresser. On its forehead is a single soft horn. It is said never to tread on or injure any living being. It is the emblem of perfect rectitude, and the incarnate essence of the five primordial elements of all things, viz. : water, fire, wood, metal, earth. It is considered the noblest form of the animal creation. Its appearance on the earth is ever regarded as a happy omen, as the harbinger of good government and the birth of good rulers. Hence the wealth of association to the Oriental mind in the kirin. The male beast is called ki and the female rin or lin. The two words combined form the general term kirin.

The tortoise is the centre of a great circle of pleasing superstitions, and hence is one of the set of symbols oftenest employed in Corean art. The practice of divination is mostly associated with tortoise-shell, the figuring of a tortoise's back having a mystic signification. In Chinese legend a divine tortoise emerged from the Yellow River, on the shell of which a sage discovered the system of numerals, and thus obtained the foundation of mathematics and the rudiments of philosophy. This tortoise was said to be the embodiment of the star in Ursa Major, and the progenitor of all the tortoise tribe. It can transform itself into other forms of life and lives to the age of ten thousand years. Hence it is the symbol of long life. It is said to conceive by thought alone. There are said to be ten kinds of tortoises, one of them being half dragon, half tortoise, and with a tail like a fringe of silver. This is the attendant of the god of waters, and hence is often used as the top of a well. The tortoise is also the symbol of immortality and strength, hence is often used over walls and places of entrance. Many Corean gateways are surmounted with huge tortoises sculptured in stone. The same idea is expressed in making the representations of this creature, cut from a single rock, the base for monumental tablets set into its back. The great seal of state, the regalia of sovereignty in Chō-sen, has the form of a tortoise. The phœnix is also represented as standing upon a tortoise. Closely connected with the Hindoo idea of the world resting on an elephant which stands on a tortoise, is the Chinese idea of "supporting the earth with the feet of a tortoise." A common idea in Chō-sen, as in China, is the huge tortoise which supports mountains on its back, and having a shell which is one thousand leagues in circumference.

The phœnix (fung-wang or hōwō), like the kirin, appears on the earth at or near the birth of a good ruler, and hence is the emblem of peace and good government. The male is called *fung*, or *ho*, and the female *wang*, or *wō*, hence the generic name fung-wang or hōwō. In its marvellous plumage the sheen of the five colors may be descried, each of which is typical of the five cardinal virtues. In figure it seems to be an ideal combination of the peacock and the golden pheasant, but with feathers wondrously curled and made into ringlets. It is not only a symbol of auspicious government, but of inseparable fellowship, and many stanzas of poetry refer to it as typical of courtship and conjugal love. In its voice are many intonations, to each of which a name is given. For this reason it is a favorite element in the decoration of musical instruments.

Another symbol often used is the Chinese lion, with marvellously curled hair and mane. Every tuft is a mass of fanciful ringlets, and the beast is so pictured as to make a masterpiece of ugliness and terror. The dog of the breed called *ngao*, so named after the earth-supporting tortoise, is also liberally furnished with tooth, nail, and hair. It usually cuts the figure of guardian on the edge or lid of vessels in which are kept treasures which, because they tempt the palate, tempt also the fingers that lift to the mouth. The marvellous creature called the Dog of Fo, or Buddha, usually associated with Chinese-Buddhist art, is believed to be of Corean origin. Jacquemart calls it the "Dog of Corea."

Other mythical creatures that have their existence in the Corean imagination are in the form of fishes and serpents. The in-é (fish-man or merman) is a sort of siren that is supposed to inhabit the Sea of Japan and the Eastern Sea, but whether partly fabulous or entirely real, we are unable to say. It is six or seven feet long, and in its head and body resembles a human being, as its nose, mouth, ears, and arms, or flippers, are covered with white skin without scales. It has a long and slender tail, like that of a horse. It suckles its young, and sheds tears when its offspring are captured. It is probable that this creature, though called a fish-man by the Coreans, is the animal of which we read, in several instances, being presented to the Manchiu emperors in Peking.

One of them inquired whether such a creature was known in Europe, and the Jesuit friar, producing a book, showed an engraving of one similar. Perhaps this "fish-man" is the same as a reported "dog-fish or shark," living in the seas around Quelpart, whose tears produce pearls.

The i-sium, a colossal marine creature, is purely imaginary, like the "earthquake-fish" of the Japanese, which causes the continent to shake. The word is pure Corean, and may answer to our symbol of vastness and uncertainty —the sea-serpent. Mr. Fergusson would doubtless find a new chapter for his "Tree and Serpent Worship" in Chō-sen, for, in the peninsula, not only are trees reverenced as the abode of spirits, but the *sa*, or snakes, are rarely, if ever, harmed. The people feed, venerate, and even worship them as the guardian genii of their households. The epkuron-gi (a pure Corean word) is the name by which they call the serpent which presides over their family Edens. Instead of being looked upon as the embodiment of the principle of evil, as in Semitic lore, their presence is hailed as an omen of blessing. They are treated like pets. In their heads they are believed to carry a precious jewel after they have lived long. A serpent often lives to be one thousand years old, and then bears in his front a glistening gem, called ya-kang-chiu, which name the people also apply to any

Battle-flag Captured by the Americans in 1871.

glittering stone, especially the diamond. The guardian serpent is represented as double-winged, with forked tongue, long and darting, flying among the clouds and protecting its worshippers by pursuing their enemies. The illustration here given is copied from one of the war-flags carried by the Corean mountaineers from their homes to the forts on the Han River, in 1871. The staff is tipped with pheasant-feathers and horse-hair.

Their fear of the serpent is the basis of their worship, and the

20

average Corean does not fail to take due precaution to guard against its sting. In addition to the ordinary *osa* or black snake, there is the venomous viper, *salmo*, which "kills its mother at birth." Its bite is considered exceedingly dangerous. The *tai-mang* is a great serpent. The flower called *kiuk-sa-wa* (snake-bane), or Eye of India, is believed by Coreans to keep away the reptiles, and hence is highly valued.

Hamel and the French missionaries agree in picturing Corea as a land well supplied with reptiles, serpents, and vermin of all sorts, and testify to the veneration of them by the people. In the folk-lore of the country, the beasts play a conspicuous part.

Another creature to whom wings rightfully belong is the *gin-sai*. This fabulous bird is capable of diffusing so venomous an influence that even its shadow poisons food.

Even the brief list of creatures which we have enumerated does not exhaust the list of the beings which are real and active to the imagination of the people. Science and Christianity are the remedies for this delirium tremens of paganism.

The ancient and still lingering belief in the powers of the air and all the creatures therein, visible and invisible, is reflected on their triangular and streamer-shaped war-banners. They believe that all these creatures and all the forces of nature are under the control of the spirits, who will give or withhold sunshine or rain, send blasting mildew and pestilence, or fertility, plenty and joy, according as they are pleased or displeased.

It will be seen at once what a soil the demagogue has for sowing dragons' teeth, and what frightful popular commotion may be stirred up by playing upon the fears of the populace. The most recent illustration of this is seen in the frightful massacre of the ministers and the Japanese, in July, 1882. The long drought having ruined the rice crop, the leaders of the anti-foreign faction persuaded the common people that the spirits were annoyed at the introduction of foreigners, and therefore withheld the rain. In this belief they were strengthened from the fact that it rained heavily for many hours after the Japanese had been driven out of Seoul.

CHAPTER XXXIV.

LEGENDS AND FOLK-LORE.

It is not difficult to appreciate or understand the history of people whose psychology is our own. We seem to look through white light in gazing at their past as told in the words of a language that grew in the same mental sunlight with our own. In eating fruit that grows on familiar intellectual soil, we may sometimes recognize a slightly strange flavor, but the pulp is good food which our mental stomach does not reject, but readily assimilates. Truth, like the moon, usually presents one side only, but the mass of mankind do not think of this, even if they know it. They go on blissfully imagining they have seen all sides, even the full orb.

With the history of the Aryan nations we are familiar, and think it is clear to us. We insist that we know we can understand what they did and that their thoughts need no translation to us.

A visitor at the American Centennial, or any exposition of the industry of all nations, sees before him for comparative study the art, symbols of religion, architecture, implements of domestic life, and all the outward expressions of inward ideas. They are the clothed or concrete soul of man under the varied civilizations of this planet. Standing before the exhibits of India—the home of the Aryan nations—the man of Western Christendom, as his mind's eye surveys the vastness of difference between him and the Hindoo, is yet able to bridge the gulf. The researches into language, art, myths, folk-lore, show him that the infancy of the two races was the same, and that modern differences are impertinent accidents. At bottom the Aryan and the Hindoo are brothers.

No such reconciliation of ideas is yet demonstrable between the Mongolian and the Aryan. Before the art, symbols, ideas, literature, language, and physical presence of the man of Cathay, no bridging of the gulf seems yet possible. He appears to be a man of another planet Language gives as yet little clue to a common origin ; art and symbol seem at the other pole, and in psychology the difference at present seems total and irreconcilable.

Hence, to attempt to write the history of a Turanian people by simply narrating bald facts in an occidental language, seems to be but putting another white skeleton in the museum of nations. Even the attempt, by a purely destructive method of criticism, to manufacture a body, or corpse, rather, of history, by hacking away all legend and tradition to get out what the critic is pleased to call "history," seems at once unnatural and false. It is like attempting to correlate the genius of Shakspeare with ounces of beef and cheese, or to measure the market value of poetry by avoirdupois. A history of an Asiatic people ought to be as much a history of mind, of psychology, as of facts or dynasties. Hence, in writing of a new and almost unknown people like the Coreans, we think it as important to tell what *they* believe to have happened, as to attempt to state what we think actually did happen. To understand a people we must know their thoughts, as well as their physical environment.

According to Corean tradition, the origin of their country and people is thus outlined:

Of old the land had neither prince nor chiefs. A Divine Being descended from heaven and took up his abode at the foot of a sandal-wood tree on the Ever-White Mountains. The people of the land became his subjects, made him their sovereign and called him Dan Kun (the Sandal Prince), and his realm Chō-sen (Morning Calm). This took place in the time of Tang Ti Yao (2356 B.C.). His first residence was at Ping-an. Later he transferred it to Pe-yo, where his descendants remained till the eighth year of the emperor Wu Ting of the Chang dynasty (1317 B.C.), when they were established in Mount Asstak. His descendants reigned in Chō-sen more than one thousand years, but nothing more is known of them after the period covered by their reign. Then followed the occupation of the country by the Chinese noble Ki Tsze.

The mythical origin and founding of Shinra is thus told in the local legends of the place. After the invasion of Chō-sen, by the Chinese emperor, many of the original inhabitants fled and scattered over the east coast. They made settlements on the mountains, in the valleys, and along the sea-shore, some of which in time grew to be cities and large towns. One day the attention of the head man of one of the villages was attracted by the neighing of horses toward a mountain. He went in the direction of the sounds, but instead of a horse he found an egg of extraordinary size, shaped like a gourd. Carefully breaking it open, he discovered a beautiful rosy boy-baby inside. The old man's heart was touched by the sight, and he took the child to his home and adopted it as his own. The boy grew up beloved of all who saw or knew him. When but thirteen years old, the elders of the six principal towns gathered together and chose him as their lord and master. They gave him a name signifying "Coming Out of the West," and to the country a name meaning "Born of the Gourd-egg." The new king took to wife a fair maiden who was reputed to be the offspring of a well-dragon. They reigned for sixty years, when their daughter succeeded to the throne.

In the fifth year of her reign she married a youth who had come from afar, whose origin was as wonderful as that of her own parents. His mother the queen had been delivered of an egg. Her husband, not enjoying such a form of offspring, threw the egg away, but the queen recovering it, carefully wrapped it in a silk napkin, and with many other treasures put it in a box and set it adrift on the sea. After many days the box was washed ashore on a distant coast. The fishermen who picked it up in their nets thought nothing of it, and threw it into the sea again. It drifted into one of the harbors of Shinra. An old woman finding it, opened the lid and found a lovely boy with a smile on his face. Carefully nourishing him, he grew up to be a man of strength, nine feet high. He excelled all other youths in bodily vigor and accomplishments. When the old woman first picked up the waif, there were a number of crows standing around the shore, and the crone gave him a name referring to the presence of these birds— "Opened in Presence of the Crows." Excelling in the knowledge of geomancy, he found a good place for a residence and built on it. Hearing of his renown, the queen of Shinra married him to her daughter.

One evening the newly made king heard a cock crow in the woods toward the west. He sent his servants after it, who found a small golden casket suspended from a tree. Under it a white cock was crowing. The servant reported the matter to his master. Another servant was despatched to the place. He returned with the box, which, being opened, was found to contain a boy baby, who was given the name signifying "The Golden Boy from the Grove in which the Cock crowed." The baby boy grew up and succeeded his father. In the reign of the twenty-second king of the line, the people of the country, then called Shin-han, changed the name of their country to Shinra.

In the "Grammaire Coréene" there are a number of speci‧ mens of folk-lore given in Corean and French, from which we extract a few of the most characteristic. The first one is an illustration of our universal human nature.

THE THREE WISHES.

There were once two old married folks who had not a single child, boy or girl. Extremely poor, they lived a pitiable life. One evening, when it was very cold in winter, after having supped, they gazed into the fire in the brazier, and sitting in their room face to face they warmed themselves a moment in silence, when the good old man thus spoke:

"For the rich the winter is an excellent season; their food is prepared in advance. Having no toil they have only to take their ease. But for the poor, it is a rough time when they have neither food for the mouth nor fuel. If they go out over the mountain through the rain or the snow to seek wood, they die of cold or frost."

The good dame replied: "They say that Heaven is just. Why then does he permit this? They say, besides, that when you pray to Heaven, it is easy to obtain that which you need. If we ask to become rich—" said she.

"You are right, do so," replied the husband.

And both prostrating themselves, prayed fervently to the Deity, when suddenly an angel appeared.

"In spite of your sin of murmuring, Heaven having pitied you, accords you three things, after which you can ask no more. Reflect well, choose, and ask." Saying this he disappeared.

The old man made this proposition: "If we ask riches, freedom from sickness, or long life—"

"No," said the old woman, "we should not enjoy these things properly if we do not have a child. What pleasure will it be?"

"Hold! I have not asked. What shall I do? If he had only said *four* things at the good moment! Why did he say only *three?* Since we wish to have a child, must we forego freedom from sickness, must we renounce riches, must we give up long life? It is hard to decide. Think, then, seriously this night, and decide to-morrow."

Breaking off their conversation, both sat plunged in reverie. At the moment of lying down to sleep, the old woman, stirring up the fire with the tongs, launched out with this reflection, "If we could have three or four feet of pudding to set to toast on this brazier, that would be royally excellent."

She spoke, and there was three feet of food placed by her side.

The husband, beside himself with rage, screamed out—

"Oh! what a woman! By one stroke you have lost all our benefits. To punish you I wish the pudding would hang itself on the point of your nose."

Immediately the pudding made a leap and attached itself to the old dame's nose.

At this the husband cried out, "Hello! Angry as I am, I have also by my fault lost a wish." Seizing the sausage to detach it, they pulled, first one, then the other, almost dislocating the nose, but the sausage held on.

"Alas!" said the woman in tears, "if this is always to remain hanging here, how can I live?"

The husband, on the contrary, without being at all disturbed, said, "If even yet our wish of fortune is fulfilled, we could make a tube of gold to hide this sausage, and then drawing it out at length, it will be only more beautiful to see."

The wife, still more miserable, cried out, "Oh, wretched me, only to think that fortune should wish to put it there. Well! whether you be rich or live long, as for me, I should like to kill myself."

Saying this she took a cord and went to strangle herself at the end of a beam. The husband, struck with fear, and touched with compassion, hastened to set her free.

"Stop," said he, "there remains one wish to us. Have your own way about it."

"If that is so, I wish that what hangs to my nose comes loose. Quick, quick, that it may go swift away. That is my chief wish."

She had hardly finished speaking when the sausage fell plump to the ground, and out of the midst of the heaven an angry voice was heard:

"You have obtained the three things which you wished for, and have you gained a great advantage? If you wish to enjoy true blessing in this world be content to live with what Heaven gives, and do not form vain desires."

The two old folks spitted the pudding, ate it, and from this night they abstained from foolish wishes.

On the morrow, agreeably to their supreme ambition, which was to have a baby, they found a little fatherless and motherless orphan. Having adopted it as their child, they gave him a good education and lived happily to extreme old age.

The following illustrates official shrewdness and rapacity:

THE HISTORY OF A NOSE.

In the chief city of Chulla, there was a politician who was in debt to the government to the amount of ten thousand strings of cash. Unable to pay the same, he was condemned to death. Cast into prison, he awaited only the orders of the king to carry out the sentence. As he had thought hard without discovering any means to get out of the affair, he bethought himself of a stratagem. So, addressing the jailer, he said:

"Helloa! you there, you'll do well to let me go free a little while."

"Helloa!" answered the jailer, "what wretched talk! After I have set free a man who ought to be put to death to-morrow or day after to-morrow, what shall *I* do?"

The prisoner replied, "Are we not friends both of us? If you do not let me go, who can save my life? Think over it a little and see. My wife, my children, my house, all I have, all my relations and friends being here, where

shall I fly ? If you set me at liberty for some moments not only will I not abscond but there will be found means for preserving my life safely. Do so."

As he thus besought him eagerly, the jailer, struck with compassion,
could not do otherwise than let him go.

So at midnight he presented himself before the door of the room where
the governor slept, and thus addressed him.

"Are you asleep ? Is your excellency sleeping ? "

Hearing the sound and astonished at recognizing the voice of the officer who
had been cast into prison and was to be executed in a short time, the governor asked.

"Who are you?"

"Your servant," answered the officer.

"A scoundrel who is at the point of being executed, how is it you are here?"

"If I may be allowed to enter to salute you," said the officer, "I have
something particular to say to you."

"Oh, well, come in and speak."

The officer entering, approached, sat down, and said :

"I pray your excellency to reflect and consider my purpose. If you put
your servant to death this will be simply one man of means less in the world,
and the money I owe will be lost to the government. What advantage will
you thus derive? If, on the contrary, you preserve my life there will be one
man more in the world, and I shall repay the whole of my debt to the government. Let me then live."

"If it ought to be so I wish you well in the matter."

"Your servant will come again, then, to-morrow, during the night, to see
you."

"Do as you will."

The morrow during the night the officer presented himself anew and asked
to be introduced. Approaching he made the prostrations before the governor,
drew from his sleeve a packet which he undid and took out a sketch representing a human nose. He immediately besought the governor to please put his
seal upon the sketch.

Agreeing to the proposal the governor imposed his seal.

The officer now associated three companions who were in the plot, and they
all assembled upon the coast of the Eastern Sea, where they found a populous
village, in the midst of which rose a high and grand mansion. Taking their
drink of spirits at a hotel in the suburbs of the next village beyond, they prepared to sup. Addressing their host they put this question :

"What is the name of the village which is just behind us? Whose is the
largest house ? "

The inn-keeper answered, "That is the house of a very rich noble. Last
year he received the degree of the doctorate and is eligible to fill very soon a
very high position under the government."

The officer taking with him one of his comrades repaired to the mansion,
where, as he noticed, everything showed abundant means, and thus spoke to
the son.

"As we have a secret affair to treat of, let us go into another room," said
the officer.

They did so. "See here, the king is very sick, and they have called all the physicians from all the eight provinces for a consultation. They have declared that the only means to obtain healing is to find the nose of a man just like this, and to concoct a remedy from it. This is why we have been commanded by the Court, where they have said to us, putting in our hand this sketch of the nose. 'Without distinction of place or person if you meet a nose similar to this, strike it off and produce it before us in this place.' Obeying this severe order we have been out many times without being able to find a nose conforming to the sketch, and thus far have made useless journeys, but now, without peradventure, your honorable father's nose exactly resembles this. We demand to see him, and wherever he may be we shall not depart till we have cut it off."

The son cried out: "*Perhaps* they do say such things!"

"Who dare oppose the government business? Hurry, hurry, strike it off and we'll go."

The son fell into a study and reflected.

"It is an affair of state. This is a matter which we cannot prevent. Cut it off, they say, but to cut off the nose of my old father, that is altogether impossible. The entire family, men, women, young and old, every one will be plunged into woe. You can bear away the half of our fortune at least, if you will go away without taking my father's nose."

The officer replied, "We had proposed to ourselves to depart only after having cut off the nose. However, as this is a matter of a son devoted to his father, and that they may not repress filial piety in others, we shall not cut off the nose. If you will give us a certain sum we will go elsewhere to procure a nose which we shall present to the king."

He accepted with thanks a sum equal to many times ten thousand strings of cash, for which he gave a receipt, told the sender of the money such a day, such a place, and on leaving offered this recommendation:

"Upon the whole, say nothing of this affair. If it should leak out, and the government comes to know that having found a proper nose we have been bribed not to cut it off, we shall be arrested and put to death, they will certainly cut off your father's nose and take your money also. Pray then be careful not to divulge this secret." Upon this they took their leave.

Overjoyed at not having his parent's nose amputated, but believing that the king on being informed would send again on this business, the son dared let no one know until the day of his father's death. Then breaking the silence he said, "I have bought my father's nose for ——— thousand strings of cash."

The story here told explains itself. Cheng-chong was the Haroun al Raschid of Corea.

AN INSTANCE OF ROYAL SOLICITUDE.

There was in Chō-sen a king called His Majesty Cheng-chong, who was celebrated in all the kingdom for his goodness. One night, disguised as a countryman, and accompanied only by a single companion, he started out from the midst of the capital to make a circuit in order to inform himself of the temper of his subjects, and to become himself acquainted with the details of their life.

Arrived at a certain point he looked in the window. There was a miser-able house, of which the outer dilapidation, extremely pitiable as it was, led him to suspect in the interior a state of things difficult to imagine. Eagerly wishing to know what it was, he punched a peep-hole in the paper door and perceived an old man weeping, a man in mourning singing, and a nun or widow dancing. Unable to divine the cause of this spectacle, he ordered his companion to call the master of the house.. The king's servant doing so, said :

" Is the proprietor of the house at home ? "

Hearing this voice the man in mourning made his appearance. His Majesty saluting him said :

" We have never before met."

" True," said the man in mourning, " but whence are you ? How is it that you should come to find me at midnight ? To what family do you belong ? "

Cheng-chong answered, " I am Mr. Ni, living at Tong-ku-an. As I was passing before your house, I was attracted by strange sounds. Then by a hole which I made in the door, I saw an old man weeping, a nun who danced, and a gentleman in mourning who sang. Why did the old man shed tears, the nun dance, and the man in mourning sing ? Unable to fathom the motive I have made my friend call the householder with the purpose of informing myself."

The man in mourning rejoined, " Have you any business to know other people's matters ? What is your reason for acting thus when it concerns you so little ? The night is well gone. Get back as quickly as possible."

" No, not at all. I acknowledge that it is not becoming to pry into the af-fairs of others, but this is such an extraordinary case I beg of you give me some light on the matter."

" Alas ! " said the man in mourning, " why is the gentleman so eager to know other people's matters ? "

Cheng-chong replied, " It is important that I should be somewhat informed."

" Since the gentleman wishes so much to know, I cannot do other than tell. This is why. My family has always been poor. In my hut one could never find sufficient grain for a meal and one flea would not have enough room upon my land to squat upon. I have no victuals for my old father. This is why, morning and evening, in default of all other resource, my wife has often cut off a tress of her hair and gone and sold it to buy a cup of bean-soup, which she graciously offers to my father. This evening she clipped and sold all of her hair that remained, and by this she has become bare-headed like a nun. My old father, seeing that for his sake his young daughter-in-law has become a nun, broke out into mourning in these terms :

" ' Why have I lived to this day ? Why am I not dead ? Why have I thus degraded my daughter-in-law ? ' And in saying this he shed tears. To con-sole him, my wife said to him, ' Do not weep,' and she danced. I, also, al-though in mourning, joined in with my wife. One danced, the other sang. This made my old father smile, and perhaps gave him solace. There ! that is why we behaved so. Do not think it strange, and go away."

Listening to this narrative the king was impressed with such a marked su-preme devotion on the part of the son and daughter-in-law, even in the time of deepest misfortune, and he said, " This is the most extraordinary thing in the world. How will it do to present you at the examination to-morrow ? "

" What examination to-morrow ? " asked the man.

"Why, certainly," said Cheng-chong, "to-morrow there will be an examination. By all means don't fail to be there."

The man responded, "But I have not heard it said that there is to be an examination."

"Whether you have heard or not," said the king, "prepare to compete, and present yourself. As I shall also present myself to-morrow I shall give you a stall in the enclosure."

Having thus spoken he took his leave, returned to the palace and awaited the stroke of the great clock-bell.

No sooner did he hear the vibration of the mighty gong than he immediately gave the order to announce promptly the examination in the city, and beyond the walls, to the utter astonishment of the literary men, who said, "Even until yesterday no one had heard of an examination, and behold it was published during the night. What does this mean ? "

The poor householder on his part made this reflection, "Although I knew nothing about it, this man knows perfectly," and he started out.

On the way he noticed a crowd of candidates. Without hesitation he entered the enclosure. The subject of the examination was: "The song of a man in mourning, the dance of a nun, the tears of an old man."

Of all the students not one could derive the sense of such a subject.

This man alone knew it perfectly well, because he had had experience of those very things in his own house. He treated the theme clearly and sent in his copy. The king having examined the essay and found it without a mistake, gave the degree of doctor and sent for him to come to him.

When they were in each other's presence the king said :

"Do you know me? It is I who yesterday recommended you to present yourself at the examination. Lift up your head and look."

Fixing his gaze attentively, the man recognized who he was—in effect the same person—and manifested his feelings in appropriate actions of gratitude.

"Go quickly," said the king to him, "go find your old father and wife."

Forthwith, with high appointment to office joined to magnificent treatment, the king recompensed the filial piety of the son and daughter-in-law.

The royal renown has been handed down from generation to generation. In truth, beyond the goodness of the king, the reward bestowed upon the filial devotion of these two married people is known to every one.

Evidently the following is a story told by metropolitans to show up the bumpkins of the provinces :

THE PRODIGIOUS EFFECTS OF A LOOKING-GLASS.

A young noble of Kiung-sang province was going on a journey to Seoul. Just as he was about to depart, his wife called him.

"He ! say now, listen to me a little. I have heard the mother of Mr. Kim speak of a very lovely thing which looks like glass and pretty metal. They say that if you look in it you will see a very curious thing. You must bring me one."

"Is it dear or cheap?" asked the husband.

"It is not dear," said she. "It will be necessary to spend some money, but if you heed the matter at all, it will be easy to pay for it." This is what the husband heard as he set out for the capital.

Having finished his business at Seoul he was on the point of returning, having almost lost sight of his wife's order. At last he recalled it, asked the name of the object in question, and made the purchase of a mirror through one of his friends. In his eagerness to get home he put his wife's commission in his wallet without even looking at it. When he arrived home, she hastened to take out the mirror. At once she perceived in it a woman. Immediately she began to weep and to berate her husband.

"Oh the villain! not only to play himself the vagabond and debauchee but to bring along a concubine! Is it possible? This woman, what is she?"

The amazed husband looked in the mirror, and at the side of his wife perceived a man. Unable to contain his wrath which made his face first dark and then blue, he uttered piercing cries.

"Is this the conduct for the wife of a noble. You have brought a libertine here," cried he.

He was about to murder his wife, when his old mother hearing the squabble came in to know what it was. At sight of the old woman the quarrel ceased on either side. Pointing at the mirror, the rivals spoke both at once. The weeping daughter-in-law raved about a concubine, the son, even more angry, talked of a paramour. As the couple had never quarrelled before, there was no way of accounting for the mystery.

"Do not be vexed," said she, and looking in the mirror she saw a woman. At once she broke out into a laugh.

"Is it because you see the old woman, your neighbor, that you dispute? The widow Pak has come to get some fire," said she, and she went out to speak to her, but she was not there.

Astonished, she called her husband and said to him

"There is in the children's room a very funny thing. You can see in it all kinds of extraordinary things and they are bickering over it. Come and see a little."

The venerable gentleman having entered the room perceived in the mirror an aged man.

"Hello! the puppy of the teacher Tsoi has come to collect his fees and I have not a penny. That is not very nice."

The people of the village, one by one, two by two, all without exception looked at the mirror, but unable to comprehend anything, they made a tumult. Curious to know what should result, they carried it to the magistrate. At sight of the instrument, the man of authority more astonished than the others, called the policemen and gave them this order:

"A new officer has arrived, why have I lost my place? Get ready men and horses for him."

Really believing that he had been cashiered he prepared to leave, when a young policeman after a careful examination of the mirror, pointed out the manner in which the visage of each individual was reflected.

CHAPTER XXXV.

PROVERBS AND PITHY SAYINGS.

SHUT off, as they are, from the rest of the world, like fish in a well, the Coreans nevertheless have coined a fair share of homely wisdom, which finds ready circulation in their daily speech. Their proverbs not only bear the mint-mark of their origin, but reflect truly the image and superscription of those who send them forth. Many, indeed, of their current proverbs and pithy expressions are of Japanese or Chinese origin, but those we have selected are mainly of peninsular birth, and have the flavor of the soil.

Do the Coreans place the seat of wisdom as they do the point of vaccination, in the nose? They ask, "Who has a nose three feet long?" which means, "If one is embarrassed, how can he put others at ease?" Evidently they have a wholesome regard for that member. A "nose of iron" describes an opinionated man and suggests unlimited "cheek." A common expression of the Christians, meaning to go to church and pray, is "to see the long nose of the father"—that feature of the French priest's face being looked upon with awe as the seat of wisdom.

Between the rivals, Japan and China, Corea probably sees herself in this proverb of the unhappy cur that wanders boneless between two kitchens—the cook in each supposing it has been fed by the other. "The dog which between two monasteries gets nothing."

Corea's isolation is "like a fish in a well," or "like a hermit in the market-place." They say of a secluded villager, "He knows nothing beyond the place which he inhabits."

"One stick to ten blind men," is something very precious.

"The cock of the village in a splendid city mansion," is the bumpkin in the capital.

"To have a cake in each hand," is to know not which to eat first—to be in a quandary.

"A volcano under the snow," is a man of amiable manners who conceals a violent temper.

"The treasure which always circulates without an obstacle," is "cash," or *sapeks*.

"An apricot-blossom in the snow," is said when something rare and marvellous happens.

"To blow away the hair to see if there is a scar," is to look for a mote in another man's eye, and to hunt for defects.

"As difficult as the roads of Thibet," is evidently a reminiscence derived from the ancient Buddhist missionaries who came from that region.

"To put on a silk dress to travel at night," is to do a good action and not have it known.

Some pithy sayings show the local gauge of sense. "He does not know silver from lead," "He has round eyes," "He can't tell cheese from wheat," He is an idiot. "Doesn't know *lu* from *yu*." This last refers to two Corean letters, jot and tittle.

"As opposed as fire and water."

"A buckskin man," is a man of no will or backbone.

"To have a big hand," means to be liberal.

"A great blue sea," refers to something very difficult, with no end to it and no way out of it.

A man who is "not known in all the eight coasts," is an utter stranger.

A very sick person is "a man who holds disease in his arms."

"A bag of diseases," is a chronic patient.

"Who can tell in seeing a crow flying whether it be male or female?" is a question referring to the impossible.

The numeral 10,000 (*man*) plays a great part in proverbial sayings as "10,000 times certain." Corea is a "land of 10,000 peaks." Certain success is "10,000 chances against one." "To die 10,000 times and not be regretted," is to be "worthy of 10,000 deaths." Ten thousand sorrows means great grief. A mountain is "10,000 heights of a man high." "Ten thousand strings of cash," is a priceless amount. *Man-nin* are 10,000 people—all the people in the universe.

"To lose one's hands," is to make a fiasco.

A comet is an "arrow star."

"A hundred battles make a veteran."

Almost as poetical as the Greek "*anarithma gelasma*" (unnumbered laughings) is this Corean description of the sea—"Ten thousand flashings of blue waves."

" To lose both at a time," is a proverb founded on a native love-story.

" When a raven flies from a pear-tree, a pear falls "—appearances are deceitful, don't hazard a guess.

" If one lifts a stone, the face reddens." The Coreans are fond of rival feats of lifting. Heavy stones are kept for that purpose. "Results are proportionate to effort put forth."

Mosquitoes are lively and jubilantly hungry in Chō-sen, yet it does not do to fight them with heavy weapons or " seize a sabre to kill a mosquito."

A very poor man is thus described : "He eats only nine times in a month," or "He eats only three times in ten days." To say he is in the depths of poverty is to mention the pathetic fact that " he has extinguished his fire ;" for " he looks to the four winds and finds no friend."

"The right and left are different," is said of a hypocrite who does not speak as he thinks.

When a man is not very bright he "has mist before his eyes ;" or he " carries his wits under his arms ;" or has " hidden his soul under his arm-pits," or he " goes to the east and goes to the west when he is bothered."

Like Beaconsfield's dictum—" Critics are men who have failed in literature and art," is this Corean echo, "Good critic, bad worker."

"On entering a village to know its usages," is our "When in Rome do as the Romans do."

" To destroy jade and gravel together," refers to indiscriminate destruction.

" Without wind and without cloud," describes a serene life.

"Go to sea," is a provincial malediction heavier than a tinker's, and worse than " Go to grass."

" I am I, and another is another," is a formula of selfish, and Corean for "*ego et non ego*," "I and not I."

"A poor horse has always a thick tail "—talent and capacity are badly located.

The large number of morals pointed and tales adorned by the tiger are referred to elsewhere.

CHAPTER XXXVI.

THE COREAN TIGER.

THE one royal quadruped associated with Corea, as the white elephant is with Siam, the bison with the United States, or the dromedary with Egypt, is the tiger. Unlike his relative in India that roams in the hot jungles and along the river bottoms, the Corean "king of the mountains" is seen oftenest in the snow and forests of the north, ranging as far as the fiftieth parallel.

Battle-flag Captured in the Han Forts, 1871.

Both actually and ideally the tiger is the symbol of power and fierceness. The flag of the tiger-hunters, from the northern provinces of Ping-an or Ham-kiung, who so bravely faced the rifles of the United States marines and sailors in "our little war with the heathen," in 1871, was a winged tiger rampant, spitting fire, holding the lightnings in his lifted fore-claws, and thus embodying the powers of earth, air, and heaven. It reminds one of the winged leopard in the vision of Daniel, "After this, I beheld, and lo another like a leopard, which had upon the back of it four wings of a fowl." It is the tutelary genius of the descendants of the aboriginal worshippers of the tiger, who even yet cling to the religion of the soil.[1]

---

[1] This flag was presented by its captors to Commodore Homer C. Blake, by whose courtesy the writer had the sketch made for the cut given above.

The caps of the body-guard of the sovereign are decorated
with the cheek and whiskers of the tiger, in order to inspire
terror among beholders. The Corean beauty carries among the
jewelry and "charms" in the reticule at her waist, a claw of the
dreaded *pem* or tiger, nor can the hardy mountaineer put in the
hand of his bride a more eloquent proof of his valor than one of
these weapons of a man-eater. It means even more than the edel-
weiss of other mountain lands. On the floors of the better class
of houses the tiger-skin rug not only adorns the best room, but
makes the children's play-ground, or the baby's cushion in lieu of
cradles, which are unknown. The soft hair of these natural rugs is
often a finger long. Curious toys are made of the fur.

The most prized articles among the tribute offerings (in these
days, rather a "bonus" or bribe, than a tax or humiliation) presented at the court of Peking, as of old at Kiōto or Yedo, are
these gorgeous pelts. One of them, which the writer saw recently,
the property of a Japanese merchant, measured twelve feet long,
exclusive of the tail. The symbol of military rank in old Japan,
as indicative as our shoulder-straps, was a tiger-skin scabbard.
Especially was it honorable to wear it if captured with one's own
hands on "frontier service." The hair of these animals seems to
have more of a woolly quality than those from India, while the
orange tint is far less predominant, white taking its place. The
black bars are, however, of equal magnificence with the tropical
product, and the tail seems to be rather longer. Some idea of the
great numbers and awful ravages of these huge *felidæ* in the two
northern provinces of the Peninsular Kingdom, may be gained
from the common saying of the Chinese that "the Coreans hunt
the tiger during one half the year and the tigers hunt the Coreans
during the other half." The Coreans retort by the proverb born
of the desolation that has so often followed the presence of a Chinese army on their soil, whether as invaders or allies : "After the
Chinese, the tigers.'" As a single man can create the gigantic
spectre of the Brocken, so in the national literature this one animal seems to have cast a measureless shadow of evil influence
upon this hermit nation. From the most ancient times it has
been an object of religious reverence. "They also worshipped the
tiger, which they looked on as a god," was written of the people
living on the sea of Japan before the Christian era. "They had
also the many-spotted leopard." A few of the national proverbs
will illustrate the amount of attention which the subject receives

21

in daily life, in art, religion, and language, and how often it serves to point the morals and adorn the tales told around Corean hearths. "A wooden tiger," is the ass in the lion's skin.

"A broken-backed tiger" describes impotent and raging malice.

"To give wings to a tiger," is to add shrewdness to force.

"If you don't enter the tiger's lair, you can't get her cubs," is said to spur on the faint heart, "to beard the tiger in his cave."

"A tiger's repast," describes excess in eating, or the gorging which follows after fasting. "To nourish a tiger, and have him devour you," probably states a common fact of history, as well as it depicts ingratitude. "If you tread on the tail of a tiger, you'll know it," explains itself. "It is hard to let go the tail of a tiger," suggests our "fire" after the "frying-pan," or the "other horn of the dilemma;" while over-cautious people "in avoiding a deer, meet a tiger." Men of irascible temper or violent disposition are given the pet name of *maing-ho*, which means an unusually ferocious tiger or "man-eater."

Corean shrewdness utilizes the phenomena of local experience, and equals the craft of the sellers of Joseph. So common is the disappearance of a villager through visitations of the tiger, that the standard method of escaping creditors or processes of law is to leave bits of one's torn clothes in the woods, and then to abscond. Obliging friends or relatives quickly report, "Devoured by a tiger," and too often it is believed that "Joseph is without doubt rent in pieces." This local substitute for our former G. T. T., or the usual trip to Europe, is especially fashionable in places where "tigers as big as a mountain" are plentiful. To drive away the dreaded *kal-pem*, the people invoke the aid of the tu-e', a fabulous monster, which is the enemy of the tiger, and which the latter greatly fears. The cry of his name *tu-e'*, *tu-e'*, is believed to act as a charm, and is often raised by villagers at night.

In art, though the native picture-maker may draw a lion in such preposterous shape and with such impossible attributes as to show at once that no living model was ever before his eyes, yet in those pictures of the tiger drawn by Corean artists which we have examined, accuracy and vigor of treatment predominate over artistic grace.

The hunters who are familiar with every habit, trait of character, and physical detail of the species, carefully distinguish his parts and varieties. *Ho-rang-i* is the generic name for the *felis tigris*. *Kal-pem* is a mature fellow in full claw, scratchy and ferocious. *Maing-ho* is a large one of unusual size and in the full rampancy of his vigor. *Mil-pal* is an old brute that can no longer scratch, and is most probably mangy, and well gouged and scarred from numerous household quarrels and frequent tussles with rivals. *Pi-ho* is one agile in turning tail to escape, rather than in showing teeth to fight—the term being sometimes applied to the leopard. *San-tol* is a huge fellow that makes annual visits to one place, making his lightning strike more than once in the same spot. *Siyo-ho* is a little, and *hal-pem* is a female, tiger. A " stone" tigress is sterile. Special terms suggestive, and even poetical, for the murders, calamities, or ravages of the beast, for traps or ditches, for the skin, tail (used for banners and spear-sheaths), beard, moustaches, and the noises of purring, growling, nocturnal caterwauling, and even for lashing the tail, enrich and vivify the Chō-sen vocabulary.

Tiger-shooting is not a favorite sport among the nobles or young bloods. Hunting in general is considered a servile occupation. Nobles, except those of a few poor families in the northern provinces, never practise it as sport. Yet it is free to all. There are no game laws, no proscription of arms, no game preserves, no seasons interdicted.

The only animal which it is forbidden to kill is the falcon, whose life is protected by stringent laws. From the most ancient times this bird of the golden wing has been held in high honor. The hunting-grounds are almost entirely among the mountains, as the valleys are too densely occupied with rice and millet fields and cultivated soil, to allow game to exist or be hunted. The chief weapon used is the flint-lock, imported from Japan. With this a single hunter will attack the huge game, although the animal, when not immediately killed, leaps right upon his enemy and easily makes him his prey. When a tiger has caused great ravages in a district, the local magistrate calls together all the professional hunters and organizes a hunt in the mountains. In such cases, the chase is usually, and of intent, without results ; for the skin is the property of the government, and the official always looks out for himself, coming in first for the spoils. Hence it is that a government hunt is usually a farce. Most of the tiger-hunters prefer to meet the royal game alone, for then the prized skin, which they sell secretly, is theirs. They eat the meat, and the bones stripped and boiled make various medicines.

The number of human lives lost, and the value of property

destroyed by their ravages, is so great as at times to depopulate certain districts. A hungry tiger will often penetrate a village in which the houses are well secured, and will prowl around a hovel or ill-secured dwelling, during several entire nights. If hunger presses he will not raise the siege until he leaps upon the thatched roof. Through the hole thus made by tearing through, he bounds upon the terrified household. In this case a hand-to-claw fight ensues, in which the tiger is killed or comes off victorious after glutting himself upon one or more human victims. Rarely, however, need this king of Corean beasts resort to this expedient, for such is the carelessness of the villagers that in spite of the man-eater's presence in their neighborhood, they habitually sleep during the summer with the doors of their houses wide open, and oftentimes even in the sheds in the open fields without dreaming of taking the precaution to light a fire.

This sense of security is especially apt to follow after a grand hunt successfully pursued. Then the prey is supposed to have been all killed off in the vicinity or driven to the distant mountains. The Coreans are as careless of tigers as the Japanese are of fires. Sometimes the tiger is caught in a snare, without danger and by very simple means. A deep pit is covered over with branches, leaves, and earth. At the bottom a sharp stake is set up. This, however, is only rarely used. During the winter the snow is half frozen over and strong enough to bear the weight of a man, but is broken through by the paws of the tiger. The beast sinks to the belly, and not being able to move fast, or escape, is as helpless as a fly in molasses. It is then apparently quite easy to approach the creature at bay, though woe be to the hunter who is too sure of his prey. To be well-equipped for this method of mountain sport, the hunter must have a short sword, lance, and snow-shoes. These *sel-mai*, or racquettes, are of slightly curved elastic board, well fitted with loops and thongs. With dogs, trained to the work, the *san-chang* (lanceman) starts the game, and following up the trail usually finishes him with a thrust of his spear ; or, in bravado, with a sword-stroke. This method of sport was the favorite one pursued by the Japanese invaders. Though occasionally a man-at-arms was chewed up, or clawed into ribbons, scores of glossy skins were carried back to Nippon as trophies by the veterans. Indeed, it may be said, to most Japanese children, the nearest country west of them has no other association in their minds than as a land of tigers. At Gensan, the merchants from Tōkiō had their dreary homesickness, about the time of their first New Year's season in the strange land, rather unpleasantly enlivened by the advent of several striped man-eaters. These promenaded the settlement at night, and seemed highly desirous of tasting a Japanese, after having already feasted on several natives. The prospect of playing Little Red Riding Hood to a whiskered man-eater was not a very pleasant experience, though a possible one at any time. A tiger ten feet long can easily stow away two five-feet Japanese without grievous symptoms of indigestion. For an untrained hand, even when armed with a Winchester breech-loader, to attempt hunting this Corean emblem of power is not attractive sport. The tiger is more apt to hunt the man, for elephants are not at hand to furnish the shelter of their backs. The Japanese do not seem to hanker after tiger-claws or skins while in the flesh, but prefer to buy for cash over their own counters at Gensan. The "crop" of these costly pelts averages five hundred a year at this one port.

Few experiences tend more to develop all the manly virtues than facing a tiger on foot in his native wilds. The Coreans know this, and in their lack of drilled troops capable of meeting the soldiers of Europe—their "army" consisting almost entirely of archers, spearmen, and jingal-firers—they summoned the tiger-hunters from Ping-an to fight the Frenchmen of Admiral Roze's expedition of 1866. Underrating their enemy, the Frenchmen, in attempting to storm a fortified monastery garrisoned by the hunt-ers, were completely defeated. When the marines and sailors of the American naval expedition of 1871 assaulted "Fort McKee," after it had been swept by the shells of the fleet, they were amazed at the stern courage of their dark-visaged enemies, who, with matchlock, spear, and sword, fought against the shells and breech-loaders to the last. The Americans speak admiringly of these brave fellows, so worthy of their lead and steel.

CHAPTER XXXVII.

RELIGION.

A. CAREFUL study of the common names applied to the mountains, rivers, valleys, caves, and other natural features of the soil and landscape of any country will lay bare many of the primitive or hidden beliefs of a people. No words are more ancient than the aboriginal names given to the natural features of a country amid which the childhood of a nation has been spent. With changing customs, civilization, or religion, these names still hold their place, reflecting the ancient, and often modified, or even vanished, faith.

Even a casual examination of the mountain, river, and other local names of places in Corea will give one a tolerably clear outline of the beliefs once fully held by the ancient dwellers of this peninsula. Against the tenets and influences of Buddhism these doctrines have held their sway over the minds of the people and are still the most deeply-seated of their beliefs. The statements of ancient Chinese, and later of Japanese writers, of foreign castaways, and of the French missionaries all concur in showing us that Shamanism is the basis of the Corean's, and especially the northern Corean's, faith. In the first historic accounts of Fuyu, Kokorai, and the Sam-han, we find the worship of the spirits of heaven and earth, and of the invisible powers of the air, of nature, the guardian genii of hills and rivers, of the soil and grain, of caves, and even of the tiger. They worshipped especially the morning-star, and offered sacrifice of oxen to heaven. From such scanty notices of early Corea, especially of the northern parts, we may form some idea of the cultus of the people before Buddhism was introduced. From the reports of recent witnesses, Dutch, Japanese, and French, and the evidence of language, we incline to the belief that the fibres of Corean superstition and the actual religion of the people of to-day have not radically changed during twenty centuries, in spite of Buddhism. The worship of the spirits of heaven and earth, of mountains and rivers and caves, of the morning star, is still reflected in the names of these natural objects and still continues, in due form, as of old, along with the sacrifices of sheep and oxen.

The god of the hills is, perhaps, the most popular deity. The people make it a point to go out and worship him at least once a year, making their pious trip a picnic, and, as of old, mixing their eating and drinking with their religion. Thus they combine piety and pleasure, very much as Americans unite sea-bathing and sanctification, croquet and camp-meeting holiness, by the ocean or in groves. On mountain tops, which pilgrims climb to make a visit for religious merit, may often be seen a pile of stones called siong-wang-tang, dedicated to the god of the mountain. The pilgrims carry a pebble from the foot of the mountain to the top.' These pilgrims are among those held in reputation for piety.

The other popular gods are very numerous. The *mok-sin*, the genii of the trees, the god of rain and of the harvest, are all propitiated, but the robust Corean, blessed with a good appetite, especially honors *Cho-an-nim*, the tutelary genius of the kitchen. To a Corean, the air is far from being empty. It is thickly inhabited with spirits and invisbile creatures. Some of these figments of imagination, and the additional powers for good and evil, which the Corean attributes to animals of flesh and blood, are treated of in a former chapter on Mythical Zoölogy. Even the breezes are the breath of spirits, and "a devil's wind" is a tempest raised by a demon intent on mischief. When a person falls dead suddenly, heart-disease is not thought of; he has been struck by a devil's arrow. There are not wanting sorcerers who seek to obtain supernatural force by magic, which they use against their enemies or for hire, direct the spirits to wreak malignity against the enemy of him who fees them. These sorcerers are social outcasts, and reckoned the lowest of humanity.

The unlucky days are three in each month, the figure of ill-omen being five. They are the fifth, fifteenth, and twenty-fifth. On all extraordinary occasions there are sacrifices, ceremonies, and prayers, accompanied with tumultuous celebration by the populace. The chief sacrifices are to heaven, earth, and to the King or Emperor of Heaven¹ (Shang Ti of the Chinese).

---

¹ This word, pronounced in a slightly different way in Corean, is the term which Dr. James Legge, in his "Religions of China," and many missionaries of Reformed Christianity, translate God (Jehovah, Theos), but which the Roman Catholic missionaries are forbidden to use. Dr. Legge holds that Shang

The various superstitions concerning the direction of evil, the auspicious or the ill-omened lay of the land, the site for the building of a house, or the erection of a tomb, will be well understood by those who know the meaning of the Chinese term, Fung Shuy, or the Corean Pung-siu. This system of superstition has not only its millions of believers, but also its priests or professors, who live by their expertness and magnify their calling. The native vocabulary relating to these pretenders and all their works is very profuse. Among the common sights in Corea are little mounds raised on eligible, propitious places, in which a pole is planted, from which little bells or cymbals are hung. These jingled by the breeze are supposed to propitiate the good spirits and to ward off the noxious influences of the demons. The same idea is expressed in the festoons of wind-bells strung on their pagodas and temples. Pung-siu means literally "wind and water," but in a broad sense is a rude cyclopædia of ideas relating to nature, and bears nearly the same relation to natural philosophy as astrology does to astronomy. Its ideas color every-day speech, besides having a rich terminology for the advanced student of its mysteries.

Upon this system, and perhaps nearly coeval in origin with it, is the cult of ancestral worship which has existed in Chinese Asia from unrecorded time. Confucius found it in his day and made it the basis of his teachings, as it had already been of the religious and ancient documents of which he was the editor.

The Corean cult of ancestor-worship seems to present no features which are radically distinct from the Chinese. Public celebrations are offered at stated times to ancestors, and in every well-to-do house will be found the gilt and black tablets inscribed with the names of the departed. Before these tablets the smoke of incense and sacrifice arises daily. In the temple also are rooms for the preservation of duplicates of the tablets in the private houses for greater safety. Like the iron atoms in his blood, the belief in ancestral piety and worship is wrought into the Corean's soul. The Christian missionaries meet with no greater obstacle to their tenets and progress than this practice. It is the source, even among their most genuine converts, of more scandals, lapses, and renunciations, than are brought about by all other causes.

Confucianism, or the Chinese system of ethics, is, briefly stated,

---

Ti is the most ancient title of Deity in the language of the Chinese, and was used by their ancestors when they held to primitive monotheism. "In the ceremonies at the altars of heaven and earth, they served God" (Confucius).

an expansion of the root idea of filial piety. It is duty based on relation. Given the five great relations, all the manifold duties of life follow. The five relations are that of king and subject (prince and minister), of parent and child, of husband and wife, of the elder brother and the younger brother, and between friends. The cardinal virtues inculcated, or "The Five Constituents of Worth," or constant virtues displayed, according to the teachings of Confucius, by the perfect man are : 1, Benevolence ; 2, Uprightness of Mind ; 3, Propriety of Demeanor ; 4, Knowledge or Enlightenment ; 5, Good Faith ; or, Affection, Justice, Deference, Wisdom, Confidence.

With the ethics of the Chinese came their philosophy, which is based on the dual system of the universe, and of which in Corean, yum-yang (positive and negative, active and passive, or male and female) is the expression. All things in heaven, earth, and man are the result of the interaction of the *yum* (male or active principle) and the *yang* (female or passive principle). Even the metals and minerals in the earth are believed to be produced through the *yum-yang*, and to grow like plants or animals.

The Confucian ethics, suiting well a state of feudalism, and being ever acceptable to the possessors of authority, found congenial soil in the peninsla, as they had already taken root in Kokorai. They nourished the spirit of filial piety and personal loyalty, of feud and of blood-revenge, by forbidding a man to live under the same heaven with the murderer of his father or master. Notwithstanding the doctrines and loftier morals of Buddha, the Chinese ethics and ancestor-worship, especially in the northern part of the peninsula, underlaid the outward adherence of the people to the religion of the Enlightened One. As the average Christian, in spite of the spirit of Jesus and the Sermon on the Mount, is very apt to base his behavior and legal procedure on the code of Justinian, so the Corean, though he may believe in Fo (Buddha), practises after the rules of Kong-ja (Confucius).

Official sacrifices are regulated by the government and are offered up publicly at the national festivals. Something of the regulated subordination in vogue among the Chinese prevails in Chō-sen when ancestors are honored. High officials may sacrifice to three ancestors, the gentry only to father and grandfather, and the common people to father only. In every province, capital, and city ranked as *Tai-mu-kan*, there are buildings containing statues of Confucius and his thirty-two disciples, which are maintained at the public expense.

Confucianism overspreads the whole peninsula, but during the prevalence of Buddhism, from the fourth to the fourteenth century, was probably fully studied and practised only by the learned classes. Under the present dynasty, or from the fifteenth century, the religion of China has been both the official and popular cult of Chō-sen, long ago reaching the point of bigotry, intolerance, and persecution. Taoism seems to be little studied.

In Corean mouths Buddha becomes *Pul*, and his "way" or doctrine *Pul-to* or *Pul-chie*. Introduced into Hiaksai in the fourth, and into Shinra in the sixth century, the new faith from India made thorough conquest of the southern half of the peninsula, but has only partially leavened the northern portion, where the grosser heathenism prevails. The palmy days of Corean Buddhism were during the era of Korai (from 905–1392, A.D.). The missionary work had been accomplished, the reigning dynasty were professors and defenders of the faith, and for these four centuries it was the religion of the state. The few surviving monuments of this era of splendor are the grand pagodas, monasteries, and temples that are found, especially in the southern provinces. The profusion of legal and ecclesiastical terms in the language which relate to lands set apart to provide revenues for the temples, and to their boundaries and rents, and the privileges of monks and priests, are more probably the relics of a past time, being only verbal shells and husks of what were once fruit and kernel.

Until the fifteenth or sixteenth century the Japanese Buddhists looked to the "Treasure-land of the West," as they termed Chō-sen, for spiritual and even pecuniary aid in their ecclesiastical enterprises. The special features of many renowned Japanese temples, libraries, collections of books, images, altar furniture, etc., are of Corean origin. This is especially noticeable in the old seats of the faith in Kiōto. Images in gold, gilt wood, bronze, and some fire-resisting material—perhaps platinum—are known and duly certified by genuine documents in temples in other cities. In a building at Kamakura is a copy of the Buddhist canon in a revolving library, said to have been obtained by Sanétomo from Corea in the thirteenth century. Among the amusing passages in the letters from Ashikaga in Kamakura, two hundred years later, is the hint given to the king of Corea that a contribution in aid of the repair of certain Japanese temples would be acceptable.

The site and general surroundings of Corean Buddhist temples and monasteries greatly resemble those of China and Japan. They are often situated on hills, rising ground, and even high mountains, and walled round by lofty and venerable trees which seem to inspire awe and veneration in the worshipper, besides acting as extinguishers to sparks drifted from neighboring fires. An imposing gateway is usually built at some distance before the temple, with massive curved roof of tiles, and flanked by a wall of masonry which, in its upper part, consists of plaster tiled at the top. On the frieze of the portal, the name of the temple is inscribed in large Chinese characters. Sanskrit letters or monograms are occasionally seen. Under a roofed shed in front hangs the drum on which the bonze beats the hours for prayer, or of the clock. On the other side stands the coffer for the cash of the faithful, or a well for the manual ablutions of pious worshippers. Boards, on which are written the names of those who have contributed money to the temple, are suspended near by, and the thatched houses of the neophytes and bonzes are close at hand.

The idols seen in a Corean temple are the same as those found throughout Buddhist Asia. The chief is that of Shaka Muni, or Buddha, the founder of the religion. In their sculpture and artistic treatment of this, the central figure of their pantheon, the image-carvers of the different countries do not greatly vary, adhering strictly to their traditions. The sage in Nirvana sits on his knees with the soles of his feet turned upward to the face. His hands touch, thumb to thumb, and finger to finger. The folds of the robes, the round bead-like caste mark of his forehead, the snails on his crown—which tradition says came out to shelter his head from the rays of the sun—and the lop or pierced ears, are substantially the same as those seen on idols from India, Siam, and Thibet. The eye is only slightly oblique, and the ear-lobes are made but slightly bulbous, to satisfy the tastes of worshippers in Chinese Asia. The throne, consisting of the fully opened calyx of a lotus flower—the symbol of eternity—with the petals around the base and seed-holes open, is the same.

In the representation of local deities the artist asserts his patriotism and displays his own taste. In the various countries overrun by Buddhism, the indigenous heroes, sages, and gods have been renamed and accepted by the Buddhists as avatars or incarnations of Buddha to these countries before the advent of the teachers of "the true religion." There are also saints and subordinate magnates in the Buddhist gallery of worshipped worthies, with whose effigies the artist does not scruple to take certain liberties. One can easily recognize an idol of Chinese, Corean, Siamese, or Japanese manufacture, though all bear the same name. The god of war in Chō-sen holds the double-bladed sword, with its tasselled cord, and wears the Chino-Corean armor and helmet. In the aureole round the head are three fiery revolving thunder-clouds. On the battle-flags captured by the American forces in 1871 were painted or embroidered the protecting deities of those who fought under them. One of these, whether representing a Buddha, as seems most probable, or, as is possible, some local hero—perhaps Dan Kun or Ki Tsze—deified, rides on one of the curious little ponies, stunted and piebald, of Ham-kiung, with which, even in ancient times, one could ride under a fruit tree. Evidently it would have been safer for Absalom in Corea than in woody Palestine.

The tutelary god on the stunted piebald horse is dressed in the peculiar winged head-dress and frilled collar which travellers on Ham-kiung soil noticed fifteen centuries ago. His armor is in scales, or wrought in the "wave-pattern" characteristic of Corean art. His shoes and saddle are of the Chinese type. He rides among the conventional clouds, which in the native technique, are different from those of either China or Japan. Evidently the Buddha and saints of Shaka Muni are portrayed by the native artist according to the strict canons of orthodoxy, while in dealing with indigenous deities, artistic licence and local color have free play. Most of the artists and sculptors of temple work are priests or monks. The principal idols are of brass, bronze, or gilded wood, the inferior sorts are of stone. The priests dress just like the Japanese bonzes. They attend the sick or dying, but have little to do with the burial of the dead, owing to the prevalence of the Pung-sui superstition, to which a Corean in life and in death is a bond-slave. This all-powerful disease of the intellect is the great corrupter of Corean Buddhism, many of its grossest ideas being grafted into, or flourishing as parasites on a once pure faith.

In its development Corean Buddhism has frequently been a potent influence in national affairs, and the power of the bonzes has at times been so great as to practically control the court and nullify decrees of the king. With the Fuyu race—that is in Chō-sen and Nihon—the history of Buddhism has a decidedly military cast. During the first centuries of its sway in the peninsula the ablest intellects were fed and the ablest men were developed by it, so that it was the most potent factor in Corea's civilization. Over and over again have the politcial and social revolutions been led by Buddhist priests, who have proved agitators and warriors as well as recluses and students. Possessing themselves of learning, they have made their presence at court a necessity. Here they have acted as scribes, law-givers, counsellors, and secretaries. Often they have been the conservers of patriotism. The shaven-pated priest has ever been a standard character in the glimpses of Corean history which we are allowed to catch.

Not always has this influence been exerted for good, for once possessed of influence at court, they have not scrupled to use it for the purpose of aggrandizing their sects. Tradition tells of high nobles won from the pleasures of the palace to the seclusion of the cloisters, and even of Corean queens renouncing the bed of their royal spouses to accept the vows of the nuns. As in Japan, the frequent wars have developed the formation of a clerical militia, not only able to garrison and defend their fortified monasteries but even to change the fortune of war by the valor of their exploits and the power of their commisariat. There seems to be three distinct classes or grades of bonzes. The student monks devote themselves to learning, to study, and to the composition of books and the Buddhist ritual, the *tai-sa* being the abbot. The *jung* are mendicant and travelling bonzes, who solicit alms and contributions for the erection and maintenance of the temples and monastic establishments. The military bonzes (*siung kun*) act as garrisons, and make, keep in order, and are trained to use, weapons. Many of their monasteries are built on the summit or slopes of high mountains, to which access is to be gained only with the greatest difficulty up the most rocky and narrow passages. Into these fastnesses royal and noble professors of the faith have fled in time of persecution, or pious kings have retired after abdication. In time of war they serve to shelter refugees. It was in attacking one of these strongholds, on Kang-wa Island, in 1866, that the French marines were repulsed with such fearful loss.

Many temples throughout the country have been erected by the old kings of Korai or by noblemen as memorials of events, or as proofs of their devotion. The building of one of these at great expense and the endowment of others from government funds, sometimes happens, even during the present dynasty, as was the case in 1865, when the regent was influenced by the bonzes. He rebuilt the temple in an unparalleled style of magnificence, and made immense presents to other temples out of the public treasury. It has been by means of these royal bounties, and the unremitting collection of small sums from the people, that the bonzes have amassed the vast property now held by them in ecclesiastical edifices, lands, and revenues. Some of these mountain monasteries are large and stately, with a wealth of old books, manuscripts, liturgical furniture, and perhaps even yet of money and land. The great monastery of Tong-to-sa, between Kiung-sang and Chulla, is noted for its library, in which will be found the entire sacred canon. The probabilities of American or European scholars finding rare treasures in the form of Sanskrit MSS. in this unsearched field are good, since the country is now opened to men of learning from Christendom. As a rule, the company of monks does not number over ten, twenty, or thirty, respectively, in the three grades of temples. Hamel tells us that they live well and are jolly fellows, though his opinion was somewhat biased, since he remarks that "as for religion, the Coreans have scarcely any. . . . They know nothing of preaching or mysteries, and, therefore, have no disputes about religion." There were swarms of monastics who were not held in much respect. He describes the festivals as noisy, and the people's behavior at them as boisterous. Incense sticks, or "joss" perfumery, seemed very much in vogue. He bears witness to their enjoyment in natural scenery, and the delightful situation of the famous temples.

Even at the present day, Buddhist priests are made high officers of the government, governors of provinces, and military advisers. Like as in Japan, Buddhism inculcates great kindness to animals—the logical result of the doctrine of the transmigration of souls, and all who kill are under its ban. Though beef, pork, and mutton are greedily eaten by the people, the trade of the butcher is considered the most degraded of all occupations, and the butchers and leather dressers form a caste below the level of humanity, like the Etas in Japan. They are beneath the slaves. They must live in villages apart from the rest of the people, and are debarred from receiving water, food, fire, or shelter at the hands of the people. The creation of this class of Corean pariahs and the exclusion of these people from the pale of recognized society is the direct result of the teachings of the bonzes. Like the Chinese, and unlike the Japanese bonze, the devotees will often mutilate themselves in the frenzy of their orgies, in order to gain a character for holiness or in fulfilment of a vow. One of these bonzes, appointed by the magistrate to dispute publicly with a Christian, had lost four fingers for the sake of manufacturing a reputation. The ceremony of *pul-tatta,* or "receiving the fire," is undergone upon taking the vows of the priesthood. A moxa or cone of burning tinder is laid upon the man's arm, after the hair has been shaved off. The tiny mass is then lighted, and slowly burns into the flesh, leaving a painful sore, the scar of which remains as a mark of holiness. This serves as initiation, but if vows are broken, the torture is repeated on each occasion. In this manner, ecclesiastical discipline is maintained.

In the nunneries are two kinds of female devotees, those who shave the head and those who keep their locks. The *po-sal* does not part with her hair, and her vows are less rigid. Hamel mentions two convents in Seoul, one of which was for maidens of gentle birth, and the other for women of a lower social grade.

Excepting in its military phases, the type of Corean Buddhism approaches that of China rather than of Japan. In both these countries its history is that of decay, rather than of improvement, and it would be difficult indeed for Shaka Muni to recognize the faith which he founded, in the forms which it has assumed in Chō-sen and Nippon; nor did it ever succeed in making the thorough missionary conquest of the former, which it secured in the latter, country. The priority of the Confucian teachings and the thorough indoctrination of the people in them, the nearness of China, the close copying of Chinese manners, customs, and materialistic spirit, the frequency of Chinese conquests, and perhaps the presence of an indigenous religion even more strongly marked than that of Shintō in Japan, were probably the potent reasons why Buddhism never secured so strong a hold on the Corean intellect or affections as upon the Japanese. Nevertheless, since Buddhism has always been largely professed, and especially if Confucianism be considered simply an ethical system and not a religion proper, Corea may be classed among Buddhist countries. Among the surprises of history is the fact that, in 1876, the Shin, or Reformed sect of Japanese Buddhists, sent their missionaries to Corea to preach and convert. Among their conquests was a young native of ability, who came to Kiōto, in 1878, to study the reformed Buddhism, and who later returned to preach among his own people. In 1880 five more young Coreans entered the Shin theological school in Kiōto, and a new and splendid Shin temple, dedicated to Amida Buddha, has been built at Gensan. Evidently this vigorous sect is resolutely endeavoring, not only to recoup the losses which Christianity has made in its ranks in Japan, but is determined to forestall the exertions of Christian missionaries in the peninsula.

So thoroughly saturated is the Corean mind with Chinese philosophy (p. 329) that when of necessity a national emblem or flag must be made, the symbol expressive of the male and female, or active and passive principles dominating the universe, was selected. Though Corea excels in the variety of her bunting and the wealth of symbolism upon her flags and streamers, yet the national flag, as now floated from her ships, custom-houses, and Legations in the United States and Europe, has an oblong field, in the centre of which are the two comma-shaped symbols, red and black, of the two universal principles. In each of the four corners of the flag is one of the Pak-wa or eight diagrams, consisting of straight and broken lines, which Fu-hi, the reputed founder of Chinese civilization, read upon the scroll on the back of the dragon-horse which rose out of the Yellow River, and on the basis of which he invented the Chinese system of writing. In these diagrams the learned men in Chinese Asia behold the elements of all metaphysical knowledge, and the clue to all the secrets of nature, and upon them a voluminous literature, containing divers systems of divination and metaphysical exegesis, has been written. The eight diagrams may be expanded to sixty-four combinations ; or, are reducible to four, and these again to their two primaries. The continuous straight line, symbol of the *yum* principle, corresponds to light, heaven, masculinity, etc. The broken line symbolizes the *yang* principle, corresponding to darkness, earth, femininity, etc. These two lines signify the dual principle at rest, but when curved or comma-shaped, betoken the ceaseless process of revolution in which the various elements or properties of nature indicated by the diagrams mutually extinguish or give birth to one another, thus producing the phenomena of existence.

Professor Terrien de Lacouperie sees in the Pak-wa a link between Babylonia and China, a very ancient system of phonetics or syllabary explaining the pronunciation of the old Babylonian characters and their Chinese derivatives. It is not likely that Morse derived the idea of his magneto-electric telegraphic alphabet from the Chinese diagrams. Possibly the Corean literati who suggested the design for a national flag intended to show, in the brightly colored and actively revolving germs of life set prominently in the centre, and contrasted with the inert and immovable straight lines in the background of the corners, the progressive Corea of the present and future as contrasted with Corea of the past and her hermit-like existence. Significantly, and with unconscious irony of the Virginia advertisers, the new Corean flag was first published to the Western world at large on the covers of cigarette packages. For centuries the energies of Coreans have been wasted in tobacco smoke, and the era of national decay is almost synchronous with the introduction of tobacco.

CHAPTER XXXVIII.

EDUCATION AND CULTURE.

COREA received her culture from China, and gave it freely to Japan. If we may believe the doubtful story of Ki Tsze, then the Coreans have possessed letters and writing, or, what is the equivalent thereto, they have had "civilization," during three thousand years. It is certain that since about the opening of the Christian era, the light of China's philosophy has shone steadily among Corean scholars. Japanese early tradition—unworthy of credence in the matter of chronology—claims that literature was brought to Nippon as early as the period 157–30 B.C. The legend of Jingu bringing back books and manuscrpts from Shinra is more probable; while the coming of Wani from Hiaksai, to teach the Chinese characters and expound the classics, is a historic fact, though the real date may be uncertain, or later than the accepted one, which is 285 A.D. While the Kokorai people may have brought letters with them, as they migrated southward, in Hiaksai the Confucian analects were not studied until the fourth century, when official recognition of education was made by the appointment of Hanken as master of Chinese literature. This is said to have been the first importation of learning into the peninsula. It was so in the sense of being formally introduced from China into the country south of the Ta-tong River.

As in most of the Asiatic countries, into which Chinese culture penetrated, popular education was for centuries a thing unthought of. Learning was the privilege of a few courtiers, who jealously guarded it from the vulgar, as an accomplishment for those about the royal person, or in the noble families. The classics and ethical doctrines seem in every case to have penetrated the nations surrounding the Middle Kingdom, and formed the basis of courtly and aristocratic education.

Buddhism furnished the popular or democratic element, which brought learning to the lower strata of society. Neophytes were

22

usually taken from the humbler classes, and thus culture was diffused. Even the idols, pictures, and scrolls, with the explanations and preaching in the vernacular, served to instruct the people and lift their thoughts out of the rut of every-day life—a result which is in itself true education. Wherever Buddhism penetrated, there was more or less literature published in the speech of the unlearned, and often the first books for the people were works on religion. China gave her language and ideographs; India sent Sanskrit and phonetic letters, from which syllabaries or alphabets were constructed, not only for vernacular writing and printing, but as aids to the easier apprehension and more popular understanding of the tenets of Confucius.

The Corean syllabary seems to have been first invented by Chul-chong, one of the ministers at the court of the king of Shinra, in the seventh century. This was the *Nido;* like the *kana* of the Japanese, purely a collection of syllables and not a true alphabet. The Nido was made by giving to some of the commoner Chinese characters a phonetic value, though the idea of having a vernacular system of writing was most probably suggested by the Sanskrit letters,[1] some of which accurately represented Corean sounds. The true alphabet of the Coreans, called *Unmun* (common language), was invented by a Buddhist priest named Syel-chong, or Sye'-chong, who is regarded as one of the ablest scholars in the literary annals of Corea. The "Grammaire Coréene" states that this took place under the dynasty of Wang, at Sunto, "toward the end of the eighth or ninth century of the Christian era." This is a palpable mistake, as the dynasty of Wang was not established at Sunto until the tenth century. Mr. Aston, whose researches are based on the statements of Corean and Japanese writers, believes that the Unmun, or true Corean alphabet, "was invented not earlier than the first half of the fifteenth century." Yet, in spite of their national system of writing, the influence of the finished philosophy and culture of China, both in form and spirit, has been so great that the hopelessness of producing a copy equal to the original became at once apparent to the Corean mind. Stimulating to the receptive

---

[1] Dr. D. Bethune McCartee, a well-known American scholar, writing on Riu Kiu, says : "The art of spelling was invented neither by the Chinese nor by the Japanese. Its introduction into both these countries (and, as we are convinced, into Corea as well) was the result of the labors of . . . the early Buddhist missionaries. In all the three countries . . . the system of spelling is most undoubtedly of Sanskrit origin."

intellect, it has been paralyzing to all originality. The culture of their native tongue has been neglected by Corean scholars. The consequence is, that after so many centuries of national life, Chō-sen possesses no literature worthy of the name. Only in rare cases are native books translated into either Chinese or Japanese.

At present, Corean literary men possess a highly critical knowledge of Chinese. Most intelligent scholars read the classics with ease and fluency. Penmanship is an art as much prized and as widely practised as in Japan, and reading and writing constitute education. From the fifth to the seventeenth century the Corean youth of gentle blood went to Nanking to receive or complete their education. Since Peking has been the Chinese capital (under the Mongols from 1279, and under the Ming emperors from 1410) few young men have gone abroad to study until within the last year, when numbers of Corean lads have entered the naval, military, and literary schools of the imperial government.

The practical democratic element pervading China was long absent from the nations which were her pupils and vassals. Of all these borrowers, Corea has most closely imitated her teacher. She fosters education by making scholastic ability, as tested in the literary examination, the basis of appointment to office. This "Civil Service Reform" was established in Chō-sen by the now ruling dynasty early in the fifteenth century. Education in Corea is public, and encouraged by the government only in this sense, that it is made the road to government employ and official promotion. By instituting literary examinations for the civil and military service, and nominally opening them to all competitors, and filling all vacancies with the successful candidates, there is created and maintained a constant stimulus to culture.

Corean culture resembles that in mediæval Europe. It is extra-vernacular. It is in Latin—the Latin of Eastern Asia—the classic tongue of the oldest of living empires. This literary instrument of the learned is not the speech of the modern Chinamen, but the condensed, vivid, artificial diction of the books, which the Chinese cannot and never did speak, and which to be fully understood must be read by the eye of the mind. The accomplished scholar of Seoul who writes a polished essay in classic style packs his sentences with quotable felicities, choice phrases, references to history, literary prismatics, and kaleidoscopic patches picked out here and there from the whole range of ancient Chinese literature, and imbeds them into a mosaic—smooth, brilliant, chaste, and a perfect unity. This is the acme of style. So in the Corean mind, the wise saws and ancient instances, the gnomic wisdom, quotations and proverbs, political principles, precedents, historical examples, and dynasties, are all Chinese, and ancient Chinese. His heaven, his nature, his history, his philosophy, are those of Confucius, and like the Chinaman, he looks down with infinite contempt upon the barbarians of Christendom and their heterodox conceptions of the universe. Meanwhile his own language, literature, and history are neglected. The Corean child begins his education by learning by voice, eye, and pen, the simple and beautiful native alphabet of twenty-five letters, and the syllabary of one hundred and ninety or more combinations of letters. He learns to read, and practises writing in both the book or square style and the script form or running hand. The syllabary is not analyzed, but committed to memory from sight and sound. Spelling is nearly an unknown art, as the vowel changes and requirements of euphony—so numerous as to terrify the foreign student of Corean—are quickly acquired by ear and example in childhood. With this equipment in the rudiments, which is all that nearly all the girls, and most of the boys learn, the young reader can master the story-books, novels, primers of history, epistles, and the ordinary communications of business and friendship. If the lad is to follow agriculture, cattle-raising, trade, mining, or hunting, he usually learns no more, except the most familiar Chinese characters for numbers, points of the compass, figures on the clock-dial, weights, measures, coins, and the special technical terms necessary in his own business. Thus it often happens that a Corean workman, like a Chinese washerman, may be perfectly familiar with the characters even to the number of hundreds relating to his trade or occupation, and yet be utterly unable to read the simplest book, or construct one Chinese sentence. With the Chinese characters, one can write English as well as Corean or Japanese, but a thorough knowledge of the terms necessary to a sailor, a jeweller, a farmer, or a lumber merchant would not enable one to read Ivanhoe or Wordsworth.

If the Corean lad aspires to government service, he begins early the study of the " true letters " or " great writing." The first book put into his hands is, " The Thousand Character Classic." This work is said to have been composed by a sage in one night— a labor which turned the hair and beard of the composer to whiteness. In it no character is repeated, and all the phrases are in two couplets, making four to a clause. The copies for children are printed from wooden blocks in very large type. At the right side of each character is its pronunciation in Corean, and on the left the equivalent Corean word. The sounds are first learned, then the meaning, and finally the syntax and the sense of the passages. Meanwhile the brush-pen is kept busily employed until the whole text of the author is thoroughly mastered by eye, ear, hand, and memory. In this manner, the other classics are committed. Education at first consists entirely of reading, writing, and memorizing. Etiquette is also rigidly attended to, but arithmetic, mathematics, and science receive but slight attention.

After this severe exercise of memory and with the pen, the critical study of the text is begun. Passages are expounded by the teacher, and the commentaries are consulted. Essays on literary themes are written, and a style of elegant composition in prose and verse is striven for. For the literary examinations in the capital and provinces, the government appoints examiners, who give certificates to those who pass. Those who succeed at the provincial tests, are eligible only to subordinate grades of employ in the local magistracies. The aspirants to higher honors, armed with their diplomas, set out to Seoul to attend at the proper time the national examination. The journey of these lads, full of the exultation and lively spirit born of success, moving in hilarious revelry over the high roads, form one of the picturesque features of out-door life in Corea. The young men living in the same district or town go together. They go afoot, taking their servants with them. Pluming themselves upon the fact that they are summoned to the capital at the royal behest, they often make a roystering, noisy, and insolent gang, and conduct themselves very much as they please. The rustics and villagers gladly speed their parting. At the capital they scatter, putting up wherever accommodations in inns or at the houses of relatives permit.

Though young bachelors form the majority at these examinations, the married and middle-aged are by no means absent. Gray-headed men try and may be rejected for the twentieth time, and grandfather, father, and son occasionally apply together.

On the appointed day, the several thousand or more competitors assemble at the appointed place, with the provisions which are to stay the inner man during the ordeal. The hour preparatory to the assignment of themes is a noisy and smoky one, devoted to study, review, declamation, or to eating, drinking, chatting, or sleeping, according to the inclination or habit of each. The examination consists of essays, and oral and written answers to questions. During the silent part of his work, each candidate occupies a stall or cell. The copious, minute, and complex vocabulary of terms in the language relating to the work, success and failure, the contingencies, honest and dishonest shifts to secure success, and what may be called the student's slang and folk-lore of the subject, make not only an interesting study to the foreigner, but show that these contests subtend a large angle of the Corean gentleman's vision during much of his lifetime.

Examination over, the disappointed ones wend their way home with what resignation or philosophy they may summon to their aid. The successful candidates, on horseback, with bands of musicians, visit their patrons, relatives, the examiners and high dignitaries, receiving congratulations and returning thanks. Then follows the inevitable initiation, which none can escape—corresponding to the French "baptism of the line," the German "introduction to the fox," the English "fagging," and the American "hazing."

One of the parents or friends of the new graduate, an "alumnus," or one who has taken a degree himself, one also of the same political party, acts as godfather, and presides at the ceremony. The graduate presents himself, makes his salute and takes his seat several feet behind the president of the party. With all gravity the latter proceeds, after rubbing up some ink on an ink-stone, to smear the face of the victim with the black mess, which while wet he powders thickly over with flour. Happy would the new graduate be could he escape with one layer of ink and flour, but the roughness of the joke lies in this, that every one present has his daub; and when the victim thinks the ordeal is over new persons drop in to ply the ink-brush and handful of flour. Meanwhile a carnival of fun is going on at the expense, moral and pecuniary, of the graduate. Eating, drinking, smoking, and jesting are the order of the day. It is impossible to avoid this trial of purse and patience, for unless the victim is generous and good-natured, other tricks and jokes as savage and cruel as those sometimes in vogue in American and British colleges follow. After this farce, but not until it has been undergone, is the title recognized by society.

The three degrees, corresponding somewhat to our B.A., M.A., and Ph.D., are *cho-si, chin-sa, kiup-chiei*. The diplomas are awarded in the king's name, the second written on white paper, and the third on red adorned with garlands of flowers. The degrees are not necessarily successive. The highest, or the second, may be applied for without the first. The holder of the second degree may obtain office in the provinces, and after some years may become a district magistrate or guardian of one of the royal sepulchres. The highest degree qualifies one to fill honorable posts at the palace and in the capital, in one of the ministries, or to be the governor of a province, or of a great city. Properly, the place of a "doctor" is in Seoul. The usual term of office is two years.

The examinations for civil titles and offices attract students of the highest social grade. The military studies are chiefly those of archery or horsemanship, the literary part of their exercises being slight. But one degree, the lowest, is awarded, and if the holder is of gentle blood, and has political influence, he may rise to lucrative office and honors, but if from the common people, he usually gets no more than his title, or remains a private or petty officer.

The system of literary examinations which, when first established, and during two or three centuries, was vigorously maintained with impartiality, is said to be at present in a state of decay, bribery and official favor being the causes of its decline.

The special schools of languages, mathematics, medicine, art, etc., are under the patronage of the government. The teachers and students in these branches of knowledge form a special class midway between the nobles and people, having some of the privileges of the former. They may also attend the examinations, gain diplomas, and fill offices. Their professions are usually hereditary, and they marry only among themselves. In most respects, these bodies of learned men resemble the old guilds of scholars in Yedo, and the privileged classes, like physicians, astronomers, botanists, etc., in Japan.

There are eight distinct departments of special knowledge. The Corps of Interpreters include students and masters of the Chinese, Manchiu, Mongol, and Japanese languages. These attend the embassy to Peking, have posts on the frontier, or live near Fusan. The treaties recently made with the United States and European powers will necessitate the establishment of schools of foreign languages, as in Tōkiō and Peking.

The School of Astronomy, geoscopy, and the choice of fortunate days for state occasions is for the special service of the king. Corea, like China, has not yet separated astrology from astronomy, but still keeps up official consultation with the heavenly bodies for luck's sake. The School of Medicine trains physicians for the royal, and for the public, service. The School of Charts or documents has charge of the archives and the preparation of the official reports sent to Peking. In the School of Design, the maps, sketches, plans and graphic work required by the government are made, and the portraits of the king are painted. The School of Law is closely connected with the Ministry of Justice, and serves for the instruction of judges, and as a court of appeals. The School of Mathematics or Accounts assists the Treasury Department, audits accounts, appraises values, and its members are often charged with the task of overseeing public works. The School of Horology at Seoul keeps the standard time and looks after the water-clock. Beside these eight services, there is the band of palace musicians.

It is evident from all the information gathered from sources within and without the hermit nation, that though there is culture of a certain sort among the upper classes, there is little popular education worthy of a name. The present condition of Chō-sen is that of Europe in the Middle Ages. The Confucian temples and halls of scholars, the memorial stones and walls inscribed with historical tablets and moral maxims, the lectures and discussions of literary coteries, and the poetry parties concentrate learning rather than diffuse it. The nobles and wealthy scholars, the few monasteries and the government offices possess libraries, but these are but dead Chinese to the common people. Nothing like the number of book stores, circulating libraries, private schools, or ordinary means of diffusing intelligence, common in China and Japan, exists in Corea. Science and the press, newspapers and hospitals, clocks and petroleum, and, more than all, churches and school-houses, have yet a mighty work to do in the Land of Morning Calm.

Paganism and superstition, Confucianism and Buddhism, having taken root in Chō-sen, each with its educational influence, Christianity entered within the last century to plant an acorn within the narrow bottle of the Corean intellect. It is needless to say that the receptacle was shattered by the spreading of the oak. The Corean body-politic, confronted by this rooted and growing influence, must be transformed. How the seed was dropped, how the tiny stem grew, how the trunk received into its bosom the lightning bolts of persecution, how the boughs were riven, and how life yet remains, will now be narrated.

III.

MODERN AND RECENT
HISTORY.

MODERN AND RECENT HISTORY.

CHAPTER XXXIX.

THE BEGINNINGS OF CHRISTIANITY—1784-1794.

CHRISTIANITY entered Corea through the gates of Rome and Peking. Though some writers have supposed that Christianity was introduced into the Corean peninsula by the Japanese, in 1592, yet it is nearly certain that this religion was popularly unknown until near the end of the eighteenth century. Then it entered from the west, and not from the east. It was not brought by foreigners, but grew up from chance seed wafted from the little garden of the church in Peking.

The soil upon which the exotic germ first lighted was in the mind of a student well-named by his father, "Stonewall," on account of his character in choosing a literary career, instead of the hereditary profession which his family wished him to adopt. During the winter of 1777, Stonewall was invited to form one of a party of students who were to spend a season of literary dalliance in company with the famous Confucian professor, Kwem.

The conference, held in a secluded temple, lasted ten days, during which time the critical study of the texts of Confucius and Mencius was indulged in with keen delight, and the profoundest problems that can interest man were earnestly discussed; but most fertilizing to their minds were some tracts on philosophy, mathematics, and religion just brought from Peking. These were translations of the writings, or original compositions in Chinese of the Jesuits in the imperial capital. Among these publications were some tracts on the Christian and Roman Catholic Religion, treating of the Existence of God, Divine Providence, the Immortality of the Soul, the Conduct of Life, the Seven Capital Sins, and the Seven

Contrary Virtues. Surprised and delighted, they resolved to attain, if possible, to a full understanding of the new doctrines.

They began at once to practise what they knew, and morning and evening they read and prayed. They set apart the 7th, 14th, 21st and 28th days of the month as periods of rest, fasting, and meditation. How long they continued this course of life is not known.

Stonewall, well knowing that his ideas of this new religion were imperfect and confused, turned his thoughts longingly toward Peking, hoping to get more books or information through a living teacher. For several years all his attempts were fruitless; though study, discussion, and practice of the new life were continued. In 1782, he moved to Seoul to live, and in 1783, to his joy, his friend Senghuni, son of the third ambassador to Peking, proceeded thither through Shing-king (Liao Tung), with a message to the bishop, Alexander de Gorla, a Portuguese Franciscan.

Senghuni himself became a docile pupil, and was, with the consent of his father, baptized. With the hope that he would become the first stone of the church in Chō-sen, he was named Peter.[1] He pledged himself to suffer all torments rather than abandon his faith, to have but one wife, to renounce worldly vanities, and finally to send his foreign friends tidings every year.

Safely passing the sentinels at Ai-chiu, he reached Seoul. Stonewall, eagerly receiving his share, gave himself for a time up to fresh reading and meditation, and then began to preach. Some of his friends in the capital, both nobles and commoners, embraced the new doctrines with cheering promptness and were baptized.

It is interesting to note the choice of baptismal names. As Stonewall had been the forerunner, he was named John the Baptist. Another called himself Francis Xavier, intending to make this saint his protector and patron. Other names of these primitive confessors are Ambrose, Paul, Louis, Thomas, Augustine, and later,

---

[1] The equipment of this first native missionary propagandist of Roman Christianity in Corea, deserves notice, as it brings out in sharp contrast the differing methods of Roman and Reformed Christianity. The convert brought back numerous tracts, didactic and polemic treatises, catechisms and commentaries, prayer-books, lives of the saints, etc., etc. These were for the learned, and those able to master them. For the simple, there was a goodly supply of crosses and crucifixes, images, pictures, and various other objects to strike the eye. It is not stated that the Bible, or any part of the Holy Scriptures, was sent for the feeding of hungry souls.

among the women, Agatha, Marie, Madeleine, Barbe, etc. The
adoption of these foreign names excited bitter feelings among the
patriotic, and became a cause of intense hatred against the Christians, who were stigmatized as "foreigner-Coreans."

A counterblast soon followed. The first, and as they were destined to be the last and most bitter enemies were the literati, who
saw at once that the new faith sapped at the base their national
beliefs and their most cherished customs. In the contest of discussion which followed, Senghuni came off victor. The pagan
champions retired from the conflict uttering memorable and prophetic words, with a final question, that became a by-word to
Americans nearly a century later : "This [Christian] doctrine is
magnificent, it is true, but it will bring sorrow to those who pro-
fess it. What are you going to do about it ? "

Among the converts were the lecturer Kwem and his brother,
both of whom propagated the faith in their district of Yang-kun,
thirty miles east of Seoul, now justly called "the cradle of the
faith." One of their converted students from the Nai-po returned
home to labor in the new cause, and from first to last, in the history of Roman Christianity in Corea, Nai-po has ever been a nursery of fervent confessors and illustrious martyrs. A second convert of the Kwem brothers laid the foundations of the faith in
Chulla. At the capital, a learned interpreter, on becoming a believer, multiplied with his own facile pen copies of the books
brought from Peking ; and it is believed translated from the
Chinese the "Explanation of the Gospels of the Sabbaths and
Feasts "—the first Christian book in the Corean language.

Thus from small beginnings, but rapidly, were the Christian
ideas spread, but soon the arm of the law and the power of the
pen were invoked to crush out the exotic faith. The first victim,
Thomas Kim, was tried on the charge of destroying his ancestral
tablets, tortured, and sent into exile, in which he soon after died.
The scholar now took up weapons, and in April, 1784, the king's
preceptor fulminated the first public document officially directed
against Christianity. In it all parents and relatives were entreated
to break off all relations with the Christians. The names of the
leaders were published ; and the example of Kim was cited.
Forthwith began a violent pressure of entreaty and menace upon
the believers to renounce their faith. Instead of peace, the sword
was brought into the household. Then began an exhibition alike
of glorious confession and shameful apostasy, but though even

Stonewall lapsed, the work went on in Nai-po, and in 1787,[1] persecution slackened.

Meanwhile, in order to cement more closely their bonds, the leaders formed a hierarchy after the model which Peter had seen in Peking, and to which their liturgical books so often referred. Francis Xavier was made bishop and others were chosen as priests. Separating to their various posts, they baptized, confessed, confirmed, and distributed the sacred elements in communion, all of which infused a new glow of faith among the converts. They robed themselves in rich Chinese silk, and erected platform confessionals. For ordinary faults confessed by the kneeling penitents alms were ordered, but for graver derelictions the priests administered one or two smart blows on the legs—a mild imitation of the national punishment, which so suggests Western methods of nursery discipline.

In perfect good faith and harmony, this curious hierarchy, so strange and even comical to a believer in the so-called "apostolical succession"—continued for two years; but in 1789, certain passages in their books suggested doubts as to the validity of their ministry. After earnest thought, and even at the risk of public ridicule, and of troubling the consciences of the faithful, they resigned their offices and took their places among the laity. A letter of inquiry was written, and sent in 1790 by the convert Paul to Peking. Surprised and overjoyed at the news from Corea, the fathers baptized and confirmed Paul, explained to him the Roman dogma of validity of ordination, and gave him a letter written on silk, to be concealed in his clothes, directed to Peter and Francis Xavier. His godfather Pansi, being an artist, painted Paul's portrait in oil, which was sent on to Paris.

The Christians at Seoul graciously submitted to the Episcopal rebuke and explanation, giving them the right only to baptize, yet

---

[1] It was during the summer of this year, 1787, that La Perouse sailed along the eastern coast of Chŏ-sen, discovered the straits which bear his name, between Yezo and Saghalin, demonstrated that the Gulf of Tartary divided Saghalin from the Asian mainland, and that Corea was not sea-girt, and named Dagelet Island and its companion Boussole. He had a copy of Hamel's book with him. He noticed the signal-fires along the coast, which from headland to headland, telegraphed to the capital the news of the stranger with his "black ships." Not as yet, however, as afterward, did the government connect the appearance of European vessels with the activity of the Christians within the realm, although La Perouse sailed under the flag which ever afterward was indissolubly associated in Corean minds with Christianity.

they yearned to receive the sacraments. Inflamed by the accounts of Paul, who pictured before them the ritual splendors, in the Peking cathedral, of altars, lights, vestments, solemn masses, music, processions, and all that enchants the eye and fires the imagination in the Roman form of Christianity, they indited another letter to the bishop, beseeching that an ordained priest should be sent them. This letter, carried by Paul, who left with the special embassy sent to congratulate the renowned emperor Kien-lung, which left Seoul September 17, 1790, contained a whole catechism of vexed questions of discipline and faith which had begun to disturb the little church.

While in Peking, Paul's companion was baptized, receiving the name of John the Baptist. The fathers gave them a chalice, a missal, a consecrated stone, some altar ornaments, and everything necessary for the celebration of the eucharist, with a recipe for making wine out of grapes, in order that all might be ready on the arrival of a priest among them. Paul and John the Baptist, after the return journey of a thousand miles through Shing-king, arrived safely in Seoul. All were filled with joy at the idea of having a priest sent them, but the episcopal decision against the worship of ancestors proved to many a stone of stumbling and a cause of apostasy. Hitherto, in simple ignorance and good faith, they had honored their ancestral shades and burnt incense at their shrines. Henceforth, all participation in such rites was impossible. After the authoritative declaration from Peking, that the worship of God and the worship of ancestors were contrary and impossible, no Corean could be a Christian while he burned incense before the tablets.

This tenet of the bishop was in the eyes of the Corean public a blow at the framework of society, the base of the family, and the foundation of the state. From this time forward, many of the feeble adherents began to fall away. In the conflict of filial and religious duty, many a soul was torn with remorse. In frequent instances the earnest believer who, for conscience sake, despoiled the family oratory and piling the ancestral tablets in his garden set them on fire, saw his aged parents sink with sorrow to the grave. For this crime Paul and Jacques Kim were put upon public trial, at which, for the first time, a clear and systematic presentation of Christian doctrine and the Roman cultus was elicited. The case, after condemnation of the prisoners, was submitted to the king, who was prevailed upon by the premier to approve the finding of the local tribunal. On December 8, 1791, the two Christians, after publicly refusing to recant, and reading aloud the sentence inscribed upon the board to be nailed over their pillory, were decapitated, while invoking the names of Jesus and Mary. Their ages were thirty-three and forty-one.

Thus was shed the first blood for Corean Christianity—the first drops of the shower to come, and the seed of a mighty church. The headless trunks, frozen to a stony rigidity which kept even the blood fresh and red, lay unburied on the ground for nine days, until devout men carried them to burial. A number of handkerchiefs dipped in their blood and preserved kept long alive the memory of these first martyrs of bloody persecution. The Nai-po now became a hunting-ground for the minions of the magistrates, who sought out all who professed themselves Christians and threw them in prison. There the tortures, peculiarly Corean, were set to work to cause apostasy. The victims were beaten with rods and paddles on the flesh and shin-bones, or whipped till the flesh hung in bloody rags. In many cases their bones were disjointed until the limbs dangled limp and useless. One man, Francis Xavier, after prolonged agonies was exiled to Quelpart, and on being removed to another place, died on the way. Peter, 61 years old, after wearying his torturers with his endurance, was tied round with a cord, laid on the icy ground at night, while pails of water were poured over him, which freezing as it fell, covered his body with a shroud of ice. In this Dantean tomb, the old martyr, calling on the name of Jesus, was left to welcome death, which came to him at the second cock-crow on the morning of January 29, 1793.

In the ten years following the baptism of Peter at Peking, in spite of persecution and apostasy, it is estimated that there were four thousand Christians in Corea.[1]

---

[1] This rapid spread of Christian ideas may be understood if we consider, as Dallet points out, the customs of the people. In every house there is the room open to the street, where everybody, friend or stranger, known or unknown, may come and talk or hear the news and discuss events. Nothing is kept secret, and being a nation of gossips and loungers, the news of any event, or the expression of a fresh idea, spreads like fire on the prairie. A doctrine so startlingly new, and preached as it was by men already famous for their learning, would at once excite the public curiosity, set all tongues running, and fire many hearts. Though in most cases the new flame would soon die out, leaving hardly enough ashes to mark a fire, yet the steady glow of altered lives would not pale even before torture and death.

CHAPTER XL.

THE first attempt of a foreign missionary to enter the hermit kingdom from the west was made in February, 1791. Jean dos Remedios, a Portuguese priest from Macao, offered himself, was accepted, and left Peking for the Border Gate with some Chinese guides. After a twenty days' journey in midwinter, he arrived on the frontier, and there awaited the precarious chances of recognition, according to certain signs agreed upon. For ten days he scanned the faces of the noisy crowd, hoping every moment to light upon friends, but in vain. The Christians, kept at home by the violence of the persecution, feared to venture to the border. The fair closed, the embassy crossed the Yalu River, while the foreigner and his Chinese guides returned to Peking. There the disappointed priest soon after died.

About the same time, the Bishop of Peking addressed a letter to the Pope detailing the origin, development, and condition of the new-born church in Corea.

Hearing no word from the Corean Christians during the next two years, it was determined to send succor. For this perilous mission, a young Chinese priest named Jacques Tsiu, twenty-four years old, of good bodily strength and pronounced piety, whose visage closely resembled a Corean's, was selected. Fortified with extraordinary ecclesiastical powers, he left Peking in February, 1794, and in twenty days arrived on the neutral ground. There he met the Christians, who urged him to wait nearly a year, on account of the vigilance of the sentinels. This he did among his fellow Christians in Shing-king, and on the night of December 23, 1794, crossed the Yalu, reached Seoul in safety, and at once began his labors. All went on well till June, when, through a treacherous visitor, the official spies were put upon his track. In spite of his removal to another place, three Christians—two who had guided him to Seoul, and one an interpreter, who in sublime self-sacrifice

23

tried to pass himself off as the Chinaman—were seized and tortured. With arms and legs dislocated, and knees crushed, they refused to betray their brother in the faith, and were put to death in prison, June 18. The three headless and battered trunks were flung in the Han River, which for the first, but not for the last time was streaked with martyr blood.

Meanwhile, the Chinese priest was at first hidden for many days under a wood-pile by a Christian lady, who, having gained over her mother-in-law, sheltered him in her house, where, protected by the law which forbids a noble's dwelling to be invaded, he remained three years. In September, 1796, he wrote a letter in Latin to the Bishop of Peking, and the native Christians writing in Chinese, the copies on silk were sewed into the garments of two believers, who, having bought positions as servants in the embassy, arrived in Peking, January 28, 1797. Among other things Jacques proposed that the King of Portugal should send an embassy to the King of Chō-sen to obtain a treaty of friendship, and allow the residence of physicians, astronomers, and scientific men in Corea.

Though no Portuguese envoy was sent out to treat with the court of Seoul,[1] a foreign vessel appeared in the autumn of this same year, off the eastern coast, floating the British flag. It was the sloop of war Providence, carrying sixteen guns, commanded by Captain W. R. Broughton, who cast anchor in Yung-hing Bay, October 4th, and touched at Fusan.[2] One of the natives who visited the ship was suspected by the government and arrested; though the English visitors were ignorant of the existence of Christians in Corea, and the local magistrates were equally uninformed as to the difference in religion and nationality between Britons and Portuguese.

The four political parties into which the Corean nobility was at this time divided, as described in Chapter XXV., were ranged into

---

[1] " Some priests proposed to the late Queen of Portugal to send an embassy hither [to Corea] with some gentlemen versed in mathematics, that they might benefit the country both in a religious and scientific way. . . . This plan never succeeded." Gutzlaff, 1834. Voyages to China, page 261.

[2] Captain Broughton was impressed with "the gorgeous Corean dresses," and the umbrella-hats, a yard in diameter. He asked for beef, but they gave him only wood, and he was tantalized with the sight of fat cattle grazing near by, which he was unable to get or purchase. He cruised in the Sea of Japan and the Gulf of Tartary, naming several places on the Corean coast. See p. 203.

House and Garden of a Noble.

two general groups, the Si-pai and the Piek-pai, "the government" and "the opposition." The Si-pai were devoted to the king,
and ready to second his views, the Piek-pai were more attached to
their special views. The king, Cheng-chong, who had ruled since
1776, was opposed to persecution of the Christians, and had done
much to restrain the bitterness of partisans. The Si-pai included the Nam-in, or "Southern" wing, in which were the Christian nobles, while all their enemies belonged to the Piek-pai.
So long as the king lived, the sword of persecution slept in its scabbard, but in 1800 [1] the king died, and was succeeded by his son,
Sunchō, a boy still under the care of his grandmother. This lady
at once assumed the conduct of national affairs,[2] and no sooner were
the five months of public mourning decently over, than the queen
regent dismissed the ministers then in office, and installed three
others of the No-ron group, all of whom were bitter enemies of the
Christians. A decree of general persecution was issued a few days
after, in the name of the king. Two converts of noble rank were
at once arrested, and during 1801, the police were busy in haling
to prison believers of every rank, age, and sex. Alexander Wang,
who had written a book in his native language on "The Principal Articles of the Christian Religion," and had begun another
on systematic theology, was arrested. From the reading of
these works, the magistrates imagined the essence of Christianity
was in hatred of one's parents and the king, and the destruction
of the human race.[3] The Church Calendar was also seized.

The Chinese priest was outlawed by the government, in a public
proclamation. On reading this, the brave man left the house of the
noble lady in which he had been sheltered, and refusing to endan-
ger longer the lives of his friends, voluntarily surrendered himself,

---

[1] See page 226.

[2] Or, as the natives say, " she proceeded to pull down the blinds." This
phrase, which is highly suggestive of American street slang, refers to the
curtain of bamboo which veils the sovereign of Chō-sen; as in Old Japan
the mikado was thus screened from the vulgar, and even noble, gaze during state councils. Whoever, therefore, is " behind the curtain," is on the
throne.

[3] This highly logical conclusion was reached by pondering upon the doctrine of Romanism that celibacy is a more perfect state than marriage; and
that " the world," which, with the flesh and the devil, was to be regarded as
one of the true believers' enemies, could mean only the king and country of
Chō-sen. To this day, most of the pagans accept the magistrates' decision as a
complete epitome of the gospel of Christ.

and received the death-stroke, May 31, 1801, at the age of thirty-two. His hostess, Colombe, thrown in prison herself, while await-ing death wrote out his life and works on the silk skirt of her dress. At her execution the noble lady begged that she might not be stripped of her clothes, as were other malefactors, but die in her robes. Her request was granted, and with the grace of the English Lady Jane Grey, she laid her head on the block. Four other women, formerly attendants in the palace, and an artist, who for painting Christian subjects was condemned, were beheaded by the official butchers, who made the "Little Western Gate" of Seoul—where a Christian church may yet be built—a Golgotha. The policy of the government was shown in making away with the Christians of rank and education, who might be able to direct affairs in the absence of the foreign priests, and in letting the poor and humble go free.

From a letter written on silk in sympathetic ink to the Bishop of Peking by Alexander Wang, and, with the aid of treachery, de-ciphered by the magistrates, they suspected a general conspiracy of the Christians ; for in his letter this Corean proposed an appeal to the Christian nations of Europe to send sixty or seventy thou-sand soldiers to conquer Corea![1] The bearer of this letter was immediately beheaded, and his body cut into six pieces; while the visitor to Captain Broughton's ship in 1799, for having said that "one such ship as that could easily destroy one hundred Corean vessels of war," was put to the torture and condemned. Alexander Wang, who had witnessed a good confession, before the king, a year before, and bore on his wrist the cord of crimson silk showing that he had touched the royal person, was likewise decapitated.

It now devolved upon the king of Chō-sen to explain to his suzerain the execution of a Chinese subject. In a letter full of Confucian orthodoxy, he declares that Chō-sen from the time of Ki Tsze, had admitted no other dogmas than those taught by the sages of China—"all other doctrine is strange to the Little Kingdom." He describes the Christians as "the monstrous, bar-barous, and infamous" "sect of brigands" "who live like brutes and birds of the vilest sort," and who in their plot, "have interlaced themselves as a serpent and knotted themselves to-gether like a cord." The plan to conquer "the Little King-

---

[1] Dallet, vol. i., p. 205.

dom at the corner of the earth" by myriads of men and vessels from Europe is detailed, with an apology for the execution of
Jacques, not as a Chinese subject, but as chief conspirator. Dallet suggests that, in answer to this letter, the Dragon Monarch
read the king a tart lecture, and hinted that a rich stream
of silver would soothe his ruffled scales. "China had not
been China had she lost so fair an occasion to fleece her cowering
vassal."

A fresh edict, made up of the usual fixed ammunition of Corean
rhetoric, was fulminated against "the evil sect," January 25, 1802.
The result was to advertise the outlawed faith in every corner of
the realm. Nevertheless, the condition of the Christians scattered
in the mountains and northern forests, or suffering poverty, hunger, and cold at home, was deplorable, under the stress of political
as well as religious hatred.

The first exchange of Muscovite and Corean courtesies took
place in 1808, when several of the commissioners from Seoul
were in Peking.[1] Presents were mutually given, which in
both cases were products of the then widely separated countries, which were destined within fifty years to be next-door
neighbors.

Out of the modern catacombs of Roman Christianity, the
Corean converts addressed two letters, dated December 9 and 18,
1811, to the Pope—"the Very High, Very Great Father, Chief of
the whole Church"—in which they invited help, not only of a spiritual nature, but aid in ships and envoys to treat with their king.
They were willing even to leave their native land and colonize the
islands in the sea, for the sake of worship and conscience. Signed
with fictitious names, copied on silk, and sewn in the clothing of
the messenger, they reached Peking and Rome, but the bishop
of neither city could afford succor. His Holiness was then a
prisoner at Fontainebleau, and the Roman propaganda was
nearly at a standstill. With a goodly supply of medals and
crosses, the messenger returned, and the church in Corea enjoyed
peace, and new converts were made until 1815, when a non-po-
litical persecution broke out for a while in Kang-wen and Kiung-
sang.

In 1817, the king and court were terrified by the appearance off

---

[1] Timkowski's Travels of the Russian Mission through Mongolia to China,
and Residence in Peking, London, 1827.

the west coast of the British [1] vessels Alceste and Lyra. They suspected that the good captain and jolly surgeon, who have given us such fascinating narratives of their cruise, were in active connection with "the evil sect;" but beyond some surveys, purchases of beef, and interviews with local magistrates, the foreigners departed without further designs against the throne.

In 1823 several of the Christians, encouraged by hopes held out by the Bishop of Peking, went to the Border Gate to meet a foreign priest, but to their dismay found none. In 1826,[2] they were troubled by a report that the shō-gun of Japan had requested their king to return six Japanese adherents of the interdicted "Jesus sect," who had fled the empire in a boat. Shortly after, in Chulla, through a quarrel instigated by a drunken potter, a convert, which led to information given in spite, a severe persecution broke out, lasting three months.

The year 1832 was noted for its rainfall and inundations. To propitiate Heaven's favor the king recalled many exiles, among whom were Christians. In this year also the British ship, Lord Amherst, was sent out by the East India Company on a voyage of commercial exploration, and to open, if possible, new markets for the fabrics of England and India. On board was a Prussian gentleman, the Rev. Charles Gutzlaff, under the patronage of the Netherlands Missionary Society, though travelling at his own cost. Reaching the coast of Chulla, July 17th, he remained one month. Being a good Chinese scholar, and well equipped with medical knowledge, he landed on several of the islands and on the mainland, he distributed presents of books, buttons, and medicines, planted potatoes and taught their cultivation. Through an officer he sent the king presents of cut glass, calicoes, and woollen goods, with a copy of the Bible and some Protestant Christian tracts. These, after some days of negotiation, were refused. A few of the more intelligent natives risked their heads, and accepted various gifts, among which were Chinese translations

---

[1] In 1793, the first British and the first European vessel entered the Yellow Sea. It was the ship of the line Lion, on board of which was Lord Macartney, the ambassador of King George III. to Peking, the first English envoy to China. The ship did not visit or approach Corean shores.

[2] This date is that given by Dallet, who perhaps refers to the uprising in 1829 at Ozaka, of suspected believers in the "Jesus doctrine," when six men and one old woman were crucified by the Japanese authorities. The leader of the so-called conspiracy fled to sea with his companions.

of European works on geography and mathematics. Mr. Gutzlaff could discover no trace of Christianity[1] or the converts, though he made diligent inquiry. The lying magistrates denied all knowledge of even the existence of the Christian faith. Deeply impressed with their poverty, dirt, love of drink, and degradation, the Protestant, after being nearly a month among the Coreans, left their shores, fully impressed with their need of soap and bibles.

The year 1834 closed the first half century of Corean Christianity.

In this chapter, the moral weakness of Roman Catholic methods of evangelization in Corea, and elsewhere in Asia, has been revealed. It must be remembered that the Corean converts were taught to believe not only in the ecclesiastical supremacy of the Pope, but also in the righteousness of his claim to temporal power as the Vicar of Heaven. Untaught in the Scriptures of the New Testament, and doubtless ignorant of the words of Jesus—"My kingdom is not of this world ; if my kingdom were of this world, then would my servants fight"—the Coreans suspected no blasphemy in the papal claim. Seeing the Pope's political power upheld by the powerful European nations then under Bourbon rule, the Corean Christians, following the ethics of their teachers, played the part of traitors to their country ; they not only deceived the magistrates, and violated their country's laws, but, as the letter of Alexander Wang shows, actually invited armed invasion. Hence from the first Christianity was associated in patriotic minds with treason and robbery. The French missionary as the forerunner of the French soldier and invader, the priest as the pilot of the gunboat, were not mere imaginings, but, as the subsequent narrative shows, strict logic and actual fact. It is the narrative of friends, not foes, that, later, shows us a bishop acting as spy and pilot on a French man-of-war, a priest as guide to a buccaneering raid ; and, after the story of papal Christianity, the inevitable "French expedition."

---

[1] While off the island of Wen-san, according to Dallet, some of the native Christians, attracted by the legend in Chinese characters on the flag "The Religion of Jesus Christ," came on board. " A Protestant minister saluted them with the words which are sacramental among the pagans, ' May the spirits of the earth bless you !' At these words the neophytes, seeing that they had been deceived, and that a snare had been laid for their good faith, retired in all haste without ever returning the salute, and made no further visits to the ships."

CHAPTER XLI.

THE French Revolution, and the wars of Napoleon following, which distracted all Europe for a period of over twenty years, completely disorganized the missionary operations of the Holy See and French Roman Catholic Church. On the restoration of the Bourbons, and the strengthening of the papal throne by foreign bayonets, the stream of religious activity flowed anew into its old channels, and with an added volume. Missionary zeal in the church was kindled afresh, and the prayers of the Christians in the far East were heard at the court of St. Peter. It was resolved to found a mission in Corea, directly attached to the Holy See, but to be under the care of the Society of Foreign Missions of Paris.

Barthelemy Brugiere, then a missionary at Bangkok, Siam, offered as a volunteer, and in 1832 was nominated apostolic Vicar of Corea. He reached Shing-king, but was seized with sudden illness, and died October 20, 1835. Pierre Philibert Maubant, his host, stepped into the place of his fallen comrade, and with five Corean Christians left Fung-Wang Chang, crossed the neutral strip, and the Yalu River on the ice. Dodging the sentinels at Ai-chiu, he entered Corea as a thread enters the needle's eye. They crawled through a water-drain in the wall, and despite the barking of a dog, got into the city. Resting several hours, they slid out again through another drain, reaching the country and friends beyond. Two days' journey on horses brought them to Seoul, from which Maubant, the first Frenchman who had penetrated the hermit kingdom, or who, in Corean phrase, had committed *pem-kiong* (violation of the frontier), wrote to his friends in Paris.

Maubant's first duty was to order back a Chinese priest who refused to learn Corean, or to obey any but the Bishop of Peking. With the couriers who escorted the refractory Chinaman to the frontier, went three young men to study at the college in Macao. At the Border Gate they met Jacques Honore Chastan a young

French priest, who, on the dark night of January 17, 1837, passed the custom-house of Ai-chiu disguised as a Corean widower in mourning, and joined Maubant in Seoul. Nearly one year later, December 19, 1838, Laurent Marie-Joseph Imbert, a bishop, ran the gauntlet of wilderness, ice, and guards, and took up his residence under the shadow of the king's palace.

Visits, masses, and preaching now went on vigorously. The Christians at the end of 1837 numbered 6,000, and in 1838, 9,000. Up to January 16, 1839, the old regent being averse from persecution, the work went on unharmed, but on that day, the court party in favor of extirpating Christianity, having gained the upper hand, hounded on the police in the king's name. The visitation of every group of five houses in all the eight provinces was ordered. Hundreds of suspects were at once seized and brought to trial. In June, before the death of the old regent, the uncle of the young king (Henchong, 1834–1849) and the implacable enemy of the Christians obtained control of power, and at an extraordinary council of the ministers, held July 7, 1839, a new decree was issued in the regent's name. The persecution now broke out with redoubled violence. In a few days, three native lay leaders were beheaded, and a score of women and children suffered death. To stay the further shedding of blood, Bishop Imbert, who had escaped to an island, came out of his hiding-place, and on August 10th delivered himself up and ordered Maubant and Chastan to do the same. The three willing martyrs met in chains before the same tribunal. During three days they were put to trial and torture, thence transferred to the Kum-pu, or prison for state criminals of rank. They were again tried, beaten with sixty-six strokes of the paddle, and condemned to die under the sword, September 21, 1839.

On that day, the inspector and one hundred soldiers took their place on the execution ground, not near the city gate, but close to the river. A pole fixed in the earth bore a flag inscribed with the death-sentence. Pinioned and stripped of their upper clothing, a stick was passed between the elbows and backs of the prisoners, and an arrow, feather end up, run through the flesh of each ear. Their faces were first wet with water and then powdered with chalk. Three executioners then marched round, brandishing their staves, while the crowd raised a yell of insult and mockery. A dozen soldiers, sword in hand, now began prancing around the kneeling victims, engaging in mock combat, but delivering their blows at the victims. Only when weary of their sport, the human butchers relieved the agony of their victims by the decapitating blow. The heads were presented to the inspector on a board, and the corpses, after public exposure during three days, were buried in the sand by the river banks.

On the day after the burial, three Christians attempted to remove the bodies, but the government spies lying in wait caught them. As of old in Rome, when the primitive Christians crawled stealthily at night through the arches of the Coliseum, into the arena, and groping about in the sand for the bones of Ignatius left after the lion's feast, bore them to honored sepulture, so these Corean Christians with equal faith and valor again approached the bloody sand by the Han River. Twenty days after the first attempt, a party of seven or eight men succeeded in bearing away the bodies of the martyrs to Noku, about eight miles north of Seoul.

Thus died the first European missionaries who entered "the forbidden land." As in the old fable of the lion's den, the footprints all pointed one way.

With the foreign leaders there perished no less than one hundred and thirty of their converts, seventy by decapitation, and the others by strangulation, torture, or the result of their wounds.[1] In November, 1839, a new edict in the vernacular was posted up all over the country. Six bitter years passed before the Christians again had a foreign pastor.

Great events now began to ripen in China. The opium war of 1840–42 broke out. The "Western Barbarians" held the chief cities of the China coast from Hong-Kong to Shanghae, and the military weakness of the colossal empire was demonstrated. The French, though having nothing to do with this first quarrel of China with Europe, were on the alert for any advantage to be gained in the far East. In 1841, Louis Philippe sent out the war vessels Erigone and Favorite, to occupy if possible some island to the south of Japan, which would be valuable for strategic and commercial purposes, and to make treaties of trade and friendship with Japan, and especially with Corea.

---

[1] By poetic justice, the chief instigators of this persecution came each to a bad end. Of the court ministers, one, having provoked the king's jealousy, was obliged by royal order to poison himself at a banquet, in December, 1845, and the other, falling into disgrace, was sent to exile, in which he shortly died. The chief informer, who had hoped for reward in high office, obtained only a minor position, with little honor and less salary. He was afterward exiled, and in 1862, having headed a local uprising, was put to death, his body was minced up, and the fragments were exhibited through the provinces.

The Erigone cast anchor at Macao, September 7, 1841, and Captain Cecile awaited events. Moving north in February, 1842, with Andrew Kim, the Corean student, as interpreter, on the Erigone, and Thomas Tsoi, his companion, on the Favorite, the French captains, hearing of the sudden conclusion of the war, gave up the idea of opening Corea.

The two Coreans, with two French priests, engaged a Chinese junk, and landed on the coast of Shing-king, October 25, 1842. On December 23d, Kim set out for the Border Gate, and within two leagues of it met the outward-bound embassy. Each of the three hundred persons had his passport at his girdle. Stopping to see them file past, he saluted one who was a Christian, and had in his belt letters from Maubant and Chastan, written before their execu-

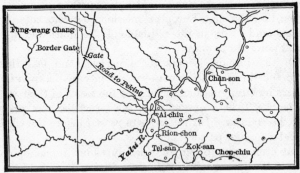

The Missionary's Gateway into Corea.

tion, and from the natives. Unable to go back with Andrew to Ai-chiu, as every name on the embassy's list was registered, the man went on to Peking. Andrew Kim, by mingling among the drovers and huge cattle returning from the fair, ran the blockade at Ai-chiu; but on the next day, having walked all night, he applied for lodgings at an inn for shelter, and was recognized as a stranger. Fearful of being arrested as a border-ruffian from the neutral strip, he took to his heels, recrossed the Yalu, and after resting at Fung-Wang Chang, rejoined his friends at Mukden.

On December 31, 1843, Jean Joseph Ferreol was consecrated Bishop of Corea, and resolved to cross the frontier, not at Ai-chiu, but at Hun-chun, on the Tumen. Andrew Kim exploring the way, after a month's journey through ice and snow, mountains and forests, reached Hun-chun, February 25, 1845. The native Christians, having been duly instructed, had arrived at Kion-wen a

month before. For recognition, Andrew was to hold a blue kerchief
in his hand and have a little red bag of tea at his girdle. At the
fair which opened at Kion-wen on the 28th, the Christians met.
The result of their conference was that Ai-chiu was declared safer
even than Kion-wen.

Since 1839, the government had tripled its vigilance, and
doubled the guards on the frontier. No one could pass the gate

Border Towns of Northern Corea.

at Ai-chiu who had not a passport stamped with the chief inspector's seal, bestowed only after the closest scrutiny and persistent
cross-questioning. On it was written the name and place of birth
and residence of the holder, and after return from China or the
fair it must be given up. The result of these stringent regulations
was to drive the missionaries to find a path seaward. In December, 1844, of seven converts from Seoul, attempting to get to the
Border Gate, to meet Ferreol, only three were able to pass Ai-
chiu. The other four, who had the wig, hair pins, and mourning
costume of a widower for Ferreol, were unable to satisfy their ques-
tioners, and so returned. At the Border Gate, Ferreol, after seeing
the caravan pass, ordered Andrew Kim to enter alone, while he
returned and sailed soon after to Macao. Andrew, with the aid of
his three friends, who met him at a lonely spot at some distance
from Ai-chiu, reached Seoul, January 8, 1845.

As soon as resources and opportunity would permit, Andrew
collected a crew of eleven fellow-believers, only four of whom had
ever seen the sea, and none of whom knew their destination, and
equipped with but a single compass, put to sea in a rude fishing-
boat, April 24, 1845. Despite the storms and baffling winds, this un-
couth mass of firewood, which the Chinese sailors jeeringly dubbed
" the Shoe," reached Shanghae in June. Andrew Kim, never before

at sea except as a passenger, had brought this uncalked, deckless, and unseaworthy scow across the entire breadth of the Yellow Sea.

After the ordeal of the mandarin's questions,[1] and visits and kindly hospitality from the British naval officers and consul, he reached his French friends at the Roman Catholic mission.

The beacon fires were now blazing on Quelpart, and from headland to headland on the mainland, telegraphing the news of "foreign ships" to Seoul. From June 25th until the end of July, Captain Edward Belcher,[2] of the British ship Samarang, was engaged in surveying off Quelpart and the south coast. Even after the ship left for Nagasaki, the magistrates of the coast were ordered to maintain strict watch for all seafarers from strange countries. This made the return of Andrew Kim doubly dangerous.

Bishop Ferreol came up from Macao to Shanghae, and on Sunday, August 17th, Andrew Kim was ordained to the priesthood. On September 1st, with Ferreol and Marie Antoine Nicholas Daveluy, another French priest, he set sail in "the Shoe," now christened the "Raphael," and turned toward the land of martyrdom. It was like Greatheart approaching Giant Despair's Castle.

The voyage was safely, though tediously, made past Quelpart, and through the labyrinth of islands off Chulla. On October 12th, the Frenchmen, donning the garb of native noblemen in mourning, and baffling the sentinels, landed at night in an obscure place on the coast. Soon after this Daveluy was learning the language among some Christian villagers, who cultivated tobacco in a wild part of the country. The bishop went to Seoul as the safest place to hide and work in, while the farmer-sailors, after seven months' absence, returned to their hoes and their native fields.

---

[1] So fearless and generous a soul as Andrew Kim, who could yet follow the ethics and example of his teachers in repeatedly practising deception and violating his country's laws at Ai-chiu, scrupled not to lie to the mandarin at Shanghae, and tell him that he and his crew had been accidentally driven out to sea. As in the later case of the robbery of the regent's tomb, "the end justified the means."

[2] The voyage of this officer, which added so much to science, resulted in making Quelpart and Beaufort Islands, Port Hamilton, and Mount Auckland as well known in geography as the names of Her Majesty's servants were known in British politics. The visitors were treated with courtesy, and even their survey-marks, stakes, and whitewashed stones were carefully set up when washed away by the storm, or disturbed by cattle. The Coreans, however, drove their beeves well away from the Englishmen, who longed for fresh meat.

CHAPTER XLII.

THE WALLS OF ISOLATION SAPPED.

WHILE the three priests were prosecuting their perilous labors, Thomas Tsoi, the Corean student from Macao with Maistre, a new missionary, were on their way through Manchuria to Hun-chun. Arriving after a seventeen days' march, they were seized by Manchiu officers, reprimanded, and sent back to Mukden.

Andrew Kim, by order of Bishop Ferreol, went to Whang-hai by water, to examine into the feasibility of making that province a gateway of entrance. The sea was full of Chinese junks, the herring fishery being at its height. Watch-towers dotted the hills, and the beach was patrolled by soldiers to prevent communication with shore. Andrew, coming ostensibly to buy a cargo of fish, was enabled to sail among the islands, to locate the rocks and sandspits, and to make a chart of the coast. Deeming the route practicable, he hailed a Chinese junk, and after conference, confided to the captain the mail-bag of the mission, which contained also the charts and two maps of Corea. Unfortunately these documents were seized by the spies, and Andrew Kim, delayed while the cargo of fish was drying, was arrested on the suspicion of being a Chinaman. He was sent to Seoul, and while in prison heard of the French ships which were at that moment vainly trying to find the mouth of the Han River and the channel to the capital. Meanwhile, from his hiding-place, Ferreol wrote to Captain Cecile, who commanded the fleet of three war-vessels.

The object of this visit was to hold a conference with the king's ministers, and demand satisfaction for the murder of Imbert Chastan and Maubant in 1839. After some coast surveys made, and the despatch of a threatening letter, the ships withdrew. Ferreol's note arrived too late, and Andrew Kim's fate was sealed.

While in prison, Andrew was employed in coloring, copying, and translating two English maps of the world, one of which was for the king, and composing a summary of geography. In a letter in Latin to Ferreol, dated August 26th, he narrated his capture and trial. On September 16th, he was led out to trial. The sentence-flag bore the inscription : "Put to death for communicating with the western barbarians," and the full programme of cruelty was carried out. Four women and four men were put to death in the persecution which followed.

Maistre and Thomas Tsoi went to Macao and there found the French frigates La Gloire and La Victorieuse, ready to sail north for an answer to Captain Cecile's letter. Gladly welcomed by Captain Pierre, they went aboard July 12th. On August 10th, while under sail in a group of islands off Chulla, in latitude 35° 45' and longitude 124° 8', in water which the English charts marked at twelve fathoms deep, both vessels grounded simultaneously. The high tides for which this coast is noted falling rapidly, both vessels became total wrecks. The largest of the La Gloire's boats was at once sent to Shanghae for assistance, and the six hundred men made their camp at Kokun Island. Kindly treated and furnished with provisions as they were, the Frenchmen during their stay were rigidly secluded, and at night cordons of boats with lanterns guarded against all communication with the mainland. Thomas Tsoi acted as dumb interpreter, with pencil, in Chinese, and though hearing every word of the Corean magistrates was not recognized. Though meeting fellow Christians, he was unable to get inland, and Ferreol's messengers to the sea-shore arrived after an English ship from Shanghae had taken the crews away.

The Corean government, fearing [1] further visits of the outside barbarians, sent an answer to Admiral Cecile, directing it to Captain Pierre at Macao, by way of Peking.[2] They explained why they treated Frenchmen shipwrecked kindly ; but sent Frenchmen disguised to execution.[3] When Admiral Cecile reached Paris in

---

[1] These were the first official relations of France with Corea ; or, as a native would say, between Tai-pep-kuk and Chō-sen ; the expression for France being Tai-pep, and for a Frenchman—curiously enough—Pepin.

[2] Inside the country, the frequent appearance of the foreign ships was the subject of everyday talk, and the news in this nation of gossips spread like a prairie fire, or a rolling avalanche. By the time the stories reached the northern provinces whole fleets of French ships lay off the coast. Their moral effect was something like that among the blacks in the Southern States during the civil war, when the " Lincoln gunboats " hove in sight. The people jestingly called the foreign vessels " The authorities down the River."

[3] For changing their name and garments, sleeping by day, going abroad at night, associating with rebels, criminals and villains, and entering the king-

1848, one of the periodical French revolutions had broken out in Paris, and a war at the ends of the earth was out of the question. The French government neglected to send a vessel to take away the effects saved from the wreck. The Coreans promptly put the cannon to use, and from them, as models, manufactured others for the forts built to resist "the Pepins" in 1866, and the Americans in 1871.

Once more Maistre and Thomas Tsoi essayed to enter the guarded peninsula, by sailing early in 1848 in a Chinese junk from Macao to Merin Island off Whang-hai, but no Christians met them. By way of Shanghae, they then went into Shing-king, and in December to the Border Gate, meeting couriers from Bishop Ferreol. On a fiercely cold, windy, and dark night, which drove the soldiers indoors to the more congenial pleasure of the long pipe, cards, and cup on the oven-warmed floors, Thomas Tsoi got safely through Ai-chiu, and in a few days was in Seoul, and later in Chulla. The work of propagation now took a fresh start. A number of religious works composed or translated into the vulgar tongue were printed in pamphlet form from a native printing press, and widely circulated. In 1850, the Christians numbered eleven thousand, and five young men were studying for the priesthood. Regular mails, sewn into the thick cotton coats of men in the embassy, were sent to and brought from China. A French whaler having grounded off the coast, the French consul at Shanghae, with two Englishmen, came to reclaim the vessel's effects, and meeting three young men sent by the ever-alert Thomas Tsoi, took them back to Shanghae, the third remaining to meet his comrades on their return with fresh missionaries to come. After still another failure to enter Corea, Maistre set foot in Chulla-dō, by way of Kokun Island, even while the fire-signals were blazing on the headlands on account of the presence of Russian ships.[1]

---

dom clandestinely, the missionaries were put to death; and no comparison could be drawn to mitigate their sentence between them and innocent shipwrecked men.

[1] Other nations besides France now began to learn something of the twin hermits of the East, Chō-sen and Nippon. During 1852, the Russian frigate Pallas sailed along the east coast up to the Tumen River, making no landing, but keeping at a distance of from two to five miles from the shore in order to avoid shoals and rocks. The object of the Pallas was to trace and map the shore line. In 1855, the French war-vessel Virginie continued the work begun by the Pallas, and at the end of her voyage the whole coast from Fusan to the Tumen was known with some accuracy, and mapped out with Euro-

Ferreol, worn out with his labors, after lying paralytic for many months, died February 3, 1853 ; but in March, 1854, Janson, making a second attempt, entered Corea, having crossed the Yellow Sea in a junk, which immediately took back three native students for Macao. Janson died in Seoul, of cerebral fever, June 18, 1854.

In these years, 1853 and 1854, Commodore Perry and the American squadron were in the waters of the far East, driving the wedge of civilization into Japan, and sapping her walls of seclusion. The American flag, however, was not yet seen in Corean waters, though the court of Seoul were kept informed of Perry's movements.

A fresh reinforcement of missionaries to storm the citadel of paganism, Bishop Simeon, François Berneux, with two young priests, Michel Alexandre Petitnicholas and Charles Antoine Pourthie, set sail from Shanghae in a junk, and, after many adventures, arrived at Seoul via Whang-hai, while Feron (of later buccaneering fame) followed on a Corean smuggling vessel, standing unexpectedly before his bishop in the capital, March 31, 1857. A synod of all the missionaries was now held, at which Berneux consecrated Daveluy as his fellow bishop. Maistre died December 20th. The faith was now spread to Quelpart by a native of that island, who, having been shipwrecked on the coast of China, was carried by an English ship to Hong-Kong, where he met a Corean student from Macao and was converted. The Roman Catholic population of Corea in 1857 was reckoned at 16,500.

Communication with the native Christians living near Nagasaki, and then under the harrow of persecution, took place. The cholera imported from Japan swept away over 400,000 victims in Corea. Thus does half the world not know how the other half lives. How many Americans ever heard of this stroke of pestilence in the hermit nation ?

In 1860, war with China broke out, the French and English forces took the Peiho forts, entered Peking, sacked the summer palace of the Son of Heaven, a few thousand European troops destroying the military prestige of the Chinese colossus. The

---

pean names, at once numerous and prophetic. The coast line of Tartary or Manchuria—at that time a Chinese province—was also surveyed, mapped, and made ready for the Czar's use and that of his ambassador in 1860.

Pallas and Virginie ! The names are suggestive of the *maiden* diplomatic victory of General Ignatieff, of whom more anon.

Chinese emperor fled into Shing-king, toward Corea. The news produced a lively effect in Chō-sen, especially at court.[1]

The utter loss of Chinese prestige struck terror into all hearts. For six centuries, China, the Tai-kuk (Great Empire), had been, in Corean eyes, the synonym and symbol of invincible power, and "the Son of Heaven, who commands ten thousand chariots," the one able to move all the earth. Copies of the treaty made between China and the allies, granting freedom of trade and religion, were soon read in Corea, causing intense alarm.

But the after-clap of news, that turned the first storm of excitement into a tempest of rage and fear, was the treaty with Russia. General Ignatieff, the brilliant and vigorous diplomatist then but twenty-eight years old and fresh on the soil of Cathay, obtained, in 1860, after the allied plenipotentiaries had gone home, the signature of Prince Kung to the cession of the whole Ussuri province. The tread of the Great Bear had been so steadily silent, that before either Great Britain or Chō-sen knew it, his foot had been planted ten degrees nearer the temperate zone. A rich and fertile region, well watered by the Amoor and Sungari Rivers, bordered by the Pacific, with a coast full of harbors, and comprising an area as large as France, was thus ceded to Russia. The Manchiu rulers of China had actually surrendered their ancestral homeland to the wily Muscovites. The boundaries of Siberia now touched the Tumen. The Russian bear jostled the Corean tiger.

With France on the right, Russia on the left, China humbled, and Japan opened to the western world, what wonder that the rulers in Seoul trembled?

The results to Corean Christianity were that, in less than a de-

---

[1] A noble of high rank presented to the council of ministers a memorial, setting forth the dangers that then menaced Chō-sen, and urging that extraordinary means be put forth to meet the emergencies. He proposed that the national policy of armed neutrality should be preserved, that the conquered emperor of China should not enter Chō-sen, that the frontier should be strengthened against a possible invasion of the border-ruffians inhabiting the neutral strip. Taking advantage of the situation, these men, banding together with Chinese adventurers and Corean refugees, might make a descent in force into the kingdom. Finally, the supreme danger that filled all minds was the threatened invasion of the French. He recommended that the castle of Tong-nai, near Fusan, and the western strongholds of Nam-an, Pu-pion, and In-chiŭn (the port opened in 1882), should be strongly garrisoned and strengthened; and that a new citadel be built on the island of Kang-wa, to command the river and the entrance to the capital. (See map, page 190.)

cade, thousands of natives had fled their country and were settled in the Russian villages.

At the capital all official business was suspended, and many families of rank fled to the mountains. The nobles or officials who could not quit their posts sent off their wives and children. All this turned to the temporary advantage of the missionaries. In many instances, people of rank humbly sought the good favor and protection of the Christians. Medals, crosses, and books of religion were bought in quantities. Some even publicly wore them on their dress, hoping for safety when the dreaded invasion should come. The government now proceeded to raise war-funds, levying chiefly on the rich merchants, who were threatened with torture and death in case of refusal. A conscription of able-bodied men was ordered, and bombs, called "French pieces," and small-bore cannon were manufactured. In a foundry in the capital heavy guns were cast after the model of those left by the wreck of the La Gloire. The Kang-wa forts were built and garrisoned. In the midst of these war preparations, the missionary body was reinforced by the arrival of four of their countrymen, who, by way of Merin Island, set foot on the soil of their martyrdom October, 1861. Their names were Landre, Joanno, Ridel, and Calais. This year the number of Christians reached 18,000.

Indirect attempts to insert the crowbars of diplomacy in the chinks of Corea's wall of seclusion were made about this time by France and England, and by Russia at another point. Japan was in each case the fulcrum. On account of the petty trade between Tsushima and Fusan, Earl Russell wished to have Great Britain included as a co-trader with the peninsula. The Russians the same year occupied a station on Tsu Island, commanding the countries on either side ; but under protest from Yedo, backed by British men-of-war, abandoned their purpose. In 1862, while the members of the Japanese embassy from the Tycoon were in Paris, the government of Napoleon III. requested their influence in the opening of Corea to French trade and residence. At this time, however, the Japanese had their hands full of their own troubles at home, nor had the court at Seoul sent either envoys or presents since 1832. They should have done so in 1852, at the accession of the new shō-gun, but not relishing the humiliation of coming only to Tsushima, and knowing the weakened state of their former conquerors, they were now ready to defy them.

One new missionary and two returned native students entered

in March, 1863.   The Ni dynasty, founded in 1392, came to an end on January 15, 1864, by the King Chul-chong, who had no child, dying before he had nominated an heir.   This was the signal for fresh palace intrigues, and excitement among the nobles and political parties.   The three widows of the kings who had reigned since 1831 were still living.   The oldest of these, Queen Chō, at once seized the royal seal and emblems of authority, which high-handed move made her the mistress of the situation.   Craftily putting aside her nephew Chō Sung, she nominated for the throne a lad then but twelve years old, and son of Ni Kung, one of the royal princes.   This latter person was supposed to be indifferent to politics, but no sooner was his son made the sovereign, than his slumbering ambition woke to lion-like vigor.   This man, to use a Corean phrase, had "a heart of stone, and bowels of iron."   He seemed to know no scruple, pity, or fear.   Possessing himself of the seal and royal emblems, he was made Tai-wen Kun (Lord of the Great Court—a rare title given to a noble when his son is made king) and became actual regent.   This Corean mayor of the palace held the reins of government during the next nine years, ruling with power like that of an absolute despot.   He was a rabid hater of Christianity, foreigners, and progress.

In spite of the new current of hostility that set steadily in, the Christians began to be bold even to defiance.   In Kiung-sang a funeral procession carrying two hundred lanterns, bore aloft a huge cross, and chanted responsive prayers.   In the capital, the converts paraded the signs of the Romish cult.   A theological training school was established in the mountains, four new missionaries entered the kingdom through Nai-po, 1976 baptisms were made during the year, and, with much literary work accomplished, the printing-press was kept busy.

The year 1866 is phenomenal in Corean history.   It seemed as if the governments and outlaws alike, of many nations, had conspired to pierce or breach the walls of isolation at many points.   Russians, Frenchmen, Englishmen, Americans, Germans, authorized and un-authorized, landed to trade, rob, kill, or, what was equally ob-noxious to the regent and his court, to make treaties.

In January the Russians, in a war-vessel, again appeared in Broughton's Bay, and demanded the right of trade.   At the same time they stated that some Russian troops were to pass the frontier of Ham-kiung to enforce the demand.   The usual stereotyped re-sponse was made, that Corea was a vassal of China, and could not

treat with any other nation without permission of that Power, and
that a special ambassador charged with the matter would be immediately despatched to Peking, etc.

The advent of the double-headed eagle was the signal for
lively feeling and action among the Christians at Seoul. The long-
cherished project of appealing to England and France to make an
alliance to secure liberty of religion was revived. The impulsive
converts now forwarded the scheme, under the plea of patriotic
defense against the Russians, with all the innocent maladdress
which characterizes men who are adults in age but children in
politics. In their exhilaration they already dreamed of building a
cathedral in Seoul of imposing proportions, and finished in a style
worthy alike of their religion and their country. Three Christian
nobles, headed by Thomas Kim, composed a letter embodying
their ideas of an anti-Russian Franco-English alliance, and had it
presented to the regent, who blandly sent Thomas Kim to invite
the bishops, then absent to a conference in the capital. On his
return to Seoul, Kim was coldly received, and no further notice
was taken of him. The anti-Christian party, now in full power at
court, clamored for the enforcement of the old edict against the foreign religion, while a letter from one of the Corean embassy in
Peking, arriving late in January, added fuel to the rising flame. It
stated that the Chinese were putting to death all the Christians
found in the empire. That lie, "as light as a feather" in its telling,
was "as heavy as a mountain" in Corea. Such an illustrious example
must be followed. Vainly the regent warned the court of the danger
from Europe. The Russian ship, too, had disappeared, and the
French seemed afraid to take vengeance for the massacre of 1839.
The cry of "Death to all the Christians, death to the western
barbarians" now began to be heard. Forced by the party in power,
the regent signed the death-warrants of the bishops and priests,
promulgated anew the old laws of the realm against the Christians,
and proceeded "to make very free with the heads of his subjects."
The minions of the magistrates sallied forth like bloodhounds un-
leashed. Berneux was seized on February 23d, and brought to
trial successively before three tribunals, the last being the highest
of the realm.

In his interview with the regent, who had formed a high idea
of the Frenchman, Berneux failed to address his Highness in the
punctilious form of words demanded by court etiquette. Forthwith the official made up his mind that the Frenchman was a man

of slight attainments, and of no personal importance—so sensitive is the Corean mind in the matter of etiquette. From the highest class prison, the bishop, after undergoing horrible tortures with club, paddle, and pointed sticks thrust into his flesh, was cast into a common dungeon, where, in a few days, he was joined by three of his fellow missionaries with several converts, faithful to their teachers even in the hour of death.

All suffered the fierce and savage beatings, and on March 8th were led out to death. An immense crowd of jeering, laughing, curious people followed the prisoners, who were tied by their hair to the chair so as to force them to hold up their faces, that the crowd might see them. Four hundred soldiers marched out with the doomed men to the sandy plain near the river. The lengthened programme of brutal torture and insult was duly carried out, after which the four heads were presented for inspection.

One day afterward, two other French missionaries and their twelve students for the priesthood were led captives into Seoul, marked with the red cord and yellow caps betokening prisoners soon to die. With like tortures, and the same shameful details of execution, they suffered death on March 11th. On this day, also, Daveluy and two other priests were seized, and on March 30th, Good Friday, decapitated, together with two faithful natives. In the case of Daveluy, the barbarity of the proceeding was increased by the sordid executioner, who, after delivering one blow, and while the blood was spouting out from the wound, left the victim to bargain with the official for the sum due him for his work of blood.

In a little over a month all missionary operations had come to a standstill. Scores of natives had been put to death; hundreds more were in prison. Ridel, while hiding between two walls, wrote to Peking, describing the state of affairs. Feron and Ridel met on May 8th, travelling all night, and on June 15th they found that Calais was still alive. Hearing that a foreign steam-vessel was cruising off the Nai-po, Ridel sent a letter begging for help. This ship was the Rona, Captain Morrison, belonging to a British firm in China, on its way back from Niu-chwang, under the direction of Mr. Ernest Oppert. The native Christians were unable to get on board the Rona; but when the same Oppert visited Haimi in the Nai-po, some months later, in the steamer Emperor, this letter was put in his hands. Meanwhile Ridel had reached the sea-coast, and in spite of the vigilant patrols, put off in a boat constructed without an ounce of iron, and manned by a crew of eleven Christian fishermen. He reached Chifu July 7th. Going at once to Tien-tsin, he informed the French Admiral Roze of the recent events in Corea, and then returning to Chifu, waited till mid-August. Feron and Calais, hearing of the presence of French ships in the Han River, reached the coast, after great straits, to find them gone. They put to sea, however, and got upon a Chinese smuggler, by which they reached Chifu, October 26th—while the French expedition was in Corea. Not one foreign priest now remained in the peninsula, and no Christian dared openly confess his faith, while thousands were banished, imprisoned, or put to death.

Thus after twenty years of nearly uninterrupted labors, the church was again stripped of her pastors, and at the end of the eighty-two years of Corean Christianity, the curtain fell in blood. Of four bishops and nineteen priests, all except four were from France, and of these only three remained alive. Fourteen were martyrs, and four fell victims to the toils and dangers of their noble calling.

In the foregoing story of papal Christianity in Chō-sen, which we have drawn from Dallet—a Roman Catholic writer—we have the spectacle of a brave band of men, mostly secular priests educated in French seminaries of learning, doing what they believed it was right to do. Setting the laws of this pagan country at defiance, they, by means of dissimulation and falsehood, entered the country in disguise as nobles in mourning. Fully believing in the dogma of salvation by works, they were sublimely diligent in carrying on their labors of conversion, ever in readiness for that crown of martyrdom which each one coveted, and which so many obtained; but the nobleness of their calling was disfigured by the foul and abominable teaching that evil should be done in order that good might come—a tenet that insults at once the New Testament and the best casuistry of the Roman Catholic Church. According to the code of any nation, their converts were traitors in inviting invasion; but if worthy to be set down as Arnolds and Iscariots, then their teachers have the greater blame in leading them astray. It is to be hoped that the future Christian missionaries in Corea, whether of the Greek, Roman, or Reformed branch, will teach Christianity with more of the moral purity inculcated by its Founder.

CHAPTER XLIII.

THE FRENCH EXPEDITION.

The preliminaries of the French expedition to Corea in 1866 may be gathered from the letters which passed between the French chargé d'affairs at Peking and Prince Kung, the Chinese premier, as published in the United States Diplomatic Correspondence, 1867–68.[1] The pyrotechnic bombast of the Frenchman may be best understood by remembering that he lived in the palmy days of Louis Napoleon and the third empire. His violent language and behavior may be contrasted with the calm demeanor and firm temper of the astute Chinaman, the greatest of the diplomats of the Middle Kingdom.

"Unfortunately for the interests of his country, M. H. Bellonet had carried into diplomacy the rude customs and unmeasured language of the African Zouaves, in whose ranks he had served at one period of his career."

[1] July 13, 1866.

M. DE BELLONET TO PRINCE KUNG.

Sir : I grieve to bring officially to the knowledge of your Imperial Highness a horrible outrage committed in the small kingdom of Corea, which formerly assumed the bonds of vassalage to the Chinese empire, but which this act of savage barbarity has forever separated from it.

In the course of the month of March last, the two French bishops who were evangelizing Corea, and with them nine missionaries and seven Corean priests, and a great multitude of Christians of both sexes and of every age, were massacred by order of the sovereign of that country.

The government of His Majesty cannot permit so bloody an outrage to be unpunished. The same day on which the king of Corea laid his hands upon my unhappy countrymen was the last of his reign ; he himself proclaimed its end, which I, in turn, solemnly declare to-day. In a few days our military forces are to march to the conquest of Corea, and the Emperor, my august Sovereign, alone has now the right and the power to dispose, according to his good pleasure, of the country and the vacant throne.

The Chinese government has declared to me many times that it has no authority over Corea, and it refused on this pretext to apply the treaties of

The best commentary upon this boast of an irate underling, dressed in the brief authority of his superior, will be found in the events of the expedition, notably in the reduction to ashes of the city of Kang-wa, which rendered 10,000 people homeless, and in the repulse of the reckless invaders even before Bellonet at Peking was settling the fate of the king.

With Bishop Ridel as interpreter, and three of his converts as pilots, three vessels were sent to explore the Han River. Equipped with charts made by Captain James of the Emperor, who had examined the western entrance one month before, the despatch-boat Déroulède leaving her consorts in Prince Jerome Gulf, steamed up the river on September 21st, as far as the narrows between Kang-wa and the mainland. The French officers were charmed with the beauty of the autumnal scenery. On the cultivated plain, checkered into a thousand squares of tiny rice-fields, all well irrigated,

---

Tien-tsin to that country, and give to our missionaries the passports which we have asked from it. We have taken note of these declarations, and we declare now that we do not recognize any authority whatever of the Chinese government over the kingdom of Corea.

I have, etc.,

H. DE BELLONET.

His Imperial Highness, *Prince Kung.*

Spurning with irritating, not to say insulting, language, the suggestion of Prince Kung that Bellonet might do well to inquire into the causes and merits of the execution of the missionaries, the representative of France, November 11th, again addressed the Chinese statesman. In this missive occurs the following: "As for the fate of the former king of Corea, it is now subject to the decision of the Emperor, my august Sovereign."

Monsieur Bellonet's method is one specimen of the manner in which the envoys of European nations are accustomed to bully the governments of Asiatic countries. In a long communication to Prince Kung, dated November 11, 1866, Mr. Bellonet charges upon the Chinese government: 1st. Complicity with Corea. 2d. That the Corean embassy, during the previous winter, had stated the project of the massacre, and had received the tacit official authorization of the Chinese government. 3d. The direct approval of several high members of it. 4th. That the recruiting and mobilization of Manchiu troops, beyond the Great Wall, was for the purpose of assisting Corea against the French. He writes, in addition to the above, an amazing amount of nonsense, which shows of what magnifying powers the human eye is capable when enlarged by suspicion.

Among other tidbits of rodomontade, is this one—which is a truthful picture of the France of Napoleon III.—"War for us is a pleasure which the French passionately seek;" and this—"The people of Corea address us as deliverers, . . . we shall inaugurate the reign of order, justice, and prosperity."

the golden-tinted grain, now full ripe, awaited the sickle and the sheaf-binder. Numerous villages dotted the landscape, and to the northwest rose the green hills on which sat, like a queen, the city of Kang-wa. A number of forts, as yet unmounted with cannon, were already built. Others, in process of construction, were rising on well-chosen sites commanding the river. No garrison or a single soldier was as yet seen. The simple villagers, at first fright-

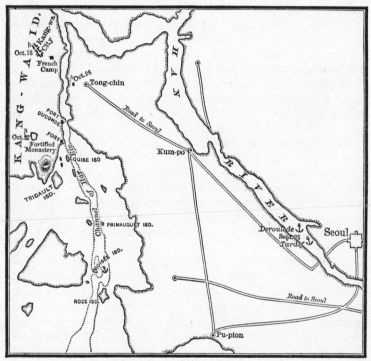

Map of French Naval and Military Operations, 1866.

ened at the sight of a mighty black ship, moving up the river against a strong current without sails or oars, collected in crowds along the banks to see this fire-pulsing monster from the western ocean.

On the 23d the Déroulède and Tardif, leaving the Primauguet at Boisée (Woody) Island, moved up the Han River to the capital, the Corean pilots at the bow, and Ridel with the men at the wheel.

One or two forts fired on the vessels as they steamed along, and in one place a fleet of junks gathered to dispute their passage. A well-aimed shot sunk two of the crazy craft, and a bombshell dropped among the artillerists in the redoubt silenced it at once. The rocks were safely avoided, and on the evening of the 25th, the two ships cast anchor, and the flag of France floated in front of the Corean capital. The hills environing the city and every point of view were white with gazing thousands, who for the first time saw a vessel moving under steam.

The ships remained abreast of the city several days, the officers taking soundings and measurements, computing heights and making plans. M. Ridel went on shore in hopes of finding a Christian and hearing some news, but none dared to approach him.

While the French remained in the river, not a bag of rice nor a fagot of wood entered Seoul. Eight days of such terror, and a famine would have raged in the city. Seven thousand houses were deserted by their occupants.

Returning to Boisée Island, having surveyed the river, two converts came on board. They informed Ridel of the burning of a "European" ship [the General Sherman] at Ping-an, the renewal of the persecution, and the order that Christians should be put to death without waiting for instructions from Seoul. Ridel in vain urged Admiral Roze to remain with his fleet, in order to intimidate the government. Sailing away, the ships arrived at Chifu, October 3d.

Tai-wen kun, now thoroughly alarmed, began to stir up the country to defense. The military forces in every province were called out. Every scrap of iron was collected, and the forges and black-smith shops were busy day and night in making arms of every known kind; even the farmer's tools were altered into pikes and sabres. Loaded junks were sunk in the channel of the Han to obstruct it. Through the Japanese at Fusan, and the daimiō of Tsushima, word was sent to the Tycoon of Japan, informing him of his straits, and begging for assistance. The Yedo government, being at that time in great straits between the pressure of foreigners on one hand, and of the "mikado-reverencers" on the other, could not then, had it been right to do so, afford any military assistance against the French, with whom a treaty had been made. Instead of this, two commissioners were appointed to go to Seoul, and recommend that Chō-sen open her ports to foreign commerce, as Japan had done, and thus choose peace instead of war with foreigners. Before the envoys could leave Japan, the Tycoon had died, and the next year Japan was in the throes of civil war, the shō-gunate was abolished, and Corea was for the time utterly forgotten.

The object of the French expedition and the blockade of the Salée (Han) River were duly announced from the French legation in China to the Chinese and foreign representatives in Peking. Without waiting to hear from his government at home, Bellonet despatched the fleet and made war on his own responsibility. The squadron which sailed October 11th, to distribute thrones and decapitate prime ministers, consisted of the frigate Guerrière, the corvettes Laplace and Primauguet, the despatch-vessels Déroulède and Kien-chan, and the gunboats Tardif and Lebrethon, with 600 soldiers, including a detachment of 400 marines from the camp at Yokohama.

One would have thought 600 men rather too small a force to root up thrones with, seeing that the days of Cortez and Pizarro were past. The Coreans were not like the Mexicans, who thought a horse and his rider were one animal. They had smelt powder and fought tigers.

On October 13th the admiral cast anchor off Boisée Island. The next day the gunboats steamed up the river, landing the marines in camp, a little over half a mile from the city. On the 15th, before any attempt was made to communicate with the government, a reconnoissance was made in force, toward Kang-hoa (Kang-wa), during which a small fort, mounting two guns, was captured.

Kang-wa was, to a modern eye, probably one of the best fortified cities in the kingdom. It was surrounded by a crenelated wall, nearly fifteen feet high! Behind this defense the native soldiery stood ready with flails, arrows, matchlocks, and jingals.

The royal residence, for pleasure in summer, and refuge in wartime, was beautifully situated on a wooded hill, from which a glorious view of the island, sea, and mainland was visible. The fertile island itself lay like a green emerald upon a greener sea. Crops of rice, barley, tobacco, sorghum, maize, various root foods, Chinese cabbage, chestnuts, persimmons, with here and there a great camellia tree just entering into bloom, greeted the view of the invaders. Kang-wa was well named "The Flower of the River."

At eight o'clock on the morning of October 16th an attack was made in force on the main gate. At the distance of one hundred yards, the infantry charged on a run, to the cry of "Vive l'Empereur." The hot fire of the jingals checked them not a moment. Reaching the wall, they set up the scaling ladders, and in a few moments hundreds of Frenchmen were inside, shooting down the flying white-coats, or engaging in a hand to hand encounter, though only a few natives were killed. The gate was soon crushed in with axes, and the main body entered easily. Firing was soon over, and the deserted city was in the victors hands. About eighty bronze and iron cannon, mostly of very small calibre, over six thousand matchlocks, and the official archives of the city were found and made trophies of.

Kang-wa was the military headquarters for western Corea and the chief place of gunpowder manufacture. Large magazines of food supplies had been collected in it. Eighteen boxes of silver, containing ingots to the value of nearly thirty eight thousand dollars, and a great many books and manuscripts were found, besides spoil of many kinds from the shops and houses. Immense stores of bows and arrows, iron sabres without scabbards, helmets, and

Breech-loading Cannon of Corean Manufacture.

breastplates, beautifully wrought, but very heavy and clumsy, were found.

The cannon had no carriages, but were fastened to logs or fixed platforms. They were breech-loaders, in that the powder, fixed in an iron cartridge, was introduced at the breech, while the ball seemed to be put in simultaneously at the muzzle. These double-ended cannon reminded one of a tortoise. A curious or rather comical thing about these cannon was that many of them had several touch-holes in a row, the cannonier firing them by applying his match rapidly along the line of vents—an "accelerating gun," of a rude kind. The Corean gunpowder is said to burn so slowly that a charge has to be lighted at both ends—a type of the national policy.

As the Coreans were fortifying Tong-chin with unusual care, the admiral sent out, October 26th, a reconnoitering party of one hundred and twenty men, who were landed on the mainland, opposite Kang-wa Island, whence the high road runs direct to the capital. Here was a village, with fortifications clustered around a great gate, having a pointed stone arch surmounted by the figure of a tortoise and a pagoda. To force this gate was to win the way to the capital.

As the marines were disembarking, the Coreans poured in a heavy fire, which killed two and wounded twenty-five Frenchmen. Nevertheless the place was stormed and seized, but as the Corean forces were gathering in the vicinity, the marines returned to the ships to await reinforcements.

Toward evening a party of Coreans defiled at the foot of the plain in gallant array, evidently elated with supposed victory. Suddenly, as they came within range, the French ships opened on them with shell, which exploded among them.

Terrified at such unknown war missiles, they broke and fled to the hill-tops, where, to their surprise, they were again enveloped in a shower of iron. Finally they had to take shelter in the distant ravines and the far plains, which at night were illumined by their bivouac fires.

Weak men and nations, in fighting against stronger enemies, must, like the weaker ones in the brute creation, resort to cunning. They try to weary out what they cannot overcome. The Coreans, even before rifled cannon and steamers, began to play the same old tricks practised in the war with the Japanese in the sixteenth century. They made hundreds of literal "men of straw," and stuck them within range of the enemy's artillery, that the Frenchmen might vainly expend their powder and iron. The keen-eyed Frenchmen, aided by their glasses, detected the cheat, and wasted no shot on the mannikins.

Meanwhile the invaded nation was roused to a white heat of wrath. The furnace of persecution and the forges of the armorers were alike heated to their utmost. Earnest hands plied with rivalling diligence the torture and the sledge. In the capital it was written on the gate-posts of the palace that whoever should propose peace with the French should be treated as a traitor and immediately executed.

On October 19th, Ni, the Corean general commanding, had sent the French admiral a long letter stuffed with quotations from the Chinese classics, the gist of which was that whoever from outside broke through the frontiers of another kingdom was worthy of death—a sentiment well worthy of a state of savagery.

The French admiral, with equal national bombast, but in direct and clearest phrase, demanded the surrender of the three high ministers of the court, else he would hold the Corean government responsible for the miseries of the war.

The Coreans in camp were ceaselessly busy in drilling raw troops and improving their marksmanship. Soldiers arrived from all quarters, and among them was a regiment of eight hundred tiger-hunters from the north, every man of whom was a dead shot either with bow or matchlock. These men, who had faced the tiger and many of whom had felt his claws, were not likely to fear even French "devils." They garrisoned a fortified monastery on the island which was situated in a valley in the centre of a circle of hills which were crowned by a wall of uncemented masonry. It could be approached only by one small foot-path in a deep ravine. The entrance was a gateway of heavy hewn stone, arched in a full semicircle, the gate being in one piece. The walls were mounted with home-made artillery.

On the same day on which this information reached the admiral, the natives attacked a French survey boat, whereupon he at once resolved to capture the monastery. For this purpose he detached 160 men, without artillery, who left at six o'clock in the morning of October 27th, with their luncheon packed on horses. The invaders, with their heads turned by too many easy victories, went in something like picnic order, frequently stopping to rest and enjoy the autumnal scenery. On several occasions they saw squads of men marching over the hills toward the same destination, but this did not hurry the Frenchmen, though a native informed them that the monastery, ordinarily inhabited only by a dozen priests, was now garrisoned and full of soldiers.

At 11.30 they arrived near the fortress, when some one proposed lunch. Others jauntily declared it would be very easy to capture "the pagoda," and then dine in the hall of Buddha himself; this advice was not, however, followed. Having arranged three parties, they advanced to within three hundred yards of the gate. All within was as silent as death. Suddenly a sheet of flame burst from the whole length of the wall, though not a black head nor a white coat was visible. In a minute the French columns were shattered and broken, and not a man was on his feet. The soldiers, retreating in a hail of lead, found refuge behind rocks, sheaves of rice, piles of straw, and in the huts near by. There the officers rallied their men lest the garrison should make a sally. The wounded were then borne to the rear. They numbered thirty-two. Only eighty fighting men were left, and these soon became conscious of being weak and very hungry, for they had been cruelly tantalized by seeing the lunch-horse kick up his heels at the first fire, and trot over to the Coreans. They learned that one of the slips 'twixt the cup and the lip might be caused by a horse in Chō-sen. Perhaps some native poet improvised a poem contrasting the patriotic nag with the steed of Kanko, which led a hungry army home.

It being madness or annihilation for eighty Frenchmen to attempt to storm a stone fortress, garrisoned by five or ten times their number of enemies, and guarded with artillery, retreat was resolved on. The wounded were hastily cared for and the mournful march began. The stronger men carried their severely injured comrades on their shoulders with brotherly kindness. The unwounded who were free formed the rear-guard. Three times the little band had to face about and fire with effect at the Coreans, who thrice charged their foes with heavy loss to themselves. They then mounted the hills, and with savage yells celebrated their victory over the western barbarians. It was not till night, hungry and tired, that reinforcements were met a half league from camp. They had been sent out by the admiral, to whom had come presentiment of failure.

There was gloom in the camp that night and at headquarters. The near sky and the horizon, notched by the hills, seemed to glare with unusual luridness, betokening the joy and the deadly purpose of the invaded people.

The next morning, to the surprise of all, and the anger of many, orders were given to embark. The work on the fortifications begun around the camp was left off. The troops in Kang-wa set fire to the city, which, in a few hours, was a level heap of ashes. The departure of the invaders was so precipitate that the patriots to this day gloat over it as a disgraceful retreat.

A huge bronze bell, from one of the temples in Kang-wa, which had been transported half way to the camp, was abandoned. The Coreans recaptured this, regarding it as a special trophy of victory. The French embarked at night, and at six o'clock next morning dropped down to the anchorage at Boisée Island. On the way, every fort on the island seemed to be manned and popping away at the ships, but hurting only the paint and rigging. To their great disgust, the men repulsed two days before, discovered the walls of the monastery from deck, and that the distance was only a mile and

25

a half from the river side. There was considerable silent swearing among the officers, who believed it could be easily stormed and taken even then. Orders must be obeyed, however, and in rage and shame they silently gazed on the grim walls. The return of the expedition was a great surprise to the fleet at Boisée Island. On his return to China, the admiral found, to his mortification, that his government did not approve of the headlong venture of Bellonet.[1]

In the palace at Seoul, the resolve was made to exterminate Christianity, root and branch. Women and even children were ordered to the death. Several Christian nobles were executed. One Christian, who was betrayed in the capital by his pagan brother, and another unknown fellow-believer were taken to the river side in front of the city, near the place where the two French vessels had anchored. At this historic spot, by an innovation unknown in the customs of Chō-sen, they were decapitated, and their headless trunks held neck downward to spout out the hot life-blood, that it might wash away the stain of foreign pollution. "It is for the sake of these Christians," said the official proclamation, "that the barbarians have come just here. It is on account of these only that the waters of our river have been defiled by western ships. It behooves that their blood should wash out the stain." Upon the mind of the regent and court at Seoul, the effect was to swell their pride to the folly of extravagant conceit. Feeling themselves able almost to defy the world, they began soon after to hurl their defiance at Japan. The dwarf of yesterday had become a giant in a day.

---

[1] The results of this expedition were disastrous all over the East. Happening at a time when relations between foreigners and Chinese were strained, the unexpected return of the fleet filled the minds of Europeans in China with alarm. It was the unanimous verdict of press and people that the return of the French in sufficient force to Corea in the spring was a measure of absolute safety to foreigners in the far East. If not, since both British and American citizens were among the crew of the General Sherman, murdered at Ping-an, the fleets of Great Britain and the United States should proceed to Seoul. This, however, was not done; the English let well enough alone, the French soon had their hands full in attending to the Germans at home, and the Americans went later only to follow Admiral Roze's example. Meanwhile the smothered embers of hostility to foreign influence steadily gathered vigor, as the report spread like a gale through China that the hated Frenchmen had been driven away by the Coreans. The fires at length broke out in the Tien-tsin massacre, June 21, 1870. "It is believed by many thoughtful observers in China that this frightful event gained its first serious impetus from the unfortunate issue of Admiral Roze's campaign in Corea."

In spite of foreign invaders and war's alarms, one peaceful event during this same year, and shortly after the French fleet had gone away, sent a ripple of pleasure over the surface of Corean society. The young king, now but fourteen years old, who had been duly betrothed to Min,[1] a daughter of one of the noble families, was duly married. Popular report credits the young queen with abilities not inferior to those of her royal husband.

According to custom, the Chinese emperor sent an ambassador, one Koei-ling, a mandarin of high rank, to bear the imperial congratulations and investiture of the queen. This merry Chinaman, cultivated, lively, poetic in mood, and susceptible to nature's beauties, wrote an account of his journey between the two capitals. His charming impressions of travel give us glimpses of peaceful life in the land of Morning Calm, and afford a delightful contrast to the grim visage of war, with which events in Corea during the last decade have unhappily made us too familiar.

---

[1] The Min or Ming family is largely Chinese in blood and origin, and, besides being pre-eminent among all the Corean nobility in social, political, and intellectual power, has been most strenuous in adherence to Chinese ideas and traditions, with the purpose of keeping Corea unswerving in her vassalage and loyalty to China. Their retainers constitute a large portion of the population of Séoul. Besides the queen, the king on his mother's side, the wife of the heir apparent, and several of the highest officers of the government belong to the house of Min. For centuries this family has practically governed the kingdom. Their social and personal influence in Peking has always been very great, while at home their relations to the treasury and the army have been very close. The plot of 1882 was in effect an ineffectual attempt to destroy their power. When China commanded, they approved of the treaty with the United States.

CHAPTER XLIV.

AMERICAN RELATIONS WITH COREA.

AMERICA became a commercial rival to Chō-sen as early as 1757, when the products of Connecticut and Massachusetts lay side by side with Corean imports in the markets of Peking and Canton. Ginseng, the most precious drug in the Chinese pharmacopœia, had been for ages brought from Manchuria and the neighboring peninsula, where, on the mountains, the oldest and richest roots are found.

The Dutch traders, at once noticing the insatiable demand for the famed remedy, sought all over the world for a supply. The sweetish and mucilaginous root, though considered worthless by Europeans, was then occasionally bringing its weight in gold, and usually seven times its weight in silver, at Peking, and the merchants in the annual embassy from Seoul were reaping a rich harvest. Besides selling the younger and less valuable crop in its natural condition, they had factories in which the two-legged roots—which to the Asiatic imagination suggested the figure of the human body they were meant to refresh—were so manipulated as to take on the appearance of age, thus enhancing their price in the market.

Suddenly the Corean market was broken. Stimulated by the Dutch merchants at Albany, the Indians of Massachusetts had found the fleshy root growing abundantly on the hills around Stockbridge in Massachusetts. Taking it to Albany, they exchanged it for hardware, trinkets, and rum. While the Dutch domines were scandalized at the drunken revels of the "Yankee" Indians, who equalled the Mohawks in their inebriation, good Jonathan Edwards at Stockbridge was grieving over the waywardness of his dusky flock, because they had gone wild over ginseng-hunting.

The Hollanders, shipping the bundled roots on their galliots down the Hudson, and thence to Amsterdam and London, sold them to the British East India Company at a profit of five hundred per cent. Landed at Canton, and thence carried to Peking, American ginseng broke the market, forced the price to a shockingly low figure, and dealt a heavy blow to the Corean monopoly.

Henceforth a steady stream of ginseng—now found in limitless quantities in the Ohio and Mississippi valleys—poured into China. Though far inferior to the best article, it (*Aralia quinquefolia*) is sufficiently like it in taste and real or imaginary qualities to rival the root of Chō-sen, which is not of the very highest grade.

Less than a generation had passed from the time that the western end of Massachusetts had any influence on Corea or China, before there was brought from the far East an herb that influenced the colony at her other end, far otherwise than commercially. Massachusetts had sent ginseng to Canton, China now sent tea to Massachusetts. The herb from Amoy was pitched into the sea by men dressed and painted like the Indians, and the Revolution followed.

The war for independence over, Captain John Greene, in the ship Empress of China, sailed from New York, February 22, 1784. Major Samuel Shaw, the supercargo, without government aid or recognition, established American trade with China, living at Canton during part of the year 1786 and the whole of 1787 and 1788. Having been appointed consul by President Washington in 1789, while on a visit home, Major Shaw returned to China in an entirely new ship, the Massachusetts, built, navigated, and owned by American citizens. At Canton he held the office of consul certainly until the year 1790, and presumably until his death in 1794. This first consul of the United States in China received his commission from Congress, on condition that he should "not be entitled to receive any salary, fees, or emoluments whatever."

Animated by the spirit of independence, and a laudable ambition, the resolute citizen of the New World declared that "the Americans must have tea, and they seek the most lucrative market for their precious root ginseng." [1]

It was ginseng and tea—an exchange of the materials for drink, a barter of tonics—that brought the Americans and Chinese, and finally the Americans and Coreans together.

---

[1] The Honorable Gideon Nye, of China, from whose article in "The Far East" these facts are drawn concerning the first consul of the United States to China, has effectually disproved the oft-quoted statement of Sir John Davis in his "History of China," that "It was in the year 1802 that the American flag was *first* hoisted at Canton." Dr. William Speer in his excellent book—fair to the Chinese as well as to foreigners—has told the story of Jonathan Edwards and his troubles over ginseng and the drink which his Indian pupils bought with it.

Cotton was the next American raw material exported to China, beginning in 1791. In 1842 the loaded ships sailed direct from Alabama to Canton, on the expansion of trade after the Opium War.

The idea now began to dawn upon some minds that it was high time that Japan and Corea should be opened to American commerce.

The first public man who gave this idea official expression was the Honorable Zadoc Pratt, then member of the House of Representatives from the Eleventh (now the Fifteenth) Congressional District of New York. As chairman of the Committee on Naval Affairs, he introduced in Congress, February 12, 1845, a proposition for the extension of American commerce by the despatch of a mission to Japan and Corea as follows:

"It is hereby recommended that immediate measures be taken for effecting commercial arrangements with the empire of Japan and the kingdom of Corea," etc. (*Congressional Globe,* vol. xiv., p. 294).

The Mexican war was then already looming as a near possibility, and under its shadow, the wisdom of sending even a part of our little navy was doubted, and Mr. Pratt's bill failed to pass.

None of the American commanders, Glyn, Biddle, John Rodgers, or even Perry, seem to have ventured into Corean waters, and Commodore Perry has scarcely mentioned the adjacent kingdom in the narrative of the treaty expedition which he wrote, and his pastor, the Rev. Francis L. Hawks, edited. In truth, the sealed country was at that time almost as little known as that of Corea or Coreæ, which Josephus mentions, or that province of India which bears the same name.

The commerce which sprang up, not only between our country and China and Japan, but also that carried on in American vessels between Shanghae, Chifu, Tien-tsin, and Niu-chwang in North China, and the Japanese ports, made the navigation of Corean waters a necessity. Sooner or later shipwrecks must occur, and the question of the humane treatment of American citizens cast on Corean shores came up before our government for settlement, as it had long before in the case of Japan.

When it did begin to rain it poured. Within one year the Corean government having three American cases to deal with, gave a startling illustration of its policy—with the distressed, kindness; with the robber, powder and iron; with the invader, death and annihilation.

On June 24, 1866, the American schooner Surprise was wrecked off the coast (of Whang-hai?). The approach of any foreign vessel was especially dangerous at this time, as the crews might be mistaken for Frenchmen and killed by the people from patriotic impulses. Nevertheless Captain McCaslin and his men with their Chinese cook, after being first well catechised by the local magistrate, and secondly by a commissioner sent from Seoul, were kindly treated and well fed, and provided with clothing, medicines, and tobacco. By orders of Tai-wen Kun, they were escorted on horseback to Ai-chiu, and, after being feasted there, were conducted safely to the Border Gate. Thence, after a hard journey *via* Mukden, they got to Niu-chwang and to the United States consul. A gold watch was voted by Congress to the Rev. Père Gillie for his kindness to these men while in Mukden.

From a passage in one of the letters of the Corean Government, we gather that the crew of still another American ship were hospitably treated after shipwreck, but of the circumstances we are ignorant. Of the General Sherman affair more is known.

The General Sherman was an American schooner, owned by a Mr. Preston, who was making a voyage for health. She was consigned to Messrs. Meadows & Co., a British firm in Tien-tsin, and reached that port July, 1866. After delivery of her cargo, an arrangement was made by the firm and owner to load her with goods likely to be saleable in Corea, such as cotton cloth, glass, tin-plate, etc., and despatch her there on an experimental voyage in the hope of thus opening the country to commerce.

Leaving Tien-tsin July 29th, the vessel touched at Chifu, and took on board Mr. Hogarth, a young Englishman, and a Chinese shroff,[1] familiar with Corean money. The complement of the vessel was now five white foreigners, and nineteen Malay and Chinese sailors. The owner, Preston, the master, Page, and the mate, Wilson, were Americans. The Rev. Mr. Thomas, who had learned Corean from refugees at Chifu, and had made a trip to Whang-hai on a Chinese junk, went on board as a passenger to improve his knowledge of the language.[2]

---

[1] These shroffs are experts in handling money. They can detect counterfeits by the touch, and, with incredible celerity, can reckon amounts to thousandths of a cent on the abacus. One or more of them are found in nearly every one of the banks and hongs in Eurasian ports.

[2] Some weeks before, he had offered to penetrate the peninsula as missionary and agent of the Scottish National Bible Society. The Coreans who had

From the first the character of the expedition was suspected, because the men were rather too heavily armed for a peaceful trading voyage. It was believed in China that the royal coffins in the tombs of Ping-an, wherein more than one dynasty of Chō-sen lay buried, were of solid gold ; and it was broadly hinted that the expedition had something to do with these.

The schooner, whether merchant or invader, leaving Chifu, took a west-northwest direction, and made for the mouth of the Ta Tong River. There they met the Chinese captain of a Chifu junk, who agreed to pilot them up the river. He continued on the General Sherman during four tides, or two days. Then leaving her, he returned to the river's mouth, and sailed back to Chifu, where he was met and questioned by the firm of Meadows & Co.

No further direct intelligence was ever received from the unfortunate party.

The time chosen for this " experimental trading voyage " was strangely inopportune. The whole country was excited over the expected invasion of the French, and to a Corean—especially in the north, where not one in ten thousand had ever seen a white foreigner—any man dressed in foreign clothes would be taken for a Frenchman, as were even the Japanese crew of the gunboat Unyo Kuan in 1875. An armed vessel would certainly be taken for a French ship, and made the object of patriotic vengeance.

According to one report, the hatches of the schooner were fastened down, after the crew had been driven beneath, and set on fire. According to another, all were decapitated. The Coreans burned the wood work for its iron, and took the cannon for models.

During this same month of August, 1866, the Jewish merchant Ernest Oppert, in the steamer Emperor, entered the Han River, and had secret interviews with some of the native Christians, who wrote to him in Latin. Communications were also held with the governor of Kang-wa, and valuable charts were made by Captain James. One month later, in September, the French war-vessels made their appearance.

The U. S. steamship Wachusett, despatched by Admiral Rowan to inquire into the Sherman affair, reached Chifu January 14,

accompanied Bishop Ridel to Chifu, and who had met Dr. Williamson, volunteered to be his guides, and he had decided to go with them. When the opportunity of going by the American vessel offered itself, he changed his plan. Against the advice of his friends, who suspected the character of the expedition, he joined the party.

1867, and is said to have taken on board the Chinese pilot of the General Sherman, and the Rev. Mr. Corbett, an American missionary, to act as interpreter.   Leaving Chifu January 21st, they cast anchor, January 23d, at the mouth of the large inlet opposite Sir James Hall group, which indents Whang-hai province.   This estuary they erroneously supposed to be the Ta Tong River leading to Ping-an city, whereas they were half a degree too far south, as the chart made by themselves shows.

A letter was despatched, through the official of Cow Island, near

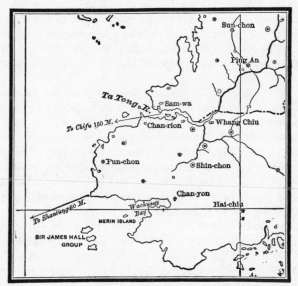

Map Illustrating the "General Sherman" Affair.

the anchorage, to the prefect of the large city nearest the place of the Sherman affair, demanding that the murderers be produced on the deck of the Wachusett. The city of Ping-an was about seventy-five miles distant.   The letter probably went to Hai-chiu, the capital of the province.   Five days elapsed before the answer arrived, during which the surveying boats were busy.   Many natives were met and spoken to, who all told one story, that the Sherman's crew were murdered by the people, and not by official instigation.[1]

---

[1] A broad streak of light was thrown upon at least one possible cause of the Sherman tragedy, by the statement of the natives that Chinese pirates frequently descend on the coast and kill and rob the Coreans.   During the pre-

On the 29th, an officer from one of the villages of the district appeared, "whose presence inspired the greatest dread among the people." An interview was held, during which Commander Shufeldt possessed his soul in patience.

To the polished American's eye, the Corean's manner was haughty and imperious. He was utterly beyond the reach of reason and of argument. In his person he seemed "the perfect type of a cruel and vindictive savage." The Corean's impressions of the American, not being in print, are unknown.

It is unnecessary to give the details of the fruitless interview. The American could get neither information nor satisfaction; the gist of the Corean reiteration was, "Go away as soon as possible." Commander Shufeldt, bound by his orders, could do nothing more, and being compelled also by stress of weather, came away.

In 1867, Dr. S. Wells Williams, Secretary of the Legation of the United States at Peking, succeeded in obtaining an interview with a member of the Corean embassy, who told him that after the General Sherman got aground, she careened over, as the tide receded, and her crew landed to guard or float her. The natives gathered around them, and before long an altercation took place between the two parties, which soon led to blows and bloodshed. A general attack began upon the foreigners, in which every man was killed by the mob. About twenty of the natives lost their lives. Dr. Williams' comment is, "The evidence goes to uphold the presumption that they invoked their sad fate by some rash or violent act toward the natives." Dr. Williams also met a Chinese pilot, Yu Wautai, who reported that in 1867 he had seen the hull of a foreign vessel lying on the south bank of the river, about ten miles up from the sea. The hull was full of water. A Corean from Sparrow Island had told him that the murder of the Sherman's crew was entirely the work of the people and farmers, and not of the magistrates or soldiery.

Still determined to learn something of the fate of the Sherman's crew, since reports were current that two or more of them were still alive and in prison, Admiral Rowan, in May, 1867, despatched another vessel, which this time got into the right river. Com-

---

vious year, several natives had been killed by Chinese pirates near the Wachusett's anchorage. As ten of the crew of the Sherman were Canton Chinamen, it is probable that the very sight of them on an *armed* vessel would inflame the Coreans to take their long-waited for revenge.

mander Febiger, in the U. S. steamship Shenandoah, besides surveying the "Ping Yang Inlet," learned this version of the affair :

A foreign vessel arrived in the river two years before.   The
local officials went on board and addressed the two foreign officers
of the ship in respectful language.   The latter grossly insulted the
native dignitaries, *i.e.*, "they turned round and went to sleep."

A man on board, whom they spoke of as "Tony,[1] a Frenchman," used violent and very impolite language toward them.   The
Coreans treated their visitors kindly, but warned them of their
danger, and the unlawfulness of penetrating into, or trading in the
country.   Nevertheless, the foreigners went up the river to Ping-an
city, where they seized the "adjutant-general's" ship, put him in
chains, and proceeded to rob the junks and their crews.   The
people of the city aroused to wrath, attacked the foreign ship with
fire-arms and cannon ; they set adrift fire-rafts, and even made a
hand-to-hand fight with pikes, knives, and swords.   The foreigners
fought desperately, but the Coreans overpowered them.   Finally,
the ship, having caught fire, blew up with a terrific report.

This story was not of course believed by the American officers,
but even the best wishers and friends of the Ping-an adventurers
cannot stifle suspicion of either cruelty or insult to the natives.
Knowing the character of certain members of the party, and remembering the kindness shown to the crew of the Surprise, few of
the unprejudiced will believe that the General Sherman's crew were
murdered without cause.

In 1884, Lieutenant J. B. Bernadon, U.S.N., made a journey from Séoul
to Ping-an, and, being able to speak Corean, learned the following from native
Christians.   The Sherman, arriving during the heavy midsummer rains, which
make the river impassable to native boats, was seen from the city walls and
caused great excitement.   When the waters subsided the governor sent officers
to inquire her mission.   Unfortunately, to gratify their curiosity, the common
people set out also in a large fleet of boats, which the Sherman's crew mistook
for a hostile demonstration, and fired guns in the air to warn them off.   Then
all the boats returned.   When the river fell the Sherman grounded and
careened over, which being seen from the city walls a fleet of boats set out
with hostile intent and were fired upon.   Officers and people, now enraged.
started fire-rafts, and soon the vessel, though with white flag hoisted, was in
flames.   Of those who leaped in the river most were drowned.   Of those
picked up one Tchoi-nan-un (Rev. Mr. Thomas), who was able to talk Corean,
explained the meaning of the white flag, and begged to be surrendered to
China.   His prayer was in vain.   In a few days all the prisoners were led out
and publicly executed.

CHAPTER XLV.

A BODY-SNATCHING EXPEDITION.

EARLY in May, 1867, the foreign settlement at Shanghae was thrown into excitement by the report of the return of an unsuccessful piratical expedition from Corea. The *ennui* of Eurasian port life was turned into a lively glow of excitement. Conversation at the clubs and tea-tables, which had wilted down to local gossip, Wade's policy, paper hunts, and the races, now turned upon the politics and geography, methods of royal sepulture, mortuary architecture, antiquities, customs, and costumes in the mysterious peninsula. The pleasures of wheelbarrow rides, and visits to the bubbling springs, now palled before the pending trial at the United States consular court.

An American citizen was charged with making an "unlawful and scandalous expedition" to Corea, and of violently attempting to land in a country with which the United States had no treaty relations. It was further stated that he had gone to exhume the bones of a defunct king in order to hold them for sale or ransom. In plain English, it was said to be a piratical and body-snatching descent upon the grave-yards of Chō-sen, to dig up royal remains, not for the purpose of dissection, nor in the interests of science or of archæology, but for the sake of money, which money was to be extorted from the regent and court of Seoul.

The idea, of course, awoke merriment as well as interest. One may well understand why Professor Marsh should make periodical descents upon the bone-yards of Red Cloud's territory, and exhibit his triumphs—skeletons of toothed birds and of geological horses as small as Corean ponies—in a museum under glass cases, well mounted with shining brass springs and iron joints. Even a school-boy can without laughing think of Dr. Schliemann rooting among the tombs of Mycenæ, and Di Cesnola sifting the dust of Kurium for its golden treasures. Even the night picture of resurrectionists, emptying graves in a Scotch kirk-yard for subjects to sell at a pound sterling apiece, has few elements of humor about it.

But to conceive of civilized "Christians," or Israelites, chartering a steamer to exhume and steal the carcase and mouldering bones of a heathen king, to hold them in pawn to raise money on them created more laughter than frowns or tears. It was thought that the sign under which the ship sailed, instead of being the flag of the North German Confederation, should have been the three golden balls, such as hang above a pawnbroker's windows.

The person on trial was formerly an interpreter at the United States consulate, and, having learned Chinese from childhood, was able to speak the language fluently, and thus converse, by means of tongue or pencil, with the many Coreans who know the standard of communication in Eastern Asia either by sound or sight. It was he also who furnished the cash for the expedition, the commander-in-chief of which was one Oppert, a North German subject; the guide was a French Jesuit priest named Farout (evidently a fictitious name) who spoke Corean, having been in the country as a missionary. These three were the leaders of the expedition.

Before going, the American had told Consul Seward that his object was to take a Corean embassy to Europe, to negociate treaties, and to explain to the governments of France and the United States the murder of their subjects in Corea. Four Coreans, with the French missionary Bishop Ridel, had been in Shanghae a short time before, April 24, 1867; and the defendant declared that it was from these four persons, whom he styled "commissioners," that he got his information as to the desire of the Corean government for treaties, etc. He also stated that this knowledge was held only by the four Coreans, himself, and a Jewish pedler, who had several times penetrated into Corea, and by whom the Corean "commissioners," had been brought to Shanghae. These "commissioners," he averred, had a new and correct version of the General Sherman affair. According to their report, some of the crew had become embroiled in a row growing out of the improper treatment of some native women, and were arrested. The crew went to rescue them. They succeeded, and took also two native officers on board for hostages. This so enraged the people that they attacked the crew, killed eight at once, and made prisoners of the others who were still alive.

Readers of our narrative will smile at discovering the poor

fishermen who brought their bishop across the Yellow Sea in their boat thus transformed into " ambassadors."

One thing seemed to be on the surface—that this modern Jason and his argonauts had gone out to find a golden fleece, but came back shorn.

On the return of the expedition, Mr. Seward questioned the American closely, sifted the matter, and finally, being satisfied that something was wrong, put him on trial, eliciting the facts which seem to be the following :

Oppert, who had been at the Naipo, and up the Han River in the Emperor and Rona, secured a steamer named the China, of six hundred and eighty tons, with a steam tender, the Greta, of sixty tons, and run the North German flag up at the fore. The complement of the ship was eight Europeans, twenty Malays from Manilla, and about one hundred Chinamen, these last were a motley crew of sailors, laborers, and coolies—the riff-raff of humanity, such as swarm in every Chinese port. With muskets in their hands —it is doubtful whether a dozen of them had ever fired off a gun —they were to form the " forces" or military escort of the expedition, which was to negotiate " treaties," embark an embassy to travel round the globe, and introduce the Hermit Nation to the world.

The "fleet" left Shanghae April 30, 1867, and steamed to Nagasaki ; in which Japanese port she remained two days, taking on board coal, water, and ten cases of muskets. The prow was then headed for Chung-chong province. They arrived in Prince Jerome Gulf at 10 P.M. on Friday, May 8th. The next day at 10 A.M. they moved farther in the river. In the afternoon they succeeded in getting two small boats, or sampans, partly by persuasion and pay, partly by force. The expedition was then organized, Oppert commanding. The mate, engineer, and regular Chinese manned the tender which was to tow the boats. The muskets were unpacked and distributed on deck, and the coolies were armed, equipped, taught the difference between the butt and muzzle of their weapons, and given their orders. Four men carried spades or coal shovels to exhume the bones and treasure.

The French priest who had been in Corea acted as guide and interpreter. Shortly after midnight, and very early on Sunday morning, the steam tender began to move up the river, stopping at a point about forty miles from the sea. The armed crowd landed, and the march across the open country to the tomb was begun. As they proceeded, the neighborhood became alive with curious people, and the hills were white with people gazing at the strange procession. A few natives being met on the way, the French priest stopped to speak with them. The party rested for a while at a temple, for the march was getting tiresome, having already occupied several hours.

Reaching the burial-place [near Totta-san?], they found a raised mound with a slab of stone on each side at the base. Beneath this tomb was the supposed treasure. Was it bones or gold?

The four men with spades now began their work, and soon levelled the mound. They had dug out a considerable quantity of earth, when their shovels struck on a rocky slab, which seemed to be the lid of the tomb proper, or the sarcophagus. This they could not move. All efforts to budge or pry it up were vain. Having no crowbars they were, after much useless labor, with perhaps not a little swearing, compelled to give up their task.

On their return march, the exasperated Coreans, plucking up courage, attempted to molest them, but the marauders, firing their guns in the air, kept their assailants at a respectful distance. The party and tender dropped down the river and rejoined the steamer at noon, the weather being foggy.

Further proceedings of the expedition are known only in outline. The steamer weighed anchor and left for Kang-wa Island. They put themselves in communication with the local magistrate during three days. On the third day a party landed from the ship, and while on shore were fired upon. Two men were killed and one wounded.

The expedition remained in Corea ten days, returning to Shanghae after two weeks' absence.

In the foregoing trial it is most evident that many details were concealed. The quantity of truth divulged was probably in proportion to the whole amount, as the puffs of steam from a safety-valve are to the volume in the boiler. The accused let out just enough to save them from conviction and to secure their acquittal.

The defendant was discharged with the Scotch verdict "not proven." Mr. George F. Seward, however, wrote to the State Department at Washington his opinion, that the expedition was "an attempt to take from their tombs the remains of one or more sovereigns of Corea, for the purpose, it would seem, of holding them to ransom."

Whether any great amount of treasure is ever buried with the sovereigns or grandees of Chō-sen is not known to us. Certain it

is that the national sentiment is that of horror against the disturbance or rifling of sepulchres. Now they had before their eyes a
fresh confirmation of their suspicions that the chief purpose of
foreign invaders was to rob the dead and violate the most holy
instincts of humanity. The national mind now settled into the
conviction that, beyond all doubt, foreigners were barbarians and
many of them thieves and robbers. With such eyes were they

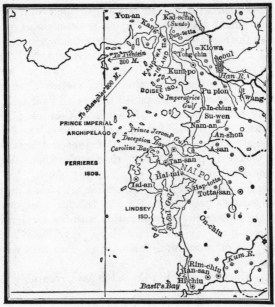

Map Illustrating the "China" Affair.

ready to look upon the flag and ships of the United States when
they came in 1871.

NOTE.—Nearly every word of the above was written in December, 1877, the
information having been derived from the United States Diplomatic Correspondence. At that time we suspected that "Farout" was the fictitious name of
Feron, the French Roman Catholic missionary, who had escaped the persecutions of 1866. It seems that three countries and three religions were represented in this body-snatching expedition, which was of a truly international
character.

In March, 1880, there was published in London and New York the
English translation of "Ein Verschlossenes Land," a work printed in Germany.
As we read "A Forbidden Land: Voyages to the Corea," it dawned upon us

that the author was none other than "the needy Hamburgh trader," "the Jewish pedler," of the Consular Court trial of 1867. It was even so. Coolly and without denial, the author tells us that the main object of his last voyage was to "remove" some buried relics held in great veneration by that "blood thirsty tyrant," the Tai-wen Kun, or regent. The project was first suggested to him by the French priest, who, as the author takes pains to tell us, was not a Jesuit, nor had ever belonged to that order (p. 295), though he gives Feron's proposition in his own words (p. 299), the italics being ours:

"If the project I am going to lay before you (*i.e.*, to rob the grave) will at first sight appear to you strange and out of the common, remember that *a great aim can never be gained by small means*, and that we must look at this affair from another point of view than that which may be taken by narrow-minded people."

The details of the landing, march [to near Totta-san?], excavation, and retreat are duly narrated, the blame of failure being laid upon one unlucky wight who was "the only disreputable character we had with us!"

After leaving Prince Jerome Gulf, the China proceeded up the Han River to Tricault Island (see map, page 379), "about twenty minutes' steam below Kang-wha." There the leader received a note from the Taiouen-goon (the Tai-wen Kun, or regent), the gist of which was, "Corea has no need of foreign intruders." While holding a parley near the wall of a town on Tricault Island, "the only disreputable character" in the party again got them into trouble. This black sheep was a German sailor, who, hungering after fresh veal, had stolen a calf; an act which drew the fire of the native soldiery on the city wall. The thief received a ball in his arm, which compelled him to drop the calf and run, while one Manilaman was shot dead. It is not known how far the statistics of a Corean warfare diverge from those elsewhere, nor how many tons of lead are required to kill one man, but owing to the incredibly bad aim of the jingal shooters, the remainder of the party of twenty or more escaped their deserts and reached the tender. The next morning the expedition set out on the return to Shanghae.

After a review of this book (in *The Nation* of April 7, 1880), which the author issued after his imprisonment, the following note appeared in the same paper of April 21st:

OPPERT'S COREAN OUTRAGE.

To the Editor of The Nation:

SIR: The notice of Oppert's book on Corea recalls some curious incidents to my mind. The raid on the King's tomb was one of the most extraordinary affairs ever known. Its inception and failure might have been concealed but for the Coreans, when they attacked the ghouls, killing an unfortunate Manilaman. Hearing of this, the Spanish consul applied to Mr. Seward (United States Consul-General at Shanghae), who at once arrested Jenkins. I was one of the four "associates" summoned to sit with the consul-general in the trial, and well remember what a perfect burlesque it was. The Chinese, who had told a plain and coherent story on preliminary examination, were as dumb as oysters on the stand. When all had been called, the defendant's counsel said that he would rest his case on their testimony. Conviction was impossible, but in the minds of those informed on the subject, the wickedness of this buccaneering expedition was remembered as surpassing even the absurdity of an attempt to destroy a granite mausoleum with coal shovels. There is a monstrous impertinence in Oppert's publishing an account of a piratical fiasco which is reported to have cost him a term of imprisonment at home.

A. A. HAYES, Jr.

NEW YORK, April 15, 1880.

CHAPTER XLVI.

"OUR LITTLE WAR WITH THE HEATHEN."

THE representations made to the Department of State at Washington by Dr. S. Wells Williams, concerning the General Sherman, and by Consul-General George F. Seward, in the matter of the China, affair, directed the attention of the Government to the opening of Corea to American commerce. The memorial of Mr. Seward, dated October 14, 1868, reviewed the advantages to be gained and the obstacles in the way. The need of protection to American seamen was pointed out, and as Japan had been opened to international relations by American diplomacy, why should not a smaller nation yield to persuasion? American merchants in China having seconded Mr. Seward's proposal, the State Department took the matter into serious consideration, and, in 1870, resolved to undertake the difficult enterprise.

The servants of the United States who were charged with this delicate mission were, Mr. Frederick F. Low, Minister of the United States to Peking, and Rear-Admiral John Rodgers, Commander-in-Chief of the Asiatic squadron. Mr. Low was directed by Secretary Fish to gain all possible knowledge from Peking, and then proceed on the admiral's flag-ship to the Corean capital. He was to make a treaty of commerce if possible, but his chief aim was to secure provision for the protection of shipwrecked mariners. He was to avoid a conflict of force, unless it could not be avoided without dishonor. "The responsibility of war or peace" was to be left with him and not with the admiral.[1]

There was at this time, all over the far East, a feeling of uncer-

---

[1] Mr. Low, who had served one term in Congress and as governor of California from 1864 to 1868, had been chosen by President Grant to be minister to China the year before, 1869, was new to his duties. He was in the prime of life, being fifty-two years of age. All his despatches show that Chō-sen was as unknown to him as Thibet or Anam, and from the first he had scarcely one ray of hope in the success of the mission.

tainty and alarm among foreigners, and many portentious signs seemed to indicate a general uprising, both in China and Japan, against foreigners. The example of Corea in expelling or beheading the French priests acted as powerful leaven in the minds of the fanatical foreigner-haters in the two countries adjoining. The " mikado-reverencers," who in Japan had overthrown the " Tycoon " and abolished the dual system of government, made these objects only secondary to the expulsion of all aliens. The cry of " honor the mikado" was joined to the savage yell of the Jo-i (alien-haters), " expel the barbarians." In China the smothered feelings of murderous animosity were almost ready to burst. The air was filled with alarms, even while the American fleet was preparing [1] for Corea.

Rear-Admiral Rodgers,[2] who had taken command, and relieved Admiral Rowan, August 20, 1869, began his preparations with vigor.

In a consultation held at Peking during November, 1870, between the admiral, minister, and consul-general, the time for the expedition was fixed for the month of May, 1871. Mr. Seward then left for a visit to India, and Mr. Low despatched, through the Tribunal of Rites at Peking, a letter to the King of Corea. After vast circumlocution, it emerged from the mazes of Chinese court etiquette, and by a special courier reached the regent at Seoul. In this, however, the Chinese were doing a great favor. No answer was received from Seoul before the expedition sailed.

Meanwhile the German minister to Japan (now in Peking),

---

[1] Admiral Rodgers left New York, April 9, 1869, with the Colorado and Alaska. The Benicia had left Portsmouth March 2d, and the Palos set sail from Boston June 20th. These vessels, with the Monocacy and Ashuelot, were to form the Asiatic squadron of Admiral Rodgers. Of our vessels on the station during the previous year, two had returned home, two had been sold, the rotten Idaho was moored at Yokohama as a store-ship, and the Oneida, which had been sunk by the British mail-steamer Bombay, lay with her uncoffined dead untouched and neglected by the great Government of the United States. Admiral Rodgers was so delayed by repairs to the Ashuelot, that finally, in order to gain the benefit of the spring tides, had to sail without this vessel.

[2] Rear-Admiral John Rodgers, who commanded the fleet, was a veteran in war, in naval science, and in polar research. He had served in the Seminole and Mexican campaigns, and through the civil war on the iron-clad monitors. He had visited the Pacific in 1853, when in command of the John Hancock. He had cruised in the China seas and sailed through Behring's Straits. He, too, was in the prime of life, being at this time fifty-eight years of age. His whole conduct of the expedition displayed consummate skill, and marked him in this, as in his many other enterprises, as " one of the foremost naval men of the age." Yet princes in naval science are not always princes in diplomacy.

Herr M. Von Brandt, had landed from the Hertha at Fusan, and attempted to hold an interview with the governor of Tong-nai. He was accompanied by the Japanese representatives at Fusan, who politely forwarded his request. A tart lecture to the mikado's subject for his officiousness, and a rebuff to the Kaiser's envoy were the only results of his mission. After sauntering about a little, Herr Von Brandt, who arrived June 1, 1878, left June 2d, and the era of commercial relations between the Central European Empire[1] and Chō-sen was postponed.

During the year 1870, Bishop Ridel, who had gone back to France, returned to China and prepared to rejoin his converts. Having communicated with them, they awaited his coming with anxiety, and we shall hear of them on board of the flag-ship Colorado.

Mr. Low, having gathered all possible information, public and private, concerning "the semi-barbarous and hostile people" of "the unknown country" which he expected to fail of entering, sailed from Shanghae, May 8th, arriving at Nagasaki, May 12th. On the 13th he wrote to the Secretary of State, Mr. Hamilton Fish. He declared that "Corea is more of a sealed book than Japan was before Commodore Perry's visit." Evidently he looked upon the pathway of the duty laid upon him as unusually thorny. The rose if plucked at all would be held in smarting fingers. While granting a faithful servant of the nation the virtue of modesty, one cannot fail to read in his letter more of an expectation to redress wrongs than to conciliate hostility.

---

[1] The first appearance of the flag of North Germany in Corean waters was at the mast-head of the China, when plunder and dead men's bones were the objects sought. Its second appearance, on the Hertha man-of-war, was in peace and honorable quest of friendly relations. Its third appearance, in May, 1871 —while, or shortly before, the American fleet were in the Han River—was on the schooner Chusan, which was wrecked on one of the islands of Sir James Hall group, the Chinese crew only, it appears, being saved. On June 6th, a party of three foreigners left Chifu in a junk to bring back salvage from the wreck. These men were not heard from until July 6th, when the Chinese crew returned without them. On the same day the British gunboat Ringdove, with the consul of Chifu, left for the Hall group. It was found that the foreigners had landed to bring away the crew of the Chusan, when the Chinamen, pretending or thinking that they had been taken prisoners, put off to sea without them. The consul found them in good health and spirits, and the Ringdove brought away for them whatever was worth saving from the Chusan. Again the Corean policy of kindness toward the shipwrecked was illustrated. The two foreigners—a Scotchman and a Maltese—had been well fed and kindly treated.

The whole spirit of the expedition was not that reflected in the despatches of the State Department, but rather that of the clubs and dinner-tables of Shanghae. The minister went to Corea with his mind made up, and everything he saw confirmed him in his fixed opinion. Of the admiral, it is not unjust to say that the warrior predominated over the peace-maker. He had an eye to the victories of war more than those, not less renowned, of peace. The sword was certainly more congenial to his nature than the pen.

The fleet made rendezvous at Nagasaki, in Kiushiu—that division of Japan whence warlike expeditions to Chō-sen have sailed from the days of Jingu to those of Taikō, and from Taikō to Rodgers. This time, as in the seventh century, the landing was to be made not near the eastern, but on the remote western, coast. The cry was, "On to Seoul."

The squadron, consisting of the flag-ship Colorado, the corvettes Alaska and Benicia, and the gun-boats Monocacy and Palos, sailed gallantly out of the harbor on May 16th, and, making an easy run, anchored off Ferrières Islands on the 19th, and, after a delay of fogs, Isle Eugenie on the 23d.

In spite of the formidable appearance of our navy, the vessels were of either an antiquated type or of too heavy a draught, their timbers too rotten or not strong enough for shotted broadsides, and their armanent defective in breech-loading firearms, while the facilities for landing a force were inadequate. The Palos and Monocacy were the only ships fitted to go up the Han River. The others must remain at the mouth. They were little more than transports. All the naval world in Chinese waters wondered why so wide-awake and practical a people as the Americans should be content with such old-fashioned ships, unworthy of the gallant crews who manned them. However, the fleet and armament were better than the Corean war-junks, or mud-forts armed with jingals. In gallant sailorly recognition of his predecessor, yet with unconscious omen of like failure, the brave Rodgers named the place of anchorage Roze Roads. The French soundings were verified and the superb scenery richly enjoyed. All navigators of the approaches to Seoul are alike unanimous in showering unstinting praise upon their natural beauty. Here for the first time the natives beheld the "flowery" flag of the United States.

Next morning the Palos and four steam-launches were put under the command of Captain Homer C. Blake, to examine the channel beyond Boisée Island. Four days were peaceably spent in this service, a safe return being made on the evening of the 28th. Meanwhile boat parties had landed and been treated in a friendly manner by the people, and the usual curiosity as to brass buttons, blue cloth, and glass bottles displayed. The customary official paper without signature, of interrogations as to who, whence, and why of the comers was displayed, and the answers, "Americans," "Friendly,"

and "Interview" re-
turned in faultless
Chinese. It was an-
nounced that the
fleet would remain
for some time.

On the follow-
ing day, May 30th,
the fleet anchored
between the Isles
Boisée and Guerri-
ére. A stiff breeze
had blown away the
fogs and revealed
the verdure and the
features of a land-
scape which struck
all with admiration
for its luxuriant
beauty. Approach-
ing the squadron in
a junk, some natives
made signs of friend-
ship, and came on
board without hesi-
tation. They bore
a missive acknowl-
edging the receipt
of the Americans'

"The Entering Wedge of Civilization."

letter, and announcing that three nobles had been appointed by the regent for conference. These junk-men were merely messen-gers, and made no pretence of being anything more. They were hospitably treated, shown round the ship, and dined and wined until their good nature broke out in broad grins and redolent vis-ages. They stood for their photographs on deck, and some fine pictures of them were obtained. One of them, after being loaded with an armful of spoil in the shape of a dozen or so of Bass' pale ale bottles, minus their corks, and a copy of *Every Saturday,* a Boston illustrated newspaper, was told in the stereotyped photographer's phrase to "assume a pleasant expression of countenance, and look right at this point." He obeyed so well, and in the nick of time, that a wreath of smiles was the result. "Our first Corean visitor" stands before us on the page.

Strange coincidence! Strange medley of the significant symbols of a Christian land! The first thing given to the Corean was alcohol, beer, and wine. In the picture, plainly appearing, are the empty pale ale bottles, with their trade-mark, the red triangle— "the entering wedge of civilization." But held behind the hands clasping the bottles is a copy of *Every Saturday,* on the front page of which is a picture of Charles Sumner, the champion of humanity, and of the principle that "nations must act as individuals," with like moral responsibility!

Promptly on May 31st, a delegation of eight officers, of the third and fifth rank, came on board evidently with intent to see the minister and admiral, to learn all they could, and to gain time. They had little or no authority and no credentials, but they were sociable, friendly, and in good humor.

"Mr. Low would not lower himself," nor would Admiral Rodgers see them. They were received by the secretary, Mr. Drew. They were absolutely non-committal on all points and to all questions asked, and naturally so, since they had no authority whatever [1] to say "yes" or "no" to any proposition of the Americans.

---

[1] These men simply acted as the catspaws for the monkey in the capital to pull out as many hot chestnuts from the fire as possible. It is part of Asiatic policy to send official men of low rank and no authority to dally and prelude, and, if possible, hoodwink or worry out foreigners. Their chief weapons are words; their main strength, cunning. When these are foiled by kindness, and equal patience, firmness, and address, the Asiatics yield, and send their men of first rank to confer and treat. Perry knew this, so did Townsend Harris in Japan; so have successful diplomats known it in China. Was it done in the American expedition to Corea in 1871 ? Let us see.

These Coreans had no right to say either "yes" or "no" to any proposition of the Americans. Had they committed themselves to anything definite, degradation, crushed shin-bones, and perhaps death, might have been their fate. The only thing for the Americans to do—who came to ask a favor which the Coreans were obstinately bent on not giving—was to feast them, treat them with all kindness, get them in excellent good humor, send them back, and wait till accredited envoys of high rank should arrive. In the light of the

A golden opportunity was here lost. The Corean envoys were informed that soundings would be taken in the river, and the shores would be surveyed. It was hoped that no molestation would be offered, and, further, that twenty-four hours would elapse before the boats began work.

"To all this they (the Coreans) made no reply which could indicate dissent." [Certainly not! They had no power to nod their heads, or say either "yes" or "no."] "So, believing that we might continue our surveys while further diplomatic negotiations were pending, an expedition was sent to examine and survey the Salée [Han] River." [1]

The survey fleet consisted of the Monocacy, Palos, the only ships fit for the purpose, and four steam-launches, each of the latter having a howitzer mounted in the bow. Captain H. C. Blake, the commander, was on board the Palos. The old hero understood the situation only too well. As he started to obey orders he remarked : "In ten minutes we shall have a row."

Exactly at noon of June 2d, the four steam-launches proceeded

---

French failure, this was the only course to pursue. There were even men of influence in the American fleet who advised this policy of patience. As matter of fact, such a course was urged by Captain H. S. Blake.

In such an emergency, patience, kindness, tact, the absence of any burning idea of "wiping out insults to the flag," and an antiseptic condition toward fight were most needed—the higher qualities, of resolution and self-conquest rather than valor. Even if it had been possible to inflict ten times the damage which was afterward actually inflicted, and win tenfold more "glory," the rear-admiral must have known that nature and his "instructions" were on the side of the Coreans, and that the only end of the case must be a retreat from the country. And the only possible interpretation the people could put upon the visit of the great American fleet would be a savage thirst for needless vengeance, a sordid greed of gain, and the justification of robbers and invaders. In spite of all the slaughter of their countrymen, they would read in the withdrawal of their armies, defeat, and defeat only.

[1] These are the rear-admiral's own words. Here was the mistake! From what may be easily known of the Corean mind, it must have seemed to them that the advance of such an armed force up the river, leading to the capital—following exactly the precedent of the French—was nothing more than a treacherous beginning of war in the face of assurances of peace. To enter into their waters seemed to them an invasion of their country. To do it after fair words spoken in friendship seemed basest treachery. Had a Corean officer counselled peace in the face of the advancing fleet, he would undoubtedly have been beheaded at once as a traitor. There were men on the American side who saw this. Some spoke out loud of it to others, but it was not "theirs to make reply."

in line abreast up the river, the Palos and Monocacy following. The tide was running up, and neither of the large vessels could be kept moving at a rate slow enough to allow the survey work to be done well, so that this part of their work is of little value.

Yet everything seemed quiet and peaceful; the bluffs and high banks along the water were densely covered with green woods, with now meadows, now a thatched-roof village, anon a rice-field in the foreground. Occasionally people could be seen in their white dresses along the banks, but not a sign of hostility or war until, on reaching the lower end of Kang-wa Island, a line of forts and fluttering flags suddenly become visible. In a few minutes more long lines of white-garbed soldiery were seen, and through a glass an interpreter read on one of the yellow flags the Chinese characters meaning "General Commanding." In the embrasures were a few pieces of artillery of 32-pound calibre, and some smaller pieces lashed together by fives, or nailed to logs in a row. On the opposite point of the river was a line of smaller earthworks, freshly thrown up, armed only with jingals. Around the bend in the river was "a whirlpool as bad as Hell Gate," full of eddies and ledges, with the channel only three hundred feet wide. The fort (Du Condè) was situated right on this elbow. Hundreds of mats and screens were ranged within and on the works, masking the loaded guns. As the boats passed nearer, glimpses into the fort became possible, by which it was seen that the cannon "lay nearly as thick together as gun to gun and gun behind gun on the floor of an arsenal." (See map, page 415.)

For a moment the silence was ominous—oppressive. The hearts of the men beat violently, their teeth were set, and calm defiance waited in the face of certain death. The rapid current bore them on right into the face of the frowning muzzles. It seemed impossible to escape. Were the Coreans going to fire? If so, why not now? Immediately? Now is their opportunity. The vessels are abreast the forts.

The Corean commander was one moment too late. From the parapet under the great flag a signal gun was fired. In an instant mats and screens were alive with the red fire of eighty pieces of artillery. Then a hail of shot from all the cannon, guns, and jingals rained around the boats. Forts, batteries, and walls were hidden for a moment in smoke. The water was rasped and torn as though a hailstorm was passing over it. Many of the men in the boats were wet to the skin by the splashing of the water over them.

Old veterans of the civil war had never seen so much fire, lead, iron, and smoke of bad powder concentrated in such small space and time. "Old Blake," who had had two ships shot under him by the Confederates, declared he could remember nothing so sharp as this.

The fire was promptly returned by the steam-launch howitzers. The Palos and Monocacy, which had forged ahead, turned back, and "Old Blake came round the point a-flying, and let drive all the guns of the Palos at them. The consequence was that they kicked so hard as to tear the bolts out of the side of the ship and render the bulwarks useless during the remainder of the fight." The Monocacy also anchored near the point, and sent her ten-inch shells into the fort. During her movements, she struck a rock and began to leak badly. After hammering at the forts until everything in them was silenced, the squadron returned down the river, sending their explosive compliments into the forts and redoubts as they passed. All were quiet and deserted, however, but the commander's flag was still flying unharmed and neglected. Strange to say, out of the entire fleet only one of our men was wounded and none was killed ; nor did any of the ships or boats receive any damage from the batteries. Two hundred guns had been fired on the Corean side. The signal coming too late, the immovability of their rude guns, the badness of the powder, and the poor aim of the unskilled gunners, were the causes of such an incredibly small damage. It was like the bombardment of Fort Sumter in 1861, or like those battles which statistics reveal to us, in which it requires a ton of lead to kill a man.

However, it was determined by the chief representatives of the civil and naval powers to resent the insult offered to our "flag" in the "unprovoked" attack on our vessels, "should no apology or satisfactory explanation be offered for the hostile action of the Corean government."

Ten days were now allowed to pass before further action was taken. They were ten days of inaction, except preparation for further fight and some correspondence with the local magistrate. What a pity these ten days had not been spent before, and not after, June 2d! Some civilians, not to say Christians, might also be of the opinion that ample revenge had already been taken, enough blood spilled, the "honor" of the flag fully "vindicated," a delicate diplomatic mission of "peace" spoiled beyond further damage, and that further vengeance was folly, and more blood spilled, murder. But not so thought the powers that be.

The chastising expedition consisted of the Monocacy, Palos, four steam-launches, and twenty boats, conveying a landing force of six hundred and fifty-one men, of whom one hundred and five were marines. The Benicia, Alaska, and Colorado remained at anchor. The total force detailed for the work of punishing the Coreans was seven hundred and fifty-nine men. These were arranged in ten companies of infantry, with seven pieces of artillery. The Monocacy had, in addition to her regular armament, two of the Colorado's nine-inch guns. Captain Homer C. Blake, who was put in charge of the expedition, remained on the Palos.

The squadron proceeded up the river at 10 o'clock, on the morning of the 10th of June, two steam-launches moving in advance of the Monocacy. The boats were in tow of the Palos, which moved at 10.30. The day was bright, clear, and warm. A short distance above the isle Primauguet a junk was seen approaching, the Coreans waving a white flag and holding a letter from one of the ministers of the court. One of the steam-launches met the junk, and the letter was received. It was translated by Mr. Drew, but as it contained nothing which, in the American eyes, seemed like an apology, the squadron moved on. At 1 o'clock the Monocacy arrived within range of the first fort and opened with her guns, which partly demolished the walls and emptied it in a few seconds.

The landing party, after a two minutes' pull at the oars, reached the shore, and disembarked about eight hundred yards below the fort. The landing-place was a mud-flat, in which the men sunk to their knees in the tough slime, losing gaiters, shoes, and even tearing off the legs of their trousers in their efforts to advance. The howitzers sank to their axles in the heavy ooze.

Once on firm land, the infantry formed, the marines deploying as skirmishers. Unarmed refugees from the villages were not harmed, and the first fort was quietly entered. The work of demolition was begun by firing everything combustible and rolling the guns into the river. Day being far spent when this was finished, the whole force went into camp and bivouacked, taking every precaution against surprise. Four companies of infantry were first detailed to drag the howitzers out of the mud, a task which resembled the wrenching of an armature off a twenty-horse power magnet.

Our men lay down to sleep under the stars. All was quiet that Saturday night, except the chatting round the camp-fires and the croaking of the Corean frogs, as the men cleaned themselves and prepared for their Sunday work. Toward midnight a body of white-coats approached, set up a tremendous howling, and began a dropping fire on our main pickets. As they moved about in the darkness, they looked like ghosts. When the long roll was sounded, our men sprang to their arms and fell in like old veterans. A few shells were scattered among the ghostly howlers, and all was quiet again. The marines occupied a strong position hàlf a mile from the main body, a rice-field dividing them, with only a narrow foot-path in the centre. They slept with their arms at their side, and, divided into three reliefs, kept watch.

While at the anchorage off Boisée Island that evening, twelve native Christians, approaching noiselessly in the dark, made signs of a desire to communicate. They had come in a junk from some point on the coast to inquire after their pastor, Ridel, and two other French missionaries whom they expected. To their great distress, the Americans could give them no information. Fearing lest the government might know, from the build of their craft, from what part of the country they came, and punish them for communicating with the foreigners, they burned their boat and returned home.

Next day was Sunday. The reveille was sounded in the camps, breakfast eaten, and blankets rolled up. Company C and the pioneers were sent into the fort to complete its destruction, by burning up the rice, dried fish, and huts still standing.

The march began at 7 A.M. The sun rolled up in a cloudless sky and the weather was very warm. It was a rough road, if, indeed, it could be called such, being but a bridle-path over hills and valleys, and through rice fields. Whole companies were required to drag the howitzers up the hills and through the narrow defiles. The marines led the advance. The next line of fortifications, the "middle fort," was soon entered. The guns were found loaded, as they had been deserted as soon as the fort was made a target by the Monocacy, every one of whose shots told. · The work of dismantling was here thoroughly done. The sixty brass pieces of artillery, all of them insignificant breech-loaders of two-inch bore, were tumbled into the river, and the fort appropriately named "Fort Monocacy."

The difficult march was resumed under a blazing sun and in steaming heat. A succession of steep hills lay before them. Sappers and miners, with picks, shovels, and axes, went ahead levelling and widening the road, cutting bushes and filling hollows. The guns had to be hauled up and lowered down the steep places by means of ropes. Large masses of white coats and black heads hovered on their flanks, evidently purposing to get in the rear. Their numbers were increasing. The danger was imminent. The fort must be taken soon or never.

A detachment of five howitzers and three companies were detailed to guard the flanks and rear under Lieutenant-Commander Wheeler. The main body then moved forward to storm the fort (citadel). This move of our forces checkmated the enemy and made victory sure, redeeming a critical moment and turning danger into safety.

Hardly were the guns in position, when the Coreans, massing their forces, charged the hill in the very teeth of the howitzers' fire. Our men calmly took sure aim, and by steadily firing at long range, so shattered the ranks of the attacking force that they broke and fled, leaving a clear field. The fort was now doomed. The splendid practice of our howitzers effectually prevented any large body of the enemy from getting into action, and made certain the capture of the cidadel.

Meanwhile the Monocacy, moving up the river and abreast of the land force, poured a steady fire of shell through the walls and into the fort, while the howitzers of the rear-guard on the hill behind, reversing their muzzles, fired upon the garrison over the heads of our men in the ravine. The infantry and marines having rested awhile after their forced march, during which several had been overcome by heat and sunstroke, now formed for a charge.

The citadel to be assaulted was the key to the whole line of fortifications. It crowned the apex of a conical hill one hundred and fifty feet high, measuring from the bottom of the ravine. It mounted, with the redoubt below, one hundred and forty-three guns. The sides of the hill were very steep, the walls of the fort joining it almost without a break. Up this steep incline our men were to rush in the face of the garrison's fire. Could the white-coats depress the jingals at a sufficiently low angle, they must annihilate the blue-jackets. Should our men reach the walls, they could easily enter through the breaches made by the Monocacy's shells. As usual, slowness, and the national habit of being behind time, saved our men and lost the day for Corea.

A terrible reception awaited the Americans. Every man inside was bound to die at his post, for this fort being the key to all the

others, was held by the tiger-hunters, who, if they flinched before
the enemy, were to be put to death by their own people.

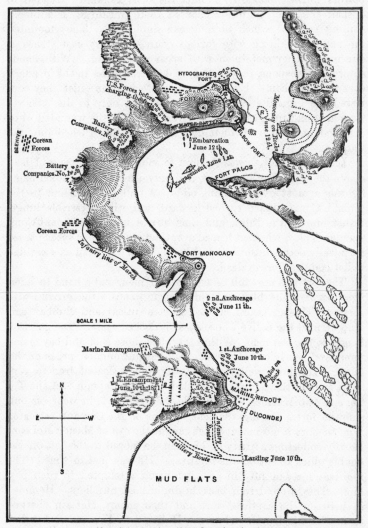

Map of the American Naval Operations in 1871.

All being ready, our men rose up with a yell and rushed for
the redoubt, officers in front. A storm of jingal balls rained over

their heads, but their dash up the hill was so rapid that the garrison could not depress their pieces or load fast enough. Their powder burned too slowly to hurt the swift Yankees. Goaded to despair the tiger-hunters "chanted their war-dirge in a blood-chilling cadence which nothing can duplicate." They mounted the parapet, fighting with furious courage. They cast stones at our men. They met them with spear and sword. With hands emptied of weapons, they picked up dust and threw in the invaders' eyes to blind them. Expecting no quarter and no relief, they contested the ground inch by inch and fought only to die. Scores were shot and tumbled into the river. Most of the wounded were drowned, and some cut their own throats as they rushed into the water.

Lieutenant McKee was the first to mount the parapet and leap inside the fort. For a moment, and only a moment, he stood alone fighting against overwhelming odds. A bullet struck him in the groin, a Corean brave rushed forward, and, with a terrible lunge, thrust him in the thigh, and then turned upon Lieutenant-Commander Schley, who had leaped over the parapet. The spear passed harmlessly between the arm and body of the American as a carbine bullet laid the Corean dead.

The fort was now full of officers and men, and a hand to hand fight between the blue and white began to strew the ground with corpses. Corean sword crossed Yankee cutlass, and clubbed carbine brained the native whose spear it dashed aside. The garrison fought to the last man. Within the walls those shot and bayoneted numbered nearly one hundred. Not one unwounded prisoner was taken. The huge yellow cotton flag, which floated from a very short staff in the centre, was hauled down by Captain McLane Tilton and two marines. Meanwhile a desperate fight went on outside the fort. During the charge, some of the Coreans retreated from the fort, a movement which caught the eye of Master McLean. Hastily collecting a party of his men, he moved to the left on the double quick to cut off the fugitives. He was just in time. The fugitives, forty or fifty in all, after firing, attempted to rush past him. They were driven back in diminished numbers. Hemmed in between the captured fort and their enemy, McLean charged them with his handful of men. Hiding behind some rocks, they fought with desperation until they were all killed, only two or three being made prisoners. Another party attempting to escape were nearly annihilated by Cassel's battery, which sent canister into their flying backs, mowing them down in swaths. Moving at full speed, many were shot like rabbits, falling heels over head. At the same time Captain Tilton passed to the right of the fort and caught another party retreating along the crest of the hill joining the two forts, and, with a steady carbine fire, thinned their numbers. At 12.45 the stars and stripes floated over all the forts. A photographer came ashore and on his camera fixed the horrible picture of blood.

The scene after the battle-smoke cleared away, and our men sat down to rest, was of a kind to thoroughly satisfy those "who look on war as a pastime." It was one from which humanity loves to avert her gaze. Two hundred and forty-three corpses in their white garments lay in and around the citadel. Many of them were clothed in thick cotton armor, wadded to nine thicknesses, which now smouldered away. A sickening stench of roasted flesh filled the air, which, during the day and night, became intolerable. Some of the wounded, fearing their captors worse than their torture, slowly burned to death ; choosing rather to suffer living cremation than to save their lives as captives. Our men, as they dragged the smoking corpses into the burial trench, found one man who could endure the torture no longer. Making signs of life, he was soon stripped of his clothes, but died soon after of his wounds and burns. Only twenty prisoners, all wounded, were taken alive. At least a hundred corpses floated or sunk in the river, which ran here and there in crimson streaks. At this one place probably as many as three hundred and fifty Corean patriots gave up their lives for their country.

On the American side, the gallant McKee, who fell as his father fell in Mexico, at the head of his men, the first inside the stormed works, was mortally wounded, and died soon after. One landsman of the Colorado and one marine of the Benicia were killed. Five men were severely, and five slightly, wounded.

The other two forts below the citadel being open to the rear from the main work were easily entered, no regular resistance being offered. The results of the forty-eight hours on shore, eighteen of which were spent in the field, were the capture of five forts —probably the strongest in the kingdom—fifty flags, four hundred and eighty-one pieces of artillery, chiefly jingals, and a large number of matchlocks. Of the artillery eleven pieces were 32,- fourteen were 24,- two were 20,- and the remaining four hundred and fifty-four were 2- and 4-pounders. The work of destruction was carried on and made as thorough as fire, axe, and shovel could make

27

it. A victory was won, of which the American navy may feel proud. Zeal, patience, discipline, and bravery characterized men and officers in all the movements.

The wounded were moved to the Monocacy. The forts were occupied all Sunday night, and early on Monday morning the whole force was re-embarked in perfect order, in spite of the furious tide, rising twenty feet. The fleet moved down the stream with the captured colors at the mast-heads and towing the boats laden with the trophies of victory. Reaching the anchorage at half-past ten o'clock, they were greeted with such ringing cheers of their comrades left behind as made the woodlands echo again.

Later in the day, Dennis Hendrin (or Hanrahan) and Seth Allen, the two men slain in the fight, were buried on Boisée Island, and the first American graves rose on Corean soil. At 5.45 p.m. McKee breathed his last.[1]

Yet the odds of battle were dreadful—three graves against heaps upon heaps of unburied slain. Well might the pagan ask: "What did Heaven mean by it?"

The native wounded were kindly cared for, and their broken bones mended, by the fleet surgeon, Dr. Mayo. Admiral Rodgers, in a letter to the native authorities, offered to return his prisoners. The reply was in substance: "Do as you please with them." The prisoners were therefore set ashore and allowed to dispose of themselves.

Admiral Rodgers having obeyed to the farthest limit the orders given him, and all hope of making a treaty being over, two of the ships, withal needing to refit, the fleet sailed from the anchorage off Isle Boisée the day before the fourth of July, arriving in Chifu on the morning of July 5th, after thirty-five days' stay in Corean waters. He arrived in time to hear of the Tientsin massacre, which had taken place June 20th. "Our little war with the heathen," as the *New York Herald* styled it, attracted slight notice in the United States. A few columns of news and comment from the metropolitan press, a page or two of woodcuts in an illustrated newspaper, the ringing of a chime of jests on going up Salt River (Salée), and

---

[1] In the chapel of the Naval Academy, at Annapolis, a tasteful mural tablet, "Erected by his brother officers of the Asiatic squadron," with the naval emblems—sword, belt, anchor, and glory-wreath—in medallion, and inscription on a shield beneath, keeps green the memory of an unselfish patriot and a gallant officer.

the usual transmission of official documents, summed up the transient impression on the American public.

In China the expedition was looked upon as a failure and a defeat. The popular Corean idea was, that the Americans had come to avenge the death of pirates and robbers, and, after several battles, had been so surely defeated that they dare not attempt the task of chastisement again. To the Tai-wen Kun the whole matter was cause for personal glorification. The tiger-hunters and the conservative party at court believed that they had successfully defied both France and America, and driven off their forces with loss. When a Scotch missionary in Shing-king reasoned with a Corean concerning the power of foreigners and their superiority in war, the listener's reply, delivered with angry toss of the head and a snap of the fingers, was : "What care we for your foreign inventions? Even our boys laugh at all your weapons."

CHAPTER XLVII.

THE PORTS OPENED TO JAPANESE COMMERCE.

THE walls of Corean isolation, so long intact, had been sapped by the entrance of Christianity and the French missionaries, and now began to crumble. With the Russians on the north, and the sea no longer a barrier, the Japanese began to press upon the east, while China broke through and abolished the neutrality of the western border. The fires of civilization began to smoke out the hermit.

The revolutions of 1868 in Japan, culminating after a century of interior preparation, abolished the dual system and feudalism, and restored the mikado to supreme power. The capital was removed to Tōkiō, and the office of Foreign Affairs—a sub-bureau—was raised to a department of the Imperial administration. One of the first things attended to was to invite the Corean government to resume ancient friendship and vassalage.

This summons, coming from a source unrecognized for eight centuries, and to a regent swollen with pride at his victory over the French and his success in extirpating the Christian religion, and irritated at Japan for adopting western principles of progress and cutting free from Chinese influence and tradition, was spurned with defiance. An insolent and even scurrilous letter was returned to the mikado's government, which stung to rage the military classes of Japan, who began to form a "war-party," which was headed by Saigo of Satsuma. Waiting only for the return of the embassy from Europe, and for the word to take up the gage of battle, they nourished their wrath to keep it warm.

It was not so to be. New factors had entered the Corean problem since Taikō's time. European states were now concerned in Asiatic politics. Russia was too near, China too hostile, and Japan too poor ; she was even then paying ten per cent. interest to London bankers on the Shimonoséki Indemnity loan. Financial ruin, and a collision with China might result, if war were declared.

In October, 1873, the cabinet vetoed the scheme, and Saigo, the leader of the war party, resigned and returned to Satsuma, to nourish schemes for the overthrow of the ministry and the humiliation of Corea. "The eagle, even though starving, refuses to eat grain;" nor would anything less than Corean blood satisfy the Japanese veterans.

In 1873, the young king of Corea attained his majority. His father, Tai-wen Kun, by the act of the king backed by Queen Cho, was relieved of office, and his bloody and cruel lease of power came to an end. The young sovereign proved himself a man of mental vigor and independent judgment, not merely trusting to his ministers, but opening important documents in person. He has been ably seconded by his wife Min, through whose influence Tai-wen Kun was shorn of influence, nobles of progressive spirit were reinstated to office, and friendship with Japan encouraged. In this year, 1873, an heir to the throne was born of the queen ; another royal child, the offspring of a concubine, having been born in 1869.

The neutral belt of land long inhabited by deer and tiger, or traversed by occasional parties of ginseng-hunters, had within the last few decades been overspread with squatters, and infested by Manchiu brigands and Corean outlaws. The depredations of these border ruffians both across the Yalu, and on the Chinese settlements—like the raids of the wild Indians on our Texas frontier—had become intolerable to both countries. In 1875, Li Hung Chang, sending a force of picked Chinese troops, supported by a gunboat on the Yalu, broke up the nest of robbers, and imbibed a taste both for Corean politics and for rectifying the frontiers of Shing-king. He proceeded at once to make said frontier "scientific" by allowing the surveyor and plowman to enter the no longer debatable land. In 1877, the governor of Shing-king proposing, the Peking Government shifted the eastern frontier of the empire twenty leagues nearer the rising sun, on the plea that "the width of the tract left uncultivated was of less moment than the efficiency of border regulations." By this act the borders of China and Corea touched, and were written in Yalu water. The last vestige of insulation was removed, and the shocks of change now became more frequent and alarming. By contact with the living world, comatose Corea was to be galvanized into new life.

Nevertheless the hostile spirit of the official classes, who tyrannize the little country, was shown in the refusal to receive envoys of the mikado because they were dressed in European clothes, in petty regulations highly irritating to the Japanese at Fusan, and by the overt act of violence which we shall now narrate.

Since 1868 the Japanese navy, modelled after the British, and consisting of American and European iron-clads and war vessels, has been manned by crews uniformed in foreign style. On September 19, 1875, some sailors of the Unyo Kuan, which had been cruising off the mouth of the Han River, landing near Kang-wa for water, were fired on by Corean soldiers, under the idea that they were Americans or Frenchmen. On the 21st the Japanese, numbering thirty-six men, and armed with breech-loaders, stormed the fort. Most of the garrison were shot or drowned, the fort dismantled, and the spoil carried to the ships. Occupying the works two days, the Japanese returned to Nagasaki on the 23d.

The news of "the Kokwa [Kang-wa] affair" brought the wavering minds of both the peace and the war party of Japan to a decision. Arinori Mori was despatched to Peking to find out the exact relation of China to Corea, and secure her neutrality. Kuroda Kiyotaku was sent with a fleet to the Han River, to make, if possible, a treaty of friendship and open ports of trade. By the rival parties, the one was regarded as the bearer of the olive branch, the other of arrows and lightning. With Kuroda went Inouyé Bunda of the State Department, and Kin Rinshiō, the Corean liberal.

General Kuroda sailed January 6, 1876, amid salvos of the artillery of newspaper criticism predicting failure, with two men-of-war, three transports, and three companies of marines, or less than eight hundred men in all, and touching at Fusan, anchored within sight of Seoul, February 6th. About the same time, a courier from Peking arrived in the capital, bearing the Imperial recommendation that a treaty be made with the Japanese. The temper of the young king had been manifested long before this by his rebuking the district magistrate of Kang-wa for allowing soldiers to fire on peaceably disposed people, and ordering the offender to degradation and exile. Arinori Mori, in Peking, had received the written disclaimer of China's responsibility over "the outpost state," by which stroke of policy the Middle Kingdom freed herself from all possible claims of indemnity from France, the United States, and Japan. The way for a treaty was now smoothed, and the new difficulties were merely questions of form. Nevertheless, while Kuroda was unheard from, the Japanese war preparations went vigorously on.

Kuroda, making Commodore Perry's tactics his own, disposed his fleet in the most imposing array, made his transports look like men-of-war, by painting port-holes on them, kept up an incredible amount of fuss, movement, and bustle, and on the 10th landed a dazzling array of marines, sailors, and officers in full uniform, who paraded two miles to the treaty-house, on Kang-wa Island, where two high commissioners from Seoul, Ji Shinken and In Jishō, aged respectively sixty-five and fifty, awaited him.

One day was devoted to ceremony, and three to negotiation. A written apology for the Kang-wa affair was offered by the Coreans, and the details of the treaty settled, the chief difficulties being the titles to be used.[1] Ten days for consultation at the capital were then asked for and granted, at the end of which time, the two commissioners returned, declaring the impossibility of obtaining the royal signature. The Japanese at once embarked on their ships in disgust. They returned only after satisfactory assurances; and on February 27th the treaty, in which Chō-sen was recognized as an independent nation, was signed and attested. The Japanese then made presents, mostly of western manufacture, and after being feasted, returned March 1st. Mr. Inouyé Bunda then proceeded to Europe, visiting, on his way, the Centennial Exposition at Philadelphia, at which also, it is said, were one or more Corean visitors.

The first Corean Embassy, which since the twelfth century had been accredited to the mikado's court, sailed in May, 1876, from Fusan in a Japanese steamer, landing at Yokohama May 29th, at 8 A.M. Two Neptune-like braves with the symbols of power—huge iron

---

[1] The Japanese refused to have the Mikado designated by any title but that of Whang Ti (Japanese Kōtei) showing that he was peer to the Emperor of China; while the Coreans would not, in the same document, have their sovereign written down as Wang (Japanese Ō) because they wished him shown to be an equal of the Mikado, though ceremonially subordinate to the Whang Ti or Emperor of China. The poor Coreans were puzzled at there being two suns in one heaven, and two equal and favorite Sons of Heaven.

The commissioners from Seoul attempted to avoid the dilemma by having the treaty drawn up in the names of the respective envoys only; this the Japanese refused to do. A compromise was attempted by having the titles of the Mikado of Japan, and the Hap-mun of Chō-sen inserted at the beginning; and, in every necessary place thereafter, "the government" of Dai Nippon (Great Japan), or of Dai Chō-sen (Great Corea); this also failed. Finally, neither ruler was mentioned by name or title, nor was reference made to either, and the curious document was drawn up in the name of the respective "Governments."

tridents—led the procession, in which was a band of twenty performers on metal horns, conch-shells, flutes, whistles, cymbals,
and drums.   Effeminate-looking pages bore the treaty documents.
The chief envoy rode on a platform covered with tiger-skins, and
resting on the shoulders of eight men, while a servant bore the
umbrella of state over his head, and four minor officers walked at
his side.   The remainder of the suite rode in *jin-riki-shas*, and the
Japanese military and civil escort completed the display.   They
breakfasted at the town hall, and by railroad and steam-cars reached
Tōkiō.   At the station, the contrast between the old and the new
was startling.   The Japanese stood " with all the outward signs of
the Civilization that is coming in."   " On the other side, were all
the representatives of the Barbarism that is going out."   On the
following day, the Coreans visited the Foreign Office, and on June
1st, the envoy, though of inferior rank, had audience of the mikado.
For three weeks the Japanese amused, enlightened, and startled
their guests by showing them their war ships, arsenals, artillery,
torpedoes, schools, buildings, factories, and offices equipped with
steam and electricity—the ripened fruit of the seed planted by
Perry in 1854.   All attempts of foreigners to hold any communication with them, were firmly rejected by the Coreans, who started
homeward June 28th.   The official diary, or report by the ambassador of this visit to Japan, was afterward published in Seoul.   It
is a colorless narrative carefully bleached of all views and opinions,
evidently satisfying the scrutiny even of enemies at court.

During the autumn of this year, 1876, and later on, in following years, the British war-vessels, Sylvia and Swinger, were engaged
in surveying portions of the coast of Kiung-sang province.   Captain H. C. Saint John, who commanded the Sylvia, and had touched
near Fusan in 1855—long enough to see a native bastinadoed simply
for selling a chicken to a foreigner—now found more hospitable
treatment.   His adventures are narrated in his chatty book, "The
Wild Coasts of Nipon."   An English vessel, the Barbara Taylor,
having been wrecked on Corean shores, an attaché of the British
Legation in Tōkiō was sent to Fusan to thank the authorities for
their kind treatment of the crew.

The Japanese found it was not wise to hasten in taking advantage of their new liberties granted by treaty.   Near Fusan, are
thousands of graves of natives killed in the invasion of 1592–97,
over which the Coreans hold an annual memorial celebration.
Hitherto the Japanese had been rigorously kept within their

guarded enclosure. Going out to witness the celebration, they were met with a shower of stones, and found the road blockaded. After a small riot in which many words and missiles were exchanged, matters were righted, but the temper of the people showed that, as in old Japan, it would be long before ignorant hermits, and not over-gentle foreigners could live quietly together.

Saigo, of Satsuma, dissatisfied with the peaceful results of Kuroda's mission, and the "brain victory" over the Coreans, organized, during 1877, "The Satsuma Rebellion," to crush which cost Japan twenty thousand lives, $50,000,000, and seven months of mighty effort, the story of which has been so well told in the lamented A. H. Mounsey's perspicuous monograph. Yet out of this struggle, with which Corea manifested no sympathy, the nation emerged with old elements of disturbance eliminated, and with a broader outlook to the future. A more vigorous policy with Chō-sen was at once inaugurated.

Under the new treaty, Fusan (Corean, Pu-san) soon became a bustling place of trade, with a population of two thousand, many of whom, however, were poor people from Tsushima. Among the public buildings were those of the Consulate, Chamber of Commerce, Bank, Mitsu Bishi (Three Diamonds) Steamship Company, and a hospital, under care of Dr. Yano, in which, up to 1882, four thousand Coreans and many Japanese have been treated. A Japanese and Corean newspaper, *Chō-sen Shimpo*, restaurants, places of amusements of various grades of morality, and a variety of establishments for turning wits and industry into money, have been established. The decayed gentry of Japan, starting in business with the capital obtained by commuting their hereditary pensions, found it difficult to compete with the trained merchants of Tōkiō and Ozaka. Great trouble from the lack of a gold and silver currency has been experienced, as only the copper and iron *sapeks*, or 'cash,' are in circulation. In Corean political economy to let gold go out of the country is to sell the kingdom; and so many rogues have attempted the sale of brass or gilt nuggets that an assaying office at the consulate has been provided. The government of Tōkiō has urged upon that of Seoul the adoption of a circulating medium based on the precious metals; and, perhaps, Corean coins may yet be struck at the superb mint at Ozaka. While gold in dust and nuggets has been exported for centuries, rumor credits the vaults at Seoul with being full of Japanese gold *koban*, the mountains to be well packed with auriferous quartz, and the rivers to run with golden sands.

Among the callers, with diplomatic powers, from the outside world in 1881, each eager and ambitious to be the first in wresting the coveted prize of a treaty, were two British captains of men-of-war, who arrived on May 21st and 28th; a French naval officer, June 16th, who sailed away after a rebuff June 18th; while at Gensan, June 7th, the British man-of-war, Pegasus, came, and saw, but did not conquer.

After six years of mutual contact at Fusan, the Coreans, though finding the Japanese as troublesome as the latter discovered foreigners to be after their own ports were opened, have, with much experience learned, settled down to endure them, for the sake of a trade which undoubtedly enriches the country. The Coreans buy cotton goods, tin-plate, glass, dyes, tools, and machinery, clocks, watches, petroleum, flour, lacquer-work, iron, hollow-ware, and foreign knick-knacks. A good sign of a desire for personal improvement is a demand for bath-tubs. Soap will probably come next.

The exports are gold dust, silver, ox hides and bones, beche-de-mer, fish, rice, raw silk, fans, cotton, and bamboo paper, ginseng, furs of many kinds, tobacco, shells for inlaying, dried fish, timber, beans and peas, hemp, jute, various plants yielding paper-stock, peony-bark, gall-nuts, varnishes and oils, and a variety of other vegetable substances having a universal commercial value.

Even Riu Kiu has seen the benefits of trade, and five merchants from what is now the Okinawa *ken* of the mikado's empire —formerly the Loo Choo island kingdom—came to Tōkiō in February, 1882, to form a company with a view to establishing an agency in Fusan, and exchanging Corean products for Riu Kiu sugar, grain, and fish.

Gensan (Corean, Won-san) was opened May 1, 1880. In a fertile region, traversed by two high roads, with the fur country near, and a magnificent harbor in front, the prospects of trade are good. The Japanese concession, on which are some imposing public buildings, includes about forty-two acres. An exposition of Japanese, European, and American goods was established which was visited by 25,000 people, its object being to open the eyes and pockets of the natives, who seemed, to the Tōkiō merchants, taller, stouter, and better looking than those of Fusan. One twenty-sixth of the goods sold was Japanese, the rest, mostly cot-

ton goods and 'notions,' were American and European. The busy
season of trade is in autumn and early winter. For the first three
months the settlers were less troubled by tigers than by continual
rumors of the approach of a band of a thousand "foreigner-haters,"
who were sworn to annihilate the aliens on the sacred soil of Chō-
sen. The bloodthirsty braves, however, postponed the execution
of their purpose. The Japanese merchants, so far from finding the
Coreans innocently verdant, soon came in contact with monopolies,
rings, guilds, and tricks of trade that showed a surprising knowledge
of business. Official intermeddling completed their woe, and loud
and long were the complaints of the mikado's subjects. Yet profits
were fair, and the first anniversary of the opening of the port was
celebrated in grand style. Besides dinners and day fireworks, the
police played the ancient national game of polo, to the great amusement of the Coreans. Among the foreign visitors in May, 1881, was
Doctor Frank Cowan, an American gentleman, and surgeon on the
Japanese steamer Tsuruga Maru, who made a short journey in the
vicinity among the good-natured natives. Besides spying out the
land, and returning well laden with trophies, he records, in a letter
to the State Department at Washington, this prophecy : "Next to
the countries on the golden rim of the Pacific, ... to disturb the monetary equilibrium of the world, will be Corea." "The
geological structure is not incompatible with the theory that the
whole region [east coast] is productive of the precious metal."

To regulate some points of the treaty, and if possible postpone
the opening of the new port of In-chiŭn (Japanese, Nin-sen) a second
embassy was despatched to Japan, which arrived at Yokohama,
August 11, 1880. The procession of tall and portly men dressed
in green, red, and pink garments of coarse cloth, with Chinese
shoes, and hats of mighty diameter, moved through the streets amid
the rather free remarks of the spectators, who commented in no
complimentary language on the general air of dinginess which
these Rip Van Winkles of the orient presented. The Coreans remained in Tōkiō until September 8th. Perfect courtesy was everywhere shown them, as they visited schools and factories, and
studied Japan's modern enginery of war and peace. The general
attitude of the Tōkiō press and populace was that of condescend-
ing familiarity, of generous hospitality mildly flavored with contempt, and tempered by a very uncertain hope that these people
might develop into good pupils—and customers.

Chō-sen did not lack attentions from the outside world—Russia,

England, France, Italy, and the United States—during the year 1880. Whether missionaries of the Holy Synod of Russia attempted to cross the Tumen, we do not know; but in the spring of 1880, a Muscovite vessel appeared off one of the ports of Ham-Kiung, to open commercial relations. The offer was politely declined. The Italian war-vessel Vettor Pisani, having on board H. R. H. the Duke of Genoa, arrived off Fusan, August 1, 1880, at 1 P.M—a few hours after the Corean embassy had left for Japan. One survivor of the Italian ship, Bianca Portia, wrecked near Quelpart in 1879, had been kindly treated by the Corean authorities and sent to Nagasaki. The duke, through the Japanese consul, forwarded a letter of thanks to the governor of Tong-nai, who, however, returned the missive, though with a courteous answer. After seven days, the Vettor Pisani sailed northward, and avoiding Gensan and the Japanese consul, anchored off Port Lazareff, where, during his six days' stay, he was visited by the local magistrate, to whom he committed a letter of application for trade. Some native cards of silk-worm's eggs were also secured to test their value for Italy. After a three days' visit to Gensan the ship sailed away, the Italian believing that negociations with the Coreans would succeed better without Japanese aid, and congratulating himself upon having been more successful than the previous attempts by the British, and especially by the French (Captain Fourmier, of the Lynx) and American (Commodore Shufeldt) diplomatic agents, whose letters were returned unread.

The Government of the United States had not forgotten Corea, and Japan had signified her willingness to assist in opening the hermit nation to American commerce. On April 8, 1878, Senator Sargent, of California, offered a resolution that President Hayes "appoint a commissioner to represent this country in an effort to arrange, by peaceful means and with the aid of the friendly offices of Japan, a treaty of peace and commerce between the United States and the Kingdom of Corea." The bill passed to a second reading, but, the Senate adjourning, no action was taken. In 1879, the U. S. steamship Ticonderoga, under Commodore R. W. Shufeldt, was sent on a cruise around the world in the interests of American commerce, and to make, if possible, a treaty with Corea. Entering the harbor of Fusan, May 14, 1880, Commodore Shufeldt begged the Japanese consul, who visited the ship, to forward his papers to Seoul. The consul complied, but, unfortunately, neither the interpreters nor the governor of Tong-nai—preferring present pay and comfort to possible future benefit—would have anything to do with such dangerous business. Japanese rumor asserts that the Coreans seeing the letter addressed on the outside to "the King of Corea," declined to receive it, partly because their sovereign was "not King of Korai" but "King of Chō-sen." Under the circumstances, the American could do nothing more than withdraw, which he did amid the usual salute from a Corean fort near by. A second visit being equally fruitless, the Ticonderoga again turned her stern toward "the last outstanding and irreconcilable scoffer among nations at western alliances," and her prow homeward.

The Corean embassy, failing in their attempts to have the Japanese go slowly, Hanabusa, the mikado's envoy at Seoul, now vigorously urged the opening of the third port, and, after much discussion, In-chiŭn,[1] twenty-five miles from Seoul, was selected; in December, 1880, Hanabusa and his suite, crossing the frozen rivers, went thither, and selected the ground for the Japanese concession.

The old questions upon which political parties in the hermit nation had formed themselves, now sank out of sight, and the new element of excitement was the all-absorbing question of breaking the seals of national seclusion. The "Civilization Party," or the Progressionists, were opposed to the Exclusionists, Port-closers, and Foreigner-haters. Heading the former or liberal party were the young king and queen, Bin Kenko, Bin Shoshoko, Ri Saiwo, and other high dignitaries, besides Kin Giokin and Jo Kohan, former envoys to Japan. The leader of the Conservatives was the Taiwen-kun, father of the king and late regent. The neutrals clustered around Kin Koshiu.

Physically speaking, the Coreans see the sun rise over Japan and set over China, but morally, and in rhetoric, their sun of prosperity has ever risen and set in China. Some proposed to buy all machinery, arms, and government material in China, and imitate her plans and policy, and conform to the advice of her statesmen. The other side urged the adoption of Japanese methods and materials. The pro-Chinese gentry imitated the Peking mandarins in

---

[1] This *fu* city, called by the Japanese Ninsen, or Nii-gawa, was well known by the Japanese, as is shown on their maps of the sixteenth century. The name means Two Rivers. The rise and fall of the tides here is very great, sometimes amounting to a difference of twenty-nine feet; and in winter the shore-water is frozen. Large vessels cannot anchor within a mile of the shore. The port Chi-mul-po is at some distance from the city.

details of dress, household decoration, and culture ; while all their books conveying Western science must be read from Chinese translations. The pro-Japanese Coreans had their houses furnished with Japanese articles, they read and studied Japanese literature and translations of European books, and when out of Corea the most radical among them wore coats and pantaloons. The long and hot disputes between the adherents of both parties seriously hampered the government, while precipitating a revolution in the national policy ; for serious debate in a despotic country is a sign of awakening life.

About this time, early in 1881, a remarkable document, composed by Kwo-in-ken, adviser to the Chinese Minister to Japan, had a lively effect upon the court of Seoul. It was entitled "Policy for Corea." It described the neighbors of Chō-sen, and pointed out her proper attitude to each of them. From Russia, devoted as she is to a policy of perpetual aggrandizement at the expense of other countries, and consumed by lust for land, Corea is in imminent danger. China, on the contrary, is Corea's natural ally and friend, ever ready with aid in men and money ; both countries need each other, and their union should be as close as lips and teeth. For historical and geographical reasons, Corea and Japan should also be one in friendship, and thus guard against "Russia the ravenous." The next point treated is the necessity of an alliance between Corea and the United States, because the Americans are the natural friends of Asiatic nations. Pointing out the many advantages of securing the friendship of the Americans, and making a treaty with them first, the memorialist urges the Coreans to seize the golden opportunity at once.

About the same time, Li Hung Chang, China's liberal statesman, wrote a letter to a Corean gentleman, in which the advice to seek the friendship of China and the United States was strongly expressed, and a treaty with the Americans urged as a matter of national safety. Many, though not all, of the members of the embassies to Japan returned full of enthusiasm for Western civilization. It soon became evident that the king and many of his advisers were willing to make treaties. In Peking, the members of the embassy, before the winter of 1881 was over, began diplomatic flirtations with the American Legation. At that time, however, neither Minister J. B. Angell, in Peking, nor John A. Bingham, in Tōkiō, had any authority to make a treaty with Corea. While the way was thus made ready, the representations of Messrs. Bingham and Angell to the State Department at Washington impressed upon our Government the necessity of having a diplomatic agent near at hand to take advantage of the next opportunity. Hitherto the only avenue of entrance seemed through the Japanese good offices ; but the apparent willingness of Coreans in Peking, the experience of the Italians in the Vettor Pisani at Fusan and Port Lazareff, the advice of Chinese statesmen to Corea to have faith in the United States, and to open her ports to American commerce, convinced the American minister at Peking that China, rather than Japan, would furnish the better base of diplomatic operations for breaking down the Corean repulsive policy.

The Government at Washington responded to the suggestion, and in the spring of 1881, Commodore Shufeldt was sent by the State Department to Peking as naval attaché to the Legation, so as to be near the American Minister and be ready with his experience, should a further attempt "to bring together the strange States of the Extreme Sea" be made.

Shortly after the presentation of Kwo-in-ken's memorial in Seoul, a party of thirty-four prominent men of the civilization party, led by Giō Inchiu and Kio Yeichoku, set out from Seoul to visit Japan and further study the problem of how far Western ideas were adapted to an oriental state.

The proposition to open a port so near the capital to the Japanese, and to treat with the Americans, was not left unchallenged. The ultra-Confucianists, headed by Ni Mansun, stood ready to oppose it with word and weapon. In swelling Corean rhetoric, this bigoted patriot from Chung-chong proved to his own satisfaction that all the nations except China and Corea were uncivilized, and that the presence of foreigners would pollute the holy land. Gathering an array of seven hundred of his followers, he dressed in mourning to show his grief, and with the figure of an axe on his shoulders, in token of risking his life by his act, he presented his memorial to the king, and sat for seven days in front of the royal palace. He demanded that In-chiŭn should not be opened, the two Bin should be deposed, and all innovations should cease.

The popular form of the dread of foreigners was shown in delegations of country people, who came into Seoul to forward petitions and protestations. Placards were posted on or near the palace gates, full of violent language, and prophesying the most woful results of Western blight and poison upon the country which had ever been the object of the special favor of the sprits.

Another party of two thousand literary men, fanatical patriots, had assembled at Chō-rio to go up to Seoul to overawe the progressive ministers, but were met by messengers from the court and turned back by the promise that the party about to visit Japan under royal patronage should be recalled. For a moment the king had thrown a sop to these cerberian zealots, whose three heads of demand would keep Chō-sen as inaccessible as Hades.

The order came too late, the progressionists had left the shores, and were in Nagasaki. Thence to Ozaka, where some remained to study the arts and sciences; the majority proceeded to Tōkiō to examine modern civilization in its manifold phases. Unlike Peter the Great, some of these reformers began with themselves, clothing mind and body with the nineteenth century. Dropping the garments of picturesque mediævalism, they put on the work-suit of buttoned coat and trousers and learned the value of minutes from American watches. The cutting off their badge of nationality —the top-knot—was accompanied with emotions very similar to those of bereavement by death.

Giō Inchiu[1] after his return from Japan was despatched on a mission to China, where his conference was chiefly with Li Hung Chang. He returned home by way of Fusan, December 29, 1881. He had now a good opportunity of judging the relative merits of Japan and China. His patriotic eye saw that the first need of Corean reform was in strengthening the army; though the poverty of the country gave slight hope of speedy success.

The results of this mission were soon apparent, for shortly after, eighty young men, of the average age of twenty, were sent to Tientsin, where they are now, 1882, diligently pursuing their studies; some in the arsenal, learning the manufacture of fire-arms, others learning the English language. A returned Chinese student—one of the number lately recalled from New England— while severely sarcastic at the Corean government's "poor discrimination in selecting the country from which her students could profit most," added, "they possess a far better physique for the navy than any of our future imperial midshipmen."

---

[1] In this and the following chapter the names of Corean noblemen have been given in their Japanese form, i.e., Bin for Min, etc., but in the Supplementary Chapter according to Corean pronunciation.

CHAPTER XLVIII.

THE YEAR OF THE TREATIES.

THE year 1882 opened ominously. A fire broke out in the royal palace in Seoul, on January 27th, in which two buildings, nearly completed for the heir apparent, were burned down. The fire was at first believed to have political significance, and the tension of the public mind was not relaxed until it was shown that the fire was the result of pure accident.

The spirit of progress made advance, but discussion reached fever-heat in deciding whether the favor of Japan or China should be most sought, and which foreign nation, the United States, France, or England, should be admitted first to treaty rights. Bin, opposed to the arbitrary spirit of the Japanese, edged his argument by proposing an alliance with foreigners in order to checkmate the designs of Japan.

An event not unlooked for increased the power of the progressionists. One Kozaikai urged the plea of expulsion of foreigners in such intemperate language that he was accused of reproaching the sovereign. At the same time, a conspiracy against the life of the king, involving forty persons, was discovered, and the sword and torture came into play. Kozaikai was put to death, many of the conspirators were exiled, and the ringleaders were sentenced to be broken alive on the wheel, the revolutions of which tore off hands and feet in succession. Six of those doomed to death were spared, through the intercession of a minister, and one, the king's cousin, who delivered himself up, was pardoned by his sovereign on the ground of the prisoner's insanity. The Progressionists had now the upper hand, and early in the spring Giō Inchiu and Riōsen left on a mission to Tientsin, to acquaint the Americans and Chinese with the information that the Corean government was ready to make treaties, and that the proper officer would be at In-chiŭn to sign the compact and complete the negotiations.

Meanwhile the reforms in military affairs were begun with en-

ergy. Japanese officers, at the head of whom was Lieutenant
Horimoto, drilled picked men in Seoul, with creditable success, in
spite of their unwieldy hats and costume, and the jeers of the anti-
foreign people, in public as well as in private. Substantial proof
of the adoption of Japan's military system was shown in an order
sent to Tōkiō for a few hundred Snider rifles with equipments—
the weapon of the British army—and one for twenty thousand of
the rifles made at the Japanese arsenal in Tōkiō, which, combining
the merits of the best-known military fire-arm, contained improvements invented and patented by Colonel Murata, of the mikado's
army. Two Corean notables later again visited Japan in April of
this year, and were annoyed to find a report spread abroad in Nagasaki that they had come to raise a money loan. Nevertheless,
they proceeded to Kiōto and Tōkiō. Some of their suite went into
the printing-offices and silk-worm breeding establishments to
learn these arts, while type, presses, and printing material were
ordered for use at home.

Affairs had so shaped themselves that even to outsiders it became evident that the Corean apple was ripe even to falling. By
March 4th it was known at the American Legation in Peking that
"Barkis was willin'," while to the Japanese envoy then in Tōkiō
it became certain that, unless he made all haste to In-chiŭn, the
American commodore would have his treaty signed and be off
without even waiting for a call. Hastily bidding his friends
good-by, he left in the Japanese steamer, Iwaki Kuan, and arrived in the harbor just one hour before the American corvette
Swatara arrived with Commodore Shufeldt on board. With the
Swatara were three Chinese men-of-war, one of them an iron-
clad.

The American diplomatic agent, Commodore R. W. Shufeldt,
having spent nearly a year in China, surmounting difficulties that
few will know of until the full history of the American treaty with
Corea is written, arrived in the Swatara off Chimulpo, May 7th. Accompanied by three officers, Commodore Shufeldt went six miles into
the interior to the office of the Corean magistrate to formulate the
treaty. Though surrounded every moment by curious crowds, no
disrespect was shown in any way. Two days afterward, the treaty
document was signed on a point of land in a temporary pavilion
opposite the ship. Thus, in the most modest manner the negotiations were concluded, and a treaty with the United States was, after
repeated failures, secured by the gallant officer who, by this act

of successful diplomacy, closed a long and brilliant professional career.[1]

Both on the American and Corean side the results had been brought about only after severe toil. The Corean nobleman Bin, a cousin of the queen, had so labored in Seoul night and day to commit the government to the policy of making treaties with the Americans, that, when the messengers had been despatched with the order for Commodore Shufeldt to appear in Imperatrice Gulf, he fell ill, and was unable to appear at In-chiŭn. The American envoy was so worn out with anxiety and toil by his efforts to have Corea opened under Chinese auspices, that on landing at San Francisco, he retired to the naval hospital at Mare's Island to recover his exhausted strength.

Four days after the signing of the American and Chinese treaties, the Corean capital was full of mirth and gayety, on account of a wedding in the royal family. The crown prince, a lad of nine years old, was wedded to the daughter of Jun, a nobleman of high rank, who had postponed a visit to Japan until the nuptials were accomplished. A brilliant procession in the streets of Seoul marked the event, and for a moment the excitement concerning foreigners was forgotten. None foresaw the bloody ending of this honeymoon so happily begun.

The British minister at Tōkiō, Sir Harry Parkes, who had left no stone unturned to secure a personal interview with the ambassador

---

[1] Commodore R. W. Shufeldt was born in Dutchess County, New York, in 1822, and entered the navy in 1839, serving ten years on foreign stations and in the coast survey. One cruise to the west coast of Africa interested him in the negro colony of Liberia, in which he has ever since felt concern. From 1850 to 1860, our navy being in a languishing state, he was engaged in the mercantile marine service, and in organizing a transit route across the Isthmus of Tehuantepec. In 1860 an article of his on the slave trade between the Island of Cuba and the coast of Africa, drew the attention of the government to him, and led to his appointment of Consul-General at Havana. The slave-trade was soon effectually broken up, and through the trying period of the first half of the civil war, he was occupied in his civil duties, at one time going to Mexico on a confidential mission to President Juarez, passing unrecognized through the French lines. He was on blockade duty during the last two years of the civil war. In 1865 he went to China, as flag-captain of the Hartford, and commanding the Wachusett visited Corea. In 1870 he organized a party for the survey of the Isthmus of Tehuantepec, his report being made the basis of Captain Eads' ship-railway project. The official history of the semi-diplomatic cruise of the Ticonderoga round the world (1878–1880) has been written, but has not yet been published.

in 1876, and, since that time, British trade with Corea, was still on
the alert. He at once ordered Admiral Willes to proceed to In-
chiŭn. Leaving his large fleet in Japanese waters, Admiral Willes
left Nagasaki in the Vigilant, May 27th, while Mr. William G. Aston, the accomplished linguist and Corean scholar, received orders
to follow. The Admiral's business was soon despatched, a treaty
was made, and his return to Yokohama was accomplished June 14th,
the U. S. steamship Ashuelot saluting him on his arrival. The French
and Germans were the next to improve the long-awaited opportunity.
The German admiral left Japan in the man-of-war Stosch, on May
31st, while a vessel of the French navy entered the port of In-
chiŭn June 5th. There had thus appeared in this sequestered nook of
creation, within a few days, two American, three British, one French,
one Japanese, and five Chinese armed vessels. All of them, except
the French, had left by June 8th, to the great relief of the country
folks and old men and women, many of whom, with the children,
had fled to the hills when the big guns began to waste their powder
in salutes, to the detriment of the thatched roofs of the houses.

China lost no time in taking advantage of the position secured
her by treaty. No vexatious delays of ratification troubled her.
Everything had been arranged beforehand with the Coreans, so
that, on the return of the vessels from In-chiŭn, officers were despatched to Shanghae to sail for Gensan and Fusan, and select land
for public buildings.

During the present year the Japanese legation in Seoul has
numbered about forty persons, including secretaries, interpreters,
military officers, policemen, students, and servants. Notwithstanding their precarious situatiòn, amid the turbulent elements at
work around them, they seemed to enjoy the spectacle before their
eyes of a repetition of the history of their own country after
Perry's arrival in 1853. The young men of the legation visited the
historic sites near the capital, enjoyed the mountain and river
scenery, and studied the Corean language and literature. At first
the common people believed that their visitors sucked the blood of
the children lured away by them ; and so carefully guarded their
little ones. By and by, however, as more liberty was afforded
them, the occasional pelting with vegetables and pebbles became
less frequent, and even the women would talk with them.

The light-hearted Japanese seemed to suspect no imminent danger, although the old fanatic and tyrant Tai-wen Kun was still alive
and plotting. To insure perfect secrecy for his plans, it is said

that he employed two or three mutes to wait on him, and act as his messengers. He was the centre of all the elements hostile to innovation, and being a man of unusual ability, was possessed of immense influence. The populace of Seoul and of the country had been taught to believe that "the Japanese were inebriated with the manners of Christian nations, and were enchanted by the Western devils, and that as a Europeanized country of the devil was being created in their immediate neighborhood, they must expel the barbarians." Every means had been used to inflame the people against foreigners. Stone monuments had been set up on the high roads and market-places which bore this inscription—"The Western barbarians will come to invade our soil, there are but two alternatives for Chō-sen ; to go to war, or to maintain peace. To submit peacefully means to sell the country ; therefore we Coreans must resort to arms." Many thousands of these inscribed stones had been set up, and an edict had been issued, commanding the ink-makers to inscribe their sticks of ink with this inflammatory declaration. When nobles of high rank would advocate progressive views, Tai-wen Kun would sneeringly dare them to remove these anti-foreign monuments.

During the nine years of his nominal retirement from office, from 1873 to 1882, this bigoted Confucianist, who refused to know anything of the outer world, bided his time and waited his opportunity, which came during the summer of the present year. Just when the populace was most excited over the near presence of the Americans and other foreigners at In-chiŭn, the usual rainfall was withheld, the wells dried up, and in the consequent drouth, the rice crop was threatened with total failure. The diviners, sorcerers, and anti-foreign party took advantage of the situation to play on the fears of the superstitious people. The spirits, displeased at the intrusion of the Western devils, were angry and were cursing the land. At the same time the soldiery of the capital were disaffected, as some say on account of arrearages of wages, or as others aver, because the old warriors of the bow and arrow hated the Japanese method of drilling as a foreign innovation insulting to the gods. A more probable reason is that on account of the failure of the rice-harvest, the soldiers' rations were cut down, and they were deprived of this choice cereal for food. Among the first Corean officers killed was the superintendent of the rice storehouses, which were pillaged by the hungry mob.

On July 23d, while the king was out in the open air praying

for rain, a mob of sympathizers with Tai-wen Kun attempted to seize his person. The king escaped to the castle. According to one account, some mischief-maker then started the report in the city that the Japanese had attacked the royal castle, and had seized the king and queen, and that the prime minister with the palace-guards in vainly endeavoring to beat back the assailants, had been defeated; and that every Corean should take up arms. Forthwith the mob rushed with frantic violence upon the legation, murdering the Japanese policemen and students whom they met in the streets and the Japanese military instructors in the barracks. Not satisfied with this, the rioters, numbering 4,000 men, attacked and destroyed the houses of the ministers favoring foreign intercourse. Before quiet was restored, the queen, Min, the heir apparent and his wife, the chief ministers of the government, Min Thai Ho and Min Yong Ik, were, as was supposed, murdered; but all these emerged alive. Many of the Mins and seven Japanese were killed.

The Japanese, by their own account, had suspected no danger until the day of the riot, when they noticed great excitement among the people, and that crowds were assembling and rushing to and fro. They sent out a policeman to inquire into the nature of the disturbance, and at two o'clock P.M. they learned from a native that the mob would attack the legation. Word was also sent to the Japanese by the Corean officer in charge of the drill-ground where the troops were trained by Lieutenant Horimoto, saying that the troops drilled in Japanese tactics had been attacked, and the legation would next be in danger. Hanabusa and his suite then arranged a plan of defence. While thus engaged, a Corean employed at the legation informed them that the mob had destroyed the houses of the two ministers Bin, and were attacking three Japanese students. Three policemen well armed then left to succor the students, but nothing was heard from either policemen or students again. A Corean officer now appeared and warned the Japanese to escape to the hill back of the legation; and being requested by Hanabusa to ask the government for soldiers, he left on this errand. At 5.50 P.M. the mob reached the legation, and raising a united yell, fired volleys of bullets, arrows, and big stones at the legation, but dared not enter the gate to face the revolvers of the policemen. In hurling stones the ruffians showed remarkable skill. The mob set on fire a house, near by, and in the rising wind—then boding a coming storm —two out-houses of the legation were burned, the police shooting down the incendiaries when they could see them. It was now about ten o'clock, and the ruffians having thrown up barricades to hem in their victims and to shield their cowardly carcases while shooting, the Japanese fired the remaining buildings, and armed only with swords and pistols, formed themselves into a circle, charged the mob, and cut their way through to the house of the chief magistrate, which they found empty. Finding no one in the official residence, they marched to the southern gate of the royal castle. Instead of opening it, the soldiers on the wall above pelted them with stones.

Hanabusa now resolved to cross the river with his party and make his way to In-chiŭn. Turning their backs on the flames, they arrived at the river and, on the ferryman refusing to convey them across, they seized the boat and crossed safely to the other side. It was now past midnight and the rain began to fall heavily, and with occasional thunderstorms continued to pour down all night. The refugees plunged on through the darkness, often losing their way, but next day at ten o'clock, they procured some raw barley to eat, and through the pelting rain pushed on, reaching In-chiŭn at 3 P.M. The governor received them kindly and supplied food and dry clothing. The Japanese officers slept in the official residence, and the servants, police, and others in a guard-house about fifteen yards distant. The governor posted his own sentinels to watch so that the Japanese could get some rest. In a few minutes the tired men were sleeping the sleep of exhaustion.

About five o'clock, Hanabusa and his officers were suddenly awakened by the shouting of a mob outside ; and in a moment more a Japanese entered covered with blood, and with a drawn sword in his hand with which he had cut his way. The mob had attacked them while they were asleep, and. the soldiers of the local garrison were joining the rioters, firing from behind fences. All the Japanese now hurried on their clothes, and charging a body of about forty soldiers, armed with swords and spears, who were blocking the gateway, made for Chi-mul-po seaport, having lost three killed and two missing.

Meeting two Japanese on horseback from the port, who reported that the road was free from ambuscades, they put the wounded man on one horse, and by another despatched one of their number to hasten forward and have a boat ready. They reached Chi-mul-po, the port, about seven o'clock, and immediately crossed over to Roze Island for safety. About midnight, having procured a junk, they put to sea, toward Nanyo Bay, where they knew the British gunboat

Flying Fish was then on survey. Encountering a southerly wind, they made little or no progress, and on the 26th a dense fog set in ; but at 11.30 A.M., it cleared up and the welcome sight of a three-masted vessel greeted their eyes. Hoisting the flag of Japan, they saw their signal answered, and soon the party of twenty-six half-naked, hungry, and cold refugees were on board the ship, where kindest treatment awaited them. That night at ten o'clock the Flying Fish sailed for Nagasaki. On August 3d a religious service in memory of their slain comrades was held by the survivors, at Shimonoséki. "The deep silence was only broken by the sobbing of the audience, overcome by deep sympathy for the murdered men." On the 8th Hanabusa had an audience with the mikado in Tōkiō.

Without hesitation, the Japanese government ordered the army to assemble at Shinonoséki and Tsushima, with naval forces to co-operate. Hanabusa and his suite were sent back, escorted by a military force. He re-entered Seoul, August 16th, and was received with courtesy. A fleet of Chinese war-vessels with a force of four thousand troops was also at hand. Apparently everything was under the control of Tai-wen Kun, who professed to be friendly to foreigners, and to ascribe the recent riot to a sudden uprising of the unpaid soldiery, which the government had not force at hand to suppress. Two Corean officers coming on board the Flying Fish, August 10th, informed Captain Hoskyn that the soldiery, dissatisfied with the unfair treatment of their superiors, had incited the peasantry to rebellion ; that by orders of Tai-wen Kun, who bitterly regretted the recent outrages, the dead Japanese had been honorably buried ; that the old regent while usurping the royal power, had professed a total change of views and was in favor of a progressive policy.

At his audience with the king, August 20th, Hanabusa presented the demands of his government. These were nominally agreed to, but several days passing without satisfactory action, Hanabusa having exhausted remonstrance and argument, left Seoul August 25th and returned to his ship. This unexpected move—a menace of war—brought the usurper to terms. On receipt of Tai-wen Kun's apologies, the Japanese envoy returned to the capital August 30th and full agreement was given to the demands of Japan, at which time it would appear, Tai-wen Kun, forcibly kidnapped by the envoy of China, had begun his travels into the country of Confucius.

The following telegram to the *New York Tribune* of October 2d, summarizes the news from Yokohama up to September 13th:

The Corean Government pledged itself to the following conditions: To arrest the insurgents within twenty days and inflict due punishment upon them, Japanese delegates to be present at the trial; to bury properly the bodies of those murdered and pay 50,000 yen (dollars) to their families; to pay Japan 500,000 yen as indemnity for expenditure, etc., in five yearly instalments; to allow Japanese troops in Seoul for the protection of the legation, and to provide proper accommodations for them; to send an apology by a special embassy to Japan; to extend gradually privileges to the Japanese residents and traders; to afford proper conveniences for travel throughout Corea for the Japanese Government officials.

While this was going on the Chinese envoy, who had remained inactive with his escort until August 25th, suddenly called up the full body of his troops, about three or four thousand, to the capital. What degree of pressure he may have exercised is not yet known, but it is certain that the chief rebel and assassin, the Tai-wen Kun, was taken on board a Chinese ship and carried to Tien-tsin. It is alleged that his departure was by no means voluntary, and that some physical effort was required to get him ashore on arriving at his destination. Whatever was the object of this proceeding, it must have been dictated by Li Hung Chang, the Chinese Viceroy at Tien-tsin, who seems to have quite abandoned his demeanor of calm stolidity during these active Corean transactions. It is declared by one Chinese party that the only purpose was to rescue the Tai-wen Kun from the dangers that threatened him, and by another that the intent was still to maintain the theory of sovereign control over Corea's rulers, which Li Hung Chang has been straining for throughout.

During the recent prospect of trouble with Corea, the Japanese Government received offers of military service from twenty thousand volunteers, and of money gifts to the value of 200,000 yen.

At this stage of affairs, when Corea ceases to be a "hermit nation," and stands in the glare of the world's attention, we bring our imperfect story to a close. The pivot of the future history of Eastern Asia is Corea. On her soil will be decided the problem of supremacy, by the jealous rivals China, Japan, and Russia. The sudden assumption of self-imposed tutelary duties by China proves her lively interest in the little country, which has been called both "her right arm of defense," and "her gloved hand"—the one to force back the ravenous Muscovite, the other to warn off the ambitious Japanese. Whether the Middle Kingdom has deliberately chosen the Land of Morning Calm to affront and humiliate "the neighbor-disturbing nation," that twice humbled her pride in the fairest islands of the sea—Formosa and Riu Kiu—the events of the not distant future will soon determine. Whether the hoary empire shall come in collision with the young northern giant, and the dragon and the bear tear each other in the slime of war in Corean valleys, may be a question the solution of which is not far off. We trust that amid all dangers, the integrity of the little kingdom may be preserved ; but whatever be the issue upon the map of the world, let us hope that paganism, bigotry, and superstition in Corea, and in all Asia, may disappear ; and that in their places, the religion of Jesus, science, education, and human brotherhood may find an abiding dwelling-place.

CHAPTER XLIX.

THE ECONOMIC CONDITION OF COREA.

For nearly a quarter of a century Corea, the once hermit nation, has been opened to intercourse with the world, and the student has had facilities for understanding the country and people and realizing what are the social and political problems of humanity in the peninsula.

As in most old Asiatic states, so in Corea, there is an almost total absence of an intelligent middle class, which in the West is the characteristic of progressive nations. In the Land of Morning Radiance there is a governing minority consisting of about one-tenth of the whole population. These, the Yangban (civil and military), living in ancient privilege and prerogative and virtually paying no taxes or tolls, prey upon the common people. The great bulk, that is, nine-tenths of the population, is agricultural and is gathered in hamlets and villages.

The typical Corean tills the soil, in which occupation, after ages of unprogressive routine, he has come to his present mental status. There is not even a distinct manufacturing class in Corea, for nearly all industry is still in the cottage. The few articles needed by the laborer for the floor, the wall, and the kitchen are made by the farmer during his winter hours, and his women-folk weave and make up the clothing. The average carpenter, blacksmith, and stone mason is simply a laborer on the land with added skill in a special line. Even the fisherman cultivates the soil. The village schoolmaster is a son of the farmer of the better class. There are groups of population-office-holders and their retainers and hangers-on, shopkeepers and traders, butchers, porters, miners, junk-sailors, and innkeepers, sorcerers, gamblers, and fortune-tellers, but, all told, the number of men who do not live on the soil form but a decimal fraction in the national household.

For these compelling reasons the problems of internal government relate almost wholly to the woe or weal of the tillers of the soil. During the summer of six months the average Corean stands bare-legged in the mud, planting or cultivating grain. His wife and children, especially his daughters, help him in the raising of rice, barley, wheat, and beans, and in the harvesting and securing of the final products. During the four cold months of the year he is at work gathering fuel or making mats, sandals, screens, or thatch. During the first and seventh moons he enjoys an easy time, doing little or nothing, and these two months are like holiday. The average income of a Corean farmer is about thirty dollars a year. The average house in Corea consists only of mud, straw, twine, and wood, above a foundation of earth faced with stone and worth but a few dollars. The price of waste land is from one to five dollars an acre, and of cultivated fertile soil from ten to sixty dollars an acre. The lots are poorly marked and boundary quarrels are incessant. The Corean farmer knows little about scientific irrigation or variety in fertilizers, dried grass being his chief manure. The mountains are greatly denuded of their forests, and alternate droughts and floods work awful disasters. With a naturally good soil and fine climate, agriculture is yet in a backward condition. It is said that the Japanese in the sixteenth century taught the Coreans the cultivation of rice, millions of bushels of which, under stimulus from the same source, they are now able to export annually. In recent years the Japanese have attempted to secure control of the waste lands of Corea so as to develop them, not only for the production of cereals, vegetable wax, paper fibre, and stuff for weaving, but also for cotton to supply the demands of the Osaka mills. Their demands, pressed too severely in July, 1904, were the cause of vigorous native protest in great public meetings.

The Corean rustic is, as a rule, illiterate. Probably only about four out of ten males of the farming class can read either Chinese or Corean, but counting in the women it is estimated that about eighty-five per cent of the people can neither read nor write, though the percentage varies greatly with the locality. As a general thing, there is more acquaintance with books and writing in the southern than in the northern provinces. It is pitiful to find in the Budget for 1904 that but $27,718 are appropriated for schools outside of Seoul, the latter receiving $135,074, of which the sum of $44,220 goes to foreign teachers in the English, French, German, Russian, Chinese, and Japanese language schools. Although since 1895 the old civil-service examinations have been abolished and there has been a Department of Education, it has thus far had little influence upon the country at large. In the central office in 1904, out of $28,617 appropriated, $19,857 went for salaries and office expenses, $6,500 being for text-book printing.

The Corean farmer is simple in his dress, food, and habits. He does not journey far from home. Although the high-roads are lively with travellers, one sees not the farmer but the literati, the traders, and the porters. Few country folks ever visit the large cities, and in regions near the capital few have seen Seoul. Custom is the eternal law to the rustic, who is patient, bearing extortion until flesh and blood can stand it no longer, when he rises in revolt against his oppressor. Yet it is against the bad man, not the system itself, that he protests. After the obnoxious officer has been recalled or driven away and temporary relief is obtained, the Corean farmer settles down into a good tax-paying subject as of yore, and unless something like the Tong Hak movement stirs him, his wheel of life quickly slips again into the rut of routine. As long as he can get enough to eat he is content. When oppression and robbery are joined to Nature's niggardliness, he and his comrades are transformed into a howling mob of starving malcontents, ready for bloody vengeance.

The son of the soil is superstitious to the last degree. He lives in constant terror of the demons and spirits that overpopulate earth, air, and water, for he is without the protection that the certainties of science or the strength of pure religion furnishes. No unifying, uplifting, and inspiring knowledge of one God is his. His thatched hut or mud-floored hovel is a museum of fetiches. Often he will give the best fruits of the fields to what seems to an alien a mass of straw or rags. The sorceress thrives like a fat parasite on the farmer, getting well paid for her songs, dances, incantations, and presence at the feasts. Yet the Corean enjoys the religious festivals. He is at least just to himself, while professing generosity to the spirits. He honors the gods but ultimately puts the well-cooked offerings far from them—even into his own interior; for above all things, the worshipper is orthodox in his belief in a well-filled stomach.

With such a people, both Confucianism and Buddhism become the grossest of superstitions. The Corean's face is toward the past. He invokes and worships the dead, and to him the graveyard contains more than the future can bring him. Besides the extortions of the nobles, officials, and other parasitic or predatory classes, the expense of offerings to his dead ancestors amounts to many millions of dollars a year, far exceeding in their total the national revenue. In Seoul alone there are three thousand sorceresses, each earning at least $7.50 a month. The farmer is poor, but he is hospitable and liberal. He has untold reverence for learning and for rank, he loves flowers and beautiful scenery, but he is stupid in the presence of an innovation. His area of vision is bounded by the hills within the circle of which he was born. His chief recreation is in going to market, for, generally speaking, there are few shops in the peninsula, but there is a market every five or six days, where the natives exchange their products and their opinions. According to the state of weather conditions, the native is happy or suffers, a large harvest making all smile, a scant crop causing famine and hunger and the outbreak of banditti and rapine. Besides buying and selling, huckstering and gossiping, there are at the markets plenty of fighting and drunkenness as diversions. Going out for wool the farmer frequently comes home shorn, but he has had his fun, or rather a variation of deadly monotony. Furthermore, he is fond of a joke and loves to chaff his fellows.

As the country itself is governed out of the graveyard, and sovereign, court, and people are driven by imaginary demons and spirits, so the farmers, both as individuals, as families, and as clans, guard jealously and in fear the ancestral mounds with superstitious reverence. Hence one large element of village excitement is in quarrelling and fighting over graves. About fifty per cent of the cases brought before the country magistrates are said to be connected with these grave fights. These bitter struggles involve whole clans and result in bloodshed and loss of life. Even the dead are not allowed to rest in peace. The digging up of corpses and the tumbling of them beyond the limits in dispute is a common occurrence. This ghoulish activity is varied by an occasional abduction of widows or by other infractions of the law. Another large element of anxiety to the farmer is the protection of the water supply for his rice-swamp. The damming of the stream above or the draining off of the water below may ruin his crop. The breaking of the mud boundaries, and the stealing of water from a neighbor's field is mirrored in proverbs and folk-lore. It is sufficiently habitual to furnish a plentiful supply of pretexts for quarrels and fighting.

There are four classes of agriculturists. The lowest tiller of the soil is a serf, owning no land, working by the day or contract, and virtually bound to the glebe. The men of the next class, though owning no lands, work the farms of others on shares. These farm-hands and farm-tenants make up the great mass of the Corean people. They live in thatched mud huts, with enough plain food to keep them alive and often fat, but with scanty change of garments and few or no comforts of life. They are occupied during the working months from daybreak to twilight in unremitting toil. The third class consists of the small owners with possessions worth from five hundred to five thousand dollars and numbering three per cent of the farming population. In the fourth or highest class are the landed proprietors, the aristocracy of the land, the richest member being worth as much as four or five million dollars, with an annual income of at least a quarter of a million. Insignificant in numbers, they are mighty in power, for it is these great landowners who rule the realm, and most of them live in Seoul.

To the great mass of the people in Corea there is no motive for much industry beyond danger of starvation, and but little incentive to enterprise. Under old normal conditions now being slowly ameliorated, the official, the yangban, and the landed aris-tocracy, in a word, the predatory classes, seize upon the common man's earnings and accumulations, so that it seems to him useless and even foolish to work for more than enough to support life, while as for the "civilization nonsense," does it not mean more taxation? On the 13th of November, 1902, the announcement was made of the increase in land tax from $10 per measure of ground to $16 per measure. So argues the average man in Corea, the land long ruled by real oppressors and imaginary demons.

The researches of scholars have also revealed the actual eco-nomic conditions of the nation in the days of hermitage. Old Corea was not, as in feudal Japan, straitened in its production of food.

In the island empire only about one-twelfth of the soil was or could be cultivated. Hence Japan was rigidly limited in her food-producing area, so that the population, besides being kept down through such natural checks as famine, pestilence, storm and flood, was further diminished to fit the food supply by such artificial means as sumptuary laws, licensed prostitution, infanticide, cruel punishments, and frequent decapitation. In Corea, also, where the fertile earth, though formed to be inhabited and abundant in area of plain and valley, was neither properly replenished nor subdued, many checks upon population existed. Local famines were frequent and often long continued, and neither religion nor the means of transportation furnished the means of saving life to any large amount. Artificial checks on too rapid multiplication of humanity operated powerfully. The lesser care and kindness given to female children resulted in a heavy death-rate as compared with that of the boys, the cruel punishments and frequent torture and decapitation and the lack of incentive to industry all wrought together to make both the land and the human life on it of comparatively slight value.

The whole situation was changed when Corea ceased to be a hermit land and began to be fertilized by foreign commerce and ideas. Confronted by new methods of trade, science, and religion, the thinking native was summoned to thought and action. Into the Corean mind, long held in bondage by Confucianism, which degrades woman and narrows man's intellect, the universal religion entered to compel the Corean man to think of other lands and people besides his own, to search his own heart, to attempt to make himself and his neighbors better, and to take a new outlook on the universe. The new doctrines delivered believers from the paralyzing thrall of demons and evil spirits, from ancestor worship, and from the sceptre held by the hand rising out of the grave. Into the Corea clamped as in iron bands by false economic notions entered the spirit of free competition. Into a land that knew no such thing as a foreign market the railway brings an eager purchaser to the farmer's door, and by carrying his goods to the seaports it enables him to give to and receive manifold benefits from the world at large.

Already, through the energy of the canny islanders from the east, the crops in Corea have quadrupled, though under native mismanagement this does not necessarily mean immediate benefit to the man on the soil, but rather to the official class, or to the landholder in the capital. It has been computed that the production of sixty million bushels of grain have thus been developed in Corea through the Japanese demand. Between the feverish enterprise of the Japanese on the one side and the tireless thrift of the Chinese on the other, " the good old days " of primitive routine are gone forever. Corea has 4,500,000 acres under cultivation, or about eight and a half per cent of her 82,000 square miles of area, so that 3,500,000 available acres await the plough. From her arable soil six millions more of population might easily find subsistence, and nearly ten millions of dollars of crops could be raised. The peninsula needs in every great valley the railway, which " quadruples the valley of every foot of land within twenty miles of its line." The line from Fusan to Seoul has already raised the value of town property in elect places hundreds of per cent and measurably all along between the terminals. This railway was begun in August, 1901, but though the work slackened for lack of capital, by December 1, 1903, thirty-one miles at either end had been built. The outbreak of the war with Russia revealed its military value and promise was at once given that by Japanese Government aid it would be completed with its thirty-one tunnels and 20,500 feet of bridges by the end of 1904. This Fusan-Seoul railway, 287 miles long, will traverse four provinces in the richest part of Corea, wherein are seven-tenths of all the houses and five-sevenths of all the cultivated area in the empire. Here also are the sites of the great fairs held six times monthly, the thirty-nine stations of the road being located at or near these places of trade, the total business of which amounts to over sixty-five per cent of the internal trade of the empire.

The Corean social and political system, sufficiently weak in hermit days, has shown itself unable to withstand the repeated shock of attack by eager and covetous foreigners, nor will it ever be able, even in a measure, to defend itself against the fierce and unrelenting greed of the strong nations intrenched upon its soil, except by complete reorganization. Both the outward forms and the inward spirit must change if the Coreans are to preserve their national identity. The nation has been the bone of contention between jealous and greedy rivals. One foreign government by crafty diplomacy secures the right of cutting timber valued at millions of dollars, another gets mining concessions, others propose this or that industry or supposed line of production which depleted the treasury. The impoverished kingdom has not only wasted many millions of treasure in foolish enterprises, but is deprived of its natural assets in timber, metals, fisheries, and industries.

The problem of bringing Corea into harmony with her modern environment is only in some features like that of Japan, for there have been wanting in the peninsula what was so effective in Japan's case. In the island empire, the long previous preparation by means of the infiltration of Western ideas during two centuries of communication with Europe through the Dutch merchants, the researches of her own scholars furnishing inspiration from their national history, the exercise during many generations of true patriotism and self-sacrifice for the public good prepared the island nation to cope with new conditions and situations. In the clash with the West, Japan came out victor. Corea has no *samurai*. She lacks what Japan has always had—a cultured body of men, superbly trained in both mind and body, the soldier and scholar in one, who held to a high ideal of loyalty, patriotism, and sacrifice for country. The island samurai enjoying the same prerogative and privilege as the Corean yangban (civil and military) not only abolished feudalism, but after giving up their hereditary pensions and privileges, joined the productive classes, while at the same time the Japanese merchants and mechanics were raised in the social scale, the pariahs given citizenship, and then all lines of promotion opened to all in the army, navy, schools, courts, and civil service. The fertilizing streams of foreign commerce, the inspiration that comes from brotherhood with other nations, and above all, the power brought to Nippon through the noble labors and object lessons of the Christian missionaries, enabled the Japanese to take equal place in the world with the nations of the West. Corea, on the contrary, by still allowing the existence of predatory classes—nobles, officials, and great landowners—by denying her people education, by being given to superstition from palace to hut and from sovereign to serf, remains still in weakness and poverty. What Corea above all needs, is that the lazy yangban cut their long finger-nails and get to work.

Yet dark as is the situation, it is not without hope. Slowly and painfully the Coreans are learning that no nation is born in a day. Under the training of Christian teachers, a generation with new motives to action and new mental horizons, and fed with food to sustain the spirit, is coming on. Christianity is, with a remnant at least, making headway against the vices so common to this mild-mannered nation—skill in lying, stealing, gambling, drunkenness, and the social evil.

For ages and until Japan humbled China in 1894, Corea was so thoroughly and in all things the vassal and pupil of the Middle Kingdom, from which most of the elements of her civilization had been borrowed, that in the tributary kingdom there could be no patriotism in its highest sense, nor could political parties and cliques have any reason for existence except as they were concerned with aims that ended in selfishness. With the people in general, there was only anxiety to pay taxes, win the favor of the local magistrate, and escape the clutches of the law. With masters and rulers, there was ever pitiful fear of the great country China, and, under Confucianism, a desire to keep things as they were, mixed with impotent dread of change. Of pure love of country, of willingness to make sacrifices for their native land—that is almost a new thought as yet nourished by a few far-seeing patriots. In the evolution of the Corean, social and psychic, his present ethical stage is not beyond that of the group, clan, or neighborhood. It has not yet reached the individual. The majority of the people have that kind of patriotism which means the instinctive desire to preserve national identity. The one thing which they now fear, being in the vortex of the great storm of war and in the centre of the economic typhoon of the twentieth century, is national extinction. Even to-day the Coreans feel that they would rather live without the new things of civilization, such as railways, education, public hygiene, or even of righteous government, than be subject to an alien Power. History to the peninsular gives no uncertain sound as to what foreign intervention has always meant, that is, more oppression and even rapine. Seeing what has happened in half a lifetime, through the coming of the alien to Corea, the native does not want civilization at the hands of foreigners, though it may be that he will have to take it. Possibly through education and a new outlook upon the universe he will be glad to get it, even struggling for it until by assimilation it becomes his own. In ancient history and the old days of the separation of nations, there were many civilizations and varying standards. In these latter days of the world's brotherhood there is but one standard of civilization, and but one body of international law, which all must obey. The nation or kingdom that will not serve and obey this standard will pass out of history and perish. The signs that Corea realizes this truth and that her best men are seeking fraternity with their fellows for help and uplift are not wanting. Naturally they turn to the great republic, which since its beginning has steadfastly followed the policy of healing, helping, teaching, and uplifting the Asiatic nations.

Corea sent a delegate to the International Postal Union, which met in Washington, and in 1896 a postal system with stamps of four kinds was established, and under French auspices has been working in excellent condition. The stamps, as well as the national flag and documents, coins and other expressions of what is essentially representative of the Coreans as a nation, illustrate their repertoire of symbolism. The flag in blue, red, black, and white contains the two great emblems of the primitive Chinese philosophy and theory of the universe. Through these, the Corean sees all things visible and invisible produced as the results of their endless working and counteraction in combination and dissolution. The forces of heaven and earth, light and darkness, the positive and the negative, the male and the female, the *in* and the *yo*, are represented as two germs or commas in constant embrace or movement. This figure occupies the centre of the field and in each corner are the broken lines of the Pal Kwai, or eight diagrams of primitive Chinese tradition concerning the origin of language and writing. On the stamps we read the Chinese characters Tai han and Corea. Like China, old Japan, Russia, Turkey and other church nations, which unite more or less closely Church and State and are governed, in spite of all outward development and manifestations, by primitive or mediæval notions, Corea is a "Tei Koku," or "divinely governed" realm, and so makes profession in Chinese characters, as does even modern Japan, though furnished with a Constitution and Diet. Besides these Chinese ideographs, we read in English, "Imperial Corean Post," and in the en-mun or native script, a sentence to the same effect. The national flower is the plum blossom, and is figured with its leaves on either side of the stem. The value or denomination of the stamp is given below both in English with Roman letters, and in Corean or en-mun. The date-mark made by the ink-stamp shows in the French spelling of the name of the country and capital the international character of the postal system. The national colors, as judged by the hangings in the royal palace, are yellow, red, and green.

Imitating other things imperial in adjoining or Western nations, the Government at Seoul established a Bureau of Decorations. These baubles, being liberally distributed, have helped handsomely to deplete the treasury of the little empire, most of whose people live in a state of semi-starvation or righteous discontent. The Emperor himself and his generals and ministers have had their breasts liberally adorned with various marks of the regard of the rulers of Japan, Great Britain, Russia, France, and Belgium, while between August 5, 1900, and December 20, 1902, the Corean Government had bestowed forty-two decorations, requiring a liberal outlay of bullion and artistic workmanship. To the Emperor of Japan, Queen Victoria, the Czar of Russia, the Kaiser of the German Empire, the President of the French Republic, the King of Italy, the King of the Belgians, the Emperor of Austria, and the Crown Prince of Japan, the Great Decoration of the Golden Measure was awarded. This contains the emblem in the centre of the flag. No Americans have been thus officially adorned, but the Great Decoration of the Golden Measure was offered to President McKinley, only to be declined; he having, happily for the American people, nothing to offer in return. The Great Decoration of the Plum Blossom has been given to Prince Kwacho of Japan and the Russian Prince Cyril, while the other decorations, containing the Pal Kwai of the eight mystic diagrams and the plum blossom or the national flower, in several grades or classes, have been offered to various servants or guests of the Government. Along with this brilliancy on foreign coat breasts, it is suggestive to read in the imperial budget for 1904 that of $19,560 appropriated to the bureau of decorations, the amount expended on bullion, medals, etc., was $7,431, and for salaries $10,130. Another interesting item, illuminating economic methods in Seoul, is that of $10,453 appropriated for the Mining Bureau. Of this amount the sum of $8,173 was spent for salaries and travelling, all the rest, except one item marked " miscellaneous $744," being for office expenses. In the Ceremonial Bureau $19,000 were used on salaries and office expenses out of a total of $21,508. Similar titbits of economic information are frequent under the heads of the Board of Generals (who supervise an army supposed to be five thousand strong) and that of Imperial Sacrifices, and others, explain very clearly the condition of a country in which there is no clear line of demarcation between the palace and the Government or administration, while eloquent in suggestions as to the reason why the larger part of Corea remains in a state of more or less chronic insurrection.

The budget for 1904 shows a total revenue of $14,214,573 made up of the following items: land tax, $9,703,591; house tax, $460,295; taxes on salt, fish, etc., $210,000; poll tax, $850,000; miscellaneous taxes, $200,000; arrears from 1903, $2,790,687.

The items of disbursement are as follows: Imperial privy purse, $1,013,359; imperial sacrifices, $186,641; household department, $327,541; war department, $5,180,614; finance department, $42,-741,999; communications, $637,648; incidentals and extras, $1,843,-503. Other items, of which the police bureau, $406,925, and the foreign department, $287,367, and educational, $205,673, are the more important, are pension bureau, board of generals, the cabinet government records, bureau of decorations, law department, department of agriculture, privy council, and special palace guard. It is pleasant to note that there is a surplus of $275, but the amount given for education and expended under the head of agriculture seems pitiful. The large items of the budget deal almost wholly with the salaries of native officials. One interesting and redeeming item among the " extras " is that " for helping shipwrecked men, $5,000."

The greatest immediate need of Corea is a uniform and stable currency. Added to ancient evils was the action of Japan in adopting the gold standard in 1899, which threw all things commercial in Corea into dire confusion. On the 15th of December, 1901, the coinage law was published, by which Corea adopted the gold standard; but this law was never put into effect. The Japanese have frequently endeavored by various means to secure a standard currency.

Under the stimulus and pressure of foreign trade, Corea has now at least nine ports open to the residence and business of foreigners besides the three or four inland places of traffic. Wonsan (Gensan), Fusan, and Chemulpo were opened by the treaties of 1876 and 1882, and have thriving settlements. The ginseng crop exported from these places is usually bought by Japanese, whose usual practice is that, for example, of May, 1902, when of the fifty thousand catties, ten thousand catties were burnt at Chemulpo, in order to keep up the price. On the 1st of October, 1898, Chinnampo and Mokpo were added to the list of open ports. The former lies on the northern shore of Ping-an inlet, twenty miles from the sea and forty miles from Ping-an city. It is now a thriving town with well laid-out streets. As the river leading to Ping-an is for ten miles or so below the city not navigable even by very small sea-going steamers, it can never be " a port " in the ordinary sense, but the returns of its trade are tabulated with those of Chinnampo, its outlet. Wiju (Ai-chiu) and Anju are almost the only other ports of value in the province of Ping-an. Anju is the landing stage of the American Mining Company for its mining materials and explosives.

Yongampo is in north latitude 38° 52' and east longitude 126° 04'. When it was opened in 1898, Russians and Japanese took up land so eagerly that a collision seemed imminent. Later it came very near being made a Russian fortress as " Port Nicholas." Mokpo, in the southwestern part of Chullado, is the natural maritime outlet of " the Garden of Corea." Soon after it was made port of entry and trade, the wisdom shown in its selection was justified, for its growth has been healthy and rapid. From this point, in the autumn of 1902, a Boston gentleman went into the interior for a hunting trip of two months, during which time he killed three large tigers, besides deer and wild boar.

On May 1, 1899, Kunsan, Masampo, and Songchin were thrown open to foreign trade and residence. Kunsan is on the west coast, and like Mokpo, long famous for its abundant export of rice paid as revenue. It lies at the mouth of the river dividing the two rich and warm provinces of Chulla and Chung Chong, about halfway between Chemulpo and Mokpo, whence the rice, wheat, beans, hides, grasscloth, paper, manufactured articles in bamboo, fans, screens, mats, and marine products of many kinds are exported. Masampo, a few miles to the southwest of Fusan, in north latitude 35° 09' and east longitude 128° 40', has one of the finest harbors

in the world, which, when well fortified, might command the
entrance to the Sea of Japan. In the negotiations between Japan
and Russia, in 1903, this spot was jealously coveted by both Powers as the prize of the future, as the party possessing it might
make it a Dardanelles, closing the sea between the island empire
and the continent and making this body of water a Euxine. Russia tried to bind Japan not to fortify this or any other place on
the east coast of Corea. Japanese, Russians, Chinese, and Coreans
soon flocked to this favored port and have made business lively.
Songchin, once the seat of an old stronghold, in the large northeastern province of Ham Kiung, bordering on Russia, which has
no long navigable rivers, as in the south, lies about 120 miles from
Wonsan and sends most of its products thither. It has a poor
harbor in a foggy region, but fertile soil, fat cattle, and mineral
riches are within reach. The Customs Reports for 1903 show a
growing trade of $328,891. Eleven other landing stages bring up
the total value of trade in Ham Kiung province to $1,676,714.
In 1902 the total imports were nearly balanced by the exports
from all Corea. Cotton is becoming an important item of sale
abroad. Gold in 1902 was exported to the amount of $2,532,053.
The total value of foreign trade has doubled during the past decade.
So far the steamer tonnage is, like the general foreign trade, over
three-fourths Japanese. Most emphatically and luminously does
the modern economic as well as political history of the peninsula
prove that the best interests of Japan and Corea are closely inter-
woven. Mutual benefit follows unity and friendship, reciprocal
injury results from estrangement.

All these open ports are the gateways of a commerce that must
steadily and healthfully increase, and which under stable and just
government would rapidly enlarge. So long as there is uncertainty
as to the political status of the Land of Morning Calm, the chief
importance of the maritime gateways into the country will be
strategic and military, rather than commercial. A permanent settlement of the political question, in debate ever since the modern
renascence of Japan, ought to act on the development of the natural resources of Corea as the warm spring rains act upon soil long
chilled and fallow under winter's frost. Few regions, whether we
consider its geographical location for commerce, the fertility of
its soil, its animal wealth, the richness of its mineral deposits, or

the abundance of its treasures in the sea, are more highly favored than Corea. When man, society, and government in the peninsula answer Nature's challenge and match the opportunity, the world will find that history's storehouse of surprises has not been empty. Toward the development of the kind of man needed, the Christian missionaries are, above all other teachers and forces, working, and with every sign of promise.

CHAPTER L.

INTERNAL POLITICS: CHINESE AND JAPANESE.

THE preponderating influence of China was the mainspring in the intricate machinery of old Corean politics, though within the two clearly defined parties in Seoul there are also factional and family differences. "From 1834 to 1864 the royal clan was shorn of much of its power, all offices were in the hands of the Kim clan, whose head, Kim Pyong-gi, was virtually ruler of the land for the years ending that epoch." The Kims hoped to continue the lease of their power, but the Tai-wen Kun humbled this clan and exalted his own, meanwhile doing much for the common people and compelling the yangban to bear a share of the burdens of government in paying a house tax. In his whole course toward these predatory gentry, he was "a blundering anticipator" of the great reforms of 1894. He began the suppression of the Tong-haks. He was a great builder of public edifices, not only in Seoul, but in the provinces. He protected the country against the foreigner. He meant well in his ignorance, but he knew nothing of the world at large. His first lease of power came to an end in 1873.

The first Corean noblemen, Kim and Pom, left their homes in 1875 to travel in lands beyond China. They went to Japan, and coming back, boldly told the King what they had seen and advocated the adoption of Western civilization. They tried to win over the powerful Min clan and the Queen to a liberal policy, but this to the Regent, Tai-wen Kun, meant nothing else than Christianity and radical reform, which involved popular education. That is exactly the sort of reform that every Confucian mandarin in any country of Asia hates most heartily, because he sees in the general enlightenment of the people the end of the power of the literati. The bold and crafty statesman, who, as Prince Parent, held his son the King as his puppet and had already shed the blood of thousands of native Christians, nearly succeeded in putting the two young champions of Western civilization to death. When the American treaty negotiations were impending, the Min clansmen held aloof until China, as represented by Li Hung Chang, gave the nod. Then they showed so much energy in the matter as to seem to foreigners the party of progress. This roused the wrath of the Regent, who determined to crush the Min clan and to nullify the treaty. We have seen how, in July, 1882, by a masterly appeal to local bigotry and superstition, he directed the soldiers' riot into a revolt against the pro-Chinese clan. After destroying, as he imagined, their leading men and the Queen, he seized the government himself, enjoying for a few days full lease of power.

When the news of the usurpation reached China and Japan, a fleet with soldiers was despatched from each country. The Chinese force landed first, marched to Seoul, built forts to command the river against the Japanese, and established their camp inside the walls. By this move China held a new lien on her " vassal state." The Chinese general made his formal call on the Tai-wen Kun, and when this lord of the land returned the courtesy, he was seized and deported to China. Meanwhile the Queen, for whom a palace maid had suffered vicarious death, together with some of her chief helpers and advisers, re-entered the palace October 9, 1882. The star of the Min clan was again in the ascendant.

Thus the results of the Regent's smart trickery were not pleasant for the Coreans, for now they had both the Chinese and the Japanese soldiers encamped in the capital and on the ground where nearly three hundred years before they had met in battle. By good discipline on both sides, collision between the soldiers was avoided, but the Government at once made provision to replace the foreign soldiery by native troops. Four battalions of Corean infantry were organized and put under Chinese drill masters, introduced by the Min leaders. Fourteen young men, mostly members of Progressive families, were sent to Tokio to study in the military school.

The treaty negotiated by Commodore Shufeldt was promptly ratified by the United States Senate, and on February 26th President Chester A. Arthur sent in the name of General Lucius H. Foote as Minister to Corea. Reaching Chemulpo May 13th in the U.S.Ss. Monocacy, the formal ratifications of the treaty were exchanged in the capital May 19th. The same cannon, and served by some of the same sailors that in 1871 had shelled the Han forts,[1] peacefully saluted the new national flag, emblazoned with the proofs of Corea's intellectual servitude to Chinese philosophy and fantastic traditions. Keeping clear of the native factions, Mr. Foote dealt as directly as possible with the sovereign. He made an earnest plea for the toleration of religion, a promise to proclaim which was secured from the King.

The Corean Government responded to the American courtesy by despatching a special mission, consisting of eleven persons headed by Min Yong Ik, which arrived in San Francisco September 2d. President Arthur being then in New York, these quaintly apparelled Oriental strangers were given audience in the parlor of the Fifth Avenue Hotel. After three months' stay in the eastern cities, one part of the embassy, headed by Han Yong Sik, returned home by way of San Francisco. A few days later, on the U.S.Ss. Trenton (afterward lost at Samoa) with Ensign G. C. Foulke (afterward of the Doshisha University, Kioto) and Lieutenant J. G. Bernadou, U.S.N. (afterward distinguished in the Spanish-American War of 1898, on the U.S.Ss. Winslow), as naval attachés to the American legation in Seoul, Min Yong Ik and two other Coreans returned home by way of Europe and the Suez Canal.

On November 27th, at the Victoria Hotel in the city of New York, I had the pleasure of spending an agreeable evening with the three Corean gentlemen, Min Yong Ik, So Kuang Pom, and Pien Su, the two latter being able to talk Japanese.[2]

---

[1] On which tablets erected to the memory of the slain have been erected by the Coreans. See the article, Kang-wha, by Rev. M. N. Trollope, (Corean) Asiatic Society Transactions, Vol. II, Part I.

[2] At that time I was engaged in editing and annotating Hamel's Narrative, which is the first account in any European language of Corea. Hamel and his party of Dutchmen were shipwrecked and spent fourteen years in Corea (see pp. 167–76). I have examined and read several copies in the original Dutch editions, printed in cheap pamphlet form at Rotterdam in Holland in 1668, and now preserved in the Royal Library at The Hague. The full narrative in English is given in the book Corea Without and Within. Philadelphia, 1884. Mr. Percival Lowell, the Secretary of the Corean Special Mission, returned with Han Yong Sik, and as the guest of the king spent a winter in Seoul, the literary fruit of which is the charming volume Chosen, the Land of Morning Calm, in which the proper names are transliterated according to Aston's Manual of Corean Geographical and Other Proper Names Romanized. Yokohama, 1883.

Though many of my questions were answered and a number of subjects discussed, nothing could be learned of Corean Christianity, or of the relics or reminders of Hendrik Hamel and his Dutchmen.[1] Before leaving, Min Yong Ik, like a true Corean gentleman, brought out a large package of choicest ginseng roots, without which no well-to-do native of the Land of Morning Calm would think of travelling abroad. He presented me with several choice specimens of the man-shaped drug, each wrapped up in its own " arms " and " legs."

On the same evening in Seoul, November 27th, a banquet was spread in the English-language-school building to celebrate the signing on the day before of two treaties, one with Great Britain and the other with the German Empire, the negotiator of the English treaty being Sir Harry Parkes.[2] The music was furnished by the band of the German man-of-war Leipsic. Seoul now began to be the residence of foreigners from Christendom, nine of whom were already in the city.

New Year's Day, January 20, 1884, dawned brightly. The little children who during the summer are " dressed in a hair ribbon," made the streets brilliant with their bright clothes of many colors, and the sky was gay with kites. In the royal palace audience was given to the envoys of China, Japan, and the United States. On February 28th the electric submarine cable between Nagasaki and Fusan was completed and messages from the once hermit nation were sent into the outside world. Han Yong Sik was appointed postmaster with power to organize a national postal system, stamps for which were engraved in Tokio. From this Japanese base of supplies many novelties from the Western world poured in, and the body politic, long insulated from other nations, thrilled with new currents of life. Treaties were made with Russia and Italy, June 25th and 26th. Later on, telegraph lines con-

---

[1] Nevertheless, in 1886 there were unearthed in Seoul two Dutch vases, as described in Mr. Scott's paper in Vol. XXVIII, 1893-94, of the Transactions of the North China Branch of the Royal Asiatic Society. The figures of Dutch farm-life told their own story, and the well-worn rings of the handles bore evidence of constant use for years. Mr. Scott suggests that the presence of these Dutchmen might perhaps explain the anomaly often noticed in Corea—namely, blue eyes and fair hair.

[2] See his biography by Lane-Poole and Dickens, 1894.

necting Seoul with Peking and with Fusan were completed. The year following the arrival home of the first Coreans who had gone round the world was a year of progress, such as Corea had never known before or has known since.

Through the advice of Ensign Foulke, several reformatory measures, political and industrial, were promulgated. The most ardent member of the reform party, Pak Yong Hio, being made mayor of Seoul, immediately set to work at sanitary and municipal improvement. Some progress was made in dress improvement. A model farm, for which California live stock had been ordered, was sown by American seeds liberally given in Washington. Edison electric lights, American rifles and Gatling guns, a powder mill, a mint, a printing office for the dissemination of useful literature for the people, together with Japanese artisans to establish or improve properties, paper factories, and other industries, not excepting the fisheries and whale hunting, gave indications of the new path of national progress upon which Corea had entered. Altogether the early days of 1884 were as a morning of bright promise, for public opinion, so far as it existed, that is, among the nobles and gentry, seemed to be entirely in favor of progress. The most hopeful felt that the Corean Government, having begun to relay the foundations of the kingdom, would persevere and possibly even excel Japan.

On the other hand, with the tide of Confucian bigotry rising and the Conservatives encouraged by Chinese reactionaries on the soil, how could there be any real advance? Yuan, the Chinese commissioner, living at the barracks in front of the palace, was ceaselessly active in the interests of his own Government, which meant active support of the Conservative party and opposition to reform. Over against enlightened liberalism, several incidents stood out in dark contrast, showing the inherent barbarism, the low state of Corean humanity, and the slight value set on human life. When the Chinese soldiery arrived, they seized ten of the rioters of 1882, court-martialled them, tied their limbs to bullocks, and tore them to pieces. Even after these men in office had returned from civilization they had eight more men, suspected of complicity with the Regent, executed by poison. Furthermore, the Kwang Wang temple was built, devoted to the interests of three thousand or more sorcerers and exorcists in Seoul, who enjoyed the direct patronage of the Queen, and sucked the vitals of the nation, making respectable government impossible.

The innovations effected by the Progressives, who thought that they had the King and Queen in full sympathy with them, led them to hope that they would be able soon to reorganize the Government, to differentiate the Court from the Administration, and to make Corea a modern state. But according to the measure of their success, so also was the suspicion and hostility of the Conservatives. Min Yong Ik while abroad might be a Liberal, an individual with personal convictions and opinions, but once back in the bosom of his family and under pressure of his clan, he lost interest in reform. The Progressive leaders began to look upon him as a traitor to their cause. He took his stand with the Conservatives and it was soon evident that the Queen was withdrawing her sympathy and support from the Liberals, whose hopes seemed about to be dashed to the ground. These men therefore turned more and more to the Japanese and to their methods and spirit. They saw the revenues for the promised industries and enterprise diverted to warlike enterprises. It looked as if Corea, as tributary vassal, was to help China against France in the Tonkin complication. Added to the fears of the Liberals was the local irritation caused by the insolent behavior of the ill-disciplined native troops who had been recruited almost wholly from the peddlers and hucksters of the country fairs. The peddler's guilds in Corea hold a truly feudal relation to the Government, often preparing the roads and escorting officials on their journeys, acting as detectives, and forming militia according to the occasion. Some astonishing proofs of their power and discipline, especially in mountain regions, were given by Min Yong Ik to Lieutenant Foulke. Instead of their being independent, as they had hoped for under the American treaty, it seemed to the progressive men that the Chinese were more than ever ruling their country, and that the Mins were their tools.

It was about October 25th that the Liberals, feeling that their heads were likely to remain on their shoulders only so long as it pleased their enemies to bring no charge against them, declared to their American friend that " for the sake of Corea, about ten of the prominent Conservatives would have to be killed." They proposed to play the same old Asiatic game of first seizing the person of the sovereign and then in his name proclaiming their own measures and reforms. The preliminaries would be a fire and a riot. Then, in the confusion, the man with a programme, knowing just what to do, would direct affairs. They believed that the Powers would condone and approve their action, make new and more favorable treaties, and loan money for national improvement. Though the Conservatives had at their call a rabble of rapacious militia eager to try their new tools of war upon their hereditary enemies, the Japanese, the Liberals knew full well the sterling qualities of the little body of Japanese infantry then in the capital, most of whom were from northern Japan and many of them deer hunters and dead shots with the rifle. There were fifteen hundred Chinese soldiers still in camp, under Yuan Shi Kai, then the lieutenant and later the successor of Li Hung Chang, but the Progressive plotters in their craft expected to secure the employment of the two hundred or more Japanese soldiers for their own purposes. The moment for action seemed to be propitious for early December. A Japanese man-of-war was expected to arrive in Chemulpo on the 5th or 6th of that month. China, pressed by France, had withdrawn half her troops. Japan with a view to strengthening her influence in Corea had, a few days before, remitted $400,000 of the indemnity exacted for the riot of 1882. The golden moment to strike off forever the chains of political slavery to China was approaching. The date was set for the 7th of December.

When, however, news arrived that the Japanese gunboat had broken down and was delayed and it was known that the Conservatives had got some intimation of what was coming, it was decided to start the fire, the riot, the *coup d'état* a few days earlier. On the night of the 4th of December, Han Yong Sik, the Postmaster-General, gave a dinner at the new post-office, situated in the very heart of the city. The guests were three Chinese, Yuan, Chin, and Wang, two Americans, General Foote and his secretary, Mr. Scudder, the British Consul-General, W. G. Aston, the German Foreign Adviser, Von Möllendorf, and a dozen or more Corean high officers, both Conservatives and Progressives, Han Yong Sik, Kim Ok Kiun, Min Yong Ik, Pak Yong Hio, and So Kwang Pom. Others also were present. The Japanese minister was absent on the plea of ill-health.

It was noticed that Kim Ok Kiun rose and left the table several times, going out into the courtyard, but nothing was thought of this action. The guests sat down at six. At seven a fire broke out, a house just in front of the post-office being in flames. Min Yong Ik, who had charge of the city fire-brigade, rose from the table, and calling on his servants to follow him, passed out. As he did so, a man dressed in Japanese clothes leaped out of the shadow of the gateway and struck at him fiercely with a sword. Min Yong Ik fell heavily, but though wounded in head and body he recovered through the skilful surgery of Dr. Horace N. Allen. The assassin escaped, and the Corean guests, instead of leaving by the door, got away over the back wall. Hastening immediately to the old palace, the leaders of the conspiracy reached the royal presence, announced that the Chinese were coming to seize the King's person and that he must hasten to a place of safety. Reaching the small gate leading into the Kiong-u Palace, Kim Ok Kiun requested the King to send to the Japanese minister for a bodyguard, but his Majesty refused. Thereupon So Kwang Pom drew out a piece of foreign note-paper and a pencil and wrote in Chinese the words " Let the Japanese minister come and give me his help." [1] This was despatched by a servant.

When the little company reached the Kiong-u Palace, the King was saluted by the Japanese minister and his interpreter, the twelve students who had been in Japan, and two hundred soldiers under Captain Murakami drawn up in line, who by some magic were all waiting there. Here then was the new Government, king, army, and counsellors. Word was sent to three of the Corean Liberals to come and receive office under the reconstructed authority. With amazing promptness they were present within half an hour. The programme had thus far been carried out with the precision of actors on a well-regulated theatrical stage. The " summoning tablet " was sent early in the morning by royal messenger to six of the Conservative leaders. Going to the palace in the expectation of losing their lives, they first sent word to the Chinese Yuan, warning him of the state of affairs and asking his

[1] See the forthcoming Korean History, by Homer B. Hulbert, in the Korean Review (April, 1904, p. 180). This work is a complete survey of the story of Chō-sen from prehistoric to recent times.

help. As soon as they had passed inside the palace gates their heads were chopped off. The royal eunuch was put to death in spite of the entreaties and remonstrances of the King himself. While the Japanese surrounded the gates of the palace, Kim Ok Kiun gave passes to those who were to be allowed to go in and out. In the reconstructed Government Yo Cha Wun and Han Yong Sik were prime ministers, Pak Yong Hio was made General-in-Chief, So Kwang Pom Minister of Foreign Affairs, Kim Ok Kiun Minister of Finance, and Su Ja Pil Lieutenant-General. The young men who had studied in Tokio were also given official positions. All these proceedings simply illustrate the Corean method of the Opposition's moving a vote of censure of the Government.

The Chinese "resident" Yuan took no immediate action, but the next morning, December 5th, great surging crowds of Coreans begged that he would interfere, because they said the Japanese were holding the King as a prisoner in his palace. Yuan sent a messenger to the Japanese minister, inquiring why he had surrounded the King with soldiers and killed the ministers, demanding that he immediately evacuate the palace. After three hours had passed, and no answer coming, Yuan moved with his Chinese troops and the Corean military, making a force of four or five thousand men, toward the old palace. He found the entrance strongly guarded with the Japanese. The battle which ensued lasted from about 3 to 4 P.M., several score of the combatants being killed. As darkness drew near, the Japanese made their way to the northeastern part of the palace grounds, whence the King escaped from them with a few of the Progressive leaders and the party of students. The Corean soldiers carried the King to the north temple, where he was saved, but Han Yong Sik and seven of the students were hacked to pieces by the mob. About 8 P.M. Captain Murakami led off his soldiers and making a masterly retreat reached the Japanese legation after forty-eight hours of absence. Pak Yong Hio, Kim Ok Kiun, So Kwang Pom, Su Ja Pil, and a half dozen or so of the military students accompanied the Japanese.

All day long on December 6th, with the cry of "Death to the Japanese," the Corean militia and the ruffians were let loose on a wild revelry of outrage, butchery, and incendiarism. The nine white foreigners in Seoul, of whom three were ladies, together with twenty-two Japanese who had escaped bullets, stones, and knives, found refuge in the American legation, which was put in a state of defence by Lieutenant Bernadou. The twenty soldiers left behind in the Japanese legation, aided by a hundred or more of their fellow refugee countrymen, defended the walled enclosure from the mob. On the afternoon of the 7th, provisions being exhausted, the Japanese with admirable coolness, discipline, and success began the march to Chemulpo. The women, children, and refugees were put inside of a hollow square formed by the soldiers, the legation buildings were fired, and despite hostile soldiers, Chinese and Corean with rifles and cannon, and armed men firing from roof and wall, they unbarred the city gates and with their wounded crossed the river. Reaching Chemulpo on the 8th, they were fed by the sailors on the Japanese man-of-war, which had happily arrived. A Japanese steamer carried the news to Nagasaki.

The short-lived Liberal Government came to an end after forty-eight hours' existence. The conspirators fled to Japan, whence most of them reached America. A month later Count Inouye, with a guard of six hundred troops, took up his quarters outside the west gate in Seoul and negotiations were opened. On January 9th a convention was signed by which the Corean Government agreed to pay an indemnity of six hundred thousand yen, and Herr Von Möllendorf and Su Sang Yu were sent to Japan to arrange terms for the renewal of friendly relations. The Coreans, to show their regret, chopped up and distributed around the streets the flesh and bones of eleven human beings supposed to have been active in the killing of defenceless Japanese in Seoul. At Tientsin, May 7, 1885, the Marquis Ito and Li Hung Chang signed a convention, by which it was agreed that the troops of both countries should be withdrawn and that neither government should land a military force in Corea without notifying the other. Early in the spring the Japanese legation was built at Corean expense in Occidental style, this being the first of the many foreign edifices which now adorn Seoul. The Chinese and Japanese troops embarked for their respective countries at Chemulpo on the 21st of May. On October 5, 1885, the Tai-wen Kun, fresh and rosy after his sojourn in Tientsin, re-entered Seoul. He was escorted by Chinese warriors and many thousands of Coreans. Most of his immediate followers being dead or in exile, his name was not often mentioned during the decade of years following. He lived in comparative seclusion until the outbreak of the Chino-Japanese war.

The Progressives of 1884 were in too much of a hurry. They had tried to hatch the egg of reform by warming it in the fire. The affair of December, in its origin an anti-Chinese uprising of Radicals, became at its end an anti-Japanese demonstration in which about three hundred lives were lost. Yet as if to show that revolutions never go backward, this bloody business pushed open the gateway through which science and Christianity entered to hasten the exit of barbarism. Dr. Horace N. Allen, an American missionary physician, had arrived in Seoul in September, 1884. When called on the night of December 4th to minister to the Min Yong Ik, he found the native doctors stopping up the sword wounds with wax. Dr. Allen, by treating the injured man in scientific fashion, saved his life. The superiority of Western methods having been demonstrated, the wounded Chinese soldiers and Coreans, with their shattered bones and torn flesh, over which they had plastered the reeking hides cut from living dogs, or had utilized other appliances of helpless ignorance, came to him in crowds. Unable to attend to all these sufferers, application was made for a hospital. The Government at once set apart the dwelling occupied by Han Yong Sik and, naming it the House of Civilized Virtue, established April 10, 1885, a hospital.

Following this event, American missionaries arrived in increasing numbers. The Government engaged three American young men, Messrs. D. A. Bunker, G. W. Gilmore, and H. B. Hurlbert, as teachers, who with thirty-five sons of noble families as their pupils opened a school September 23, 1885. Missionaries with unquenchable patience began the instruction of a people much better acquainted with malevolent demons than with beneficent beings or with one living and true God, whose only idea of sin is that it is a civil offence, and whose language has no word for the love of a superior to an inferior. In apathetic faces they were to light the fire of a new hope. To become a Christian in Corea means a complete revolution in a man's life, especially in that of a yangban, who has the intellectual power of a man with only the actual knowledge of a child. Nevertheless, with orphanages, Sunday-schools, Christian women's work in the home, organized Christian churches, hospitals, schools for boys and girls, and a printing establishment, most of the forms of active Christianity were soon visible in Corea, the country which, in 1904, with its tens of thousands of believers, is the most hopeful of missionary fields.

A treaty with France, negotiated in the summer of 1886 and ratified May 30, 1887, enabled the French Roman Catholic missionaries to come forth into open day. They at once made preparations for the erection of a cathedral, which, when completed and dedicated, May 29, 1897, was the tallest and most imposing edifice in the capital. It is 202 feet long and from 60 to 90 feet wide, and cost $60,000. The French minister endeavored to secure the same magisterial rights for the bishops and priests in Corea which have been long enjoyed by prelates of the Roman form of Christianity in China. Although at first the Government resisted, yet these claims have been virtually validated, and France acts in Corea, as elsewhere in Asia, as the protector of Roman Catholics. Much disquiet and local disorder in various parts of the country, especially in Quelparte and the provinces of Whang Hai, may be traced to popular notions and the procedure of the priests based on this peculiarity of French foreign policy.

Corea soon found that diplomacy could not be one-sided. Having dealings with foreign nations, it was not sufficient that Western governments should have their representatives in Seoul, while there were no Corean legations or consulates abroad. An episode arising from international jealousies soon caused this desire to take tangible form, despite active opposition from China. On April 14, 1885, the British Government, in view of eventualities with Russia, ordered the temporary occupation of Port Hamilton in the Nan How group of islands, about thirty-five miles from the northeastern end of Quelparte. Corea at once protested against this seizure of territory, and, in spite of all offers of gold for purchase, and all diplomatic pressure, she secured, after voluminous correspondence and the assurance that Russia would not occupy any part of Corea, the evacuation of Port Hamilton by the British. The flag of the double cross was hauled down February 27, 1887. At once the Government at Seoul prepared to send embassies to Japan, Europe, and the United States to establish permanent legations. This plan was of course opposed by Yuan Shi Kai, the Chinese " resident," as he called himself, in an active, impudent, and villainous manner, he acting at the beck of his chief,

Li Hung Chang. The right to make a treaty carries with it the right of a legation abroad, and the American minister, the Honorable Hugh N. Densmore, by order of the Government of the United States, invited the embassy to take passage in the U.S.Ss. Omaha, which was done. With his secretary, Dr. H. N. Allen, Pak Chung Wang, envoy plenipotentiary, arrived in Washington and had audience of President Cleveland in January, 1888. A minister of equal rank went also to Europe and another to Japan. The Chinese " resident " then planned, by transferring his headquarters three miles from Seoul, to get all other foreigners removed from Seoul in order to have more power, but the scheme was frustrated in good season.

The road out of fetichism, superstition, and ignorance into light and civilization was not an easy one and had many a drawback. Until schools dispel ignorance, and the certainties of science dominate the minds of the natives terrorized by superstition, Corea, long intoxicated with sorcery, will suffer from continual attacks of the *delirium tremens* of paganism. Even the importation of condensed milk acted on the diseased imagination of the people to develop the disease. In 1888 what is known as the " baby war " agitated the people. The report was spread abroad that Americans and Europeans were stealing children and boiling them in kettles for food, and that foreigners caught women and cut off their breasts. The absence of cows led the Coreans to believe that the condensed milk, so much used among them, came wholly from a human source. For a time there was imminent danger of an uprising, but a proclamation from the King couched in strong language calmed the excitement, which gradually died away. The local revolts against unjust taxation and dishonest officials occurred with the usual regularity of such events in Corea.

Provision was made for a stable revenue in a system which was organized under Herr Von Möllendorf on an independent Corean basis, but after his dismissal in July, 1885, the customs service was put under the management of Sir Robert Hart, and an entirely new staff of men was sent from China. Mr. H. N. Merrill was made chief commissioner and the three open ports were given in charge of men directly from the Chinese customs staff, one of the most able and valuable among whom was Dr. McLeavy Brown. Financially promising as this movement seemed and has proved, it gave China her great prestige and furnished the strongest lever for carrying out her ambitious plans in the peninsula, which some Coreans suspected of going even so far as to dethrone the King and to set up a new heir—a plot which Min Yong Ik exposed. Yuan, the Chinese resident, made himself practically a Chinese mayor of the palace. In ostentatious display of gorgeous costume, palanquin and retinue, as he vibrated between the royal residence and the Chinese legation, he and his procession formed one of the notable sights of the Corean capital. In a word, Li Hung Chang's policy, working in conjunction with the Mins at court, headed by the Queen, resulted in a vigorous and undisputed reassertion of Chinese control, so that in the emergency which was soon to arise, the Peking Government felt perfectly safe in speaking of Corea as " our tributary state." Apparently the influence of Japan had become a cipher, while that of the United States had dwindled into a merely academic theory of Corean independence. Potentially Japan was insulted and defied by her old rival and modern enemy. To make her grip on Corea sure, China massed her forces on the frontier, bought large quantities of Nagasaki coal for her steel-clad fleet at Port Arthur, and with her German-drilled army and great fortresses on the promontories guarding the sea-gates to the capital, she seemed herself defiantly ready to maintain her prestige regained in the peninsula which she called her " tributary state."

Thus stood, or rather, thus crouched, in the early days of 1894, the pigmy, Corea, between the continental colossus on the one hand and the insular athlete on the other. To add to troubles imported from abroad, the long-standing intestine disturbances again broke out and the Tong Hak rebellion culminated in civil war, at the local causes of which we may now glance. This uprising of sectarians became not the cause, but the occasion of the clash between China and Japan, which ended in the destruction of China's claim of suzerainty over Corea, and the independence of the peninsular state.

CHAPTER LI.

THE WAR OF 1894: COREA AN EMPIRE.

IN Asia and in semi-civilized states, as in the old European world, each sovereignty is a church nation. Religion and the state are one. China, Corea, and Japan, in their normal oriental condition, are all acute illustrations of the evils of the union of church and state. Like Turkey and Russia, they are persecuting nations, allowing no freedom of conscience to the subject. Any attempt to think differently from the orthodox and established cult, or philosophy, is sure to call down persecution, torture, and death. Modern Japan, by ceasing to be oriental and adopting freedom of conscience, has simplified the relations between ruler and ruled. China still persecutes in bigotry, and during the course of her history has shed more blood in the name of religion and government than probably the mediæval states of Europe.[1] In all Asiatic countries in which religious despotism still flourishes, practical Christianity, especially that form of it which is founded on the Bible in the vernacular, is the great disturbing force, even as it is the hope of the future. It comes at once into collision with the theory of the union of Church and State. Giving the common man a new outlook on the universe makes him exactly the kind of man that despots and men of privilege and prerogative most bitterly fear, hate, and oppose. Of this truth Corea is a striking illustration.

The religious history of the people in the Corean peninsula is first that of fetichism and shamanism, then of Buddhism, which brought in culture and made a nation, giving also to the land its permanent monuments, its art, manners, and most of its folklore and general traditions. In the intellectual clash which, in every country in eastern Asia, has at one time or another taken

---

[1] See Sectarianism and Religious Persecution in China, by J. J. de Groot. Amsterdam, 1904.

472

place between Confucianism and Buddhism, Buddhism remained victorious. Running a splendid career for over a thousand years, it finally reached corruption through wealth, worldliness, and political ambition. Yet intrenched in office and revenue, it held its own until overthrown with the dynasty in 1392, when Confucianism, after a long struggle, became the state church system. Buddhism, left to stagnation and decay, and as the religion of the peasants, remained in a frightfully corrupt form, while the scholars and thinking men were almost wholly devoted to Confucianism. As this system of Chinese ethics lends itself most admirably to despotism and the continuance in power of the privileged classes over the masses, so also under stereotyped Confucianism, Corea's type of civilization, as we see it to-day, seems to mean for the nation at large only a general degradation as compared with the splendor of the mediæval Buddhist age. Allied with Chinese bigotry of race and ignorance of the world, Corean Confucianism degenerated still further into the savagery of conceit, of which the Tai-wen Kun seemed an incarnation, and made Chō-sen, as a body politic, a country eaten up with parasites— one-tenth of the population living on the other nine-tenths. In the persecution of the Christian converts to that form of Christianity which entered in 1777, Corean Confucianism showed itself as barbarous and as devilish as the Spanish Inquisition, or anything else in history which masks man's lower nature under the garb of noble pretexts. Nevertheless, the very patience of the Christians under their tortures, the zeal and consecration of both the natives and their foreign priests, so impressed a Corean scholar named Choi, that in 1859 he set himself to ponder the question whether, after all, Christianity, though foreign, were not the true religion.

After severe sickness and a revelation, as he believed, from the Lord of Heaven, Choi felt himself called to found a new religion. He proceeded to do so after the time-honored manner most fashionable in China, Corea, and Japan, where originality is not too common, that is, make an eclectic system. From the ethics of Confucius and the philosophy of his commentators, from the writings of Lao-tsze and his interpreters, and from the Buddhist sutras and their accretions, he composed a book entitled the Great Holy Scripture and wrote out the brief prayer which his followers still daily repeat. As Christianity was a Western sect, he gave to his new religion the name of Tong Hak, Eastern Doctrine or Culture. Many, perhaps most, of his followers laid their emphasis in the new religion upon the idea of maintaining Orientalism as against Occidentalism. Beginning in the town of Kion Chiu, forty-five miles north of Fusan, the movement spread quickly into the provinces of Chung Chong and Chullado. Entering the sphere of politics, it gave the downtrodden peasants hope and new life, in the midst of the awful night of ever-increasing official corruption and oppression. It was about this time that the tenure of office by the provincial governors was changed from three years to one year. This move, made in the interests of the official class, vastly increased the burdens laid upon the people, since the political spoilsman, who usually bought his office, having now less time wherein to recoup and fill his own chest, became threefold more grasping than before.

The influence of Christianity is very manifest in the history of the Tong Haks and in the literary, dogmatic, and devotional manifestations of their leader. Within six years, under the fierce initiative of the Tai-wen Kun, Choi and his disciples were officially charged with being "foreigner Coreans" and followers of the Lord of Heaven, that is, Roman Catholic Christians. Choi was tried, tortured, and beheaded, and his doctrines were outlawed. As with the Boxer and other common delusions among the ignorant, the Tong Haks believed that "by the influence of their god they could dance the sword dance and ascend into the air." The sect kept on spreading year after year, its animus blending with that spirit of revolution and resistance to intolerable official oppression then rampant in the southern provinces, the two movements melted into each other and became one.

Early in 1893, before the palace gate at Seoul, there was a wonderful sight. With pathetic ceremonies and long and patient waiting, fifty of Choi's followers presented a petition that their founder be rehabilitated and their sect be tolerated even as the Christians were. They intimated that if they were kept under ban they would drive all aliens out of the country. Their prayer for toleration was refused, and they were driven away by the palace guards. In the springtime the Tong Haks led a great uprising of the peasantry in the southern provinces. The soldiers sent to

Seoul to put down the insurrection were scattered like chaff before the wind. The insurgents occupied the chief city of Chullado and the danger seemed to threaten the whole kingdom. The Corean general, Hong, notified the Court of his inability to cope with the situation. Then the pro-Chinese faction in Seoul, instigated by Yuan, applied to Peking asking for military aid to put down the Tong Hak rebels. According to the Li-Ito convention of May 7, 1885, neither China or Japan could send soldiers into Corea without first notifying the other Power.

Meanwhile Kim Ok Kiun was in Japan. Though the Government at Seoul repeatedly demanded his extradition and both in Corea and Japan assassins continually plotted to kill him, he received the same asylum and protection which, under the laws of civilization, the Government in Tokio gave to all foreigners. Finally, in 1894 Kim Ok Kiun was lured to Shanghai by a false telegram and a forged bank-draft. On his arrival at the hotel he was promptly murdered. His assassin was rewarded with honor, fame, and money from Seoul, and in China looked on as a hero. With indecent haste, but following its ancient barbarous traditions, the Chinese Government made itself the express company which carried the victim's body in a man-of-war to Corea, where it was cut to pieces and the head and limbs exposed on the public highway. This action of China raised a storm of popular wrath in Japan, while about the same time, China, first on June 7th forwarding .her troops into Corea, in violation of the treaty of 1885, sent a defiant insult to the Tokio Government. Following this action, a despatch was sent to the Japanese legation in Peking, in which were the words which we italicize: " It is in harmony with our constant practice to protect *our tributary states* by sending our troops to assist them. . . . General Weh has been ordered to proceed to Zenra . . . to restore the peace of *our tributary state.*" Thus by force of arms China defied Western diplomacy, and, trampling on the treaties, asserted her ancient claims of suzerainty over Corea as her vassal state.

The reply of the Tokio Government was the announcement, on June 12, 1894, of the despatch of a body of the Mikado's troops under strict discipline to Chō-sen. On June 17th China was invited to co-operate with Japan in financial and administrative reforms in Corea, in order to preserve the peace of the Far East.

China curtly refusing this request, demanded the immediate return to Japan of her soldiers, at the same time ordering her Tartar forces in Manchuria to cross that ancient Rubicon of eastern Asia —the Yalu River. Chartering the British ship Kow Shing, she put on board eleven hundred soldiers with ammunition and artillery to reinforce the Chinese camp at Asan in the northwest of Chung Chong province. The reply from Tokio was, that, pending an amicable settlement of the questions in dispute, any further despatch of Chinese troops into Corea would mean war.

As soon as it was known in Tokio that the Tartar forces had been mobilized and that the Kow Shing was being loaded, the Japanese fleet sailed and orders were given to the troops, railways, and steamers to be ready for the embarking of an army. Within twelve days a Japanese army corps was landed at Chemulpo, marched to Seoul, the Han River bridged by pontoons in twenty minutes, and the military cordon around Seoul completed. On the 20th of July Yuan fled the Corean capital, leaving his nationals to shift for themselves. On the 23d Mr. Hoshi Toru, envoy of the Mikado, with a military guard entered the palace and demanded of the King an answer to the question of Corea's independence and willingness to stand by her treaty with Japan. The royal answer was in the affirmative. The King called in the Tai-wen Kun to allay his fears and aid him in the formation of a new cabinet, to which he invited, for the most part, the Liberals exiled in 1884. Prince Pak Yong Hio, who had been declared an archtraitor and his house razed to the ground, was again received into royal favor.

On July 25th the Japanese cruiser Naniwa, under Captain, now Admiral, Togo, met the Kow Shing. After four hours of parley and refusal to surrender, the transport was sunk by the guns of the Naniwa. On July 29th and 30th the Japanese met the Chinese forces at Asan, routed them and occupied their stronghold. The declarations of war between the emperors of China and Japan, the old rival Sons of Heaven, were published to the world on the same day, August 1, 1894. The former was full of arrogance and ignorance, the latter was clear in phrase and temperate in tone. The Chinese lady then on the throne called on her soldiers to " root the pigmies out of their lair." With the conceit and stupidity of the giant, China went to war against the intelligent

and splendidly armed Jack of the islands. In results it was an
affair of Goliath and David over again. Ancient and overweening
orthodoxy met culture and intelligence in the field and on the wave,
to be confronted by what was despised as too small to do harm.
At bottom the Chino-Japanese war meant the right of a nation
to change its civilization. Japan, already a signatory to the Geneva
Convention and her officers trained in the ways of civilization,
even though her people were dubbed heathen by some semi-en-
lightened folks of the West, went to war in Christian style. The
Japanese had a superb Red Cross organization, a corps of surgeons, and a body of fifteen hundred trained nurses, while their
hospitals were equipped according to scientific ideas. With each
army corps and fleet went a lawyer versed in international law,
to see that nothing should be done against the laws of nations.
The literary fruits of these precautions and this loyalty to the
high standards of civilization are seen in Mr. Takahashi's masterly work " International Law During the Chino-Japanese War,"
and in Mr. Ariga's " La guerre Sino-Japonaise au point de vue
du droit internationale." The Chinese had not yet (or before the
year 1904) recognized the laws of civilization and had scarcely the
beginning of hospital corps, hospitals, or surgeons. It was not
wonderful, therefore, that her wounded usually crawled away to die
like dogs, or that her ignorant soldiers frequently fired upon those
bringing succor to the wounded. The official organization of the
Chinese was honeycombed with corruption, but with their thirty
thousand drilled troops and fleet, including battle-ships, of which
the Japanese had none, they expected easy victory. Occupying
Ping-an, they built between fifty and sixty forts. At sea their
fleets were busy in convoying transports full of soldiers to the
mouth of the Yalu River to prevent the Japanese from advancing
beyond Corea and in the hope of overwhelming them at one onset.
On the site of their previous victory three centuries before, they
expected to rout the Japanese and then to drive them southward
and out of Corea.

The Japanese, centuries ago, learned the difference between
bulk and brain, and are but slightly overawed in the presence of
mere weight or size. They knew that the military reputation of
China only existed on paper, and their excellent system of *jiu-jitsu*
had taught them how to turn an enemy's strength against him-

self. Her soldiers had grown up in the new era of ideas which had come to fruit under Christian civilization. Borrowing these ideas and forces and combining them with their own resources and informing them with their own genius, they gave the world a surprise. They had long grieved in spirit over their non-recognition by the world at large of their peaceful ambitions and of the principles that lie at the basis of their civilization. They mourned that war and bloodshed were necessary to impress the world and secure respect. Within six months they humbled China and compelled her to sue for peace.

In three divisions, up from the south, eastward from the mouth of the Ta Tong River, and westward from Gensan, the three columns of the Japanese army marched and met at Ping-an (Ping Yang). After two days' fighting, September 15th and 16th, the Chinese hosts were routed. The next day, at sea, off the mouth of the Yalu River, the Chinese fleet, in the first great battle of modern steel ships, was disabled and was never afterward able to resume the offensive. Before October 1st Corea was entirely cleared of Chinese. On the continent of Asia, chiefly in Manchuria, they held an area larger than their own empire. Port Arthur fell on November 21st, and the great fortress of Wei-hai-wei was surrendered January 31, 1895.

Then Russia unmasked. Calling to her aid France and Germany, this triple alliance compelled Japan to give up all claims upon the continent and to be content with an indemnity and the island of Formosa. Had the Japanese possessed a fleet of battleships, they would have refused this insolent demand and declared war on Russia. As it was, the treaty of Shimonoseki, between Li Hung Chang and Ito and Mutsu, was signed. The Japanese spent the indemnity money on a new navy and proceeded to gird themselves for their next war with another giant, and to show again the difference between bulk and brain.

Corea suffered surprisingly little from the presence of two great armies on her soil. Her people were paid liberally for labor and materials which they so grudgingly furnished to the Japanese, who were not, in this instance, sufferers on account of their own excess of politeness, while the Chinese troops were within her borders too short a time to be a very heavy tax. Only around Ping-an was there much public or private suffering.

In Seoul, the Mikado's envoy, as early as August, began to insist upon a programme of reforms, which, had they been carried out, would have amounted virtually to a new constitution.

In the reconstruction of the administration of the seven departments, that of Public Works was broadened to include Agriculture and Commerce, and in place of the Department of Ceremonies there was created one of Education co-ordinate with the others. A mighty programme of reforms, twenty-three in number, was prepared, but enough to make up several social tornadoes, some of which were possible, while others seemed too radical and absurd on their faces. A new mint began to issue coins in European form.

The second son of the King was sent to Tokio to bear the thanks of the nation and Government for having secured the independence of Cho-sen. The Corean sovereign, on January 8, 1895, with tremendous picturesqueness of procession, pomp, and circumstance, proceeded to the temple of his ancestors and with imposing ceremonies solemnly adjured all vassalage and dependence upon China. The official name of the new empire is Dai Han or Ta Han, that is, the Great Han, single and sovereign, as contrasted with the three (San Han) of ancient history. With this royal act vanished from history the strangest anomaly in diplomacy, and one of the last of the dual sovereignties in Asia. Furthermore, from this time forth, the whole tissue and complexion of Corean politics altered. The native scholars began to seek a new intellectual climate and the culture of the West. Scores of students were sent abroad and many foreigners were employed, as in the new Japan of 1868.

When, however, Count Inouye, one of the purest and best statesmen in Japan, in co-operation with the Reform Committee of the Corean Government began his labors, the old chronic difficulties at once presented themselves and in legions. There seemed to be no real patriotism in the country. Rare indeed was the native of ability who was not hopelessly inoculated with the vices of the old clans and noble families, whose only idea of the relation between government and office holders was that of the udder and the sucking pig. Plots and jealousies continually hampered reform. The real problem was to separate the functions of the Court from those of the Government, which in Corea, as in China, had never been fully done. In Japan the holding of office by females in the palace had been abolished. In the palace at Seoul their influence could secretly nullify public business. The question of succession to the throne without Court intrigue through the influence of the Queen and the mob of palace underlings, and the reconstruction of the military system and that of civil and criminal law were grappled with. Over one hundred young men were sent to Japan to study. On June 20, 1895, a royal ordinance was issued dividing the kingdom into thirteen prefectures, five of the large provinces being divided into two parts, with 151 districts and 339 magistracies. A cabinet, with nine boards of administration, was organized, and a judiciary system for the entire country formed, a postal system inaugurated, and the army, consisting of 5,000 men, was put under the instruction of Japanese and American officers. For all these enterprises, money was of the first necessity. Attempts, therefore, were made to reform the revenue, making taxes payable in money instead of in kind, while lands illegally seized were restored to their rightful owners.

All seemed to promise well, notwithstanding that many of the old-style gentry, who saw in the change a lessening of their income, still opposed what they called the "civilization nonsense." The Chinese merchants gradually returned after the war and resumed business. Foreign trade in 1895 amounted to nearly thirteen million dollars. Commercial prosperity seemed to be general and increasing. A fitful insurrection of the Tong Haks, in the summer of 1895, was completely subdued by Japanese troops. All was proceeding auspiciously until Count Inouye left Corea for a visit home. The Queen, who feared that her father-in-law, the Regent, might make a bad use of the Japanese troops, was anxious. Count Inouye assured her that the Mikado's Government "would not fail to protect the royal house of Corea." Thus allaying her well-grounded suspicions, Count Inouye left Seoul about September 15th.

There were still living in the peninsula the two ablest characters, man and woman, in modern Corean history; the Queen, bound to overcome, and nullify by her craft and the power of the Min clan, the reforms begun by the Japanese, and the old Regent, who was bent on getting his son's wife out of the way, by fire, sword, poison, or dynamite. Nominally about seventeen thousand

useless persons in Government employ and pay had been discharged,
and the Queen's palace attendants reduced from hundreds to a
dozen.   But after Inouye had gone away, these parasites gradually returned at her invitation, until the palace was crowded again
as of old with her women, eunuchs, servants, and underlings of all
sorts, while her clansfolk prepared for another of those plots so
characteristic of unregenerated Corea.   At the signs of danger,
Prince Pak Yong Hio, minister of Home Affairs, fled the capital.
It looked to the Japanese as if all their work and influence were to
come to nothing.   They had been foiled by a woman.

The Tokio Government had appointed as its envoy, in place of
Count Inouye, a military officer named Miura, who, like the French
Zouave de Bellonet, of whom we have read before, brought to his
work in Seoul the habits of the camp and the methods of the soldier, rather than the patience, tact, and civil abilities of his immediate predecessor.   About this time there were in Seoul many
Japanese, of all grades of character, especially *soshi*, political bul-
lies or "heelers" from Tokio, angry at the Queen, who, as they
professed to believe, was the friend of Russia.   These men gathered
many other spirits like unto themselves from among the native soldiers who had been discharged through the Queen's influence.   Soon
both the native and the foreign worthies concluded, with the Tai-
wen Kun, that for the good of Corea the Queen would have to be
killed.   On the early morning of October 8th the Japanese troops
were conveniently and purposely posted so as to make possible the
entrance into the palace of a motley band of ruffians, some sixty in
number.   Seizing the Queen in her own apartments, they murdered
her, dragged her corpse into one of the areas outside, poured
petroleum over the rice straw mats and clothing and set the heap
on fire.   Thus perished one of the ablest women in Corean annals.
A new Government was quickly formed under the instigation of
the Tai-wen Kun.   A radical programme of reforms was published,
new officers were appointed at home and envoys sent abroad.   With
horrible mockery of history and justice, this "rebel cabinet"—
as the King later stigmatized it in public documents—pretended
that the Queen was alive and forthwith conducted an absurd trav-
esty of publicly trying some native accused of her murder.   In the
name of his Majesty a proclamation was forged degrading the
Queen to the level of a servant.   All this was done by men, some

of whom, it seems impossible to doubt, were implicated in the palace slaughter. When on November 27th some ultra-patriotic Coreans, opposed to the Japanese and the policy of the Tai-wen Kun, made an effort to drive out their new rulers by an attack on the palace and failed, the chief participants, as well as those alleged on trumped-up charges to have been in the affair of October 8th, were executed December 8th. Meanwhile there were anti-Japanese riots in many parts of the country.

On hearing of the strange use of the Mikado's soldiery in Seoul, the Japanese Government promptly recalled Miura and arrested forty-seven persons supposed to have taken part in the assault on the palace in Seoul. Nevertheless, in the court at Hiroshima, technical evidence against them was lacking and the whole band of this new I-ro-ha of modern Japanese heroism was discharged free of blame, or at least without the stigma of condemnation. It is probable that the whole affair of October 8th was connived at by a reckless diplomatic blunderer, to the regret and mortification of the Mikado's ministers and the national sentiment of Japan. In any event, it proved the death-blow, for a time at least, of Japanese prestige in Corea. In December the troops of Japan evacuated the country.

This was almost the last appearance in public of "Yi Haeung, Prince of Heung Song," the Tai-wen Kun, or Prince Parent. He emerged fitfully on one occasion before the police authorities to secure the release of one of his retainers, and then retired to his estate in Kiodang. He died peacefully, on the 22d of February, 1898, and was buried with due ceremonies. His mausoleum, made according to all the proprieties of Corean taste and mortuary art, makes an attractive sight on the landscape of Corea. On August 18, 1900, Corea being now an empire, he was by imperial decree raised to the rank of Wang, or King. He will ever be remembered by the Coreans as one of the most powerful personalities in the modern history of their nation. According to traditional usage, Corean princes cannot hold office, and for that reason many of them decline the title, in order to avoid the poverty which acceptance of it brings, and get Government appointments to office with salary. The Tai-wen Kun, born in Seoul, January 22, 1811, made good use of his opportunity, which came both with his title and his office. Besides doing a great many bad things, to the injury of his country, he made some great improvements. He was, according to his lights, a statesman and a patriot, and he foresaw to some extent the designs of Russia. In methods he never rose above the atmosphere of the environment within which he had been educated. In person he was five feet six inches in height, but looked a leader of men. He was the great-grandson of one king, the nephew of another, and the father of a third. " He became the leader of the small remnant of the imperial clan left, and really preserved it from extinction." [1]

The passing away of these two eminent characters, Queen Min and Tai-wen Kun, marked the end of an era.

---

[1] See in the Korean Repository for July, 1898, a sketch of his life by Rev. G. H. Jones.

CHAPTER LII.

JAPAN AND RUSSIA IN CONFLICT.

FROM the night of the murder of his consort until his escape, four months later, to the Russian legation, the sovereign of Corea was to all intents and purposes a prisoner in his own palace. Unable to trust anybody and feeling in constant danger, he sought the American missionaries for food, for companionship, and even for protection.[1] To him the new Government consisted of his jailers. The Corean people, sympathizing with their King, hated the Japanese all the more, for they felt that their sovereign was a virtual prisoner in the hands of the Tai-wen Kun and the pro-Japanese conspirators. Under these circumstances, he determined to break the palace jail. On the morning of February 11, 1896, according to a plan elaborated by the women and arranged with the Russians, he entered one of the ordinary box chairs in which female servants are carried. A few minutes later, pale and trembling, the King of Corea knocked at the north gate of the legation of Russia and was promptly admitted. It has been insisted that "no Russian had been to the palace or near it, nor had any Russian been to any of the public offices," yet by some curious coincidence the Russian legation guards had been increased on the evening of the 10th by nearly one hundred men from the Czar's men-of-war at Chemulpo. Furthermore, the Russians welcomed not only the King but later also the Crown Prince and the Queen Dowager.

His Majesty was scarcely within the walls of his new shelter before he issued an edict against his "rebel cabinet," ordering his soldiers to "cut off their heads at once and bring them," but in the afternoon another edict decreed that the six traitors should be degraded and delivered to the courts for trial. This royal order was the signal for another outburst of riot, savagery, and bloodshed. The Corean prime minister and the Minister of Agriculture were

---

[1] See Fifteen Years Among the Topknots, by L. H. Underwood (1904).

killed and their corpses mutilated and dragged round the streets. The prisons were emptied and the innocent and guilty alike released. Sixty-six Japanese, mostly workmen on the telegraphs, were murdered and the line partially destroyed.

The pro-Japanese party, beginning with the bloody morning of October 8, 1895, when Queen Min was murdered, had been in power during four months, during which time a tremendous blow was dealt to the prestige of Japan in Corea. For eleven months the King transacted the national business in the Russian legation buildings, going only occasionally to the palace to give audiences to the foreign envoys. One of these from the Mikado presented a claim of indemnity for $146,000 for his subjects slain during the riot.

The flight of Corea's sovereign was like that pictured in the proverb " from the frying pan into the fire." In fierce reality, it was escape from bloody to inky tyranny, from an iron to a silken chain; but in both cases it was humiliation and slavery. While the guest of the Russians, the King paid well his bill as tenant by signing a concession to his hosts, permitting them to cut timber " in the Yalu valley." The Russian Government liberally interpreted this document, according to the vast scale of Muscovite geography, as meaning the whole basin drained by the Yalu and its tributaries, that is, a region half as large as Corea. The Russians thus obtained for a year's rent of part of their legation buildings a lien on Corean property valued at fifty millions of dollars.

Revolutions do not go backward, and the general proceeding of the Government was along the line of progress. The external reforms are particularly noticeable in the capital, in which Corean officers trained in Washington have greatly improved the streets, the methods of cleaning and the drainage. The police and soldiery were uniformed and disciplined, and preparations made for a national census. The untrustworthy " census " of Seoul showed a population of 144,626 in 27,527 houses, and in the suburbs 75,189 in 18,093 houses, or a total of 219,815, and of houses 45,350, in which district are 36 Buddhist temples with 442 priests and 204 nuns. The original width of the streets, as laid out in 1392, of 55 feet, has been regained over many miles of the city thoroughfares. Foreign trade steadily increased. American capital and energy helped to make what was once one of the filthiest and most unprogressive cities of the Far East a clean and attractive place, bright with electric lights and railway and modern water-works. A railroad was built from the seaport to the capital and opened for traffic September 1, 1899. The steel bridge, made at Chattanooga, Tenn., spanning the Han River is nearly a mile long. The electroliers give light to the palace and to part of the city of Seoul. The trolley line, besides traversing the city, runs to the mausoleum of the Queen, which has been built in superb style. There her scant remains, escorted by a vast procession characterized in all its features by the old barbaric grandeur of Corea, were laid with appropriate ceremonies.

In the spring of 1896 the Independence Club, with a membership of over 2,000, was formed. It was composed entirely of natives actively interested in social and material development as well as in the independence of Corea. On October 21st the cornerstone of Independence Arch was laid on a site but a few yards distant from the old Chinese Gate under which the ambassadors of China had for centuries received the vassalage of the Corean sovereign. It is a structure in stone, alike of architectural beauty and of political significance. The subsequent history of this club and of the general movement, in which the publication of a daily newspaper in both English and native script, *The Korean Independent*, were prominent features, is not a happy one. It showed clearly that independence or freedom must be something more than a word, in order to bring forth the fruits seen in America or among the nations that have most cultivated liberty, safeguarded by law. In this Seoul movement the seed may have been good, but good and well prepared soil did not exist. Rock, brambles, and the beaten road of bad precedent, in which Corea is so rich, received the sower's hopes. The movement ended in sedition or evaporated. Nevertheless, it was vastly better than the Seoul mobs that so often dictated imperial policy to the ministers of the Government. As late as May, 1902, the former members of the Independence Club were being arrested and executed. More promising in ultimate results was the celebration on September 2d of the forty-fifth birthday of the King by a great gathering of Corean Christians in the pavilion near the old Chinese Gate.

After a stay of one year and nine days, the King left his Russian quarters and took up his residence in the new palace of Kyengwun, built in 1896 in the western part of the city, where are gathered the foreign legations and residences, some of them very handsome and substantial.

Corea, being now free and independent, between the two great empires of Japan and China, and Corean conceit of national history and antiquity, real or supposed, being never at any time lacking, it was thoroughly appropriate and financially very profitable for the yangban and palace officials to take measures to proclaim the once "little outpost state" an "empire," and their sovereign an "emperor." Besides suffering from imperialism in an acute form, the Corean office-holders knew well the significance of this nominally political act, in relation to their own fortunes; for in the assumption of the King of Corea of the title of Emperor, $100,000 was taken out of the treasury to celebrate the event, most of which, as a matter of course, went into the pockets of the King's faithful servants. His Majesty protested in vain against the proceedings, but finally yielded gracefully. At 3 A.M. on October 12, 1896, with great pomp and state, before the altars of the Spirits of the Land, the King assumed the title of Emperor of Ta Han, or the Great Han—in distinction from the ancient San Han. "The King is dead, long live the Emperor."

This, too, was the time of Russia's political dominance, when a Russian military commission of fourteen were drilling the Corean military and when the Minister of Foreign Affairs at Seoul and the Russian envoy, Mr. Speyer, signed an agreement, November 5th, by which Dr. McLeavy Brown, the Englishman in charge of the national finances—able, faithful, and unterrified—should be ousted and a Russian, Mr. Kuril Alexieff, put in his place. Mr. Brown's contract not having expired, he refused to vacate his post, and a large British and Japanese fleet having appeared off Chemulpo, he was able to maintain his ground. The three countries, Russia, Great Britain, and Japan, made an agreement that Mr. Brown should remain in office and that a Russian and a Japanese commissioner of customs should share in the collection of foreign duties at the ports. On December 23, 1897, a telegram was received from the Czar of Russia recognizing the Emperor of Corea, whereat the imperial party in Seoul was greatly elated. This whole incident illustrates the rather theatrical methods of Russian diplomacy in Corea during the past twenty years, showing how entirely her interests were military and strategic, but not commercial, she having usually scarcely a score, and never at any time a hundred, of subjects in the empire commercially engaged, and only a few fishermen who are whale hunters on the coast. One Baron Guntzburg was busy as a promoter of Russian interests, and the wife of the Russian minister was not inactive in social affairs and even as an influencer of political action.

It was not long before there were signs of a popular reaction against Russia. On January 22, 1898, an attempt was made to assassinate Kim, the native Russian interpreter. By March 10th this feeling had taken form in a great anti-Russian demonstration, which ended in the apparently total though not real withdrawal of Russian influence in the peninsula. The military commission soon after departed and the Russo-Corean Bank was closed. After much excitement, Russia and Japan, on April 25th, agreed on a *modus vivendi*, both recognizing the sovereignty of Corea and engaging to refrain from direct interference in her internal affairs. No military or financial adviser was to be nominated without mutual agreement, and Russia bound herself not to impede the commercial relations between Japan and Corea. It was evident (probably in large measure on account of Russia's new interests in Manchuria) that she considered Corea for the present beyond her sphere of influence. No serious revival of the claims of Russia to any part of Corea were made again openly until 1903. When the correspondence between Tokio and St. Petersburg, leading to the war of 1904, opened, the ambitions of Russia were seen to be serious and all-embracing.

The first year of the Corean empire was completed after the celebration of the King's birthday with unusual demonstrations of loyalty. The founder's day (that of Ki-tsze, or Ki-ja, whose tomb and temple are at Ping-an and which suffered during the war of 1894) and the 506th anniversary of the establishment of the dynasty, as well as the celebration of the coronation, were honored with unusual demonstrations, including the illumination of the capital. This year was noted for a revival of Confucianism among the yangban, Buddhism having already enjoyed a " recrudescence "—both systems being galvanized into a similitude of life by the powerful induction, and evidences, both in leaven and bloom, of the new faith. On the whole, the year 1898 was characterized by an intense conservative reaction in the Government and by an absence of important diplomatic or political events, except the chronic local rebellions in the provinces and the plots of rivals and partisans in the capital. Notwithstanding that the solar calendar had been adopted in 1895, and had been officially observed, the people still celebrate New Year's Day with a fortnight of oldtime rejoicings, merrymakings, and customs according to the lunar calendar.

The year 1899 was one of comparative quiet in the capital and provinces. During the Boxer agitation in China, there was danger of eruptions across the border which were duly guarded against, and a Russian escort of fifty soldiers to the refugee Danish missionaries from China was given free passage. Corea virtually joined the allies marching to Peking, by giving aid and comfort in the form of a thousand bags of cleaned rice, two thousand bags of flour, and several hundred cases of cigarettes.

In August, 1899, the written constitution of the kingdom was issued, the nine articles of which declare the absolute power of the King. It cannot be said that either the Coreans, the foreign diplomatic corps, or the world at large took this giving of a constitution as a very serious matter. To the special "imperial" envoy despatched from Seoul to Tokio, Japan flatly refused to promise the complete neutrality of Corea. Nevertheless, Corean subjects are expected to bow down and worship (either in the old English sense of the term or with more profound significance) the picture of the Emperor as in other pagan or semi-civilized countries. A memorial tablet and pagoda "to commemorate the virtues of his Majesty" was begun—on a day significant in the West—April 1, 1902. These will be in the main street at the junction of Palace Street in Seoul.

It was noted as a great event in the history of a country that has never given very serious attention to its high-roads, that Dr. W. B. Magill, an American missionary, drove a horse and carriage from Gensan to Seoul. A system of lighthouses was decided upon October 31, 1901.

The fiftieth anniversary of the Emperor's birthday was celebrated December 7th, silver commemorative medals being given to each guest at the palace. A Corean band of musicians, trained by Mr. Franz Eckhart, a German, who arrived in the country February

19, 1901, played two pieces of foreign music very creditably to themselves and their instructor. On July 1, 1902, the Corean national hymn, an adaptation by Franz Eckhart, was published. This German musician had already made a good record in Japan.

On May 30, 1902, the Emperor entered the Society of the Hall of Aged Men, having completed the first year of the sixth decade of his life (51 years), the foreign representatives being entertained at breakfast. Prominent among these, in influence and ability, was the American minister, Dr. Horace Newton Allen, born in Delaware, Ohio, in 1868, and resident in Corea since the summer of 1884, when he introduced modern methods of healing and surgery. He accompanied the first legation of Chō-sen in Washington. There he was appointed secretary to the American legation in Seoul, and since 1890 has been the chief guardian of American interests in Corea, being made minister in July, 1896. During the time of the Boxer insurrection in China, when the movement threatened to spread into Corea, he was especially alert in precautionary measures of safety. Previous to the outbreak of the Russo-Japanese war, he secured the presence of a guard of American marines in Seoul by which American rights, personal and commercial, were thoroughly secured.

Events during the year 1903 showed a steady movement toward an inevitable end and pointed to the impending crisis between Russia and Japan. The situation in Seoul was dominated by Yi Yong Ik and Yi Keun Tak, who were in close communication with Port Arthur and the Russian authorities at that place. Their highhanded financial and other schemes, in opposition to the Japanese efforts at securing a stable currency, came to naught after severe pecuniary loss to natives and foreigners and the serious disturbance of trade. The Russians, on April 11, 1901, had secured a twenty-year extension of timber cutting and prosecuted vigorously their advances in the north. They now refused to allow the Corean Government any supervision over their work of denuding the forests in the Yalu valley. In May one of the Czar's gunboats anchored in the harbor of Yongampo, which the Russians called Port Nicholas, and soon after began what were believed to be fortifications. A guard of twenty-six Russian marines reinforced the legation in Seoul, shortly after the violation by Russia of her pledge to evacuate Manchuria. A serious riot in November between

Nipponese and Muscovite soldiers at Chemulpo foreshadowed the impending clash on a large scale in 1904. During December Russia's influence at Seoul blocked all attempts of the foreign representatives to have Wiju (Ai-chiu) opened as a port of trade.

At this stage in the nation's history, the once white-coated hermits who had hitherto lived under their own top-knots, and often under hats that were as big as a haycock, began numerously to go abroad as students. Scores of them have been in America and Europe and hundreds in Japan. In December, 1902, a party of nearly one hundred emigrants, men, women, and children, started for Hawaii. All of these were admitted, except eight who were sent back because of contagious eye disease. Other incidents showed healthful movement in a long-stagnant mass of population. Light and vision are coming to a people blind to nearly everything modern.

Of all the moral and reformatory forces at work, that of active Christianity leads. The missionary pioneers, Allen, Underwood, Scranton, Appenzeller, Heron, Gale, Jones, Hulbert, and others, mastered the language and opened the treasures of native literature and history. Already the list of aids to the vernacular and of their writings descriptive of country and people is a very respectable one. These works, the fruit of earnest toil, contrast superbly in the quality of truthfulness with the sketchy and ephemeral writings of tourists and hasty travellers. With other scholars and civil servants of various governments, they sustain the editor in furnishing the richly freighted pages of the *Korea Review*, and have formed the Korea Branch of the Royal Asiatic Society, from which already several creditable volumes of " Transactions " have appeared to delight the serious student, who values perspective and tone in his mind-pictures of this once hermit nation.

Already the representatives of the Christian brotherhoods of English-speaking peoples have their row of graves in which sleep heroes, veterans, and some who " fell at the first fire." Beginning in 1884, their prospective celebration of a double decennial, in September, 1904, was postponed under the clouds of war. Besides healing and helping, translating the Scriptures, and teaching the great uplifting truths which centre around the idea of one living and true God, gathering thousands of souls into churches and furnishing Gospel nurture, they have taught the natives the grand lesson of self-support and self-propagation through a first-hand knowledge of the Bible. War, persecution, and manifold trials have tested and proved the quality of the converts, who in sincerity and power to stand in the midst of temptations are perhaps second to none in any field.

It was evident at the opening of the year 1904 that Japanese armies were once again to tread the soil of Corea, this time the war being not between China and Japan, but between Japan and Russia. Against the Colossus of the North and Russian rapacity, the Island Empire had a long list of grievances. As far back as 1861 a Russian man-of-war had, not without shedding the blood of its defenders, landed marines on the Island of Tsushima. There they had planted seed and begun the formation of a settlement looking to permanent occupation. In those days of hermitage, weakness, and fear, nothing could be done by the Japanese authorities at Yedo; but Katsu Awa, the Shogun's most far-seeing statesman, called the attention of the British minister at Peking to this invasion, and a British naval force was sent to compel the Russians to retire. A few years later Russia took possession of Saghalien, after the usual preliminary of " joint occupation," compelling the Japanese to be satisfied with the Kurile Islands below 50° 56′ of north latitude. This was in the year 1875, but long before that, Japanese statesmen, especially Okubo, had penetrated the designs of Russia. The formation, out of feudal elements, of her national army in 1871 and the first of this character since the twelfth century, was largely with a view of defending Japan against Russian and other aggressions. On the return of the Japanese embassy from its trip round the world in 1873, Okubo, Kido, and others opposed the Corean war project (as we have seen in Chapter XLVII), because a war with Corea then meant playing into Russia's hands. Something of the popular fear of Russia over the Japanese nation, which hung like an advancing black cloud, was seen in the attack by a fanatical policeman on the Crown Prince, now the Czar of Russia, during his visit to Japan in 1891, but the Government in Tokio, even in the person of the Mikado, besides making ample apology, scrupulously maintained propriety in all dealings with Russia, at home and in Corea, living on terms of perfect friendship. It was therefore a stunning disappointment, though a not wholly unexpected procedure, when Russia, in 1895, summoning to her aid the French and Germans, deprived the Japanese of the fruits of their victories in the war with China, by compelling the islanders to relinquish all territory on the mainland of Asia, and to be content with Formosa and an indemnity. Exhausted as they were by the war with China, yet had the Japanese been possessed of five battle-ships, they would have declared war upon Russia as an abominable intermeddler and aggressor. The force of circumstances required them to swallow their humiliation, but as the Japanese, any more than certain Christian nations, never forgive an injury, they began immediately to gird themselves for the coming and inevitable struggle with the Power that seemed bent upon their destruction. When the Boxer uprising in 1899 called forth the military energies of eight nations, the Japanese Government at first held back, lest its motives in being too forward might be questioned. When finally urged to lead the van of the allied armies of rescue, Japan sent 21,000 of her ablest and best equipped soldiers into the campaign. Their experiences on the march to Peking were invaluable to the Japanese, for through becoming comrades with the *mujiks* in the camps and on the battle-field, they learned that they had nothing to fear from such foes when arrayed against them in anything like an equality of numbers in war. The Japanese officer found himself a modern man in the presence of his equals, who were men steeped in mediæval methods of thought.

Steadily enlarging their navy and perfecting in every detail arms, ammunition, field equipment, army hygiene, and the physical development of their soldiers, the Japanese determined to stand for their rights, even though this might seem like Jack challenging the giant. No longer hermits on an island, which, having but a small fraction of arable fertile soil, could not feed its inhabitants, so that population had to remain stationary, the Japanese had become a nation of traders and manufacturers, with an annual increase of population of over 500,000 a year, with a total population of fifty millions, and with a foreign trade that had increased 543 per cent since 1890, with a total export trade consisting of 84.6 per cent of manufactured articles. With nearly thirty thousand Japanese subjects in Corea, most of them married and with homes, and with 10,000 of their people in Manchuria, they took an interest in the affairs of Corea and Manchuria which was not like that of the Russians, chiefly military and strategic, but which, on the contrary, was commercial and vital. During the Boxer troubles, Russia sent a large army into Manchuria and finally took possession of the whole of that portion of the Chinese Empire. She promised solemnly to all the governments interested, to vacate the country on the 9th of October, 1903.

The world knows how this promise was broken. The correspondence between Tokio and St. Petersburg reveals the exasperating delays of the Russian Government, and its intention not only to remain permanently in Manchuria but to prevent if possible Japan from having anything to do with the matter. Russia even desired " recognition by Japan that Manchuria is outside her sphere of special interest" and requested a mutual engagement to establish " a neutral zone on the Corea-Manchuria frontier, extending fifty kilometers each side into which neutral zone neither of the contracting parties shall introduce troops without the consent of the other," and " the engagement on the part of Japan not to undertake on the coast of Corea any military works capable of menacing the freedom of navigation in the straits of Corea."

In a word, what Japan claimed is, that " Japan has a perfect right to demand that the independence and territorial integrity of China shall be respected and the rights and interests of Japan in that region shall be formally guaranteed."

After innumerable delays and the situation growing more serious every day, the Russians continually reinforcing their naval and military forces in the far East, Mr. Kurino, the Mikado's minister to St. Petersburg, having waited for an answer since the 13th of January, called on Count Lamsdorff at 8 P.M. February 4th for a definite reply, which was not forthcoming. Finding that in all probability there would be no changes in Russia's claims of control over Manchuria and her demand for " a buffer region between confines of direct influence and action of the two countries in the far East," being out of the question, the Japanese legation was on the 10th of February withdrawn from St. Petersburg and war began.

The Russians were already on Corean soil with three hundred Cossacks guarding their timber cutters on the left bank of the Yalu River. Since June, 1903, they had reinforced their army with 40,000 men and their navy with 26 vessels, ranging from battle-ship to torpedo boat, thus adding 83,000 tons to their sea power. Five days before, the Russian commander at Vladivostok had notified the Japanese commercial agent that a state of siege might be declared at any moment. With steam up, decks cleared for action, and search-lights in use for night work, the Russian seamen instantly replied to the fire and torpedoes of Admiral Togo's attack. The Japanese thus anticipated a naval raid from the Russians, which was afterwards successfully carried out from Vladivostok. To the Czar's advisers in Europe actual war may have come as a surprise. It did not come thus to his servants in the far East. Nevertheless, within three days after the rupture of peaceful relations the Russian war ships Variag and Koreetz had been sunk outside of the harbor of Chemulpo by the guns of Admiral Uriu and an army landed to begin its march northward. At Port Arthur three battle-ships and four cruisers had been sunk or damaged by Admiral Togo's torpedoes. The first idea of the Japanese was to eliminate the sea power of Russia from the scene of the seat of war. Landing her armies in Corea, at Chemulpo, the march was made without serious opposition, until near Wiju, the Mikado's hosts once more stood on the banks of the Yalu, the Rubicon of eastern Asia, confronting the forces of the White Czar.

Meanwhile, a new protocol between Japan and Corea was signed, in March, 1904, in which the stronger Power bound itself to reform the weaker country without annexing it and to protect it without impairing its sovereignty. Corea pledged herself, as distinctly under Japan's protection, to repose confidence in and to accept advice from the Japanese Government, and to make no agreement with a third Power which might seem to contravene the principles of the protocol. This document made Japan the champion of Corean independence, and is in spirit and letter the antipodes of Russia's action in Manchuria.

The new model army in Asia, and the most modern of all armies, was in its fitness of body and mind to cope with the problems of war in the twentieth century, the creation of the public schools of Japan. These soldiers, both veterans and youth, set a new standard of resourceful valor, celerity of movement, temperance in living, ability to endure hunger and hardship, and of self-abnegation in the presence of death. To a Japanese patriot, life, apart from duty, has no value. On the 1st of May, this "public school army," under Kuroki, having crossed the Yalu under fire, won a brilliant victory, capturing many guns and prisoners. They had met European troops and beaten them in fair fight.

Then began the Japanese march through the old Border Gate and Feng-Wang Chang or Phœnix Castle, and over the mountain range dividing the Yalu from the Liao valley. The fortified passes were one after the other carried in victorious assault, and in the early days of September both Russian and Japanese main armies were marshalled before Liao Yang city, southwest of the ruins of the ancient Corean stronghold, for one of the great decisive battles of modern times and perhaps of human history.

During this time other armies were landed in Manchuria and by May 15th Oku was in possession of the railway leading to Port Arthur. Dalny was occupied May 26th, and later Yinkow and Niu Chwang came under the sun banner. On August 25th Field-Marshal Oyama took command of all the Japanese forces and the armies of Kuroki, Nodzu, and Oku.

After the great pitched battle in the early days of September, the Mikado's flag floated over Liao Yang, and Kuropatkin fell back on Mukden, in masterly retreat.

From Port Arthur, girdled by a wall of fire and under a rain of shells, the Czar's battle-ships and cruisers made desperate efforts to escape, only to be sunk, driven back, or, torn and riven, to seek shelter in the ports of China, and elsewhere, their presence giving rise to perplexing questions in international diplomacy.

As we close again, in the autumn of A.D. 1904, our story of the once "hermit nation," the Japanese, confronted with the practical difficulties of assuming a real protectorate over Corea, while nominally but sincerely striving to maintain her independence, are still determined to control the peninsula as a vital possession. One hundred miles of the Seoul-Fusal railway are in operation. The sound of the blasting night and day in the deep rock-cuts near Seoul announce their purpose to finish speedily a highway of steel to the Chinese frontier. The real purpose of the war is the integrity of China, upon which depends the safety of Japan, perhaps even the political salvation of Asia.

CHAPTER LIII.

COREA A JAPANESE PROTECTORATE.

HAVING been responsible for two great foreign wars fought by Japan, it was natural that at the end of each campaign the position of Corea among nations should be notably altered. The war with the Middle Kingdom blew to pieces the Chinese doctrine of universal sovereignty, besides making the once vassal state independent. In name, at least, Corea was made an empire. The war with Russia annihilated the dogma so long held in Europe, that Asiatic nations exist for conquest and spoliation, with the corollary that "the break-up of China" was imminent. Japanese success in the war of 1894–95 was a vindication of the American doctrine as expounded by men from the United States during a century, and formulated by John Hay—"China for the Chinese."

Had Corea been a state fitted, by the power of unselfish patriotism and love of industry among her leaders, to survive amid modern political and economic conditions, Japan's triumph over Russia would have made her all the stronger. Her independence would have been assured, had the virtue of her own sons responded to the opportunity.

On the contrary, the history of Corea since 1866, as outlined on these pages, reveals the fatal weakness of the ruling class in Corea. Instead of giving themselves to patriotic sacrifice and personal industry, the yang-ban, or men of privilege, have made their capital a hot-bed of intrigue and Corea the storm centre of the Far East. Instead of developing their own strength and the nation's resources, they have plied the arts of cunning and the crafts of the weak. Yet modern civilization, rich in powerful governments, has no place for the weak. Least of all is self-chosen weakness allowable.

Being neither skilful merchants like the Chinese, nor brave warriors like the Japanese, the Corean noblemen—on whom lies

497

the burden of responsibility—might at least have imitated the good example of their island neighbors. In Japan the outstanding event of modern times was the renunciation, in 1871, by 400,000 knights or gentry, of their hereditary pensions paid out of the public treasury.[1] After this sacrifice, made in the interests of true patriotism, they put off their swords and silk petticoats, got to work, paid taxes, and began to earn an honest living. Even China has broken with her unsocial past and conceit of perfection, and has entered upon the path of modern civilization.

The Corean yang-ban abused their independence by intrigue. They failed to discern that the petty arts of the plotter endangered their existence as a nation. After her second great war, Japan saw clearly that to allow her neighbor state, wherein there was no sharp distinction between the Court and the Government, to remain, as of old, the hot-bed of intrigue, would jeopard her own existence. She therefore did for Corea what Great Britain has done for Egypt, the United States for Cuba, and the French for Annam. Corea is now numbered among protectorates.

When our narrative closed in September, 1904, the Japanese were building a trunk line of railroad, nearly six hundred miles long, which should traverse the whole peninsula from Fusan to Wiju (Ai-chiu, pp. 181, 364). Port Arthur had not surrendered. The real goal of the Japanese armies, the city of Mukden, containing the mausoleums of the Manchiu dynasty now ruling in Peking, "the possession of which would put the heart of China in the palm of Japan's hand," was yet unreached. Yet those who in the early seventies had helped to train the boys who made the public-school army of Japan, had no fear of its ultimate triumph.[1]

On the 3d of January, 1905, Port Arthur was formally surrendered, and its evacuation completed January 7th. The main Japanese army fronting Mukden was quickly reënforced by Nogi's division on the left, or west, and by Kawamura's army, out of Corea, on the right, or east. The great campaign of hard fighting, destined to last nearly a month, opened amid a snow-storm on the 23d of February. By the 28th the fighting was general along the whole front of nearly one hundred miles. On the 10th of March

---

[1] See "The Mikado's Empire," pp. 533–535, and p. 682, of the eleventh edition, 1906, for the five points of prediction made at Hartford, Conn., February 8, 1904.

Oku's columns entered, by the southern gate, the city of Mukden. The Russians lost nearly thirty thousand in dead and over forty thousand prisoners. The Japanese pursuit northward lasted until April 14th.

On the 27th and 28th of March "the battle of The Sea of Japan" took place, in which the Russian armada of thirty-eight modern ships of war was, "by the grace of Heaven and the help of the gods," annihilated.

By invitation of President Roosevelt, the envoys of the two warring nations, de Witte and Rosen for Russia, and Komura and Takahira for Japan (both of the latter the writer's former pupils in Tokio), met at Portsmouth, N. H.; whence, in the thirties, had sailed Captain Edmund Roberts, commissioned by President Jackson, and the first American diplomatist in the Far East. The Japanese won a signal diplomatic victory, securing the main points of their contention.

The peace treaty which was signed recognized in the first article Japan's predominant position in Corea, political, military, economic, as well as her right to supervise that country's affairs and to protect it, Russia agreeing not to obstruct Japan's proceedings in any respect. One of the first and worst results for Corea was the immediate entrance within her borders of a horde of low-class, insolent Japanese adventurers, who, by their cruelties and spoliations of natives, nearly neutralized the well-meant plans of good men in Tokio.

Following up the results of the decisive war, the Mikado sent his highly honored servant, Baron Komura, to Peking to arrange matters amicably with China, and then turned his attention to Corea. The protocol of March, 1904 (p. 495), had been quickly followed by the abolition of the Pedlers' Guild (so long used by pro-Russian intriguers) and by the visit of Marquis Ito, who bore a reassuring message of fraternity and good-will. Mr. I. Megata, one of the most experienced and skilful officers of the Treasury Department in Tokio, was sent to Seoul as financial adviser, and Mr. Durham Dwight Stevens, an American gentleman, who united ability and tact to long and varied experience in diplomacy in the Far East, accepted the post of assistant at the Corean Foreign Office. These gentlemen, like all their predecessors, encountered insuperable difficulties in dealing with a government that was nominally carried on at the Council Board, but in reality directed from the harem or by clan factions in secret intrigue.

Occupied so seriously with other matters, few attempts were made at first by the Japanese Government in the interest of real reforms that could benefit the Corean people. Meanwhile, it must be repeated, tens of thousands of the Mikado's subjects, many of them of the most truculent temper and disreputable character, crowded into the peninsula, committing acts of rapine and brutality which neutralized many of the best measures of wise statesmen. When the proposition, approved of in Tokio, was made that all uncultivated land in the peninsula should be open to Japanese occupation and enterprise, and the water rights and supply be shared by these aliens, the Corean people, as a body, made systematic protest. All the circumstances considered, this sudden act of virtual spoliation was a colossal blunder. In the eyes of the Coreans it was not only " stealing water from another man's field "—so terrible a crime in lands of rice culture, where irrigation is a vital necessity—but the theft of the very soil itself. At once a storm of opposition arose that swept the peninsula from end to end. The Corean Emperor was besieged with petitions to resist the Japanese demands. A society called Po-an, for the preservation of safety and peace, was formed, which met in Seoul in excited discussion, and began the propagation of what seemed to the Japanese authorities a campaign of sedition. The meetings of the Po-an were broken up by the police, and the Japanese garrison of Seoul was augmented to six thousand men. Though other Corean societies were formed, the excitement died out, the Japanese not pushing their scheme, the Corean noblemen showing little or no real patriotism, and the people little power of persistent unity. On October 13, 1904, General Hasegawa took control of the military situation.

Yet it is the simple truth to state that while the Japanese soldier, superb in discipline and noble in human qualities, is respected by the Corean, the low Japanese, who so often proves himself a rascal, is feared and despised. It is unfortunate that these disreputable characters were so long under such slight control from Tokio. On the other hand, notwithstanding that Japan, in the treaty of 1904, had guaranteed the independence of Corea, yet the Government in Seoul, choked by palace cliques, languished in chronic feebleness. Unable to keep order at home, to pay its legation bills abroad, or to separate itself from that " Forbidden Interior " of mystery in the boudoir inhabited by a mob of women, eunuchs and hangers-on, which curses China, Corea, and so long cursed old Japan in both Yedo and Kioto, what guarantee was there for the peace of Asia and the world? For the preservation of this, the Mikado's Government was responsible, while every complication in Corea involved Japan also.

After long deliberation, the statesmen in Tokio agreed that the surest exit out of the labyrinthine difficulty was to take charge of Corea's foreign relations and place a controller-general at the capital, with subordinates at the chief cities and seaports, leaving internal affairs to be directed from Seoul. The Mikado despatched Marquis Ito—" patient, able, and authoritative "—to Seoul.

On the 17th of November, 1905, the Corean Emperor's minister, Pak Che Soon, and the Mikado's representative, Hayashi, signed a treaty, of which the following is the official translation into English :

The Governments of Japan and Corea, desiring to strengthen the principle of solidarity which unites the two Empires, have with that object in view agreed upon and concluded the following stipulations to serve until the moment arrives when it is recognized that Corea has attained national strength :—

Article I. The Government of Japan, through the Department of Foreign Affairs at Tokio, will hereafter have control and direction of the external relations and affairs of Corea, and the diplomatic and consular representatives of Japan will have the charge of the subjects and interests of Corea in foreign countries.

Art. II. The Government of Japan undertake to see to the execution of the treaties actually existing between Corea and other Powers, and the Government of Corea engage not to conclude hereafter any act or engagement having an international character, except through the medium of the Government of Japan.

Art. III. The Government of Japan shall be represented at the Court of His Majesty the Emperor of Corea by a Resident General, who shall reside at Seoul, primarily for the purpose of taking charge of and directing matters relating to diplomatic affairs. He shall have the right of private and personal audience of His Majesty the Emperor of Corea. The Japanese Government shall also have the right to station Residents at the several open ports and such other places in Corea as they may deem necessary. Such Residents shall, under the direction of the Resident General, exercise the powers and functions hitherto appertaining to Japanese Consuls in Corea, and shall perform such duties as may be necessary in order to carry into full effect the provisions of this agreement.

Art. IV. The stipulations of all treaties and agreements existing between Japan and Corea not inconsistent with the provisions of this agreement shall continue in force.

Art. V. The Government of Japan undertake to maintain the welfare and dignity of the Imperial House of Corea.

In faith whereof the undersigned, duly authorized by the Governments, have signed this agreement and affixed their seals.

[Signed]   HYASHI GONSUKE,
                        Envoy Extraordinary and Minister Plenipotentiary.

[Signed]   PAK CHE SOON,
                                        Minister for Foreign Affairs.
November 17, 1905.

Whatever may be the real history of the transfer thus made or the means taken to secure the document, it is certain that the governments of Europe and America were very prompt in withdrawing their legations from Seoul and in acknowledging Japan's supremacy. In Washington the minds of the President and Secretary of State were quickly made up, because of the local eccentricities of Corean envoys, unable to pay their grocery bills, and despite the representations of more than one private emissary. On the accession of Theodore Roosevelt to the presidency by the election of the people and his change of diplomatic assistants, Minister Horace N. Allen, long our able representative in Seoul, was succeeded, in 1905, by Mr. Edwin Vernon Morgan, who had had experience in Samoa, Corea, Russia, and China. He being appointed to another position, the American legation in Seoul ceased, while the consul-general and consuls were retained as before.

Meanwhile, under the energetic action of the Resident General Ito, real reforms were inaugurated and disorderly Japanese characters arrested and either sent out of the country or made to give pledges for good behavior. The whole prospect of things brightened.

At a banquet given in his honor by his countrymen in Seoul, April 8, 1906, the Marquis Ito spoke as follows:

"According to what His Corean Majesty has repeatedly condescended to say to me, I may be permitted to believe that I have the honor to enjoy his confidence and trust in no small measure. He has on more than one occasion been pleased to assure me that he wished to rely upon my loyal services for the regeneration of the Corean Administration. His Majesty has also given orders to his Ministers to carry out this work of regeneration under my direction and guidance. As for the Corean Ministers, they have assured me of their determination to do their utmost to this end; they say that an opportunity like the present will not occur again, and, as a matter of fact, they are now actively engaged in the work of regeneration."

Apparently these words were as honestly applauded by the Corean Emperor's servants as they were believed to be true by the speaker himself. In mutual confidence, Corean military officers were duly appointed, and both General Hasegawa and the Marquis Ito left with them for Japan, to witness the grand review of the returning victorious Japanese armies from Manchuria, which was held in Tokio April 30th.

The opportunity for intrigue and conspiracy created by the absence of the two great men was too tempting to be lost by the factions of the boudoir and its inmates. The Corean Conservative and Progressive parties kept warring among themselves, hatching plots in which even the emperor's privy councillors, palace eunuchs, and officers of the Imperial household were active. Two lines of policy looking to domestic and foreign disturbance were mapped out by the conspirators. One utilized the distress and almost chronic troubles in the southwestern provinces, the other was based on the hope of Russian intervention. The plot was planned by yang-ban in the palace itself.

In Chung Chong Do (p. 194) a Min and in Chulla Do (p. 199) a Choi nobleman led the insurrections. Antiquated muskets, matchlocks, swords, and spears were laid in store against the Japanese. In Kang-wen Do (p. 208), also, troubles were reported. Four police (out of the 350 then in all Corea) were sent from the Residency in Seoul, but they were killed or driven away. The Corean provincial troops being supine, two companies of Japanese infantry were sent to the city. Attacking in daylight in order to spare the peaceful non-combatants, the soldiers blew up the gates with dynamite. After some street fighting the city was in the hands of the military, 69 Coreans being killed and 145 made prisoners. It was hoped that this affair would end further insurrection.

But in a land so long governed by the sorcerer, where the

means of communication are slight and the people lack education and mental initiative, news travels slowly. Choi, in the more southern city, held out. Murderous attacks on Japanese settlers and fishermen continued. The Wi-pion party, representing inveterate conservatism, sided with the insurgents, while the Il Chinghoi, or Liberal Progressive, set to work to unearth evidence and expose the Conservative plotters. Giving information at the Residency in Seoul, five high officers, Kim, Choi, Min, Hong, etc., of the Corean Court or Government, including a eunuch, were arrested. The twofold plan, first, to make the world believe that the whole Corean people was opposed to the Japanese protectorate, and second, to enlist Russian cooperation, was exposed. One immediate result of forcing the Japanese military hand was the quick surrender of Choi to Corean soldiers in Chulla Do. In his camp was found authorization from Seoul, sealed with the vermilion seal of the palace, to raise troops. Thus collapsed the plot for internal disturbance.[1]

The prospect of drawing Russia again into hostilities which might free Corea from the Japanese yoke shows the weak spot in the Russo-Chinese negotiations of Ignatieff in 1860 (p. 371). In the delimitation of frontiers then made, a strip of country containing nearly 3,000 square miles, called Han-do, or Island Circuit, between the Tumen and its affluent, the Hai-lan River, which, beginning about seventy-five miles from the sea, flows nearly parallel, was left as neutral territory to be uninhabited. This region is shown on the maps (pp. 210, 365), and though the Chinese characters describe an island, it is interfluvial only. In reality the land, being very fertile, did in course of time attract many settlers, both Chinese and Corean. When Russia began to assert her strenuous policy in the Far East, she demanded that this neutral strip should be cleared of Coreans, or that all settlers in this region between the rivers should be enrolled as Chinese subjects. The Japanese War coming on in 1904, nothing further was done. Since Russia, by the Portsmouth treaty, controls the railways of Kirin, she may by holding this region control the trade routes to the seaboard.

---

[1] See the long letter in the London Times of August 8, 1906, from an unimpeachable authority—the author of the Oriental Series, nearly forty years in the Far East.

Here then was the bait to make the Russian bear bite. One of the Kims, an anti-Japanese ultra-conservative, secured a commission from the Corean Emperor appointing him virtually governor of this Hai-lan region. At Vladivostok, through the infamous pro-Russian Li Yong Ik and M. Pavloff, the late envoy of the Czar in Corea, the Court of St. Petersburg was to be sounded on the possibility of gaining control of this strategic territory.

If it be asked, what ground of hope Kim Hseung-mun had of success, it must be remembered that while all other foreign consuls in Corea, under the new order of things, had received their *exequaturs*, or authorizations, from the Emperor of Japan, the new Russian Consul-General, M. Plancon, claimed that he should be recognized by the Corean and not the Japanese emperor, thus ignoring Corea's denunciation of her old treaty with China and the convention of November 17, 1905. The Russian envoy, for a little while or until he withdrew his contention, consciously or unconsciously, gave encouragement to the Corean conspirator, Kim. This whole plot to embroil Russia and Japan was frustrated, getting no further than the palace, while the surrender of Choi in Chulla Do was made sure by the arrest, on the night of June 8th, of the chief conspirators as they were leaving the palace. The Liberals had turned state's evidence.

Without impeaching the Corean Emperor, the Japanese Government removed his evil advisers and resolved to persevere in using what authority he still possesses for the good of the Corean people—as their protectors see it.

That policy requires the public finance of Corea to be known in ledgers and budgets, with strict accountability for every dollar; the purging of the palace, and the thorough differentiation of Court and Government, and of the "boudoir" from the council table; the creation of a public school system; the building of a railway from Ping An to Gen san; a coinage and stable monetary system; the reform of prison methods and the judiciary; the reclamation of the vast quantities of waste land; the encouragement of all moral forces; the development of trade, commerce, and industry; and last, but not least, the severe handling of unprincipled and truculent Japanese; or, in general, a policy of righteousness and conciliation that must overcome the traditional hatred between the Coreans and the Japanese. To make the yang-ban get to work and earn their own living will be the great blessing to this long-oppressed land. If Japan can satisfy the enlightened judgment of the world that Corea is exploited for the good primarily of the Coreans and not the Japanese, humanity will approve and rejoice. The accomplished author of "The Passing of Korea," which contains the severest arraignment of the Japanese thus far made, passes this verdict on the situation:

"The Koreans have awakened to the fact that this, which should have been their first consideration many years ago, is now their last resort, and they are clamoring for education. . . . Korea can gain nothing by holding back and offering to the plans of Japan a sulky resistance. They are face to face with a definite condition, and theories as to the morality of the forces which brought about the condition are wholly academic."

CHAPTER LIV.

CHŌ-SEN: A PROVINCE OF JAPAN.

CHŌ-SEN is the official name of the country described in this volume and now a province of Japan, as declared in the Act of Annexation of August, 1910. Thus its oldest name, now to be better known to the world, is also its newest. Since 1392 the natives have known no other. The Chinese characters for Chō-sen, or Morning Calm, were stamped on the first and earlier editions of this book. The Japanese name of the capital is Kéijo.

By the Russo-Japanese war, Corea was saved from being a Russian province and the king and court given the supreme occasion of reform, which, if carried out, would mean new national life. Corea would have remained a sovereign state, had the chief ruler and the governing classes risen to their opportunity.

It was not to be. With despotism in the palace and a lettered class bound in cast-iron traditions, but profoundly ignorant of the world and the century, there lay beneath an oppressed populace, steeped in superstition, for which the Government did nothing. Lacking an intelligent middle class between, reform in Corea, except from without, was perhaps morally impossible.

Old Corea, an unreformed Oriental state, with all the features inseparably associated with such a society, was thus described by Lord Curzon in 1894:

"A royal figure-head, enveloped in the mystery of the palace and the harem, surrounded by concentric rings of eunuchs, Ministers of State, officials and retainers, and rendered almost intangible by the predominant atmosphere of intrigue; a hierarchy of office-holders and office-seekers, who are leeches in the thinnest disguise; a feeble and insignificant army, an impecunious exchequer, a debased currency, and an impoverished people—these are the invariable symptoms of the fast-vanishing *régime* of the older and unredeemed Oriental type. Add to these the first swarming of the flock of foreign practitioners who scent the enfeebled constitution from afar and from the four winds of Heaven come pressing their pharmacopæia of loans, concessions, banks, mints, factories, and all the recognized machinery for filling Western purses at the expense of Eastern pockets, and you have a fair picture of Korea as she stands after ten years of emergence from her long seclusion and enjoyment of the intercourse of the nations."

Corea as represented by the yang-ban, or ruling class, numbering with their families 200,000 souls, was dragged suddenly out into the world's light and confronted with vital problems. Without that long interior intellectual preparation which enabled Japan in the nick of time to meet her new duties, the Coreans were neither able nor willing to grapple with the colossal tasks awaiting them. Yet this was no fault of the plain people, for it is to their credit that they welcomed foreigners. Except a morbid curiosity as to alien persons and ways, they have ever shown kindness, and politeness so far as they knew it. With amazing promptness the spiritually hungry and thirsty masses have responded with grateful appreciation to what their foreign teachers brought them. One secret of their readiness and docility lies in the fact that they were glad to be delivered from the oppression of rulers, whose one idea of government meant the grinding of the people for private benefit.

After the treaty of November 17, 1905, by which a Resident-General from Japan was established in Seoul, and which took control of the foreign relations and affairs of the little kingdom, it was found that few of those who could have effected national reform gave any indication of their desire to do so. In 1907 a fresh agreement was made, "with the object of speedily providing for the wealth of Corea and of promoting its welfare," and the Japanese Government spent millions of dollars in schemes of practical advantage to the Coreans. When, after four years, it was found that the age-old abuses continued, and reform by natives seemed impossible, the formal annexation of Corea was consummated on August 29, 1910. The full text of the treaty, in eight articles, with preamble, etc., and English translation, is printed in the

Journal of International Law (Revue de Droit International) for December, 1910, published in Tokio.

The Amalgamation Convention provides :[1]

" (1) The Emperor of Corea shall concede to the Emperor of Japan the Corean sovereignty, together with all territorial rights.

" (2) The Sovereign Imperial Household is to be treated as a quasi-Imperial Family of Japan, continuing to have the annual allowance of 1,500,000 *yen*, while members of the Imperial Family and meritorious persons of the country are to be created peers, or endowed with certain grants.

" (3) The name Corea shall be changed into 'Chō-sen.'

" (4) The Corean Cabinet being abolished, the Residency-General shall be changed into a government of Governor-General, while as to the administrative business and customs tariff, there will be no change for the present."

The cost to Japan of the amalgamation is estimated at *yen*, 30,000,000, or $15,000,000. Seventy-five Coreans of distinguished families were created peers of Japan, and the monetary grants in *yen* were conferred as follows: to a baron, 50,000; to a viscount, 100,000; to a count, 150,000; and to a marquis, 200,000. As with the kugé, or court nobles, to prevent waste, the principal is retained in the Imperial Treasury, and the interest promptly paid at frequent intervals. Provision has been made for other meritorious persons, and the military conscription will not be put in force for ten years yet. Meanwhile, besides thousands of Corean students in Tokio, delegations of leading men and women of Chō-sen have visited and travelled in Japan.

It has always been a sore spot with the Coreans that the United States refused to intervene, though in the first article of the treaty of May 22, 1882, promise was made that "if other Powers deal unjustly or oppressively with either Government, the other will exert their good offices, on being informed of the case, to bring about an amicable arrangement, thus showing their friendly feeling." Yet apart from the settled policy of non-intervention in the affairs of foreign nations, the United States was but one of several nations that, with a significant promptness and unanimity,

---

[1] *The Japan Mail.* August 27, 1910.

gladly called home their legations and handed over the control of Corea to Japan.

There is nothing mysterious to the student in the loss of Corea's sovereignty and her absorption in the Japanese Empire. A survey of her history and a view of the world's movement since 1866 shows inexorably the law of cause and effect. It was the weakness of Corea to be not only shut off from the world, but in her hermitage so to exaggerate antiquity and its importance as to leave the nation helpless in the modern clash of civilizations, when Orient and Occident are meeting to merge into one world society. The first infirmity of the Coreans of insular mind arises from long contact with the history and literature of the Chinese. Stimulating to the intellect, this has paralyzed mental initiative and swamped originality. The Corean imagined that China's was the beginning and end of all wisdom. Added to this was the delusion that a knowledge of letters was in itself sufficient to preserve both society and national sovereignty.

Old Japan suffered frightfully, but not fatally, from the same disease. In Corea's case, this insanity of literary pride was exaggerated into a crime when, after 1392, the popular religion was ruthlessly destroyed, the people robbed of their teachers, and the country given over to superstition and ignorance by a Government which Lieutenant Foulk, in 1883, after prolonged tours within the country and study of the details of administration, declared was but armed robbery.

There was no political or social unity in the Corean peninsula until the tenth century. The chief force in welding together the various tribes and peoples into the astonishing unity and similarity now visible among the people and villages from Quelpart to the Ever White Mountain was Buddhism. The missionaries of this faith, coming from Thibet and China, gave the peninsulars art, architecture, literature, folk-lore, a noble path of morals for guidance in this life, vast consolations for the future, and pretty much everything that means culture, refinement, and civilization. In very early days, before Mikadoism in Japan was formulated into a militant dogma, the islanders and the peninsulars, the Japanese and the Coreans, were virtually one and the same people, and in about the same stage of civilization. In the reaction of nature upon man and of man upon nature, during ten centuries, the two peoples were differentiated, and the two languages—almost exactly the same in structure, thus proving their common origin—developed their vocabulary and local pronunciation. The two nations, according to their ethnic mixtures, heredity and environment, grew further and further apart. Nevertheless, to-day, after a millennium of separation, the underlying elements are so much greater than the surface differences that the prospects of an amalgamation of the two peoples are decidedly promising.

In the main, the history of Corea is like its landscape. Her political annals, as thus far studied, seem like monotonous undergrowth among which loom indistinct figure-heads. As bare as her desolated coast or denuded mountains, the scene in historic perspective reminds one of the peninsula's lava beds, her square leagues of disintegrated granite, or her waste lands, out of which rise sculptured rocks, and whence emerge the Miryeks, or stone colossi, amid ruins surrounded with forests. To a native scholar his nation's chronicles are not without a rugged grandeur of their own, besides a rich coloring that recalls the rock-scenery of Corea when looked at in the sunlight.

To the alien student, Buddhism looms as the chief civilizer and the mother of popular culture. It is certain that during its thousand years of growth and prosperity in the peninsula the people were as one flock led by one shepherd. They were trained in what was at least beautiful and human. Corea's debt to Buddhism is unspeakable. Even to-day, in the land so often invaded, desolated, peeled, and scraped by Tartar, Chinese, and Japanese marauders, and raided by men from countries called Christian, almost everything that remains to touch the imagination, whether in architecture, rock sculpture, stone colossus, pagoda, in art, and even in literature, apart from erudition, is of Buddhist origin.

When, after A.D. 1392, the popular faith was banned, its temples, schools, monasteries, and works of art destroyed or doomed to decay, its priesthood socially outlawed and oppressed even to beggary, the people were left to ignorance and superstition and were as sheep without shepherds. They became the prey alike of the ruling classes and of sorcerers and fortune-tellers, who, though densely ignorant, lived by their wits and wickedness. Parasitic spoilers of all sorts, from the palace to the hovel, thrived, while the people, the foundation of the state, existed on life's narrowest margins. Confucianism, as made into a state ritual since 1392, and as interpreted and developed by the yang-ban, or educated and office-holding classes, meant neglect of the land, the grinding of the people's faces, the permanent destruction of popular wealth and comfort, the paralysis of the motives to industry, and the creation of a standing army of inquisitors, office-seekers, and office-holders, and their satellites and hangers-on, with headquarters in Seoul. In place of the spiritual bread of Buddhism, the new régime offered a stone. In government, instead of the egg for nourishment, they proffered a scorpion—even chronic extortion. A great gulf was fixed socially between the men to whom education meant the stifling of original thought, a ban on mental initiative and the oppression of the people. Monopoly of office and privilege, as held by one class, meant systematic robbery of the populace, the Government itself being an engine of oppression by which fewer than one-quarter million yang-ban subsisted upon eleven million of the common folk.

When reform was called for which meant public benefit, apart from private rapine or individual advantage, manual as well as clerkly labor, continuous and unselfish toil with only slight pecuniary reward, the average high-class native proved a total failure. Despite the purging from the palace of several hundred women, and over a thousand male persons who drew salaries, the remainder within, or parasitic to royalty, proved worthless for the remaking of the nation.

Ever under the spell of the Chinese characters, saturated with the ideas of Confucianism run to seed, having only one ideal of life—selfish advantage and the subordination of the lower classes—devoted to their sensual enjoyments, their long pipes, and their liquor, to checker-playing, gossip, and elaborate idleness, the yang-ban during five centuries did nothing to develop the soil or the resources of the country. On the contrary, the office-holding class systematically hindered the development of wealth, or even thrift, by extortion, unjust taxes, and dishonest manipulation of imposts, which were paid in kind instead of in coin, by exactions or forced loans never repaid—usually under the menace and reality of beating, torture, and imprisonment. One innovation under the Japanese rule, which made taxes payable in cash and not in kind, wrought infinite blessing to the people and carried consternation to the army of extortioners.

In the modern world-life, Japan and Corea are as necessary to each other as are man and woman. It soon became evident to the Tokio Government, after every step, that some stronger remedy than advice would be necessary to heal the age-old and deep-seated Corean disease that seemed as incurable as leprosy. Hence the measures of 1907, which put into the hands of the Mikado's Resident-General still greater powers.

To this work of reforming Corea, Nippon gave her ablest son, one who, both in feudal and constitutional Japan, had dedicated his life to promoting the evolution of the modern man. The statesmanship of Ito was that of a lover of humanity, who might well, after long and multifarious labors, have taken the rest which he craved and which his physical condition demanded. Nevertheless, with his unique experience and amazing abilities, he applied himself with unremitting toil to lead the once hermit nation into the twentieth century. According to Ito's motto, "The secret of statesmanship consists in securing the contentment of the people." He was all the better fitted for his colossal task by having known so well the late feudal Nippon with its political diseases. Neglect of the people and of the soil, official falsehood, and class oppression were characteristic of both countries. Ito took all the more encouragement because life in Chō-sen was but the mirror of that in old Japan. Having fought belated feudalism and grappled with the new problems of a modern state in Asia, none was better equipped than he for the task of making a progressive nation out of a people whose mental eyes were set even further back in their heads than those of the Chinese.

For while China boasts of Confucius, Corea penetrates further into the primitive. She hails as the founder of her social order, Kija (Ki-Tsze, or Kishi, pp. 11–15), the distant ancestor of the Chinese sage. On this nursery fairy tale of the nation—since the peninsulars knew nothing of writing until, long after the Christian era, they obtained the Chinese ideographs—every Corean for a thousand years or more has been brought up. The early myth-

ology and legend of the peninsulars are about as trustworthy as
those of the neighboring islanders, whose conceit of antiquity was
once fully as great and whose official and orthodox chronology was
fixed and published so long ago as A.D. 1872!

This myth of Kija, as the actual founder of civilization east of
the Yalu, took its literary form only in the eighth century, when
the Coreans had become saturated with Chinese ideas. Then the
peninsulars, made acquainted with Chinese historiography, and
having but one model before them, faithfully followed it (as did
the Japanese also), the Coreans surpassing even the greater nation
in pride of antiquity and in the glorification of heroes, who loom up
in vaster proportions according as the unrecorded centuries mul-
tiply and recede into the past. Historical science has already begun to change this perspective of antiquity as surely as hospitals
have furnished object-lessons in the law of cause and effect. Corean
gods and demons, more numerous even than old Japan's mythical
menagerie and pantheon, are being steadily banished to the realms
of fairy-land.[1]

Ito, scorning delights and living laborious days, continued the
labors, but vastly enlarged the plans of his predecessors. First of
all, having deported hundreds of the bad subjects of the Mikado
and curbed the rapacity and brutality of his own countrymen, he
applied himself unceasingly to healing the wounds of war, to in-
demnifying the unjustly impoverished natives, and to giving Corea
what she never had—or, if possessed of, had allowed to lapse
during the five hundred years of the dynasty that had destroyed
the people's religion and had done nothing for national development. A system of good roads, honest coinage and currency, courts
and justice, popular education, afforestation of the mountains, improvement of the soil through scientific agriculture and reclamation of waste land, preventive hygiene, honest taxation and collection now exists. Ito cleansed the palace, separating the functions
of Court and Government, lessening by fifty per cent. the number
of persons paid from the public treasury, both male and female,
removing as far as possible the king and his advisers from the
great mob of sorcerers, fortune-tellers, geomancers, and others who

[1] See "The Unmannerly Tiger and Other Korean Fairy Tales," by W. E.
Griffis, New York, 1911.

prey upon the Corean people. The deposition of the incompetent emperor and the installation of his son in power were followed by the education of the crown prince in Tokio.

The difficulties in the way of reform were appalling. The principal obstacles existed in the two classes of which Corean society is composed—oppressors and oppressed. The yang-ban, or privileged men, with more or less scholarship of a Chinese kind, seemed to have no conception of patriotism apart from pelf. Their chief trait was political vampirism. On the other hand, the supine attitude of the common people, accustomed for centuries to systematic oppression, was discouraging. To them even decent government, that is, the kind which could be tolerated to the point of rebellion, meant the grace of their masters and rule without robbery. One of the striking features of nearly every Corean town or city is seen in the long rows of tablets in stone or iron that celebrate the merits of "good," that is, fairly decent, governors. A collection of all the local instruments of torture, stacked in one museum, would be impressive and furnish fuel for a vast conflagration.

In education, progress was hampered by the general prevalence of fanaticism on the subject of "race suicide" and in the absurd measures taken for its prevention—measures that largely tend to hinder the end in view. In Corea the marriage and birth rate may possibly be in excess of that of any country in the world, while, almost as matter of course, and as a scientific corollary, the same may be said of the death rate, which, owing to superstition, ignorance, and dirt, is appalling. Corea, despite shining white clothes, is not a land of bath-tubs. In the schools, nearly all the boys were found to be married, and to girls older than themselves. These over-mature youths, of antediluvian frame of mind, too often seem to have eyes set too far back in their heads, which fix their gaze on duties appropriate to the time of Confucius rather than of the twentieth century.

We have glanced at this subject before. Yet even to-day, with all the advantages afforded them, there is danger. Expecting, like their fathers before them, to be verse-makers, to quote from the ancient Chinese, to be literary, and to hold office, because of a knowledge of the characters, the young Corean yang-ban are indifferent to useful progress and scorn manual labor. Having already lost nearly everything, they will, unless radically changed in mind, lose all. The one hope of Chō-sen is the raising up in a generation, now under new influences, of a new type of humanity. The Christian schools and churches are supplying this need.

Indeed, the fall of yang-banism and the extinction of Corea's sovereignty means Buddhism's opportunity. It will be both logical and natural that one of the first effects of Christian missions will be, as in Japan, to quicken the spirit and improve the form and power of the older religion. Nor ought missionaries fear its vigorous competition, should it become potent for the abolition of demon-worship and the moral uplift of the masses otherwise neglected, especially in out-of-the-way places.

Unfortunately, Corea of mediæval mind, like barbarous Japan of not so many years ago, sought a remedy for supposed wrongs in assassination. Rashly unintelligent, sword and bullet were resorted to in order to stop the car of progress. Quick to misjudge and impatient to wait for results, the assassin selected as his first victims his country's best friends. The weak and disappointed tried suicide as a remedy and deterrent. The insurgents in the so-called Righteous Army, too often were robbers of their own people. In the name of patriotism they attempted redress, seeking to turn back "modern civilization which rides on a powder cart." The list of Coreans who in cowardice or discouragement died by their own hands, who were slaughtered by their own compatriots, who fell beneath the bullets or the swords of rebels in civil strife, or who were mown down by the resistless fire of the Japanese infantry, is sadly great.[1]

The Mikado's soldiers were perhaps frequently unable to distinguish between the deserving and the undeserving. Their actions are not absolutely free from criticism. Yet with unrestrained frankness the statistics of the military operations are given in the Annual Reports on Reforms and Progress in Korea, in 1907, 1908–9, and 1909–10. From July, 1907, when the riots broke out in Seoul, on account of the disbanding of the Corean army, to the end of 1908, there were of Japanese soldiers 179 killed and 277 wounded, besides 67 Japanese residents killed in 1907 and 16 in 1908. Of Corean

---

[1] See also " The Tragedy of Korea," by H. A. McKenzie, London, 1908.

insurgents, 14,566 were "killed." Besides positive military measures, the Corean Emperor's rescripts urging those in arms to submit quietly were effective, and the total of those who surrendered and were pardoned to December 13, 1907, was 8,728. During the fiscal year 1909 the Japanese lost 38 men, but the number of insurgents killed (3,001), wounded, captured, or surrendered was 6,131. Those in arms who yielded or asked pardon were given employment in road-making and other useful occupations. By 1911, most of the activity of native insurgent bands had degenerated into the work of mere banditti. Military movements on a large scale were not required, and much of the desolation of villages was repaired with better hope of more comfortable existence. Frightful as is this frank showing, it is doubtful whether more lives were lost in the suppression of rebellion, from 1907 to 1911, than in the nearly chronic anarchy that prevailed in the southern provinces during the previous decade and a half.

The Annual Reports above referred to show by text, pictures, and statistics, not only the purpose and results of the Japanese Government, but also the fearful cost of restoring order, a cost of life and treasure aggravated both by natives who have not scrupled to use the torch, the mulct, and the assassin's weapon on their own native soil, and by foreigners who, in the name of liberty, abused the freedom of the press and kept the useless and dangerous embers of sedition in a flame. Not satisfied with murder at home, Coreans have made the United States, already the happy hunting ground of the Black Hand and the lyncher, the arena of their cowardly exploits.

After Mr. Durham White Stevens, an American of long experience in the Far East, and Diplomatic Adviser to the Corean Government, had been shot and killed in San Francisco by a Corean, the most shining mark was Corea's best friend, Ito. Made a prince and rewarded with every mark of honor possible to a subject by the Emperor of Japan, this man who, in unquailing discharge of his duty, had already braved the Japanese feudal sword wielded by cowards in Choshiu, and the infuriated Tokio mob in constitutional Japan, and who seemed immune from the assassins of which old Japan raised such a luxuriant crop, fell in Manchuria at the Harbin railway station, on October 26, 1909, before the bullets of the petty revenger, who shot from behind. Amid the grief and the honor of the whole world, on November 4, 1909, Ito was given a State funeral such as has been bestowed upon few subjects of Japan. Ito shed his blood in the cause of peace. Whether these assassinations hastened the absorption of Corea by Japan, and the blotting out of a sovereignty unknown to the world until Japan, by peaceful diplomacy, conferred it in 1876, is not known. The Emperor at once appointed General Viscount Terauchi, then Minister of War, and already famous for his brilliant military record and notable organizing abilities, to be the successor of Ito in Corea. The record for energetic action, consummate tact, and ceaseless toil already made by Terauchi places his name very near that of Ito as a modern civilizer and lover of the victories of peace even more than those of war.

Despite all the instances of individual wrong, private injustices, and public mistakes made by the Japanese in Corea, and in view of the severe criticisms of Terauchi by such leading Japanese newspapers as the *Kokumin* and *Kochi,* it is nevertheless manifest that the policy of the Tokio Government is antipodally the reverse of that of Hidéyoshi. Instead of the Ear-tomb, and the scooping of Corea clean of her artists, artisans, potters, and art treasures, there rise to-day the school, the hospital, and the temples of justice and finance. Plans are being perfected for the development of the soil and of the wealth of the nation, in the interest of the people, while to the missionary and alien philanthropist is given all encouragement. A new land survey is in operation for the equalization of taxes. Light-houses have reduced the dangers of a foggy and treacherous coast. Harbor works are in course of construction; well-made common roads are decreasing the difficulty of transport; while these and the highways of steel continually increase the value of the arable lands and of town lots. Rivers, even the wide Yalu and Han, are spanned by bridges. Many a place, historic because of war, is now famous for its commercial and industrial development. Piracy gives way before policemen in steam launches, and chronic brigandage is dying out. In all that relates directly to humanity, the reform of the judiciary methods of justice, prison procedure, the codification of laws, etc., the progress is marvellous. At the head of the judicial department is a Christian, Judge Watanabé, and many men of this faith, Japanese and Corean, fill other high offices. Special schools, of medicine, surgery, nursing, scientific agriculture, forestry, live-stock improvement and manual training, are preparing young men and women to raise the standard of human life in Chō-sen and to reclaim the sixty-six per cent. of the arable land in the peninsula which has lain waste.

The absorption of Corea by Japan has given the astonishingly successful Christian missionary work a new environment, and one for the better, despite the manifest dangers of misunderstanding arising temporarily from the political situation and the eager readiness of a few Japanese press correspondents to misrepresent. With full religious liberty, and under the protection of a firm, orderly, and impartial government, the great work of raising up the new type of man and woman in Chō-sen, now one of the most promising of mission fields, proceeds. In the Christian household, numbering roughly about 200,000, we discern the best promise for Chō-sen's future. Into his new world of hope and cheer, the native, when enlightened and converted, brings the richest inheritances of the national culture, the best results of his training, and the most winning traits of his character. This is strikingly shown in the general eagerness to read and study the Holy Scriptures, in the wonderful powers of memory, and in the committing of large portions of the Bible, which is now accessible in the vernacular. The native's generosity, good-nature, power of self-support, mutual desire and practice of helpfulness, patience, and power to endure persecution of any and all sorts fit him admirably for Christian service.

Christianity has come to Corea to reveal the national treasures that are enduring. For centuries the beautiful phonetic alphabet, en-mun, and syllabary Nido (p. 47), lay neglected and scorned by the learned. Yet this was but one of many elements of potency for good that lay unused like barren rocks. At the smiting of the missionaries' hand of faith gushed forth the waters of life and healing. The new messages of hope and salvation came to the people not only in their own tongue, but in their own script. Christian teachers, after long years of discouragement, have made, through the patience of hope, of love and sympathy, a real conquest of the Corean heart. The faces of men and women are lighted up with a new glow of interest in life here and hereafter as they find both body and soul ministered to by their friends from afar. With this spiritual invitation and challenge to enter into the promised land fully accepted by the Coreans, it is not too wild a dream to imagine even the strong conqueror conquered by the weaker. Samson's experience and his riddle may be the Corean's. Chō-sen may yet be to Nippon what Palestine was to Greece and Rome. Bereft of political sovereignty, from the land of the Hebrews went forth that salvation which "is of the Jews" to conquer Europe and the world. Already, by closer contact of the humbler classes of the two nations on Corean soil, the paganism of rustic Japan—hitherto almost untouched by the gospel—begins to disintegrate and ferment because of the leaven brought from Christian Chō-sen. This has the Corean left—and perhaps more abundantly than ever before—"power to become" the spiritual regenerator of Japan.

INDEX.

521